Fodor's upCLOSE

CENTRAL AMERICA

the complete guide, thoroughly up-to-date

SAVVY TRAVELING: WHERE TO SPEND, HOW TO SAVE

packed with details that will make your trip

CULTURAL TIPS: ESSENTIAL LOCAL DO'S AND TABOOS

must-see sights, on and off the beaten path

INSIDER SECRETS: WHAT'S HIP AND WHAT TO SKIP

the buzz on restaurants, the lowdown on lodgings

FIND YOUR WAY WITH CLEAR AND EASY-TO-USE MAPS

Previously published as *The Berkeley Guide to Central America*

FODOR'S TRAVEL PUBLICATIONS, INC.

NEW YORK • TORONTO • LONDON • SYDNEY • AUCKLAND

www.fodors.com

ISBN 0–679–00311–8

FODOR'S UPCLOSE™ CENTRAL AMERICA

EDITOR: Anto Howard

Editorial Contributors: Michele Back, Olivia Barry, Jennifer Brewer, Christine Cipriani, Mark Cutmore, David Dudenhoefer, Tim French, Melisse Gelula, Julie Le Duff, Mara Loveman, Carlos Pineda, Ian Singer, Wendy Smith, Simon Worrall
Editorial Production: Linda K. Schmidt
Maps: David Lindroth, *cartographer*; Steven Amsterdam, *map editor*
Design: Fabrizio La Rocca, *creative director*; Allison Saltzman, *cover and text design*; Jolie Novak, *photo editor*
Production/Manufacturing: Rebecca Zeiler
Cover Art: © Michael Evan Sewell

CONTENTS

3. GUATEMALA 83

4. EL SALVADOR 171

5. COSTA RICA 222

6. PANAMA 303

INDEX 346

TRAVELING UPCLOSE

Hike through virgin cloud forest. Dive down to a coral reef. Climb a Mayan Temple. Go to a festival. Shop in a native market. Commune with nature. Memorize the symphony of the streets—then get lost. And if you want to experience the heart and soul of Central America, whatever you do, don't spend too much money.

The deep and rich experience of Central America that every true traveler yearns for is one of the things in life that money can't buy. In fact, if you have it, don't use it. Traveling lavishly is the surest way to turn yourself into a sideline traveler. Restaurants with white-glove service are great—sometimes—but they're usually not the best place to find the perfect tamale. Doormen at luxury hotels have their place, but not when your look-alike room could be anywhere from San Salvador to Seattle. Better to stay in a more intimate place that gives you the atmosphere you traveled so far to experience. Don't just stand and watch—jump into the spirit of what's around you.

If you want to see Central America up close and savor the essence of the region and its people in all their various glory, this book is for you. We'll show you the local culture, the offbeat sights, the bars and cafés where tourists rarely tread, and the B&Bs and other hostelries where you'll meet fellow travelers—places where the locals would send their friends. And because you'll probably want to see the famous places if you haven't already been there, we give you tips on losing the crowds, plus the politics, the history, and all the quirky and obscure facts you want as well as the basics everyone needs.

OUR GANG

Who are we? We're artists and poets, slackers and straight arrows, and travel writers and journalists, who in our less hedonistic moments report on local news and spin out an occasional opinion piece. What we share is a certain footloose spirit and a passion for all things Central American, which we celebrate in this guidebook. Shamelessly, we've revealed all of our favorite places and our deepest, darkest travel secrets, all so you can learn from our past mistakes and experience the best part of Central America to the fullest. If you can't take your best friend on the road, or if your best friend is hopeless with directions, stick with us.

Freelance hack **David Dudenhoefer** has spent the better part of the past decade in Central America. Based in San José, Costa Rica, he travels regularly within the isthmus, writing about everything from surfing to presidential summits. A regular Fodror's contributor, he is also author of *The Panama Traveler.* David updated the Costa Rica and Panama chapters.

Melisse Gelula, the El Salvador updater, grew up skipping back and forth across the Canadian-American border, residing in Toronto, Chicago, New York, San Francisco, and Iowa City. Using her lack of geographical allegiance and her MA in English, she set to work as a travel writer, traipsing across El Salvador in search of the best pupusería and the black sand beaches filmed by Oliver Stone. Melisse has worked on several Fodor's guides, most recently, Fodor's *New York City.*

A native of Dublin, Ireland, **Anto Howard** now lives in New York where he is a freelance editor and writer. He has traveled widely in Europe and North and Central America. He is also the editor of *Fodor's UpCLOSE Ireland* and *Fodor's Hong Kong 1999.*

When writer **Wendy Smith** isn't chasing down multicolored chicken buses for a living, she leads the good citizen life of a mild-mannered writer and editor. Previous assignments for Fodor's have led her through Europe, Latin America, and her own home base, San Francisco. Wendy updated the Guatemala chapter.

Simon Worrall is a British-born journalist whose long list of publishers includes the *Sunday Times Magazine* (London), the *Observer,* the *Independent, Islands,* and *Harper's.* Along with his wife, Kate, he has hiked the jungle, swam with dolphins, rode horseback, and dived the canyons and walls of Belize's barrier reef while he was updating this chapter.

A SEND-OFF

Always call ahead. We knock ourselves out to check all the facts, but everything changes all the time, in ways that none of us can ever fully anticipate. Whenever you're making a special trip to a special place, as opposed to merely wandering, always call ahead. Trust us on this.

And then, if something doesn't go quite right, as inevitably happens with even the best-laid plans, stay cool. Missed your bus? Stuck in the airport? Use the time to study the people. Strike up a conversation with a stranger. Study the newsstands or flip through the local press. Take a walk. Find the silver lining in the clouds, whatever it is. And do send us a postcard to tell us what went wrong and what went right. You can E-mail us at: editors£fodors.com (specify the name of the book on the subject line) or write the upCLOSE Central America editor at Fodor's upCLOSE, 201 East 50th Street, New York, NY 10022. We'll put your ideas to good use and let other travelers benefit from your experiences. In the meantime, bon voyage!

INTRODUCTION

BY TIM FRENCH, UPDATED BY ANTO HOWARD

This book is being published in the shadow of Hurricane Mitch. Our writers visited Central America only weeks before the region was ravaged by its worst natural disaster in living memory. Nicaragua and Honduras took the brunt of the damage; by the latest estimate, more than 10,000 people died and 2 million were left homeless. The extent of the damage to these two small nations forced us to omit them from this book. The magnitude of the catastrophe makes touring in these countries almost impossible for the foreseeable future. Many of the major charities are still accepting donations to aid victims. Of the five countries still in the book, Belize, El Salvador, and Guatemala also suffered serious damage from the hurricane, but nothing like the devastation in Honduras and Nicaragua. Mitch may have suddenly made some of the information in this book dated—especially when it refers to matters of infrastructure and navigability of smaller roads. Calling the tourist board or embassy of the country you want to visit is a good idea.

Central America has always been a land both blessed and cursed: saturated with natural beauty and a rich cultural heritage, yet simultaneously plagued by an unstable and volatile political legacy. It is these types of provocative contradictions that exemplify Central America's allure. The ordinary and the inconceivable are so deeply intertwined that they become indistinguishable, leaving visitors dumbfounded by an unbelievable history, mind-blowing natural beauty, and politically vehement, ethnically diverse peoples.

No other area in the world exists where the waters of the Pacific and Atlantic oceans bleed into one another. The land itself—a seven-country isthmus fusing North and South America—is overwhelmingly surreal. The sun beats down over lowland fields of sugarcane and cotton that seem to expand, then melt away in the wavy, dreamlike heat. In the highlands, the invigorating mountain air provides a respite from the taxing equatorial climate. The fertile volcanic soils of these looming cones yield most of the region's material wealth. Evanescent clouds hover over the agricultural patchwork, lending an opaque, mystical twist. On a clear day, climb high enough and you may be treated to a view of two oceans so stimulating it leaves your knees weak.

Central America's Caribbean or Mosquito coast might as well be another continent. Here lives a polychromatic mix of indigenous, Ladino, and Afro-Caribbean offspring who proceed at their own, slightly more sedate pace, professing more of an allegiance to their own tribal heritage than to any nation or political entity. The fate of this region has historically been linked to a yellow, oblong fruit—this is the original banana republic. Foreign interests, such as the United Fruit Company, laid claim to the provinces and enlisted locals to build their empire. Today, the presence of the banana companies has

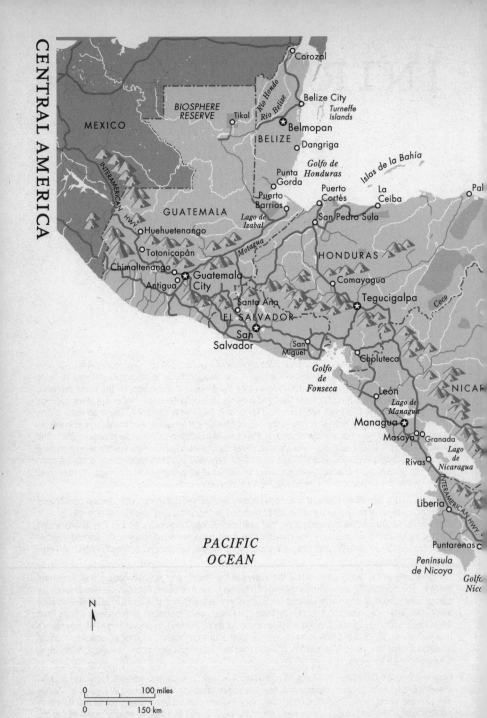

CENTRAL AMERICA

MEXICO

BIOSPHERE
RESERVE

INTERAMERICAN HWY

GUATEMALA

Huehuetenango

Totonicapán

Chimaltenango

Antigua

Guatemala
City

Santa Ana

EL SALVADOR

San
Salvador

San
Miguel

Corozal

Río Hondo

Río Belize

Tikal

Belize City

Turneffe
Islands

Belmopan

BELIZE

Dangriga

Golfo de
Honduras

Punta
Gorda

Puerto
Barrios

Puerto
Cortés

La
Ceiba

Islas de la Bahía

Pal

Puerto
Barrios

Lago de
Izabal

San Pedro Sula

Motagua

HONDURAS

Comayagua

Tegucigalpa

Coco

Choluteca

Golfo
de
Fonseca

León

NICAR

Lago de
Managua

Managua

Masaya

Granada

Lago
de
Nicaragua

Rivas

Liberia

INTERAMERICAN HWY

Puntarenas

PACIFIC
OCEAN

Península
de Nicoya

Golf
Nic

N

0   100 miles

0   150 km

JAMAICA

Palacios

Puerto
Lempira

*Caribbean
Sea*

Puerto
Cabezas

ARAGUA

Rama

*Islas del
Maiz*

*Isla de
San Andrés*

Bluefields

*Bahía
Punta Gorda*

*Río
San Juan*

Chirripó

Tortuguero

COSTA
RICA

Alajuela   Heredia

Puerto
Limón

San
José   Cartago

Bocas
de Toro

El Porvenir

Colón

Ciudad de
Panama

CORDILLERA
TALAMANCA

*Golfo de los
Mosquitos*

*Panama
Canal*

*Lago
Bayano*

o de
oya

*Bahía de
Coronado*

PANAMA

*Bahía de
Panamá*

Puerto
Obaldia

Chucunaque

*Península
de Osa*

David

INTERAMERICAN   *HWY*

Santiago

Chitré

*Golfo de
Chiriquí*

Las Tablas

*Isla del
Rey*

*Golfo de
Panamá*

Yaviza

*Río
Sambú*

*Isla de
Coiba*

COLOMBIA

RESPONSIBLE TOURISM

Tourism is one of the world's largest industries, so as a traveler it's important to recognize the influence you exert, particularly in developing countries. Although tourism injects much-needed hard currency into struggling nations, a sudden influx of cash can upset fragile economies, introducing greed and resentment where there was once harmony and interdependence. Tourists, with all their glittering toys and wealth, can alter locals' self-perceptions and accentuate the division between those who have and those who don't. Natives may end up feeling inferior and denigrate themselves and their unique culture in their attempts to become "Westernized." Too often, tourism ends up damaging that which it seeks to discover. Walk lightly, with a sense of humility and respect.

The Center for Responsible Tourism (Box 827, San Anselmo, CA 94979, tel. 415/258–6594) works with various organizations that promote mindful traveling. What follows are some excerpts from their Code of Ethics for Tourists:

Travel in a spirit of humility and with a genuine desire to meet and talk with local people.

Learn about local customs; respect them.

Be aware of the feelings of the local people; prevent what might be offensive behavior. Photography, particularly, must respect persons.

Cultivate the habit of listening and observing rather than merely hearing and seeing or knowing all the answers.

Instead of seeking only the exotic, discover the richness of another culture and way of life.

When shopping by bargaining, remember that the poorest merchant will relinquish a profit rather than give up their personal dignity.

Make no promises to local people or to new friends that you cannot implement.

Spend time each day reflecting on your experiences in order to deepen your understanding. What enriches you may be robbing others.

And remember: The contents of your luggage may be worth more than what many of the people you meet will own in a lifetime. Be aware, be awake.

THE OTHER AMERICANS

The influence of the United States permeates almost perversely in Central America: the good things in life are unilaterally "made in the U.S.A." The majority of Central American's impressions of life in the United States are gleaned from secondhand stories or programs beamed in from Hollywood. These accounts of far-off utopia inspire awe and respect, while consistently borderline Orwellian foreign policy decisions will always conjure bitterness and disdain.

toned down considerably, rendering the local economy increasingly dependent upon less traditional sources of revenue, principally tourism and the illicit drug trade. Cargo ships from Columbia—loaded to the hilt with contraband—ritually drop anchor in port towns before making their way north to the United States. But such illicit activity has yet to stem the tide of tourists, who flock here lured by the occasional waft of ganja and the arresting blue-green sea. For all its turmoil, this region remains the ideal place to take a vacation from your Central American vacation.

Big cities in Central America are paradoxical in their very nature. These are capitals of entire nations, yet there is nothing thriving nor cosmopolitan about them. Central American cities belie the rigid distinction between urban and rural. Most of the cities are but concentrated extensions of the countryside. Most *ciudadanos* (city dwellers) retain ties to the agricultural sector, routinely migrating in search of seasonal labor. The stress, crime, and grime of city life assure that the majority of the population lives in a degree of squalor that would put any first-world ghetto to shame. The rich—the other 1%—reign as the distributors of all things agricultural. They can be spotted speeding through poverty-stricken streets in their BMWs on their way to exclusive fringe neighborhoods that accentuate the extreme dichotomies between affluence and indigence.

Religion and gender politics play prominent roles in the cultural blueprint of Central America. Catholicism is still the largest social institution, and the church has long held sway over the daily lives of the Central American faithful. In a world where your father can be suddenly "disappeared" by a clandestine military faction and where you must improvise daily to feed your family, the church is a necessary source of stability and spiritual sustenance. The regimen, the rules, and the guarantee of a better life after death bring structure to a region lacking in just that. The Christian model of family dictates that men are the bread-winners, the ones in charge, superior to "their women." The majority of men subscribe to this old-line custom of machismo at least mildly. Machismo is, however, just one facet of a society that is largely traditional culture: change, if any, is slow and not received taken all that well.

The history of Central America lies on a tumultuous foundation of rape, pillage, and plunder. The statues of Spanish conquistadores that adorn plazas throughout the continent serve as constant reminders of the roots of Central America's "civilization." An abundance of silver, gold, indigo, and obedient natives was Central America's constitutional curse. Spanish fortune seekers began colonization in the early 1500s and Catholic priests followed in their footsteps, seeking to convert native souls. A central cathedral—constructed by the indigenous people themselves—was always the first building erected in a newly founded community. History textbooks will tell you that independence was reinstated some 300 years later, but U.S. intervention soon became its functional equivalent. The persistent filibuster William Walker was only the most outlandish in a subsequent parade of unsavory Americans characters who sought to transform Central America into their own personal Land of Opportunity.

In the early 1960s Central America was thrust into a grisly descent of apocalyptic revolutionary violence. Caught up in a complex web of poverty, rapid urbanization, Uncle Sam's fatherly love, and wicked dictatorships for the next 20 years, Central America grabbed headlines throughout the world. By the late 1970s and throughout the 1980s, the situation was dangerous in Nicaragua, El Salvador, and Guatemala, and incipiently volatile in Honduras and Panama. Costa Rica was the only secure country because a stable democracy and equitable economy had permitted it to dismantle its army in 1948. In

1979, U.S. television audiences watched ABC journalist Bill Stewart's execution by the Nicaraguan National Guard, while the CIA used Honduran and Costa Rican soil as a covert training ground for counterrevolutionaries. The site of a civil war pitting the extreme military right against the campesino "communist" left, El Salvador played host to nightmarish body dumps and death squads. While delivering an antiviolence Sunday Mass in 1980, Archbishop Oscar Romero was murdered in cold blood. The early '80s for Guatemala, too, meant torture and mutilation for some 100,000 people—most indigenous—during the government's "scorched-earth" counterinsurgency campaign.

But a new, gentler wind has blown across the region in recent years. The slow transformation from AK-47s to ballots and guerrilla warfare to the political dialogue has given Central America a desperately needed break from the violence. What remains is widespread, crippling poverty and several nations struggling to reconstruct themselves and their democracies, *de cabo a rabo* (from head to toe). Panama and El Salvador, due to a backlog of past due debts, entered the 1990s ineligible for World Bank loans. Considering these statistics, it's safe to say that most of Central America will continue to feel the crippling effects of economic instability well into the next millennium. And yet the visitor will not find a defeated people. Life does not only go on in this troubled isthmus, it positively vibrates with humor and vitality. The tourist is usually welcomed with open arms; well, the local thinking goes, things must be getting better if the gringos are coming here to holiday.

If you exercise healthy amounts of patience and sensitivity, you might have the privilege of discussing Central America's intriguing history with those who have experienced it. Few life experiences can compare to knowing the people, understanding why passion for their homeland runs so deep, and sharing their pain resulting from years of enduring warfare, commercial oppression, and slavery. Taking this all into consideration, an appreciation of their unparalleled enthusiasm and genuine respect for life itself is enough to monumentally shake your world view.

BASICS

f you've ever traveled with anyone before, you know the two types of people in the world: the planners and the nonplanners. Travel brings out the worst in both groups. Left to their own devices, the planners will have you goose-stepping from sight to sight, with no more noble aim than crossing each one off a list; while the nonplanners will have you sitting on a bench in the train station, waiting for a missed connection. This chapter suggests a middle ground; we hope it provides enough information to help you plan your trip to Central America without nailing you down. Be flexible, and hold on to your sense of humor—the most hair-pulling situation abroad can turn into the best travel studies back home.

AIR TRAVEL

MAJOR AIRLINE OR LOW-COST CARRIER?

Most people choose a flight based on price. But there are other issues to consider. Major airlines offer the greatest number of departures; smaller airlines—including regional, low-cost and no-frills airlines—usually have a more limited number of flights daily. Major airlines have frequent-flyer partners, which allow you to credit mileage earned on one airline to your account with another. Low-cost airlines offer a definite price advantage and fewer restrictions, such as advance-purchase requirements. Safety-wise, low-cost carriers as a group have a good history, but **check the safety record before booking** any low-cost carrier; call the Federal Aviation Administration's Consumer Hotline (*see* Airline Complaints, *below*).

MAJOR AIRLINES • American (tel. 800/433–7300). **Continental** (tel. 800/231–0856). **Delta** (tel. 800/221–1212). **United** (tel. 800/827–7777). **US Airways** (tel. 800/428–4322).

SMALLER AIRLINES • Aviateca Guatemala (tel. 800/327–9832). **Lacsa Costa Rican** (tel. 800/225–2272). **LTU** (tel. 800/888–0200). **Mexicana** (tel. 800/531–7921). **TACA** (tel. 800/535–8780).

FROM THE U.K. • American Airlines (tel. 0345/789–789) flies from Heathrow via Miami, one of the fastest options given that there are no nonstop flights to Costa Rica from the United Kingdom. **British Airways** (tel. 0345/222–111) flies direct to Panama City, and also offers flights to Madrid, changing to an **Iberia** (tel. 0171/830–0011) flight to Costa Rica, Honduras, and Nicaragua. **Virgin Atlantic** (tel. 01293/747–747) travels from Gatwick to Miami, where you can catch a flight to any of the major cities in Central America.

DON'T STOP UNLESS YOU MUST

When you book, **look for nonstop flights** and **remember that "direct" flights stop at least once.** International flights on a country's flag carrier are almost always nonstop; U.S. airlines often fly direct. Try to **avoid connecting flights,** which require a change of plane. Two airlines may jointly operate a connecting flight, so ask if your airline operates every segment—you may find that your preferred carrier flies you only part of the way.

USE AN AGENT

Travel agents, especially those who specialize in finding the lowest fares (*see* Discounts & Deals, *below*), can be especially helpful when booking a plane ticket. When you're quoted a price, **ask your agent if the price is likely to get any lower.** Good agents know the seasonal fluctuations of airfares and can usually anticipate a sale or fare war. However, waiting can be risky: the fare could go *up* as seats become scarce, and you may wait so long that your preferred flight sells out. A wait-and-see strategy works best if your plans are flexible, but if you must arrive and depart on certain dates, don't delay.

GET THE LOWEST FARE

The least-expensive airfares to Central America are priced for round-trip travel. Major airlines usually require that you **book in advance and buy the ticket within 24 hours,** and you may have to stay over a Saturday night. It's smart to **call a number of airlines, and when you are quoted a good price, book it on the spot**—the same fare may not be available on the same flight the next day. Airlines generally allow you to change your return date for a fee of $25–$50. If you don't use your ticket, you can apply the cost toward the purchase of a new ticket, again for a small charge. However, most low-fare tickets are nonrefundable. To get the lowest airfare, **check different routings.** If your destination or home city has more than one gateway, compare prices to and from different airports. Flexibility is the key to getting a serious bargain on airfare. If you can play around with your departure date, destination, and return date, you will probably save money. Ask which days of the week are the cheapest to fly—weekends are often the most expensive. Even the time of day you fly can make a big difference in the cost of your ticket. Also look into discounts available through student- and budget-travel organizations (*see* Student Travel, *below*).

CHECK WITH CONSOLIDATORS

Consolidators, also sometimes known as bucket shops, buy tickets for scheduled flights at reduced rates from the airlines, then sell them at prices that beat the best fare available directly from the airlines, usually without advance restrictions. Sometimes you can even get your money back if you need to return the ticket. Carefully read the fine print detailing penalties for changes and cancellations, **confirm your consolidator reservation with the airline,** and be sure to check restrictions, refund possibilities, and payment conditions

CONSOLIDATORS • Airfare Busters (5100 Westheimer St., Suite 550, Houston, TX 77056, tel. 713/961–5109 or 800/232–8783, fax 713/961–3385). **Globe Travel** (507 5th Ave., Suite 606, New York, NY 10017, tel. 212/843–9885 or 800/969–4562, fax 212/843–9889). **United States Air Consolidators Association** (925 L St., Suite 220, Sacramento, CA 95814, tel. 916/441–4166, fax 916/441–3520). **UniTravel** (1177 N. Warson Rd., St. Louis, MO 63132, tel. 314/569–2501 or 800/325-2222, fax 314/569–2503). **Up & Away Travel** (347 5th Ave., Suite 202, New York, NY 10016, tel. 212/889–2345 or 800/275–8001, fax 212/889–2350).

CONSIDER A CHARTER

Charters usually have the lowest fares but are not dependable. Departures are infrequent and seldom on time, check-in can be chaos, schedules are often erratic, and flights can be delayed for up to 48 hours or can be canceled for any reason up to 10 days before you're scheduled to leave. Moreover, itineraries and prices can change after you've booked your flight, so you must **be very careful to choose a legitimate charter carrier.** Don't commit to a charter operator that doesn't follow proper booking procedures. Be especially careful when buying a charter ticket. Read the fine print regarding refund policies. If you can't pay with a credit card, **make your check payable to a charter carrier's escrow account** (unless you're dealing with a travel agent, in which case his or her check should be made payable to the escrow account). The name of the bank should be in the charter contract.

CHARTER CARRIERS • DER Tours (tel. 800/782–2424). **MartinAir** (tel. 800/627–8462). **Tower Air** (tel. 800/348–6937). **Travel CUTS** (tel. 416/979–2406). **Council Travel** and **STA** (*see* Student Travel, *below*) also offer exclusively negotiated discount airfares on scheduled airlines.

GO AS A COURIER

Courier flights are simple: you sign a contract with a courier service to baby-sit their packages (often without ever laying eyes on them, let alone hands), and the courier company pays half or more of your airfare. On the day of departure, you arrive at the airport a few hours early, meet someone who hands you a ticket and customs forms, and off you go. After you land, you simply clear customs with the courier luggage, and deliver it to a waiting agent.

It's cheap and easy, but there are restrictions: Flights are usually booked only a week or two in advance—often only a few days in advance—and you are allowed carry-on luggage only, because the courier uses your checked luggage allowance to transport the shipment. You must return within one to four weeks, and times and destinations are limited. If you plan to travel with a companion, you'll probably have to travel a day apart. And you may be asked to pay a deposit, to be refunded after you have completed your assignment.

COURIER CONTACTS • **Discount Travel International** (169 W. 81st St., New York, NY 10024, tel. 212/362–3636, fax 212/362–3236). **Now Voyager** (tel. 212/431–1616, fax 212/334–5243).

AVOID GETTING BUMPED

Airlines routinely overbook planes, knowing that not everyone with a ticket will show up, but sometimes everyone does. When that happens, airlines ask for volunteers to give up their seats. In return these volunteers usually get a certificate for a free flight and are rebooked on the next flight out. If there are not enough volunteers, the airline must choose who will be denied boarding. The first to get bumped are passengers who checked in late and those flying on discounted tickets, so **get to the gate and check in as early as possible,** especially during peak periods.

Always **bring a photo ID to the airport.** You may be asked to show it before you are allowed to check in.

ENJOY THE FLIGHT

For more legroom, **request an emergency-aisle seat**; don't, however, sit in the row in front of the emergency aisle or in front of a bulkhead, where seats may not recline.

If you don't like airline food, **ask for special meals when booking.** These can be vegetarian, low-cholesterol, or kosher, for example.

To avoid jet lag try to maintain a normal routine while traveling. At night **get some sleep.** By day **eat light meals, drink water (not alcohol), and move about the cabin** to stretch your legs.

Some carriers prohibit smoking throughout their systems; others allow smoking only on certain routes or even certain departures from that route, so **contact your carrier regarding its smoking policy.**

COMPLAIN IF NECESSARY

If your baggage goes astray or your flight goes awry, complain right away. Most carriers require that you file a claim immediately.

AIRLINE COMPLAINTS • U.S. Department of Transportation **Aviation Consumer Protection Division** (C-75, Washington, DC 20590, tel. 202/366–2220). **Federal Aviation Administration (FAA) Consumer Hotline** (tel. 800/322–7873).

WITHIN CENTRAL AMERICA

Flying from one Central American city to another is quite cheap (although not when compared to the bargain-basement bus fares) and flights are regular. Air travel can save you heaps of time, a real plus if you are only visiting for a week or two. The **Taca Group** (tel. 800/840–0129) consists of a number of small airlines and covers all the major cities in the region, plus some of the bigger tourist attractions that have airfields. Government regulations ensure that all airlines charge the same rates. Buying a ticket is wonderfully uncomplicated; just go to a travel agent or the airline's office and pay your money. With the exception of holiday time, you don't have to book in advance at all.

The **Visit Central America Program** is a system of coupons offered by TACA that you can buy only outside Central America. Each coupon is good for one flight and you must buy between three and 10 coupons. The price depends on how many coupons you buy, where you start and end up, and the time of year, but usually you save up to 40%.

BUS TRAVEL

Bus travel in Central America is the functional equivalent of trains in Europe and private cars in the United States. They are a tremendous value (often less than a dollar for 100 km [60 mi]) and run with impressive regularity. However, comfort is minimal; roads tend to be bumpy, seats lumpy, and on longer trips, people grumpy. It's a bit of a gamble because seats on buses can be scarce during prime traveling hours, and drivers don't always stop where they should, although most depart promptly. In most places, you can flag down a bus on the road; if there's room, the driver will let you on and give you a pro-rated fare.

Most local buses are salvaged school buses from the United States; their new owners often like to paint them in wonderful displays of brash colors. The long-distance buses that run between countries are more expensive, but tend to have many more comforts including guaranteed seating, toilets, and (thank the Lord) air-conditioning.

Its a good idea to keep a close eye on your stuff on crowded buses; pickpockets like nothing better than to ply their trade in these cramped circumstances. But most passengers are very patient, friendly, and open to a chat to pass the time.

CAMERAS & COMPUTERS

EQUIPMENT PRECAUTIONS

Always **keep your film, tape, or computer disks out of the sun.** Carry an extra supply of batteries, and **be prepared to turn on your camera, camcorder, or laptop** to prove to security personnel that the device is real. Always **ask for hand inspection of film,** which becomes clouded after successive exposure to airport X-ray machines, and **keep videotapes and computer disks away from metal detectors.**

PHOTO HELP • Kodak Information Center (tel. 800/242–2424). *Kodak Guide to Shooting Great Travel Pictures,* available in bookstores or from Fodor's Travel Publications (tel. 800/533–6478; $16.50 plus $4 shipping).

CAR RENTALS

Renting cars is not common among Central American travelers. The reasons are clear: in capital cities, traffic is bad and car theft is rampant (look for guarded parking lots or hotels with lots); in rural areas, roads are often unpaved, muddy, and dotted with potholes; and the cost of gas can be steep. However, with your own wheels you don't have to worry about unreliable bus schedules, and you have a lot more control over your itinerary and the pace of your trip.

Decide which type of vehicle you want to rent: a *doble-tracción* (four-wheel-drive) vehicle is often essential to reach the more remote parts of Central America, especially during the rainy season. They can cost roughly twice as much as an economy car and should be booked well in advance. Most destinations are easily reached with a standard vehicle. **Reserve several weeks ahead of time if you plan to rent any kind of vehicle in peak season or during holidays.**

All the countries of Central America have local rental outfits as well as the major U.S. companies, and they may sometimes be cheaper and more friendly than the mulitnational competition. For a list of these agencies in each country, try the local yellow pages or tourist office.

Rates in Central America begin at around $30 a day and $150 a week for an economy car with air-conditioning, a manual transmission, and unlimited mileage.

MAJOR AGENCIES • Budget (tel. 800/527–0700; 0800/181181 in the U.K.). **Dollar** (tel. 800/800–4000; 0990/565656 in the U.K., where it is known as Eurodollar). **Hertz** (tel. 800/654–3001; 800/263–0600 in Canada; 0345/555888 in the U.K.; 03/9222–2523 in Australia; 03/358–6777 in New Zealand). **National InterRent** (tel. 800/227–3876; 0345/222525 in the U.K., where it is known as Europcar Inter-rent).

CUTTING COSTS

A recent proliferation of companies has led to competitive pricing in parts of Central America. **Look for discount coupons in the tourist papers** (and ads for rentals of privately owned vehicles as well) and call around for prices.

You can often get a better rate by booking your rental car from home. To get the best deal, **book through a travel agent who is willing to shop around.**

Also **ask your travel agent about a company's customer-service record.** How has the company responded to late plane arrivals and vehicle mishaps? Are there often lines at the rental counter? If you're traveling during a holiday period, does a confirmed reservation guarantee you a car?

INSURANCE

When driving a rented car you are generally responsible for any damage to or loss of the vehicle. You also are liable for any property damage or personal injury that you may cause while driving. Before you rent, **see what coverage you already have** under the terms of your personal auto-insurance policy and credit cards.

REQUIREMENTS

In all Central American countries your own driver's license is acceptable. You will also need a valid passport and credit card.

SURCHARGES

Before you pick up a car in one city and leave it in another, **ask about drop-off charges or one-way service fees,** which can be substantial. Note, too, that some rental agencies charge extra if you return the car before the time specified in your contract. To avoid a hefty refueling fee, **fill the tank just before you turn in the car,** but be aware that gas stations near the rental outlet may overcharge.

CAR TRAVEL

Driving in developing nations may be a bit of a challenge, but it's a great way to explore certain regions. Keep in mind that mountains and poor road conditions make most trips longer than you would expect. If you want to visit several far-flung areas, domestic flights may be a better option.

AUTO CLUBS

In Australia, **Australian Automobile Association** (tel. 06/247–7311). In Canada, **Canadian Automobile Association** (CAA, tel. 613/247–0117). In New Zealand, **New Zealand Automobile Association** (tel. 09/377–4660). In the United Kingdom, **Automobile Association** (AA, tel. 0990/500–600), **Royal Automobile Club** (RAC, tel. 0990/722–722 for membership, 0345/121–345 for insurance). In the United States, **American Automobile Association** (tel. 800/564–6222).

BETWEEN COUNTRIES IN CENTRAL AMERICA

It is possible to drive between countries in Central America, but it must be done in a private vehicle, since a car rented in one country cannot be taken into the next. There will often be a vehicle tax of up to $20 for taking your car across a border.

EMERGENCY SERVICES

See the Basics section for each chapter for emergency numbers. There are unreliable traffic police scattered around the region, but locals are usually very good about stopping for people with car trouble. Car-rental companies provide customers with a list of numbers to call in case of accidents or car trouble, although these may not always lead to a rapid response.

GASOLINE

Gasoline costs somewhere between $1.40 and $2.00 per gallon.

INSURANCE

Don't leave home without valid insurance: Check your personal auto insurance to see if it covers you; if not, you may have to insure through a Mexican company.

INSURANCE AGENTS • Sanborn's (tel. 210/686–0711), in McAllen, Texas, will write insurance for trips of any length south of the border—talk to "Mexico" Mike Nelson.

PARKING

Car theft is not rare in Central America. Be certain to **park overnight in a locked garage or lot,** because Central American insurance may hold you liable if your rental car is stolen. Most hotels, except for the least expensive, offer secure parking with a guard or locked gates.

ROAD CONDITIONS

Road conditions throughout Central America can be lamentable: you'll run into plenty of potholes and many stretches with no paving at all. But things are slowly improving, and if you stick to the main roads, you should be all right.

There are plenty of would-be Mario Andrettis on Central American highways; **be prepared for hare-brained passing on blind corners, tailgating, and failures to signal.** Watch out, too, for two-lane roads that feed into one-lane bridges with specified rights of way. And finally, look out for potholes, even in the smoothest sections of the best roads.

CONSUMER PROTECTION

Whenever possible, **pay with a major credit card** so you can cancel payment or get reimbursed if there's a problem, provided that you have documentation. This is the best way to pay, whether you're buying travel arrangements before your trip or shopping at your destination.

If you're doing business with a particular company for the first time, **contact your local Better Business Bureau and the attorney general's offices** in your state and the company's home state, as well. Have any complaints been filed?

Finally, if you're buying a package or tour, **always consider travel insurance** that includes default coverage (*see* Insurance, *below*).

BBBS • Council of Better Business Bureaus (4200 Wilson Blvd., Suite 800, Arlington, VA 22203, tel. 703/276–0100, fax 703/525–8277).

CUSTOMS & DUTIES

When shopping, **keep receipts** for all your purchases. Upon reentering your home country, **be ready to show customs officials what you've bought.** If you feel a duty is incorrect, appeal the assessment. If you object to the way your clearance was handled, get the inspector's badge number. In either case, first ask to see a supervisor, then write to the appropriate authorities, beginning with the port director at your point of entry.

IN AUSTRALIA

Australia residents who are 18 or older may bring back $A400 worth of souvenirs and gifts (including jewelry), 250 cigarettes or 250 grams of tobacco, and 1,125 ml of alcohol (including wine, beer, and spirits). Residents under 18 may bring back $A200 worth of goods.

INFORMATION • Australian Customs Service (Regional Director, Box 8, Sydney, NSW 2001, tel. 02/9213–2000 or 02/9213–4000).

IN CANADA

Canadian residents who have been out of Canada for at least seven days may bring in C$500 worth of goods duty-free. If you've been away less than seven days but more than 48 hours, the duty-free allowance drops to C$200; if your trip lasts 24–48 hours, the allowance is C$50. You may not pool allowances with family members. Goods claimed under the C$500 exemption may follow you by mail; those claimed under the lesser exemptions must accompany you. Alcohol and tobacco products may be included in the seven-day and 48-hour exemptions but not in the 24-hour exemption. If you meet the age requirements of the province or territory through which you reenter Canada, you may bring in, duty-free, 1.14 liters (40 imperial ounces) of wine or liquor *or* 24 12-ounce cans or bottles of beer or ale. If you are 16 or older, you may bring in, duty-free, 200 cigarettes and 50 cigars.

You may send an unlimited number of gifts worth up to C$60 each duty-free to Canada. Label the package UNSOLICITED GIFT—VALUE UNDER $60. Alcohol and tobacco are excluded.

INFORMATION • Revenue Canada (2265 St. Laurent Blvd. S, Ottawa, Ontario K1G 4K3, tel. 613/993–0534; 800/461–9999 in Canada).

IN NEW ZEALAND

Although greeted with a "Haere Mai" ("Welcome to New Zealand"), homeward-bound residents with goods to declare must present themselves for inspection. If you are 17 or older, you may bring back $700 worth of souvenirs and gifts. Your duty-free allowance also includes 4.5 liters of wine or beer; one

1,125-ml bottle of spirits; and either 200 cigarettes, 250 grams of tobacco, 50 cigars, or a combination of all three up to 250 grams.

INFORMATION • New Zealand Customs (Custom House, 50 Anzac Ave., Box 29, Auckland, New Zealand, tel. 09/359–6655).

IN THE UNITED KINGDOM

From countries outside the EU, including those of Central America, you may import, duty-free, 200 cigarettes or 50 cigars; 1 liter of spirits or 2 liters of fortified or sparkling wine or liqueurs; 2 liters of still table wine; 60 milliliters of perfume; 250 milliliters of toilet water; plus £136 worth of other goods, including gifts and souvenirs.

INFORMATION • HM Customs and Excise (Dorset House, Stamford St., London SE1 9NG, tel. 0171/202–4227).

IN THE UNITED STATES

U.S. residents may bring home $400 worth of foreign goods duty-free if they've been out of the country for at least 48 hours (and if they haven't used the $400 allowance or any part of it in the past 30 days).

U.S. residents 21 and older may bring back 1 liter of alcohol duty-free. In addition, regardless of your age, you are allowed 200 cigarettes and 100 non-Cuban cigars. Antiques, which the U.S. Customs Service defines as objects more than 100 years old, enter duty-free, as do original works of art done entirely by hand, including paintings, drawings, and sculptures.

You may also send packages home duty-free: up to $200 worth of goods for personal use, with a limit of one parcel per addressee per day (and no alcohol or tobacco products or perfume worth more than $5); label the package PERSONAL USE, and attach a list of its contents and their retail value. Do not label the package UNSOLICITED GIFT, or your duty-free exemption will drop to $100. Mailed items do not affect your duty-free allowance on your return.

INFORMATION • U.S. Customs Service (Inquiries, Box 7407, Washington, DC 20044, tel. 202/927–6724; complaints, Office of Regulations and Rulings, 1301 Constitution Ave. NW, Washington, DC 20229; registration of equipment, Resource Management, 1301 Constitution Ave. NW, Washington, DC 20229, tel. 202/927–0540).

DISABILITIES & ACCESSIBILITY

ACCESS IN CENTRAL AMERICA

Accessibility in Central America is extremely limited. Wheelchair ramps are practically nonexistent, and outside major cities, roads are unpaved, making wheelchair travel difficult. Exploring most of the area's attractions involves walking down cobblestone streets and, sometimes, steep trails and muddy paths, though there are some attractions that require little or no walking. Buses are not equipped to carry wheelchairs, so wheelchair users should hire a van to get about and have someone with them to help out. There is a growing awareness of the needs of people with disabilities, and some hotels and attractions have made the necessary provisions.

MAKING RESERVATIONS

When discussing accessibility with an operator or reservations agent, **ask hard questions.** Are there any stairs, inside *or* out? Are there grab bars next to the toilet *and* in the shower/tub? How wide is the doorway to the room? To the bathroom? For the most extensive facilities meeting the latest legal specifications, **opt for newer accommodations,** which are more likely to have been designed with access in mind. Older buildings or ships may have more limited facilities. Be sure to **discuss your needs before booking.**

TRANSPORTATION

Central America presents serious challenges to travelers with disabilities. Although the more developed areas can be managed in a wheelchair, most rural areas are tougher. The tour company Vaya con Silla de Ruedas, Spanish for Go with Wheelchair, provides transportation and guided tours for travelers in wheelchairs in Costa Rica and neighboring countries and specializes in accessibility, with emphasis on comfort and safety.

TOUR COMPANY • Vaya con Silla de Ruedas (Apdo. 1146-2050, San Pedro Montes de Oca, Costa Rica, tel. 225–8561, 253–0931).

COMPLAINTS

Disability Rights Section (U.S. Department of Justice, Civil Rights Division, Box 66738, Washington, DC 20035–6738, tel. 202/514–0301 or 800/514–0301, TTY 202/514–0383 or 800/514–0383) for general complaints. **Aviation Consumer Protection Division** (*see* Air Travel, *above*) for airline-related problems. **Civil Rights Office** (U.S. Department of Transportation, Departmental Office of Civil Rights, S-30, 400 7th St. SW, Room 10215, Washington, DC 20590, tel. 202/366–4648 or 202/366–9371) for problems with surface transportation.

TRAVEL AGENCIES & TOUR OPERATORS

As a whole, the travel industry has become more aware of the needs of travelers with disabilities. In the United States, the Americans with Disabilities Act requires that travel firms serve the needs of all travelers. Note, though, that some agencies and operators specialize in making travel arrangements for individuals and groups with disabilities.

TRAVELERS WITH MOBILITY PROBLEMS • **Access Adventures** (206 Chestnut Ridge Rd., Rochester, NY 14624, tel. 716/889–9096), run by a former physical-rehabilitation counselor. **Accessible Journeys** (35 W. Sellers Ave., Ridley Park, PA 19078, tel. 610/521–0339 or 800/846–4537), for escorted tours exclusively for travelers with mobility impairments. **Flying Wheels Travel** (143 W. Bridge St., Box 382, Owatonna, MN 55060, tel. 507/451–5005 or 800/535–6790), a travel agency specializing in customized tours and itineraries worldwide. **Hinsdale Travel Service** (201 E. Ogden Ave., Suite 100, Hinsdale, IL 60521, tel. 630/325–1335), a travel agency that benefits from the advice of wheelchair traveler Janice Perkins.

DISCOUNTS & DEALS

Be a smart shopper and **compare all your options** before making any choice. A plane ticket bought with a promotional coupon may not be cheaper than the least expensive fare from a discount ticket agency. For high-price travel purchases, such as packages or tours, keep in mind that what you get is just as important as what you save. Just because something is cheap doesn't mean it's a bargain.

CLUBS & COUPONS

Many companies sell discounts in the form of travel clubs and coupon books, but these cost money. You must use participating advertisers to get a deal, and only after you recoup the initial membership cost or book price do you begin to save. If you plan to use the club or coupons frequently, you may save considerably. Before signing up, find out what discounts you get for free.

DISCOUNT CLUBS • **Entertainment Travel Editions** (2125 Butterfield Rd., Troy, MI 48084, tel. 800/445–4137; $20–$51, depending on destination). **Great American Traveler** (Box 27965, Salt Lake City, UT 84127, tel. 801/974–3033 or 800/548–2812; $49.95 per year). **Moment's Notice Discount Travel Club** (7301 New Utrecht Ave., Brooklyn, NY 11204, tel. 718/234–6295; $25 per year, single or family). **Privilege Card International** (237 E. Front St., Youngstown, OH 44503, tel. 330/746–5211 or 800/236–9732; $74.95 per year). **Sears's Mature Outlook** (Box 9390, Des Moines, IA 50306, tel. 800/336–6330; $19.95 per year). **Travelers Advantage** (CUC Travel Service, 3033 S. Parker Rd., Suite 1000, Aurora, CO 80014, tel. 800/548–1116 or 800/648–4037; $59.95 per year, single or family). **Worldwide Discount Travel Club** (1674 Meridian Ave., Miami Beach, FL 33139, tel. 305/534–2082; $50 per year family, $40 single).

CREDIT-CARD BENEFITS

When you use your credit card to make travel purchases you may get free travel-accident insurance, collision-damage insurance, and medical or legal assistance, depending on the card and the bank that issued it. American Express, MasterCard, and Visa provide one or more of these services, so **get a copy of your credit card's travel-benefits policy.** If you are a member of an auto club, always **ask hotel and car-rental reservation agents about auto-club discounts.** Some clubs offer additional discounts on tours, cruises, and admission to attractions.

DISCOUNT RESERVATIONS

To save money, **look into discount-reservations services with toll-free numbers,** which use their buying power to get a better price on hotels, airline tickets, even car rentals. When booking a room, **always call the hotel's local toll-free number** (if one is available) rather than the central reservations number—you'll often get a better price. Always ask about special packages or corporate rates.

When shopping for the best deal on hotels and car rentals, **look for guaranteed exchange rates,** which protect you against a falling dollar. With your rate locked in, you won't pay more, even if the price goes up in the local currency.

AIRLINE TICKETS • Tel. 800/Fly–4–less.

PACKAGE DEALS

Packages and guided tours can save you money, but don't confuse the two. When you buy a package, your travel remains independent, just as though you had planned and booked the trip yourself. Fly/drive packages, which combine airfare and car rental, are often a good deal. The local airlines in Central America offer multitrip passes that can save you money if you intend hopping from country to country (*see* Air Travel, *above*).

ECOTOURISM

Ecotourism, green tourism, environmental tourism: these buzzwords and catch phrases have been flying around Costa Rica, Panama, and Belize for more than a decade. Many of the tour companies currently operating in these three countries have evolved a high level of environmental awareness in their business practices. More recently the ideas have spread to the other, less tourist-developed countries in the region. **Find out whether or not a tour company you're interested in practices "eco-friendly" policies,** such as hiring and training local people as guides, drivers, managers, and office workers; teaching people as much as possible about the plant and animal life, the geography, and the history they are experiencing; controlling the numbers of people allowed daily onto a given site; restoring watersheds or anything else damaged by trail-building, visitors, or overuse; or discouraging wildlife feeding or any other unnatural or disruptive behavior (i.e., making loud noises to scare birds into flight). All of this can mitigate the effects of intense tourism; and, after all, it is better to have 100 people walking through a forest than to cut the forest down.

ELECTRICITY

With the exception of Belize, the electrical current in Central America is 110 volts (AC), and plugs are the same as in the United States.

To use your U.S.-purchased electric-powered equipment in Belize, **bring a converter and adapter.** The electrical current in Belize is 220 volts, 50 cycles alternating current (AC); some wall outlets in Belize take Continental-type plugs, with two round prongs.

If your appliances are dual-voltage, you'll need only an adapter. Don't use 110-volt outlets, marked FOR SHAVERS ONLY, for high-wattage appliances such as blow-dryers. Most laptops operate equally well on 110 and 220 volts and so require only an adapter.

FOOD

Although Central American cattle rustlers are very proud of their beef, and the general population consumes lots of it, vegetarians can find refuge in produce markets, Chinese restaurants, and a smattering of vegetarian restaurants. Expensive restaurants are spreading throughout the region, but price is certainly not a guarantee of quality. Often the pricier places try to do an "international menu," which, more often than not, turns out to be a bland selection of imitation gringo meat and fish dishes. You have to search for the gems, but they are there, especially when it comes to seafood. Lunch is the day's biggest meal. The *comida típica* or *comida corriente* usually consists of a combination of rice, beans, eggs or meat, greens, and a beverage. A plethora of seafood dishes and other specialities ensures that you'll never get stuck in a beans-and-rice rut.

GAY & LESBIAN TRAVEL

Harassment of gays and lesbians is infrequent in Central America, but so are public displays of affection—discretion is advised. As a result of its history of tolerance, Costa Rica has attracted many gays from other Latin American nations and, consequently, has a large gay community. The rest of the region, on the other hand, doesn't have as extensive a gay population, and gays should practice discretion.

GAY- AND LESBIAN-FRIENDLY TOUR OPERATORS • Toto Tours (1326 W. Albion Ave., Suite 3W, Chicago, IL 60626, tel. 773/274–8686 or 800/565–1241), for groups.

GAY- AND LESBIAN-FRIENDLY TRAVEL AGENCIES • Corniche Travel (8721 Sunset Blvd., Suite 200, West Hollywood, CA 90069, tel. 310/854–6000 or 800/429–8747). **Islanders Kennedy Travel** (183 W. 10th St., New York, NY 10014, tel. 212/242–3222 or 800/988–1181). **Now Voyager** (4406 18th St., San Francisco, CA 94114, tel. 415/626–1169 or 800/255–6951). **Skylink Travel and Tour** (3577 Moorland Ave., Santa Rosa, CA 95407, tel. 707/585–8355 or 800/225–5759), serving lesbian travelers. **Yellowbrick Road** (1500 W. Balmoral Ave., Chicago, IL 60640, tel. 773/561–1800 or 800/642–2488).

HEALTH

For up-to-the-minute information about health risks and disease precautions in all parts of the world, call the U.S. Centers for Disease Control's 24-hour **International Travelers' Hotline** (tel. 404/332–4559). You can listen to recorded information or receive faxes of current reports. The **Department of State's Citizens Emergency Center** (Bureau of Consular Affairs, Room 4811, N.S., U.S. Dept. of State, Washington, DC 20520, tel. 202/647–5225, modem 202/647–9225, or 202/647–3000 for return fax information) provides written and recorded travel advisories. The "return fax line" offers you several prompts and will return information immediately to your fax number.

BEFORE YOU GO

Use your upcoming trip as an excuse to update routine immunizations. These include measles, mumps, rubella, diphtheria, tetanus, pertussis, polio, haemophilus influenza, and hepatitis A and B. You should also consider updating your pneumococcal vaccines. Immune globulin (IG) is suggested if you are traveling to underdeveloped countries with dubious sanitation. Other required vaccines will be determined by your specific destinations and a careful weighing of the vaccines' effectiveness versus their side effects. Check with your physician, or even better, a travel clinic (sometimes located in international airports) for details and a complete list of all the shots you need. If you're not familiar with a travel clinic in your area, ask your doctor to suggest one.

Finally, compared to the risks of malaria and dengue fever, sunburn may not seem very important, but you're much more likely to suffer from a painful sunburn than any exotic disease. Even if you have a dark complexion, bring plenty of powerful sunscreen, and slather it on at every opportunity.

DISEASES FROM FOOD AND WATER

In Central America disease spread through contaminated food and water is the primary cause of illness to travelers. Standards vary throughout the region. Although the Costa Rican and Panamanian food and water supplies are sanitary for the most part, in rural areas there is some risk posed by the contamination of drinking water, fresh fruit, and vegetables by fecal matter. Throughout the rest of the region, **watch what you eat and drink.**

CHOLERA • This distressing intestinal infection is caused by a bacterium carried in bad water or food. Cholera is characterized by profuse diarrhea, vomiting, cramping, and dehydration. If you think you may have contracted cholera, seek medical attention right away. Most people recuperate with simple fluid and electrolyte-replacement treatment. Cholera is relatively quiet in the region, but outbreaks are common in Guatemala and El Salvador and can happen in any country.

Like diarrhea, cholera is best avoided by eating only cooked foods that are still warm; drinking only bottled, boiled, or chemically treated water; and peeling fresh fruits. Avoid seafood, food sold by street vendors, and ice. The vaccine, in the form of a series of injections, is only 50% effective, and the U.S. Centers for Disease Control does not recommend it as a standard vaccine for all travelers.

DIARRHEA • For many people, traveling in Latin America means an extended case of the ever-unpopular *turista* (tourists' disease). Contaminated food and drink are the major causes. Diarrhea, sometimes accompanied by nausea, bloating, and general malaise, usually lasts from a few days up to a week. The best way to treat it is to take in lots of fluids (not dairy products). Drugs such as Bactrim and Septra (available in the United States) may help shorten the time you suffer. Lomotil or Imodium may decrease the number of trips you make to the toilet; however, if you have a serious infection, these drugs can cause more serious complications. In severe cases, doctors will suggest an oral rehydration liquid that you can concoct yourself by mixing purified water with a few pinches of salt and a couple of teaspoons of sugar. If you're hungry, stick to small portions of dry toast or rice; avoid greasy, spicy foods. The best cure for diarrhea is just to let it pass, but if you are very uncomfortable or need to travel, ask a local doctor for prescription drugs or tell a pharmacist you need something for turista. If you maintain a fever over 102°F, if you have persistent vomiting, if you cannot rehydrate, if your stool is bloody, or if your bout lasts longer than a week, seek immediate medical attention.

To avoid this nasty annoyance, **be sure to drink only boiled (20 minutes in higher elevations) or chemically disinfected water.** Don't even brush your teeth with water that hasn't been treated. You can purchase water disinfectants such as Globaline and Potable-Aqua in the United States before you leave. If your boiled water seems flat and tasteless, add a pinch of salt to bring back some taste. And, it may seem self-evident, but do not add untreated ice cubes to boiled water.

Also **be careful in selecting your foods.** Raw foods are often contaminated, so be wary of salads, uncooked produce, milk, and milk products. Meats and shellfish are usually suspect as well. To be on the safe side, **peel fruit yourself, don't eat any cooked foods that have been allowed to cool,** and **avoid raw dishes** such as ceviche. Many fish, such as reef fish, red snapper, amberjack, grouper, sea bass, barracuda, and puffer fish, should be avoided at all times due to the high levels of toxins in the areas they inhabit. Think twice about consuming suspect foods just because you see people of the region doing so. These folks may have developed immune systems to combat sicknesses you aren't prepared for, or they may live with chronic illness themselves. That said, if you spend your whole trip consuming only what appears sterile, you'll miss out. The best strategy is to **give your body a little time** to get used to the new challenges it faces by exercising restraint during the first week or so of your trip.

HEPATITIS A • Hepatitis A is a viral infection that attacks the liver. It is transmitted through contaminated food and water or between people. Hepatitis A causes exhaustion, fever, loss of appetite, queasiness, dark urine, jaundice, vomiting, light stools, and achiness. It is prevalent in Central America, especially in rural areas, and there is no specific treatment available.

Be sure to drink only treated water and thoroughly cooked foods. It is also a good idea to receive a dose of immune globulin (formerly known as gamma globulin) before traveling. **Check with your doctor regarding dosage requirements** for the length of your stay. Also, when you are in another country, be aware that what they advertise as immune globulin may not be equivalent to what you would receive in the United States.

TYPHOID FEVER • Typhoid, a bacterial infection, can be spread through contaminated food and water and through contact with contaminated people. Fever, headaches, exhaustion, loss of appetite, and constipation all indicate an onslaught of typhoid. If you think you have contracted typhoid, seek medical attention immediately. Typhoid is a risk throughout Central America, but it is most common in Mexico.

A typhoid vaccine is available in oral form, taken over a week, and as a series of injections spread over a month. The vaccine is only about 70%–90% effective, so it is important to stick to bottled, boiled, or treated water and foods that have been cooked thoroughly.

INSECT-BORNE DISEASES

Central America is teeming with mosquitoes, flies, fleas, ticks and lice—all ready to give travelers a melange of foul diseases. For starters, you should reduce your exposure to mosquitoes by using mosquito netting and wearing clothes that cover most of your body. Beyond that, **bring the strongest insect repellent you can find and use it.** The CDC recommends products with DEET—get the highest percentage available. Other nontopical spray insecticides like Perrnethrin are worth a try. You'll probably still get nailed, but why surrender to the critters without a fight?

If all of this sounds a bit too much like chemical warfare to you, you can try a few other options. Thanks to modern science, we know mosquitoes don't like the taste of vitamin B. By megadosing (using two to four times the recommended daily allowance) on B-complex vitamins daily for at least a month before your trip, you'll put enough of the stuff in your blood to make you a less delectable dish than your friends. It won't completely solve the problem, but most people who try it notice the difference. Be warned, though, that taking large doses of vitamin B (or any other vitamin) can have side effects and may harm you in the long run. Your urine will be bright orange, too. Another option is to apply Avon Skin-So-Soft Moisturizer, which bugs can't stand. The Marines have been using it for years.

DENGUE FEVER • Dengue fever is transmitted by the *aedes* mosquito, which, unlike other mosquitoes, is most active during the day and around dawn and dusk. Dengue usually flourishes during and after rainy seasons. It is most common in urban areas, especially below an elevation of 4,000 feet, but it's found in rural areas as well.

Dengue manifests itself suddenly with flu-like symptoms, a high fever, severe headache, joint and muscle aches, nausea, and vomiting. About three or four days after the fever appears, a rash develops. There is no vaccination for dengue, and treatment consists simply of rest, fluid intake, and over-the-counter fever-reducing medications. Avoid aspirin. Dengue lasts for up to 10 days, and full recovery may take as long as a month. There are more intense and rare forms of dengue that are characterized by faintness, shock, and general bleeding. If you develop any of these symptoms during your trip or up to a month after your return, visit your doctor immediately.

Since there is no vaccine, the best way to avoid dengue is to protect yourself from mosquito attacks: wear clothes that do not leave you exposed, sleep under mosquito netting, and slather on that insect repellent.

MALARIA • Malaria thrives year-round in most areas of Central America. It is transmitted by the bites of *anopheles* mosquitoes, which are out and hungry from sundown to sunup. Malaria usually resembles a feverish flu at the onset. The symptoms can develop to include chills, aches, and fatigue. It can lead to anemia, kidney failure, coma, and death if neglected. If you experience any of the telltale symptoms while traveling or up to a year after exposure, seek medical attention.

Unfortunately, the antimalarial drugs available aren't 100% effective. If you are going to a risk area, chloroquine or mefloquine is the recommended deterrent. Most travelers take chloroquine, but if you plan to travel east of the Canal Zone in Panama or to the San Blas Islands, where mosquitoes are resistant to this treatment, mefloquine is preferable. Both drug regimens begin two weeks before you enter the malarious zone; ask your doctor about side effects before starting either one.

YELLOW FEVER • Yellow fever, a viral disease spread by the bite of evening-feeding mosquitoes, is a very rare problem for tourists these days. Characterized by headaches, chills, fever, and vomiting, yellow fever can develop into jaundice, internal bleeding, and kidney failure, and in about 5% of all cases death occurs. There is no specific drug to treat this disease, so you may want to consider getting a vaccine before you leave.

Some countries require yellow fever vaccination certificates before allowing entry, depending on the country you are traveling from and the status of yellow fever at your destination. Fewer than 5% of those vaccinated experience the side effects of headaches and muscle aches. Still, you should consult your doctor before receiving this one-dose shot. These aches and pains show up 5 to 10 days after the vaccine has been administered, so get your shot and certificate at least 10 days before you plan to enter the country. This will help you get through the side-effect window, and your certificate won't be valid until this 10-day period passes. Your certificate is good for 10 years, and you must carry it with you when traveling. Currently, the countries of Central America do not require a yellow-fever certificate unless you are traveling from a country infected with the disease.

OTHER INSECT-BORNE DISEASES • If we haven't yet convinced you to avoid insect bites like the plague, so to speak, here are a few of the other diseases (albeit rare) that you can pick up in Central America. **Flariasis** is contracted from mosquitoes that transfer a parasitic worm, which then inhabits the lymph nodes and tissues. It can occasionally lead to enlargement of the extremities (elephantiasis). There is no vaccine available.

Leishmaniasis is contracted through the bite of a sand fly. It causes fever, weakness, and in some cases a swollen spleen or skin sores. There is no vaccine, but treatment is available, so seek medical attention if you encounter these symptoms. **American trypanosomiasis** or **Chagas' disease** is contracted from the excrement of the reduviid bug, also known as the cone nose assassin or kissing bug. This bug lives in mud, adobe, and thatched abodes. You may have no symptoms or only a fever in the early stages of this disease, but it could lead to heart disease, an enlarged intestine, or possible paralysis. There is no vaccine available, and treatment is limited, so avoid staying in buildings infested with this nasty critter.

Oropouche virus disease, carried by gnats, is distinguished by a sudden high fever, a severe headache, aches and pains, nausea, and diarrhea. There is no vaccine, and treatment is limited. To date, Panama is the only Central American country reporting this disease.

OTHER AFFLICTIONS

PARASITES • In addition to all the diseases and viruses Central America has to offer, parasites abound. They are transmitted through bad food and water, through direct contact with infected water and soil, or by insect bites. Again, take precautions against insect bites, drink and eat foods you know are safe, and be sure to wear shoes to avoid direct penetration.

RABIES • Rabies is a concern in most Central American countries. It is a viral infection (contracted by the bite of a rabid animal) that attacks the central nervous system. In Central America, do not handle any animals, and be especially wary of dogs. If you are bitten, wash the wound thoroughly with soap and water and seek immediate medical attention. You can be vaccinated before you leave the United States, but you'll still have to seek medical attention and get injections after you are bitten. The vaccine only lessens the amount of post-exposure care.

MEDICAL PLANS

No one plans to get sick while traveling, but it happens, so **consider signing up with a medical-assistance company.** Members get doctor referrals, emergency evacuation or repatriation, 24-hour telephone hot lines for medical consultation, cash for emergencies, and other personal and legal assistance. Coverage varies by plan, so **review the benefits of each carefully.**

MEDICAL-ASSISTANCE COMPANIES • **International SOS Assistance** (8 Neshaminy Interplex, Suite 207, Trevose, PA 19053, tel. 215/245–4707 or 800/523–6586; 12 Chemin Riantbosson, 1217 Meyrin 1, Geneva, Switzerland, tel. 4122/785–6464; 10 Anson Rd., 14-07/08 International Plaza, Singapore, 079903, tel. 65/226–3936).

INSURANCE

Travel insurance is the best way to **protect yourself against financial loss.** The most useful plan is a comprehensive policy that includes coverage for trip cancellation and interruption, default, trip delay, and medical expenses (with a waiver for preexisting conditions).

Without insurance, you will lose all or most of your money if you cancel your trip, regardless of the reason. Default insurance covers you if your tour operator, airline, or cruise line goes out of business. Trip-delay covers unforeseen expenses that you may incur due to bad weather or mechanical delays. It's important to compare the fine print regarding trip-delay coverage when comparing policies.

For overseas travel, one of the most important components of travel insurance is its medical coverage. Supplemental health insurance will pick up the cost of your medical bills should you get sick or injured while traveling. U.S. residents should note that Medicare generally does not cover health-care costs outside the United States, nor do many privately issued policies. Residents of the United Kingdom can buy an annual travel-insurance policy valid for most vacations taken during the year in which the coverage is purchased. If you are pregnant or have a preexisting condition, make sure you're covered. British citizens should buy extra medical coverage when traveling overseas, according to the Association of British Insurers. Australian travelers should buy travel insurance, including extra medical coverage, whenever they go abroad, according to the Insurance Council of Australia.

Always **buy travel insurance directly from the insurance company**; if you buy it from a cruise line, airline, or tour operator that goes out of business, you probably will not be covered for the agency or operator's default, a major risk. Before you make any purchase, **review your existing health and home-owner's policies** to find out whether they cover expenses incurred while traveling.

TRAVEL INSURERS • In the United States, **Access America** (6600 W. Broad St., Richmond, VA 23230, tel. 804/285–3300 or 800/284–8300). **Travel Guard International** (1145 Clark St., Stevens Point, WI 54481, tel. 715/345–0505 or 800/826–1300). In Canada, **Mutual of Omaha** (Travel Division, 500 University Ave., Toronto, Ontario M5G 1V8, tel. 416/598–4083; 800/268–8825 in Canada).

INSURANCE INFORMATION • In the United Kingdom, **Association of British Insurers** (51 Gresham St., London EC2V 7HQ, tel. 0171/600–3333). In Australia, the **Insurance Council of Australia** (tel. 613/9614–1077).

LODGING

Lodging, although often a bargain in Central America, will probably be your second-largest expense after transportation. Central American lodging is a far cry from that in the United States, where your only choices are usually a bland motel or a posh hotel. In Central America the possibilities range from dirt-cheap cabanas by the beach to multistory luxury hotels in the capitals, plus pretty much everything in between. If there is one shortage, it might be in the quality medium-price range. If you'll be arriving during the high season, you may want to **reserve your first few nights' lodging in advance** to avoid the stress of looking for a room on a few hours of sleep.

CAMPING

Many, though not all, national parks have camping areas. Some popular beaches have private camping areas with bathrooms and showers. If you camp on the beach or in other unguarded areas, you risk being robbed if you turn your back on your tent. Also, be warned; there's nothing the insect world loves more than a couple of plump, unprotected campers.

HOSTELS

Compared to the rest of the world, Central America has a real dearth of hostels, but there are a few, and they're usually well worth the effort it takes to find them. No matter what your age, you can **save on lodging costs by staying at hostels.** In some 5,000 locations in more than 70 countries around the world, Hostelling International (HI), the umbrella group for a number of national youth hostel associations, offers single-sex, dorm-style beds and, at many hostels, "couples" rooms and family accommodations. Membership in any HI national hostel association, open to travelers of all ages, allows you to stay in HI-affiliated hostels at member rates (one-year membership is about $25 for adults; hostels run about $10–$25 per night). Members also have priority if the hostel is full; they're eligible for discounts around the world, even on rail and bus travel in some countries.

HOSTEL ORGANIZATIONS • Hostelling International—American Youth Hostels (733 15th St. NW, Suite 840, Washington, DC 20005, tel. 202/783–6161). **Hostelling International—Canada** (400-205 Catherine St., Ottawa, Ontario K2P 1C3, tel. 613/237–7884,). **Youth Hostel Association of England and Wales** (Trevelyan House, 8 St. Stephen's Hill, St. Albans, Hertfordshire AL1 2DY, tel. 01727/855215 or 01727/845047); membership in the United States $25, in Canada C$26.75, in the United Kingdom £9.30.

HOTELS

There are a few big, luxury hotels in the major cities of each country and also at the biggest tourist resorts, but most hotels are smaller affairs, offering more personalized service. Remember that most hotels drop their rates during the "green season": from May to December.

MAIL

Mail from the States or Europe can take two–three weeks to arrive in a Central American country (occasionally it never does); within these countries, mail service is even less reliable. Outgoing mail is marginally quicker, especially when sent from the capitals. **Always use airmail for overseas cards and letters**; delivery may take anywhere from five days to two weeks or more. Mail theft is a chronic problem, so **do not mail checks, money, or anything else of value.**

RECEIVING MAIL

You can have mail sent to your hotel or use poste restante at the post office (Lista de Correos). Most Central Americans have to go to the post office to pick up their mail, because of the absence of house-to-house service. Apartado (abbreviated *apdo.*), which you will see in many addresses, means post-office box.

Anyone with an American Express card or traveler's checks can have mail sent to them at the American Express offices in major cities.

A faster and more functional alternative for business letters, particularly those confirming reservations and the like, is the fax machine, which is nearly ubiquitous throughout the region.

If you need to send important documents, checks, or other noncash valuables, you can use one of the courier services, such as Federal Express, DHL, or one of the less expensive airline courier services.

MONEY

CREDIT & DEBIT CARDS

Major credit cards are accepted at most of the larger hotels and more expensive restaurants throughout Central America. As the phone systems improves and expands, many budget hotels, restaurants, and other facilities are accepting credit cards. Still, **don't count on using plastic**—it is essential, especially when traveling away from the major cities, to **carry enough cash or traveler's checks** for the many businesses without phones or credit-card capabilities. Some hotels, restaurants, tour companies, and other businesses will give you a 5%–15% discount if you pay cash.

Should you use a credit card or a debit card when traveling? Both have benefits. A credit card allows you to delay payment and gives you certain rights as a consumer (*see* Consumer Protection, *above*). A debit card, also known as a check card, deducts funds directly from your checking account and helps you stay within your budget. When you want to rent a car, though, you may still need an old-fashioned credit card. Although you can always *pay* for your car with a debit card, some agencies will not allow you to *reserve* a car with a debit card.

Otherwise, the two types of plastic are virtually the same. Both will get you cash advances at ATMs worldwide if your card is properly programmed with your personal identification number (PIN). For use in Central America, your PIN must be four digits long. Both offer excellent, wholesale exchange rates. And both protect you against unauthorized use if the card is lost or stolen. Your liability is limited to $50, as long as you report the card missing.

CURRENCY

All prices in this guide are quoted in U.S. dollars, because of constant inflation and shifting exchange rates in the region.

EXCHANGING MONEY

For the most favorable rates, **change money through banks.** Although fees charged for ATM transactions may be higher abroad than at home, Cirrus and Plus exchange rates are excellent, because they are based on wholesale rates offered only by major banks. You won't do as well at exchange booths in airports or rail and bus stations, in hotels, in restaurants, or in stores, although you may find their hours more convenient. To avoid lines at airport exchange booths, **get a bit of local currency before you leave home.**

It's best to **avoid people on the city streets who offer to change money:** most of the people who change money at the airports are legit, althought they might not be above shortchanging you. The money changers in the streets of major cities are notorious for shortchanging people and passing counterfeit bills.

EXCHANGE SERVICES • Chase *Currency to Go* (tel. 800/935–9935; 935–9935 in NY, NJ, and CT). **International Currency Express** (tel. 888/842–0880 on the East Coast; 888/278–6628 on the West Coast). **Thomas Cook Currency Services** (tel. 800/287–7362 for telephone orders and retail locations).

GETTING CASH

Cash advances on your credit card are available from many ATMs in cities and through Credomatic offices throughout the region.

There are ATMs connected to the Cirrus system in many of the major cities, especially in San José and Panama City. The Plus system is less prevalent, but can be found with a little effort.

ATM LOCATIONS • Cirrus (tel. 800/424–7787). **Plus** (tel. 800/843–7587) for locations in the U.S. and Canada, or visit your local bank.

REPORTING LOST CARDS • American Express (tel. 336/393–1111 collect to United States). **Diners club** (tel. 303/799–1504 collect to United States). **MasterCard** (tel. 0800/011–0184 toll-free to United States). **Visa** (tel. 0800/011–0030 toll-free to United States; tel. 410/581–9994 collect to United States).

TRAVELER'S CHECKS

Do you need traveler's checks? It depends on where you're headed. If you're going to rural areas and small towns, go with cash; traveler's checks are best used in cities. Lost or stolen checks can usually be replaced within 24 hours. To ensure a speedy refund, buy your own traveler's checks—don't let someone else pay for them: irregularities like this can cause delays. The person who bought the checks should make the call to request a refund.

Travelers who have an american express card and money in a U.S. checking account can purchase traveler's checks at the American express offices in the major cities; there's a 1% service charge.

PACKING

LUGGAGE

How many carry-on bags you can bring with you is up to the airline. Most allow two, but the limit is often reduced to one on certain flights. Gate agents will take excess baggage—including bags they deem oversize—from you as you board and add it to checked luggage. To avoid this situation, try to make sure that everything you carry aboard will fit under your seat. Since big, bulky baggage attracts the attention of gate agents and flight attendants on a busy flight, make sure your carry-on is really a carry-on. Finally, a carry-on that's long and narrow is more likely to remain unnoticed than one that's wide and squarish.

If you are flying internationally, note that baggage allowances may be determined not by piece but by weight—generally 88 pounds (40 kilograms) in first class, 66 pounds (30 kilograms) in business class, and 44 pounds (20 kilograms) in economy.

Airline liability for baggage is limited to $1,250 per person on flights within the united states. On international flights it amounts to $9.07 per pound or $20 per kilogram for checked baggage (roughly $640 per 70-pound bag) and $400 per passenger for unchecked baggage. You can buy additional coverage at check-in for about $10 per $1,000 of coverage, but it excludes a rather extensive list of items, shown on your airline ticket.

Before departure, **itemize your bags' contents** and their worth, and label the bags with your name, address, and phone number. (If you use your home address, cover it so potential thieves can't see it readily.) Inside each bag, **pack a copy of your itinerary.** At check-in, **make sure that each bag is correctly tagged** with the destination airport's three-letter code. If your bags arrive damaged or fail to arrive at all, file a written report with the airline before leaving the airport.

PACKING LIST

Pack light: baggage carts are scarce at airports, and luggage restrictions are tight. Bring comfortable, hand-washable clothing. T-shirts and shorts are acceptable near the beach and in heavily touristed areas. Loose-fitting long-sleeve shirts and pants are good in smaller towns (where immodest attire is frowned upon) and to protect your skin from the ferocious sun and mosquitoes. **Bring a large hat to block the sun from your face and neck.** Pack a light sweater or jacket for cool nights and early mornings in higher areas and trips up volcanoes. Sturdy sneakers or hiking boots are essential, especially if you plan to do a lot of sightseeing and hiking. Waterproof hiking sandals or other footwear that lets your feet breathe are good for strolling about town, and also for beach walking, fording streams, and navigating the myriad mud holes you'll find on rain- and cloud-forest trails. Of course, you should be careful about leaving your feet exposed to mosquitoes.

Insect repellent, sunscreen, sunglasses, and umbrellas (during the rainy season) are musts. Other handy items—especially if you will be traveling on your own or camping—include toilet paper, facial tissues, a plastic water bottle, and a flashlight (for occasional power outages or use at campsites). Snorkelers should consider bringing their own equipment unless traveling light is a priority, though gear can be rented at most beach resorts. Some beaches do not have shade trees, so if you're planning a stay at the beach, you might consider investing in a large beach umbrella or a shade-making tarpaulin. For long-term stays in remote rural areas, *see* health, *above.*

In your carry-on luggage **bring an extra pair of eyeglasses or contact lenses** and **enough of any medication you take** to last the entire trip. You may also want your doctor to write a spare prescription using the drug's generic name, since brand names may vary from country to country. **Never put prescription drugs or valuables in luggage to be checked.** To avoid customs delays, carry medications in their original packaging. And don't forget to copy down and carry addresses of offices that handle refunds of lost traveler's checks.

PASSPORTS & VISAS

When traveling internationally, **carry a passport even if you don't need one** (it's always the best form of id), and **make two photocopies of the data page** (one for someone at home and another for you, carried separately from your passport). If you lose your passport, promptly call the nearest embassy or consulate and the local police.

PASSPORT OFFICES

The best time to apply for a passport or to renew is during the fall and winter. Before any trip, be sure to check your passport's expiration date and, if necessary, renew it as soon as possible. (Some countries won't allow you to enter on a passport that's due to expire in six months or less.)

AUSTRALIAN CITIZENS • Australian Passport Office (tel. 131–232).

CANADIAN CITIZENS • Passport Office (tel. 819/994–3500 or 800/567–6868).

NEW ZEALAND CITIZENS • **New Zealand Passport Office** (tel. 04/494–0700 for information on how to apply, 0800/727–776 for information on applications already submitted).

U.K. CITIZENS • **London Passport Office** (tel. 0990/21010), for fees and documentation requirements and to request an emergency passport.

U.S. CITIZENS • **National Passport Information Center** (tel. 900/225–5674; calls are charged at 35¢ per minute for automated service, $1.05 per minute for operator service).

STUDENT TRAVEL

Central America is a fantastic place for students and youths on a budget. Although prices are on the rise, it is still possible to travel on less than $20 a day. With the exception of Costa Rica, there are not that many hostels in the region, but it has more than its share of inexpensive hotels. One of the cheapest ways to spend the night is camping. As long as you have your own tent, it's easy to set up camp anywhere. (If it looks like you're near someone's home, it's always a good idea to inquire first.) Central America is popular with adventurous backpackers, so you'll have no problem hooking up with other likeminded travelers in major cities or along popular travel routes. To get good tips and advice on traveling within a budget, chat with other backpackers.

To save money, **look into deals available through student-oriented travel agencies** and the various other organizations involved in helping out student and budget travelers. Typically, you'll find discounted airfares, rail passes, tours, lodgings, or other travel arrangements, and you don't necessarily have to be a student to qualify.

STUDENT TRAVEL ORGANIZATIONS

The big names in the field are STA Travel, with some 100 offices worldwide and a useful Web site (www.sta-travel.com), and the Council on International Educational Exchange (CIEE or "Council" for short), a private, nonprofit organization that administers work, volunteer, academic, and professional programs worldwide and sells travel arrangements through its own specialist travel agency, Council Travel. Travel CUTS, strictly a travel agency, sells discounted airline tickets to Canadian students from offices on or near college campuses. The Educational Travel Center (ETC) books low-cost flights to destinations within the continental United States and around the world. And Student Flights, Inc., specializes in student and faculty airfares.

Most of these organizations also issue student identity cards, which entitle their bearers to special fares on local transportation and discounts at museums, theaters, sports events, and other attractions, as well as a handful of other benefits, which are listed in the handbook that most provide to their cardholders. Major cards include the International Student Identity Card (ISIC) and Go 25: International Youth Travel Card (GO25), available to nonstudents as well as students age 25 and under; the ISIC, when purchased in the United States, comes with $3,000 in emergency medical coverage and a few related benefits. Both the ISIC and GO25 are issued by Council Travel or STA in the United States, Travel CUTS in Canada, at student unions and student-travel companies in the United Kingdom, Australia, and New Zealand. The International Student Exchange Card (ISE), issued by Student Flights, Inc., is available to faculty members as well as students, and the International Teacher Identity Card (ITIC), issued by Travel CUTS, provides similar benefits to teachers in all grade levels, from kindergarten through graduate school. All student ID cards cost between $10 and $20.

STUDENT IDS AND SERVICES • **Council on International Educational Exchange** (CIEE, 205 E. 42nd St., 14th floor, New York, NY 10017, tel. 212/822–2600 or 888/268–6245, fax 212/822–2699), for mail orders only, in the United States.

Council Travel in the United States: Arizona (Tempe, tel. 602/966–3544). California (Berkeley, tel. 510/848–8604; Davis, tel. 916/752–2285; La Jolla, tel. 619/452–0630; Long Beach, tel. 310/598–3338; Los Angeles, tel. 310/208–3551; Palo Alto, tel. 415/325–3888; San Diego, tel. 619/270–6401, San Francisco, tel. 415/421–3473 or 415/566–6222; Santa Barbara, tel. 805/562–8080). Colorado (Boulder, tel. 303/447–8101; Denver, tel. 303/571–0630). Connecticut (New Haven, tel. 203/562–5335). Florida (Miami, tel. 305/670–9261). Georgia (Atlanta, tel. 404/377–9997). Illinois (Chicago, tel. 312/951–0585; Evanston, tel. 847/475–5070). Indiana (Bloomington, tel. 812/330–1600). Iowa (Ames, tel. 515/296–2326). Kansas (Lawrence, tel. 913/749–3900). Louisiana (New Orleans, tel. 504/866–1767). Maryland (College Park, tel. 301/779–1172). Massachusetts (Amherst, tel. 413/256–1261; Boston, tel. 617/266–1926; Cambridge, tel. 617/497–1497 or 617/225–2555). Michigan (Ann Arbor, tel. 313/998–0200). Minnesota (Minneapolis, tel. 612/379–2323). New York (New York, tel. 212/822–

2700, 212/666–4177, or 212/254–2525). North Carolina (Chapel Hill, tel. 919/942–2334). Ohio (Columbus, tel. 614/294–8696). Oregon (Portland, tel. 503/228–1900). Pennsylvania (Philadelphia, tel. 215/382–0343; Pittsburgh, tel. 412/683–1881). Rhode Island (Providence, tel. 401/331–5810). Tennessee (Knoxville, tel. 423/523–9900). Texas (Austin, tel. 512/472–4931; Dallas, tel. 214/363–9941). Utah (Salt Lake City, tel. 801/582–5840). Washington (Seattle, tel. 206/632–2448 or 206/329–4567). Washington, DC (tel. 202/337–6464).

Council Travel elsewhere: France (Paris, 22 rue des Pyramides, 1er, tel. 01–46–55–55–65; Nice, 37 bis rue d'Angleterre, tel. 04–93–82–23–33). **Educational Travel Center** (438 N. Frances St., Madison, WI 53703, tel. 608/256–5551 or 800/747–5551). **French Government Tourist Office**: California (Beverly Hills, tel. 310/271–6665 or 900/990–0040 [50¢ per minute]). Illinois (Chicago, tel. 312/751–7800 or 900/990–0040 [50¢ per minute]). New York (New York, tel. 212/838–7800 or 900/990–0040 [50¢ per minute]). **Maison de la France:** Canada (Montréal, tel. 514/288–4264; Toronto, tel. 416/593–4723). France (Paris, tel. 01–42–96–10–23).

STA in the U.S.: California (Berkeley, tel. 510/642–3000; Los Angeles, tel. 213/934–8722; San Francisco, tel. 415/391–8407; Santa Monica, tel. 310/394–5126; Westwood, tel. 310/824–1574). Florida (Miami, tel. 305/461–3444; University of Florida, tel. 352/338–0068). Illinois (Chicago, tel. 312/786–9050). Massachusetts (Boston, tel. 617/266–6014; Cambridge, tel. 617/576–4623). New York (Columbia University, tel. 212/865–2700; West Village, tel. 212/627–3111). Pennsylvania (Philadelphia, tel. 215/382–2928). Washington (Seattle, tel. 206/633–5000). Washington, DC (tel. 202/887–0912).

STA elsewhere: Argentina (Buenos Aires, tel. 01/315–1457). Australia (Adelaide, tel. 08/223–2434; Brisbane tel. 73/229–2499; Cairns, tel. 70/31–41–99; Canberra, tel. 06/247–8633; Darwin, tel. 89/41–29–55; Melbourne, tel. 39/349–2411; Perth, tel. 09/227–7569; Sydney, tel. 29/368–1111 or 29/212–1255). Belgium (Brussels, tel. 02/524–0178). Brazil (Rio de Janeiro, tel. 21/259–0023; Sao Paulo, tel. 11/816–1500). Canada (Calgary, tel. 403/282–7687; Edmonton, tel. 403/492–2592; Montréal, tel. 514/284–1368; Toronto, tel. 416/977–5228; Vancouver, tel. 604/681–9136). Chile (Santiago, tel. 02/334–5167). Colombia (Bogotá, tel. 01/214–4308). Czech Republic (Prague, tel. 02/26–64–66). Denmark (Copenhagen, tel. 33/55–75–33; Holstebro, tel. 97/42–67–33). Fiji (tel. 679/72–27–55). France (Nice, tel. 04/93–13–10–70; Paris, tel. 01/43–43–46–10). Germany (Berlin, tel. 30/285–9826 or 30/311–0950; Cologne, tel. 22/144–2011; Frankfurt, tel. 69/70–30–35 or 69/43–01–91; Hamburg, tel. 40/450–3840; Heidelberg, tel. 62/212–3528). Greece (Athens, tel. 01/322–1267). Holland (Amsterdam, tel. 20/624–0989 or 20/626–2557). Hong Kong (Kowloon, tel. 2730–9407). Hungary (Budapest, tel. 01/111–9898). India (Bombay, tel. 22/218–1431; New Delhi, tel. 11/332–5559). Indonesia (Bali, tel. 361/75–11–40; Jakarta tel. 21/230–0336). Israel (Haifa, tel. 04/67–02–22; Jerusalem, tel. 02/25–24–71; Tel Aviv, tel. 03/524–6322). **Student Flights** (5010 E. Shea Blvd., Suite A104, Scottsdale, AZ 85254, tel. 602/951–1177 or 800/255–8000). **Travel Cuts** (187 College St., Toronto, Ontario M5T 1P7, tel. 416/979–2406 or 800/667–2887) in Canada.

TELEPHONES

Telecommunication services in Central America are reasonably dependable, notwithstanding the usual quirks (delays, echos, and strange alien-infiltration beeps). Most public phones are clustered in central telecommunication buildings that often double as post offices. Pay phones and phonebooks have become much more common in recent years. *See* individual country chapters for country codes, USADirect access codes, and specifics on how to deal with operators.

TOUR OPERATORS

Buying a prepackaged tour or independent vacation can make your trip to Central America less expensive and more hassle-free. Because everything is prearranged, you'll spend less time planning.

Operators that handle several hundred thousand travelers per year can use their purchasing power to give you a good price. Their high volume may also indicate financial stability. But some small companies provide more personalized service; because they tend to specialize, they may also be more knowledgeable about a given area.

BOOKING WITH AN AGENT

Travel agents are excellent resources. In fact, large operators accept bookings made only through travel agents. But it's a good idea to **collect brochures from several agencies,** because some agents' suggestions may be influenced by relationships with tour and package firms that reward them for volume sales. If you have a special interest, **find an agent with expertise in that area**; ASTA (*see* Travel Agencies, *below*) has a database of specialists worldwide.

Make sure your travel agent knows the accommodations and other services. Ask about the hotel's location, room size, beds, and whether it has a pool, room service, or programs for children, if you care about these. Has your agent been there in person or sent others you can contact?

Do some homework on your own, too: local tourism boards can provide information about lesser-known and small-niche operators, some of which may sell only direct.

BUYER BEWARE

Each year consumers are stranded or lose their money when tour operators—even very large ones with excellent reputations—go out of business. So **check out the operator.** Find out how long the company has been in business, and ask several travel agents about its reputation. If the package or tour you are considering is priced lower than in your wildest dreams, **be skeptical.** Try to **book with a company that has a consumer-protection program.** If the operator has such a program, you'll find information about it in the company's brochure. If the operator you are considering does not offer some kind of consumer protection, then ask for references from satisfied customers.

In the United States, members of the National Tour Association and United States Tour Operators Association are required to set aside funds to cover your payments and travel arrangements in case the company defaults. It's also a good idea to choose a company that participates in the American Society of Travel Agent's Tour Operator Program (TOP). This gives you a forum if there are any disputes between you and your tour operator; ASTA will act as mediator.

TOUR-OPERATOR RECOMMENDATIONS • American Society of Travel Agents (*see* Travel Agencies, *below*). **National Tour Association** (NTA, 546 E. Main St., Lexington, KY 40508, tel. 606/226–4444 or 800/755–8687). **United States Tour Operators Association** (USTOA, 342 Madison Ave., Suite 1522, New York, NY 10173, tel. 212/599–6599 or 800/468–7862).

COSTS

The more your package or tour includes, the better you can predict the ultimate cost of your vacation. Make sure you know exactly what is covered, and **beware of hidden costs.** Are taxes, tips, and service charges included? Transfers and baggage handling? Entertainment and excursions? These can add up.

Prices for packages and tours are usually quoted per person, based on two sharing a room. If you are traveling solo, you may be required to pay the full double-occupancy rate. Some operators eliminate this surcharge if you agree to be matched with a roommate of the same sex, even if one is not found by departure time.

GROUP TOURS

Among companies that sell tours to Central America, the following have a proven reputation and offer plenty of options. The classifications used below represent different price categories, and you'll probably encounter these terms when talking to a travel agent or tour operator. The key difference is usually in accommodations, which run from budget to better, and better-yet to best.

DELUXE • Globus (5301 S. Federal Circle, Littleton, CO 80123-2980, tel. 303/797–2800 or 800/221–0090). **Maupintour** (1515 St. Andrews Dr., Lawrence, KS 66047, tel. 913/843–1211 or 800/255–4266). **Tauck Tours** (Box 5027, 276 Post Rd. W, Westport, CT 06881-5027, tel. 203/226–6911 or 800/468–2825).

FIRST-CLASS • Brendan Tours (15137 Califa St., Van Nuys, CA 91411, tel. 818/785–9696 or 800/421–8446). **Caravan Tours** (401 N. Michigan Ave., Chicago, IL 60611, tel. 312/321–9800 or 800/227–2826). **Collette Tours** (162 Middle St., Pawtucket, RI 02860, tel. 401/728–3805 or 800/340–5158).

BUDGET • Cosmos (*see* Globus, *above*).

PACKAGES

Like group tours, independent vacation packages are available from major tour operators and airlines. The companies listed below offer vacation packages in a broad price range.

AIR-HOTEL • American Airlines Vacations (tel. 800/321–2121). **United Vacations** (tel. 800/328–6877).

FROM THE U.K. • **South American Experience** (47 Causton St., London SW1P 4AT, tel. 0171/976–5511). **Journey Latin America** (16 Devonshire Rd., Chiswick, London W4 2HD, tel. 0181/747–8315). **Steamond Holidays** (278 Battersea Park Rd., London SW11 3BS, tel. 0171/924–4008).

THEME TRIPS

ADVENTURE • **American Wilderness Experience** (Box 1486, Boulder, CO 80306, tel. 303/444–2622 or 800/444–0099). **Himalayan Travel** (110 Prospect St., Stamford, CT 06901, tel. 203/359–3711 or 800/225–2380). **Mountain Travel-Sobek** (6420 Fairmount Ave., El Cerrito, CA 94530, tel. 510/527–8100 or 888/687–6235). **Safaricentre** (3201 N. Sepulveda Blvd., Manhattan Beach, CA 90266, tel. 310/546–4411 or 800/223–6046).

ART AND ARCHAEOLOGY • **M.I.L.A.** (100 S. Greenleaf Ave., Gurnee, IL 60031-3378, tel. 847/249–2111 or 800/367–7378).

BIKING • **Backroads** (801 Cedar St., Berkeley, CA 94710-1800, tel. 510/527–1555 or 800/462–2848).

CUSTOMIZED TOURS • **Avanti Destinations** (851 SW 6th St., Suite 1010, Portland, OR, 97204, tel. 503/295–1100 or 800/422–5053). **4th Dimension Tours** (7101 S.W. 99th Ave., #106, Miami, FL 33173, tel. 305/279–0014 or 800/343–0020). **Ladatco Tours** (2220 Coral Way, Miami, FL 33145, tel. 305/854–8422 or 800/327–6162).

FISHING • **Anglers Travel** (1280 Terminal Way, #30, Reno, NV 89502, tel. 702/324–0580 or 800/624–8429). **Cutting Loose Expeditions** (Box 447, Winter Park, FL 32790, tel. 407/629–4700 or 800/533–4746). **Fishing International** (Box 2132, Santa Rosa, CA 95405, tel. 707/539–3366 or 800/950–4242). **Rod & Reel Adventures** (566 Thomson La., Copperopolis, CA 95228, tel. 209/785–0444).

HORSEBACK RIDING • **Equitour FITS Equestrian** (Box 807, Dubois, WY 82513, tel. 307/455–3363 or 800/545–0019).

HORTICULTURE • **Expo Garden Tours** (70 Great Oak, Redding, CT 06896, tel. 203/938–0410 or 800/448–2685).

LEARNING • **Earthwatch** (Box 9104, 680 Mount Auburn St., Watertown, MA 02272, tel. 617/926–8200 or 800/776–0188) for research expeditions. **National Audubon Society** (700 Broadway, New York, NY 10003, tel. 212/979–3066). **Natural Habitat Adventures** (2945 Center Green Ct., Boulder, CO 80301, tel. 303/449–3711 or 800/543–8917). **Nature Expeditions International** (6400 E. El Dorado Cir. #210, Tucson, AZ 85715, tel. 520/721–6712 or 800/869–0639). **Naturequest** (934 Acapulco St., Laguna Beach, CA 92651, tel. 714/499–9561 or 800/369–3033). **Oceanic Society Expeditions** (Fort Mason Center, Bldg. E, San Francisco, CA 94123-1394, tel. 415/441–1106 or 800/326–7491). **Questers** (381 Park Ave. S, New York, NY 10016, tel. 212/251–0444 or 800/468–8668). **Smithsonian Study Tours and Seminars** (1100 Jefferson Dr. SW, Room 3045, MRC 702, Washington, DC 20560, tel. 202/357–4700). **Wilderness Travel** (1102 Ninth St., Berkeley, CA 94710, tel. 510/558–2488 or 800/368–2794). **Victor Emanuel Nature Tours** (Box 33008, Austin, TX 78764, tel. 512/328–5221 or 800/328–8368).

SCUBA DIVING • **Rothschild Dive Safaris** (900 West End Ave., #1B, New York, NY 10025-3525, tel. 212/662–4858 or 800/359–0747). **Tropical Adventures** (111 2nd Ave. N, Seattle, WA 98109, tel. 206/441–3483 or 800/247–3483).

WALKING/HIKING • Backroads (*see* Biking, *above*). **Country Walkers** (Box 180, Waterbury, VT 05676-0180, tel. 802/244–1387 or 800/464–9255). **Walking the World** (Box 1186, Fort Collins, CO 80522, tel. 970/498–0500 or 800/340–9255) specializes in tours for ages 50 and older.

TRAVEL AGENTS

A good travel agent puts your needs first. Look for an agency that has been in business at least five years, emphasizes customer service, and has someone on staff who specializes in your destination. In addition, **make sure the agency belongs to a professional trade organization,** such as ASTA in the United States. If your travel agency is also acting as your tour operator, *see* Buyer Beware *in* Tour Operators, *above*).

LOCAL AGENT REFERRALS • **American Society of Travel Agents** (ASTA, tel. 800/965–2782 24-hr hot line,). **Association of Canadian Travel Agents** (Suite 201, 1729 Bank St., Ottawa, Ontario K1V 7Z5, tel. 613/521–0474). **Association of British Travel Agents** (55–57 Newman St., London W1P 4AH, tel. 0171/637–2444). **Australian Federation of Travel Agents** (tel. 02/9264–3299). **Travel Agents' Association of New Zealand** (tel. 04/499–0104).

TRAVEL GEAR

Travel catalogs specialize in useful items, such as compact alarm clocks and travel irons, that can save space when packing. They also offer dual-voltage appliances, currency converters, and foreign-language phrase books.

CATALOGS • Magellan's (tel. 800/962–4943). **Orvis Travel** (tel. 800/541–3541). **TravelSmith** (tel. 800/950–1600).

VISITOR INFORMATION

TOURIST INFORMATION

See Basics *in* individual chapters for national tourist agencies.

U.S. GOVERNMENT

Government agencies can be an excellent source of inexpensive travel information. When planning your trip, **find out what government materials are available.**

ADVISORIES • U.S. Department of State (Overseas Citizens Services Office, Room 4811 N.S., Washington, DC 20520, tel. 202/647–5225 or 202/647–3000 for interactive hot line; 301/946–4400 for computer bulletin board); enclose a self-addressed, stamped, business-size envelope.

PAMPHLETS • Consumer Information Center (Consumer Information Catalogue, Pueblo, CO 81009, tel. 719/948–3334 or 888/878–3256) for a free catalog that includes travel titles.

VOLUNTEER & EDUCATIONAL TRAVEL

Volunteer programs typically provide room and board in exchange for labor. Most exact application fees and many require significant contributions or fund-raising commitments to defray program costs. Plan ahead: the best (and cheapest) programs and placements are booked solid up to a year in advance.

ORGANIZATIONS

Amigos de las Americas (5618 Star La., Houston, TX 77057, tel. 800/231–7796) runs well-established programs throughout Latin America, with projects focused on improving health and education. Volunteers live with families and work in communities for four to eight weeks. **Casa Alianza,** a branch of the New York–based Covenant House, works for the defense of children's rights and has offices in Mexico, Guatemala, and Honduras. The organization works with street kids aged seven to 18 (they're about 90% male; most of the homeless girls end up being forced into prostitution) and runs a homeless shelter, five group homes, a transitional home, foster families, and a farm where youth can learn new and marketable skills.

Council's **International Voluntary Services Department** (205 E. 42nd St., 14th Floor, New York, NY 10017, tel. 212/822–2600, ext. 2695) offers two- to four-week environmental or community-service projects in 22 countries around the globe. Participants must be 18 or older and pay a $165 placement fee. Also, Council publishes *Volunteer! The Comprehensive Guide to Voluntary Service in the U.S. and Abroad* ($12.95, plus $1.50 postage), which describes nearly 200 organizations around the world that offer volunteer positions.

At one time or another everyone considers joining the **Peace Corps** for two years of volunteer service abroad. You don't have to be an expert in your field, but you do need a college degree and a strong sense of commitment. Room and board are provided, along with a small monthly stipend. *1990 K St. NW, Washington, DC 20526, tel. 800/424–8580.*

Volunteers for Peace (VFP) sponsors two- to three-week international work camps in the United States, Europe, Africa, Asia, and Central America for around $150. Send for their *International Workcamp Directory* ($10); it lists more than 800 volunteer opportunities. *43 Tiffany Rd., Belmont, VT, 05730, tel. 802/259–2759, fax 802/259–2922.*

WorldTeach, a program run by Harvard University, offers excellent volunteer opportunities for those who want to teach in Europe, Africa, Latin America, and parts of Asia. Subjects range from English and science to carpentry, forestry, and sports. You'll need a college degree and must be willing to commit for at least one year. WorldTeach provides housing, a monthly stipend, and unlike the Peace Corps, allows their volunteers to make extra money through private tutoring. *WorldTeach, c/o Harvard Institute for*

International Development, 14 Story St., Cambridge, MA 02138, tel. 617/495–5527 or 800/483–2240, fax 617/495–1599.

ENVIRONMENTAL PROGRAMS

Some, but not many, Central Americans have smartened up of late in realizing the need to preserve the area's precious, eye-opening biodiversity. Volunteer and educational efforts have been created by natives and far-flung environmentalists, and you, too, can have an impact. You do, however, pay for the privilege.

OPERATORS • CCC (4424 Northwest 13th St., Suite A-1, Gainseville, FL 32609, tel. 800/678–7853). **Earthwatch Institute** (680 Mt. Auburn St., Box 9104, Watertown, MA 02272–9104, tel. 800/776–0188).

PUBLICATIONS

The Archaeological Institute of America annually publishes *Archaeological Fieldwork Opportunities* ($16 including shipping), a very detailed listing of field projects around the world. *656 Beacon St., Boston, MA 02215-2010, tel. 617/353–9361, fax 617/353–6550.*

Another good bet is Bill McMillon's *Volunteer Vacations* ($13.95), which lists hundreds of organizations and volunteer opportunities in the United States and abroad. Look for it in your local bookstore.

WHEN TO GO

CLIMATE

Central Americans divide their year into two seasons: *invierno* (hot and rainy) and *verano* (hot and dry). Invierno (literally, winter) takes place during what most of us would consider summer, generally April through November. If you crave natural beauty, the vegetation is at its most splendiferous during this period. Keep in mind, however, that a few places may be inaccessible, and more than a few roads will be washed out—don't expect to drive on any nonasphalt surface. Expect to get rained on every day. Verano, the dry "summer" season (November–April), is more popular for travelers, with correspondingly higher airfares and hotel prices. Cities of the highlands and central plateaus are mild year-round; some, like San José in Costa Rica, are known as cities of eternal spring. Towns at higher altitudes are cooler during the day and can be downright chilly at night. Temperatures vary radically within short distances, too: one minute you're sweating so much your thighs and the vinyl bus seat become one; next, you're turning a corner, heading up a mountain, and making a mad scramble for that pullover.

NATIONAL HOLIDAYS

Do not plan on conducting any official business on the following days: **January 1,** New Year's Day; Thursday and Friday of Holy Week (the week before Easter) and Easter itself; Labor Day; **October 12,** Columbus Day (Indigenous People's Day); **November 1,** All Saints' Day; **November 2,** All Souls' Day; **December 24–25,** Christmas Eve and Christmas. *See* individual country Basics for their unique celebrations.

FESTIVALS

Most communities have annual **patron saint festivals,** replete with parades, food, drink, and dance. **Semana Santa** (Holy Week, the week before Easter) is a serious subject to Central Americans: it's one big party, and whole families join in. Beaches, islands, and hotels are packed, restaurants are usually closed Thursday and Friday of that week, and prices skyrocket. It's a lot of fun provided you don't mind getting plastered and dancing in the streets. Check out Semana Santa in Antigua, Guatemala—travelers from all over the world come for it, so make reservations in advance or you'll end up sleeping curbside. **Carnaval** usually refers to the Tuesday before Lent, aka "Mardi Gras" in other parts of the world. Bizarre costumes, booze, decadent food, and general hedonism are the order of the day. Las Tablas, Panama, reputedly hosts the most glorious carnavals in Central America.

BELIZE

BY JENNIFER BREWER, UPDATED BY SIMON WORRALL

I   f freakish plate tectonics had sheared the nation of Belize from its skinny stretch of continent 400 years ago and sent it drifting into the Caribbean Sea, it couldn't seem more different from the rest of Central American than it does today. Squeezed onto the Yucatán
Peninsula south of Mexico and east of Guatemala, this lilliputian, English-speaking nation is
physically isolated from its Latin neighbors by the rugged, nearly impassable Maya Mountains to the south and west and by a spectacular barrier reef along its coast. The result is a
country more Caribbean than Latin American, one blessed with probably the most peaceful political climate in the entire region. Even though its citizenry includes a potentially volatile mix of Latinos, blacks,
and whites, Belize doesn't make big headlines like neighboring Guatemala. In fact, Belize, the size of
Massachusetts but with a total population of less than 250,000 (i.e., half that of Boston), rarely makes
any kind of headlines at all. This might explain why many travelers greet the phrase "Let's visit Belize"
with a vacant stare.

Those who can pinpoint Belize on the map are a growing number of ecoconscious and adventure
tourists. The most visited feature of Belize is its 282-km-long (175-mi-long) barrier reef, which lies about
40 km (25 mi) off the coast in the emerald 75° waters of the Caribbean Sea. Famed French marine
explorer Jacques Cousteau studied the reef (it's the largest in the Western Hemisphere and second-
largest in the world, next only to Australia's Great Barrier Reef) in the 1970s, blazing a trail for thrill-seek-
ing scuba divers. Today the cays (rhymes with "Belize")—dozens of small coconut palm- and
mangrove-covered islands strewn along the reef—are a favorite destination of snorkelers, sun worshipers, and big-fish anglers, although the smallest remain uninhabited and wholly wild. None offer
wide white-sand beaches, but the point of Belize isn't parking your ass under an umbrella—it's sea
kayaking, diving, spelunking, canoeing, hiking, snorkeling, and manatee- or bird-watching.

In the difficult-to-reach south and central regions of the country, you can explore vast tracts of old-
growth rain forest and immense limestone-cave networks. The jungle and pine forest of western Belize
used to be the exclusive domain of luxury resorts owned by the likes of Francis Ford Coppola (filmmaker
and U.S. special consul to Belize); budget ranches and reliable transportation now make it a well-trod
stop for backpackers. The north isn't as spectacular, but the flat countryside, dominated by mangrove
swamps and sugarcane fields, includes several important wildlife reserves and Mayan ruins.

The magic of Belize has as much to do with the people who live here as it does with the sensational
countryside. About half are Creoles, descendants of African slaves, whose patois is a pidginized medley

that sounds remotely like English but blends elements from Spanish, French, and Indian languages. The Creoles consider themselves the heirs of the colonial era and hold most university, police, and government positions. In Belize City, they form approximately 70% of the population. They share cultural ties (and a passion for Bob Marley) with the nearby Caribbean isles, and, traditionally, Belize has always identified more with the British Caribbean than with Central America, more with Trinidad or St. Kitts than with Mexico or El Salvador.

A third of Belize's population are mestizos (mixed blood); the rest are Garifuna/black Caribs (*see box* 100% Garifuna, *below*), German-descended Mennonites (*see box* The Mennonites: Mavens of Modesty, *below*), or Mopan and Kekchi Mayan Indians. Smaller numbers of Chinese and Middle Eastern immigrants have recently settled throughout the country, and you can count on seeing shiny, happy expatriate Americans or Brits behind the counter of every new cappuccino, granola, or burger stand in the more touristed areas. Just about every native is bi- or trilingual, speaking English, Spanish, Creole, and maybe a Mayan dialect or two; and national holidays include celebrations of Mexican heritage, the Garifunas' arrival, and the Queen of England's birthday.

All of these peoples, like Belize's most recent refugees—the thousands of Salvadorans and Guatemalans who fled their countries' death squads and torture chambers in the 1970s and 1980s—have mixed and married, producing an extraordinary rainbow coalition of peoples. You're likely to see facial structures and skin colors you haven't encountered before—blacks with blue eyes and half-Mayan, half-Creole folks with green eyes. To declare ethnically diverse Belize one of the friendliest, most harmonious countries on the planet would not fall too far short of the truth. Locals joke gently about anything, including race, and the humor seems to diffuse tension. Undercurrents of resentment do exist against newcomers who violate the unwritten "Belize for Belizeans" code; and vociferous claims that the Americans buy up all the land or that the Chinese take up all the jobs are commonplace. But the fact is, on a cosmic scale almost everyone in Belize is a newcomer: the Garifunas first arrived in 1832, Mayans from Mexico and Guatemala arrived seeking refuge from oppression beginning in the mid-1800s, and the Mennonites arrived in the 1950s and 1960s.

For the past two decades, development in Belize has been swift but uneven, making this a nation of contradictions. It has one of the best telecommunications systems in Central America, yet thousands still live in wooden shacks. Utility poles march up and down the country, bringing electricity to even the smallest settlements, but there are currently only two decent paved roads—the Northern and Western highways. Although more than 50% of the population owns land and can afford to visit the United States on a regular basis, the government says it does not have the funds to build a national museum for its priceless collection of Mayan artifacts. Traveling by bus in Belize will give you plenty of time to contemplate these ironies. In the north and west, service is cheap, frequent, and reliable. To the south, dirt tracks (referred to as "highways") are often impassable in the rainy season; look for the rusting skeletons of vehicles abandoned in the quagmire.

So far, the democratic political system has prevented the kind of endemic corruption that afflicts so many Caribbean countries, but in recent years there have been worrying signs that drug money is beginning to find its way into the country. Two of the nation's most expensive resorts, Blackbird Caye and Manta Reef Resort, are now owned by a businessman who is persona non grata in the U.S. because of his well-established drug connections.

Belize lies along *La Ruta Maya,* the ancient network of Mayan cities and outposts that at one time stretched from Mexico to El Salvador. Estimates put the ancient Mayan population of Belize at close to 2 million in its heyday—about 10 times greater than the present-day population. More than 600 ruins large and small have been found throughout the country, and the archaeological evidence increasingly suggests that far from being a minor tributary of the great Mayan civilization that flourished in Central America 1,000 years ago, Belize was one of its heartlands. Indeed, Caracol, deep in the jungle of western Belize, may have been the greatest classic-period (AD 300–900) ceremonial center in Latin America. No other Mayan center has been uncovered to rival its size, and deciphered hieroglyphs tell stories of military victory over the great Tikal in Guatemala. A new site in southern Belize, currently being excavated in conjunction with the National Geographic Society, promises to be as impressive.

The Spanish conquistadors who ravaged 16th-century Central and South America in search of gold and silver skipped Belize because of the absence of valuable minerals and overwhelming abundance of swampland. Ever acquisitive, Spain claimed the area anyway in the 1520s and lumped it together with Guatemala. Settlement—an accident—came over a century later with a motley crew of shipwrecked British sailors, and British-led piracy and logging dominated the history of colonial Belize for the next

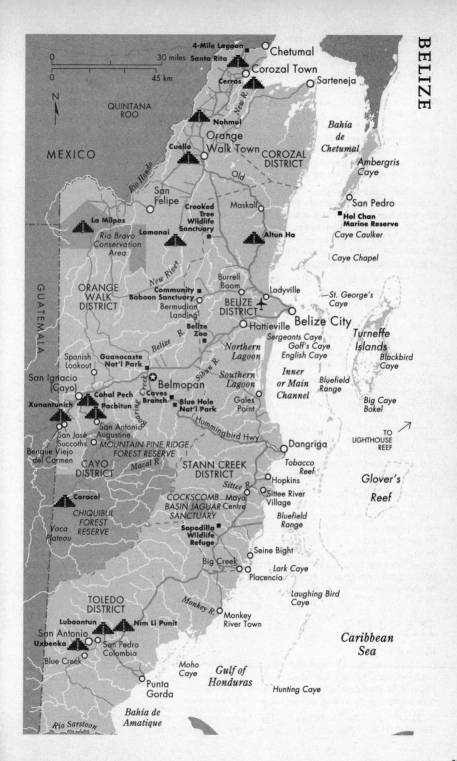

BELIZE

0 ————— 30 miles
0 ————— 45 km

N

4-Mile Lagoon
Santa Rita
Chetumal
Corozal Town
Cerros
Sarteneja

QUINTANA
ROO

Bahía
de
Chetumal

Nohmul
Orange
Walk Town
COROZAL
DISTRICT

Cuello

Ambergris
Caye

MEXICO

San
Felipe

Maskall

San Pedro

Hol Chan
Marine Reserve

Caye Caulker

Crooked
Tree
Wildlife
Sanctuary

Lamanai

La Milpas

Rio Bravo
Conservation
Area

Altun Ha

Caye Chapel

New River

ORANGE
WALK
DISTRICT

Community
Baboon Sanctuary
Bermudian
Landing

Burrell
Boom

Ladyville

St. George's
Caye

GUATEMALA

BELIZE
DISTRICT

Belize
R.

Belize
Zoo

Hattieville

Belize City

Turneffe
Islands

Sergeants Caye
Goff's Caye
English Caye

Blackbird
Caye

Spanish
Lookout

Guanacaste
Nat'l Park

Northern
Lagoon

Inner
or Main
Channel

Bluefield
Range

San Ignacio
(Cayo)

Belmopan

Southern
Lagoon

Big Caye
Bokel

Xunantunich

Cahal Pech
Pacbitun

Caves
Branch

Blue Hole
Nat'l Park

Gales
Point

TO
LIGHTHOUSE
REEF

San José
Succoths
San Antonio
Augustine

Hummingbird Hwy.

Benque Viejo
del Carmen

MOUNTAIN PINE RIDGE
FOREST RESERVE

CAYO
DISTRICT

Macal R.

Dangriga

Glover's
Reef

STANN CREEK
DISTRICT

Tobacco
Reef

Hopkins

Caracol

CHIQUIBUL
FOREST
RESERVE

COCKSCOMB
BASIN JAGUAR
SANCTUARY

Sittee R.

Maya
Centre

Sittee River
Village

Bluefield
Range

Vaca
Plateau

Sapodilla
Wildlife
Refuge

Seine Bight

Big Creek

Lark Caye

Placencia

Laughing Bird
Caye

TOLEDO
DISTRICT

Lubaantun

Nim Li Punit

Monkey R.

San Antonio
Uxbenka

San Pedro
Columbia

Monkey
River Town

Caribbean
Sea

Blue Creek

Moho
Caye

Gulf of
Honduras

Hunting Caye

Punta
Gorda

Bahía de
Amatique

Rio Sarstoon

200 years. In Belize's interior, loggers (called Baymen) in search of valuable mahogany trees set up rough-and-tumble outposts with fanciful names like Millionario, Moses Head, and Go-to-Hell Camp. On the cays lurked miscreants who navigated the dangerous barrier reef in shallow boats, attacking homeward-bound Spanish galleons laden with gold and silver.

Great Britain tacitly encouraged piracy in an effort to break the Spanish monopoly on trade in the New World. In the 17th and early 18th centuries, renegade British adventurers hungry for a taste of easy fortune flocked to the Caribbean to exploit the people and their land. Throughout the 18th century, Spain harassed the British settlers, and a slew of government-to-government treaties consistently failed. Finally, on September 10, 1798, England defeated Spain for the final time at St. George's Caye. The battle, which pitted 32 Spanish ships against five sailboats, seven gun rafts, and the Royal Navy ship HMS *Merlin,* lasted only 2½ hours. The date is now a cut-loose national holiday, and from this point on Britain officially laid claim to Belize by right of conquest.

The military presence, so pervasive in most of Central America, is all but invisible in modern Belize. Known as British Honduras until 1972, Belize became self-governing in 1964 and achieved full independence from Britain on September 21, 1981. It remains a member of the Commonwealth of Nations (basically meaning that the queen's birthday is celebrated with an annual bike race). Its government, one of the only true democracies in Latin America, is based on the two-party British parliamentary system: the UDP (United Democratic Party) and the PUP (Peoples United Party), both centrist, constantly battle for primacy. There is a healthy free press.

Historically, the only real threat to national security has come from Guatemala. For years, the Guatemalan government claimed Belize as one of its own territories, and Guatemalan maps drew no boundaries drawn between the two. In 1991, Guatemalan president Serano announced diplomatic relations with the nation of Belize. Although he was subsequently thrown out of office, affairs stabilized sufficiently for Great Britain to remove its 1,500 troops. Relations between Britain and Belize remain close. Belize's defense force is still trained by the Brits, and Harrier jump-jets, which used to inspire gasps of amazement from arriving tourists by flying backwards over the airport, are still on call in case Guatemala should try to reassert its claim to what it has called its 13th province.

Since independence, this unassuming little nation has established itself as a world leader in ecotourism. Flourishing jungle, rugged pine forest, lush swampland, and the mighty barrier reef host hundreds of species of wildlife. Belize has developed a program of conservation and protection almost unheard-of in the Third World—or any other world for that matter. Eighty percent of the country's forests are still intact; compare that to El Salvador, which has less than 2% of its virgin forest remaining. As a developing nation, Belize is taking an impressive economic risk by attempting to preserve its valuable natural resources instead of cutting them down for short-term gain. With community-based projects like the Baboon Sanctuary and Crooked Tree Wildlife Reserve, the country is successfully using tourist dollars to help save its fragile ecosystems.

Unfortunately and perhaps inevitably, the government's commitment to the environment is occasionally compromised. Much of the acreage in the undeveloped southern region is being developed by the powerful timber industry. Locals along the Northern Highway grumble about the number of Taiwanese-backed developments plowing into the savanna. Sustainable agriculture is a priority to many Belizeans, yet slash-and-burn farming is still rampant. Still, with tourism growing in leaps and bounds, the delicate balancing act of developing enough resources for visitors while maintaining the integrity of the countryside is becoming a real issue. If conservation measures prove economically successful, irreplaceable tropical forests may have a chance for survival—and Belizean inhabitants (human and otherwise) will be a lot happier.

BASICS

MONEY

Compared to the rest of Central America, Belize is no bargain. It has plenty of budget accommodations, cheap restaurants, and a low-priced public transportation system, but most of the spectacular sights and exciting adventures carry high price tags. You can live on less than $20 a day, but if you want to see or do anything really unique, prepare to spend a lot more.

Credit cards are almost worthless to budget travelers in Belize, except to get cash advances. Some banks will do the transaction for free, while others (particularly those on the edges of civilization) will charge $7.50–$15; if you do find a business that takes credit cards, expect to pay a 5% surcharge. All prices in this chapter are in U.S. dollars. Belizeans, though usually honest, may not be so explicit. Before you pay, always make clear whether the price you've been quoted is in Belizean or U.S. "dollars."

CURRENCY • The currency of choice in Belize is Uncle Sam's. The Belize dollar is tied to the U.S. dollar at a fixed rate of BZ$2–U.S.$1. Businesses that deal with tourists (restaurants, hotels, tour guides) usually take U.S. cash and traveler's checks—some even prefer them. An exchange rate of BZ$1.98 is standard at most banks. (Other currencies are usually changed first to U.S. dollars and then to Belizean dollars.)

COMING AND GOING

You can enter Belize from Guatemala by plane, bus, or boat, and from Mexico by plane or bus. Currently, there is a $10 exit tax (plus $1.25 security tax) for all visitors leaving Belize.

BY PLANE • International flights arrive at Philip Goldson International Airport, 13 km (8 mi) north of Belize City and probably the only airport in the world with a mahogany roof. Airlines serving Belize from the United States are **American** (tel. 800/624–6262 in the U.S.), daily nonstop flights from Miami; **Continental** (tel. 800/231–0856), daily nonstop flights from Houston; and **TACA International** (tel. 800/535–8780), regular flights from Los Angeles, New Orleans, Miami, and San Francisco. Taca International offers special baggage concessions to divers and has the most modern fleet; the snag is that flights are often late in arriving, which can be a nuisance if you have to make connections later on. There are no direct flights from the United Kingdom or Canada; most travelers connect with U.S. flights.

Practically the only international news to come out of Belize this decade was when the country—together with the Caribbean trio of Jamaica, Barbados, and Trinidad—volunteered 266 troops to the 1994–95 peacekeeping operation in Haiti.

A cheaper option is to arrive via Cancún in Mexico. There are hundreds of charter flights and package deals into Cancún (just 323 km [200 mi] up the Yucatán Peninsula) for as little as $250 round-trip. Ask a travel agent, or contact **Aero México** (tel. 800/237–6639) or **Mexicana Airlines** (tel. 800/531–7921). From Cancún, you can bus (*see below*) into Belize or catch a flight on **Bonanza Airline** (tel. 027/0219) or **Aerocaribe** (tel. 027/5213). The price is around $190 round-trip. Another option is to fly into Guatemala City (*see* Coming and Going *in* Chapter 3). From Guatemala City, you can fly to Belize City with **Aerovías** (tel. 305/885–1775) or TACA for around $100 one-way. **Tropic Air** (tel. 026/2012 or 800/422–3435 in U.S.) flies regularly between Belize City and Flores, Guatemala, for $61 one-way.

BY BUS • Crossing the borders on the west and north is easy: Belize's bus companies go directly to Chetumal, Mexico, and Melchor de Mencos, Guatemala, where you can connect with each country's own bus lines. From Chetumal, you can catch a direct bus to Cancún (5 hrs, $10). If you're entering Belize on its western border, **Pinitas** buses depart from Santa Elena (at the Hotel San Juan) in northern Guatemala to Belize City (7 hrs, $10) daily at 5 AM. To reach Belize City from the United States by bus though Mexico is cheap but long and exhausting: it's about two days from the U.S.–Mexico border to Mexico City, and another two days to the border with Belize.

BY CAR • It's a three-day drive from Brownsville, Texas, to Chetumal, Mexico, on the border with Belize, and then about another 3½ hours to Belize City. On arrival from Mexico, you'll have to hand in your Mexican Tourist Card (and/or car papers, if you have them). On the Belizean side, make sure you get a Temporary Import Permit for your car, or you may be delayed when leaving the country. Car insurance for Mexico is sold at the border, and **Belinsco** (21 Regent St., Belize City, tel. 02/77–025) handles car insurance in Belize. If you're flexible about your start date, **Crystal Auto Rental** (Northern Hwy., Mile 1½, Belize City, tel. 02/31–600) has a Houston–Belize City drive-away deal for drivers age 25 or older. Crystal delivers the car to you in Houston and you're given two weeks to get through Mexico, at your own expense; contact them at least a month in advance. In Belize, customs will make you prove you're not importing the car you're driving (or smuggling drugs). Depending on how suspicious they are, they might ask for a return ticket or other proof that you're not going to stay forever.

BY BOAT • You can leave the country by boat from three towns in southern Belize: (1) from Dangriga, a boat leaves once weekly for Puerto Cortés, Honduras ($30); (2) from Placencia, you can charter a water taxi ($40–$45) to Livingston or Puerto Barrios, Guatemala, or to Puerto Cortés; and (3) from Punta Gorda, water taxis will make runs to the same two towns in Guatemala for $7–$10. There's also ferry service ($6.50) twice weekly to Puerto Barrios, where you can catch a bus inland to Guatemala City.

GETTING AROUND

The easiest and cheapest way to get around Belize is by bus, though for remote areas you'll need to consider hitching or renting a car. If you're in a hurry and have the extra cash, you can hop from town to town by plane. For information on catching a boat to the cays, *see* The Cays, *below*.

BY BUS • Belize has no railroad network, so its bus service is the main way to get around. The quality of the buses and the roads on which they travel varies considerably. Expect anything from air-conditioned, TV-equipped luxury coaches (which run the express route north to Mexico) to wheezing, yellow U.S. school buses (your most likely ride on shorter routes). However, the buses do run according to reliable schedules, are extremely cheap (Belize City to Placencia costs only $18), and remain an excellent way of experiencing Belize as the Belizeans do. Outside the cities you can flag buses down like cabs, and the driver will let you off whenever you want. There are four main companies: **Batty Bros** (15 Mosul St., Belize City, tel. 027/2025) covers most northern and western bus routes, with stops in Corozal, Belmopan, and San Ignacio; **Novelo's** (W. Collet Canal, Belize City, tel. 027/7372) makes an afternoon run to San Ignacio; **Venus Bus Service** (Magazine Rd., Belize City, tel. 027/7390 or 027/3354) heads north to Orange Walk and Corozal; and **Z-Line Bus Service** (Magazine Rd., Belize City, tel. 027/3937) runs to Belmopan, Dangriga, and Punta Gorda, among others.

BY CAR • If you're expecting the New Jersey Turnpike, fugedaboudit. Only the Northern Highway, to Orange Walk and Corozal, and the Western Highway, to Belmopan and San Ignacio, are paved, but even these can be badly potholed after rains. After the first 32 km (20 mi), the Hummingbird Highway, to the south, is a difficult road in any season. In the rain it turns to orange slop; when dry, to bumpy concrete. Once you get off the main highways, distances don't mean that much—it's time that counts. You might have only 20 km (12½ mi) to go, but it can take you 90 minutes. If you bring your own car, you'll need to buy insurance in Belize. Gasoline costs $2.40 per gallon, and remember, it's leaded gas. Fill up whenever you see a gas station.

A half-dozen car-rental agencies serve Belize City, including internationals **Avis** (tel. 800/331–1212 in U.S.), **Budget** (tel. 800/527–0700 in U.S.), and **Hertz** (tel. 800/654.3131 in U.S). Of the local companies, we recommend **Crystal Auto Rental** (tel. 023/1600) and **Jabiru** (tel. 024/4680). Prices vary from company to company, but all are expensive by U.S. standards. A four-wheel-drive Suzuki with unlimited mileage from Avis, for instance, costs about $68 per day; weekly rates are considerably cheaper (about $400). For serious safaris, a four-wheel-drive vehicle (preferably a Land Rover or an Isuzu Trooper) is invaluable. Most major hotels offer all-terrain vehicles with guides for about $200 per day.

BY PLANE • Travelers with only a week or so to spare may want to consider flying from Belize City to the cays ($20) or down the coast ($40–$60), as opposed to wasting an entire day on bus or boat. Like everything good in Belize, flying—in twin-engine island-hoppers—comes with a bit of adventure. Most domestic flights leave from the **Municipal Airport,** 2 km (1 mi) or so from the Belize City center. The most modern domestic carriers are **Tropic Air** (tel. 024/5671 or 800/422–3435 in the U.S.) and **Maya Island Air** (tel. 024/4032), both of which fly to Ambergris and Caye Caulker as well as Dangriga, Placencia, Punta Gorda, and nearby Mexican towns to the north. The flight to San Pedro, on Ambergris Caye, costs approximately $84 round-trip; to Placencia, $115; and to Punta Gorda, $160. If you have just won the lottery, **Javier Flying Service** (tel. 023/5360) will take you pretty much anywhere for $170 per hour.

WHERE TO SLEEP

Belize has little in the way of standardized, Holiday Inn–style accommodations. Large hotels are the exception rather than the rule. The best lodgings are small, highly individual resorts with personalized service and rooms; these are very much shaped by the tastes and interests of their owners, who are mostly American or British. Most have traveled widely themselves and are excellent hosts, but the quality of the facilities they provide varies greatly. Because of the salt and humidity, operating a hotel in the tropics is an art in itself, the closest thing to keeping house on the deck of a ship. Without constant maintenance, things start to rust, the palapa (a frequently used natural building material) leaks, and the charms of paradise quickly fade.

There are budget hotels and guest houses everywhere in Belize, but *budget* is a relative designation. Hostels don't exist, and dormitory-style accommodations are rare. A clean, simple double room is $10–$14 (shared bath) or $15–$22 (private), depending on location and season. In western Belize or out on the cays, you can score your own two- to four-person cabana for around $25. Bathrooms in Belize are all fitted with standard Motel 6–style flush toilets, and even the cheapest places will typically supply you with toilet paper, towel and soap, clean sheets, an electric fan, and hot water. Wheelchair accessibility is rare in Belize, and most places are constructed with the rooms on the second floor. Only the most expensive resorts and hotels in Belize accept credit cards. All hotels tack a 7% government tax onto room rates.

In reserves and small villages, you'll find host-family programs ($6–$10 per night) in place of hotels. This can mean a room in the family's house or a bed in a separate cabana, and usually includes home-cooked meals. Camping in Belize is heavily restricted, but when possible it's a great way to beat hotel prices and have an adventure at the same time. Reserves, ranches, and some resorts have primitive camping facilities (i.e., a patch of grass and an outhouse) for about $5 per night. If you ask nicely, landowners will often let you pitch a tent or hang a hammock on their land for free. Those who are considering roughing it, be warned: small insects may crawl into your underwear and call it home unless you get busy with some mosquito netting and bug spray.

FOOD

Belizean cuisine is not one of the world's greatest. Although there are tasty local treats—like the john-nycake, a sconelike bread roll fried to a golden crisp and served at breakfast—rice and beans, fried chicken, and tasty creole chicken are the staple entrées. Added to these are such acquired tastes as iguana (known as "bush chicken") and gibnut, a small rodent christened "the queen's rat" after Her Majesty dined on it during a state visit, and oddities of the British culinary heritage, like bread-and-butter pudding and cow-foot soup. But with the world's second-largest coral reef running the length of the coast, Belize whips up seafood as tasty as any in the Caribbean. Belizean chefs have learned how to prepare fish for a lighter northern palate (no deep-frying), and at their best, dishes like grilled grouper or red snapper in a citron sauce, shrimp and coconut, or blackened shark steak squirted with fresh lime can be sublime. Just be aware that there is no fresh lobster during spawning season (March 1–June 15), and no conch July through September. Throughout the country, meals are washed down with delicious fresh-squeezed juices, such as lime, watermelon, and orange.

Creoles are fond of saying "First vex he lose" (The first person to get angry loses out), and this might explain Belize's good vibe. For travelers, this means no hard sell and no hustling; you'll never feel like a pocketbook on legs.

Most of the best restaurants are in hotels and resorts, and they bear comparison with good, though not first-class, eateries in North America or Europe. Ambergris Caye has established itself as Belize's epicenter of fine dining with the opening of several excellent establishments. More and more restaurants now carry substantial wine lists. Be careful not to judge a restaurant by the way it looks; some of the best cooking comes from the humblest-looking cabanas. Follow your nose. Belize is a casual place and demands little in the way of a dress code. The most expensive restaurants prefer, but do not require, a jacket and tie for men; otherwise, you'll probably get served if you're wearing shoes and a shirt. Reservations are advisable at high-end places.

Prices vary considerably between the interior, Belize City, and the cays. Because it's the most developed, Ambergris Caye is the most expensive; here, a meal for two at one of the best restaurants costs a whopping $50–$70. You can, however, eat well for much less. Lobster runs $10–$15, depending on the restaurant. A fish like grilled grouper usually costs about $10; a substantial American-style breakfast, $5; and a hamburger, $3. Many restaurants charge about $3–$5 for the omnipresent rice, bean, and meat combination, which vegetarians can request without the meat. To look like a local, douse your meal with Marie Sharp's Habanero Pepper Sauce (a bottle is on *every* Belizean table).

Islanders will split a few coconuts if you ask, but don't overindulge; it's a natural laxative. In town markets, look for papaya, bananas, mangoes, sliced watermelon, and soursop (a prickly fruit that tastes like a mixture of pineapple, lime, and pear). You can also fill up cheaply at snack stands and street carts selling *garnaches* (fried corn tortillas topped with beans, salsa, and wisps of cheese) or *panades* (sort of like ravioli, but deep-fried and filled with fish). Fearless travelers may embrace the mystery-filled tamales available everywhere. Nowhere in Belize will you find milk (other than powdered or condensed) or coffee (beyond Folger's Crystals); you will, however, find delicious cheeses made by the country's Mennonite farmers. Belize is the only nation in Mezoamerica free of U.S. fast-food chains, but HL's Burger fills the gap with its eight locations.

DRINKS • All regional capitals have water-treatment plants, making most tap water drinkable. (The only exception is the cays, which rely on briny, ill-tasting well water). Bottled water is available all over the country in restaurants and groceries. The local beer is Belikin, regular or stout, at about a buck a bottle. Rum is served up with a plethora of mixers: Coke, coconut juice, condensed milk, and even sea-weed and sugar. Several brands are available, from the cheap Cane Juice to the smooth Caribbean.

TIPPING • Although Belizeans themselves don't usually tip in restaurants, they know that foreigners do. Let your conscience be your guide. Tour guides of any sort expect (and appreciate) a tip of a few dollars. You don't need to tip cab drivers.

OUTDOOR ACTIVITIES

If you're planning a trip to Belize to plant your ass on a beach, think again. From diving, snorkeling, and sea kayaking on the barrier reef to canoeing or tubing down inland rivers to trekking through jungles and ancient caves, outdoor activities will dominate your stay. In almost any town, you can rent bikes ($10–$15 per day) to explore the surrounding area, although heat and humidity will likely humble your Iron-man dreams. But it is for the spectacular snorkeling and scuba diving on the majestic Barrier Reef that thousands of visitors flock to Belize each year. Dive destinations can be divided into two broad categories—the reef and the atolls. Most reef diving is done on the northern section, particularly off **Ambergris Caye.** Here the reef is just a few hundred yards from shore, making access to your dive site extremely easy: the journey by boat usually takes 10–30 minutes. The farther south you go, the farther apart are coast and coral, and longer boat trips make for greater dependence on weather. On Ambergris, in contrast, you might be stuck inside for a morning storm, but still have a good chance of getting out in the afternoon. Most of the cays' dive shops are attached to hotels, and the quality of dive masters, equipment, and facilities vary considerably.

Many resorts offer diving courses. A one-day basic familiarization course costs between $125 and $175. A four-day PADI certification course costs $400. A popular variant is a referral course, in which you do the academic and pool training at home, then complete the diving section here; the cost, for two days, is $250.

If you want to experience something truly dramatic, head to the atolls, which make for some of the greatest diving in the world. The only problem is that they're awfully far from where you're likely to stay. If you're based on Ambergris Caye, Glover's Reef is out of the question for a day trip by boat, and getting to Lighthouse Reef's Blue Hole—even when the weather is perfect, which it often isn't in winter—is at least a two- to three-hour boat trip. Turneffe is more accessible, but even that is a long and comparatively costly day trip, and you're unlikely to reach the atoll's southern tip, which has the best diving. Another option is to head south to Dangriga and take a boat out to one of the cheap dive camps on Glover's Reef. Live-aboard dive boats and atolls resorts are prohibitively expensive.

If snorkeling, fishing, or sea kayaking are what float your boat, you're better off heading to the less expensive destinations like Caye Caulker or the town of Placencia (on the mainland). Snorkeling equipment runs about $5 per day. Boat trips out to the reef are about $10–$15 per person (all-day excursions to more remote spots can be $25 or more); Caye Caulker's Rasta crews are famous for partying it up on their boats. Sea kayaks rent for $5–$10 per hour and allow you to paddle out to the reef where you can snorkel on your own. In almost any seaside town, you'll find locals happy to take you sportfishing ($50–$100) for tarpon, black grouper, mutton, and yellowtail snapper.

Inland, a host of other adventures await you. Hiking is not wildly popular in Belize; trails through the jungle are usually short, hot, and filled with a variety of blood-ingesting insects lying in ambush. If hike you must (or if you're a bird-watcher intent on checking out Belize's 300-plus species), the Cockscomb Basin Jaguar Sanctuary (*see* Near Dangriga, *below*) in the southern half of the country has well-maintained trails through a portion of its 100,000 acres. In northern Belize, the **Community Baboon Sanctuary** and the **Crooked Tree Wildlife Sanctuary** both offer hiking trails, although you must initially explore with a guide ($5 an hour or $15 a half-day). After your first hour you can venture off on your own or remain with the guide. An easier way to explore is on horseback; you can rent the beasts for around $20 per hour in many towns. You can rent canoes (often dugouts constructed from a single tree trunk) almost anywhere in Belize for less than $15 a day to cruise the jungle's rivers and lagoons.

In the mountainous west and south, Belize has many fascinating, eerie cave systems to explore. The most popular tours are run by Ian Anderson's Caves Branch Adventure Co. (*see* Near Belmopan, *below*), which takes you deep into ancient river cave systems in rubber inner tubes for about $60 per day, guide and lunch included.

BUSINESS HOURS

BTL offices and other places of business are generally open weekdays 8–noon and 1–5, Saturdays 8–noon (hours are severely curtailed in smaller towns and on the cays). Bank hours are typically Mondays,

Tuesdays, and Thursdays 8–noon; Wednesdays 8–1; and Fridays 8–1 and 3–6. Post offices are open weekdays 8–5. Almost everything (including many restaurants) is closed on Sundays.

VISITOR INFORMATION

Belize Tourist Board. Their official visitor magazine, *Destination Belize,* puts a glossy spin on everything Belizean. *In the U.S.: 421 7th Ave., Suite 1110, New York, NY 10001, tel. 212/563–6011 or 800/624–0686, fax 212/563–6033. In Belize: Box 325, Belize City, Belize, C.A., tel. 02/77–213. In the U.K.: 10 Harcourt House, 16A Cavendish Sq., London WIM 9AD, tel. 0171/499–9728.*

The **Belize Audubon Society** oversees most of the country's parks and reserves. Contact them for information on home-stay and volunteer programs. *12 Fort St., Belize City, Belize, C.A., tel. 02/34–985 or 02/34–987.*

VISAS AND TOURIST CARDS

All visitors to Belize must have a valid passport. Visas are not required for citizens of the United States, Canada, Australia, New Zealand, and the United Kingdom. Nationals of certain other countries, as well as visitors with one-way tickets, must obtain visitor's permits in advance. Visitors rarely need to show proof of return tickets or sufficient funds, although those with a less polished appearance may be harassed. Technically, you need a return or onward ticket and about $50 per day. Maximum stay is 30 days, although you may extend your visit up to six months (in one-month increments) by visiting the immigration office in Belize City or in Belmopan (*see* Basics for either city, *below*). The charge is $12.50 per month. For more information, contact the **Belize Embassy** (2535 Massachusetts Ave. NW, Washington, DC 20008, tel. 202/332–9636), the **Consulate of Belize** (5825 Sunset Blvd., Suite 206, Hollywood, CA 90028, tel. 213/469–7343), or the embassy in your home country.

HEALTH

The major health risk for travelers to Belize is Montezuma's Revenge, or traveler's diarrhea, caused by eating contaminated fruit or vegetables or drinking contaminated water. The country is not considered a major risk for the serious diseases (malaria, cholera, typhoid fever, etc.) found throughout the rest of Central America. Belizeans fly to the United States for treatment of serious medical problems, but you can receive 24-hour emergency medical care from hospitals in all the major cities; pharmacies are prevalent in the big cities and on Ambergris Caye.

PHONES AND MAIL

In almost every town and village around the country there is a **BTL** (Belize Telecommunications Limited) office where you can make direct, calling-card, and collect international calls, or send a fax. Most towns also have at least one pay phone. To reach an international operator from most phones, dial 115. Direct-dial costs are about $3 per minute to North America, $6 per minute to Europe, and $8 per minute to Australia and New Zealand. From the international airport, Belize City BTL, and San Pedro BTL, you can hook up with "home country direct service," which makes collect and calling-card calls *much* cheaper. For USA Direct, dial 555 (AT&T), 556 (Sprint Express), or 557 (MCI World Phone). For UK Direct, dial 552; for Canada Direct, dial 558. The country code for Belize is 501.

Belize's **postal service** is one of the quickest and most expensive in Central America. Mail between Belize and the United States takes about two weeks. A postcard to the United States costs 15¢ (to Europe, 20¢). A letter to the United States costs 30¢ (to Europe, 40¢). The main post office in Belize City is the only place you can receive mail; address mail to: Poste Restante, Belize City, Belize, C.A. They hold stuff for three months, after which it may be returned to sender (or disappear forever). If you're an American Express cardholder, you can also receive mail at their office in Belize City: c/o Belize Global Travel, 41 Albert St., Belize City, Belize, C.A.

WHEN TO GO

Despite popular opinion, Belize is a year-round destination, but some seasons are better than others. The dry season, from March to May, can be the least attractive time for inland trips, because of dust and wilting vegetation. The hottest months are March–September, when temperatures are around 80°–90° on the coast and cays and over 100° inland. There is a wet season in June and July, and you may find yourself battling flooded towns and mucky roadways, especially in the less-developed and rainier south, where as much as 160 inches of rain falls annually, On the cays, the wet season can be accompanied by lashing northerly winds, known in Creole as Joe North. Humidity in Belize is 75%–80% throughout the year, and temperatures never dip below 50°.

HOLIDAYS AND FESTIVALS • National holidays are celebrated with parades, block parties, and jump-ups (huge street dances). Banks, most businesses, and some restaurants close; bus lines and hotels usually continue to operate. Almost the entire country shuts down for a four-day weekend around **Easter.** Unique Belizean celebrations include **Baron Bliss Day** (March 9), honoring the country's greatest benefactor with a regatta and horse and cycle races in Belize City; **Commonwealth Day** (May 24), which commemorates the queen's birthday with a cycle race from Belize City to San Ignacio and horse racing in Belize City; **St. George's Day** (September 10), which begins a week of countrywide carnivals, parades, and pop concerts celebrating Britain's defeat of Spain at St. George's Caye in 1798; and **Independence Day** (September 21), which begins another week of street jump-ups and flag-raising ceremonies with music, dance, and food. **Garifuna Settlement Day** (November 19), celebrated mainly in the south, honors the first arrival of the Garifuna (Black Carib) people to Belize in 1832 with several days of dancing, punta rock, drumming, and traditional feasts.

Some of the Spanish- and Mayan-speaking villages in southern and western Belize celebrate their patron saints' days with traditional food, music, and dance. In southern Belize, the village of San Antonio holds a colorful Mayan celebration that begins in late August and culminates in the **Feast of St. Luis** (September 25). The Kekchi Mayan village of San Pedro Columbia fetes **San Luis Rey** (August 5) with religious ceremonies and dancing. In northern Belize, **Mexican National Day** (celebrated every September) recognizes ancestors who fled Mexico's caste wars in the 1800s.

FURTHER READING

Sastun: My Apprenticeship with a Maya Healer, by Rosita Arvigo (Harper Collins San Francisco). *Jaguar: One Man's Battle to Establish the World's First Jaguar Preserve,* by Alan Rabinowitz (Doubleday). *Cuello: An Early Maya Community in Belize,* by Norman Hammond (Cambridge University Press). *The Formation of a Colonial Society: Belize from Conquest to Crown Colony,* by Nigel Bolland (Johns Hopkins). *Spirit Possession in the Garifuna Community of Belize,* by Byron Foster (Cubola Productions).

BELIZE CITY

Don't believe the rumors about Belize City. Nothing here will cause you to lose your hair, your lunch, your sanity, or your life—unless you go looking for it. This peninsula, where the meandering Belize River finally meets the Caribbean Sea, was originally settled during the 17th and 18th centuries by log-rolling, hell-raising British pirates-turned-lumberjacks looking for a nice place to drink rum; its reputation as the lair of miscreants and laggards has persisted to the present day. Many natives still speak about Belize City as if it were truly a village of the damned, but this is a matter of perspective: on the vice scale, it's closer to Tulsa than Detroit.

Rumor has it that Belize City sits on a foundation of wood chips, loose coral, and rum bottles that were used to fill in what was once a huge swamp. In 1961, Hurricane Hattie claimed the lives of 300 residents, destroyed several million dollars' worth of property, and hastened the governmental exodus to Belmopan. This robbed Belize City of its middle class and so began a long, dark night, culminating in the arrival in the late 1980s of crack cocaine, which swept through the city leaving a trail of destruction even worse than Hattie's. So bad was Belize City's rap that press accounts of street crime made the place sound like south-central Los Angeles. It was never quite that bad, but in the mid-1990s both the government and private sector began a concerted effort revitalize the city. In 1995, $45 million was set aside for a new waterfront walkway along Eve Street. Open drains were replaced with septic tanks. Most importantly, the government came down heavily on the bad boys. A Tourism Police Unit was created, and their black-and-white jeeps and armed foot patrols are now a familiar sight. Stiff mandatory sentences on all offenders, and a speedy trial procedure (muggers are tried immediately, so their tourist victims are still in the country to testify against them) means that Belize City is now off the U.S. State Department's traveler's advisory list.

Although it's near impossible to visit Belize without spending at least a few hours making transportation connections in Belize City, don't look at a stop in town as penance for a week on the cays. There is a common beauty to life here. Street vendors hawk fried plantain chips and slices of watermelon from overloaded carts; groups of schoolchildren wearing matching uniforms parade the streets; elegant century-old colonial houses bristle with awkward hand-lettered signs advertising homemade tamales for sale. And it is still the only place in the country where you can pick up Stay-Puft marshmallows and

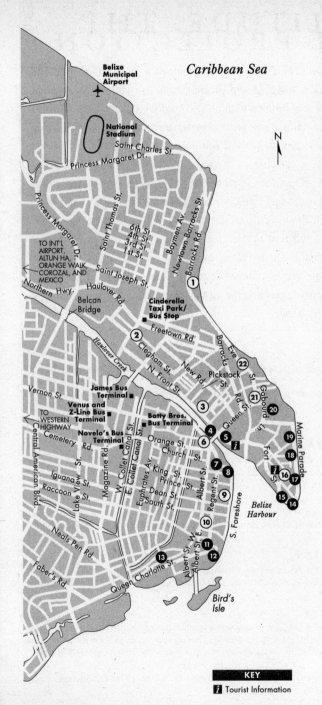

Caribbean Sea

Belize Municipal Airport

National Stadium

Saint Charles St.

Princess Margaret Dr.

N

TO INT'L AIRPORT, ALTUN HA, ORANGE WALK, COROZAL, AND MEXICO

Princess Margaret Dr.

Saint Thomas St.

6th St.
4th St.
3rd St.
1st St.

Baymen Av.

Newtown Barracks St.

Barracks Rd.

Saint Joseph St.

Haulover Rd.

Northern Hwy.

Belcan Bridge

Cinderella Taxi Park/ Bus Stop

Freetown Rd.

Clegham St.

Haulover Creek

Barracks St.

Eve St.

New Rd.

Pickstock St.

N. Front St.

Gabourd St.

Queen St.

Marine Parade

Fort St.

Vernon St.

James Bus Terminal

Venus and Z-Line Bus Terminal

TO WESTERN HIGHWAY

Novelo's Bus Terminal

Central American Blvd.

Cemetery Rd.

Iguana St.

Lake View St.

Raccoon St.

Magazine Rd.

W. Collet Canal St.

E. Collet Canal

Orange St.

Church St.

Euphrates Av.

King St.

Prince St.

Dean St.

South St.

Albert St.

Regent St.

Albert St. W.

Albert St. E.

S. Foreshore

Batty Bros. Bus Terminal

Neals Pen Rd.

Faber's Rd.

Queen Charlotte St.

Belize Harbour

Bird's Isle

1
2
22
21
3
20
4
5
19
6
18
7
16 17
8
9
15 14
10
11
12
13

Sights ●

American Embassy, **20**

Baron Bliss Memorial, **15**

Bliss Institute, **8**

Chateau Caribbean, **19**

Fort George Lighthouse, **14**

Government House, **12**

Memorial Park, **18**

Mona Lisa Hotel, **7**

Paslow Building, **5**

Radisson Fort George Hotel, **17**

Saint John's Cathedral, **11**

Swing Bridge, **4**

Yarborough Cemetery, **13**

Lodging ○

Bakadeer Inn, **2**

Colton House, **16**

Downtown Guest House, **21**

Fiesta Inn, **1**

Freddie's Guest House, **22**

Hotel Mopan, **10**

Isabel Guest House, **6**

North Front Street Guest House, **3**

Seaside Guest House, **9**

KEY

i Tourist Information

ATTITUDE: THE BEST PROTECTION

Like almost any urban area, Belize City has problems with crime, poverty, and drugs. Petty crime like mugging and pickpocketing are your main worries, although women will also contend with oh-so-appealing whistles, catcalls, and stares. Combat these with a few commonsense precautions: leave glittering jewels at home, stow expensive camera equipment out of sight, and keep the amount of cash you're carrying to a minimum (most hotels will lock up valuables if you ask). At night it's safest to stick to the main tourist areas north and south of the Swing Bridge. If you're traveling to the bus stations and other out-of-the-way places, catch a cab. Obvious fear and naiveté are magnets for trouble, and women will find that acting defensive or angry only increases verbal abuse. Be friendly, act streetwise, and keep your cool when hassled or approached. It's not uncommon for people on the street to try to sell you drugs; be careful, because tourists get suckered all the time. If you're caught with one joint, the fine is a hefty $500.

Ragu Extra-Chunky. The population is the most diverse of any Latin American city: a swirl of Creole, Garifuna, mestizo, Mayan, East Indian, and Chinese. Stick around for a while, and you're guaranteed to meet all kinds of colorful locals and expatriate gringos.

BASICS

VISITOR INFORMATION

The **Belize Tourist Board** has a friendly, helpful staff who distribute free up-to-date bus schedules, city maps, and a comprehensive list of hotels. *83 N. Front St., Box 325, tel. 02/77–213. North of Swing Bridge, across from post office. Open Mon.–Thurs. 8–noon and 1–5, Fri. 8–noon and 1–4:30.*

The **Belize Audubon Society** oversees most of the country's parks and reserves. Drop by for brochures, or call to book accommodations in park cooperatives or with home-stay programs. *12 Fort St., tel. 02/34–985 or 02/34–987. 1 block SE of Fort Street Guest House (see Food, below). Open weekdays 8–noon and 1–5.*

AMERICAN EXPRESS

Belize Global Travel is the local AmEx affiliate, where card members can receive mail. It's also a full-fledged travel agency. *41 Albert St., at King St., tel. 02/77–185. Open weekdays 8–noon and 1–5, Sat. 8–noon.*

CHANGING MONEY

Banks all give a rate of BZ$1.98 to US$1, usually with a minimal per-transaction charge (around 50¢). The black market gives you the full 2:1 rate, but the risk of having your money stolen in the process may not be worth the few extra cents. All banks are just south of the Swing Bridge (*see* Getting Around, *below*).

Atlantic Bank. Cash advances on Visa cards only. *6 Albert St., tel. 02/77–124. Open Mon., Tues., Thurs. 8–noon and 1–3; Wed. 8–1; Fri. 8–1 and 3–6.*

Barclay's Bank. No charge for credit-card advances. *21 Albert St., tel. 02/77–211. Open weekdays 8–1.*

Belize Bank. Charges $7.50 for credit-card advances. *60 Market Sq., tel. 02/77–132. Open Mon., Tues., Thurs. 8–noon and 1–3; Wed. 8–1; Fri. 8–1 and 3–6.*

EMBASSIES AND CONSULATES

Great Britain, Costa Rica, and El Salvador have their diplomatic headquarters in Belmopan.

British High Commission. *Embassy Sq., Belmopan, tel. 082/2146. Open weekdays 8–noon and 1–5.*

Canadian Consulate. *29 Southern Foreshore, tel. 02/31–060. Open weekdays 9–1.*

Guatemalan Embassy. Issues visas. *6A Saint Matthews St., tel. 02/33–150. Open weekdays 9–1.*

Panamanian Consulate. Issues visas. *2 Princess Margaret Dr., tel. 02/34–282. Open weekdays 9–1.*

United States Embassy. *29 Gabourel La., tel. 02/77–161. Open weekdays 8–noon and 1–5.*

IMMIGRATION

The **Office of Immigration and Nationality** extends visas in monthly increments ($12.50 per month). *Pickstock and N. Front Sts., 2nd floor, tel. 02/33–505. Open weekdays 8:30–11:30 and 1:15–3:30.*

EMERGENCIES

Dial 90 for **fire** and **ambulance** and 911 for **police.** The Belize Tourism Industry Association (BTIA) maintains a 24-hour hotline, **Crime Reporter** (tel. 02/72–464), to which you should also report theft or harassment. **Belize Medical Associates** (5791 St Thomas St., tel. 023/0303) and **Karl Heusner Memorial** (Princess Margaret Dr., tel. 023/1548) have 24-hour emergency rooms.

MAIL

The **main post office** (Paslow Building, Queen and N. Front Sts.) is open Monday–Thursday 8–5 and Friday 8–4:30. On the first floor, you can pick up mail (addressed to: Poste Restante, Belize City, Belize, C.A.). The parcel office, for mailing packages, is right next door. Mail between the United States and Belize can take as long as two–three weeks.

PHONES

The **BTL** office (1 Church St., near Albert St., tel. 02/77–179) is the place to make local and long-distance calls or send faxes. They have several direct Sprint and AT&T lines to the United States, United Kingdom, and Canada, although you may be asked to show a calling card before using them. The office is open Monday–Saturday 8 AM–9 PM and Sunday 8–noon. Pay phones are common south of the Swing Bridge on Albert Street; north of the bridge you'll find one at the post office.

COMING AND GOING

BY BUS

Four major bus companies (*see* Getting Around *in* chapter Basics, *above*) have terminals along **Collet Canal,** about 10–12 blocks west of the commercial center of town. This is not one of Belize City's more stellar neighborhoods. You're fine walking west from the Swing Bridge on Orange Street during busy daylight hours, but you'll probably want to cab it in the early morning, after dark, and on Sundays. Each region is served by several companies with complementary schedules; all are fairly uniform in terms of price, speed, comfort, and reliability. The Belize Tourist Board (*see* Visitor Information, *above*) can furnish you with up-to-date schedules for all bus companies except James, which is headquartered in Punta Gorda. At most terminals you can store oversize luggage for a small fee (50¢ each piece per day).

BY CAR

Although expensive, rental vehicles are often the most convenient—and sometimes the only—way to reach many of Belize's Maya ruins and forest preserves. Most companies (*see* Getting Around *in* chapter Basics, *above*) rent only to drivers age 25 and up; all offer unlimited mileage and free pickup and delivery at Belize City airports and hotels.

BY BOAT

Boats depart daily for the cays from three locations: the dock at the Bellevue Hotel; the landing immediately adjacent to the Swing Bridge; and the A&R Texaco Station, on North Front Street. (For times and rates, *see* The Cayes, *below.*)

BY PLANE

The **Phillip S. W. Goldson International Airport** (tel. 025/2014) is in Ladyville, 18 km (11 mi) north of Belize City off the Northern Highway. The **Municipal Airport** is located on the northern outskirts of Belize City. Remember to keep $11.25 for exit taxes when departing Belize by air. (For more information on international and local airlines, *see* chapter Basics, *above*.)

AIRPORT TRANSPORT • From the international airport you can take a taxi ($15), or walk 3 km (2 mi) to the Northern Highway and catch a southbound Batty or Venus bus (20 min, $1). From the Municipal Airport, your only option is a taxi ($2.50).

GETTING AROUND

Belize City is divided in half by **Haulover Creek**; spanning the creek near the harbor is the **Swing Bridge,** which marks the center of town. Running south from the Swing Bridge, **Regent** and **Albert streets** are where you'll find banks, government offices, many cheap restaurants, and Brodie's, the nation's only supermarket-cum-department store. All are within five or six blocks of each other, about 10–12 blocks east of the bus terminals.

Just north of the Swing Bridge (and parallel to Haulover Creek), **North Front Street** has the post office, tourist office, and the city's only traffic light. Follow **Queen Street** north from the Swing Bridge to the sea (about 10 blocks) and you'll reach the more exclusive and less frenzied part of town, with embassies, luxury hotels, and the city hospital. You'll find little reason to stray very far west on either side of the Swing Bridge—it's primarily residential and occasionally possessed by street gangs.

Because Belize City has no urban buses, **taxis,** recognizable by their green license plates, are the only alternative to moseying around town. Use them to get to the bus terminals, airports, and a handful of out-of-the-way restaurants, particularly at night or if you are traveling alone. The fixed price is $3 for one person between any two points in the city, plus $1 for each additional person. Outside the city, you're charged by distance, but there are no meters, so be sure to set a price before you leave. Pick up a taxi at Market Square, by the Swing Bridge, or call Cinderella Taxi (tel. 024/5240) or Caribbean Taxi (tel. 027/2888).

WHERE TO SLEEP

Most travelers end up staying in Belize City at least a night or two before or between escapes to more pleasant locales. Accommodations abound at every price level, from dorm beds to posh rooms at the city's two chain hotels ($90–$130 double), the **Radisson Fort George** (2 Marine Parade, tel. 02/33–333) and the **Fiesta Inn** (Newtown Barracks Rd., tel. 02/32–670). What you'll find worth paying most for in Belize City isn't necessarily a clean toilet seat (though that's nice, too) but safety. When trudging from the bus stations you may be tempted by cheap nearby digs—keep walking. Presumably you're lugging that stuff around in your backpack because you want to keep it. North of the Swing Bridge is a budget-hotel area that's close to buses and boats. The best deals are small, family-run affairs—if possible, call a few days ahead to ensure you'll get a room. Many hotels will do your laundry for a small fee. Those who can't will steer you toward the closest Laundromat (usually $5 per load to wash and dry).

UNDER $15 • Downtown Guest House. Opened in 1994, this new-kid-on-the-block has yet to be ravaged by the backpacking hordes—perhaps because it's nowhere near downtown. Simple whitewashed rooms are clean, bright, and airy at $7.50 (single) or $10 (double) with shared bath. All have access to a pleasant second-floor veranda and indoor common room. The only double with private bath goes for $17.50. *5 Eve St., near Queen St., tel. 02/32–057. From Swing Bridge, walk 4 blocks north on Queen St. and turn left. 15 rooms, 11 with shared bath. Cash only.*

North Front Street Guest House. The best of the bunch on North Front Street, it has reasonably clean, comfortable singles ($7.50) and doubles ($12.50), plus a small common room and a bulletin board cluttered with tourist info. Although the neighborhood is sketchy, Mrs. Speer, the proprietor, keeps the building secure. This place is a magnet for backpackers, so call ahead. *124 N. Front St., tel. 02/77–595. 3 blocks west of Swing Bridge. 8 rooms with shared bath. Laundry.*

UNDER $25 • Freddie's Guest House. They have only three rooms, but each of them is immaculate. Those with shared bath are $17.50 (single) or $21 (double), and the room with private bath is $24. The surrounding residential neighborhood is quiet and very safe. Mrs. Griffith, the proprietor, is the closest thing to a mother away from home; this keeps her loyal guests flocking back. It's often full, so ring ahead. *36 Eve St., near Belize City Hospital, tel. 02/33–851. From Swing Bridge, walk north on Queen St. 5 blocks, turn left, and walk 3 blocks. Cash only.*

Isabel Guest House. A friendly, family-run place, Isabel has three pleasant, clean, safe rooms at $17 (single) or $22.50 (double) in an ideal upstairs location immediately south of the Swing Bridge. *3 Albert St., tel. 02/73–139. Above Matus Drug Store in Market Sq. Entrance is behind drug store: follow signs up stairs. 3 rooms with private bath. Cash only.*

UNDER $40 • Hotel Mopan. This aging colonial building radiates a sort of dilapidated charm. Decent rooms start at $35 (double), plus $10 if you'd like air-conditioning instead of fans. The hotel operates a small travel agency, bar, and restaurant serving reasonably priced Belizean dishes. The location in the historical district, just south of the city's commercial center, is terrific. *55 Regent St., at Palm La., tel. 02/77–351. From Swing Bridge, walk about 8 blocks south on Regent St. 12 rooms with private bath. Laundry.*

Seaside Guest House. This is, hands down, the most popular value spot in Belize City. The house is a good-looking, two-story quasi-colonial, and the owner, Fred Prost, is intent on making your stay an agreeable one. Rooms are $25 (double). A space in the seven-bed dorm is $8. Grab a beer at the small bar downstairs, or escape to the shaded porch and upstairs common room. It's usually full, so call before arriving. No advance reservations accepted. *3 Prince St., at Regent St., tel. 02/78–339. From Swing Bridge, walk south 5 blocks on Regent St. and turn left. 7 dorm beds and 4 rooms with shared bath.*

UNDER $90

Bakadeer Inn. The surrounding area is drab, but this new Belizean-run hotel has very agreeable rooms built along a quiet, secure courtyard set back from the street. All rooms have a well-stocked minibar, phone, TV, and private bath. There is a cheery breakfast room and a reassuringly large night watchman. *74 Clegham St., tel. 023/1400. 12 rooms with bath.*

Colton House. This beautiful colonial house with a white wraparound veranda is a real find. Inside are fancy antiques and cool, polished wooden floors. The English family who run the place give it the charm of a traditional B&B (without the breakfast, alas). Reservations are essential. *9 Cork St., tel. 024/4666. 5 rooms with bath.*

FOOD

Although it's possible to eat cheaply in Belize City, to eat well is a task. Several of the more pleasant restaurants lie on the outskirts of town, requiring a cab, especially at night. Others are clustered south of the Swing Bridge, along Regent and Albert Streets. Very few places are open on Sunday.

If it's merely a snack you're in search of, you've plenty of options. Two **indoor markets,** just north and south of the Swing Bridge, operate daily, offering produce, nuts, and freshly squeezed juices. There are also two supermarkets in town: **Brodie's** (Bishop and Albert Sts., tel. 02/77–070) and **Ro-Mac's** (27 Albert St., at Church St., tel. 02/77–022), both open weekdays 9–6, Saturday 8–5, and Sunday 9–12:30, as well as numerous corner grocers. Along Regent, Albert, and Queen Streets, look for **street vendors** selling delectable tacos (two for 50¢) or mystery-content tamales, as well as fresh fruits and juices. For cheap burgers, hot dogs, sandwiches, and other snacks, visit the **Elbow Room** (22 Albert St., no phone), **Scoops Ice Cream** (Eve St. and Gaol La., no phone), or **Blue Bird Ice Cream Parlor** (35 Albert St., at Church St., no phone). **Pete's Pastries** (41 Queen St., between Barrack and New Rds., no phone) serves slices of the sweet stuff, as well as sandwiches, meat pies, and savory soups. Milkshakes, fruit frosties, and credible iced cappuccinos can be found at the **Juice Connection** (14 New Rd., north of Queen St., tel. 02/72–289).

UNDER $10 • Chon Saan III. One of the best Chinese restaurants in town, Chon Saan dishes out filling portions of fried rice, chop suey, egg rolls, and various meat dishes, all around $3–$8; a quarter of a chicken with fries is only $4. The drawback: it's in a rough neighborhood, so consider taking a cab here, especially at night. Takeout available. *166 N. Front Street, tel. 02/35–706. Other locations in Belize City: Chon Saan Palace, 1 Kelly St., near Cinderella Taxi Park, tel. 02/33–008; New Chon Saan Restaurant, 55 Euphrates Ave., between King and South Sts., tel. 02/72–709.*

Dit's Saloon. Dit's is a Belize City institution. More pastry café than restaurant, it's a simple place, with cheery striped tablecloths and a homey feel. (Like many other older Belizean restaurants, it's got a sink right in the dining room.) The cakes—try the three-milks cake or the coconut tarts—are sticky and sweet, and breakfasts—toast, eggs, and beans washed down with ample mugs of tea—are excellent value. The fresh-squeezed juices are just right. *50 King St., 1 block west of Albert St., tel. 02/73–330.*

BONA FIDE
BUSH MEDICINE

Feeling poorly? Pepto failed you? For more than 30 years, Aunt Barbara, certified herbalist, has dispensed bush remedies from her stall in the Belize central market on Queen Street. She can set you up with a steaming herbal brew made from jackass bitters (a favorite of the Maya), plus 11 other secret herbs and spices. It works as well as Western medicine (or better), but don't expect a pleasant peppermint taste.

G & G's Cafe and Patio. The umbrella-topped tables in the shady courtyard are a pleasant place to indulge, and the food is delicious. Burgers and fries are $3–$5, Creole dishes like stewed chicken with beans and rice are $7–$9. This is a popular lunch spot for local businessmen, although there's rarely a crowd for dinner. *2-B King St., just east of Regent St., tel. 02/74–378. Closed Sun. and the first 2 wks of July.*

Macy's Cafe. The photo of Harrison Ford, who ate here during the making of *The Mosquito Coast,* and the sign above the door in Greek, German, Japanese, and Arabic shows how popular this small restaurant has become. If you're an ecofreak or a vegetarian, some of the fare may make you shudder. You've seen the wildlife? Now you can eat it. Wrap your mouth around such game as stewed armadillo, brocket deer, gibnut, and stewed iguana. Luckily, Macy, the Jamaican proprietor, also serves Creole dishes ($5–$7), usually featuring fresh-caught fish. There's a takeout window next door. *18 Bishop St., just west of Albert St., tel. 02/73–419. Closed Sun.*

UNDER $15 • Fort Street Restaurant and Guest House. For consumers weary of beans and rice, this gracious colonial mansion is a welcome haven. Lodging prices may be steep (though quads go for $85), but dinners here are within reach ($9–$15) and feature a changing array of international specialties—Thursday is pasta night. There are excellent full breakfasts (try the Mosquito Toast, cinnamon french toast stuffed with cream cheese, honey, and pineapple), sandwiches and salads for lunch, and a constantly changing chalkboard menu in the evening. *4 Fort St., near Memorial Park, tel. 02/30–116. Closed Sun.*

UNDER $30 • Quarterdeck. Getting here at night is an adventure in itself. A free boat picks you up at Maya Landings, and you head out across the black water to Moho Caye. The food includes steaks, from finest Cayo beef that has been "hung" for 15 days for maximum tenderness. The fish specials (gouper and blue marlin) are famous. *Moho Caye, tel. 02/35–499.*

WORTH SEEING

Belize City's streets are filled with fine examples of colonial architecture, although much of it is in varying stages of decay. Some of the best surviving examples lie south of the Swing Bridge on **Regent Street**: the **courthouse** is a cement reconstruction of the original wood structure that burned down in 1926. Just north of the courthouse, what is now a modest two-story office building used to be the home of the **Mona Lisa Hotel**; it was a set in Peter Weir's 1985 film *The Mosquito Coast.* Seven blocks south you'll find the beautiful **Government House,** which is said to have been designed by the illustrious British architect Sir Christopher Wren. It was once the residence of the Governor General, the queen's representative in Belize. It was refurbished in 1995 and is now open to the public; you can peruse archival records, check out silver, glassware, and furniture, or just mingle with the tropical birds in the beautiful gardens. Walk one block west to **Albert Street** to view **Saint John's Cathedral,** the oldest Anglican church in Central America. The kings of the Mosquito Coast were crowned here from 1815 to 1845. One block southwest of the cathedral stretches **Yarborough Cemetery,** where the inscriptions on the headstones once hinted at tales of deceit, murder, and derring-do, though you'd be hard-pressed to find any legible inscriptions after the passing of a century.

Immediately north of the Swing Bridge is the somewhat dowdy **Paslow Building,** built in 1842 and named after an early 19th-century magistrate and slave owner. Presently it houses the postal service. Continue southeast along the water on **Front Street** to reach the **Fort George Lighthouse** and **Baron Bliss Memorial** (*see below*). You'll find a view of the bustling city harbor and open sea just over the promontory. Walk north on **Marine Parade** and behold the Radisson Fort George Hotel, with its luxury rooms and polite, white-helmeted lobby attendants. (Slip up to the top floor for a spectacular view of the city and even the nearby cays.) Next door is the **Chateau Caribbean,** a beautiful colonial mansion that was once Belize's only private hospital. Both adjoin **Memorial Park,** a tranquil respite with welcome sea breezes. Farther inland are most of the embassies, housed in well-preserved mansions; the impressive **American Embassy** (*see* Basics, *above*) is on Gabourel Lane, just south of Queen Street.

THE SWING BRIDGE

As you may have guessed, the Swing Bridge spanning **Haulover Creek** *swings.* Daily at 5:30 AM and 5:30 PM, four men hand-winch the bridge a quarter-revolution so a bevy of waiting seacraft can continue their journeys upstream. (When it was the only bridge in town, this snarled traffic for blocks.) The bridge, made in Liverpool, England, opened in 1923; it's the only one of its kind left. Before the Swing Bridge arrived, cattle were "hauled over" Haulover Creek in a barge. Clever, huh?

BLISS INSTITUTE

Overlooking the harbor from the south bank of Haulover Creek is Bliss Institute, the cultural center of Belize. The center's namesake was the eccentric Baron Bliss, the country's greatest benefactor. The baron was an avid fisherman who fell in love with Belize without ever setting foot on the mainland. When he died he left most of his estate to the people of Belize. The money has been used on many important projects such as roads, markets, and cultural centers. March 9, the day Baron Bliss died, is now a national holiday. The institute houses the **National Arts Council** and hosts events such as a drama series (end of April), Children's Festival of the Arts (May), dance festival (June–July), and a variety of musical and cultural performances during the month-long celebration of independence in September. All events are inexpensive ($1.50–$5) or free. A few Mayan artifacts from Caracol are on display in the entryway. *2 Southern Foreshore, between Church and Bishop Sts., tel. 02/72–110. Open weekdays 8:30–noon and 1–5.*

SHOPPING

Belize is a good place to cure your shopping addiction: there is not much to buy. Most of the crafts you see come from over the border, in Guatemala, where they are half the price. That said, the **National Handicraft Center** (Fort St., just past Fort Street Guest House) stocks Belizean products of all kinds, including handwoven baskets, black coral jewelry, pottery, slate carvings, and carved hardwood figures. The **Fort Street Guest House** (*see* Food, *above*) has a good gift shop as do Belize City's poshest hotels, the **Radisson Fort George** (2 Marine Parade) and the **Fiesta Inn** (Newtown Barracks). Belize's beautiful stamps are available from the **Philatelic Society** (Queen St., behind post office). **Go Tees** (23 Regent St.) has T-shirts for adults and children and a good selection of crafts. The new **Save-U** supermarket (Belikin Area Plaza) is a good place to browse for local bargains. Bibliophiles should head for the **Book Center** (4 Church St.) and the **Belize Bookshop** (Regent St).

AFTER DARK

Lots of bars and discos exist for moneyed travelers, and every corner of the city has a divey watering hole for local men, but places where backpackers will feel comfortable are scarce. Cost and safety are major factors: because muggings are a threat, you'll need to cough up money for a cab even before you raise your first Belikin. The **Villa Hotel** (15 Cork St., near Memorial Park, tel. 02/32–803) has a bar with a cool view, and the **Belize Biltmore Plaza** (Northern Hwy., Mile 7 near international airport, tel. 02/32–302) has karaoke on Thursday nights. The **Ramada Hotel** (*see* Where to Sleep, *above*) offers happy-hour drink specials daily 5–9 PM.

Bellevue Hotel. When the bands start rocking, join the crowd (mostly tourists) for some sweaty, exhilarating dancing, from punta (dirty dancing) to disco. *5 Southern Foreshore, tel. 02/77–051. Live music Thurs.–Sat. nights.*

Hard Rock Cafe. Unaffiliated with its international namesake, this juke joint is the spot to mix with young locals and dance to recorded music in air-conditioned comfort, or chill out with a beer ($2) on the roof. Weekends get jumping after 11 PM. *35 Queen St., at Handyside St., tel. 02/32–041.*

Lindbergh's Landing. Is that Belizean or Polynesian decor? You decide. In any case, it's a favorite with gringos and the local upper class and often has an excellent sax player working the dance floor. *162A Newtown Barracks, across from Ramada, tel. 02/30–890.*

NEAR BELIZE CITY

THE BELIZE ZOO AND TROPICAL EDUCATION CENTER

If the word " zoo " conjures images of iron bars and miserable critters, this one will surprise and delight you. Like everything in Belize, it has a story. After the shooting of a wildlife film, *Path of the Rain Gods,* in 1983, Sharon Matola, their handler, was left with 17 semitame animals. They wouldn't have survived in the wild, so she decided to set up a backyard zoo. In 1991, in consultation with the great British zoologist and writer Gerald Durrell, whose zoo on the island of Jersey is a Noah's Ark of endangered species, she moved them here. Today, about 100 blissed-out animals—all Belizean natives and many endangered species—live in a natural setting. The national animal, the tapir (locally known as the "mountain cow"), along with the national bird, the keel-billed toucan, and Belizean's favorite oversized rodent, the gibnut, all reside here. Although they're sometimes camouflaged by the undergrowth, you'll also see jaguars, ocelots, pumas, and jaguarundis; as for the birds, don't miss the scarlet macaws, spectacled owl, and vultures. There are plans to add a butterfly exhibit, reptile center, and large aviary as soon as money becomes available. To visit the zoo, catch any of the hourly westbound Batty or Novelo buses (*see* Coming and Going, *above*) and ask the driver to drop you off. Camping is available at the zoo's Tropical Education Center ($5 per night), or you can stay overnight in the dorms ($10 per person). *Western Hwy., Mile 29, tel. 081/3004. Admission $7.50.*

About a mile from the zoo on the Western Highway is **Monkey Bay** (tel. 08/23–180), a small, privately owned ecocenter, research station, and school. They maintain a pair of short trails to the savanna and the river. Here you can camp in thatched palapas ($5 per night) and enjoy delicious organic vegetarian food ($4 a meal).

THE CAYES AND ATOLLS

The moment your boat speeds away from Belize City and out to sea, a certain air slowly but surely begins to assert itself. Although all Belize is generally laid-back, on the cays, it seems, they've unraveled the mystery of life—which apparently has something to do with hammocks, rum punch, and an ocean breeze. No fewer than 175 cays (the word comes from the Spanish *cayo,* "low island or reef," but is pronounced "key," as in Key Largo) dot the coastline like punctuation marks in a long, liquid sentence. Most cays lie inside the Barrier Reef, which over the centuries has acted as a breakwater, allowing them to form and develop undisturbed by the tides and winds that would otherwise sweep them away.

Belize's reef is the second-longest barrier reef in the world (the longest is Australia's Great Barrier Reef). It was first explored centuries ago by the Maya, who used the tiny islands as way stations on their arduous trading journeys around the Yucatán Peninsula to the eastern coast of modern-day Mexico. In the 17th and 18th centuries, the reef became the focal point of Belize's colorful colonial history. Caribbean pirates—*real* pirates, not the patch-on-the-eye Disney variety—skulked the sandy beaches, looking to plunder vessels groaning with booty bound for the Old World. Most notorious of these pirate residents was Edward "Blackbeard" Treach. With his greasy black hair and gross neglect of personal hygiene, Treach was the maritime equivalent of a Hell's Angel, except instead of riding an Harley and smashing up bars, he cruised up and down the coast plundering ships. Home base was St. George's Caye (now a resort), which you'll whip by on the way to Ambergris or Caye Caulker. This is also the island where the Spanish and English duked it out in 1798 to settle control of Belize. Great Britain won, in a battle that lasted 2½ hours.

Some of the cays are no more than a Band-Aid™–size patch of sand with a few shady palms and a weird name: Funk Caye, Hatchet Caye, Wee-Wee Caye. Some names suggest the kind of company you should expect: Mosquito Caye, Sandfly Caye, and even Crawl Caye, which is infested with boa constrictors.

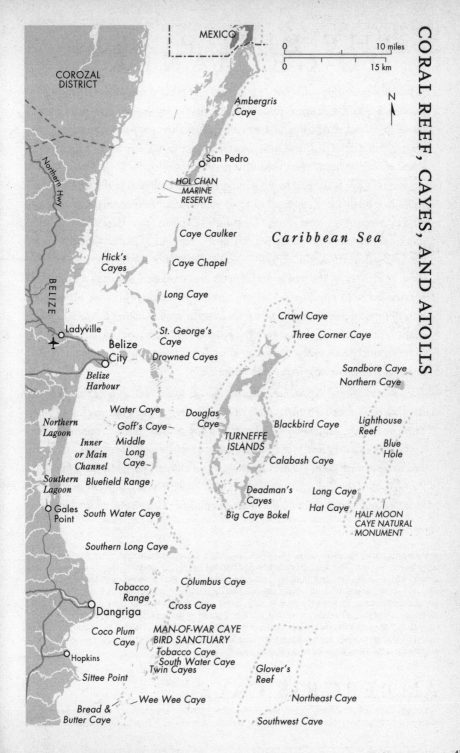

MEXICO

COROZAL
DISTRICT

0   10 miles
0   15 km

N

*Ambergris
Caye*

Northern Hwy

San Pedro

*HOL CHAN
MARINE
RESERVE*

Caribbean Sea

BELIZE

Caye Caulker

Caye Chapel

*Hick's
Cayes*

Long Caye

Crawl Caye

Three Corner Caye

Ladyville

*St. George's
Caye*

Belize
City

Drowned Cayes

Sandbore Caye
Northern Caye

*Belize
Harbour*

Water Caye

*Douglas
Caye*

Blackbird Caye

*Lighthouse
Reef*

*Northern
Lagoon*

Goff's Caye

*TURNEFFE
ISLANDS*

*Blue
Hole*

*Inner
or Main
Channel*

*Middle
Long
Caye*

Calabash Caye

*Southern
Lagoon*

Bluefield Range

Gales
Point

South Water Caye

*Deadman's
Cayes*

Long Caye

Hat Caye

Big Caye Bokel

HALF MOON
CAYE NATURAL
MONUMENT

Southern Long Caye

Columbus Caye

*Tobacco
Range*

Cross Caye

Dangriga

*Coco Plum
Caye*

MAN-OF-WAR CAYE
BIRD SANCTUARY

Tobacco Caye
South Water Caye
Twin Cayes

*Glover's
Reef*

Hopkins

Sittee Point

Wee Wee Caye

Northeast Caye

*Bread &
Butter Caye*

Southwest Caye

THE BEST PLACES TO GET TANKED

Belize has more than 560 km (347 mi) of reef just waiting to be dived, more than in Bonaire, Cozumel, and all the Caymans put together. In all, several hundred species of Caribbean tropicals frequent the reef, including grouper, squirrel fish, parrot fish, and such colorful aquatic characters as the damselfish, a bolt of blue no bigger than your little finger known locally as the "disco fish." Ambergris Caye is the best base for budget divers: it's closest to the reef (only a 10-minute boat-ride, as opposed to 30 or 40 minutes in the south) and has the biggest selection of dive shops. Sergeant's, English, and Goff's Cayes—all minuscule islands with sandy beaches and a handful of palms—are popular snorkeling day-trip destinations from either Caulker or Ambergris, because all three lie directly on the barrier reef. Divers and snorkelers both will appreciate Mexico Rocks (a point on Ambergris Caye's eastern shore), which attracts a bevy of tropical fish and includes an underwater cave. Another hot spot is Hol Chan Marine Reserve, a 13-square-km (5-square-mi) area approximately 6 km (4 mi) south of San Pedro. Barren and overfished when it was named a reserve in 1987, Hol Chan now teems with aquatic life.

The ultimate diving experience, however, awaits to the east, outside the Barrier Reef, at one of Belize's three atolls: Glover's Reef, Lighthouse Reef, and the Turneffe Islands. Although they all require a day or more to reach, these are well worth the extra time and money. There are spectacular wall dives, coral caves, as well as cartoonish giant yellow tube sponges and zillions of brightly hued fish. Of the two atolls, the Turneffes are closer (and cheaper to visit); popular dive spots include Rendezvous Point on the north end and Big Caye Bokel on the south.

Many, like Cockney Range or Baker's Rendezvous, simply express the whimsy or homesickness of the early British settlers. The vast majority are uninhabited except by possum, frigate birds, pelicans, brown- and red-footed boobies, and lewd-sounding creatures called wish-willies (a kind of iguana). A very few at one time supported fishing villages, like Caye Caulker and Ambergris Caye, the two most popular destinations. Expect your costs to be in direct proportion to how far behind you want to leave civilization. That said, wherever you end up you'll be dazzled by the populations of colorful fish and tropical plants that cohabit in one of the richest marine ecosystems on Earth. There is tons to do: swimming, scuba diving, snorkeling, fishing, kayaking, horseback riding, or canoeing. Or you can just kick back with a rum punch and a book and do absolutely nothing.

AMBERGRIS CAYE

Ambergris Caye is Belize's only type-A personality, where police make their rounds in black-and-white golf carts, beaches are groomed every morning at dawn, and drinks with umbrellas are served without irony. But at 40 km (25 mi) long and 7 km (4½ mi) wide at its widest point, Ambergris is the queen of the cays. It has the best dive shops, the most restaurants, and the biggest selection of accommodations from budget simplicity in San Pedro, the main town, to splashy resorts like Mata Chica, where Mick Jagger recently rented a villa for $400 per night. At night, water taxis zip up and down the coast like New York cabs, taking people bar- and restaurant hopping. Ambergris is also virtually the only place in the country where, if so inclined, you can party all night to the jumping sounds of punta, soca, and reggae. But remember; to enjoy Ambergris you will have to dig deeper in your wallet than elsewhere.

The Maya traded here thousands of years ago, and on early maps it was referred to as Costa de Ambar, or the Amber Coast, a name derived from a blackish, marbled substance secreted by the sperm whale and often washed up on the beach. For centuries it was used in perfumery and medicine. For most of its existence, San Pedro, the main town, was a sleepy fishing village. But in the past 10 years, it has been transformed into a sort of Belizean Sausalito (this is the San Pedro that Madonna sang about in her 1986 song *La Isla Bonita*, which San Pedroites practically treat as their official anthem). Although everyone grumbles about how commercial it has become (and they're right), San Pedro is no Cancún. The heart of the town is still a couple of streets of brightly painted, mostly two-story wooden houses, where old men still lean over their balconies in the evenings watching the world go by, most people go barefoot, and the stores and restaurants have names like Lily's, Alice's, and Martha's. The local population of 3,000 (mostly mestizo) islanders who live here is also intensely proud of its success

Every year there are more cars, more souvenir shops, and a little less innocence, but La Isla Bonita is still a charming, laid-back place; and there's still no McDonald's!

story. Tourism means flush toilets and good schools for their kids. San Pedro has one of the highest literacy rates in the country and an admirable level of ecological awareness about the fragility of the reef from which it now makes its living.

BASICS

San Pedro has two banks: **Belize Bank** (49 Barrier Reef Dr.; open Mon.–Thurs. 8–1 and Fri. 8–1 and 3–6) and **Atlantic Bank** (Front St.; open Mon., Tues., Thurs., and Fri. 8–noon and 1–3, Wed. 8–1, and Sat. 8:30–noon). You won't have any trouble cashing traveler's checks at most local establishments. **BTL** (open weekdays 8–noon and 1–4, Sat. 8–noon) is on Pescador Drive, at the far north end of town past the electricity plant. The **post office** (open weekdays 8–noon and 1–5) is on Barrier Reef Drive around the corner from Belize Bank. Seek medical attention at the **San Carlos Medical Clinic and Pharmacy** (Pescador Dr., tel. 026/2918; open weekdays 8–noon and 1–5, Sat. 8–1) or **Lion's Clinic** (next to the hyperbaric chamber, near the airstrip). **J's Laundromat** (Pescador Dr., tel. 026/2373) can take care of your stinky clothes for 50¢ a pound (they'll even iron for 50¢ per item); it's open Monday–Saturday 8–8 and Sunday 8–2.

COMING AND GOING

San Pedro enjoys frequent service by plane and boat to and from Belize City, Corozal, and Caye Caulker. Be warned: when winds are high, the crossing by boat from Belize City can be a jolting experience.

BY BOAT • A variety of boats connect Belize City with Ambergris. The most dependable leave from the **Belize Marine Terminal** (on N. Front St., near the Swing Bridge, tel. 023/1969). The quick open boats leave Belize City at 9 AM, noon, and 3 PM, then return from San Pedro at 8 AM, 11:30 AM, and 2:30 PM. The cost is $15 one way. Kiosk shops and the Belize City Marine Museum help kill the time before departure. The *Andrea* and *Andrea II* depart from the Southern Foreshore, by the Bellevue Hotel, weekdays at 4 PM and Saturday at 1 PM, and return from San Pedro at 7 AM weekdays and 8 AM on Saturday. The journey takes 75 minutes and costs $20 round-trip. Private charter boats also make the round-trip, leaving from the docks around the Swing Bridge, but they've been known to rip folks off—pay the fare only when you've reached your destination. The *Thunderboat* (tel. 026/2217) runs Monday–Saturday to both San Pedro and Caye Caulker, departing from Cesario's Dock in San Pedro at 7 AM and returning from Belize City at approximately 1 PM. The fare is $10 round-trip.

BY PLANE • Because an increasing number of travelers transfer directly to Ambergris Caye upon arrival in Belize City, there are regular flights to San Pedro from both the municipal and international airports. You'll always find taxis at the airstrip, and the hotels run courtesy coaches. If you're proceeding on foot, it's about two minutes, around the edges of the soccer field, to the main street. There are no buses.

Tropic Air (tel. 026/2012 or 800/422–3435 in the U.S.) and **Maya Island Airways** (tel. 023/1140) both fly to Ambergris. Round-trip fares for the 20-minute flight are about $40 (municipal) and $77 (international). Flights leave all day long from the Municipal Airport. They also stop at Caye Caulker, by request.

GETTING AROUND

In the years B.T. (Before Tourists), the three streets in San Pedro that ran parallel to the shore were called simply Front, Middle, and Back streets. Now, they're officially **Barrier Reef Drive** (Front), **Pescador Drive** (Middle), and **Angel Coral Street** (Back), although residents often use the no-frills originals. Many hotels, restaurants, and services are within a few blocks of each other on Barrier Reef and Pescador drives, and even the airstrip is in easy walking distance south of town. **Central Park** on Barrier Reef Drive, though not much to look at (unless there's a heated pickup game on the basketball court), marks the middle of town. Golf carts are the preferred mode of transportation. **Caribbean Golf Court Rental** (Barrier Reef Dr., tel. 026/3171) rents them by the hour ($15) or day ($70), offering discounts for extended use.

WORTH SEEING

A good place to cool off is the air-conditioned **Ambergris Museum & Cultural Center** (Island Plaza, tel. 026/2298). Local grannies have emptied their trunks and families have researched their histories to create this simple and pretty museum. Among other things, you'll see deer-horn tools that were used here up until deer hunting stopped in the 1960s.

WHERE TO SLEEP

North and south of San Pedro are dozens of exclusive beachside resorts that are prohibitively expensive. Fortunately, within town there are a few good-value hotels to be found—though only a handful. Don't expect any to be left if you waltz into town late in the day. Make reservations in advance, or at least arrive on the island early in the morning.

UNDER $30 • Milo's Hotel. The cheaper, basic rooms have ceiling fans, but they share two overwhelmed and often vengeful toilets. A small consolation is the view of the sea from the second-floor balcony. Rooms with private bath are $30. *North end of Barrier Reef Dr., tel. 026/2033. 15 rooms, 8 with bath. Cash only.*

UNDER $40 • Martha's Hotel. This large, white house on Pescador Drive gets shabbier every year, but it's still one of the few moderately priced places on Ambergris (doubles are $22.50). All rooms have private baths and ceiling fans, and guests have access to a phone in the first-floor office. Owner Martha Perez can set you up with all manner of tours. *Middle of Pescador Dr., tel. 026/2053. 14 rooms with bath. Cash only.*

Ruby's (Rubie's) Hotel. Rooms with private bath in this family-run hotel are $26–$36, depending on proximity to the (noisy) street. All are upstairs from the hotel's small private beach and dock. *Far south end of Barrier Reef Dr., tel. 026/2063. 18 rooms, 10 with bath.*

San Pedrano. Painted mint-green, blue, and white, this is the cheeriest hotel in San Pedro. Each of the spotless rooms has crisp linens and its own bathroom. The owners, the Gonzalez family, are friendly and hardworking. There is even a sea view from some rooms. *Barrier Reef Dr., north end, tel. 026/2054. 6 rooms with bath. Cash only.*

UNDER $75 • Spindrift Hotel. Centrally located, this family-run hotel and restaurant is something of a meeting place for locals (a hilariously funny game, known as Chicken Drop, is played on the beach outside on Wednesdays; *see* Cheap Thrills, *below,* for details) and is a favorite with divers. The rooms, some of which overlook the ocean, are grouped around an inner courtyard and vary considerably in price. *Front St., tel. 026/2251. 22 rooms with bath.*

FOOD

You can eat well without breaking the bank in San Pedro if you skip places that have the word *resort* in their names and target instead the smaller, more interesting restaurants and numerous stands and corner stores along Pescador and Barrier Reef drives that sell freshly squeezed juices and tropical fruits.

UNDER $5 • Many bars and snack counters, such as **Tarzan's Club** (Barrier Reef Dr., across from Central Park, tel. 026/2947) and **Ruby's Café** (Barrier Reef Dr., between Black Coral and Tarpon Sts., tel. 026/2063), sell vegetarian, chicken, and fish burritos ($1.50–$3) for lunch and dinner; Ruby's concocts highly addictive cinnamon rolls ($1) for breakfast. **Micky's,** just across the street from Tropic Air, is a good place for a hearty, inexpensive Belizean breakfast; fry jacks (a type of pancake) are $1.50.

UNDER $10 • Perhaps the best local cooking is at the **Reef Restaurant** (Barrier Reef Dr., no phone) where stewed fish with rice and beans is $6. A modern supermarket, **Rock's Shopping Center** (Pescador Dr. at Black Coral St., tel. 026/2044) stocks necessities like tortillas and beer, plus gourmet items like marinated mushrooms. In Fido's courtyard, the **Pizza Place** (Barrier Reef Dr., tel. 026/2444) dishes them up at $5.50–$10 for a small or $11–$19 for a large; they have salads and deli sandwiches ($3–$5), too.

Ambergris Delight. Delight in knowing that ambergris (whale bile) never appears on the menu as the plat du jour. Rather, you'll find decent Creole dishes at good prices: stew chicken with beans and rice ($3), fish ($5), and salads ($3). The atmosphere here is less "here we are in paradise" and more down-to-earth. *North end of Pescador Dr., tel. 026/2464. Open daily 11–2 and 6–10.*

Sweet Basil. It's a bit of a trek to this new bistro-cum-deli in a quiet residential area 2 km (1 mi) north of San Pedro; that's half its charm. Take a bike or a golf cart up Pescador Drive (you could walk, but it's quite a long way) until you come to the "cut," a cross-cay channel where a hand-pulled ferry will take you across the 60 ft of water for 50¢. A ½ km (¼ mi) later, you will be relaxing on the upstairs veranda of a two-story pink-and-green house. The deli offers all those things that gringos far from home suddenly crave, like lox, prosciutto, and Swiss cheese. There are also light bites like salade niçoise with fresh mozarella ($3.50) or tapenade ($2). *Tres Cocos, tel. 026/3870. Closed Mon.*

UNDER $15 • **Elvi's Kitchen.** When Elvi, a savvy, local Creole woman, opened her restaurant in 1964, she had a few tables on the sidewalk under a flamboyant tree and a take-out window. Today, she has San Pedro's equivalent of Planet Hollywood. It's easy to be cynical about the plastic tree in the corner or the gringos who flock here for the "local color," but Elvi's success mirrors the larger success of Ambergris Caye. And, unlike Planet Hollywood, it has retained a certain innocent charm. Dinner entrées are mostly seafood ($7.50 and up), although you can always choose the omnipresent stew chicken with beans and rice ($4.50). Don't miss the *liquados* (blended drinks of watermelon, soursop, pineapple, and banana). *Pescador Dr., near Ambergris St., tel. 026/2176. Closed Sun.*

Estel's. Estel's father-in-law was a World War II flier with a squadron called "Di Nah Might." (His flying jacket is up on the wall.) So if you are feeling nostalgic for the "YouEssofA," this is a good place to get an American-style breakfast ($4.50) as well as burgers ($2.50), sandwiches ($1.75), and excellent seafood ($5 and up). The little white-and-aqua building is right on the beach and has a sand floor and porthole-shape windows. There's a terrace outside, where you can sit under an umbrella of palapa leaves and watch pelicans splat into the water. And Estel has a great collection of CDs. *Front St., tel. 026/2019. Closed for dinner.*

CHEAP THRILLS

For those ardent fans of David Letterman's Stupid Pet Tricks, the Pier Lounge at the **Spindrift Hotel** (*see* Where to Sleep, *above*) has the perfect evening's entertainment. The Wednesday night **Chicken Drop** is a bizarre gambling game in which you put your money on circled numbers spread out on a piece of cardboard. The game begins when a chicken is held over the board and an audience member is asked to blow on its butt. When the chicken eventually takes a dump on the board, the lucky number wins the pot (the winner is also responsible for clean-up duty). Monday is another special game night, featuring the **Crab Race**. Put down $5, pick a crab, and win $100 if it scuttles to the finish line first. The games begin at 8:30 PM.

Under Belizean law, all beaches, including those at the ritziest resorts, are open to the public. You may make yourself unpopular by parking yourself on the well-raked sand of an four-star hotel, but, technically, you are within your rights. Two resorts immediately north and south of town, the **Paradise Hotel** and **Ramon's Village,** offer fancy lounge chairs, hammocks, shady palm trees, enclosed swimming areas, and tropical drinks. Farther north, out of town, you will find the bucolic splendor of **Victoria House.** The room prices are expensive, but you can sit under a palm tree and fantasize about that Hollywood movie you want to write.

AFTER DARK

San Pedro doesn't have the sort of drink-till-you-drop nightlife of some tropical resort towns, but it can be lively. You'll find plenty of open-air bars, cheap tropical drinks, and locals (mostly dive instructors and boat captains) who talk about "supporting San Pedro wildlife"—meaning they'd like another rum and Coke. North of town, next to Paradise Village Resort, **Sandals Pub** (Barrier Reef Dr., tel. 026/2281) is a friendly dive where tourists and locals mix to play a little pool or sway to reggae. So is the oceanfront bar at the **Sunbreeze Hotel** (Barrier Reef Dr., tel. 026/2191). At the south end of town, the **Tackle Box Bar** (on pier at Barrier Reef Dr. and Black Coral St.) is one of the most popular in town, with free live music some weekends. **Celi's,** at the San Pedro Holiday Hotel (Barrier Reef Dr., tel. 026/2014), does a barbecue on Wednesday night for $7. **Big Daddy's** (Barrier Reef Dr., just south of Central Park, tel. 026/2050) is the only disco in town (it's a favorite with posses of teenage Belizeans), and it has happy-hour specials daily 5–9 PM. In the evening there's always a mellow crowd at the **Purple Parrot** (Barrier Reef Dr. at Pelican St., tel. 026/2056) on the beach at Fido's Courtyard. The bar at the **Spindrift Hotel** (see Cheap Thrills, above) is also a popular watering hole. Every Tuesday, Belikins are $1.50, and on Thursday and Sunday, $1.25 buys you a rum and Coke.

SHOPPING

The best gift shops in Belize are in San Pedro. At Lindsay Hackston's **Belizean Arts** (Fido's Courtyard, off Barrier Reef Dr., tel. 026/3019) and its sister shop, **Arts and Crafts of Central America** (Pescador Dr., tel. 026/2623), you'll find a fine selection of works by local painters plus jewelry and crafts from the region, including hand-painted animal figures from Mexico, masks and fabrics from Guatemala, and brilliantly colored tropical fish made of coconut wood. British Honduras, as Belize was known until independence, supplied the mahogany used by many of the greatest English cabinetmakers, like Thomas Chippendale. Although standards have regrettably slipped since then, you can still find some fine mahogany furniture at **Best of Belize** (Barrier Reef Dr., tel. 026/3412), including clam chairs, boxes, salad bowls, and some beautiful chopping boards.

OUTDOOR ACTIVITIES

This water world offers a plethora of aquatic pleasures, including sea kayaking, snorkeling, sailing, and some of the world's best, and certainly the most accessible, scuba diving.

DIVING • Scuba diving—that's why San Pedro's streets are filled year-round with visitors from all over the world and why dive shops in San Pedro are as plentiful as chicle trees in a Belizean rain forest. In terms of the number of dive shops, quality of dive masters, and range of equipment and facilities, Ambergris Caye remains the most obvious base for diving. San Pedro even has a hyperbaric chamber, paid for by contributions from all the dive shops and fees attached to diver insurance—which is highly recommended, since emergency services and transportation costs could wipe out your savings in a hurry.

Diving trips are generally run from fast, maneuverable speedboats. There's no bouncing around in Zodiacs here: many of these boats are hand-built out of solid mahogany. Because they represent the dive masters' major assets, having cost as much as $14,000 each, the boats tend to be lovingly maintained. Power generally comes from two hefty outboards mounted on the back, and with the throttle open, it's an exhilarating ride. If you don't want to get splashed, sit in the middle.

Most of these dive masters are ex-fishermen, locals from San Pedro who started diving as an adjunct to their work as lobstermen and went on to get certified as dive masters. The best of them are immensely personable and have an intimate knowledge of the reef and a superb eye for coral and marine life. They also have an unusually developed ecological awareness, knowing full well that the destruction of the reef would not only be a great tragedy in itself, but economic suicide for them. It was a group of dive masters who fastened a network of buoys to the bedrock to prevent further destruction of the coral by anchors dropped directly into it. In bad weather, one anchor dragged across the bottom can destroy more coral than 1,000 divers.

Dives off Ambergris are usually one-tank dives at depths of 50–80 ft, giving you approximately 35 minutes of bottom time. The general pattern is two one-tank dives per day—one in the morning at 9 and one in the afternoon at 2, but you can vary this depending on your budget. At press time, the following were the prices for diving and snorkeling from Ambergris. Snorkeling: $15–$20 for two hours or $40–$50 for a day trip with lunch; diving: $30–$35 for a single-tank dive, $35–$55 for a double-tank dive, $35–$40 for a single-tank night dive, and $125–$200 for day trips with three-tank dives to Turneffe Atoll or to the Blue Hole at Lighthouse Reef.

Diving is similar all along Ambergris Caye, with only slight variations. You always dive on the windward side of the reef, and the basic form is canyon diving. For wall diving, you have to go out to the atolls (see below). The highlight of the reef is the **Hol Chan Marine Reserve** (Maya for "little channel"), 6 km (4 mi) from San Pedro at the southern tip of Ambergris (a 20-minute boat ride). Basically, Hol Chan is a break in the reef about 100 ft wide and 20–35 ft deep through which tremendous volumes of water pass with the tides. Varying in depth from 50 to 100 ft, Hol Chan's canyons lie between buttresses of coral running perpendicular to the reef, separated by white, sandy channels. Some sides are very steep; others comprise gently rolling undulations. You'll occasionally find tunnellike passageways from one canyon to the next. Not knowing what's in the next "valley" as you come over the hill is one of Hol Chan's thrills.

Although Belize doesn't have quite the rainbow variety of coral you'd find on the Great Barrier Reef in Australia—much of it is biscuit-colored—there is a dizzying array of marine life. Stellar attractions include the majestic spotted eagle ray, parrot fish, and queen angelfish as well as Nassau groupers, barracuda, and large shoals of yellowtail snappers. Because the reef is so close to the surface of the sea, you can experience most of the marine reserve's highlights with a snorkel and mask. A recent addition to the reef's attractions is **Ray and Shark Alley,** a sandbar where you can snorkel with nurse sharks and rays (who gather here to be fed) and even larger numbers of day-trippers from Ramon's resort.

As well as containing rich marine life and exciting corals, the 13-square-km (5-square-mi) park has a miniature Blue Hole, a 12-ft-deep cave whose entrance often attracts such fish as the fairy basslet, an iridescent purple-and-yellow fish frequently seen here. The reserve is also home to a large population of the gloomily named *Gymnothorax funebris,* better known as the moray eel. A **night dive** here is a special treat: the water lights up with bioluminescence, and many nocturnal animals emerge, such as octopus and spider crabs. You need above-average swimming skills, especially at night; the strong tidal current has caused at least one drowning.

San Pedro is the jumping-off point for trips to Hol Chan, but before you go, stop in at the Hol Chan office on Barrier Reef Drive for information on Belize's marine flora and fauna. The dive shops cater to virtually every kind of customer. Most offer trips to Hol Chan that generally last about two hours and are reasonably priced (about $15 for snorkeling, $30 for a single-tank dive). A full four-day open-water certification course—usually PADI, although some shops have NAUI instructors as well—runs about $350. Referral courses (where you do the first half of the course at home in a pool and the second, open-water half here) are $200, and resort courses (where you don't get certified and you can only dive with the person who instructs you) cost $125. At all shops, dive prices include

The waters around Ambergris Caye are teeming with plenty of beautiful tropical fish and, unfortunately, damaged coral— killed by contact with careless snorkelers' fingers and fins. The rule of thumb while on the reef: look but don't touch.

tanks, weights, and belt, but not other equipment; you can rent each piece separately (around $6), or get a full package (regulator; BCD; mask, snorkel, and fins; wet suit) for about $25 per day.

Among the numerous local operations, there are some real cowboys. So, if you don't want to end up in the hyperbaric chamber, choose carefully. Recommended local shops are **Amigos del Mar** (on pier at north end of town, tel. 026/2706 or 026/32–39); **Blue Hole Dive Center** (Barrier Reef Dr., tel. 026/ 2982); and **Coral Beach Dive Club** (on pier at center of town, tel. 026/2013). It might be worth paying a few extra bucks and hooking up with the dive shops at the resorts. The dive shop at **Ramon's Village** (1 km [½ mi] north of San Pedro, tel. 026/2071) is crowded with tourists, but reliable. For enthusiasm and knowledge, you can't beat **Rebecca McDonald,** at the palatial Victoria House (1 km [½ mi] north of San Pedro, tel. 026/2067). She runs the best dive shop and PADI instruction center on the cay. Another extremely capable gringo is Hugh Parkey, of **Belize Dive Connection** (tel. 023/4526). *Skindiver* Magazine described him as "one of the most knowledgeable dive masters in Belize." And they should know.

SNORKELING • Thinking they can save the bucks for the boat trip, a few unknowing travelers have waded into the sea grass that fringes Ambergris beaches and tried to swim out to the reef, only to find themselves in hospital, having been speared by a Spanish ray, a particularly nasty critter that lurks in the grass. Snorkeling trips on the cays are not so much sport as they are an excuse to party under full sail, though bottomless cups of rum punch and a lunchtime beach barbecue come at a price. Your cheapest option is to board a slow-moving glass-bottom boat and head for the nearby reef: **Captain Badillo** (Barrier Reef Dr., blue house next to Milo's, tel. 026/2264) will take you out for $10 (3 hrs). Otherwise, **Island Adventures** (on pier at Fido's Courtyard, tel. 026/2697 daytime or 026/3205 evenings) is one of the least expensive operations in town. They run three-hour trips in regular skiffs to popular nearby snorkel spots Hol Chan and **Mexico Rocks** for $15 (four-person minimum). They also offer night snorkeling with underwater lights ($17.50) and a full-day excursion with beach cookout ($35). For those who want to experience the reef without getting wet, **Ramon's Dive Shop** (tel. 026/ 2071) and **Amigos del Mar** (tel. 026/2706) run glass-bottom-boat tours of the marine reserve.

FISHING • For those who prefer to see their fish out of water, the **Belize Visitor & Tours Company** (Pescador Dr., tel. 026/2728) can hook you up with a half-day expedition ($90) on reef or flats, tackle or fly-fishing for 3- to 12-pound tarpon, as well as black grouper, mutton, and yellowtail snapper. Most hotels, resorts, and some dive shops also run fishing trips inside the reef for about $100 (half-day) to $150 (full).

KAYAKING AND CANOEING • Independent types will love the fact that Island Adventures (*see* Diving, *above*) rents canoes and sea kayaks for $5 per hour (2-hr minimum)—perfect for exploring the island's beaches or for a do-it-yourself day of snorkeling on the reef. Rentals include life vests, ice chest, and water jug (with optional attachable umbrellas for canoes).

HORSEBACK RIDING • Not every enjoyable activity on Ambergris Caye involves wearing a wet suit or snorkel. **Isla Equestrian Stables** (Middle St., behind Paradise Hotel, tel. 026/2895) has "healthy, responsive, well-mannered" horses to take you on beach rides, nature rides, or sunset rides; for a few extra bucks they'll throw in a picnic lunch, too. Rates are $20 per hour or $65 for a halfday trip.

CAYE CAULKER

Signs posted along the sandy streets of Caye Caulker reiterate the obvious: You'll find little else to do but GO SLOW and STOP. It's a mystery *why* these signs were erected, since most people amble around on foot or putter along in golf carts. The truck that delivers Belikins and Cokes is apparently the only combustion-engine vehicle on the island. Caulker is the nearest caye to Belize City, and the cheapest to reach, which is why, before independence, it used to be the destination of choice for British "squaddies" (soldiers) on leave, who used to regularly trash the place on a Saturday night. For many years, it only catered to the dirt-cheap category of traveler, but recently the island has started to offer a greater variety of accommodations and eateries. As the grunge recedes, the attractions of Caye Caulker are coming to the fore. With its brightly painted houses on stilts, bougainvillea, and hibiscus, it can be a delightful place to spend a few lazy days.

Caye Caulker is about 6 km (4 mi) long, but the Split, a channel formed when Hurricane Hattie sliced the island in half in 1961, emphatically marks the end of the inhabited portion less than 2 km (1 mi) up from the southern tip of the island. Three main streets run the length of town: Front Street, Center Street, and Back Street, with the "front" side of the island the one closest to the reef. Numbered addresses don't exist, but everything is within walking distance and easy to spot. Two public piers, on the front and back sides of the island respectively, mark the center of town. The locals—a mellow community of Belizeans (mostly of Spanish descent), Creole families, and expat gringos—are equally amiable. Lobster fishing has been the primary source of income for most islanders since the early 1900s, but dwindling lobster populations—and rising visitor populations—in the past decade have prompted fishermen to switch to the tourist trade. You'll find the island full of snorkel and scuba outfits (of variable quality) as well as affordable lodging, food, and tour operators.

If you have an hour or two between snorkeling expedition and dinner, there are one or two stops worth making in town. At **Sea-ing is Belizing** (Front St., near north end of town, tel. 022/2189), check out the display of beautiful underwater and wildlife photos by owner Jim Beveridge, or take advantage of the paperback-book swap. Slide shows on conservation and natural habitats are held every Tuesday and Friday at 8 PM (high season) or by request (low season); admission is $2.50. At **Hicaco Tours and Travel Agency** (Front St., near south end of town, tel. 022/2073), admire Belizean handicrafts and chat about reef conservation with the knowledgeable Ellen McRae. The gallery hosts a variety of ecoconscious tours, slide shows, and lectures.

BASICS

Atlantic Bank (Back St., across from Center's Grocery, tel. 022/2207) is open weekdays 8–noon and 1–2, Saturday 9–noon. For $2, they give cash advances on credit cards. **BTL** (Front St., next to Emy's Grocery, tel. 022/2168) is open weekdays 8–noon and 1–4, Saturday 8–noon. Postal services can be had at **Celi's Market** (Back St., south end of town) weekdays 8–noon and 3–6, Saturday 9–noon. You can wash your grungies at the **Coin Laundry** (between Front and Back Sts., west of Public Pier) daily 7 AM–9 PM, or **Marie's Laundry Mat** (Back St) Cost at both is $2 to wash and $2 to dry; bring your own soap and dollar coins.

COMING AND GOING

BY BOAT • The **Caye Caulker Water Taxi Association** (tel. 022/2992) operates a fast (when the engines do not break down) speedboat service from Belize City to Caye Caulker. Boats leave from the new Belize Marine Terminal on N. Front Street, near the Swing Bridge. The journey takes 45 minutes and costs $7.50 one way. Departures are every hour and a half from 9 AM to 5 PM, and the return from the Public Pier in Caulker from 6:30 AM to 3 PM. The *Thunderboat* (tel. 026/2217) runs Monday–Saturday to both San Pedro and Caye Caulker. The boat leaves the Marine Terminal at 1 PM and docks at the Lagoonside Marina on Caye Caulker. The fare is $10 round-trip.

BY PLANE • Both **Tropic Air** (tel. 022/2040) and **Maya Island Air** (tel. 022/2013) have hourly service (daily 7 AM–5 PM) between Caye Caulker and the Municipal Airport in Belize City. The journey takes 10 minutes and costs $84 return. The airstrip is a 10-minute walk south of town, on the back side of the island.

WHERE TO SLEEP

Caye Caulker is your basic low-budget island with plenty of affordable rooms and no luxury resorts. The digs right on the water tend to be a little more expensive, but they're worth it.

UNDER $20 • Housed in a funky, red colonial house, **Castaways Hotel** (tel. 022/2294) has lots of atmosphere, hearty breakfasts, and rock music in the bar. Next door is **Hotel Mira Mar** (tel. 022/2157). Both have clean, no-frills rooms with shared bath and cold water for $14 a double. Just around the corner is **Sandy Lane Hotel & Cabanas** (Center St., tel. 022/2217), with similarly priced rooms as well as two cabanas for $22. Another good deal is **Deisey's (Daisy's) Hotel** (Front St., tel. 022/2150). Rooms with shared bath and hot water are $12.50 (downstairs) and $16 (upstairs), or three can share a room for $21. Rooms with private bath are $5 more.

Everywhere in Belize is laid back, but the Cayes are laaaiiiid baaaaaack, mon.

UNDER $30 • **Ignacio's Beach Cabins.** This miniresort is a great deal for two or more people, although the management sometimes seems suspicious of new arrivals. For $26 you score a simple cabin on stilts, right at the water's edge. A private pier and shady palm trees complete the picture. *Far southwest end of island, tel. 022/2212. 17 cabins with bath. Cash only.*

Jimenez Cabanas. Thatched-roof cabanas and a lush garden setting of coconut palms and flowering plants give this family-run place a cool jungle feel. So friendly and helpful are the Jimenezes that you might almost forgive them the painful mattresses that lurk in some rooms. Otherwise, delightful cabins ($28 doubles) all have private baths with hot water. It's on the back (leeward) side of the island. *Back St., south end of town, tel. 022/2175. 6 cabanas with bath. Laundry. Cash only.*

Marin's. Often full, Marin's is popular with travelers. Rooms encircle a colorful garden with shady palm trees, and the hammocks seem to beckon at siesta time. Doubles with shared bath go for $14–$19 (with private bath $27–$30); all have hot water. The management strictly enforces a no-visitors rule. *South end of town, between Front and Center Sts., tel. 022/2110. 14 rooms, 8 with bath. Cash only.*

Treetops. Anglo-German husband-and-wife team Doris and Terry, and their three miniature security guards (Jack Russell terriers), are wonderful hosts at this charming guest house. The rooms are a good size and have ceiling fans, TVs, and refrigerators; one has a private bath. The white-sand garden has bougainvillea, hibiscus bushes, and palm trees, and is a peaceful place to curl up on a chaise longue and read. Doris runs a tight ship and is a mine of information on the island. *South end of town, just off Front St., tel. 022/2008. 3 rooms with shared bath, 1 with private bath. Cash only.*

Vega's Inn and Gardens. The Vegas are extremely enthusiastic, and their interest in their guests borders on doting. Their beachfront property and pier are well-maintained, with plenty of shade and tight security. Rooms with hot water and shared bath are $22.50 for a double or $18 for a single. Camping, including use of showers and toilets, is allowed here for $7 per person. *Front St. at public pier, tel. 022/2142. 10 rooms with bath. Cash only.*

FOOD

Caye Caulker is that much more pleasant during **lobster season** (June 15–Feb. 15), when the tasty crustaceans are available by the plateful. In the off-season make do with killer seafood or chicken burritos ($1–$2). Tons of pastry and ice-cream shops dispense sumptuous goodies, notably coconut bread (50¢) baked fresh and fragrant every morning.

UNDER $5 • **Glenda's,** run by the eponymous owner out of her brilliant blue–painted house on Back Street, serves good breakfasts, burritos, and garnaches, as well as delectable juices. Behind the unassuming appearance of **Pinx Fast Food,** on Front Street, lie the considerable culinary skills of the mar-

LOBSTERS IN LOVE

To give the poor things a chance to breed, lobster fishing is strictly forbidden February 16–June 14: watch for posters bearing ridiculous drawings of pie-eyed lobster couples "in love" tacked up all around Caye Caulker, reminding locals not to catch them and tourists not to eat them. You'll also see wooden lobster traps—or "pots," as they're called by lobstermen—stacked head-high in town. Fines for off-season possession run $25–$30 per lobster.

velously named Ms. Pinx. She keeps irregular hours, but that doesn't prevent folks standing hungrily in the street, waiting for more delicious burritos ($1.50), fried fish with slaw, beans, and rice ($4), or whatever else she feels like whipping up.

UNDER $10 • To experience real home cooking (in a Belizean home), visit **Claudette's Kitchen** (near Split, tel. 022/2079) for shrimp and lobster ($7.50), conch ($6), fish ($5), or vegetarian ($4) dinners. Reservations are required.

Cindy's Cafe. Cindy swapped the snows of British Columbia for the sun on Caye Caulker, married a local, and now runs the cutest café in town on the veranda of her brightly painted cottage on stilts. It's open only for breakfast, but there's no bacon and eggs here, just organic muesli, fresh-squeezed orange juice, waffles, and the best cappuccino in town. Cindy is also the town's unofficial librarian, and, if you promise to bring it back, she'll lend you a tome from her well-stocked shelves. Once you've finished breakfast, Cindy's Belizean husband, Carlos, the best (and most ecologically conscious) snorkeling guide in town, will show you the fish. *Front St. at the public pier, tel. 022/2337.*

Marin's Restaurant & Bar. A cheap restaurant specializing in seafood, Marin's has a classy dining room, fine garden patio, and wicked banana daiquiris. Lobster dinners start at $7 and lobster breakfast is a mere $3. Conch, shrimp, and fish dishes are $4–$9. Excellent seafood soups are $3. *Center St., south end of town, tel. 022/2104.*

The Sandbox. Whether outside under the palms or indoors in the hardwood room with overhead fans, you'll have your feet in the sand in this bustling hot spot. Open from 7 AM–10 PM, the Sandbox menu includes a lobster omelet for breakfast, a roast-beef sandwich for lunch, and red snapper in mango sauce for dinner. The chowders are very good, the conch fritters spicy, the jerk chicken lip-smackin' tasty. Prices are reasonable (shrimp lasagna stuffed with cheese and spinach is $7) and the portions are enormous. At night the joint jumps to the sound of the American owner's extensive blues collection. *Front St. at the public pier, tel. 022/2200. Closed Wed.*

Syd's. Sick of the heat? Then cool off at Syd's, an air-conditioned restaurant with Mexican masks on its white walls and a small bar in one corner. The food is inexpensive and includes good seafood for dinner, and burgers or burritos for lunch. On Saturday nights there's a special barbecue for $4 a person, and on both Fridays and Saturdays you can have a late-night snack here from 10 PM on. *Back St., no phone.*

AFTER DARK

If you want to boogie all night, head for the resort playland of San Pedro on Ambergris Caye (*see above*). If, however, your idea of a good time is a mellow evening on the beach with a cold beer and warm friends, then Caye Caulker is the place to be. Local boys congregate for pool and tunes at the **Martinez Bar & Restaurant** (Front St., north end of town, tel. 022/2113). The **I & I Cafe and Lounge** (south end of town, between Front and Center Sts., tel. 022/2206) has a multilevel outdoor garden with trippy lights and cool swings, plus great mixed drinks. If none of these sounds appealing, round up a few friends and stumble over to the **Caye Caulker Belikin Distributor** at the back public pier, where cases of Belikin are $21.

OUTDOOR ACTIVITIES

Travelers during the off-season should beware that many tour and boat operators require a minimum of four–six participants, often leaving frustrated singles and pairs stranded. That said, there are plenty of friendly locals eager to show you the best fishing, snorkeling, or sightseeing (for a price, of course). Swimming, best at the Split (far north end of town), is the only free activity on the island. There's a small dock here for sunning—it fills fast—and the island's only real strip of sand. To explore the cay by bike, head to **Island Sun Gift Shop** (Back St., tel. 022/2215), where you can rent a bike for $10 (half day). It's open daily 9–noon and 1–5.

DIVING • Caye Caulker has numerous dive shops, of extremely varying quality, so be choosy. The best of them, located at the north end of town just off Front Street, is **Frenchie's Diving Services** (tel. 022/2234). A two-tank dive on the reef costs $48, equipment included. *See* Ambergris, *above* for details on nearby diving sites.

FISHING • Although expensive ($100 and up), a day of reef fishing for grouper or snook can be an exhilarating experience. The real McCoy here is deep-sea fishing for the prized blue marlin. A 492-pound monster caught off Caye Caulker by an angler from New Orleans in 1997 set a new Belizean record. **Porfilio Guzman** (tel. 022/2152) will take groups of three or more out for a day ($100) of reef fishing.

KAYAKING • A kayak is your ticket to independent exploration beyond the confines of the village; paddle out to the reef for a snorkel session or make a day of circling the island. Both **Deisey's Hotel** (*see* Where to Sleep, *above*) and **Hicaco Tours and Travel Agency** (Front St., south end of town, tel. 022/2073) rent one-person kayaks for $7.50 per hour or two-person kayaks for $10 per hour, though the more seaworthy crafts are at Deisey's.

One of the largest underwater, ultramarine caverns in Belize is located directly beneath Caye Caulker.

SNORKELING • Take your pick of boat operators—motor or sailboat, Rasta crew or not. Sailing is a slow and easy way to go, while Rasta crews love to party it up on the boat. Trips out to the reef are about $10–$15 per person; all-day excursions to more remote spots like Goff's Caye or the Turneffe Islands run $25–$70. If it's the Rasta experience you seek, **Creek** and his trusty *Reggae Muffin* can be found at the front public dock most mornings around 11 AM. Of the other operators, two stand out from the rest. **Carlos** (*see* Cindy's Cafe in Food, *above*) does ecotours to the reef, the Hol Chan Marine Reserve, and Shark Alley (*see* Ambergris Caye, *above*). **Chocolate** (Front St. at the north end of town, tel. 022/2151) is a very fit, 60ish Belizean and one of nature's gentlemen. Although his tours are more expensive than some ($17–$35 for a whole day), they are well worth it. As well as snorkeling, there is a wonderful manatee-watching trip to Goff Caye and a river and coastal-lagoon trip that comes complete with alligators, spoonbills, and orchids. With his Minnesota-born wife, Annie, he also offers the most beautiful room on the Caye, complete with four-poster bed.

SHOPPING

There are any number of shops selling island souvenirs. Two stand out from the rest. **Annie's Boutique** (*see* Chocolate, under Snorkeling, *above*) has the best women's and children's clothes not just on the Caye, but in the whole of Belize, including dresses and sarongs made with fabrics from Bali, some unique silver jewelry, and Guatemalan bags that somehow don't make you look like a resident of Haight Ashbury circa 1968. **Galeria Hicaco** (Front St. south end, tel. 022/2178) has Belizean arts and crafts, including jewelry, dolls, carvings, and pottery.

THE ATOLLS

From the air, they appear improbably beautiful. At their center, the water is mint green as the white sandy bottom reflects the light upwards and is flecked with patches of mangrove and rust-colored sediments. Around the fringe of the atoll, the surf breaks in a white circle before the color changes abruptly to ultramarine as the water plunges to 3,000 ft. The origin of Belize's atolls, which lie between 48 and 96 km (30 and 60 mi) off the coast, is still something of a mystery, but evidence suggests that unlike the Pacific atolls, which formed by accretion around the rims of submerged volcanoes, these grew from the bottom up, as vast pagodas of coral accumulated over millions of years on top of limestone fault blocks. The Maya were probably the first humans to discover and use the atolls, as stopovers on their trading routes. Piles of seashells and rocks, known as "shell maidens" and thought to have been placed there as markers, have been found on the Turneffe Islands.

Early in Belize's colonial history, the atolls were known by their Spanish names. But with the rout of the Spanish at the Battle of St. George's Caye, in 1798, English won the day: Terre Nef became Turneffe, Quattro Cayos became Lighthouse Reef, and Longorif became Glover's Reef. Until recently they were sparsely inhabited; lobster fishing, sponge gathering, and coconut plantations provided the small population with a precarious living. Then divers discovered the atolls and erected spartan dive camps, which, in turn, became some of Belize's most expensive resorts.

LIGHTHOUSE REEF

The atoll is about 29 km (18 mi) long and less than 2 km (1 mi) wide and is surrounded by 67 km (42 mi) of coral reef. The Lighthouse Reef system has two of the country's five-star dives: the Blue Hole and the vertiginous walls off Half Moon Caye. Loggerhead turtles, iguanas, and one of the world's two large colonies of red-footed boobies are protected here.

At its center is the great **Blue Hole,** made famous in the 1970s by French marine explorer Jacques Cousteau. Once upon a time this was a dry cavern beneath the sea floor. When its roof collapsed, it created a perfectly circular sinkhole more than 100 yards wide and 400 ft deep. The name of this natural wonder arises from the intense blue tint of the water in the depths of the shaft, in contrast to the light blues of the shallows that surround it. The cool thing about diving the Blue Hole isn't the marine life—there isn't much inside the hole—but the spacey moonscape of gigantic stalactites and the thrilling chance to explore at freaky depths of up to 130 feet, the maximum for recreational diving. The coral reefs surrounding the sinkhole are a spectacular snorkeling spot, though the money and effort required to get here makes simply flapping around on the surface seem silly.

At the southern end of the lagoon, **Half Moon Caye National Monument** was designated Belize's first national reserve in 1982. The island is a protected breeding ground for one of Belize's silliest sounding birds: the red-footed booby. It's an endangered species, and no wonder: it is so complacent that it won't budge even if you walk right into it. Some 4,000 of these rare seabirds hang their hats on Half Moon Caye, along with more than 90 other bird species, including the magnificent frigate bird (with a wingspan of 7 ft) and many migrants. You can observe the boobies' nests, on the lush western side of the island, from a viewing platform constructed by the Audubon Society. Climb up, and you're suddenly in a sea of birds that fill the branches of the surrounding trees so completely that it's hard not to be reminded of a certain Hitchcock movie. On the island's southern beaches, endangered loggerhead and hawksbill turtles come ashore to lay their eggs in the spring. On the eastern half of the island—mostly sand and coconut palms—camping is permitted; interested parties must register at the island lighthouse and bring their own water and food.

The best diving on Lighthouse is also at Half Moon Caye. The Half Moon Caye Wall is a classic wall dive, beginning at 35 ft and dropping almost vertically to blue infinity. Floating out over the edge is a bit like free-fall parachuting. Magnificent spurs of coral jut out to the seaward side, looking like small tunnels; they're fascinating to explore and invariably full of fish. Because of the great variety of ocean-floor terrain, an exceptionally varied marine life hovers around this cay. On the gently sloping sand flats behind the coral spurs, a vast colony of garden eels stirs, their heads protruding from the sand like a field of periscopes. Spotted eagle rays, turtles, and other pelagics also frequent the drop-off. Offshore, look for the rusting hulk of a tanker that wrecked on the reef in the 1970s.

TURNEFFE ATOLL

This chain of tiny islands and mangrove swamps makes up an atoll the size of Barbados. It's the largest and, at 40 km (25 mi) east of Belize City, the closest of the three atolls, making it within day-trip range of both Belize City and Ambergris Caye. Turneffe's highlight, and probably the most exciting wall dive in Belize, is **The Elbow,** at the southernmost tip of the atoll. It's generally considered an advanced dive because of the strong currents here, which want to sweep you out toward the deep water beyond the reef. The drop-off is dramatic: you have the feeling of flying in blue space, your likely traveling companions large groups of eagle rays. As many as 50 have been known to congregate here, forming a rippling herd that will take your breath away.

Turneffe's western, leeward side, where the reef is wide and gently sloping, is good for shallower dives and snorkeling; you'll see large concentrations of tube sponges, soft corals such as forked sea feathers and sea fans, and varied fish, including plentiful permit. Also on the leeward side is the wreck of the *Say-*

onara. No doubloons to be scooped up here—it was a small passenger and cargo boat that went down in 1985—but it's a good place to practice wreck diving.

GLOVER'S REEF

Named after the pirate John Glover, this coral necklace strung around a 208-square-km (80-square-mi) lagoon, 113 km (70 mi) southeast of Belize City, is the southernmost of Belize's three atolls. The diving rates as some of the best in Belize, and there is excellent fishing for permit and bonefish. Like the other atolls this one now has a splashy property, Manta Reef Resort, which, according to rumor is owned by Belize's leading drug dealer (he is certainly persona non grata in the United States). But there are several dive camps that make Glover's the best bet for an extended atoll stay.

Although most of the finest dive sites are along the atoll's southeastern limb, on the windward side, the one exception is **Emerald Forest Reef,** named for its mass of huge green elkhorn coral. Because the most exciting part of the reef is only 25 ft down, it's excellent for novices and snorkelers, and it abounds in healthy corals and fish. It also proves the important point that depth isn't everything. **Southwest Caye Wall** is a typically dramatic drop-off—an underwater cliff that falls quickly to 130 ft. As with all wall dives, this one makes it easy to lose track of depth and time with the exhilaration of flying in blue space, so both ascent and descent require careful monitoring. **Long Caye Wall** is yet another exciting wall, with a dramatic drop-off to hundreds of feet. Overhangs covered in sheet and boulder coral make it a good place to spot turtles, rays, and barracuda.

Glover's Reef is the only one of the atolls that has moderately priced accommodations. **Slickrock Adventures** (Box 1400, Moab, UT 84532, tel. 800/390–5715 in U.S.) used to run white-water trips in Utah: they now have a sea-kayaking camp on Long Caye, on Glover's Reef. Tents have mattresses and are pitched under palapa covers. There is only solar power, but a Belizean cook conjures seafood feasts on a propane stove. There are daily sea-kayaking and snorkeling trips around the atoll, as well as windsurfing and fly- fishing on the flats. For travelers with a week or two to spare, **Glover's Atoll Resort** (Box 563, Belize City, tel. 08/23–048), on 15-acre **Long Caye,** offers the quintessential deserted-isle experience at unbelievable beans-and-rice prices. It's one of only two guest facilities at Glover's Reef, where clear waters and pristine conditions guarantee amazing snorkeling, scuba diving, and fishing. The handful of beach cabins ($95 per person per week, transportation included) are outfitted with kerosene-powered kitchen, cold-water shower, candles, private outhouse, and all the rainwater you can drink; you can also camp ($70 per person per week). Basic groceries or seafood-and-rice meals are available. Rent canoes or snorkel gear, take a four-day scuba certification course ($295, gear included), or fish ($75 half-day) for wahoo, barracuda, and tarpon. You are required to eventually leave.

COMING AND GOING

Most people come to the reefs on either live-aboard dive trips or day trips. Scuba divers can contact **Out Island Divers** (tel. 026/3154 or 026/2151), who run trips from both San Pedro and Caye Caulker. Snorkelers should contact the Caye Caulker outfit **Sunrise** (tel. 022/2195), which organizes day trips to Lighthouse Reef twice weekly. **Coral Beach Dive Club,** in San Pedro (tel. 026/2013), runs overnight trips to the outer atolls from $230 (one night, four dives). **Amigos Del Mar** (*see* Ambergris Caye, *above*) offers day or overnight trips to Turneffe or Lighthouse Reef.

All these outfits are weather dependent, and in bad weather, it can be a four-hour barf-marathon to Lighthouse Reef, that is if the boat does not turn back. **The Blue Hole Express** (Barrier Reef Dr., San Pedro, tel. 026/2982) cannot change the weather: but its 40-foot, custom-built dive boat, equipped with massive diesel engines and GPS, will get you out to the atolls on days that other outfits cannot. Trips depart San Pedro at 6:15 AM and return at 4:15 PM, making dive stops at Lighthouse Reef and Turneffe Islands. The price—$165 for divers and $110 for snorkelers—includes everything from the gear to lunch and drinks.

There are no scheduled boats to Glover's Reef, but the two operations on the atoll, Slickrock Adventures and Glover's Atoll Resort, run their own boats, once weekly, departing from Sittee River Village, 48 km (30 mi) south of Dangriga. To reach Sittee River from Dangriga, take a Z-Line bus south to G & G Cool Spot (90 min, $2) in the village of Kendal, where you will get a minibus ($10) to Sittee River. If you arrive a day early, you can spend the night at **Glover's Guest House** (tel. 05/23–048); all bunk beds are $5.

THE CAYO

Many visitors have blown off the beach scene altogether after a taste of the Cayo, Belize's wild western region and the nation's second most popular tourist destination. Comprising more than 5,200 square km (2,000 square mi) of rugged, mountainous land, and over 35,000 inhabitants, the Cayo—whose name originally referred to the peninsula of land between the Macal and Mopan rivers, on which San Ignacio grew up—is full of surprises for the adventurous visitor. In the Mountain Pine Ridge area you can drop, ecologically speaking, from South Carolina to Brazil in the space of a few miles. One minute you're in pine savanna; the next, in lush, subtropical rain forest. "Cayo," as Belizeans call it, is also filled with good food, quality budget hotels, and a diverse but consistently friendly population. Add to this stands of jungle and the cool green Macal River and you'll see why many gringos plan to stay for a week, delay their return for a month, then settle for good at the end of the year.

National Geographic filmed *Journey to the Underworld* in the Cayo's Caves Branch River area, and most of the critters featured on Belize's $20 bill live in the Cayo—mountain lions and jaguars, ocelots, margays, and tapirs, plus most of Belize's 300-plus bird species. Even if you've never been birding before, setting off through the jungle in search of masked tityras, violaceous trogons, and the improbably named scaly-throated leaf-tosser will soon have you hooked.

Remnants of the ancient Maya are omnipresent here. Most Cayo residents have discovered house mounds (the rubble of ancient peasant dwellings), pottery shards, or carved-rock fragments on their property. And then there's the big stuff: the ancient metropolis of Caracol, in the heart of the Vaca Plateau wilderness, is one of the most dramatic Mayan centers in the country if not in all Central America. Almost as impressive are **Xunantunich** (Stone Maiden), near the Guatemalan border; Cahal Pech, an ancient royal residence on the outskirts of San Ignacio; and El Pilar. The alien-infiltration stories in Von Däniken's *Chariots of the Gods* almost seem plausible when you marvel at these great stone temples, which were built without the aid of the wheel.

SAN IGNACIO

Modest San Ignacio is the rarest surprise: a tourist town that refuses to sell out. Although it's one of the most popular destinations in Belize, there are no ugly souvenir T-shirts here and very few attempts to sell cappuccino. With its well-preserved vernacular architecture, bustling Spanish ambience, and dusty charm, it is also one of the few Belizean towns where you might wish to linger. Evenings are cool and mosquito-free, and there are a few funky and interesting bars and restaurants. Although hotel, restaurant, bus, and taxi operators all speak English with tourists, Spanish is the dominant language and mestizo is the dominant ethnicity. You'll also find plenty of Mayans, Creoles, Mennonites, Chinese, and East Indians; after a week you're likely to know most residents by their first name. Maybe the beans and rice are spiked, because San Ignacio is the friendliest damn town in Belize.

The salient feature of San Ignacio is its proximity to the wonders of western Belize: caves, ruins, and rain forests, all of which are accessible by a variety of means. An excellent introduction is the 20-minute walk from San Ignacio to **Branch Mouth,** where the Macal and the Mopan join to form the Belize River. The track leads north out of town past a soccer field. From the riverbanks you can watch wild parrots, lazing iguanas, and local boys washing their racing ponies—or the occasional four-wheel-drive truck in the river. In town, pause long enough to admire the Hawkesworth Bridge, straddling the river between San Ignacio and her sister city, **Santa Elena.** Built in 1949, and modeled after New York City's Brooklyn Bridge, it's the only suspension bridge in the nation and one of six bridges that appear on the back of the dollar bill.

BASICS

Eva's Restaurant (22 Burns Ave., tel. 092/2267) is a Cayo institution—bulletin board, information center, trading post, and meeting place for travelers and locals. Presiding over the colorful chaos is Bob Jones, a garrulous British ex-serviceman, who can tell you everything from where to score a canoe to what to do if you get bitten by a fer-de-lance (say your prayers) to where to find a room.

The **BTIA** (28 Burns Ave., on alley at West St., tel. 092/3596) distributes brochures and maps of Cayo (25¢) Monday–Saturday 8:30–noon and 1:30–5. **Belize Bank** (16 Burns Ave.) is open weekdays 8–1

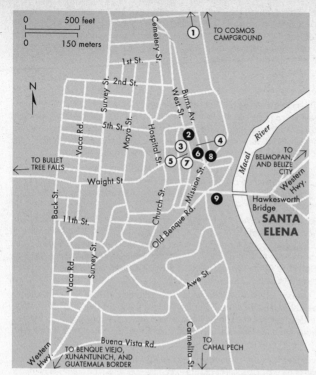

Sights ●
BTIA Office, **2**
Bus Station, **8**
Eva's Restaurant, **6**
Post Office, **9**

Lodging ○
Central Hotel, **4**
HI-ET Hotel, **5**
Martha's, **7**
Mida's Eco Resort, **1**
Pacz Hotel, **3**

(with additional hours Fri. 3–6). **Atlantic Bank** (4 Burns Ave.) is open Monday–Tuesday and Thursday–Friday 8–noon and 1–3, Wednesday 8–1, Saturday 8:30–noon. Local restaurants will change small denominations themselves, or point you toward black marketeers. The **BTL** office is on Burns Avenue north of Eva's (open weekdays 8–noon and 1–4, Sat. 8–noon). The **post office** (open weekdays 8–noon and 1–5, Sat. 8–1) is in the government building next to the bridge. **August Laundromat** (10 West St.), next door to Martha's Kitchen, charges $2.50 per wash and $2 per dry; it's open daily 6:30 AM–9 PM.

COMING AND GOING

San Ignacio is on the Western Highway, 18 km (11 mi) east of the Guatemalan border. **Batty** and **Novelo's** buses connect San Ignacio with points west and east. Buses leave for Belize City (3 hrs, $3) hourly 5 AM–5 PM, with a stop at Belmopan (45 min, $1.75). Batty does the morning run; Novelo's the afternoon trip. The return schedule is similar. Trips to San José Succotz (15 min) and Benque Viejo del Carmen (20 min) are 50¢, with hourly departures 7:30 AM–10:30 PM. Returns are hourly 1–5 PM. Many westbound buses continue across the border to the Guatemalan town of Melchor de Mencos (40 min, $3); inquire at the bus station for current schedule. The bus depot is in the center of town, where Waight and Burns avenues meet.

GETTING AROUND

Use what the Chinese call the No. 11 bus (i.e., your legs) to get you around town or across the bridge to Santa Elena. Besides buses, **taxis** are an option for destinations along the Western Highway (such as Bullet Tree Falls and San José Succotz), although they have been known to gouge tourists; settle on a price before you get in. Taxis hover around the bus depot and bridge. Fare to the border is about $4 per person. A limited number of **four-wheel-drive vehicles** are available for rent at the Venus Hotel (*see* Where to Sleep, *below*) for $65–$75 per day. Reserve a few days in advance for weekend rentals. Know that cars rented anywhere in Belize are not allowed across the Guatemalan border.

You can usually catch rides by **hitching** with locals to and from the border just by walking out along the main road. It is more difficult to reach Mountain Pine Ridge attractions and Caracol, since traffic is sparse and forest-service vehicles (the most frequent traffic in this area) are not permitted to pick up passengers. Try to hook up with fellow tourists in town, or get in on a guided tour—about $18 per person for a full day. **Jute Expeditions** (tel. 092/2076) are the pros. Women traveling alone can safely hitch in the area during the day—although, as always, use caution and common sense. If *you* are the lucky driver, tie down loose objects and tank up on gas. Roads in the area are steep, graded but unpaved, and impossibly slippery in the rainy season.

WHERE TO SLEEP

There are plenty of interesting budget rooms to be found in the center of San Ignacio (along Waight Ave., between Burns Ave. and West St.), a mere two blocks from the bus depot. You can easily walk around to a few to check prices and availability, although the best fill early in the day, so spare yourself the hassle by calling ahead for reservations. Beware of too-cheap-to-be-true deals near Hawkesworth Bridge and Blue Angels disco, unless you don't mind late-night and early morning noise.

If you have any extra cash, take the opportunity to stay at one of the ranches or resorts outside town: for $20–$50 a night you'll get a private thatched cabana right on the river. Several also allow **camping** for about $10 per night. Two campgrounds are within walking distance of town, and a few excellent sites exist in or near Mountain Pine Ridge.

UNDER $15 • Central Hotel (24 Burns Ave.) has small, clean, safe rooms at $9.50 (single) or $11 (double), all with shared bath. **HI-ET Hotel** (12 West St., at Waight Ave., tel. 092/2828) is a family-run establishment and an especially good place for women alone: Junior and Beatrice are diligent about monitoring comings and goings from their living room. Clean and basic doubles with fans are $10. Another cheapie is **Venus Hotel** (29 Burns Ave., tel. 092/3203 or 092/2186), across from Eva's. Doubles are $12.50, or $20 with private bath.

UNDER $30 • Martha's. Owners John and Martha August are extremely friendly and committed to providing a homey atmosphere at reasonable rates. If you want to be a couch *patata* in tropical paradise, watch soap operas on cable TV or catch some sun on the spacious veranda. Rooms are $17 (double). Discounts at August Laundromat and Martha's Kitchen nearby. *10 West St. 3 rooms with shared bath. Cash only.*

Pacz Hotel. A block or two farther from the center than other budget hotels, Pacz is clean and quiet, save the early morning cackle of parrots. Doubles ($18) are extremely spacious. The common room has cable TV, porch, and a fridge stocked with cheap beer and sodas. Peter Pacz is an ex-mountaineering guide for the British army and runs some serious spelunking tours to the jungle (*see* Outdoor Activities, *below*) as well as renting mountain bikes and arranging tours. *4 Far West St., tel. 092/2110. From bus depot walk up Waight Ave. and turn right on Far West. 7 rooms with shared bath. Cash only.*

CAMPING • There are a few camping options in and around San Ignacio, offering varying degrees of civilization. The cheapest and most convenient are both a short walk from the bus depot. **Mida's Eco Resort,** about ½ mi (¼ mi) north of town (Branch Mouth Rd., tel. 092/3172 or 2101), has 38 tent sites ($3.50 per person) and six thatched-roof cabanas ($20–$23) located near a sandy beach on the Macal River. Your hosts, the Preston family, can help arrange tours. About 1 km (½ mi) farther north, **Cosmos Camping** (Branch Mouth Rd.) has tent sites ($4) and a deluxe swimming hole. They rent hammocks ($2) to tentless travelers. To reach either from the bus depot, walk north past the soccer field and follow signs.

Hilltop Camping. The least touristy campground, it also offers the best way to see Mountain Pine Ridge Reserve (*see* Near San Ignacio, *below*) on the cheap. It's located in the tiny village of San Antonio, 3 km (1½ mi) from the reserve boundary. Sites are $2.50 each; hammocks or palapas are available at no extra charge. Best of all, caves, pools, and falls are all within hiking distance. The 10 or 10:30 AM "San Antonio taxi" (really a former cattle truck) from San Ignacio ($1) will get you here—check with the Sand Castle Bar (*see* Food, *below*) for more info. If you have your own ride, you can stay in Mountain Pine Ridge Reserve at the rangers' outpost in **Augustine.** A space in one of their bunk houses is $7.50, and camping is $1. To camp you'll need to pick up a permit (free) at the rangers' outpost when you arrive. Don't think about straying into the forest with your tent unless you'd like your hide crisped in a flash fire. It happens.

RANCHES AND RESORTS • Deny yourself a few weeks in the Cayo countryside and you're missing one of Belize's greatest pleasures. If you stay in town, the only wildlife you'll see will be sweating wildly, beer in hand, at the Blue Angels disco. Spend the extra money and time on the (unpaved) road and you'll see giant iguanas, toucans, and parrots, and possibly the tracks of a furtive tapir or jaguar—literally at your palapa doorstep. Most lodges are family-run and serve home-cooked meals; almost all offer tours and activities like swimming, canoeing, and horseback riding (though the budget-conscious will probably want to check prices in San Ignacio first). Most listed below are accessible by some form of shuttle service. (Check at Eva's for more info.) Bacadia Resort and Parrot Nest, both in the village of **Bullet Tree Falls,** are easily reached by taxi for about $5.

Built on an ancient Maya house mound, **Clarissa Falls** (tel. 092/3916) has four basic thatched cabanas with shared bath ($30 per person) overlooking waterfalls. The open-air bar and dining patio serves home-cooked meals ($6), and leftovers are much appreciated by the friendly family cow. Clarissa Falls is located 3 km (2 mi) west of San Ignacio, just off the Western Highway. **Du Plooy's** (tel. 092/3101) is a homey, laid-back operation with swimming hole and bar. Rooms with shared bath are $45 (double) or $35 (single) in the "Pink House," their budget lodge, breakfast included. The resort is down a 6-km (4-mi) unpaved road, 8 km (5 mi) west of San Ignacio. Nearby, **Black Rock River Lodge** (tel. 092/2341 or 092/3296) is popular with backpackers and has riverside shared-bath cabanas for $42 (double) or $36 (single). Meals are $6–$13. In the village of Cristo Rey, 5 km (3 mi) south of San Ignacio on the road to Mountain Pine Ridge, **Crystal Paradise Resort** (tel. 092/2823) has 14 cabanas with private bath ($75 and up), dinner and breakfast included. The Tut family's 340-acre property includes a nice beach on the Macal River, plenty of trails, groves of coconut palms and orange trees, and even homegrown coffee. Finally, if you want to feel like a million dollars, without actually spending them, treat yourself to a night at the luxurious tented camp at **Chaa Creek,** a superb jungle lodge not far from San Ignacio. Rooms cost more than $200, but for $45 per night you can sleep in a state-of-the-art tent on an individual wooden platform a stone's throw from the Macal River. The price also allows you to chow down on three meals a day prepared by a Belizean chef on a traditional fire hearth, known as a *fogon*. The hiking trails and swimming holes on the resort's 300-acre property are some of the very best.

The bird-watching at the Parrot Nest cabins is excellent, especially in those rooms that rest on stilts at treetop level. The record claim for sighting parrots is 125 species in 2½ days.

Five km (3 mi) north of San Ignacio, the village of Bullet Tree Falls offers lodging in a less lushly forested but more economical setting. **Bacadia Resort,** run by artist Marcos Manzanero, has three thatched-roof cabanas with shared bath ($30–$40) set in a garden of flowering native plants. Below, a rope swing is the best way to reach the Mopan River. **Parrot's Nest** (tel. 093/7008), which is run by Fred Prost, creator of Belize City's Seaside Guest House, has four thatched-roof cabanas on the banks of the Mopan River, each with two single beds for only $20 a night for two. Breakfasts ($3) and dinners ($6) can be tailored for vegetarian, vegan, and lactose-intolerant diners.

Far from San Ignacio but well worth the trek is **Martz Farm** (tel. 092/3742), the working ranch of the friendly Martinez family. Cabins or rooms are $12.50 (single) or $20 (double). One of 14 brothers and sisters will happily saddle a horse, show you around their nature school for local youngsters, or lead you down the steep 5-km (3-mi) trail to the river. Meals ($3) are back-a-bush (home) style; after tasting Felicita's barbecue chicken you may decide to stay forever. Taxis to the ranch, 19 km (12 mi) south of Benque Viejo del Carmen (*see* Near San Ignacio, *below*) on Hydro Dam Road, are prohibitively expensive, so unless you've got a four-wheel-drive, call ahead to inquire about getting picked up from San Ignacio.

FOOD

San Ignacio has several Chinese restaurants, and one of the best spots in town is a Sri Lankan joint. The **Maya Café** (26 Burns Ave.) serves cheap snacks and a drink more precious than gold: real, freshly brewed coffee. Carts assembled around the bus depot sell produce and delicious barbecue chicken. Just across the bridge in Santa Elena, **Fruit a Plenty** (Western Hwy. at High St., tel. 092/2755) has packaged granola and dried fruits that health nuts will cherish. Come dinnertime, follow your nose to Santa Elena's barbecue stands. For $3, you get a giant meal—just make sure the meat has been thoroughly cooked.

Eva's Restaurant and Bar. Eva's is home base for everyone in town, from Peace Corps volunteers to local cab drivers, archaeologists, Mennonite farmers, Rastas, backpackers, and tour guides. The food is honest-to-goodness Belizean fare, with some bacon and eggs, omelets, and sandwiches thrown in for good measure. Mugs of wickedly strong black tea are always available, and a bowl of yogurt and granola for breakfast is only $2.50. No one is in much of a hurry, making this an excellent place to write postcards or catch up on your journal. *22 Burns Ave., tel. 092/2267.*

Martha's Kitchen. Martha is just as proud of her pizza (slice, $1.50; whole pies from $9) as she is of her Belizean dishes and hearty burritos ($1.50). The decor is homey and the grub delicious. *10 West St., no phone.*

Sand Castle Bar-n-Grill. The open-air tables, sand-covered floors, and river views make this the perfect place to enjoy daily fish specials ($6) or fuel up on breakfast ($2.50–$5) before canoeing. Evenings there's music and a variety of drink specials. Ask for Remo if you are interested in checking out day-trip options. *Manza Plaza, by river, tel. 092/3213.*

Serendib Restaurant. Let serendipity be your guide: excellent Sri Lankan curries are served up at affordable prices ($4–$8) in a quiet atmosphere. *27 Burns Ave., tel. 092/2302. Closed Sun.*

CHEAP THRILLS

Sandy Beach Rope Swing. Local kids are usually around to, well, show you the ropes. Also check out the 15-ft, trilevel rock jump. The preliminary climb is treacherous—you may want to follow the lead of one of the agile youths. *From town, walk under bridge and follow path to right, heading south about ½ km (¼ mi) to Sandy Beach. Swim across river to swing.*

AFTER DARK

Many restaurants double as bars: locals and tourists alike usually stop at Eva's to see what's up and have a beer. At the Sand Castle, listen to blues on Monday or reggae on Thursday while enjoying drink specials and cool river breezes. The tavern at **Cahal Pech Village** (Cahal Pech Hill, tel. 092/3203) has sweeping views of San Ignacio and late-night dancing to reggae and soca beats. Friday evenings showcase "local talent," and all karaoke participants are broadcast live on local TV. Take a taxi ($2) at night; the walk uphill is long and unsafe. At the center of town the **Western Bar** and **Blue Angels** are locals' favorite spots to drink and do the fandango. The crowd sometimes raises a ruckus, but gringos are always welcome.

OUTDOOR ACTIVITIES

Whether hiking through the jungle, riding horseback, canoeing down jade-green rivers, inner tubing through caves, or clambering about in ancient Mayan ruins, the Cayo is the place to live out your Indiana Jones fantasies. Lots of locals have some kind of adventure trip to offer, equipment to rent, or vehicle and guide service for hire, so spend a few hours asking around at Eva's and other restaurants before you cement your itinerary.

BIRDING • Harboring everything from great blue herons to Amazon parrots and "Belizean roadrunners" (the gawky gray-necked wood rail), the forests around Cayo are a birder's paradise. Canoe trips (*see below*) are excellent for observing waterfowl. Some of the best sightings can be had simply by staying at one of the area's many resorts and ranches. Crystal Paradise offers nighttime tours led by a local expert.

CANOEING • The Cayo's many rivers, especially the Mopan and Macal, make it an excellent place for canoeing. Myriad birds and giant iguanas populate the treetops, and villagers still wash clothes on the rivers' banks. The going rate for full-day guided trips is around $12.50, but prices and destinations vary, so shop around. **Toni Canoes,** at Eva's (tel. 092/2267), comes highly recommended. It's also possible to rent your own canoe through **Float Belize** (tel. 092/3213), at the Sand Castle, for the same price. Especially in the dry season, you'll need a guide or extra-strong arm muscles to paddle through shallow rapids.

CAVING • Over the millennia, as dozens of swift-flowing rivers bored through them, the soft limestone of the Maya Mountains became pitted with caves, à la Swiss cheese. The Maya used them as burial sites and, according to one theory, as subterranean waterways that linked the Cayo with communities as far north as the Yucatán. Cayo residents joke that on every property there's a cave, and in every cave there are Mayan artifacts: pottery shards, ceremonial altars, sometimes even human remains.

Two companies have staked out the caves as their own. First on the scene was Ian Anderson, Canadian owner of **Caves Branch Adventure Co.** (tel. 082/2800). Based at a Spartan jungle camp (pit toilets, rustic cabanas, kerosene lamps), 19 km (12 mi) south of Belmopan, you'll ride rubber inner tubes deep into ancient river cave systems (about $60 per day, guide and lunch included). It's a day trip from San Ignacio by catching an 8 AM eastbound bus, changing at Belmopan, and ultimately arriving at 10:30 AM. (For more info, *see* Near Belmopan, *below*.) Peter Pacz, of **Pacz Tours** (tel. 092/2110), is a former mountain-expedition guide for the British Army, with a wealth of experience in both jungle survival and caving. He calls his two-night, three-day hike up the Roaring River ($100 per person) to a series of remote caves dotted with Maya burial sites "the ultimate expedition"—if you're lucky, he'll even cook you some termites. Closer to town is **Che Chem Ha Cave,** accessible only by car or taxi ($30). It's on the Morales family's land; admission ($25 for one–three people) includes a guide who will point out the cave's 1,000-year-old Mayan ceremonial artifacts. Flashlights and food are available for an extra charge. The cave is several miles south of Benque Viejo del Carmen, on Hydro Dam Road; ask at Eva's for more info.

MENNONITES:
MAVENS OF MODESTY

A devout Christian denomination named after Menno Simons, a Dutch religious reformer, the Mennonites are descendants of 16th-century Swiss Anabaptists. Separation from the outside world and conformity to scripture are essential to their belief system. The Mennonite people converse in German or German-accented English and maintain small, insular agrarian communities throughout Belize. Men dress in dark pants with suspenders, white shirts, and hats, and women wear simple cotton dresses and head scarves. Orthodox "horse-and-buggy" Mennonites are completely averse to modern technology, while other sects may have a few electrical appliances and drive cars. The Mennonites are famous for their elegant hand-carved furniture, and locals sometimes grumble about the Mennonites' perceived monopoly on the cheese market. Other than that, the Mennonites are well received; they're treated as just another one of the many groups of people who immigrated to Belize for its warm climate, social and otherwise. If you'd like to visit the Mennonite farming community at nearby Spanish Lookout (dubbed by locals as "mechanites," because its members embrace modern technology), take a bus east from San Ignacio to Holdfast Camp (8 km [5 mi]) and walk or hitch the 5-km (3-mi) road north.

HORSEBACK RIDING • Exploring on horseback is the ideal way to tour Cayo, and many resorts willingly supply steeds—though sometimes at outrageous prices. The best options for budget travelers are **Easy Rider** (tel. 092/3110), ½ km (¼ mi) west of town on Waight Avenue (becomes Bullet Tree Falls Rd.) and **Blue Ridge Mountain Rider** (tel. 092/2322) for exploration of the jungle, Mayan ruins, and river valleys. Rates start at $30 per half-day. Blue Ridge also offers a two-hour ride ($15) to Pacitbun (*see* Near San Ignacio, *below*). **Crystal Paradise Resort** (*see* Ranches and Resorts, *above*) does half-day rides to waterfalls or ruins ($40) and night rides ($35 per person, two-person minimum) complete with barbecue dinner. Arrange transportation to Crystal Paradise at Eva's. The undisputed equestrian experts, however, are the folks at **Mountain Equestrian Trails** (tel. 082/3310). Superbly trained and conditioned Texas quarter horses pick their way over the resort's 97 km (60 mi) of jungle trails, on the edge of the Mountain Pine Ridge Park. Tours are $40 per person for a half-day.

MOUNTAIN BIKING • The steep hills, heat, and humidity make mountain biking around San Ignacio and Mountain Pine Ridge Reserve seem like a nutty thing to do—but hey, it's your vacation. There are several good day-long rides (to the Mennonite community at Spanish Lookout, the Mayan ruins of Xunantunich, or a nearby river lodge for a swim) and two outfitters in town, both of which rent bikes for $2.50 an hour. **B&M** (26 Burns Ave., tel. 092/2382) charges $15 a day and offers great deals on weekend or week-long rentals. **Pacz** (4 Far West St., tel. 092/2110) charges $10 a day and also does organized tours, although they're pricey. Both can help you plan routes and will furnish maps and helmets.

NEAR SAN IGNACIO

Guatemala traditionally regarded itself as the cradle of Mayan civilization, much as the Attic Greeks view themselves as the keepers of the flame of classical Greek culture, and has spent millions of dollars restoring ruins like Tikal to prove it. But in recent years, as more and more Mayan ruins have been discovered in Belize and it became clear that Belize was not a spoke on the wheel of ancient Mayan civilization, but one of its hubs, the history books have had to be revised, much to Guatemala's chagrin.

Of the more than 600 Mayan ruins discovered in Belize thus far, a large proportion are in and around in the Cayo. Without your own wheels some of them will be hard to reach, although Xunantunich is easily reached by bus, and the small ruins of Cahel Pech are only a short hike from San Ignacio. Pacitbun and El Pilar are more difficult; and as for Caracol (the most impressive), you'll need to join a tour or rent a jeep. If you want to see Tikal, across the border in Guatemala, tours cost from $65 per person.

CAHAL PECH

Although not as imposing as many other ruins in the area, Cahal Pech is easily reached from town, and the visitor center and museum make for a good introduction to things Mayan. Occupied from 1200 BC up until the end of the Classic period, this site was the hilltop residence of a royal Maya family, a group of middle-class citizens, and their attendants—totaling no more than 40–50 people at its height. *From San Ignacio, walk about 2 km (1 mi) up Buena Vista Rd., pass the San Ignacio Hotel, and turn left on Carmelita St. The ruins are just up the steep hill from Cahal Pech Village* (see *After Dark,* above). *The 30-min walk is safe during daytime, but cab back ($2) if you stay past sunset. Admission $2.50. Open Tues.–Sat. 9–noon and 1–4:30, Sun. 9–noon.*

XUNANTUNICH

Perhaps the best part of a visit to Xunantunich (pronounced shoo-NAN-too-NEECH) is the spectacular 360° panorama over Guatemala and the Mopan River Valley from the top of El Castillo, the massive 120-ft-high main pyramid. If you manage to sneak in after the site officially closes (5 PM), sunset and moonrise are breathtaking. Little is known about the history of Xunantunich, despite extensive excavations earlier in the century and some renovation of the site's glorious stucco friezes; translated, the name means "Stone Maiden." It flourished as a ceremonial center during the Classic period; witness the ball court, several plazas, and numerous temples. Three well-preserved stelae are also on display. Evidence of a large earthquake around AD 900 probably explains its eventual abandonment. On the eastern wall is a reproduction of one of the finest Maya sculptures in Belize, a frieze decorated with jaguar heads, human faces, and abstract geometric patterns. Sweep the frieze with your eyes, then pan out across the jungle. *Take one of many westbound buses daily from San Ignacio and get off at the thriving Maya village of San José Succotz (15 min, $1); a hand-cranked ferry (closed noon–1) will take you across the river. From there, walk the 3-km (2-mi) trail through the jungle to the ruins. Admission $2.50. Open daily 8–5, weekends 8–4.*

EL PILAR

Officially known as the El Pilar Archaeological Reserve for Mayan Flora and Fauna, the site is still being excavated under the direction of Anabel Ford, an archaeology professor at U.C. Santa Barbara who's known for her unconventional views. Excavations of Maya ruins have traditionally concentrated on public architecture and "guy things" like ball courts and pyramids. At El Pilar, the emphasis is on domestic architecture—reconstructing houses, replanting a garden with crops used by the ancient Maya, and generally creating a sense that people actually lived here. They did so, according to Professor Ford, for 15 centuries, although most of the 25 small plazas and temples date from the last 300 years of occupation, AD 700–AD 1000. Evidence of sentry posts and the inaccessibility of parts of the site suggest that this was a community of high-ranking officials surrounded by a hostile population. Two well-marked trails take you around the site. Because the structures have not been stripped of vegetation, you may feel like you're walking through a series of shady orchards. The creation of a 4,940-square-mi nature reserve in 1995 around the site means you will see zillions of brilliantly colored tropical birds as you walk the excellent loop trails. At a lookout point by the main plaza is a spectacular view across the rain forest to El Pilar's sister city, Pilar Poniente, on the Guatemalan border. An ambitious cross-border project aims to excavate the causeway that links the two sites in 1999. You'll need a four-wheel-drive vehicle, a guided tour, or a lot of stamina on a mountain bike to get here. *Follow the signs from the bridge in Bullet Tree Falls, approximately 13 km (8 mi) west. Admission free. Open daily 8–5.*

CARACOL

Awesome, amazing, mind-blowing: these are just some of the words used to describe Caracol, Belize's grandest Mayan site and one of the most impressive in Central America. For centuries, until it was discovered in 1937 by Rosa Mai (a logger of Mayan descent), Caracol ("the snail" in Spanish) lay buried under the jungle of the remote Vaca Plateau. Excavation was sporadic for the first few decades after its discovery, and many of the site's treasures were looted until patrols were initiated in the 1980s. Only with intensive new archaeological work did the full scale of the city become clear. A set of hieroglyphs found at the site suggest that Caracol gained a crushing victory over its rival, Tikal, an idea that Guatemala has still not quite gotten used to. In its heyday, it was a Maya Manhattan, with five plazas and 32 large structures covering nearly a square mile, with a population of 250,000, slightly less than that of modern-day Belize. The pyramid of **Canaa,** or "sky house," is, at 138 ft, still the tallest human-made structure in the country. Why Caracol, and the rest of Mayan civilization, suddenly collapsed 1,000 years ago is still a riddle. One theory is that Caracol exhausted its water supply. For the latest information on the ruins themselves, call John Morris of the Archaeological Commission (tel. 082/2106). *Caracol is a 3-hr drive south of San Ignacio, off the Mountain Pine Ridge Rd., deep in the Chiquibul rain forest. Follow signs from the ranger outpost at Augustine (where you'll also need to pick up a free permit). Admission free. Open daily 9 AM–5 PM.*

PACITBUN

Once a massive Maya ceremonial center with more than 20 pyramids and raised pathways, Pacitbun saw its glory days in the Preclassic period—and is now one of the oldest known sites in Belize. Little excavation or research has been completed here; besides the mute 1,000-plus-year-old grassy mounds, you'll find a plaque bearing historical details. Pacitbun is on private land, so if you're not with a tour group, be sure ask for permission at the landowner's house before traipsing about. If you stay at Hilltop Camping (*see* Where to Sleep, *above*), it's within hiking distance. *Mountain Pine Ridge Rd., 21 km (13 mi) southeast of San Ignacio and 2 km (1 mi) east of the Maya village of San Antonio, this site is accessible by car (follow signs), by horseback, or by van tour. Admission free.*

The folks here are serious about tourists having a good time: only those tour guides who pass strict requirements—including a background check for any criminal record—are allowed to wear the official ID badge.

PANTI MEDICINE TRAIL

The Maya were masters at utilizing the jungle's natural resources for their practical and medicinal needs. **Ix Chel Farm's** self-guided Panti Medicine Trail, named for the celebrated Mayan healer Dr. Eligio Panti (who died at age 103 in 1995), winds gently along the bank of the Macal River, past medicinal plants and native hardwoods. You'll see and learn about the healing properties of such indigenous plants as the "give and take" tree, which coagulates blood; the gumbo-limbo, which provides a cure for poison wood rash; the negrito tree, the bark of which cures dysentery (it was worth its weight in gold in 17th-century Europe); and the "man vine" that stores fresh, drinkable water inside its tendrils. Cures that Mayan healers have relied on for centuries are finally being taken seriously by the Western medical community. The wild yam, for example, already has 14 known uses (including contraception and antiinflammation), and chemical analysts in the United States predict that as many as 20 more uses will be found in the coming decades. The trail, under the capable direction of Dr. Rosita Arvigo (who apprenticed with Dr. Panti), is an excellent place to get an overview of this new intersection of the ancient and the modern. Her small shop stocks teas, salves, and Maya medicinal products like Belly Be Good and Flu Away, as well as Dr. Arvigo's excellent books. For those who want a real immersion in the subject, Dr. Arvigo offers a five- to 10-day seminar in natural healing and herbalism for $125 per day. *Tel. 092/3870. Paddle upstream from San Ignacio in a canoe. By car, follow signs south from town to Chaa Creek Cottages. Admission $5. Open daily 8–noon and 1–5:30.*

MOUNTAIN PINE RIDGE RESERVE

Place *Bonanza*'s pine trees on the set with palms from *Gilligan's Island* and you've re-created Mountain Pine Ridge, a preserve 25 km (16 mi) southeast of San Ignacio that protects stands of pine forest as well as tracts of jungle. This mountainous, 780-square-km (300-square-mi) nature reserve, a rugged dome of granite and limestone containing some of the most ancient rocks in Central America, is a highlight of any journey to Belize. And, after the heat and humidity of lowland Belize, the cool air and the shady pine woods are a real treat. The incredibly out-of-place ecosystem is thought to be the remnants of a Caribbean island that collided with the peninsula millions of years ago, and as your vehicle rattles through the mountains, the scenery changes from rain forest to Ticonderoga and back again with startling quickness. You'll see lilac-colored mimosa, Saint-John's-wort, and occasionally a garish red flower known as hotlips. There's also a huge variety of ferns, ranging from the tiny maidenhair fern to giants the size of small coconut trees, and a fair selection of Belize's 154 species of orchid. Look out, too, for a wild tree called craboo, whose berries are used to make a brandy-like liqueur believed to have aphrodisiac properties.

There are several things to see and do within the reserve: **Hidden Valley Falls,** also known as the 1,000 Foot Falls (though they're in fact nearly 1,600 ft high) are the highest in Central America. A thin plume of spray plummets over the edge of a rock face into a seemingly bottomless gorge below. You'll find a shelter, some benches, and a public rest room, though the distance from viewing platform (admission $1.50) to falls lessens the effect, particularly during the dry season. Not included on van tours are the spectacular **Five Sisters Falls,** accessible only by hiking from nearby campgrounds (see Where to Sleep, above). On the southern spur of the Mountain Pine Ridge Road are the **Rio On Pools and Falls,** great places to stop for a picnic and swim, as well as the impressive **Rio Frio Cave.** Cathedralesque in its grandeur, the cave was once used by the Maya as a ceremonial center. A river runs right through the center of the cave, and it has carved the rock into fantastic shapes over the centuries. Swallows fill the place and at night, ocelot and margay pad silently across the cold sand floor in search of slumbering prey. From the cool, dark interior, the light-filled world of mosses, birds, and plants outside seems more intense and beautiful than ever. Bisecting the circle of light and rising vertically through the mouth of the cave, like a spar propping up the whole mountain, is a giant hardwood tree, *Pterocarpus officialis,* its massive paddle-shape roots anchored in the sandy soil of the riverbank and its green crown straining toward the blue sky. You can approach the cave via a nature trail (45 min), or drive to within 400 yards of the entrance. Both sites are located near the ranger's headquarters in Augustine. Worth a stop on the way in or out of MPR, is the **Green Hills Butterfly Farm** (tel. 092/3310), created by two Dutch lepidopterists. A one-hour tour takes you through a netted house full of breeding butterflies of all sorts and the flowers that sustain them. The gift shop sells butterfly-patterned quilts made by local Mennonites (open Christmas–Easter, daily 9–4; after Easter, call for appointment).

The Mountain Pine Ridge Reserve can be reached from the road running southeast from San Ignacio that passes through the Maya villages of **Cristo Rey** and **San Antonio.** Or take the slightly more direct route south from **Georgeville,** a town 10 km (6 mi) west of San Ignacio on the Western Highway. Either way, the entrance gate is approximately a 45-minute drive over rough and hilly roads. If you are driving, Caracol (see above) and Pacitbun ruins (see above) are in the area and worth a visit. Without a car, your best option is to join a tour group leaving from San Ignacio (about $18 per person); a full day's trip usually includes 1,000-Foot Falls, Rio Frio Cave, and the Rio On Pools and Falls.

BELMOPAN

The best way to see Belize's capital is through the rear-view mirror, as you head toward the Cayo. The brainchild of Belize's longest-serving prime minister, Vincent Price, Belmopan was to be Belize's answer to Brasília—a resplendent, modern capital city in the interior. Instead, Belmopan calls to mind the mortifying question: what if you throw a party and nobody comes? Blame Hurricane Hattie. After Hattie destroyed Belize City in 1961, the thought was to create an inland administrative and cultural center that wouldn't be as vulnerable to tidal waves and hurricanes. The result was designed to look like an ancient Mayan city—instead, it is a drab collection of box-like concrete buildings. And the town now faces the same pitiful image problem as Sacramento, California, and Canberra, Australia—it's got the title but none of the glory. Many foreign countries—including the United States—have opted to keep their diplomatic headquarters in Belize City. Most of the 6,000 residents are grumpy government apparatchiks who'd rather be somewhere else. You, too, will be bored. Even the one thing that used to make a visit worthwhile—the so-called Archaeological Vault, where Belize's Mayan treasures were stored in a giant Chubb safe—has closed. And until a long-planned (but never executed) National Museum is built, the best thing to do, unless you have to change buses or renew a visa, is keep on going to the Cayo or other points of interest nearby (see Near Belmopan, below).

BASICS

The **British High Commission** (Embassy Sq., tel. 08/22–146) is open weekdays 8:30–noon and 1:30–4. The embassies of **Costa Rica** (Hummingbird Hwy., tel. 08/23–801) and **El Salvador** (23rd St., tel. 08/23–404) issue visas weekdays 9–1. **Barclay's** and **Belize Bank** (open Mon.–Thurs. 8–1, Fri. 8–1 and 3–6) both have offices behind the market, near the bus station. **BTL** is by the satellite dish, and the **post office** is in the main square (marked by the ugly contemporary art piece). The **immigration office** (Half Moon Ave., tel. 08/22–423) charges $12.50 per month for visa extensions. It's open weekdays 8–noon and 1–5.

COMING AND GOING

Belmopan lies 81 km (50 mi) southeast of Belize City at the junction of the Western and Hummingbird highways. **Batty** and **Novelo's** buses ply the Western Highway with hourly departures to several locations, weekdays 7:30 AM–9 PM and weekends 7:30–7. Destinations include Belize City (1 hr, $1.50) to the east, and San Ignacio (2½ hrs, $2) and Melchor de Mencos, Guatemala (3¼ hrs, $2.50), to the west. **Z-Line** buses pass through on their way to Dangriga (3 hrs, $4) and Punta Gorda (8 hrs, $10). Six southbound buses head out daily 9–4, but only three of those travel beyond Dangriga. All buses passing through Belmopan stop at the parking lot just south of the government offices and outdoor market, making transfers a breeze.

WHERE TO SLEEP

The only reason you'd need to spend the night in Belmopan is if you're comatose from heat stroke and in desperate need of an air-conditioned hotel with cable. The **El Rey Inn** (23 Moho St., tel. 08/23–438) has clean rooms with private bath, hot water, and ceiling fans at $22.50 a double. The bonus is extra-friendly management.

NEAR BELMOPAN

GUANACASTE NATIONAL PARK

Named for the mammoth 150-year-old guanacaste, or "monkey's ear" tree, growing near the park entrance, the park contains dozens of orchids and flowering bromeliads, along with reptiles, small mammals, and approximately 100 species of birds. At the park's western boundary, **Roaring Creek** flows into the Belize River, making for ideal swimming (there's also a rope swing for Tarzan types). Pick up a leaflet, which will lead you on a tour of the park's botanical wonders, from the **visitor information center.** *3 km (2 mi) north of Belmopan, at the junction of the Western and Hummingbird highways. Open daily 8:30–5, last tour 3:30 PM.*

BLUE HOLE NATIONAL PARK

Not to be confused with the offshore Blue Hole (*see* Lighthouse Reef, *above*), the inland Blue Hole National Park encompasses some 575 acres of mountainous terrain with limestone deposits pocketed by underground streams, sinkholes, and ancient cave systems. Hidden within dense jungle are the **Blue Hole** and **St. Herman's Cave,** a popular picnicking and swimming spot. The Blue Hole was created when water on its way to the Sibun River emerged from underground to fill a collapsed karst-rock sinkhole. The resulting pool is crystal-clear, cold, and an intense sapphire color. Farther downstream the river flows underground again, into a cave with incredible natural acoustics (use caution when swimming in the cave, because currents can be swift). Some years ago, there were some nasty incidents at the site, with tourists robbed and, in one case, raped; but a full-time attendant was subsequently appointed to patrol the area, and the problem has been resolved. The imposing St. Herman's Cave is at the end of a strenuous 3-km (2-mi) trail north of the swimming hole. Mayan artifacts such as pots, spears, and torches have all been recovered here. The concrete steps you'll use to descend are constructed over those originally created by the Maya. It's one of few caves in Belize you can enter without a guide or permit. Any bus heading south from Belmopan or north from Dangriga will drop you off (20 min, $1), and there are six daily in each direction. When you've had enough, either flag another bus or hitch, although you may have a wait because traffic is fairly sparse. *19 km (12 mi) south of Belmopan, on the Hummingbird Hwy. Open daily 8–4.*

CAVES BRANCH

On either side of the Caves Branch River—just across the Hummingbird Highway from Blue Hole National Park—stretches a 3,000-acre private wildlife preserve that is **Ian Anderson's Caves Branch Adventure Co. and Jungle River Camp** (Box 356, Belmopan, Belize, tel. 08/22–800). Here you can explore four river cave systems and dry-land crystal caves, in addition to 40 km (25 mi) of jungle trails. Tours start at $55 per person. Cave exploration is either on foot or in rubber inner tubes: the longest is an all-day, 13-km (8-mi) float on a subterranean river—certainly not an excursion for the meek. Inside the caves are giant stalagmites, crystal flows, and evidence of ceremonial and sacrificial use by the Maya (such as pottery shards, crystallized footprints, and carved altars). Overnight stays run $20 (single), $35 (double) in one of seven immaculate thatched cabanas, or $10 for a spot in the bunkhouse. You can also camp ($5). Meals, served family style with the friendly staff (and a pet spider monkey), are $8 (breakfast or lunch) and $12 (dinner). Make reservations as far in advance as possible.

SOUTHERN BELIZE

Because it is underrated and out-of-the-way, many tourists either blow off or blow through this part of Belize; for this reason, the rugged south is the country's closest thing to a tropical paradise. Here's your best chance to see a wild jaguar, visit old-growth rain forest, explore an ancient Mayan ceremonial cave, or camp on a deserted island. Just getting to the southlands can be a struggle: the **Hummingbird Highway** (which connects Belmopan to Dangriga) is one of the most spectacular bus rides in the country. It's also a potholed mess. The **Southern Highway** picks up at Dangriga; this hellish track is the reason why many travelers avoid the Toledo district unless they're catching a water taxi from Punta Gorda to Livingston or Puerto Barrios, Guatemala. But there is good news: the road is currently being upgraded. To the west, the 3,000-ft-tall Maya Mountains are so thickly forested they make crossing the Himalayas seem like a stroll in the park. To this day, parts of the southland remain unexplored.

Southern Belize has the largest concentrations of Garifunas (Black Caribs) and Maya, all of whom live in villages still untainted by *Dallas* reruns, NFL merchandising, and 24-hour CNN. You'll find these are friendly, generous people who welcome visitors rather than resent them. The town of Dangriga (in the Stann Creek District) is the Garifuna cultural center, but smaller, more traditional villages scattered up and down the coast, like Hopkins or Seine Bight, make terrific day trips. Farther south in the Toledo District, Maya from the Mopan and Kekchi tribes, in search of refuge from Guatemalan repression, have established villages in the hills above Punta Gorda; many of the villages belong to home-stay programs that help raise money for health and education programs. If it's the cays and the sea that you seek, the town of Placencia, with its long sandy beach, is a choice spot from which to launch your exploration.

DANGRIGA

Dangriga is like death and taxes for travelers in southern Belize: sooner or later you'll have to face it, to change buses, catch a boat, or hop a plane. Streets here feel vaguely like the Western frontier, with ramshackle wooden buildings alongside once-ornate colonial structures. Recently, drug dealers and gangs, chased out of Belize City during the crackdown on crime, have decamped to Dangriga, making it a crime hot spot.

There's another side to the town: it's the center of Garifuna culture (*see box* 100% Garifuna, *below*), a close-knit community with a rich cultural history, currently being torn apart by drugs. The best time to visit is on **Garifuna Settlement Day** (Nov. 19), when the whole town cuts loose for a weeklong celebration with traditional food, music, and Waribagabaga dance. You can drop in on local Garifuna drum maker **Austin Rodriguez** (32 Tubroose St., tel. 05/22–308) any time of year to watch him craft a drum or shape the *matta*, an instrument used to beat plantains. **Mercy Sabal** (22 Magoon St., tel. 05/23–018) is another townsperson hoping to preserve the old ways of life; she welcomes visitors to her home to see her handmade Garifuna dolls.

BASICS

Dangriga is a one-road town with everything a backpacker could wish for along an eight-block span. North of the bridge at town center, the main drag's called **Commerce Street**; to the south its name changes to **St. Vincent Drive. Barclays Bank** and **Scotia Bank** are one block north of the bridge on Commerce Street; **Belize Bank** is one block south. All are open weekdays 8–1, with additional hours Fridays 3–6. The **Stann Creek Medical Center and Pharmacy** (tel. 05/23–237 or 05/22–138) is south of the bridge adjacent to the Belize Bank. It's open Monday–Saturday 7–3. **BTL** (tel. 05/22–065) is north of the bridge at the corner of Courthouse Road, across from the police station. To reach the **post office** (Mahogany Rd. at Caney St.), walk south from the bridge two blocks on St. Vincent Street and turn left. Both BTL and the post office are open weekdays 8–noon and 1–4. The town's lone **laundromat,** at the Affordable Corner Store (129 Commerce St.), is a four-block walk north of the bridge.

COMING AND GOING

If you're seeking nirvana at one of the southern cays or simply heading south along the coast, prepare to wait for a while in Dangriga.

BY BUS • Dangriga is connected to the rest of Belize by **Z-Line Bus Service** (tel. 05/22–211 or 05/22–748), which makes stops immediately north and south of the Commerce Street bridge. The Z-Line ter-

100% GARIFUNA

The Garifuna (pronounced Ga-RIF-una), or Black Caribs, are a unique cultural and ethnic group. They first appeared in this area more than 300 years ago, when escaped and shipwrecked slaves mixed with the native Caribs who had given them refuge on Saint Vincent Island. Garifuna adopted the Carib language but kept their African musical and religious traditions, against the demands of the island's colonial masters. In 1795, the Garifuna people rebelled against the British; the crown punished them for their insolence by deporting them to the island of Roatán, off Honduras. In the years that followed, the Garifuna slowly established fishing villages on islands and along the coast of southern Belize, Guatemala, and northern Honduras. Belize's independence from Great Britain in 1981 sparked a revival of the Garifuna culture in the Stann Creek District. Its capital was renamed Dangriga (a Garifuna word meaning "standing waters") and today is home to the largest Garifuna population in the country.

The Garifuna's African spirituality so mystified and terrified Europeans that, during the days of slavery, drums were banned throughout most of the Caribbean—their powerful rhythms were thought to cause madness. Today, drumming and chants are a core part of Garifuna rituals, coupled with fervent dancing and speaking in tongues. As young Garifuna are swept up in a world of ganja, Marley, and MTV, some elders wonder if the old ways will survive. "After it all, from Africa to the English, we're still here today," they say. "The language is on our tongues, we're born with it in our blood—100% Garifuna."

minal—clean, efficient, and expertly air-conditioned—is seven blocks south of town on the main road, near the Texaco and Shell stations.

BY BOAT • Generally, boats tie up daily at the river mouth, either at the fish market or on either side of the Commerce Street bridge. Stroll around to secure a favorable price and departure time—or make a reservation with an island guest house and they'll send someone to fetch you. Departures are usually between 10 AM and 3 PM. To Coco Plum Caye (30 min), Man-O'-Way Caye Bird Sanctuary (45 min), Tobacco Caye (1 hr), or South Water Caye (2 hrs) cost is $15–$30 one way, depending on distance. You can also reach the village of Hopkins (45 min, $20). Once weekly a boat departs Dangriga for Puerto Cortés, Honduras (4 hrs, $30), though this requires good weather and a minimum of eight passengers; inquire at Soffie's Hotel.

BY PLANE • **Maya Island Air** (tel. 024/4032) and **Tropic Air** (tel. 024/5671 or 800/422–3435 in the U.S.) have regular service north to and from Belize City or south to Placencia or Punta Gorda. Buy tickets at Treasured Travels (64 Commerce St., three blocks north of bridge, tel. 05/22–578), open weekdays 8–noon and 1–4; or at the Bonefish Hotel (15 Mahogany St., next to post office, tel. 05/22–165). The airstrip is a brisk 25-minute walk away, on the far north end of town past the cemetery. Sure, you can be masochistic about it, or you can pay $2.50 to catch a ride from Neal's Taxi (1 St. Vincent St., just south of bridge, tel. 05/23–309).

WHERE TO SLEEP AND EAT

To most travelers Dangriga is a fleeting stop on the way to somewhere better, but those with imperfect timing can catch some shut-eye at **Río Mar Hotel** (990 Chatuye St., tel. 05/22–201), located at the river mouth south of the Commerce Street bridge, or **Pal's Guest House** (868-A Magoon St., tel. 05/22–095). Doubles start at $12.50 with shared bath; upstairs doubles, which have private baths and cable TV, are $20–$30. Slightly more upsacle is the **Riverside Hotel** (135 Commerce St., tel. 05/22–168), just north of the bridge, where large, airy second-floor rooms cost $20.

You will never dine to the strains of violins in Dangriga, but you can find plenty of greasy spoons offering food that's tasty, filling, and cheap. Most popular in town is **Burger King** (135 Commerce St., just south of bridge, tel. 05/22–476). It is unaffiliated with its American namesake, but burgers, fries, and coleslaw are still on the menu, plus hearty breakfasts and fresh-squeezed juices. Several reasonable Chinese restaurants can be found north of the bridge, including **Sun Rise** (96 Commerce St., tel. 05/22–482) and **Sea Flame** (42 Commerce St., near Church St., tel. 05/22–250). **Melly's Homemade Ice Cream** (66 Sawai St., at Commerce St., tel. 05/22–477) has pastries and delicious ice cream flavors Ben and Jerry have never dreamed of—try the soursop. Be aware that most restaurants close 2–6 PM for unofficial siesta time and reopen in the evening, and virtually everything is closed on Sunday.

NEAR DANGRIGA

Although Dangriga itself offers as much beauty and excitement as an unwashed sock, within easy distance lie some of Belize's treasures: sleepy fishing villages, tiny coconut-palm cays, and wildlife reserves where you actually stand a chance of seeing animals more interesting than your travel partners.

GALES POINT

Forty-eight km (30 mi) north of Dangriga, at the tip of a narrow, sandy peninsula that juts into the Southern Lagoon, the unspoiled lagoons, rivers, and swamps surrounding this sleepy fishing village have recently been targeted as a wildlife protection area. The area is home to the largest population of manatees in Central America, and it is the main breeding ground for the endangered hawksbill turtle. Human activity here is fairly low-key; you can laze on the beach or ask around town if you're interested in going out manatee-watching. Or whip yourself into a frenzy at the **Maroou Creole Drumming School,** where rhythm master Emmeth Young gives lessons ($5 per hour), demonstrates drum making, and dishes out Creole history. You can camp on the grounds for $6. There's one guest house in town, **Gentle's Cool Spot,** which has three simple, clean rooms ($15 per double) on the beach. Another option is the town's host-family network; cost per night (including meals) is about $12. Make arrangements in advance for any of these by calling the Gales Point **community telephone** (tel. 05/22–087).

COMING AND GOING • Z-Line (tel. 05/22–211 or 05/22–748) has a bus that departs Dangriga for Gales Point (2½ hrs, $3) once daily at 1 PM, with an additional bus Friday at 5 PM. It continues north to the Western Highway, ending up at Belize City (3 hrs, $3). The bus makes the return journey to Dangriga the following morning. From Gales Point, buses depart for Dangriga Monday–Saturday at 5 AM and 9 AM and Sunday at 9 AM.

TOBACCO REEF

Several cays off the coast of Dangriga remain secreted away from the general wash of the vacationing masses. Two here make great day trips from Dangriga: **Coco Plum Caye** for snorkeling and **Man-O'-Way Caye Bird Sanctuary** for peering through binoculars at nesting brown boobies and magnificent frigate birds. The tranquillity and beauty of tiny **Tobacco Caye** is slowly being displaced by beach-volleyball courts, but the reef is still a big draw here. Only 20 yards offshore, it offers truly fantastic snorkeling. There are several guest facilities (and little else) on the coconut palm–covered island; most reasonable is **Gaviota Coral Reef Resort** (tel. 05/22–085), where a kerosene-lit cabana (shared bath) by the sea is $45 per couple or $25 for single travelers, all meals included. They'll catch your dinner, including delicious conch, fish, and when in season, lobster, daily on the reef. **Island Camps** (Box 174, Belize City, tel. 02/47–160) has private cabanas with bath ($65), or without ($45), all meals included. Most outfits rent snorkel gear (around $5 per day) or canoes (around $20 per day) and can arrange fishing trips. Also right on Tobacco Reef, **South Water Caye** is outrageously overpriced (beach cabins are around $100 per night). It is, however, the only island with scuba diving, and its reefs—currently under consideration for designation as a marine reserve—are pristine. Save your cash by staying on Tobacco Caye and boating over for a day's diving. When you arrive, look for **Junior,** a friendly independent dive master who'll take you out for as little as $25 plus equipment rental. For information on taking a boat from Dangriga to the cayes near and along Tobacco Reef, *see* Coming and Going in Dangriga, *above*.

HOPKINS

A peaceful Garifuna fishing village 32 km (20 mi) southwest of Dangriga, Hopkins is just like the cays were prior to the invasion of "You Better Belize It!" T-shirts. Palm trees, sandy beachfront, and villagers who lavish warmth and hospitality on arriving travelers make this town—the soul of Belize's Garifuna community—an ideal place to chill for a few days. The **BTL** and **post office** (both open weekdays 8–noon and 1–4) are at the center of town. There's also a restaurant and bar, some small stores, and three places to stay. The **Sandy Beach Lodge** (tel. 05/22–033), a women-owned cooperative at the far south end of town, has simple double-occupancy thatched-roof cabanas ($20) on the beach; ask anyone on the street to point you in its direction and they'll reply, "The women are waiting for you." The **Caribbean View** (tel. 05/22–083) has rooms for $18 per person. The **Hopkins Inn** has single rooms for $7.50 and doubles for $12.50. It's also fairly easy to find a patch of ground for camping if you get permission from the owner first. When you grow restless from so much relaxation, ask around about sightseeing and fishing expeditions by boat. For more information or to make reservations, call the Hopkins **community telephone** (tel. 05/22–033 or 05/22–803).

COMING AND GOING • Promised Land Bus Service (tel. 05/23–012) provides transportation to Hopkins from Dangriga (1 hr, $1.50), continuing south to Placencia (90 min, $2). From Dangriga you can also hire a boat ($20 one way) to make the 45-minute trip down the coastline. For more information, *see* Coming and Going in Dangriga, *above*.

COCKSCOMB BASIN JAGUAR SANCTUARY

Boat service between Dangriga and the cayes is a lackadaisical affair. There are no fixed schedules or prices, most vessels look like elongated bathtubs, and a few salty old captains are fond of a beer or four before weighing anchor. Ships ahoy, mate!

Up to 6 ft long and weighing in just below Mike Tyson, *Felis onca*—or *El Tigre*, as it's known in Spanish—is nature's great loner, a supremely free creature that shuns even the company of its own kind. The term jaguar comes from the Indian word *Yaguar* meaning "he who kills with one leap," and that's exactly what a jaguar does, falling on deer, peccaries, or gibnut with a deadly leap and severing the vertebrae in the neck. Except during a brief mating period, and the six short months the female spends with her cubs before turning them loose, jaguars live alone, roaming the rain forest in splendid isolation. By day, they sun themselves to sleep; by night, they stalk gibnut, armadillo, and curassow, a kind of wild turkey, with the deadly efficiency of a serial killer. To the ancient Maya, the jaguars were intermediaries between this world and the world of the gods.

Once the undisputed king of the Central and South American jungles, the jaguar is now extinct or endangered in most of its original range. But it has a haven in the Cockscomb Basic Wildlife Sanctuary, which covers 102,000 acres of lush rain forest in the Cockscomb Range of the Maya Mountains. There are an estimated 25 to 30 jaguars—8 to 10 mature males, 9 to 10 adult females, and the rest young animals—spread over about 400 square km (154 square mi). This is the largest jaguar population in the world and one of Belize's most significant contributions to conservation. In contrast, the jaguar was hunted to extinction in the United States by the late 1940s.

You are not likely to see a jaguar; they have exceptionally good senses of smell and hearing. If you do, you'll be far too close. But walking along the 12 well-marked loop trails you may come across a paw print in a patch of dry mud. And you are likely to see many other endangered flora and fauna: 300 species of birds, including the keel-billed toucan, the king vulture, several species of hawks, and the scarlet macaw; other cats, like pumas, margays, and ocelots; plus coatis, kinkajous, deer, peccaries, anteaters, red-eyed tree frogs, and boa constrictors. Search the treetops for bizarre and beautiful blooms of orchids.

If you plan to hike extensively, pick up a trail map at the visitor center and make sure you have some serious bug spray with you—Cockscomb is alive with no-see-ums (tiny biting flies) and mosquitoes. The most strenuous trail takes you up a steep hill, from the top of which there is a magnificent view of the entire Cockscomb Basin. Keep in mind that the best times to hike anywhere in Belize are early morning and early evening, when temperatures are lower and more animals are out. Near the preserve's northwest boundary is **Victoria Peak,** the highest mountain in Belize at 3,675 ft; for information on climbing permits contact the Belize Audubon Society (12 Fort St., Belize City, tel. 02/34–985 or 02/34–987). You can camp inside the reserve for $2 per person, or stay in a bunkhouse for $10 per person. Kitchen facilities are available but you'll need to bring your own food, water, and artificial light—there's no electricity, and the best time to see wildlife is on a night hike. *Admission $2.50. Open daily 8–5.*

COMING AND GOING • The sanctuary headquarters lie at the end of a rough 10-km (6-mi) unpaved road leading off the Southern Highway. Take a Z-Line bus south 23 km (14 mi) to the village of **Maya Centre** (1 hr, $2.50), where the entrance road begins. You can walk (difficult in the heat), hitch (challenging with so little traffic), or make arrangements in advance with the Audubon Society (*see above*) for a ride ($20). When you're ready to leave, take note that the last northbound bus passes at around 3 PM and the last southbound one at about 9 PM.

SAPODILLA LAGOON WILDLIFE REFUGE

Like the Cockscomb Sanctuary, this new 30,000-acre private preserve prides itself on its resident population of big cats—sightings are more frequent here, since it's not as heavily visited by tourists. The refuge's **Black Cat Lodge** (tel. 05/22–006) has dorm beds and one double room for $18–$25 per person, all meals included. For an additional price you can rent horses or canoes to explore the surrounding forest. To reach the refuge, take a Z-Line bus to Mile 16 (just south of Maya Centre) on the Southern Highway and look for the entrance sign. You can either walk in (20–25 min) or call ahead to arrange for pickup.

PLACENCIA

If you want to get "blissed out in Belize," this is the place to do it. Set in a sheltered half-moon bay, at the end of a peninsula with crystal-clear green water and almost 5 km (3 mi) of palm-dotted white sand, this balmy fishing village is straight out of a Robert Louis Stevenson novel. To the west, the Cockscomb Range ruffles the tropical sky with its jagged peaks; to the east, a line of uninhabited cays dots the Caribbean horizon. Originally founded by pirates, it is now peopled with an extraordinary mélange of races. Everyone looks different; Placencia is one of the few places in the world where you'll see black people with blue eyes. There's lots to do: canoe up the Monkey River, go snorkeling and diving, or just lie in a hammock under a palm tree, read, sleep, and perhaps get up long enough to swim.

Placencia's main thoroughfare is recorded in the *Guinness Book of Records* as the narrowest street in the world. In fact, it is less a street than a path, just wide enough for two, that meanders past wooden cottages on stilts overrun with bougainvillea and festooned with laundry. Along the path are most of the village's guest houses, and little palapa-covered cafés serving mainly burgers, rice and beans, and a bit of seafood.

Five years ago, the village stopped less than 3 km (2 mi) north of the town, at the exclusive **Rum Point Inn** resort, one of only four resorts in the area. Now, there are 11, stretching up the coast from Placencia. Thankfully, none of them are large, Florida-type operations. But if things continue as they are, Placencia looks set to become a southern Ambergris Caye. For the moment, there is still plenty here for the adventurous traveler (local restaurants, modest guest houses, fun bars), making it a great base for offshore excursions and inland adventures. Shop around town for the best prices; anyone with a boat or a car may be willing to do a trip.

BASICS

Getting around Placencia is straightforward: there's the road and there's the sidewalk. Most services are clustered at the end of the Split, where road and sidewalk meet. There's no bank in town, but **Wallen's Market** (open Mon.–Sat. 8–noon and 1–5), by the curve in the road near the end of the peninsula, cashes traveler's checks. Your only alternative is a boat ride to the mainland town of Big Creek, where a **Belize Bank** (tel. 06/22–079) is open weekdays 8–1. The Placencia **post office** and **BTL,** at the tip of the peninsula near the public docks, are open weekdays 8–noon and 1–4. The **Placencia Laundromat** (north end of sidewalk) will take care of your smelly stuff daily 8–5. For medical attention you must return to the mainland.

COMING AND GOING

Two bus lines connect Placencia to mainland Belize. The **Z-Line** (tel. 05/22–211 or 05/22–748) bus departs Placencia for Dangriga (2½ hrs, $3.50) Monday–Saturday at 6 AM; from Dangriga, you can pick up Z-Line buses going north to Belmopan and Belize City. **Promised Land Bus Service** (tel. 05/23–012) also shuttles between Dangriga and Placencia, with a stop at the village of Hopkins (90 min, $2). There is no direct service between Placencia and Punta Gorda. If you're arriving from the south, get off at the town of Independence or at Big Creek Village, where the *Hokey-Pokey* **boat** (yes, that's its name) will take you across the lagoon for $5.

If you have limited time, both **Tropic Air** (tel. 024/5671 or 800/422–3435 in the U.S.) and **Maya Island Air** (tel. 024/4032) have regular services to and from Belize City (½ hr., $35). Purchase tickets at the BTL office or at one of the resorts. The airstrip is about 3 km (2 mi) north of the center of town, so you'll probably want a taxi ($3). If you wish to escape Belize entirely, check in with **Deja Vu Charters** (tel. 06/ 23–338), on the pier near the BTL office. They provide one-way water-taxi service to Livingston ($45) and Puerto Barrios ($40) in Guatemala, and to Puerto Cortés, Honduras ($40).

WHERE TO SLEEP

You'll find plenty of places to snooze in Placencia, although the guest houses are all in town and luxury resorts dominate the beachfront. The best lodgings fill fast during the high season (especially on weekends), so book a room early in the day.

UNDER $20 • **Conrad and Lydia's Rooms** (tel. 06/23–117) is a comfortable, clean, and friendly place at the north end of town. They charge $12 for a double, and Lydia will cook breakfast on request. **Coconut Cottage** (tel. 06/23–234) has two small cabanas ($26 single, $35 double) near the beach. Both have a fridge and private bath with hot water. The **Paradise Vacation Resort** (tel. 06/23–179 or 06/23–260) at the end of the Split near the BTL office, is a great deal: beach access, a pleasant veranda, and doubles for $20 (shared bath) or $28 (private). For a funky alternative, **Dr. Ted** (tel. 06/ 23–172) rents houses for about $80 per week (sleeping up to four people); showers are rustic (basically buckets of rainwater), and cooking facilities are equally simple. Inquire at the Acupuncture Center, on the road near Wallen's Market. Many locals will rent out a room in their house for less than official guest houses; ask around and look for signs. You can camp for $2 at **Mr. Clive's,** on the beach at the north end of town.

A century ago, loggers worked the Cockscomb Basin and obviously loved every minute of it. Old maps of the area are marked with names like Go-to-Hell Camp and Sal Si Puede (Leave if You Can).

UNDER $50 •

Barracuda and Jaguar Inn. Tucked behind the hardware store, this little cluster of wooden buildings belongs to Canadian Wendy Bryan, owner of the Pickled Parrot, one of Placencia's most popular watering holes. The cabanas are elegant for the price ($40 double), with hardwood fittings, private baths, refrigerators, coffee makers, and small porches with hammocks. You'll get some sleep: Wendy shuts down the bar at 10 PM and doesn't open the restaurant until noon. *The sidewalk, southern end of town, tel. 06/23–330. 2 rooms with bath.*

Sonny's. The larger cabanas with sea views are more expensive, but the smaller ones, set back from the water, are only $30 for a double. The restaurant serves good local dishes. *The sidewalk, southern end of town, tel. 06/23–103. 14 rooms with bath.*

FOOD

Just about every restaurant in town is affordable, and all serve excellent seafood. **Sonny's Resort** (tel. 06/23–103), on the sidewalk at the south end of town, is probably the most popular eatery, serving tasty breakfast ($4), lunch ($2–$4), and dinner ($4–$15) with slothlike speed. Farther up the sidewalk, **Omar's Fast Foods** (tel. 06/23–236) features burrito breakfasts ($1.50), homemade brownies (50¢), and delicious seafood dinners. Good for breakfast is the **Driftwood Café** (tel. 06/23–248), near Omar's. If you need a sugar high, there are several good pastry and cookie shops in Placencia: **John the Baker Man** has fresh bread rolls most mornings, while **Miss Lizzy** has homemade yogurt and granola as well as fresh juice; look for their signs on the sidewalk. Betty, the cook at **BJ's Restaurant** (tel. 06/23–108), on the road at the north end of town, makes wonderful *serre* (a local dish with lobster, cassava, and coconut cream), as well as burgers, seafood, and fresh-squeezed juices from her own trees. If you want to feel the breeze blowing through your hair, head for the **Kingfisher Restaurant and Bar** (tel. 06/23–175), a large, thatched building on the beach, for seafood and local standards like chicken and beans and rice. **The Pickled Parrot** (tel. 06/2330) is more upmarket (seafood pasta: $6.50), but the ambience is great, and Canadian host Wendy Bryan is good company. On Thursday, there is a limbo contest and on Friday, a full pizza menu. If you like Chinese, head for **Kowloon,** at the far end of the football field in town. The charming owner, Susanne Mak, used to run a popular restaurant in Punta Gorda, as evidenced by her letters of thanks from the British consul and the American embassy. Once you have tasted the curried shrimp or conch with vegetables, you will understand why.

Most of the resorts north of town are prohibitively expensive, but if you want to splurge, head for the bar and restaurant at **Kitty's Place** (tel. 06/23–237), a midpriced resort on its own white-sand beach 3 km (2 mi) north of town. The breakfast menu (until noon) features treats like homemade breads, tropical fruits, and burritos; for lunch there are Belizean dishes plus burgers and sandwiches. At night, the **Sand Bar,** built by local Mayans using rain-forest materials, has a great view of the sea (or, for sports events, a giant TV); while the candlelit veranda is a place to get intimate with your significant other. On Sundays, there is a three-course Mayan Pibil barbecue for $14. If you decide to stay, there are rooms from $55 to $135.

AFTER DARK

Placencia is fun in a laid-back, beach-town kind of way, and it's easy to stumble up and down the sidewalk in search of the action. Women travelers will feel safe because the attitude here is more similar to the cays than to the male-dominated mainland. One of the best bars in town is the **Pickled Parrot,** with its mahogany counter and candlelit tables, where the ambience is relaxed. To do some serious drinking, head for the **Lagoon Saloon,** where American ex-pats Mike and Bonnie will ply you with concoctions like Lagoon Monsters (triple-decker rum punches), sliced meat sandwiches, and some of the best/worst jokes you'll ever hear. The satellite TV is usually tuned to rock-and-roll, and there is also a dartboard and backgammon. **The Sand Bar,** at Kitty's Place is always packed. At the far south end of town, there are two popular waterfront joints. **Dockside** often busts out with live music and free parties and is a great place to meet seafaring adventurer types or hitch a ride to Belize City by yacht. The more upscale **Tentacles,** as well as serving shots of rum, has seafood and Belizean dishes. For a really funky, local experience and a game of pool, try the **Corner Pocket,** at the north end of town. If you feel dancing fever coming on after a few shots of cane juice, the **Cozy Corner Disco** (on the sidewalk near the center of town) gets going after 10 PM, with the best boogie nights on Wednesday, Friday, and Saturday.

OUTDOOR ACTIVITIES

Fly-fishing on the flats off the cays east of Placencia is some of the best in Belize. You'll encounter plentiful tarpon—they flurry 10 deep in the water at times—as well as permit fish, bonefish, and snook. Many locals will offer to take you out. Three of them are real experts: David Westby (tel. 06/23–234), Kurt Godfrey (tel. 062/3277), and Egbert Cabral of P & P Sport Fishing (tel. 06/23–132). If you're seeking a more boisterous activity, you can rent **sea kayaks** for $13 (half day) or $24 (full day) at Conrad and Lydia's Rooms (*see* Where to Sleep, *above*) or at Kitty's Place (*see* Food, *above*). Or explore the peninsula by **bike** with a rental ($7.50) from Sonny's Resort (*see* Food, *above*).

One of the most exciting and underrated trips in Belize is up the **Monkey River.** The wildlife, including howler monkeys, iguanas, and dozens of species of birds, is spectacular. You can arrange short day trips or extended camping trips. Some of the operators running tours are Seahorse Guides (tel. 06/23–116) and P.I. Tours (tel. 06/23–291), or you can check around town for a deal.

SCUBA DIVING • By the time you get this far south, the reef is as much as 33 km (20 mi) offshore, which means boat rides of 45 minutes to an hour to reach dive sites. Because this part of the reef has fewer cuts and channels, it's also more difficult to get out to the seaward side, the best one for diving. As a result, most diving in this region is done from the offshore cays, which have minireefs around them, usually with gently sloping drop-offs of about 80–100 ft. If you want spectacular wall dives, this isn't the place; you're better off staying in the north or going to the atolls. But there are other pluses here—off Moho Caye, southeast of Placencia, are brilliant red and yellow corals and sponges that rarely appear elsewhere in Belize.

Diving costs more in Placencia than elsewhere. All-day trips, including two-tank dives and lunch, run $65 with a few people in the boat, including gear. Snorkeling is about $40 per day. Nearly all snorkeling or diving trips will end up at beautiful **Laughing Bird Caye.** This little sliver of paradise is now a national reserve, and though heavily frequented by the folks from resorts along Maya Beach, it's still a top-class spot. Other popular destinations include Lark Caye, Silk Caye, and out on the reef, **Hunting Caye.**

There are several dive shops in town, of varying proficiency and safety. Recommended is **Seahorse Dive Shop** (tel. 062/3166), which also has manatee-watching tours and jungle and river trips. **Southern Guide** (tel. 06/23–166), run by the Godfrey brothers, also offers fly-fishing trips. For snorkeling trips and gear, head for **Ocean Motion,** near the Co-op grocery store (tel. 062/3363).

SHOPPING

Orange Peel Gift Shop (next to Wallen's Market) has T-shirts and local crafts. The best gift shops are at the resorts, north of town. **Rum Point Inn,** halfway between Placencia and Seine Bight, has everything from aloe to T-shirts to Belizean music, books, and film. **Kitty's Place** has T-shirts, swimsuits, toys, hats, and sarongs.

TOLEDO AND THE DEEP SOUTH

For many years, the horrendously potholed Southern Highway, spotty communications, and the country's highest annual rainfall—as much as 160 inches—kept Belize's "Deep South" off-limits to all but the most adventurous. The rain still falls (mostly in typically tropical downpours that last only a few minutes), but with improvements to the Southern Highway, the beauty of Toledo is finally becoming accessible. This is the new frontier. It is rather like the Cayo district 10 years ago, except that the flora and fauna here are even more dramatic. Toledo is the only part of Belize that has *real* rain forest. No, the rest isn't Styrofoam: it's secondary rain forest, meaning it's been logged at some point. This is what is known as climax rain forest. Sadly, in a rare act of environmental irresponsibility, the Belizean government has granted vast concessions to several logging companies. This is being strongly opposed by the local Mayan population (*see* The Mayan Heartland, *below*).

For the moment, Toledo is the most species-rich part of Belize, with an abundant supply of all your favorite wildlife stars, including jaguars and tapirs. If you want to laze on the beach, you will have to travel away from Punta Gorda, because the waters of the Gulf of Honduras are invariably muddy from silt deposited by the numerous rivers flowing down from the Maya Mountains. But the cays off the coast are prime snorkeling, diving, and sunning spots. The closest are the Snake Cayes; farther out are the Sapadillo Cayes, the largest of which is Hunting Caye,

> *Punta Gorda averages 168 inches of rain annually, making it one of the wettest spots on Earth.*

which has beaches of white coral where turtles nest in late summer. The mountains to the west of Punta Gorda hide, beneath them, one of the longest cave systems in the world. The area is also one of the richest in Belizean Mayan ruins (*see* The Maya Heartland, *below*).

PUNTA GORDA

Most journeys south begin in what is known locally as "PG," the region's administrative center. Its early modern history reads like a Peter Mathiesson novel. Founded in 1867 by immigrants from the United States, and subsequently settled by Methodist missionaries from Mississippi, Punta Gorda once boasted 12 sugar estates, each with its own mill. By 1910, however, the town had almost reverted to jungle, and the missionaries had abandoned it. Its fortunes revived after World War II, when Britain built an important military base here. When this closed in 1994, the linchpin of the local economy disappeared, businesses closed, and people moved out. When the tourist dollars start to flow PG will pick up again, but at the moment it feels a bit like a town in limbo.

Most travelers see no more of Punta Gorda than the ferry dock, customs office, and bus stop; those who stay a day or two will find that the southernmost town in the country is one of the friendliest and safest places in Belize, where locals will go out of their way to greet you and learn your name. Physically and spiritually, it is the closest you can come to Guatemala while still in Belize. While the people in town are mostly Garifuna fisherman (and a surprising number of expat Americans and Brits), Kek'chi and Mopan Maya live and farm in the various nearby villages. On market days, Wednesday and Saturday, women come to town in traditional embroidered dresses, often with intricately woven reed baskets and colorful bracelets to sell.

BASICS

Most of Punta Gorda's business establishments are at the north end of town, along Middle, Main, and Front streets. **Belize Bank** (43 Front St., tel. 07/22–183), just opposite the town square, is open Monday–Thursday 8–1, Friday 8–4:30. It's the only bank in town and charges a whopping $15 for a cash advance. The **BTL** office is north of town square, at the corner of Main and King streets; the **post office** is adjacent to it on Front Street; both are open weekdays 8–noon and 1–4. A **pharmacy** can be found on Main Street, one block south of the town square, and the **hospital** is at the south end of town, on Main Street near Cemetery Lane. If you need someone to drive you around, **Clive Genus' Taxi, Tour, and Car Rental** (30 Wahima Alley, tel. 072/2068) is a reliable local outfit. Clive is the perfect companion for jostling around on bumpy roads visiting ruins.

Several private organizations dispense advice (not always impartial) on activities in the area. Most helpful is the **Toledo Visitors Information Center (TVIC)** (at ferry dock, tel. 07/22–470). Friendly owners

Alfredo and Yvonne Villoria can supply you with district maps ($1 each) and all the local info—as well as the scoop on their village home-stay program and their ecofarm (*see* Near Punta Gorda, *below*). The **Belize Tourism Centre** (11 Front St., tel. 07/22–834) can help with bus or ferry schedules and will make room reservations free of charge.

COMING AND GOING

Until the Southern Highway is fully paved, Punta Gorda will remain only marginally connected to the rest of the country. Bus service is infrequent and other road traffic a mere trickle. Hitching is the quickest, safest, and sometimes only way to get around Toledo District. It helps if you're carrying a copy of *War and Peace*; long hours of waiting by the side of the road for a lift are not uncommon. At the end of a ride, drivers may ask for a small fee—it's customary to ask, "How much do I have for you?" In town, **Hines Taxi Service** (tel. 07/22–233) can take you door-to-door late at night and during drenching downpours for $2.

BY BUS • Z-line (53 Main St., tel. 07/22–165) makes the spine-jarring trek up the Southern Highway to points north: buses depart daily for Dangriga (5 hrs, $6.50), Belmopan (8 hrs, $10), and Belize City (9 hrs, $11). Road conditions are unpredictable in the rainy season, June–September. Traveling to villages in the Toledo District is not so straightforward. Each village runs a bus (or truck) to Punta Gorda on market days only: Wednesday and Saturday. Generally these depart for town between 3 and 5 AM and return to the village around noon; drivers charge whatever they feel like. All buses (and village trucks) stop in PG on Main Street next to the Civic Center auditorium, just north of the town square.

BY BOAT • To cross the Gulf of Honduras to Puerto Barrios, Guatemala, you have two options: a **ferry** departs from the Punta Gorda pier Tuesday and Friday at noon; the 2½-hour trip is $6.50 one way. Purchase tickets (preferably a day in advance) at **Tienda La Indita Maya** (26 Middle St., tel. 07/22–065) and allow about an hour before departure for border formalities. The ferry returns from Puerto Barrios Tuesday and Friday at 7 AM. If you've missed the boat, you can charter a **water taxi** to Puerto Barrios or Livingston, Guatemala, for approximately $7–$10 per person. **Frank Tate** (tel. 07/22–858) will make the crossing Monday–Saturday. Or ask around at the fish market or the Toledo Visitors Information Center (*see* Basics, *above*).

BY PLANE • Maya Island Air (tel. 023/1348) and **Tropic Air** (tel. 026/2012 or 800/422–3435 in the U.S.) both have regular services to Punta Gorda, via Dangriga and Placencia. The **airstrip** is on the west side of town: from the town square, walk four blocks west on Prince Street. Purchase tickets at the airlines' offices on the strip, or at many of the hotels and shops in town.

WHERE TO SLEEP

Punta Gorda has lots of hotels, many dating from the days when the town was full of "squaddies" (British soldiers). Some feel very neglected and run-down. You can pitch a tent almost anywhere—if the spot looks inhabited, just ask the landowner.

UNDER $20 • Mahung's Hotel (11 Main St., North St., tel. 07/22–044 or 07/22–016), at the north end of town, has clean but cramped and dark doubles ($17.50) with TV and private bath. **Verde's Guest House** (22 Middle St., north end of town, tel. 07/22–069) may also do in a pinch, with plenty of stripped-down doubles for $12.

UNDER $30 • Arvin's Landing Guest House. Experience a few days of British hospitality at this mini ecoresort on a creek just outside town. Doubles ($15) share cold-water showers and organic dry toilets. Or bring a tent and camp ($2.50 per person) on 4 acres of orchard and lawn. Meals ($2.50–$5) are served family-style. The charming hosts also run day and overnight snorkeling, fishing, and camping expeditions. *Joe Taylor Creek, tel. 07/22–873. 4 rooms sharing 2 baths. Laundry.*

Nature's Way Guest House. Although it's a 10-minute walk from the center of town, backpackers flock here for a reason: it's steps from the sea, the rooms (with bunk beds) are clean and airy, and the shared bathrooms are even hygienic. Doubles are $13 (shared bath) or $22 (private). *83 Front St., tel. 07/22–119. 10 rooms, 6 with bath. Laundry.*

UNDER $70 • Sea Front Inn. When it opened in 1998, this impressive new hotel immediately became a magnet for travelers. The 14 excellent rooms are not cheap ($60 and up), but they're worth it. The roof is supported by rosewood tree trunks etched with Maya carvings. The view, across the Gulf of Honduras, is breathtaking (if you are lucky, you may even see a pod of passing porpoises). If you need any local information, especially about dive sites, American owner Larry Smith will be happy to oblige. He was once a missionary, but thankfully saw the error of his ways. Later, he trained the British army's dive teams. *Front St., tel. 072/2682. 14 rooms with bath.*

FOOD

UNDER $5 • A funky culinary odyssey awaits in PG. At the north end of town (past Texaco), the **Punta Gorda Bakery** cranks out delicious breakfast sweets, and you can get plenty of papayas at the **market** (Wednesday and Saturday) along Front Street, south of the ferry dock. For cheap local grub, like beans and rice, fried fish, pork chops, and stew chicken, served in a local home, head for **Man-Man's Five Star Cook House** (Far West St., between King and Queen Sts.) or **Lucille's Kitchen** (3 North St., by Texaco Station). For Chinese, it's the **Mira Mar Hotel** (2 Front St., across from ferry pier, tel. 07/22–033). Unrepentant sweet tooths will appreciate the **Ice Cream Parlour** (Main St., 1 block south of town square), which dispenses burritos and burgers in addition to mango milkshakes.

UNDER $10 • Angie's Bar and Restaurant. This tiny four-table restaurant is a family affair: Angie cooks up your order while her British husband pours the Guinness and fills you in on local happenings. Typical Belizean dinners are $5–$9. *115 Jose Maria Nunez St., between Church and George Sts., tel. 07/22–668.*

Punta Caliente Restaurant. *Se habla español* at this modest hotel restaurant crowded with working-class locals and decorated with a colorful wall mural (and last year's Christmas spangles). For such delicious breakfasts ($2–$4), with beans, bacon, eggs, and homemade tortillas, you may stick around another day; lunch and dinner items like conch ($5), stew pork ($4), or whole panfried snapper ($7) are excellent. *108 Jose Maria Nunez St., tel. 07/22–561.*

Sea Front Inn. The breakfast buffet at this hotel, complete with delicious fresh-squeezed juices, costs $6 and will keep you going all day. For lunch, there is seafood and burgers. In the evening, you can sit with a Belikin and look out at the sea. *Front St., tel. 072/2682.*

AFTER DARK

Punta Gorda used to have a lot of pretty grungy discos and bars, where British squaddies would down too much Belikin and practice being hooligans in preparation for the soccer season back home. These days it's much quieter. There are a half-dozen lively pool halls and dive bars along the waterfront at the center of town—fun, unless you're a woman alone. Fortunately, the bar and pool tables at the **Mira Mar Hotel** (*see* Food, *above*) draw a less macho crowd. **Dreamlight** and **Bobby's Bar** (Main St., across from Mahung's) are swell places to toss back Belikins with locals. At the south end of town, the **Southside Bar & Disco** (José Maria Nunez St., near George St.) and **Massive Rock Disco** (José Maria Nunez St., near Cemetery La.) are the places to party to punta rock on weekend nights.

NEAR PUNTA GORDA

BLUE CREEK CAVE

Next to the small Mopan Mayan village of Blue Creek is the Blue Creek river cave. Some claim it is one of the largest underground cave systems in the world, and with an experienced guide it's even possible to make a two-day journey through its maze of tunnels and come up in Guatemala. If you're on your own, you can catch the Blue Creek village market bus (*see* Coming and Going, *above*), then follow a short, marked trail upriver from the road to a small campsite ($1) and the cave entrance. Spectacular waterfalls, rock-lined pools, and super-cool stalactites are fun even if you aren't a spelunker. The hike can be treacherous if the rocks are wet, so climb carefully.

DEM DATS DOIN'

Hardworking Alfredo and Yvonne Villoria have spent almost 10 years building their own ecoconscious self-sufficient Eden, and they'd like you to visit. During a two-hour tour ($5), you'll see medicinal plants, perfume trees, a crafts center, and an insect dryer (you can purchase dried rhinoceros beetles here). They also serve organically homegrown meals ($5) and have room for one or two overnight guests ($15–$20). To get here, take a Z-Line or James bus to the Southern Highway Shell Station (about 23 km [14 mi] northwest of town). For $10 per carload, the station owner will drive you the 6 km (3¾ mi) to the farm.

THE MAYA HEARTLAND

The Toledo District is the heartland of the Maya in Belize. Half the population is Mayan, and this group is more cohesive and better organized politically than any other Mayan population anywhere else in Belize. The Toledo Maya Cultural Council has created an ambitious network of Maya-run ecolodges (*see below*), and in 1995 it initiated the **Mayan Mapping Project** (MMP), in conjunction with the University

SKULLDUGGERY!

Lubaantun became the scene of the biggest hoax in modern archaeology. After it was excavated in the 1920s, a British adventurer named F. A. Mitchell-Hedges claimed to have stumbled upon what became known as the Crystal Skull. Mitchell-Hedges described the incident in a potboiler, Danger, My Ally, in 1951. According to the book, the Crystal Skull was found under an altar at Lubaantun by his daughter, Anna "Sammy" Mitchell-Hedges. She was not, actually, his daughter. He had adopted her as a 13-year-old orphan in Québec and, given the fact that she became his lifelong companion, his relationship to her was most likely everything other than paternal. Mitchell-Hedges made himself out to be a serious archaeologist and explorer: in truth, he was a magazine hack, who was later exposed in England as a fraud and a grave robber. His accounts of Mayan civilization are the worst kind of imperialistic, racist nonsense. At one point, he fabricates a story of a village leader coming to his tent with a virgin girl, begging him to inseminate her so the degenerate genes of the Maya could receive an infusion of potent, Anglo-Saxon DNA. For armchair travelers in suburban England, the Crystal Skull made good copy. Also known as the Skull of Doom, it was supposedly used by Maya high priests to zap anyone they did not care for. Mitchell-Hedges claimed it was 3,600 years old and had taken 150 years to fashion by rubbing a block of pure rock crystal with sand. In truth, it was a complete rip-off. A similar skull, in the possession of the British Museum, shows signs of having been manufactured with a dentist's drill. Anna Mitchell-Hedges, who today lives in Ontario, has promised to one day reveal the secret, but so far, she has adamantly refused to allow the Crystal Skull to be tested and has denied all requests by the Belizean government to return it. Recently, well into her nineties, she tottered back down to Belize in the company of two publishers, so it seems there may be life in this dead horse yet. With millions of people believing they have been abducted by aliens, it might just be that a windy tale like this is soon coming to a movie house near you.

of California-Berkeley. By collating oral history and evidence of ancient Maya settlements, the MMP hopes to secure rights to land that the Maya have occupied for centuries but that the Belizean government has seen fit to cede to multinational logging companies. The case has been before Belize's Supreme Court for a number of years.

In keeping with the Toledo District's original settlement by religious zealots from the United States, the Deep South has become a magnet for (mostly white, mostly Evangelical) missionaries. They come mostly from the southern United States, and their favorite ploy, as they vie for the souls of the Maya, is to offer the villagers free dentistry and medicine: so don't be surprised to find a brand-new medical center in the middle of a dusty village. They are here, in the south, because Catholic missionaries operating out of Mexico have a lock on the north. Many villagers are converting. The good news is that they only do so to get the goodies. At home, they continue to adhere to their own ancient belief systems.

The Maya divide into two groups: Mopan Maya and Kek'chi-speaking Indians from the Guatemalan highlands. Most of the latter are recent arrivals, refugees from repression and overpopulation. Each group tends to keep to itself, living in its own villages and preserving its own traditions. The village of **San Antonio,** a market town 58 km (35 mi) west of Punta Gorda and the second-largest town in Toledo, is a Mopan Maya center. It was settled by people from the Guatemalan village of San Luis, who revere their former patron saint. The village church, built of stones carted off from surrounding Mayan ruins, has a stained-glass window donated by another city with a Luis connection: St. Louis, Missouri. The people of San Antonio have not forgotten their ancient heritage, though, and each year on June 13 they take to the streets for a bacchanalian festival that dates back to pre-Columbian times. Nearby are waterfalls and a swimming hole. You can overnight at **Bol's Hill Top Hotel** for $10, and Mr. Bol will cook meals on request. A little farther west is the Kek'chi Indian village of **San Pedro Columbia,** a cheerful cluster of brightly painted buildings and thatched houses. One of the most eye-catching points is a raspberry-red grocery with the delightful name "People Little Store."

If you are into Mayan ruins, there is plenty to see here. Much still lies buried beneath the ground, including a major site in the jungle to the northwest of Punta Gorda that is currently being excavated by a team from the National Geographic Society and which, by all accounts, dwarfs even Caracol. Two of Toledo's major Mayan sites have already been excavated: Nim Li Punit and Lubaantun. **Nim Li Punit** (once spoken aloud, this name will go round and round in your head) is 73 km (45 mi) northeast of Punta Gorda, off the Southern Highway. A late

Legend has it Crooked Tree got its name from three local white slave owners notorious for their slippery behavior. They were dubbed the "crooked three," written and pronounced "tree" in Creole.

Classic site, it was discovered in 1976. Twenty-five stelae (inscribed stone slabs) were unearthed, including one 30 ft tall, the largest ever found in Belize. In 1986, a royal tomb was excavated. Sadly, none of these artifacts remain on-site.

Lubaantun, which lies beyond the village of San Pedro Columbia, is also a late Classic site. Lubaantun's construction is unique in the Mayan world: unlike most sites, where mortar binds stones together, everything at Lubaantun was made by fitting the stone blocks together like pieces in a giant jigsaw puzzle. Archaeologists have theorized that the Mayans were forced to build without mortar here because they'd clear-cut the entire forest to plant crops; no trees were left to burn into ash (the key ingredient). The site's knowledgeable caretaker has assisted with excavations and will answer questions or show you around free of charge.

The site was discovered in 1924 by German archaeologist Thomas Gann, who coined the name, which means "Place of Fallen Stones." Before they fell, Lubaantun must have been an awe-inspiring sight: situated on top of a conical hill, with views to the sea in one direction and the Maya Mountains in the other, its stepped layers of white-plastered stone would have towered above the jungle like a wedding cake. No one knows exactly what the structure served, but the large number of miniature masks and whistles found here suggest that it was a center of ceramic production. The central plaza, with tiered seating for 10,000 spectators, and three adjacent ball courts give rise to images of a Maya Madison Square Garden.

COMING AND GOING • The site is 2 km (1 mi) north of the village of San Pedro Colombia (32 km [20 mi] north of Punta Gorda). Catch a ride on the village market bus (*see* Coming and Going, *above*). Or you can take a Z-Line or James bus to the Southern Highway Shell Station and for $10 the station owner will take you out to the site.

VILLAGE VISITATION PROGRAMS

Two competing organizations offer visitors to the Toledo District an opportunity to experience everyday life in a Kek'chi or Mopan Mayan village. A portion of your money goes toward village health and education projects. Most villagers carry on a traditional lifestyle (if you don't count their battery-powered boom boxes): women wash clothes in the river and cook over fire, men tend to livestock and the family plots of corn. Visitors are similarly treated according to gender. There are no flush toilets, no electricity, and no running water. For some this is a rare opportunity to learn about a culture as an anthropologist might. For others, chickens running in and out of the house and pit toilets may be a bit too spartan an experience.

BRAVO FOR THE RAIN FOREST

Far northwestern Belize is home to the ambitious **Rio Bravo Conservation and Management Area,** *a 229,000-acre tract of rain forest (42,000 acres of which were donated by Coca-Cola, Inc.) managed by the private organization* **Programme for Belize** *(2 South Park St., Belize City, tel. 02/75–616). It joins Guatemala's Maya Biosphere Reserve and Mexico's Calakmul Biosphere Reserve in forming a trinational peace park, where conservationists hope to turn locals on to agricultural practices that don't destroy the forest—like farming chicle, the stuff that puts the chew in gum. A visit to Rio Bravo is a chance to visit a working research station and encounter biologists, archaeologists, and botanists roaming free in their natural habitat. Its remoteness means plenty of wildlife: more than 300 species of birds, 200 kinds of trees, and 12 endangered animal species. It also encompasses 60 Mayan sites. The largest of them is the ceremonial center,* **La Milpa.** *The Great Plaza, flanked by four temple-pyramids, is one of the largest public spaces in the Mayan world. Although many of the tombs, which date from 400 BC to AD 800, were looted in the 1980s, a survey by researchers from Boston University has unearthed many of La Milpa's secrets. You'll need to make reservations with the Programme for Belize at least a few days in advance to visit Rio Bravo. From Orange Walk Town, take the 1 PM bus to San Felipe village (90 min, $3.50), where a ranger will pick you up and transport you to the reserve. The research station's dorm-style accommodations are $65 per person and include three meals and two activities (hikes, archaeology expeditions, field lectures) per day.*

With the nonprofit **Mayan Village Homestay Network,** overseen by the Toledo Visitors Information Center (*see* Basics, *above*), families in seven participating villages take visitors into their homes. Lodging is $5 per night, meals are $2 each. Depending on your interests and the availability of transportation, you can explore Mayan ruins, help with planting, hike in the jungle, or visit a bush doctor. For more information, contact Alfredo and Yvonne Villoria (TVIC, Box 73, Punta Gorda, tel. 07/22–470). The more ambitious **Toledo Eco-Tourism Association** (Box 75, Punta Gorda, tel. 072/2680) arranges stays in one of 13 participating Mopan and Kek'chi villages. You live with one family in bunkhouse-style guest cabins ($10 per person) in five participating villages. Visitors take meals ($4 each) in the villagers' houses, and the association will arrange vegetarian or special meals. There's lots to do, but watch out—*everything* has a price tag.

NORTHERN BELIZE

As you approach the northern coast of Belize, the blue waters of the Caribbean seem to rise out of the omnipresent sugarcane fields. These endlessly expansive fields are the region's biggest employer and the source of the nation's main exports. Here you'll find ambitious nature reserves—the **Community Baboon Sanctuary,** Belize's answer to *Planet of the Apes,* and the **Crooked Tree Wildlife Sanctuary,** an ornithologist's fantasy land. You'll also find two of the most impressive Mayan ruins in the country, **Altun Ha** and **Lamanai,** as well as several smaller sites. These major settlements once controlled trade in jade, obsidian, cacao, honey, and salt all along the coast of the Yucatán Peninsula and on waterways deep into the Petén region of Guatemala. Most backpackers blow through northern Belize in air-conditioned express buses to Mexico, because transportation between the various attractions is nonexistent—although Crooked Tree and the Baboon Sanctuary lie only a few miles apart, each has separate bus service originating in Belize City. For those who feel comfortable hitchhiking, there's a week's worth of sightseeing in this part of the country, and it's virtually free of tourists.

Northern Belize is a patchwork of Mayan, Creole, British, and Spanish settlers, and its multiculturalism is reflected in its globally inspired village names: Caledonia, Calcutta, San Francisco, Cowpen, Concepcíon, Xaibe, and Patchchacan. Until the Northern Highway was built in 1930, the region's ties were stronger to Mexico than to its own country. Many Spanish-speaking northerners are descendants of the thousands of refugees who fled the brutal Caste Wars, which ravaged Mexico's Yucatán Peninsula in the 1840s. The conflict, not formally settled until 1935, began when disenfranchised Mayans rose up against their mestizo landlords; colonial retaliation resulted in the extermination of entire Mayan villages. On **Mexican National Day,** held in mid-September, families in the towns of **Corozal** and **Orange Walk** cross the border to reunite with relatives for festivities and remembrances.

Lamanai means "submerged crocodile," and it's one of few sites where the original Mayan name is known today. Earlier efforts had mistakenly produced a different interpretation, "drowned bug."

COMMUNITY BABOON SANCTUARY

"Baboon" is the local term for the endangered black howler monkey, and these babies *really* howl. It's hard to believe that all that racket, a cross between a donkey braying and a gorilla, is coming from such a (comparatively) small monkey. The best time to hear the ruckus is at dawn or dusk. During the day the monkeys travel around the forest in groups of four to eight, foraging for their vegetarian diet. It's not difficult to get a glimpse of the jet-black monkeys, and you'll also see plenty of beautiful birds, reptiles, and fellow mammals like the coati, agouti, peccary, and deer.

The sanctuary was established in 1985 with help from the Worldwide Fund for Nature to protect the endangered monkeys and their habitat along the Belize River. It's a private community effort involving eight riverside villages. Broadleaf forest and farmland coexist, with local farmers taking active measures to preserve crucial vegetation and to maintain corridors of forest around farmland and along riverbanks. These land-use measures not only protect the howlers' habitat but also benefit the farmers by reducing erosion and keeping the rivers free of muck.

COMING AND GOING

Three bus lines offer service between Belize City and the sanctuary's visitor center in the village of **Bermudian Landing**: both **Russell's** and **Young's** buses leave from the corner of Orange and George streets, two blocks west of the Swing Bridge. **McFadean's** bus (sometimes a truck) departs from the corner of Orange and Russell streets, behind the Pacific Store. If you're leaving from somewhere other than Belize City, it's possible to hop off a bus at Mile 13 on the Northern Highway and hitch the 21 km (13 mi) west on the Burrell Boom cutoff. Or, of course, you can drive; it's 45 km (28 mi) from Belize City.

WHERE TO SLEEP AND EAT

Accommodations with a local family, a wonderful way to meet the friendly Belizean people, cost $12 (double); register with the visitor center in Bermudian Landing and they'll set you up. An extra $8 gets you three home-cooked meals. Camping is possible for $2.50. Make reservations through the **Belize Audubon Society** (12 Fort St., Belize City, tel. 02/34–985 or 02/34–987). Thatched-roof private cabanas run by knowledgeable Belizean hosts within the sanctuary can be had at **Jungle Drift Lodge** (Box 1442, Belize City, tel. 02/32–842) for $15 (single) or $20 (double).

OUTDOOR ACTIVITIES

Plenty of affordable activities will keep you busy for a day or three, including numerous **hiking** trails scattered throughout the sanctuary. You must initially explore the trails with a guide ($5 an hour or $15 a half day). Wildlife, botany, and river ecosystems are just some of the special interests that lie in wait here. **Canoeing** and **kayaking** trips can be found for the same price, while **horseback riding** is available for $10 an hour.

ALTUN HA

Once thought peripheral to the Mayan empire, Altun Ha was actually an important link in coastal trading routes between the southern lowlands and the Yucatán and has yielded some of the richest artifacts yet uncovered in the Mayan world. The site was also a minor ceremonial center during the Classic period, though settlement dates back to 200 BC. The central ceremonial precinct is made up of two plazas and some interesting temples, unique in that they were the tombs of priests rather than warlords. The Temple of the Green Tomb (Temple A-1) contained the remains of a Mayan book, as well as jade, jewelry, and hundreds of other artifacts. The tallest temple on the site is the Temple of the Masonry Altars (Temple B-4), where a carved jade head representing the sun god Kinich Ahau was discovered; at 9¾ pounds it's the largest piece of worked jade ever discovered in the Mayan region. Unfortunately, this famous head and other valuable objects are locked away where no one can see them—although a tiny reproduction of the *Kinich Ahau* carving is on the corner of every Belizean dollar bill.

COMING AND GOING • Unfortunately, Altun Ha lies off the old Northern Highway, where road traffic (including buses) has all but disappeared. Practically the only way to see it is with a tour group: **Mayaland Tours** (67 Eve St., Belize City, tel. 02/30–515) takes small groups on half-day tours ($45 per person), with lunch, guide, entrance fee, and transportation from Belize City included. **Native Guide Systems** (1 Water La., Belize City, tel. 02/75–819) charges $12.50 per person for a basic half-day tour departing from Mile 19 on the Northern Highway, though they're sometimes unreliable. Book tours at least two or three days in advance. Consider organizing your own group of merry travelers and hiring a cab ($75) from **Lady Vida Taxi Service** (tel. 02/77–913). If you must check out Altun Ha on the cheap, do it on Saturday. A bus ($1) leaves Vernon Street, near the Batty Bus Terminal in Belize City, for the town of **Maskall** at 11 AM and returns at 3 PM. The walk from Maskall to Altun Ha is about 2 km (2 mi), so you'll have to move it.

CROOKED TREE WILDLIFE SANCTUARY

Crooked Tree Wildlife Sanctuary is one of the least appreciated treasures of Belize. An island village surrounded by a shallow lagoon and lush wetlands, it is guardian to approximately 300 migratory and resident bird species, as well as other wildlife like black howler monkeys, Morelet's crocodiles, and several species of turtles and iguanas. During the dry season (October–March), thousands of birds congregate in the network of inland waterways and logwood swamplands. Even if you've been traumatized by Hitchcock or could care less about the difference between a bare-throated tiger heron and a black-bellied whistling duck, it's an amazing sight. The most famous visitor to the reserve, the rare jabiru stork, has a wingspan of 10 to 12 ft and is the largest flying bird in the Americas. An incredible variety of other birds nest and feed here year-round: great blue herons, snowy egrets, snail kites, kingfishers, ospreys.

That the Crooked Tree sanctuary exists at all is pretty close to miraculous. In 1978, a prominent local businessman and a visiting American naturalist united to begin persuading villagers to protect the birds for visitors rather than shooting them for sport. Six years later, in 1984, the 3,000 acres surrounding Crooked Tree village were finally dedicated as a reserve. The first few years brought only a handful of curious tourists, but townspeople continued to believe they made the right decision.

COMING AND GOING

Two bus lines offer direct service to Crooked Tree Sanctuary (75 min, $1.75) from Belize City: **Jex Bus Service** (Crooked Tree Village, tel. 021/2032) and **Batty Brothers** (15 Mosul St., Belize City, tel. 02/72–025). Crooked Tree Village and the sanctuary headquarters are at the end of a 5-km (3-mi) causeway, at Mile 33 on the Northern Highway. To hitch, take any of the frequent buses going north or south of the highway and hop off at the turnoff.

WHERE TO SLEEP AND EAT

Crooked Tree Village is an unspoiled paradise: the sandy lanes are lined with cashew trees, and houses are small but tidy. It is one of the oldest inland villages in Belize, with a population of 800; the community has a church, a school, and even a cricket pitch. Most villagers get around on horseback or foot, so traffic noise is nil. Several families operate bed-and-breakfasts for $20 (double), plus $5 a day for meals: **Rhaybum's** has four rooms with shared bath (they will heat water on their stove, if you ask), and **Molly's** has seven charming, immaculate thatched cabanas with lanterns, outdoor shower, and latrine. You can also camp at either for $3.50. Arrange your stay in advance with the Belize Audubon Society (tel. 02/34–985 or 02/34–987) or drop in at the **Visitor Center** (open daily 8–5), where they'll set you up on the spot. The village also has two hotels: **Sam Tilletts Hotel** (tel. 021/2026) has three rooms with private bath, in a palapa on stilts, for $30 (double), including meals. It's an ideal place for bird-watchers going on one of Sam's tours (*see* Outdoor Activities, *below*). The Crawfords' **Paradise Inn** (tel. 02/4433) is the kind of place you want to stay for a week. Beautiful thatched cabanas with private bath are $55 (double) plus $14 a day for meals. All sit right on the lagoon and offer sweeping views. Camping ($10 per night) on the grounds is also allowed.

A mural on the wall of Corozal's town hall depicts the history of some of its most recent settlers, the refugees from the Yucatán Caste Wars of 1849.

OUTDOOR ACTIVITIES

Numerous exploring options make the reserve worth an overnight stay. Rent **canoes** to cruise the lagoon on your own for $10 a day, or take a full-day guided tour for $35. For $15, you can hire **horses** for half a day (guides run $10 an hour extra). Half-day boat tours are offered for a flat fee of $70, for up to six people. **John Jex** (tel. 021/2032), one of the sanctuary's founders, may give discounts to students. **Sam Tilletts** (tel. 021/2026) is an expert bird-watcher; in addition to boat tours, he does jeep and walking excursions ($20 hr). Brothers **Glenn** and **Robert Crawford** of Paradise Inn (tel. 02/4433) run river and land tours, including trips to the unexcavated Chaa Hix and, during nesting season, to a family of jabiru storks.

ORANGE WALK TOWN

The first thing you'll notice when you enter town is the sugarcane fields; like a tropical Topeka, Orange Walk is surrounded on all sides by farmland. The second thing you'll notice—as you lie in bed trying to sleep—is the sugarcane trucks: they start wheezing and rumbling through town before dawn and continue their trips to the refinery well past nightfall. Although other agricultural areas of Belize have diversified (citrus is fast becoming the big moneymaker in the south and west, followed by bananas and mangoes) cane is still king in this district; Orange Walk Town is its working-class citadel. There's nothing appealing about its dirty unmarked streets bracketed with shops selling cut-rate polyester clothing and junk electronics, and there's something vaguely menacing about the number of unshaven men who walk around carrying machetes. Then factor in the stories about Orange Walk's other big money maker: marijuana—rumored to be concealed inside nearby cane fields. When sugar prices plummet, the drug industry supposedly keeps the town's economy afloat.

You can hook up here with a river tour to Lamanai (*see below*), but Orange Walk isn't the kind of place that makes you think "vacation." Two interesting Mayan ruins lie within a few miles of Orange Walk Town, though neither is spectacular. Just west of town, the **Cuello** ruin is a small unrestored ceremonial center dating to 2500 BC. You'll need permission from the folks who make Caribbean Rum to see it, because it's on their property: contact **Cuello Brothers Distillery** (tel. 03/22–183). Just off the Northern Highway, approximately 34 km (21 mi) north of town, the partially excavated, larger **Nohmul** ruin stands on an acropolis and is actually twin sets of plazas and structures connected by a raised walkway.

COMING AND GOING

Orange Walk Town is on the Northern Highway, 92 km (57 mi) northwest of Belize City. Bus service by **Batty's** and **Venus** is half-hourly. The Batty's depot is ½ km (¼ mi) north of the town plaza on Queen Victoria Avenue (a.k.a. Northern Hwy.). Venus buses stop at the northwest corner of the plaza. Traffic on the Northern Highway is brisk, so hitching shouldn't be a problem, but use caution—Orange Walk seems to attract some unsavory characters.

WHERE TO SLEEP

The few hotels you'll find here offer rooms that are either cramped, depressing, and cheap, or roomy, depressing, and overpriced. The best value in town is the **Taisan Hotel** (30 Queen Victoria Ave., tel. 03/22–752), two blocks north of the town's plaza on the main road. Bed down in one of six small but clean doubles with shared bath for $14. (Don't plan on sleeping late—cane trucks begin rumbling by around dawn.)

FOOD

There are lots of Chinese restaurants in Orange Walk—**Lee's,** on San Antonio Road, even has air-conditioning—and there are plenty of produce and snack carts around the **plaza.** But the bright spot on an otherwise bleak culinary horizon, and one of the few reasons to come to the town at all, is the **Diner** (37 Clark St., tel. 03/22–131). It serves gourmet Creole food ($6–$10.50) in an engaging atmosphere and is one of the best small restaurants in Belize. The original one is a 20-minute walk north of town, so you will need a cab ($3), but because of the Diner's popularity, there's also a downtown branch.

LAMANAI

The great Mayan ceremonial center of Lamanai lies on a beautiful lagoon in the middle of a 980-acre reserve. Rare pristine tracts of jungle and savanna—never cleared or tilled for sugarcane—lie within its boundaries. Several troops of chattering black howler monkeys hang about the ruins, and colorful birds, such as the collared aracan and northern jacana, live here, too.

Lamanai was occupied from 1500 BC until Spanish encroachment in the late 16th century; it reached its height in the late Preclassic period with an estimated population of 40,000. The 112-ft Temple N10-43 is the largest Preclassic temple yet discovered, and the view of the surrounding countryside from its top is spectacular. The 6th-century Temple P9-56 has a beautiful, excavated 13-ft mask of Mayan sun god Kinich Ahau at its front. Nearby, restorations are nearing completion on a temple once dedicated to the jaguar god. A ball court, numerous dwellings, and several other fine temples remain. One of Belize's finest stelae is also here, an elaborately carved depiction of the ruler Smoking Shell, as well as Belize's only archaeological museum, where caretakers will be glad to show you a 2,500-year progression of pottery, carvings, and small statues. In a sense, it is lucky that many structures at Lamanai have been only superficially excavated. Trees and vines grow from the tops of the temples, the sides of one pyramid are covered with vegetation, and another rises abruptly from the forest floor. More people are tramping through here each year, but the magic remains.

South of the temple complex are the ruins of two Catholic churches, a reminder of the repeated Spanish attempts to convert the 16th-century "Indians" to Christianity. There are also remains of a 19th-century sugar mill built by wayward Confederates after the U.S. Civil War. Admission $1.50. Open daily 8:30–5.

COMING AND GOING

One of the most impressive sites in Belize, Lamanai is fully worth the time and money it takes to make a visit. The easiest approach is by boat trip on the New River and through New River Lagoon, itself a pleasant day on the water, complete with bird-watching and a good chance of seeing crocodiles. **Jungle River Tours** (20 Lovers La., Orange Walk Town, tel. 03/22–293 or 03/20–348) does all-inclusive tours for $35 per person (four-person minimum). During the high season (Nov.–Mar.), they can accommodate smaller parties at the same price by putting together a group. **Batty Brothers** (15 Mosul St., Belize City, tel. 02/74–924) can put you aboard the 10-passenger *Lamanai Lady* for $35 (with lunch) or $28 (without), no minimum. Call in advance for best chance of hooking up with a group. Trips are generally 9:30–4, including a 1½-hour boat ride each way. All departures are from the river landing at the **Tower**

Hill Toll Bridge, 10 km (6 mi) south of Orange Walk Town on the Northern Highway. Batty and Venus buses will stop here from either Belize City (1¾ hrs, $2) or Orange Walk (15 min, 50¢). (For schedules, *see* Coming and Going in Orange Walk Town, *above*.)

COROZAL TOWN

The seaside town of Corozal is like a 7-Eleven with marble-topped counters: sure, it's beautiful, but nobody cares. Once upon a time, when the Northern Highway resembled a dangerously cratered lunar landscape capable of making ordinary travelers feel like dazed prizefighters, Corozal—named after the cohune palm, a Mayan symbol of fertility—was a marvelous place to relax and recover for a few days before continuing north up the Yucatán Peninsula into Mexico, or for those heading south, a chance to grit their teeth and grab their *cajones* before making a trail to Belize City and beyond. Since the paving of the highway, Corozal has lost a lot of its attraction for backpackers—although it still offers a shortcut to the cays for travelers arriving from Mexico.

But don't cry for Corozal. As the several nearby ruins will attest, it was a continuously thriving Mayan settlement from about 1500 BC until the Spaniards rode into town in the 1500s; for centuries, trade routes along the coast and down the New River to Lamanai (*see above*) were controlled by the Mayan people of Corozal Bay. More recent settlers include Mexican refugees from the Yucatán Caste Wars of 1849, who have contributed to Corozal's Latin feel: a spacious, typically Spanish plaza—with clock tower, fountain, and plenty of inviting benches—is physically and spiritually the heart of town, and most residents speak Spanish when not dealing with monolingual Americans. This is probably the most picturesque town in Belize, despite the post–Hurricane Janet (1955) encroachment of ugly cinderblock buildings and the growth of gringo retirement communities nearby. A good place to get oriented is at the new **Corozal Cultural Center & Amphitheatre,** on the Old Market Square (admission $1.50; closed Sun. and Mon.).

Most impressive is the 73-ft-tall temple at Cerros, which sits at water's edge. A Texas company once had dreams of creating a Disney-style Mayaland here, with on-site museum, hotel, and pool.

COMING AND GOING

Corozal Town is on the Northern Highway, 156 km (97 mi) north of Belize City and 26 km (16 mi) south of the Mexican border. **Batty Brothers** (4th Ave. and 3rd St. N, tel. 04/23–034) and **Venus** (7th Ave. and 1st St. S, tel. 04/22–132) buses connect Corozal with Orange Walk, Belize City, and the Mexican town of Chetumal to the north, with a stop at the border-crossing point (Santa Elena–Subteniente López) for paperwork. Black marketeers at the border give fairly good exchange rates.

Maya Island Air (tel. 04/22–874) and **Tropic Air** (tel. 026/2012) fly from Corozal's tiny airstrip to San Pedro, Ambergris Caye (20 min, $30 one way). Both offer two or three flights daily. The airstrip is about 3 km (2 mi) south of town—a $4 cab ride. Purchase tickets at Hotel Maya or the Caribbean Motel and Trailer Park (*see* Where to Sleep, *below*).

WHERE TO SLEEP

Corozal is a small town, and hotels (besides one or two pricey resorts) are few but reasonably priced.

UNDER $20 • The **Caribbean Village Resort** (2 km [1 mi] south of town on Northern Hwy., tel. 04/22–045) has six not-quite-idyllic stucco-and-thatch cabins at $20 (double), or camping for $5 per person. Although it is not on the coast, another good deal is **Nestor's Hotel** (123 5th Ave., at 4th St., tel. 04/22–354), where a small but spiffy double with private bath (cold water only) is $12.50.

UNDER $30 • **Hotel Maya.** The Maya is just across the highway from the sea. Rooms are large, airy, cheerfully painted, and spotless. There's an inviting patio with table and chairs out front, and a cheerfully decorated restaurant on the ground floor. Doubles are $30. *Northern Hwy., 1 km (¾ mi) south of town, tel. 04/22–082. 15 rooms with bath.*

FOOD

There are at least half a dozen nearly indistinguishable Chinese restaurants in town, all serving mediocre food at reasonable prices. **Nestor's Restaurant and Bar** (123 5th Ave., at 4th St., tel. 04/22–354) is owned by a Canadian who pines for Texas: note the Garth Brooks posters and blackjack machines (which do accept Belizean coins). Enjoy American and Belizean fare for $3–5. Farther down the road at

Hailey's (tel. 04/22–725), located on the Caribbean Village Resort's premises, you'll find egg-and-beans breakfasts, sandwiches, and fried fish or chicken. The Corozal **market,** at the pier (between 2nd and 3rd Sts. S), offers fresh produce and homemade tamales daily, as do stalls along the town plaza.

Jo-Mel-In. No big signs or fancy menus here—in fact, no menus at all. Most of the customers are regulars who drop by for a soda, a chat, and more of the delicious food. Look for specials on the chalkboard, or just let the kitchen fix you up with fry jacks, eggs, beans, coffee, and a giant goblet of fresh OJ ($4). Stewed chicken or fish with beans and rice ($3.50) are reliable daily specials. The friendly proprietor is full of advice. *5th Ave. and 2nd St. S, tel. 04/22–526. Closed Sun.*

OUTDOOR ACTIVITIES

The coast is swimmable at most points, the water is clear and shallow, but the sandy bottom provides little interest to snorkelers. Although there are no beaches, the town's **waterfront park** (3rd St. S–8th St. S) offers benches, swings, a slide, and plenty of grass and palms. If you feel like rubbing your toes in some fine imported sand (it feels like walking in flour), head to the ritzy **Tony's Inn and Beach Resort** (tel. 04/22–055), about 2 km (1¼ mi) south of town on the Northern Highway. Their restaurant is pretty cheeky, but if you purchase a drink ($2–$4), you can loaf around the small beach for a few hours. For solitude and clean, clear water, head to 4-Mile Lagoon.

AFTER DARK

Most of the time Corozal is very mellow—and generally safe for women traveling alone, even at night. When the area's sugarcane workers get paid (at the end of a harvest) they come to town to party. The Capri Hotel (South St., between 4th and 5th Aves.) is popular, with a cavernous dance hall, a bar, and a pool table on the ground floor. Backpackers, when there are any, congregate at Nestor's (*see* Where to Sleep, *above*), though it closes nightly at 10.

NEAR COROZAL

4-MILE LAGOON

The best swimming in the area is in the clean, clear azure waters of this palm-fringed lagoon, 10 km (6 mi) northeast of town on the Northern Highway. There's a string of private RV campgrounds along the lagoon, but **Godfrey's** is open to all. Weekdays Godfrey's is deserted; weekends it's packed with frolicking Belizean families. Northbound buses (15 min, 15¢) will drop you at the entrance (it's on the right, past the RV turnoffs), then walk ½ km (¼ mi) to the water. The road is heavily traveled, so hitching is also safe and easy. Entrance is $1.50; if you bring a tent and want to camp, it's $5 per person. There are thatch-covered picnic areas, a volleyball net, fire rings, and toilets, but you'll need to bring food and water (and a Spanish phrasebook if you want to make yourself understood by the caretaker).

CERROS

Across the bay from Corozal Town is the largely unexcavated late Preclassic trading center of Cerros. Tombs, ball courts, several plazas, and former residences for the elite have all been unearthed here. Cerros had close ties with the spectacular settlement at Lamanai (*see above*), via the nearby New River, and also received jade and obsidian by sea.

COMING AND GOING • The pleasant boat ride across the bay from Corozal to Cerros is half the fun of a visit, and fishermen at Corozal's dock, adjacent to the public market, know it. They charge a highly negotiable $25–$50 to ferry up to three people. A resident naturalist, **Stephan Moerman** (37 1st Ave., 1 block east of plaza, tel. 04/22–833) will make the trip for $10 per person, even on short notice. The journey takes a half hour each way. It's also possible to reach Cerros by car, though only during the dry season. Drive 23 km (14 mi) south on the Northern Highway to the rough and circuitous 40-km (25-mi) northwesterly track through the scenic villages of Caledonia, Progresso, and Copper Bank.

SANTA RITA

Within easy walking distance of Corozal Town is what was probably the ancient Mayan city of Chetumal, inhabited from 2000 BC until the arrival of the Spaniards. At its height the settlement covered 3 square km (1.2 square mi) and controlled trading routes all along the coast and south along the Rio Hondo (now marking the border with Mexico) and the New River. Sadly, its beautiful and unusual frescoes were destroyed after discovery; remaining is a Classic-period temple with corridors, chambers, and some wall carvings. The site is 2 km (1 mi) north of town: take Santa Rita Road (the Northern Highway) toward Mexico. When you reach the fork in the road, go left, pass the hospital, then turn right. Admission is free.

GUATEMALA

BY JULIE LEDUFF AND MARA LOVEMAN, UPDATED BY WENDY SMITH

Guatemala's appeal as a travel destination is its mind-boggling diversity of people, culture, religion, and landscape. With the largest indigenous population in Central America, Guatemala is home to more than 100 distinct ethnic groups who speak more than 20 languages, from the Afro-Guatemalan Garifuna of the Caribbean Coast to the Highland Quiché. Flanked by the Pacific and Atlantic oceans and bordering Mexico, Belize, Honduras, and El Salvador, Guatemala is, in the words of poet Pablo Neruda, the "sweet waist" of the Americas.

The first stop on most itineraries through Guatemala is the Western Highlands, the center of *indígena* (indigenous) culture. The most popular highland destinations include Antigua Guatemala, the charming colonial capital of Sacatepéquez; Panajachel, on the shore of beautiful Lago Atitlán; and Chichicastenango's market, arguably the biggest and best market in all of Central America. Hundreds of smaller villages are strewn through the mountains, each with its own distinct style of brilliantly colored dress, its whitewashed colonial church, and teeming market days. Separated by towering volcanoes and kilometers of steep, winding dirt roads, many smaller pueblos see few tourists. In the far northern reaches of the country is the Petén, where dense jungle shrouds the majestic ruins of Tikal and other Mayan lost cities.

The central and eastern regions of Guatemala comprise an astounding amalgam of everything from Kekchí villages to Caribbean beaches, expansive farms, and dusty Ladino frontier towns. The Pacific coast is one of the least attractive parts of Guatemala, littered with sleazy ports filled with drunken sailors and vacationing *guatemaltecos*. It's a breeding ground for mosquitoes, and the sun blazes relentlessly on the black-sand beaches—a gift from the volcanoes. The Biotopo Monterrico–Hawaii, a coastal nature reserve near the Salvadoran border, is a notable exception, where stretches of beautiful coastline and lush mangrove swamps make the heat and humidity more bearable. Inland from the coast are marshy lowlands diced into large fincas (farms) growing sugarcane, bananas, and coffee. Lacing it all together is the nation's capital, Guatemala City, crammed with belching buses, cheap pensions, in-your-face pollution, and all the amenities a traveler could ever want—or want to pass up.

For all its culture and beauty, Guatemala has a dark side of enormous exploitation and pain. From conquest to the present day, Guatemala's indigenous majority has labored under the injustices of an often ruthless ruling class. Until recently, Guatemala suffered the daily nightmare of Latin America's longest running civil war, which lasted for 36 years until peace talks between the guerrillas and the government finally ended the conflict on December 31, 1996. The war claimed the lives of some 200,000 people, largely poor and indígena—more people than in the more widely publicized conflicts in El Salvador and Nicaragua. But years of stalled peace talks finally resulted in a treaty, the provisions of which are falling slowly into place as this scarred country attempts to heal itself.

As you explore the fascinating culture and magnificent natural beauty of Guatemala, you'll soon discover why it's a budget traveler's paradise. What might buy you a sleazy hotel room and greasy food for a week in London can get you a month or two of comfortable rooms, healthy food, and thrilling adventures in Guatemala. More than anything, traveling here means preparing yourself for sights and events like nothing you could encounter in the first world: from a little girl sleeping in a cardboard box on the filthy streets of Guatemala City, to a view of the seemingly endless rain forest from the top of Temple IV at Tikal, to an incense-filled pagan shrine in a destroyed colonial church. Almost every place has a story to tell—of a bloody massacre, a flamboyant Mayan ruler, or a priest who used hymns rather than swords to conquer the native people. Today, modern and traditional, *Ladino* (Spanish-speaking descendants of Spaniards and indigenous groups) and indígena, rich and poor continue to coexist in a relationship nearly as rocky as when the Spanish first encountered the Maya almost 400 years ago.

Guatemalans have a long relationship with exploitation and war. As early as 600 BC, the great city centers of the Maya rose out of this soil, using the sweat of thousands of laborers to build temples and palaces for a ruling class of priests and lords. Among the most dramatic of their achievements was Tikal, a brilliant city whose temples rise hundreds of feet above the thick, humid jungle. While Europe was in the throes of the Dark Ages, the Mayan elite were drinking hot chocolate from the top of these towering architectural marvels. But in the 9th century AD, their great cities met a mysterious end. The immense centers that had once controlled nearly all of Guatemala began to crumble. The people scattered into tribes that duked it out with each other until the Spanish joined the fun in 1524. A hot-blooded conquistador named Pedro de Alvarado played on old rivalries and, with his meager army, helped the divided and warring Maya to defeat themselves. Today, indigenous Guatemala remains divided, but not conquered. The Quiché, Mam, Cackchiquel, Kekchí, and many other tribes continue to speak their languages and celebrate a culture that predates Columbus.

Alvarado established the Kingdom of Guatemala in Ciudad Vieja, the first of the colony's many ill-fated capitals. Many of the Spanish colonists had children by indígena women, and the resulting Ladino class benefited from the Spanish wealth that flowed into the Spanish New World. The Ladinos chafed under Spanish rule and, in 1821, declared themselves the Independent Federation of Central America. Although independence granted new freedom and power to the upper classes, it worsened the lot of the Maya. For the next century, Mayan lands were annexed and sold to plantation owners, and the indígena became virtual slaves on their own land. In fact, some anthropologists claim that the striking traditional garb unique to each village was actually introduced by the ruling classes as a way to identify their human "property."

By 1839, the loose ties of the Central American union had been severed, and Guatemala began to take its present geographic shape (though it claimed Belize within its borders until 1990). The next century saw a series of unspectacular and downright corrupt dictators who looked after the interests of the small Ladino ruling class, all the while oppressing the indigenous majority. A ray of hope briefly shone through in 1944, when an army coup replaced the dictator Jorge Ubico Castañeda with Juan José Arevalo, who gave an ear to the indigenous voices of his country. His successor, Jacobo Arbenz Guzmán, continued reforms but went a bit too far for the reactionary right and the United States. He began to redistribute idle land belonging to the United Fruit Company (which, at the time, was the largest landowner in Guatemala) and use the company's tax returns (which vastly underestimated the true value of the land) to calculate compensation. United Fruit didn't like this one bit and in 1954 helped to finance a CIA-organized coup. The tired and frightened president resigned, leaving coup leader Castillo Armas to became the first in a string of dictators that dragged Guatemala to its lowest depths. By the 1960s, Guatemalan society was drastically polarized: paramilitary death squads answered leftist guerrilla activity with brutal force. An unsuccessful 1961 coup is considered the beginning of the civil war, but the most tragic period in Guatemala's history was yet to come.

In the early 1980s, the Guatemalan government mounted a series of "scorched-earth" counterinsurgency campaigns. The military destroyed hundreds of villages throughout the country in an effort to flush out a handful of suspected guerrillas. The victims—largely poor rural indígena—were raped, tortured, shot, mutilated, and often walled into their homes and burned alive. By 1985, the military had murdered 70,000 people and was responsible for the "disappearance" of 40,000. An additional 75,000 Guatemalans fled into Mexico to escape the violence, while some 30,000 others hid in the hostile mountains in the north. The situation in Guatemala was widely considered the region's most extreme example of state-sponsored human-rights abuses. The wholesale butchery subsided in the mid-'80s, but the military remained a constant presence, and antigovernment guerrillas continued to operate, particularly in the northern highlands.

Things first began to look up in 1985, when Guatemala elected its first civilian president in almost 40 years. U.N.-monitored peace talks between the army and the Guatemalan National Revolutionary Unity (UNRG) began in 1990. Guatemala saw a huge step back in May of 1992, when civilian president Jorge Serrano Eliás abruptly suspended parliamentary activity in what may have been an effort to stifle growing political and economic protest. Several days later, the Guatemalan military forced Serrano from office, replacing him with the government's human-rights ombudsman, Ramiro de León Carpio. Peace talks continued off and on over the next several years. When President Alvaro Arzu entered office in January 1996, one of his first promises was to forge a peace treaty before the end of his first year of office. True to his word (but barely), a peace treaty was achieved on December 31, 1996.

Guatemala has entered a period of slow recovery. The peace accord provides for greater legal, linguistic, and educational rights for the indigenous communities, scales back the military and police, and establishes a land bank and national property survey to address the claims of landless peasants forced from their communities by the army. To the dismay of human-rights advocates, however, the accord also includes a controversial amnesty that prevents prosecution of most of the government and military officials responsible for the atrocities. With peace have come increased international investment and economic growth. Evidence of this growth can be found throughout the country in the form of new and improved roads, increased electrification, and better communications systems, all of which make Guatemala a more tourist-friendly and less frustrating destination.

With transition, however, comes a certain level of uncertainty and chaos. Kidnapping for ransom, armed robbery, and violent bandits pose a growing security problem that some associate with the uncertainty of a dismantled military and police force. The January 1998 roadside assault and rape of a group of American university students brought Guatemala's security issue under an international spotlight. All visitors to Guatemala should take reasonable precautions, especially along highways after dark and along footpaths to more remote tourist sights. Visitors should also be aware of current security issues and consider that reasonable precautions may not be enough to allow for comfortable and safe travel in all regions. Despite its troubles, Guatemala remains an incredible country that, perhaps better than any other, represents the beauty and diversity that is the New World.

BASICS

MONEY

Traveling in Guatemala is awfully cheap, even by budget standards. In most parts of the country, a single traveler can live fairly well on under $20 a day, less if you travel with a friend. Guatemala City, Tikal, and the heavily touristed parts of the Western Highlands will cost more, especially during popular festivals (*see below*).

CURRENCY • The *quetzal* (also the name of the national bird) is one of the most stable currencies in Latin America. In fact, Guatemala is one of the few places in Latin America where the smallest unit of money (1 *centavo*) still has value and is readily used. There are 100 centavos to a quetzal. Prices quoted in this chapter are based on an exchange rate of 6 quetzales to U.S.$1. The word *peso* is sometimes used in place of quetzal, and *len* in place of centavos. Guatemala is one country where people use their money—no matter how ripped, torn, taped, and scribbled on they get, they're still accepted everywhere. The main thing to avoid is 100-quetzal bills—everyone hates to accept them.

General banking hours are weekdays 9–4 and Saturday 9–1, but most branches of **Banco del Quetzal** (tel. 251–2053) and **Banco del Ejército** (tel. 230–0856) stay open weekdays until 8 and Saturdays until 2. Most national banks will change American traveler's checks, but none change Australian traveler's checks, and only **Banco de Guatemala** (tel. 251–3263) deals in Canadian traveler's checks. You can get a cash advance on Visa or MasterCard from **Credomatic** (tel. 331–7436) and at branches of **Banco Industrial** (tel. 334–5111), which also has ATMs with the Plus System in their offices, as well as in the Camino Real and El Corado Hotel lobbies in Guatemala City (*see* Money in Guatemala City). If all else fails, **Banco Del Agro** (tel. 251–4026) works with **Western Union** wire services (tel. 800/325–6000 in U.S.). **Banco Del Café** (tel. 331–1311) is the official American Express affiliate, so you can get money from home via an **American Express Moneygram** (tel. 800/929–9400 in U.S.).

GUATEMALA

N

0 ——— 0
20 miles
30 km

PACIFIC OCEAN

La Mesilla

SIERRA LOS CUCHUMATANES

El Carmen
Quetzaltenango
Totonicapán
Momostenango
Huehuetenango
Todos Santos
Cuchumatán
Nebaj
Chajul
Cotzal
San Juan
Cobán
San Pedro
Carchá
Lanquín
Cahabón
ALTA VERAPAZ
SIERRA DE SANTA CRUZ

Retalhuleu
Mazatenango
Panajachel
Lago
Atitlán
Chichicastenango
Mixco Viejo
Santa Cruz
del Quiché
EL QUICHE
Taclic
BAJA VERAPAZ
Río Cahabón
SIERRA DE SANTA CRUZ
IZABAL

Santa Lucía
Cotzumalguapa
Antigua
Chimaltenango
San Juan
and San Pedro
Sacatepéquez
Salamá
Río Hondo
Lago de
Izabal
El Estor

Puerto
San José
Escuintla
Guatemala
City
El Progreso
Río Hondo
Río Hondo
Zacapa
Mariscos
Lago de
Izabal
Río Dulce

Iztapa
Taxisco
Esquipulas
Chiquimula
El Florido
Quiriguá
Río Motagua
barrios

La Hachadura
Biotopo
Monterrico-
Hawaii
Antiguatu
Agua Caliente
Copán
HONDURAS

San Salvador
EL SALVADOR

86

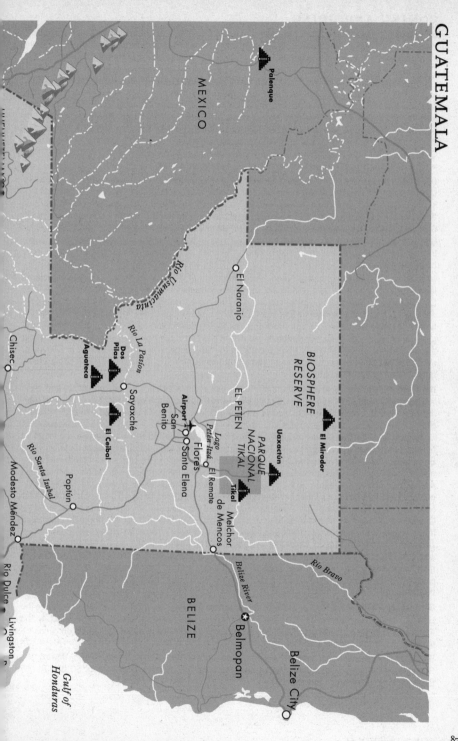

GUATEMALA

MEXICO

Palenque

El Naranjo

Río Usumacinta

Río La Pasión

BIOSPHERE
RESERVE

Chisec

Dos
Pilas

Aguateca

Sayaxché

San
Benito

Airport
Santa Elena
Flores

Lago
Petén Itzá
El Remate

EL PETÉN

PARQUE
NACIONAL
TIKAL

Uaxactún

El Mirador

El Ceibal

Río Santa Izabal

Poptún

Melchor
de Mencos

Tikal

Modesto Méndez

Río Bravo

Belize River

BELIZE

Belmopan

Belize City

Río Dulce

Livingston

Gulf of
Honduras

COMING AND GOING

BY PLANE • The cheapest and easiest way to get to Guatemala from the United States is by plane. Guatemala has two airports, one in Guatemala City (international and domestic) and one in Flores (domestic). Almost every airline arrives in the capital city, although you can take flights from Cancún (Mexico) or Belize City to Flores. Airlines flying from the United States include **American** (tel. 800/433–7300), **Aviateca** (tel. 800/327–9832), **Continental** (tel. 800/231–0856), **TACA** (tel. 800/535–8780), and **United** (tel. 800/538–2929). Round-trip airfares fluctuate from around $400 to $600 and more, but Aviateca and TACA usually have the best deals. Flights to Guatemala City either pass through or originate in Los Angeles, Miami, Houston, New Orleans, or Dallas/Fort Worth, and often pass through San Salvador. From Europe, weekly connecting flights usually stop in New York City, Miami, or Mexico City. You can easily fly to most Central American capitals from Guatemala City. TACA has flights from Guatemala City to Belize ($125), San José ($130), Managua ($189), and Panama City ($250). Upon leaving Guatemala by plane, you will be charged a $15 departure tax.

BY BUS • It's no easy project to bus it all the way from the United States to Guatemala, although it certainly makes for a great American adventure and possibly the subject of your first novel. **Greyhound** (tel. 800/231–2222) will take you as far as Mexico City, where you'll have to find a series of second-class buses to take you to the Guatemalan border. The entire trip from the U.S.–Mexico border to Guatemala City can take four–five days (or longer) and will cost about $200. The two main border crossings to enter Guatemala from Mexico are La Mesilla and El Carmen. From either crossing, it's about seven hours through the Western Highlands to Guatemala City if you take a Pullman (private) bus, and much longer by public bus.

Most buses to neighboring Central American countries leave from Guatemala City. **Melva Internacional** leaves daily once an hour from Guatemala City to San Salvador (5 hrs, $6; see Guatemala City, *below*). One way to get to Mexico from Guatemala City is to take a bus to Huehuetenango and then catch a connecting bus from there. **Velasquez** (*see* Huehuetenango, *below*) has buses from Huehuetenango to the border at La Mesilla (2 hrs, $1.25). From Esquipulas, the Salvadoran border is just a hour away and costs about $1. To get to Belize, **Pinitas** buses depart daily from the Hotel San Juan in Santa Elena (in the Petén) to Belize City (7 hrs, $10). At the border the bus connects with a Novelo bus. For $10 more, minibuses (which are much more comfortable) do this same route to Belize City. See Santa Elena, *below*, for more info on minibuses.

BY CAR • If you decide to drive through Mexico, make sure your car can take a beating, and leave yourself tons of time for the trip. Gas is quite expensive: you could pay up to $500 in gas driving from the México–U.S. border to Guatemala City, and the whole trip can take as long as a week. An added expense are the toll roads, which set you back $4–$5 a pop. The best and most popular route into Guatemala is via the Pan-American Highway along the coast of Mexico, entering Guatemala through La Mesilla. From there, you can go through Huehuetenango to the capital. Another popular route begins in Brownsville, Texas, going along the Gulf coast to Veracruz, and then to the Guatemalan border at El Carmen. It's very unusual to enter Guatemala through the isolated Petén region—it's dangerous, the roads are horrible, and resources (for fixing a car, etc.) are few and far between. Mexico and Guatemala do not recognize international insurance coverage, so you'll need to purchase additional car insurance for both Guatemala and Mexico—it's available at the border for about $6 per day. At the border entering Guatemala, officials will often fumigate your car and make you foot the bill. It's not quite clear what they're spraying for, but it's definitely a good way for them to make a few extra dollars. This doesn't happen when returning to Mexico. No matter what route you take, make sure to tote spare car parts, tools, and a mechanic's manual so you can take care of car breakdowns on your own. One consolation for road warriors willing to take the trip: beat-up cars are de rigeur in Central America; a barely running clunker that can't sell for $500 in the United States will bring you at least that in Guatemala, enough to fly you home in style.

BY TRAIN • **Amtrak** (tel. 800/872–7245) and **Southern Railways** (tel. 800/233–8564) go as far as the U.S.–Mexico border. From there, you can catch a Mexican train to the capital. South of Mexico City, the trains are exceptionally slow, unreliable, and unsafe, and all rail service within Guatemala unceremoniously bit the dust within the past few years.

BY BOAT • Boats head between Punta Gorda (in southern Belize) from Puerto Barrios (on Guatemala's Caribbean coast) twice weekly. The trip takes 2½ hours and costs about $6. *See* Puerto Barrios for info on where to buy tickets.

GETTING AROUND

BY BUS • *Everyone* rides the bus in Guatemala. Unfortunately, robberies by roadside bandits occur frequently and randomly. Always a traveler's concern in Guatemala, these bus robberies have become more common and more violent in recent years, a phenomenon commonly tied to the dissolution of the armed forces. Avoid traveling at night, and talk to locals and other travelers to gain information on the latest hot spots. Obviously, carry little cash and valuables on your body to minimize potential loss. Bus schedules are approximations. Private (or Pullman) buses are more expensive, more comfortable, and more direct than public buses mainly because they don't stop at every third shady tree along the highway. Public buses are packed until people smash up against the windows. It's fairly easy to figure out the bus system: signs advertising the main destinations are on the front of the bus, and tickets are generally purchased aboard. A bus will stop anywhere along the road; just whistle, wave, or pound the sides of the bus to get the driver's attention. Excluding the remote Petén region, most destinations are less than five hours from the capital. Ticket prices for public buses are generally about 40¢–60¢ per hour, but private buses are considerably more expensive ($6–$12 per ride). City buses cost about 10¢.

BY PLANE • **Aviateca** (tel. 334-7722) has daily flights to Flores (near Tikal) from Guatemala City, and the fare is about $35 each way. **Tapsa** (tel. 331–9108) and **Aerovías** (tel. 331–9663) also fly to Flores. Because it's a long, long bus ride (11–20 hrs, depending on service) and not especially safe, you should definitely consider flying if you can afford it.

> *Scrunched seven to a row, Guatemalan bus passengers take it all in stride. In most places, people would be screaming, "Turn off that music!" and "Get that animal's butt out of my face!" Here, they just laugh.*

BY MOTORBIKE • Traveling by motorbike is an excellent way to see Guatemala, and bikes are easy to rent in the more touristed areas. In Guatemala City, you can rent bikes from **Rental** (12a Calle 2–62, Z10, tel. 332–6911) for a day, week, or month for about $15 a day, plus about $2 per day for insurance. A deposit is usually required. Make sure to inspect the bike before you leave to avoid being charged for existing damages.

BY BIKE • Bicycles aren't prevalent in the more developed areas of the country, because most roads have little or no shoulders, lots of hairpin turns, steep up-and-down grades, and obnoxious macho drivers. If you chose your route carefully and you're in shape, a sturdy mountain bike can be a great and economical way to cruise around Guatemala. If you get tired, you can always throw your wheels on the roof of a bus until you recuperate. You'll need to be able to fix your own flats, and you should bring basic spare parts, because they can be hard to come by. In Guatemala City, **Villeda Bicishon** (7a Av. 6–34, Z4, tel. 334–1451) has parts for most brands of mountain bikes and a decent selection of accessories. Most bigger cities have bike-rental places, but they normally rent just for the day ($5). In Antigua Guatemala, you can rent bikes for up to a week. You might be able to work out a deal for longer, but you should consider buying a bike or bringing yours from home.

BY CAR • For obvious reasons, it's great to cruise the country in a car. You can see a lot more of Guatemala in a much shorter time and you don't have to rely on Latin time schedules and buses that never show. On the downside, gas is expensive ($1.50 per gallon) and many roads really and truly suck. One notable exception is the amazingly smooth Pan-American Highway. Be sure to ask locals which roads to take and not take; they often know the scoop on the current favorite haunts of hijackers and bandits. Driving at night ain't smart, period. Another Guatemalan car problem is that vandalism and theft are rampant in the big cities—to be safe, look for guarded parking lots or hotels with lots. Guatemala City has awful traffic, and on a Friday afternoon you can be stuck in a traffic jam for hours. Be sure to travel with your passport, driver's license, and an extra $10 to clear up any "unofficial fines" if you get pulled over. The capital has a bunch of car-rental places (*see* Getting Around in Guatemala City, *below*), as do other major cities. Renting usually comes to $60–$95 a day, including insurance. Be aware that in Guatemala, car insurance will generally cover only about 90% of the value of the car for collision or theft—you will be liable for the rest if someone decides what's yours temporarily is theirs permanently. If you're planning to visit the Petén or other remote areas, or explore the Highlands during the rainy season, a four-wheel-drive is a must.

HITCHING • Hitching is one of the cheapest ways to get around Guatemala (and the only way in many of the more isolated areas). Here everyone—both gringos and Guatemalans—pays for the ride. It's good to figure out the average price of a ride to your destination before you hop in the back of a truck. Police checkpoints have large speed bumps and often require drivers to stop—a perfect opportunity to ask for a ride. Also, the roads in many areas are so bad that a slow jog will be enough to catch up and ask for a ride through the window. To catch a ride, just wave a vehicle down. Hitching at night is not recommended, and, sadly, women hitching alone run a much greater risk than their male counterparts.

WHERE TO SLEEP

Guatemala is the land of cheap sleeps, but in the more built-up areas you'll find accommodations to suit every wallet and required comfort level. In most regions, simple rooms with shared (public) bath are about $5; cleaner, more comfortable rooms run $5–$10; rooms with private bathrooms will set you back no more than $10; and $15 will usually get you ice water, a towel, toilet paper, shampoo, and hot water. If you pay any more than that expect air-conditioning and a TV. Hotels are required to display the latest "approved rates," which are the maximum amount any establishment can charge for its rooms. A 17% tax is always added to the listed price. Look behind the front desk or on the door in your room for the rates. In small villages where there are no hotels, search out the *alcalde* (mayor), who can usually set you up in an empty office or church courtyard if there are no private homes willing to take you in.

CAMPING • Most camping in Guatemala is free, and there are lots of places to put up a tent or hang a hammock and a mosquito net. While Guatemalans don't camp much, they're getting used to seeing tourists who do, so you won't get looked at funny. Bring a warm jacket or blanket for higher altitudes. You can get water and supplies like mosquito repellent, sun block, and batteries for your flashlight in towns. Most regional parks and other official campgrounds have guards at night, so you can rest assured, at least in theory. If you are camping in the tropical areas, be sure to check your shoes for unwanted stowaways like scorpions. If you camp and cook your own food, you can live on about $5 a day. The cities rarely have campgrounds—Panajachel and Tikal are the main exceptions. Tikal is one of the few places where you're charged to camp (about $6). Campers will have the most luck in Cobán and the Alta Verapaz region (*see* Where to Sleep in Cobán). In Cobán itself is the Parque Nacional Las Victorias, with 203 acres perfect for exploring and camping. Cobán's surrounding villages also offer tons of parks where you can camp for free. San Pedro Carchá, Lanquín, and Tactic all have palapas (campsites covered by a thatched roof; *see* Near Cobán, *below*), and you can find similar camping possibilities throughout Alta Verapaz.

FOOD

Standard fare throughout the country consists of rice, beans, eggs, cheese, tortillas, *carne asada* (roast beef), and chicken. Luckily, many areas also have delicious regional specialties, and in all the major cities you can chow down on a variety of eats from Mickey D's to Spanish paella. Street stands sell ridiculously cheap food; just keep an eye out for the hygiene—if it's grilled right in front of you, it's probably okay. A hot *empanada* (meat turnover) or tamale runs about 25¢, a piece of chicken with tortillas 50¢, and a hot beef sandwich 75¢. *Comedores* are cheap and simple restaurants that usually serve only *comida típica,* a basic menu of beans, rice, and meat. If you're going to get the runs, it'll probably be from a comedor. The best you can do is watch them prepare the grub and not eat anything that's obviously spoiled. Do not drink nonbottled water—it's a serious health risk. In most places, you'll find agua purificada for about 50¢ a bottle. The town market is the place to get fresh fruits, vegetables, and other goodies. A well-balanced lunch of bread, nuts, fruit, and juice can be bought at a market for under a buck.

TIPPING • Tipping is becoming more customary in Guatemala. If you're served at a table, 10% is standard.

OUTDOOR ACTIVITIES

Guatemala's varied topography and tremendous diversity of climates give you a lot to do in the great outdoors. **Hiking** is one of the easiest and most rewarding activities, especially in the highlands where moderate temperatures, small mountain villages, and beautiful vistas accompany your meanderings. You can almost always find a hike to suit your ability—from serious mountain treks to half-hour strolls on flat footpaths. Around Todos Santos, three hours from Huehuetenango, hiking is really the best way to enjoy the breathtaking greenery, and a number of easy-to-find trails crisscross the area. Also, hiking up volcanoes is popular among tourists and locals. Make sure to heed the warnings of this guidebook and of locals because there have been many robberies on volcano trails. In the Petén and in Central and Eastern Guatemala, you can explore remote **caves,** like the caves of Lanquín (near Cobán) and the caves of Actun Can, south of Santa Elena. **Rafting,** especially on the Río Cahabon (near Semuc Champey), is a fantastic adventure. Not only do you crash through white-water rapids, but you can also check out ancient Mayan cities that lie just off the river's banks. For **water sports,** try Lake Atitlán. Although this area is a tourist magnet, prices are still fairly cheap. You can rent a boat or kayak for $2 an hour, or for the whole day.

VISITOR INFORMATION

GOVERNMENT TOURIST OFFICES • INGUAT, the national tourist commission, publishes numerous colorful guidebooks and brochures focusing on Guatemala's many natural and cultural wonders, while carefully avoiding discussion of its unpleasant politics. You'll find branches in Antigua Guatemala, Guatemala City, Panajachel, and Quetzaltenango, as well as in the airports of Guatemala City and Flores. In towns without an INGUAT office, the *municipálidad* (usually on or near the main plaza) can usually point you toward hotels and comedores or private citizens who house and feed visitors.

If you write or call **INGUAT's U.S. branch** before you leave, they'll gladly send you a packet of introductory material including a great map of the country. *Guatemala Tourist Commission, 299 Alhambra Circle, Suite 510, Coral Gables, FL 33134, tel. 305/442–0651 or 800/742–4529, fax 305/442–1013.*

INFORMATION BUREAUS • The Network in Solidarity with the People of Guatemala is an umbrella organization connecting more than 150 solidarity organizations across the United States. They can help you get in touch with one of seven regional centers in California, Illinois, Kentucky, Massachusetts, New York, and Washington, DC. *1500 Massachusetts Ave. NW, Room 241, Washington, DC 20005, tel 202/223–6474.*

The **Guatemala News and Information Bureau** maintains an office and library with extensive files, periodicals, and other resources on Guatemala. Their *Report on Guatemala* ($12 for four issues) is an excellent quarterly news magazine with in-depth coverage of current political trends, insightful commentary, book reviews, and interviews with important figures. *Box 28594, Oakland, CA 94604, tel 510/835–0810.*

VISAS AND TOURIST CARDS

To visit Guatemala, citizens of the United States, Canada, and most European countries receive a tourist card upon arrival—it's actually just a stamp in your passport. Depending on your nationality, you'll get either 30 days (Australia, Canada, New Zealand, and the United Kingdom) or 90 days (United States) of travel within the country. Tourist cards are issued at the airport and at any border crossing, as well as at Guatemalan embassies and consulates. Regulations change often, however, so you would be wise to check with a Guatemalan consulate before heading off.

To extend your stay, apply for tourist card renewals at the **immigration office** in Guatemala City (41 Calle 17-36, Z8, tel. 475-1302; open weekdays 8–4), but it may be more fun and just as quick to pop over to El Salvador. You have to be out of the country at least 72 hours before you're allowed back into Guatemala. If you're planning an extended stay, though, consider applying for a visa—they're free and good for five years of travel in and out of Guatemala.

HEALTH

Guatemala poses pretty much the same health risks as every other developing country in the world. Be careful of what you eat and be sure to drink only *agua purificada* (purified water) even in larger towns, so as to avoid Montezuma's revenge (traveler's diarrhea) and other nasties like cholera and giardia. Of course, the big word on everyone's mind is malaria. There are occasional outbreaks in the mosquito-infested humid regions, especially in the Petén and the Caribbean and Pacific coasts. Use insect repellent containing DEET, take chloroquinine (Aralen is the most common brand name), and hope for the best.

The Guatemalan medical system isn't exactly High-Tech General, so you're best off avoiding getting sick here entirely (*see* Health in Chapter 1). For minor boo-boos, most larger towns have some kind of medical personnel around to help you out, but oftentimes a pharmacist is the best and most convenient option.

VOLUNTEERING

If you're interested in volunteering and you're not hooked up with a specific program, you can travel to Guatemala and wing it. If you want to volunteer at a hospital or clinic, go to the smaller towns and ask around. The same goes for other areas of interest; you're sure to find some organization or hard-hit village that would welcome assistance.

Casa Guatemala is an organization dedicated to addressing the needs of Guatemala's undernourished and orphaned children, who are often victims of poverty and urban displacement. Volunteers help out at one of three assistance centers: one is an orphanage on the banks of the Rio Dulce. It's the ideal place for the socially minded to work with young Guatemalans who are really in need. Those who stay only a short time can expect to help with the daily chores, but long-term volunteers may get to work closely with the children. The minimum volunteer time is two weeks. *Write to: 14a Calle 10-63, Zl, Apdo. Postal 5-75-A, Guatemala City, Guatemala, tel. 232–5517.*

Proyecto Ak' Tenamit also puts volunteers to work with Kekchí communities in the Rio Dulce area, assisting with medical clinics, educational projects, and family-income generation. The organization has recently begun to concentrate on literacy projects for women and girls. *Write to: Apdo. Postal 2675, Guatemala City, Guatemala, tel. 254–1560. In U.S.: The Guatemalan Tomorrow Fund, Box 3636, Tequesta, FL 33469, tel. 561/747–9790.*

STUDYING ABROAD

Guatemala has earned a well-deserved reputation for its excellent Spanish-language courses. The two main hot spots are Antigua Guatemala and Quetzaltenango, both of which offer programs of every type including courses in local indígena languages. **Proyecto Linguítico** (tel. 763–1061, 800/963–9889 in the U.S.) in Quezaltenango is a top-notch, nonprofit institution. Most programs offer home stays with local families, organized excursions, and intensive courses with individualized instruction, all for about $100–$150 per week. The most popular programs fill up quickly, so it's best to call a few weeks ahead to reserve a spot, especially during the Highlands' high tourist season (Oct.–May).

PHONES AND MAIL

It's really, really cheap to send mail home (about 5¢ for a letter to the United States), but you'll hear stories about letters getting lost before they even leave Guatemala. Mail usually takes one–two weeks to get to the United States. To receive mail, just have your pen pals address it to your name, Lista de Correos, the city, and the department (region). Sometimes you'll be charged a small fee for each letter held in your name, and you have to show your passport or other ID to receive your mail. Post office hours all over the country are generally weekdays 8–4, although the central office in the capital has longer hours (open weekdays 8–7, Sat. 8–6). The capital's **American Express** office (*see* American Express in Guatemala City, *below*) will hold mail for members.

The national phone company, **TELGUA,** has offices across the country. In smaller towns the TELGUA office is often the only place to make local, long-distance, international, collect, or credit-card calls. Local calls cost 10 centavos (2¢). Hold the money above the slot and drop it in when the phone beeps, and always keep more coins ready. From some public phones you can reach an **AT&T** operator by dialing 190, which will give you direct person-to-person service to the United States only. The direct number to Canada is 198. In some cities, you can get hold of an **MCI** operator by dialing 189. Practically anything—including calling collect—is cheaper than calling internationally with local operators. Try to get a calling card, wealthy friends, or write a letter. In August 1996, Guatemala changed all the country's phone numbers to a seven-digit format. You'll still see the outdated six-digit numbers all over the place: if you need to convert an outdated number, the nice TELGUA people can help.

WHEN TO GO

During Easter Week, Guatemala is overrun with tourists. and you may be hard-pressed to find a place to stay. May and June are the country's slowest tourist months—hotels and restaurants often offer discounts.

CLIMATE • The tourist brochures that tout Guatemala as "The Land of Eternal Spring" are doubtless referring to the moderate, comfortable climate of the capital and Western Highlands, where most of the tourists go. In truth, Guatemala's varied geography makes it impossible to characterize the climate of the whole country. Guatemala is in a tropical zone, but it also has the highest mountains in Central America. Guatemala City and the Western Highlands are the only regions with a true dry season (Oct.–May) and rainy season (June–Sept.). Temperatures in and around Guatemala City average 57°F–76°F. In highland areas, temps can drop to a chilly 42°F, so you might need a heavy sweater. Along the humid Pacific and Caribbean coasts, temps rarely get below 88°F, and can reach 102°F. Hotter still, the sticky Petén region sees temps of 110°F and above. Eastern Guatemala's dry weather averages 60°F–80°F. The cooler valleys and mountains of the Central Verapaces average about 52°–75°F.

HOLIDAYS AND FESTIVALS • There's a festival for practically every day of the year somewhere in the country; pick up the "Directorio de Fiestas" booklet at INGUAT's Guatemala City branch (*see* Visitor Information in Guatemala City, *below*). Some of the most famous nationwide festivals are Semana Santa (Easter Week, late March or early April) and Christmas (Dec. 25) in Antigua Guatemala; Independence Day (Sept. 15) and Our Lady of the Assumption (Aug. 15) in Guatemala City; and the festival of the Black Christ in Esquipulas (Jan. 1–15th). Other diverse celebrations include Cobán's national folklore festival (last week of July), Chichicastenango's Dia de Santo Tomás (Dec. 13–21), and Livingston's Garifuna Celebration (Nov. 15).

FURTHER READING

The following books are excellent sources of info on the political and cultural history of Guatemala. *Men of Maize,* by Nobel laureate Miguel Angel Asturias, Guatemala's most prominent fiction writer. *After the Bombs,* by Arturo Arias (Curbstone Press; 1990). *Guatemala: Eternal Spring, Eternal Tyranny,* by Jean-Marie Simon (W.W. Norton, 1987). *I, Rigoberta Menchú: An Indian Woman in Guatemala,* the memoir of Nobel laureate Rigoberta Menchú (Verso Editions, 1984), is a controversial rendition of the indígena experience. Michael Coe's *The Maya* and *Mayan Folktales,* edited by James D. Sexton (Doubleday, 1992), are both difinitive books on the ancient Maya. *Time Among the Maya: Travels in Belize, Guatemala, and Mexico,* by Ronald Wright (Henry Holt & Co., 1991), is an important travelogue. If you like movies, try to rent the feature film *El Norte* (1984).

GUATEMALA CITY

The enormous contrasts in Guatemalan society are laid bare in the capital's sprawling tangle of grimy streets and fume-choked alleyways. Trouble in the highlands sparked a migration into Guatemala City—often referred to as Guatemala or Guate—which now holds around 2¼ million residents or about a quarter of the country's entire population. Not surprisingly, overpopulation has led to desperate poverty, and the split between rich and poor slaps you in the face the moment you begin your exploration of the various neighborhoods. Women in traditional dress pawn plastic windmills on the street while the elite fill the shopping malls, spending quetzales in denominations that the poor have never seen. Not surprisingly, street crime is a serious and endemic problem in the capital. Be especially vigilant in the bus terminals, on city buses, in the market, and at night. Try to leave valuables at your hotel reception, and use a money belt tucked inside your shirt or pants. Also, many people carry some "mug money"—about 20 quetzales—in a pocket separate from the rest of their cash, to hand over if robbed. Welcome to your local developing nation.

When Guatemala's colonial capital, now called Antigua Guatemala, was devastated by an earthquake in 1773, the Spanish searched for a more protected location for their new capital. They chose a nearby valley, which centuries before had been home to the center of the Mayan highland groups, Kaminal Juyú. As the northernmost city of the Kingdom of Central America, Guatemala City linked the countries farther south to Mexico City and rapidly became the wealthiest and most important center of the region. For all its fortune, the new capital was not spared the fate of its predecessor—earthquakes in 1917 and 1918, and then again in 1976 nearly leveled the city, and the colonial majesty of "the jewel of Central America" was destroyed forever. Now, quasimodern architecture lines charmless streets swimming in neon, forming something of an architectural curio cabinet lacking in style, subtlety, and continuity.

Few travelers will spend time here on purpose, but Guatemala City is useful as the economic and bureaucratic crossroads of the country, and you'll most likely find yourself here at one time or another. With a huge range of restaurants, hotels, and shopping facilities, the capital city will bend or stretch to any budget. When you're not tied up in red tape at the embassy, searching the Sunday artisan's market at Plaza Mayor for a tiny *huipil* (a locally made hand-embroidered blouse), or arranging tomorrow morning's flight to the Petén, you can entertain yourself with a variety of city sights. The excellent Museo Nacional de Arqueología y Etnología helps illuminate the mysteries of the ancient Maya, the Palacio Nacional offers a quick lesson in contemporary political history, while an afternoon in Parque Concordia is just plain fun. As you walk through the city, you'll get an taste of the third world, and the flavor, while usually not pleasant, is authentic.

BASICS

VISITOR INFORMATION

INGUAT will give you all the propaganda you could ever want, as well as useful advice about bus routes and hotels throughout Guatemala. Some of the staff speaks English. *Centro Cívico: 7a Av. 1–17, Z4, tel. 331–1333. From any even-numbered avenida, take any bus marked* TERMINAL *to the Teatro Nacional; walk east toward the towering buildings. Look for the little blue "I" across the bridge over 7a Av. Open weekdays 8–4, Sat. 8–1.*

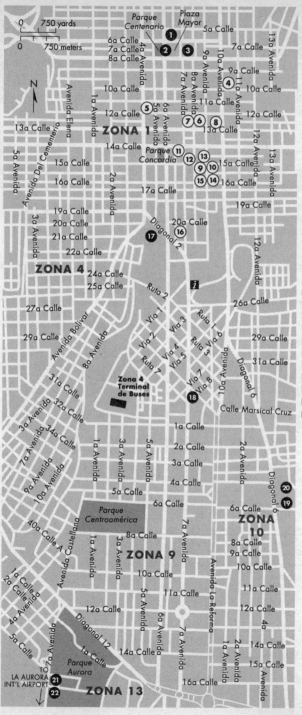

GUATEMALA CITY

Sights ●

Catedral Metropolitana, **3**
Centro Cultural Miguel Angel Austrias, **17**
Iglesia Yurrita, **18**
Museo Ixchel, **19**
Museo Nacional de Arqueología y Etnología, **21**
Museo Nacional de Historia Natural, **22**
Museo Popol Vuh, **20**
Palacio Nacional, **1**
Plaza Mayor, **2**

Lodging ○

Fortuna Royal, **7**
Hotel Ajau, **13**
Hotel Belmont, **9**
Hotel Capri, **14**
Hotel Centroamérica, **15**
Hotel Chalet Suizo, **11**
Hotel España, **10**
Hotel Fuente, **16**
Hotel Lessing House, **5**
Hotel San Diego, **12**
Hotel Spring, **6**
Pensión Mesa, **4**
Poseda Belem, **8**

The **Guatemalan telephone directory** has a section for tourists in both English and Spanish with information about banks and transportation and a list of festivals and sights in Guatemala City and throughout the country. You can find one at the main TELGUA office next to the main post office. Look in the pink pages near the front.

AMERICAN EXPRESS

The American Express office is in the Banco del Café building in Zona 9. They hold mail and cash personal checks for cardholders, as well as replace lost or stolen cards. *Send mail care of American Express, Av. La Reforma 9–00, Z9, Ciudad de Guatemala, tel. 331-1311. From 10a Av., Z1, take Bus 82 to glass Banco del Café Bldg. Open weekdays 8:30–4:30.*

CHANGING MONEY

Zona 1 has a lot of banks and they're always crowded, so expect to wait at least 20–30 minutes in line. You shouldn't have any trouble changing U.S. dollars and traveler's checks at any of them, but **Banco de Guatemala** (7a Av. and 22a Calle, Z1, tel. 251–3263; open Mon.–Thurs. 8:30–2, Fri. 8:30–2:30) and **Lloyd's Bank** (11a Calle 8–20, Z1, tel. 251–4789) are two of the biggies. After hours, try **Banco del Quetzal** (10a Calle 6–28, Z1, tel. 251–2053). They're open weekdays 8:30–8, Saturday 9–1, and their airport branch (tel. 334–7508) is also open Sundays and holidays 8–6. **Banco Industrial** (7a Av. 5–10, Z4, tel. 334–5111; open weekdays 8–5:30, Sat. 8–2:30) processes credit-card advances and has ATMs on the Plus system in each of their branches. The financially strapped will appreciate **Banco del Agro** (9a Calle 5–39, Z1, tel. 251–4026), because it's the local Western Union representative. Some hotels change money, but it's generally a service for guests only, and they often charge a hefty commission.

BLACK MARKET • Banks are often hesitant to change cash other than American dollars, so if you're desperate, you can try the **black market** in Zona 1 on 7a Avenida, between 11a and 13a calles. Money changers generally offer a slightly poorer exchange rate than the banks and will deal in Canadian dollars, Mexican pesos, and any Central American currency. Be extremely careful—it's easy to get ripped off.

EMBASSIES

Guatemala's recent political upheavals have made security an uncertain issue, so it is a good idea to check in with your embassy when you arrive for recent news and travelers' advisories.

United States. *Av. La Reforma 7–01, Z10, tel. 331–1541. Open weekdays 8–noon and 1–5.*

Canada. *Edificio Edyma Plaza, 13a Calle 8–44, Z10, 8th Floor, tel. 333–6102. Open Mon.–Thurs. 8–4:30, Fri. 8–1:30.*

United Kingdom. Australians, New Zealanders, and other Commonwealth affiliates can get help here with lost passports and other problems. *Edificio Centro Financiero Torre II, 7a Av. 5–10, Z4, 7th Floor, tel. 332–1601. Open Mon.–Thurs. 8:30–12:30 and 2–4:30, Fri. 9–11:30.*

EMERGENCIES

Call the **police** (tel. 120) for help or the **Red Cross** (tel. 125) for an ambulance.

LAUNDRY

A few hotels have a *pila* (a washboard and sink) or washing machine, but most don't, so your best bet is to take your clothes to a local *lavandería* (laundromat). You can wash and dry one load of clothes for $2 at **Lavamática El Siglo** (12a Calle 3–42, Z1, tel. 230–0223), open Monday–Saturday 8–6. If you're feeling busy or lazy, pay Reina a few more quetzales to do your wash for you.

MEDICAL AID

Although the **Centro Médico Hospital** (6a Av. 3–47, Z10, tel. 332–3555) and **Herreta Llerandi** (6a Av. 8–71, Z10, tel. 334–5955) have doctors who speak English, they charge mucho dinero. The public **Hospital General San Juan de Dios** (1a Av., at 11a Calle, Z1, tel. 332–3741) provides care free or for a very small fee. Most hospitals are open 24 hours.

For less urgent ailments, a pharmacist can usually help you out; most drugs are cheap and available over the counter. **Farmacias Godoy** has a branch at 21a Calle 1–87 in Zona 1 (tel. 232–9240). For tampons, condoms, and other necessities, try **Farmacias Klee.** There's one in Zona 1 on 6a Avenida at 9a Calle (tel. 331–0475). **Farmacia Sinai, S.A.**(4a Av. 12–74, Z1, tel. 251–5276) is open 24 hours, and other pharmacies take turns staying open all night; look on the door of a closed one to find the nearest one open.

LOCATING GUAT CITY ADDRESSES

Guat is arranged on a grid: avenidas run north–south, calles run east–west. Each is numbered in order from a central point. The first part of the address is the calle or avenida the building is on. The second part lists the cross street closest to the central point, followed by the building number, and, most important, the zone it falls into. Say you're looking for 7a Avenida 19–24, Z1. This means the entrance is on 7a Avenida between 19a and 20a calles in Zona 1; the building number is 24.

PHONES AND MAIL

TELGUA has offices throughout the city. Their headquarters, next to the main post office, is by far the most crowded—you might want to bring along a few volumes of Dostoyevsky to read while you simmer in the waiting room. Dial 171 for a TELGUA international operator, 190 for **AT&T**, 189 for **MCI**, or 195 for **Sprint**. You can also send and receive faxes here. This is the only spot in Zona 1 to make international calls, so it attracts a lot of pickpockets—watch your valuables. *8a Av. at 12a Calle, Z1, tel. 232–0498. Open weekdays 7 AM–midnight.*

The main **post office** is in a beautiful pink-and-white colonial building. You can buy postcards, paper, and envelopes on the street just outside. If you want to receive mail in Guatemala City, have it addressed to you at Lista de Correos, Ciudad de Guatemala, Guatemala. You'll need picture ID to pick up your letters in Room 110 on the ground floor. **Telegrams** are a popular means of communication throughout Guatemala. To reach the telegraph office, turn right just inside the main building. *7a Av. 12–11, Z1, tel. 232–6101. Post office open weekdays 7–7, Sat. 8–6. Telegraph office open daily 24 hrs.*

TRAVEL AGENCIES

A fairly complete list of tour operators and the services they provide is available at INGUAT (*see* Visitor Information, *above*). Prices and packages vary widely, from $24 city tours to $1,000 jungle expeditions. If you want to get way off the beaten track and you're willing to pay for it, try **Maya Expeditions** (15a Calle 1–91, Z10, tel. 363–4955), which specializes in adventures such as white-water rafting, journeys to obscure archaeological sites, and diving expeditions in remote areas. One-day trips to Montagua, Naranjo, and Cahabon cost $69. If your wallet's feeling a little light, try one of the following companies.

Delta Travel advertises "the lowest prices in town." Yeah, right. In any case, their rates are competitive, and they are centrally located. Delta will arrange car rentals, airline tickets, and tours of Tikal ($148), Río Dulce, and Quiriguá ($100). They also have shuttle service to Antigua Guatemala ($7) and Panajachel. *6a Av. 10–36, Z1, tel. 332–8661 or 332–1478 after 8 PM. Open daily 9–8.*

Swiss Travel, in the Hotel Chalet Suizo (*see* Where To Sleep, *below*), can arrange volcano and river expeditions, trips to highland markets, and tours to the Petén. These bilingual tours cost about $35 for one day and $120 for two days, and their Mixco Viejo ruins tour (*see* Near Guatemala City, *below*) is much less jarring to your nerves than taking public transportation. You can also purchase plane tickets to Flores here. *14a Calle 6–82, Z1, tel. 253–2342 or 251–3786. Open daily 9–1.*

COMING AND GOING

If you're traveling in Guatemala, you'll probably have to pass through Guatemala City at some point. The Pan-American Highway runs right through, so you can easily zip in and out if you choose. Hitching is dangerous and difficult but also unnecessary, because buses run so frequently that all you have to do is stand at the side of the road and wave desperately and you'll get picked up.

BY BUS

City buses to destinations around Guatemala City leave from the **bus terminal** in Zona 4. To get to the terminal from Zona 1, take any bus marked TERMINAL. Watch for pickpockets in and around the terminal. For longer distances, each region of the country is served by a different bus company (*see below*), and buses depart from the company's office. Most long-distance buses don't cross borders, but you can easily transfer and continue into Mexico, El Salvador, or Belize. Keep in mind that bus robberies are not uncommon. Keep your pack in sight when possible, carry traveler's checks instead of cash, choose direct buses to the Petén, and never, never travel at night.

TO/FROM THE NORTHWEST • **Transportes Unidos** (15a Calle 3–75, Z1, tel. 232–4949) goes to Antigua Guatemala (1 hr, 50¢) every half hour between 8 AM and 6:30 PM daily. **Veloz Quichelese** (20a Calle, at Av. Bolívar, Z1) stops in Chimaltenango on the way to Chichicastenango (3½ hrs, $2). Buses leave every half hour between 5 AM and 6 PM daily. **Rebulli** (21a Calle 1–34, Z1, tel. 251–3521) leaves hourly every day from 5 AM to 4 PM for Panajachel (4 hrs, $1.75). **Transportes Galgos** (7a Av. 19–44, Z1, tel. 232–3661) serves Quetzaltenango (4 hrs, $3), with buses daily at 5:30 AM, 8:30 AM, 11 AM, 2:30 PM, 5 PM, and 7 PM. Galgos also has connections to Mexico.

TO/FROM THE SOUTH • **Cubanita** leaves from the Zona 4 bus terminal three times daily for Monterrico (5 hrs, $2). **Melva Internacional** (3a Av. 1–38, Z9, tel. 331–0874) heads to San Salvador (5 hrs, $6) once an hour from 5:30 AM to 4:30 PM every day. For faster, more comfortable service, try **Tica Bus** (11a Calle 2–72, Z9, tel. 331–4279), which leaves for San Salvador (4½ hrs, $9) daily at 12:30 PM.

Be sure to pick up a map at the front desk of Hotel Chalet Suizo. It's one of the best you'll find of Guatemala City—even the tourist office uses it.

TO/FROM THE PETÉN • You'll need to reserve a seat for **Fuentes del Norte** (17a Calle 8–46, Z1, tel. 251–3817), which heads to Flores/Santa Elena (about 14 hrs, $8) at 7:30 AM, 11 AM, noon, 1 PM, 3 PM, and 5 PM. Do yourself a big favor and choose the faster direct service (about 11 hrs, $11).

TO/FROM THE EAST • **Escobar/Monja Blanca** (8a Av. 15–16, Z1, tel. 238–1409) leaves daily about every hour from 4 AM to 5 PM for Cobán and the Biotopo del Quetzal (4 hrs, $4). **Litegua** (15a Calle 10–42, Z1, tel. 232–7578) runs comfy buses to Puerto Barrios (6 hrs, $6) hourly every day between 6 AM and 5 PM.

BY PLANE

In Zona 13, **La Aurora International Airport** (tel. 332–6084) services all domestic and international flights. The airport's **INGUAT** office is open daily 7 AM–8 PM, and **Banco del Quetzal** is open weekdays 7 AM–8 PM and weekends 8–6. **TELGUA** is on the second floor. The car-rental agencies **Avis** (tel. 331–0017), **Budget** (tel. 331–0273), **Dollar** (tel. 331–7185), and **Hertz** (tel. 331–1171) also have offices in the airport. **American** (tel. 334–7379), **Continental** (tel. 335–3341), **Lacsa** (tel. 331–8222), **Mexicana** (tel. 333–6001), **TACA** (tel. 334–7722), and **United** (tel. 332–2995) have counters in the airport. **Aviateca** (10a Calle 6–20, Z1, tel. 332–7722), **Aerovías** (Av. Hincapié, 18a Calle, Z13, tel. 331–9663), and **Tapsa** (Av. Hincapié, Hangar 14 at the airport, tel. 331–9180) are domestic airlines that fly to and from Flores. Don't forget to save cash for the departure tax—$15 for international flights, $5 for domestic trips—or you may end up staying longer than you planned.

AIRPORT TRANSPORTATION • The cheapest way to get to the airport from Zona 1 is to take either Bus 5 from 4a Avenida or Bus 83 from 10a Avenida. Make sure that the sign in the front window says AEROPUERTO and allow at least half an hour to get there. Leaving the airport, take either Bus 5 or Bus 83 from just outside the terminal to Zona 1. If you have a departure or arrival before 6 AM or after 9 PM, you'll have to take a taxi, because the buses do not run outside those times. You should also consider a taxi if you have lots of luggage—it's easier and more secure. INGUAT publishes an official list of authorized fares between the airport and various locations in the city, so ask at the INGUAT counter before leaving the terminal. A taxi ride from the airport to the budget hotels of Zona 1 with up to four passengers costs about $7 (40 quetzales), while $25 (150 quetzales) will get you to Antigua Guatemala. Taxis aren't allowed to charge more than these fares, but you might try to barter for less. Your driver will expect a tip: offer about 5 quetzales for each passenger with luggage.

GETTING AROUND

The capital has the same basic plan as all other Guatemalan cities—numbered *calles* (streets) and *avenidas* (avenues) radiate from a central plaza to the different parts of town. Here, as in other larger

ZONE IN ON GUAT CITY

In large cities like Guatemala City, the grid system of avenidas and calles gets kinda wacky, so cities are divided one step further into zonas (zones). Because Guatemala City has 21 zonas, you absolutely have to know the zone in which your address is located. Even a taxi driver can't find the corner of 5a Avenida and 7 Calle because 21 corners in the city have that exact address. You'll probably spend most of your time in the zonas listed below.

Zona 1 is a crowded tangle of beggars, street vendors, shops, restaurants, and budget accommodations. The Palacio Nacional, Mercado Central, Catedral Metropolitana, Plaza Mayor, and Parque Concordia are all here. At night, avoid 18a Calle and the red-light district on 9a Avenida between 12a and 20a calles.

Zona 2 is the place to go if maps turn you on. Take Bus 45 or 46 to the Mapa En Relieve, a relief map that shows the country at a scale of 1:10,000. It's the only point of (questionable) interest in Zona 2.

Zona 4 is where you'll find INGUAT, the local bus terminal, the National Theater, and the main food market.

Zona 7 basically makes up the burbs of Guat City. Here you'll stumble upon a few grassy hills that are the ruins of Kaminal Juyú, an extremely important but sadly neglected Mayan Center. If you want to go picnicking, check out these few blocks of greenery.

Zona 9 is the home of the Popul Vuh Museum. You can recognize Zona 9 by the huge Torre del Reformador, a bad imitation of the Eiffel Tower on 12a Calle at 7a Avenida.

Zona 10 is where you'll find the American and Canadian embassies and the new Museo Ixchel. Zona 10 is also known as "La Zona Viva" (the Live Zone) for the upscale bars and discotheques where the rich have their fun. Big open spaces, immense mansions, and the occasional carjacking characterize this zone.

Zona 13 is dominated by the Parque Aurora, which combines a military base, a zoo, three national museums, and the international airport.

cities, these gridded sections are divided into several zones (see box). If you can master this system in Guatemala City, with 21 zones of up to 30 calles and avenidas each, you'll instantly be able to find any address in any major Guatemalan city (but there's no money-back guarantee).

BY BUS

By far the most entertaining and economical way to see Guatemala City is through the dirt-coated windows of a public bus. Doors of Guatemalan buses are literally always open. Your best bet is to wait on a street corner and hope that the bus you want hits a red light. Or, when you see it barreling down the street, stick out your hand, with an optional whistle or hiss, and the driver will stop as soon as he can. Fares to anywhere within the city are 10¢. Buy tickets from the attendant on board; just take a seat and he'll come around. Remember to watch out for pickpockets.

Infinite routes snake through the city, and each bus has its own peculiar variation, but the routes listed below should get you just about anywhere you'll want to go in the city. To be sure of a particular bus's destination, check the sign in the lower left corner of the front window.

Bus 17 will take you from 4a Avenida in Zona 1 to Zona 7 and the ruins of Kaminal Juyú. Be sure to look for the sign in the window, because not all buses numbered 17 pass the ruins.

Buses 45 and **46** go from 5a Avenida in Zona 1 to the Mapa En Relieve in Zona 2.

Bus 82 passes by INGUAT and Zona 4 on its way from 10a Avenida in Zona 1 to Avenida La Reforma in Zonas 9 and 10.

Bus 83 also passes through Zona 4, but heads to and from Zona 13's Parque Aurora, stopping at the airport and zoo.

BY CAR

Parking and traffic are such a nightmare in Guatemala City that it's not always worth it to have your own wheels. If you do, park in a guarded parking lot or garage near the city center (look for a sign with a big "E" for *estacionamiento*). You can rent a car for $60–$90 per day (including insurance) at the airport or at one of numerous rental agencies. Remember that you will need a four-wheel-drive if you're headed into the backcountry. **Avis** (12a Calle 2–73, Z9, tel. 331–2750), **Budget** (Av. La Reforma 15–00, Z9, tel. 331–6546), and **Tabarini** (2a Calle A 7–30, Z10, tel. 331–9814) are just a few of the many agencies in Zonas 9 and 10. **Dollar** (6a Av. A 10–13, Z1, tel. 232–3446) has the advantage of its convenient location in the lobby of Zona 1's Hotel Ritz.

The best lunch deal at basic restaurants is the "menú del día" (menu of the day). It usually includes bread, soup, salad, beans, rice, a simple main dish, a drink, coffee, and dessert for about $2.

BY TAXI

You can catch taxis on most streets or in Zona 1 at Plaza Mayor and Parque Concordia or in Zona 4 at the bus terminal. Most city rides cost at least $4, but you should always agree on a price before jumping in. Metered cabs cost less, but they only come when you call first (tel. 332–1515).

BY FOOT

To get a mouthful and eyeful of smoggy Zona 1, you absolutely have to walk. Grab your most comfortable shoes and join the throngs of people on 5a and 6a avenidas, south from Plaza Mayor. The crowded streets are overflowing with fruit stands, blue jeans for sale, watches, weavings, pornography, and plastic toys. Above all, watch your belongings: lots of poor people with nothing may want your somethings. No one, especially women, should go out alone at night. The streets are desolate after dark for a reason: they are *muy peligroso* (very dangerous).

WHERE TO SLEEP

All hotels must register their prices with INGUAT, and they should have their approved rates posted in quetzales or U.S. dollars. Many of the cheapest digs have only double rooms, which they'll usually offer to a single traveler for a lower price. Get the most for your quetzales by getting a room as far above and away from the busy, noisy streets as possible. Zona 1 is the place to look for budget hotels, especially on and around 9a Avenida in the heart of the red-light district. Although you'll share the neighborhood with prostitutes, beggars, and thieves, it's jammed with restaurants, stores, and nonstop action. It's not a good idea to come here at night on your own, especially if you're a woman. On the other end of the spectrum, the towering hotels (and towering prices) of Zonas 9 and 10 might be worth checking into if you want to soak your feet and watch TV. All hotels in Guatemala City are most crowded at the end of December, in August, and during Semana Santa. Because of Guatemala's high inflation rate, the prices of all types of accommodations continue to rise, especially in the capital.

UNDER $10 • Hotel San Diego. The staff may not be the friendliest in Central America, but the clean bathrooms, hot water, and fairly clean sheets make up for their lack of social skills. A real bargain at $4.75 a double ($8 with private bath). *15a Calle 7–37, Z1, tel. 232–2958. 25 rooms, 14 with bath. Cash only.*

UNDER $15 • Hotel Ajau. This basic hotel is built in the Spanish style, with an interior courtyard and three floors of balconied rooms. The rooms ($9) are clean and have tile floors and a few pieces of cheap wooden furniture; those with bath ($14) also have cable TV. Rooms facing away from the street are quieter. *8a Avenida 15-62, Z1, tel. 232–0488. 38 rooms, 19 with bath. Cash only.*

Hotel Belmont. Rooms are dark and dingy, but the place is brightened by abundant plant life in the hallways. Rooms near the back of the hotel are very quiet. The sweet maid may ask you if you know her relatives in New York City—no matter where you're from. Doubles are $8, $8.50 with bath. *9a Av. 15–30, Z1, tel. 251–1541. 64 rooms, 25 with bath. Cash only.*

Hotel España. This place is simple but clean, and they provide fresh towels daily and there's actually toilet paper in the bathrooms. In the central lounge you can watch TV or schmooze with other guests. Avoid getting a room near the street—it's a major bus route. Doubles without bath are $9, with bath $11. *9a Av. 15–59, Z1, tel. 230–0502. 82 rooms, 10 with bath. Laundry. Cash only.*

Hotel Fuente. Rooms here are large but musty. Get one with a private bath to avoid the perennially backed-up and seatless toilets of the communal bathrooms. Hot water is provided by an electric heater attached to the showerhead (after all those years of making sure not to bring your hair dryer in the bathtub . . .) Padlocks secure the doors, but for extra safety consider bringing your own. Next to the Galgos bus station, this is the place to crash if you've got an early morning bus to Quetzaltenango or the Mexican border. *7a Av. 20–16, Z1, tel. 232–3723. 8 rooms with bath. Cash only.*

Pensión Mesa. Known affectionately to many backpackers as "the mesa," this hotel has a very youth-hostelish atmosphere and is a great place to meet young travelers. Join a game at the Ping-Pong table or check out the bulletin board listing everything from dentists to jungle excursions to personal messages. It's not the cleanest pensión in the world, but beds come pretty cheap—$6 for a double with one bed, $7.50 with two beds, or $2.50 for a bed in a dorm. *10a Calle 10–17, Z1, tel. 232–3177. 27 rooms, 1 with bath. Cash only.*

UNDER $20 • Hotel Capri. Although rooms are small, musty, and plain, the TV lounge has comfy couches and a social atmosphere. The luggage storage looks especially safe—it's in a locked room near the front desk. Get a room away from the street to escape the heavy-duty bus noise; rooms near the top floor offer a view of the city. Doubles are $10, $16 with bath. *9a Av. 15–63, Z1, tel. 232–8191. 63 rooms, 58 with bath. Laundry.*

Hotel Centroamérica. This hotel seems out of place on seedy 9a Avenida. Guests are greeted with a mint on the pillow, free shampoo, and wonderfully clean towels. Rooms are spotless and bright, and most face onto a central corridor with fountains and hanging ferns. Doubles are $14, $17 with bath. Sanitary napkins, aspirin, Band-Aids, and other last-minute necessities are theoretically available from the dusty cabinet by the front desk. *9a Av. 16–38, Z1, tel. 232–6917. 52 rooms, 22 with bath. Laundry.*

Hotel Chalet Suizo. This place has the cleanest bathrooms of any hotel in Central America, no contest. The staff is extremely friendly and can give advice about everything in Guatemala. The hotel's quiet courtyard, café, and recently opened travel agency (*see Basics, above*) are other pluses. Doubles are $18, $30 with bath. *14a Calle 6–82, Z1, tel. 251–3786. 47 rooms, 26 with bath.*

Hotel Lessing House. Several blocks from Plaza Mayor, this hotel has fairly clean rooms decorated with hand-woven textiles. Rooms to the left as you walk in have windows and are brighter than those across the hall. Doubles with bath are $14. *12a Calle 4–35, Z1, tel. 251–3891. 8 rooms with bath. Laundry.*

Hotel Spring. Most rooms open onto a bright and comfortable central patio, where tons of greenery and plenty of tables and chairs await you for lounging, reading, writing, or chatting. The small kitchen serves breakfast and lunch at moderate prices ($1–$2), and you can buy expensive soft drinks and beer at the front desk. Hot water in the downstairs units is unpredictable, but it's a good place to meet people. Reservations are recommended because it's always packed with Peace Corps volunteers. Plain doubles are $14, $19 with bath. *8a Av. 12–65, Z1, tel. 232–6637. 27 rooms, 16 with bath.*

UNDER $45 • Fortuna Royal. Somehow the Fortuna pulls off the trick of combining American-style comfort and decent prices in the middle of grimy Guate. Comforts include marble floors in the lobby, and wall-to-wall carpeting and floral wallpaper in the rooms, all of which are spotless and have phones and cable TV. A tip: prices are lower if you don't need a receipt. *12 Calle 8–42, Z1, tel. 251–7887. 20 rooms with bath. Restaurant.*

Poseda Belem. This little bed-and-breakfast on a quiet side street is run by a warm, friendly couple. The 1873 building is the family's former home. Rooms have tile floors, walls decorated with Guatemalan paintings and weavings, and modern private baths. The owners are a font of info and will help you make travel arrangements. *13a Calle 10–30, Z1, tel. 232–9226. 10 rooms with bath.*

FOOD

Guatemala City is full of international restaurants and fast-food joints. The cheapest comida típica can be found at street vendors or in the grimy comedores in the Mercado Central, but unless you have bowels of steel, it's better to eat in restaurants to avoid a nasty case of the runs. The majority of restaurants are in Zona 1's commercial district, just south of Plaza Mayor on 5a and 6a avenidas. The variety is not great, but you'll get more for your dollar than in other Central Amnerican cities. **Pollo Campero,** Guatemala's KFC, offers greasy and good three-piece chicken dinners for about $3, including coffee, salad, a drink, and fries. They have two branches in Zona 1, including one on 5a Avenida near Plaza Mayor and another just across from Parque Concordia on 6a Avenida and 14a Calle. For wonderful fresh fruits and vegetables, go to the **central food market** in Zona 4 (*see* Shopping, *below*).

UNDER $5 • El Mesón de Don Quijote. A colorful restaurant in the heart of the old city, Don Quijote serves respectable northern Spanish cuisine—from Asturias to be precise—at moderate prices. It's a favorite late-night spot (open until 2 AM) of Guatemalan old-timers. The restaurant has a long bar and several adjacent dining rooms, and live music is played at night under a flashy painting of a flamenco dancer. The large menu is filled with such palate pleasers as seafood casserole, cold cuts of Spanish hams, lentils with sausage, baked lamb, and paella (for four people or more). On weekdays, a four-course executive lunch can't be beat. *11 Calle 5–27, Z1, tel. 253–4929. Closed Sun.*

American fast-food joints are so popular with well-to-do Guatemalans that security guards have to let you in the jam-packed eateries. A burger and fries costs twice a rural worker's daily wage ($4).

Frutti Licuados. This squeaky-clean white-tiled restaurant has plastic-covered chairs and tables—the whole package may remind you of a hospital cafeteria. Boost your immune system with a healthy fruit shake (80¢) or try a tasty vegetarian meal for less than $3, like a veggie burger ($1) or chili rellenos stuffed with rice and vegetables (70¢). *11a Calle 7–60, Z1, no phone.*

Fu Lu Sho. This is one Chinese restaurant in Guatemala that's discovered there is more to Chinese food than rice and bean sprouts. The *carne de res con jengibre* (beef with ginger; $2.50) and the huge plate of *camarón chow mein* (shrimp chow mein; $3.50) taste like they came straight out of China. The portions are gargantuan; you should starve yourself for a few hours ahead of time if you plan to clean your plate. Don't confuse this place with Fu Sun Lo, a mediocre Chinese joint nearby. *6a Av. 12–09, Z1, tel. 232–3456.*

Restaurante Capri. Right next to Hotel Capri on 9a Avenida, this is yet another place to enjoy comida típica. The menú del dia is only slightly more expensive than at other spots, and it's much better, with juicy chicken and chunky vegetable soup. Also tasty is a meal of *plátanos fritos* (fried bananas), eggs, beans, and coffee for $2.50. *9a Av. 15–63, Z1, tel. 511–062.*

Restaurant Piccadilly. If you're craving Italian delights, load up on lasagna ($2.50), tortellini ($2.50), or one of Piccadilly's tasty pizzas. At the full-service bar downstairs you can get toasted for pretty cheap. *6a Av. 11–01, Z1, tel. 251–4268.*

UNDER $10 • Delicadesas Hamburgo. The atmosphere and food is reminiscent of a small-town U.S. diner. Steaks, shish kebabs, and chicken all go for about $8. This is the place to chow down on a mongo breakfast ($4) or a late-night ice cream ($2). Sit near the window to watch the nonstop action across the street in Parque Concordia. *15a Calle 5–34, Z1, tel. 238–1627. Across the street from Parque Concordia to the south.*

El Gran Pavo. Right between Plaza Mayor and Parque Concordia, this brightly colored restaurant serves authentic food from various regions of Mexico. Try one of the seafood dishes typical of Veracruz or Yucatecan fare for about $8 a plate. The enchiladas verdes ($3) or one of a number of soups ($3) will satisfy a smaller appetite, while excellent larger meals cost about $5–$8 a plate. *13a Calle 4–41, Z1, tel. 251–0933.*

Los Cebollines. A wide selection of delicious Mexican food is the attraction at Los Cebollines, one of the best restaurants in Ciudad Vieja. Two menus are available: a drinks menu that includes cocktails, Mexican beers, and sangria; and a food menu that lists traditional tacos, burritos, fajitas, and, less predictably, *caldo tlalpeno de pollo* (a chicken stew with chickpeas and avocado). *6 Avenida 9–75, Z1, tel. 232–7750; 1 Avenida 13–42, Z10, tel. 368–0663.*

DESSERT/COFFEEHOUSES

Guatemala City's "Zona Viva" is overrun with cosmopolitan (read, expensive) cafés where the affluent repose in style. If you happen to be in the neighborhood and feel like playing high society, **Nais** (1a Av. 2–47, Z10, tel. 232–6705) is a snazzy patio café with green-and-white awnings, glass tables, and excellent coffee. Accompany one of their devilish desserts with an espresso ($1) or a cappuccino ($1.50), or try the cheese fondue ($5) with crisp breadsticks. Don't worry, the waiters are too refined to let on that they're painfully aware of your grungy travel attire. Although Zona 1 cafés lack the artful pseudo-European coffee drinks, they're good places to hang out like a normal person.

Cafetería y Pastelería Royal. This place is spacious and inviting, perfect for a chat. You can't leave without trying one of the delicious pastries—check out the strawberry shortcake, Black Forest cake, or chocolate cream pie for less than 75¢, coffee included. *7a Av. 20–80, Z1, tel. 232–4223.*

Pastelería Lutecia. Tasty pastries and hot fresh-brewed coffee welcome the footsore traveler in need of respite from the city's chaotic and noisy streets. *11a Calle 4–40, Z1, no phone.*

Restaurant y Panadería Maxipán. The moment you step out of smoggy Zona 1 and into this breezy oasis, you're really going to feel bad that you snickered at its name. Relax and have a cup of Guatemalan coffee (40¢) while black-and-white-clad waiters cater to your every whim. *6a Av. 15–22, ½ block from Parque Concordia, Z1, tel. 253–4488.*

WORTH SEEING

As you've probably already gathered, Guatemala City is not somewhere you want to spend too much time. But since you're here you might as well check out the city's tossed salad of curiosities, ranging from Zona 1's bright pink post office to the Kaminal Juyú in Zona 7 (although it looks more like a vacant lot than a major archaeological site).

PLAZA MAYOR

This large plaza in Zona 1 is divided into two parks by 6a Avenida. To the east (toward the Catedral Metropolitana) is the Parque Central and to the west is Parque Centenario, which has a huge amphitheater. By far the most interesting time to visit the park is Sunday 8–6, when brightly clad indígena women sell *huipiles* (traditional woven or embroidered blouses) and *cortes* (woven wraparound skirts) from all parts of the country. You may also catch a third-rate salsa singer or a children's chorus in the amphitheater on the west side plaza. *Between 5a and 7a Avs., 6a and 8a calles, Z1.*

CATEDRAL METROPOLITANA

Built between 1782 and 1809, this cathedral is one of the few colonial buildings in Guatemala City that has survived the area's myriad earthquakes. It has suffered considerable damage, though, and the walls are riddled with cracks, making the interior look centuries older than it really is. For 5¢ you can buy a votive candle to place in front of your favorite saint. Sunday masses are every two hours from 8 to 4, but if you want to explore the church, it's better not to come when mass is in session. *Between 7a and 8a Avs., 6a and 8a calles, on the east side of Plaza Mayor, Z1. Open daily 9–6.*

PALACIO NACIONAL

The imposing National Palace was built between 1939 and 1943 under the orders of the egotistical president Jorge Ubico Castañeda. After you get frisked and your bag is searched, you can wander at your leisure through the compound's lush vegetation and around the impressive fountains. Find a guide near the top of the stairs on the second floor for access to the **Salón de Recepción,** an opulent ballroom with a Bohemian crystal chandelier and a giant Guatemalan coat of arms that has a real stuffed quetzal. The Regional Telecommunications Center on the second floor near the back was reputedly the headquarters for organizing and directing the assassinations and "disappearances" of key political figures since 1966. *6a Calle, on the north side of Plaza Mayor, Z1. Admission free. Open weekdays 8–4:30, Sat. 8–noon.*

A DEADLY VANISHING ACT

The term "desaparecidos" (the disappeared ones) refers to the many victims of ruthless counterinsurgency programs all over Latin America. In an effort to eliminate all traces of guerrilla activity, anyone under suspicion was kidnapped—that is, "disappeared"—under cover of darkness and whisked off to a distant outpost for torture and interrogation. Over the past 25 years, literally tens of thousands of Guatemalans (mostly poor and indigenous) have "been disappeared." Because the victims are not officially listed as dead, families cannot inherit their property. As a result, countless indígena women and children flock to Guatemala City to sell their labor—and often their bodies. The traditional lives of the Maya are quickly being swept away as widows of desaparecidos leave their looms for a grueling and alienating life in the city.

In a letter (smuggled out of an army prison in 1984) to his wife, a desaparecido captured the horror and tragedy of Guatemala's political situation: "I am on the brink of life and death because they accuse me of being a guerrilla. I am not the first or the last such case in this world; after a while you come to realize anything can happen. I am very sad because I only think of death, and the mother I will never hug again. A kiss for them all. Please face life like a real woman. You are not the first woman in the world to become a widow. Goodbye forever." (Excerpted from "Guatemala: Eternal Spring, Eternal Tyranny" by Jean-Marie Simon, published by W.W. Norton, 1987.)

CENTRO CULTURAL MIGUEL ANGEL ASUTRIAS

This cluster of buildings is dominated by the futuristic **Teatro Nacional.** A number of military police guard the periphery, and one will take you to the top and show you inside the theater for a "voluntary" tip of 1 or 2 quetzales. The top of the theater offers a fantastic view of the sprawling city. A short walk through a cement park will take you to the **Teatro del Aire Libre,** an open-air theater. Sitting in the bleachers of this military amphitheater, it's easy to imagine camouflaged guards in the round gun turrets guarding the dictator of your choice as he shouts proclamations from center stage. Leaving the theater through the main parking lot to the right, you descend from this playground of the rich and powerful to a vomit-stained alley housing the desperately poor—yet another reminder of the capital's rich/poor dichotomy. *Take any bus marked* TERMINAL *to Zona 4 and make your way up the hill to the funky blue and white Teatro.*

IGLESIA YURRITA (NUESTRA SENORA DE LA ANGUSTIAS)

One of the wildest buildings in Guatemala City, this overly ornate church with bizarre stained-glass windows and weird carvings looks like somewhere the Addams Family would go for Sunday mass. The church and the adjoining colonial home were built by the wealthy Yurrita family in the mid-19th century. If you're lucky enough to get in, you may be able to see the carved-wood interior. Try at 8:30 AM or at 4:30 PM, when the priest opens the gates to let people in for mass (if he's in the mood). *Ruta 6, between 7a Av. and Av. La Reforma, Z9. Take Bus 82.*

MUSEO POPUL VUH

This private museum of ancient Mayan and colonial-era artifacts has a new home at the University of San Carlos. You'll find Mayan pottery, dusty colonial costumes, and a copy of the *Dresden Codex*, an ancient Mayan book that helped scholars to decipher the writing system of the ancient Maya. At the entrance, buy the guidebook ($1) that explains all the pieces on display. The small library is open to anyone who wishes to study the ancient Maya in depth. *Universidad Francisco Marroquín, end of 6a Calle, Z10, tel. 334–7121. Take Bus 82 or 102 to Av. La Reforma, get off at the U.S. Embassy, and walk 6 blocks east. Admission $1.75. Open weekdays 8–6, Sat. 9–1.*

MUSEO IXCHEL

This private museum takes its name from the goddess of the moon and weaving, and it's devoted to cataloging and preserving the weaving traditions of Guatemala. The collection is small but well presented, and the various native textile and weaving techniques are explained by signs in both English and Spanish. *Universidad Francisco Marroquín, end of 6a Calle, Z10, tel. 331–3739. Take Bus 82 or 102 to Av. La Reforma, get off at the U.S. Embassy, and walk 6 blocks east. Admission $1.75. Open weekdays 8–6, Sat. 9–1.*

MUSEO NACIONAL DE ARQUEOLOGIA Y ETNOLOGIA

If you have limited time in the city, come here: it's better than Ixchel and Popul Vuh combined. According to one of the few employees who take care of the massive collection, this museum is "perhaps as popular as Tikal itself." Because it's state-run, it lacks the fancy brochures and gift shops of the private museums, but most of the amazing artifacts are presented in a logical order. The first part of the museum traces Mayan archaeological history through the Preclassic, Classic, and Postclassic periods. Some of the collection's many highlights include an intricately carved human skull, a replica of a wood lintel from Tikal, and some of the most famous stelae (upright engraved stone slabs) in the Mayan world. Also extra special is a vault filled with jade masks, jewelry, and a reconstructed grave site of a Mayan ruler. The pieces basically speak for themselves, but try to stay within earshot of vacationers with a professional guide to learn even more. The second part of the museum focuses on modern Guatemalan ethnology. The fairly complete display of men's and women's costumes from different villages is complemented by a map showing the location of each village. *Salón 5, Finca La Aurora, Z13, tel. 472–0489. Take any bus with a sign in the lower left corner reading AEROPUERTO or LA AURORA to the large pink colonial building just south of the National Zoo. Admission 20¢. Open Tues.–Fri. 9–4.*

MUSEO NACIONAL DE HISTORIA NATURAL

For the most part all you'll see is a collection of mangy stuffed mammals and birds in dusty glass cases in this natural history museum. Turn to the left when you enter and look at the diorama of the quetzal (Guatemala's national bird and currency namesake) on the far wall. For a 50¢ "donation," someone at the front desk will take you to a small room filled with enough live poisonous snakes to kill an elephant. Gila monsters (stout, poisonous lizards) saunter around the room—you can even pet one—and a number of velvety tarantulas paw the glass of their small terrariums. The security guard, Isai, may even play a request on the guitar while you view the vipers. *In Finca La Aurora, Z13. Take any bus marked AEROPUERTO or LA AURORA to the Museo de Arqueología y Etnología; the museum is across the street and to the south. Open Tues.–Fri. 9–4.*

CHEAP THRILLS

Sizzling comedores dot the periphery of grimy Parque Concordia, between 5a and 6a avenidas and 14 and 15a calles in Zona 1. You can sit and watch the preachers, magicians, tin-pan musicians, and fortune-tellers that make this park a happenin' spot. At night it becomes even seedier than during the day and you should avoid it.

FESTIVALS

On August 15, Guatemala City celebrates the feast day of its patron saint, the **Virgen de La Asunción.** A special mass is held in churches all over the city and there is a fair in the Hipódromo del Norte with games for children and raffles. Both Semana Santa and the days near Christmas are busy, fiesta-filled times in the capital as in the rest of Guatemala.

SHOPPING

Guatemala City is the place to buy anything and everything you may have left at home. Most stores are closed on Sunday. Listed below are some of the best (and cheapest) places to buy traditional and other goodies.

MAIN FOOD MARKET

This huge warehouse, near the bus terminal in Zona 4, is piled high with familiar and exotic fruits of all shapes and sizes. You'll probably be the only gringo pushing your way through the hordes of shoppers. Remember to buy only fruits you can peel—melons, mangoes, bananas—or risk the consequences! You'll also see rows upon rows of new and old leather shoes, religious paraphernalia, and witchcraft items like love potions, blessed elixirs, and copal, the sacred incense used by the Maya. Be sure to visit the statue of the Virgin, whose presence blesses each sale, in the center of the marketplace. *Diagonal 2 between 5a and 6a Avs., Z4. Take any bus marked* TERMINAL *to the end of the line, look for the large yellow and blue warehouse north of the bus terminal.*

MERCADO CENTRAL

This cement box looks more like a parking garage than a market, but once inside, you'll be ducking through narrow hallways bursting with *artesanía* like woven backpacks, leather, and silver, right beside more Grateful Dead clothing than you could ever want. Prices here are sometimes 50% cheaper (before bargaining) than in Antigua Guatemala and Chichicastenango. Downstairs is a large market selling basketry, dried goods (here's where you can buy that famous Guatemalan coffee), meats (you'll know 'em when you smell 'em), and fruits. *Between 7a and 9a Av., behind the Catedral Metropolitana, Z1. Open Mon.–Sat. 6–6, Sun. 9–noon.*

If you lose your luggage, or just need that extra jacket, sweater, or raincoat, Ropa Americana stores sell high-quality secondhand clothing donated by the United States for 50¢ to $2 per piece.

AFTER DARK

Guatemala Weekly, the nation's main English-language newspaper, has an events calendar. You can pick one up at Hotel Spring or Hotel Chalet Suizo.

BARS

If you're heading to the *discotecas* in Zonas 9 and 10, you might want to grab a few cheap(er) drinks in Zona 1 before you go. Try one of the restaurants with full bar service in the center of town, such as **Picadilly** (6a Av. 11–01, Z1) or **Los Cebollines** (6a Av. 9–75, Z1). If you're looking to make an evening of it in Zona 1, try one of the following bars.

Bar Europa. This bar is one of the few places in Zona 1 where you'll feel right at home in the friendly and open atmosphere. The crowd is informal. You can eat a good meal for less than $5, or just hang out and nurse a beer at the bar. The bartender loves to talk with foreigners and might watch your baggage for free if you have to catch that odd afternoon flight and can't leave it in your hotel. *11a Calle 5–16, Z1, tel. 253–4929. Next to the large spiral driveway.*

El Encuentro. This bar is tucked away in an unmarked room on the top floor of a shopping mall in crowded Zona 1. Head here to relax and talk with *amigos de ambiente* (Central America's largely hidden gay population). Sip a drink and listen to soothing light-rock hits by Karen Carpenter and Barbra Streisand. The owner, Mario, speaks excellent English and if this is your gig, you'll find him an invaluable source of information. *Centro Capital, 5th level, Local 321, 6a Av. between 11a and 12a calles, Z1. Upstairs on the left side of the mall, toward the movie theater. Listen for music coming from a doorway with a Chinese screen.*

El Mesón de Don Quixote. Full bar service and live music in an Andalusian setting, complete with pictures of Spanish ships, the spirit of Don Quixote on a horse, and red stripes everywhere. Come here for the atmosphere but not for cheap prices. *11a Calle 5–27, Z1, tel. 253–4929.*

CLUBS

To escape the dirty old men who plague the nightspots in Zona 1, boogie on down to La Zona Viva in Zona 10. Most clubs are clustered around the luxurious **Camino Real Hotel** (Av. La Reforma and 15a

Calle, Z10). **El Jaguar** (tel. 333–4633), a disco within the hotel itself, offers your typical flashing colored lights, overpriced drinks, and crowded dance floor. Be prepared to shell out the bucks, at least by Guatemalan standards, since drinks are $4–$6 a pop. To make the most of your money, come on a Tuesday night, when the music is salsa caliente and the drinks are two for one until 10 PM.

At **Pandora's Box** you can get down with the capricious younger generation of amigos del ambiente.. Disco balls flash overhead as people pack the dance floor and rock out to the latest American pop hits. Your $6 cover charge gets you two tickets that you can exchange for any two drinks at the bar until 1 AM. The place usually keeps rocking until 3 AM. Live shows add to the party atmosphere. *Ruta 3, 3–08, Z4, tel. 332–2823. Open Fri.–Sat. 9 PM–3 AM, or until the place empties out.*

LIVE MUSIC

The traditional music of Guatemala is played on the marimba, a wood xylophone with an African name that Guatemalans insist they invented first. The **Mercado Central** often blasts marimba tunes.

La Bodegita del Centro. This laid-back joint was once a big ol' warehouse. Now, it's a superhip nightclub with a full bar downstairs and a music store on the second floor. Most importantly, it has live music Tuesday–Saturday 9 PM–1 AM, featuring everything from acoustic folk music to rock and roll. The cover charge is $4 on Fridays and Saturdays. *12a Calle 3–55, Z1, tel. 230–2976.*

NEAR GUATEMALA CITY

SAN PEDRO AND SAN JUAN SACATEPÉQUEZ

Although less than an hour's bus ride from the capital, the sister cities of San Pedro and San Juan Sacatepéquez remain far off the beaten gringo trail through the Western Highlands. If you come during the week, you're sure to stand out among the pigs, chickens, and women with huge baskets of goods balanced skillfully on their heads. The air rings with the guttural sounds of Cakchiquel, and you may be hard-pressed to find someone who speaks Spanish. San Pedro's market is smaller than the one in San Juan, but the town's quaint church and outrageous multicolored huipiles are worth a stopover. Both the market and the church are just down 4a Avenida from where the bus lets you off. The women of neighboring San Juan wear unique huipiles with bold geometric designs in lavender and yellow, embroidered on multicolored handwoven cloth. You'll see this kind of finery on sale at the indoor artisans' market, just across from the town's main plaza. Neither town has any lodging, but San Juan has a couple of food stands and comedores where you can grab a cheap meal.

COMING AND GOING • From Zona 1, take any bus marked TERMINAL to the Zona 4 terminal. From there, the bus marked SAN JUAN SAC passes through San Pedro (30 min, 25¢) before reaching San Juan (45 min, 30¢). The bus leaves every half hour from 6 AM to 7 PM daily.

MIXCO VIEJO

Perched on a plateau overlooking the secluded highlands north of Guatemala City, the sparkling temples and paved ball courts of Mixco Viejo (admission 20¢) are so beautifully restored they don't deserve the title "ruins." Here, more than 120 pyramids, palaces, and temples glisten with silvery mica, and from the top of any one you can peer off steep cliffs into cultivated fields far below. This dramatic city was once the capital of the Pocomam Maya, who occupied it until the Spanish broke up the party in 1542. The city is a formidable fortress, surrounded on three sides by sharp precipices, and is accessible only by a single causeway that winds steeply up a mountain on the north side. Pedro de Alvarado launched several full-frontal attacks in his attempts to conquer this city, but never succeeded. Unable to win the city fair and square, he wound up sneaking in a secret entrance and murdering all its inhabitants by night. Spared the moist heat and enveloping jungle of the Petén, the abandoned city remained largely intact. In fact, the largest part of its damage occurred during the earthquake of 1976. The Guatemalan government has put a tremendous amount of effort into Mixco Viejo's restoration and is committed to developing the site for tourism. For now, though, it remains a real bitch to get to. Just one daily bus braves the winding, unpaved road that passes the entrance to the ruins, and it doesn't return to Guatemala City until 3 AM. But anyone who dares to make the journey will be well rewarded: three roofed enclosures overlook the ruin and each has its own barbecue pit; you can camp for free.

COMING AND GOING • Although people will try to convince you otherwise, you do not want a bus for Mixco, which is basically a Guatemala City suburb. You want the bus to Pachalum ($1) that leaves the Zona 4 terminal around 9:30 AM—make *sure* it's the one that passes *las ruinas de Mixco Viejo*. You'll arrive at the ruins in the early afternoon and then you're on your own until 3 AM, when the bus returns to Guatemala City. If you don't want to wait around, you should try to flag down a passing car or truck a couple of hours before dark. If you wait too long, though, you might get stuck walking a long and lonely road. Make it to San Juan Sacatepéquez before 7 PM, and you can hop on one of the buses back to Guatemala City.

WESTERN HIGHLANDS

The Western Highlands contain one of the most intact indígena cultures in existence in Latin America. This beautiful land of mountains and volcanoes is home to the living Maya, whose ancestors settled here thousands of years ago. A large percentage of the indígena population continues to speak their own languages, including Cakchiquel, Mam, Tzutujil, and Quiché. Children learn Spanish in school, so most of the younger folks are bilingual. Some villages still follow the ancient 260-day Tzolkin Mayan calendar, and ashes and melted candles from recent religious ceremonies can be found at Mayan ruins throughout the highlands. Most women still practice the old weaving arts, incorporating brilliant colors and elaborate depictions of animals, flowers, and abstract symbols into the cloth. For the all the richness of the indigenous culture, an assuredly colonial infrastructure is cemented into the highland lifestyle. Each village has it's whitewashed adobe church, and

From May to June, the market in San Juan Sacatepéquez sells "sanpopos de mayo," roasted giant ants with salt and lemon. Just a tip: remove the head and wings before you chow down.

local pagan customs were long discouraged by the Catholic Church. Now, the bizarre mix of Catholicism and ancient local practice is readily apparent in most highland towns. In Chichicastenango, indígena ceremonies unfold on the church steps. San Simón, the smoking and drinking saint, hears prayers and receives symbolic offerings from faithful believers, indígena and Ladinos alike.

Highland village life is, for the most part, a steady round of hard work and daily routine. That is, until market day, when villages explode with color and activity. Towns generally have one market a week, although some have two or three. Most villagers survive on subsistence farming, carting to market what little is left over. Entire families pack fruit, vegetables, weavings, and household goods onto their backs and truck the whole shebang to the village center. Market day is as much a social gathering as a shopping and selling spree. Activity starts in the wee, chilly morning hours. Bargaining and transactions are carried out in hushed, amicable tones. The momentum wanes around late afternoon as everyone crowds the buses to get home before the sun disappears. The only other time the towns are this happening is during the annual festival in honor of each town's patron saint. Added to the bustle of the market are Ferris wheels, carnival games, foosball tables, live music, dancing, and plenty of alcohol.

Highland markets were once a local affair, but in the past 10 years or so they began to attract international attention. The international market for Guatemalan textiles grows in leaps and bounds, and tourist demand for típico clothing has grown so great that villagers are literally willing to sell the clothes off their backs to make a buck. They then buy cheaper *ropa americana* (Western clothing) for themselves. Unfortunately, many of the finer points of the weaving tradition are being left by the wayside to accommodate the frenzied shoppers. The traditional back-strap loom is speedily being replaced with gleaming sewing machines so garments can be churned out faster to meet tourists' demands—the handmade, intricate huipiles sometimes take as long as six months to weave. The woven patterns once related personal info like marital status, the number of male children in a family, and what village the owner was from. But as the law of supply and demand came into effect, patterns began conforming more and more to gringo aesthetics. Despite the effects of tourism, you can still witness some symbols that speaks volumes about the culture: for example, if a woman's apron is finished with jagged edges, it means she is from the mountains.

This richly cultured land has a long history of conquest and repression. The Spanish colonists capitalized on fierce rivalries between the indigenous tribes to settle the heavily populated area. Today, the unobtrusive ruins of the Quiché capital of Utatlán lie fallow just outside the city of Santa Cruz del Quiché, and Zacaleu, the ancient Mam capital sits right by the predominantly Ladino city of Huehuetenango. The Spaniards constructed their own capital at Antigua Guatemala. Since independence, the government and military have been dominated by Ladinos. Throughout highland history, the indígena have been treated as second-class citizens.

Not surprisingly, much of the guerrilla activity from the 1970s until recently was centered in the highlands. Highland villages paid cruelly for their proximity to supposed rebel strongholds, whether or not they actually supported the rebel activities. During the "scorched earth" campaigns of the early 1980s, entire towns were burned to the ground and thousands of people were murdered and "disappeared" by paramilitary forces. The violence was designed to terrify the indigenous populations so they would be too afraid to assist the guerrillas with so much as a loaf of bread. And terrify them it did. Thousands fled into the mountains or across the border into Mexico, where many still live as refugees.

Political tensions and armed conflict flagged in the early part of this decade, but the anticipation of the November 1995 elections brought about a new uncertainty. The guerrillas increased their presence, occupying towns, barricading central plazas, giving antigovernment speeches and collecting food and supplies. Fortunately, the new military official line was to avoid confrontations with civilians. Since the 1996 peace treaty, it is generally safe to travel throughout the touristed highlands. This includes the Cuchumatán Mountains at least as far as Todos Santos Cuchumatán, and the Department of Quiché as far as Nebaj. The Ixil Triangle has also become relatively safe. Currently, several international organizations are working with returning refugee populations. Even in this new climate of reconciliation, it's always a good idea to stay abreast of the news if you'll be straying from the usual tourist trail.

On a map, the Western Highlands look like they're only a hop, skip, and a jump away from the capital. But the moment you begin your trek to the highlands, it feels like one hell of a journey. The air is remarkably cooler, and temperatures can drop to near freezing at night. At these high altitudes, however, you can also get burned to a crisp by the sun during the day. The rainy season begins in May and lasts until October, wreaking havoc on the already poor road conditions. With a good umbrella, a devil-may-care attitude about getting wet, and a lot of patience, you'll find the rain need not put a damper on your travels. The Pan-American Highway cuts north through the highlands until it reaches the border of Mexico. All buses travel this highway, and **Los Encuentros,** about two hours from the capital, and **Cuatro Caminos,** about five hours from the capital, are the two main pit stops along the way. Almost every bus traveling through the highlands will stop at one of these junctions to unload and collect passengers. Other roads are often unmarked and unpaved mountain switchbacks. Public buses are the cheapest and most convenient (if not the most comfortable) way to get around the highlands; if you're traveling on a budget, you'll get to know them all too well. They'll take you just about anywhere you'd want to go, miraculously covering roads you'd presume to be impassable. The downside is they're consistently slow, prone to breakdown, and almost always crammed to bursting with people who are packed in like livestock to make room for more passengers.

ANTIGUA GUATEMALA

Set in a valley surrounded by the looming (and sometimes spewing) Agua, Acatenango, and Fuego volcanoes, Antigua Guatemala was Guatemala's colonial capital from 1543 to 1773. In the mid-18th century it had a population of more than 50,000, a university, one of the first printing presses in the region, and a newspaper. All this collapsed in 1773, when two earthquakes severely damaged the town and the capital was moved to Guatemala City. The local government has taken great pains to preserve and restore the city's colonial charm—massive churches, restored colonial mansions, and crumbling ruins sit side by side along the cobblestone streets—while banning modern distractions like hanging signs and billboards. To ensure the safety of Antigua Guatemala's many tourists, a recent innovation has been introduced: a nonmilitary police force, called the "tourist police," patrols the streets during the day. Since its introduction, the effect has been amazing—Antigua Guatemala's streets are the picture of security during the day; but at night, the delinquents reemerge, and travelers, especially women, should be leery of walking alone.

Travelers and urbanites flock to Antigua Guatemala to relax in the small-town atmosphere. By Guatemalan standards, Antigua Guatemala is very amenable: hotels have plenty of hot water, and most bathrooms are stocked with toilet paper. The Semana Santa (Holy Week) celebrations are Antigua Guatemala's biggest event of the year. Thousands pour in from all over, and the area explodes with magnificent parades attended by purple-robed believers, red-clad "Roman soldiers," and dolorous women in black. The celebration begins on Palm Sunday and ends on Good Friday, but elaborate parades are held on several Sundays before Palm Sunday. Make reservations months in advance for Holy Week itself, because Antigua Guatemala is *the* tourist hotspot during that week.

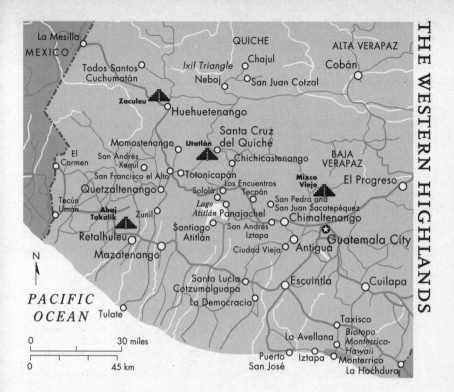

With respected language schools and hotels and restaurants, Antigua Guatemala is a popular meeting ground for travelers of all sorts. Semiresident students, retired Americans, wealthy Guatemalans, Ladinos, and indigenous people live together here, participating in a sort of cultural swap meet. Tourists dress in embroidered huipiles and carry colorful bags stuffed with Guatemalan trinkets, while indígenas can be seen in solid colors, blue jeans, and high heels. Antigua Guatemala's slow pace is occasionally overshadowed by bus loads of tourists: as the first stop on the gringo shopping trail, Antigua Guatemala is often mobbed by Westerners on an adrenaline rush from their first contact with indigenous people. It's also a good place to network and exchange tips with other travelers. After a few days, however, Antigua Guatemala may get a little too cozy.

BASICS

VISITOR INFORMATION • At **INGUAT** (Palacio de los Capitanes General, next to the police station; open daily 8–6), pick up a list of "approved" Spanish schools, a decent map, and a copy of the biweekly *Classifieds REVUE,* an English-language publication for residents and travelers. Also look at notice boards in many hotels and restaurants—the biggest and most widely read is at Doña Luisa Xicotencatl (*see* Food, *below*).

BOOKSTORES • Antigua Guatemala has a number of excellent bookstores with good collections in English. **Casa del Conde** (5a Av. Norte 4, west side of Plaza Mayor) has detailed maps and books on Antigua Guatemala and Mesoamerica in both English and Spanish. It's open Monday–Saturday 9–7, Sunday 10–7. A few doors down, **Un Poco de Todo** (5a Av. Norte 10A, tel. 832–0729) buys, sells, and trades used novels in English; it's open Monday–Saturday 9–6:30, Sunday 10–6. Other bookstores worth checking out are **Librería del Pensativo** (5a Av. Norte 29, tel. 832–5055) and **Casa Andinista** (4a Calle Oriente 5).

CHANGING MONEY • **Banco Agro** (4a Calle Poniente 8, north side of Plaza Mayor, tel. 832–0793) is open weekdays 9–6 and Saturday 1–6. At **Banco Industrial** (5a Av. Sur 4, tel. 832–0957) use ATM cards with the Plus system, or get a cash advance on your Visa card weekdays 8–7, Saturday 8–5.

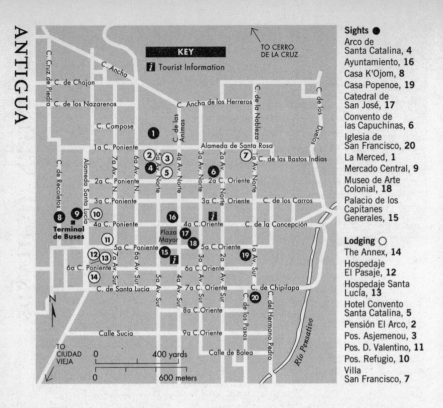

ANTIGUA

KEY

i Tourist Information

TO CERRO
DE LA CRUZ

C. Cruz de Piedra
C. de Chajon
C. Ancha
C. de los Nazarenos
C. Ancha de los Herreros
C. Compose
C. de las Ánimas
C. de la Nobleza
C. de los Duelos
1a C. Poniente
Alameda de Santa Rosa
4a Av. Norte
3a Av. Norte
2a Av. Norte
C. de los Bastos Indias
2a C. Poniente
7a Av. N.
6a Av. Norte
5a Av. Norte
C. de Recoletos
Alameda Santa Lucía
3a C.Poniente
2a C. Oriente
C. de los Carros
3a C. Oriente
Terminal
de Buses
4a C. Poniente
Plaza
Mayor
4a C.Oriente
C. de la Concepción
5a C. Poniente
5a C.Oriente
6a C. Poniente
6a C.Oriente
1a Av. Sur
C. de Santa Lucía
7a C. Oriente
C. de Chipilapa
5a Av. Sur
4a Av. Sur
3a Av. Sur
2a Av. Sur
8a C.Oriente
C. de los Pasos
C. del Hermano Pedro
N
Calle Sucia
9a C.Oriente
Río Pensativo
TO
CIUDAD
VIEJA
Calle de Balea
0   400 yards
0   600 meters

Sights ●
Arco de
Santa Catalina, **4**
Ayuntamiento, **16**
Casa K'Ojom, **8**
Casa Popenoe, **19**
Catedral de
San José, **17**
Convento de
las Capuchinas, **6**
Iglesia de
San Francisco, **20**
La Merced, **1**
Mercado Central, **9**
Museo de Arte
Colonial, **18**
Palacio de los
Capitanes
Generales, **15**

Lodging ○
The Annex, **14**
Hospedaje
El Pasaje, **12**
Hospedaje Santa
Lucía, **13**
Hotel Convento
Santa Catalina, **5**
Pensión El Arco, **2**
Pos. Asjemenou, **3**
Pos. D. Valentino, **11**
Pos. Refugio, **10**
Villa
San Francisco, **7**

EMERGENCIES • The **tourist police** are stationed in the Palacio de los Capitanes Generales on the south end of Plaza Mayor. The officers speak broken English at best, so bring a translator if your problem is serious and your Spanish is *muy mal*. **San Rafael Private Hospital** (Calle Ancha 7, tel. 832–0884, 832–0317, or 832–2785 in emergency) has 24-hour medical care. English and German are spoken at **Servicios Médicos de Sacatepéquez** (3a Av. Norte 1, behind cathedral, tel. 832–4134), a family medical practice that offers vaccines, adult medicine, gynecology, and obstetrics; it's open weekdays 8:30–12:30 and 2:30–4:30, Saturday 9–noon.

LANGUAGE SCHOOLS • Antigua Guatemala is known internationally for its Spanish-language schools, more than 30 of which are scattered throughout the city. For about $100 a week, most schools will give you one-on-one instruction plus room and board with an Antiguan family. Some families may house more than one student, which can be a serious deterrent to learning fluent Spanish. There's generally no need to sign up before arriving in Antigua Guatemala (it's best to check out a few schools when you get here to see what best suits you). Excellent unaffiliated teachers can also be found by checking the board at Doña Luisa Xicotencatl (*see* Food, *below*) or Café Opera (6a Av. Norte, at 2a Calle Poniente). One popular school is the **Centro Lingüístico Maya** (5a Calle Poniente 20, tel. and fax 832–0656). Slightly cheaper is **Cervantes** (5a Calle Poniente 42A, tel. and fax 832–0635). At only about $35 weekly, **Don Pedro Alvarado** (1a Calle Poniente 24, tel. 832–2266) offers little formal training, but it is a cheap way to garner a captive audience for practicing conversation.

The **Proyecto Lingüístico Francisco Marroquín** is the oldest school in Antigua Guatemala and has an excellent reputation. A group of linguists and indigenous Guatemalans started the school in 1971, earning money to support the preservation of Guatemala's many indigenous languages. Today, part of the school's income goes to support the linguistic project. *7a Calle Poniente 31, tel. and fax 832–2–886 or tel. 800/552–2051 in the U.S. Mailing address: PLFM, Apdo. 237, La Antigua, Guatemala.*

PHONES AND MAIL • **TELGUA** (5a Av. Sur and 5a Calle Poniente, southwest of Plaza Mayor) has AT&T direct-dial phones and is open daily 7 AM–10 PM. Fancy **Hotel Posada de Don Rodrigo** (5a Av. Norte 17, 1½ blocks north of Plaza Mayor, tel. 832–0291) has an MCI direct-dial phone.

Post office. To recieve mail in Antigua Guatemala, have it addressed to: Lista de Correos, Antigua, Guatemala 03001. *Alameda Santa Lucía, at 4a Calle Poniente, across from bus station. Open weekdays 8–4.*

Conexión is a one-stop communication shop. Here you can send and receive mail and faxes and check, send, or receive E-mail; it's also the best place in town to leave a message for another traveler. It's more expensive than the public services, but it's more reliable and the staff speaks English well. *4a Calle Oriente 14, in La Fuente shopping center, tel. 832–3768, fax 832–0082. Open weekdays 8:30–7, weekends 9:30–5:30.*

COMING AND GOING

Antigua Guatemala's **bus terminal** is at the corner of Alameda Santa Lucía and 4a Calle. Buses leave every half hour for Guatemala City (1 hr, 50¢) and several times daily for Panajachel (via Chimaltenango, 2½ hrs, $1.25). To explore the highlands, take a bus to Chimaltenango (45 min, 50¢); from here you can catch a bus to almost anywhere. **TURANSA** (5a Calle Poniente 11B, tel. 832-3316) runs convenient shuttle buses to Panajachel (2 hrs, $8) and Guatemala City (45 min, $7). Although expensive, shuttles offer door-to-door service and are a great way to get to the airport without spending a night in Guate. To reach Antigua Guatemala from Guatemala City by car, follow the Pan-American Highway to San Lucas Sacatepéquez and look for the turnoff to Antigua Guatemala. The smooth 45-km (28-mi) drive takes less than an hour, but watch for the wicked curves as you descend into the valley—several busloads of visitors have had their last glimpse of Guatemala on this road.

The Tzolkin Maya calendar, still used in many villages, is one of the most accurate ever created. Each year is divided into 13 periods of 20 days each and each day has its own "nahual," an animal, element, or divinity that influences people born on that day.

GETTING AROUND

Antigua Guatemala is relatively small and easily negociated on foot. Orient yourself at **Plaza Mayor** (between 4a and 5a Avs., 4a and 5a calles), which has plenty of banks, pharmacies, restaurants, and tourist shops. Numbered calles are labeled *poniente* from the plaza west to the bus station, and *oriente* to the east. Numbered avenidas are called *sur* south of the plaza toward Volcán Agua, and *norte* to the north. In the dead center of town is Plaza Mayor, and the four blocks bordering Plaza Mayor don't receive the east–west or north–south treatment.

WHERE TO SLEEP

The cheapest pensions are within a few noisy blocks of the bus station. Pay a little more to distance yourself from the constant stream of buses and experience Antigua Guatemala's charm, slow pace, and tranquillity. Hot water and use of a laundry sink is generally available and should be included in the price of a room. And don't hesitate to bargain—hotel managers will often try to charge you a few extra quetzales over the INGUAT-approved rate, which should be posted in each room. Many places have curfews, so if you want to partake in Antigua's nightlife, choose a place that won't cramp your style.

UNDER $5 • The Annex. This tiny, exceptionally clean hotel is just three blocks from the bus station. No sign marks the spot, but it's easy enough to find and at $3.50 a person it's a good deal if you're traveling alone. Keep in mind that, because of its size, the Annex fills quickly. *6a Calle Poniente, at Alameda de Santa Lucía, no phone. First door on right-hand side across from the cutesy store A Pie del Volcán. 6 rooms, none with bath. Cash only.*

UNDER $10 • Hospedaje El Pasaje. Only three blocks from the bus station, this hospedaje has clean and sparse doubles for $7. A nice terrace on the roof invites you to meditate at sunrise, which may very well be the only quiet time in this neighborhood. Curfew is 11:30 PM. *Alameda Santa Lucía, at 5a Calle Poniente, 2 blocks south of bus station. 16 rooms, none with bath. Cash only.*

Pensión El Arco. This pension is quiet, secluded, and away from the budget lodging area. The manager keeps the place spotless, and the door to the street is locked 24 hours a day for added security. Ring the bell to be let in. Curfew is 11 PM. Doubles are $7 ($11 with private bath). *5a Av. Norte, tel. 832–2701. Just north of Santa Catalina arch. 9 rooms, 1 with bath. Cash only.*

Posada Refugio. Conveniently located between the bus station and Plaza Mayor, this hotel is extremely popular with travel-weary backpackers. Big windows let in plenty of light but also limit your privacy—make sure the window locks before you choose a room. The roof is an outdoor patio of sorts: a pleasant spot to read the paper early in the morning. Doubles are $7 ($9 with private bath). *4a Calle Poniente 30, no phone. 30 rooms, 20 with bath. Cash only.*

Villa San Francisco. Only slightly more expensive than the budget hotels, this charming colonial "villa" is probably the best deal in town. The carefully decorated rooms are clean and cozy, and a quiet garden in back is a tranquil refuge. The rooftop sundeck is an added bonus—there's a great view and your laundry will dry in no time flat. The door to the street is kept locked to ensure security, but the friendly management will let you in at any hour, day or night. Other services include fax, telephone, E-mail, and TV. Doubles are $8 ($10 with private bath). *1a Av. Sur 15, at Calle de la Nobleza, tel. 832–3385. 9 rooms, 5 with bath. Cash only.*

UNDER $20 • Hospedaje Santa Lucía. This lovely, quiet two-story colonial home is the best lodging of its kind in town. It has attractive whitewashed walls, beamed ceilings, and clean, cozy rooms with bed, table, and reading lamp. It's even near the bus station. Doubles go for $12. *Calzada de Santa Lucía 7, no phone. 12 rooms with bath. Cash only.*

Hotel Posada Don Valentino. Reasonably priced, this place does a decent job of mimicking Antigua Guatemala's high-end hotels. Immaculate and well-furnished rooms surround a pleasant garden patio. Doubles are $15 ($20 with bath). *5a Calle Poniente 28, tel. 832–0384. 12 rooms, 7 with bath. Cash only.*

Posada Asjemenou. It's a cheery, tile-roofed, brightly painted place set around a well-kept courtyard with a fountain in the center. The clean rooms are decorated with heavy Spanish colonial furniture and indigenous art. The attached restaurant serves a quality breakfast for $2. Doubles are $12 ($18 with bath). *5a Av. Norte 31, just north of Santa Catalina arch, tel. 832–2670. 8 rooms, 4 with bath. Cash only.*

UNDER $45 • Hotel Convento Santa Catalina. Built on the ruins of an old convent, this property's front rooms are spacious and face a verdant courtyard with an ancient fountain, perfect for cocktail sipping. The more modern rooms in the annex are less authentic, but they're bright and have small kitchenettes. *5 Av. Norte 28, tel. 832–3080. 18 rooms with bath. Cash only.*

FOOD

Antigua Guatemala is well known for its specialty restaurants, with everything from upscale comida típica to Chinese, Italian, Tex-Mex, and even good ol' American hamburgers. A few vegetarian and health-food restaurants cater to the tastes of international travelers. Comedores serving comida típica for less than $1 are in the mercado central (central market), directly in front of the bus station.

Café Flor. This cheerful family-run restaurant with friendly service switched from Mexican cuisine to Thai in 1996 but kept the same low prices. Try the filling Thai curry, but watch out—it's very spicy by Guatemalan standards. *4a Av. Sur 1, tel. 201–3934. Closed Sun.*

Doña Luisa Xicotencatl. Named after the adored mistress of Spanish conquistador Pedro de Alvarado, this is the most popular place in town to hang out, sip Guatemalan coffee, eat a pastry, and peruse the popular notice board that occupies an entire wall. A multitude of tables are scattered throughout a dozen rooms and on the balcony and terrace of this former colonial residence, but it's still not easy to get a seat. A hearty ham-and-egg breakfast with freshly made bread, coffee, and juice costs $2, or you can get healthy with homemade granola and fresh fruit for $2.50. Salads and sandwiches are less than $4. After your meal, visit the happy couple's joint gravesite in the cathedral. *4a Calle Oriente 12, 2 blocks east of Plaza Mayor, tel. 832–2578.*

La Fonda de la Calle Real. An Antigua favorite, this place now has two locations serving the same menu of Guatemalan and Mexican cuisine. In both places, the house specialty is *caldo real* ($2.50), a hearty chicken and rice soup that you season to taste. If you haven't tried *pepian* ($5), a traditional fiesta dish, this is the place to do it: it's a delicious spicy stew of chicken or vegetables served with rice, tortillas, and a mini tamale. Save room for desserts like fried bananas with honey and cinnamon ($2), egg creole custard ($1.25), or a steaming cup of whipped hot chocolate (75¢). *5a Av. Norte 5, ½ block north of Plaza Mayor, tel. 832–2696; 3a Calle Poniente 7, tel. 832–0507.*

Peregrinos Restaurante. Mosey on down to Tex-Mex in Antigua Guatemala. The tasty *burrito chicano* ($3.50) is a stuffed flour tortilla served with rice, beans, and salad. Come during happy hour (6–7 PM) for mini pizzas baked in a brick oven ($1), drink specials, and free chips and salsa. *4a Av. Norte 1, next to Lloyd's Bank, tel. 832–0431.*

Quesos y Vino. Both of these small Italian restaurants serve homemade pasta, pizzas baked in a wood-burning oven, and a variety of cheeses and home-baked breads. The newer location on 2 Calle Oriente offers a more polished atmosphere than the original but is less intimate. Choose from an impressive selection of imported wines sold by the bottle. *5a Av. Norte 32, no phone. Closed Tues.*

Rainbow Café. This bohemian patio café is usually crammed with young travelers and hippie expatriates. Relax in the shade with a fresh fruit shake and peruse something from the eclectic collection of used books in English. Delicious breakfasts ($2–$3) are served all day. Lunch and dinner specials ($3), like spinach and ricotta cannelloni or tofu chili, include salad and a drink. *7a Av. Sur 8, behind Rainbow Reading Room, no phone.*

WORTH SEEING

The best way to experience Antigua Guatemala is to meander through town, checking out side streets and climbing around colonial ruins.

Plaza Mayor. In the center of town, this is the perfect spot to stretch out on one of the many park benches and laze away the day. It's also as good a place as any to check out what Antigua Guatemala has to offer: facing the south side of the park is the **Palacio de los Capitanes General**; once home to the colonial rulers of the kingdom of Guatemala, it now houses the national police and a bank. (New world order, same old shit.) The **Ayuntamiento,** north of the plaza, was the city hall until the capital shifted to Guatemala City; it now houses the **Museo de Santiago,** which contains a boring collection of cheesy paintings and Spanish weapons and torture tools, as well as the **Museo del Libro Antigua,** which displays the first printing press in Central America. Both museums are open Tuesday–Friday 9–4, weekends 9–noon and 2–4, and cost 40¢ to enter. East of the plaza is the partially restored **Catedral de San José,** which was destroyed in the 1773 earthquake; the gigantic crumbling walls and fallen columns look more like a set from *Clash of the Titans* than a reminder of the glory days of the Spanish empire.

Casa Popenoe. In 1932, Señor Popenoe restored this old mansion and fully decorated it with authentic furniture and art from the 17th–19th centuries. If you're totally intrigued by colonial decor, check it out. *1a Av. Sur, at 5a Calle Oriente. Admission 50¢. Open Mon.–Sat. 2–4.*

Convento de las Capuchinas. This is the largest and best-preserved convent in Antigua Guatemala. The Capuchin nuns arrived from Madrid in 1726, and their new convent quickly grew in size because, unlike at other convents, the women did not need to pay dowries to undertake the religious life. *2a Av. Norte and 2a Calle Oriente. Admission $2 (includes the Santa Clara convent). Open Tues.–Sun. 9–5.*

Iglesia de San Francisco. The attraction of this church is neither its grace nor its beauty (it has none), but the remains of Pedro de Betancourt, the most beloved of Guatemalan holy men. After an intense religious experience with a wooden Virgin Mary who came to life before his eyes, Betancourt settled in Antigua Guatemala, founded a hospital and a school, and became known as a great healer. The church is now a shrine for the sick and desperate, drawing believers from all over Central America in need of a miracle or two. Decorating the walls are marble, wood, and metal plaques and photographs and letters thanking Hermano Pedro for his divine intervention. Don't miss the **Museo de San Francisco** inside, which displays the skull that Hermano Pedro meditated over, the rags he wore, tokens of gratitude bequeathed to him, and a stash of abandoned crutches. *7a Calle Oriente, between 1a Av. Sur and Calle del Hermano Pedro. Museum admission 30¢. Museum open daily 8–noon and 2–4:30.*

La Merced. Spanning an entire block starting at 6a Avenida Norte and 1a Calle Poniente, La Merced is a massive church with the most elaborate facade in town. Unfortunately, earthquakes damaged the interior and it's barely worth the 15¢ admission charge to look inside. As you leave, walk along 5a Avenida Norte to catch a glimpse of the beautiful Arco de Santa Catalina (Arch of Santa Catalina), framing Volcán Agua far off in the distance.

Museo de Arte Colonial. The exhibit of antique colonial furniture is excellent and worth checking out— you'll really get a feel for life in colonial Antigua. *5a Calle Oriente 5, 1 block east of Plaza Mayor. Admission 25¢. Open Tues.–Fri. 9–4, weekends 9–noon and 2–4.*

Casa K'ojom. If you've grown tired of stuffy colonial artifacts, visit this lively museum honoring Mayan musical ceremonies with an assortment of photographs, instruments, traditional masks, and an audiovisual show. *Calle Recoletos 55, behind the bus terminal. Admission 85¢. Open Mon.–Sat. 9:30–12:30 and 2:30–6.*

CHEAP THRILLS

Adjacent to the bus station is the **mercado central,** where you can meander through a maze of stalls selling fresh produce, screwdriver sets, miraculous love potions, live chickens, handwoven baskets, made-for-tourist "típica" clothing, and lots more. Mondays, Thursdays, and Saturdays are the busiest market days, when indígenas and Ladinos commute to Antigua Guatemala from surrounding pueblos. On Sundays, get sweaty with Antiguans at local soccer tournaments held behind the central market.

Games begin at 10 AM and last well into the afternoon. If you don't want to play, cheering from the sidelines can be just as entertaining. A great place to end a long day (or begin a long night) is the beautiful **Hotel Posada de Don Rodrigo** (5a Av. Norte 17), where you can hear authentic live marimba for free at 8 PM nightly.

AFTER DARK

Bar hours fluctuate depending on the mood of the owner—in general no place is kicking until 10 PM, but things tend to close around midnight. **Café Picasso** (7a Av. Norte 3, between 3a and 4a calles Poniente) plays country music that will make you forget you ever left your home on the range. **El Bistro** (5a Av. Norte, just beyond Arco de Santa Catalina) sports a jock-bar image with live CNN sports coverage of all the biggest games. **La Chimenea** (7a Av. Norte and 2a Calle Poniente) doubles as a video-cinema, with daily video screenings; a schedule is posted on the wall outside. No-fuss **Macondo** (5a Av. Norte and 2a Calle Poniente), near the arch, has a pub-like atmosphere and allows patrons to drink in peace.

OUTDOOR ACTIVITIES

HIKING • Because of a number of robberies and assaults against tourists in recent years, INGUAT advises against hiking. Incidents are most common on the 20-minute hike to **Cerro de la Cruz,** a lookout point over all of Antigua Guatemala; take 4a Calle Oriente east to Calle de la Nobleza, then turn left. Ask around for current safety info before you head for the hills. Local tourist agencies have responded to concerns about safety with guided climbs to the peaks of the active **Volcán Pacaya** and the sleeping **Volcán Agua.** For $10, you and up to 30 other people take a minivan halfway up Pacaya, followed by a fairly rigorous two-hour hike and an almost vertical final ascent up the ashy peak—how close you can get will depend upon how active the volcano is and how daring your guide feels. Sign up with one of the many agencies surrounding Plaza Mayor, such as **King Travel Bureau** (5a Av. Norte 9, tel. 832–0142) or **ICO'S Volcano Expeditions** (5a Av. Norte 20B), which also offers tours to Volcán Agua. There have been numerous robberies along this route, too: don't take anything of value with you. Tours leave daily at 2:30 PM and return around 11 PM, dropping you at Plaza Mayor. Bring food, water, a flashlight, a raincoat, and something warm to wear.

BIKING • For guided rides to local villages, ruins, and coffee farms, try **Mayan Mountain Bike Tours** (6a Av. Sur 12B, tel. 832-2768), open Monday–Saturday 9–12:30 and 2–5:30. Bilingual tours start at $9 for two–three hours; overnight trips are also available. At **La Casa de Las Gargolas** (5a Av. Norte 14) you can rent bikes for $2 an hour to explore on your own. If you plan to leave Antigua Guatemala, it's best to ride with a friend. Make sure you know where you're going before you leave—trailblazing on private property is not a good idea.

NEAR ANTIGUA GUATEMALA

CIUDAD VIEJA

Ten minutes away by bus, this is a good place to come if you're feeling claustrophobic in Antigua Guatemala. Besides, it has such an entertaining past that it's worth a look. It's the original site of the first capital, Santiago de los Caballeros. Conquistador Pedro de Alvarado brought his wife, Doña Beatriz, to a newly built mansion in the city, soon leaving her to continue his pillage of the New World. Along the way, he was crushed by a horse. When the news reached Doña Beatriz, she went wacko, painting all the mirrors and furniture in her stately home black. She also commanded officials to appoint her governess—the first female leader of the Americas. But her rule was short-lived: a raging storm caused one side of Volcán Agua to erode, and water from the mouth of the crater flooded the capital, killing Doña Beatriz on her second day in office. Buses leave Antigua Guatemala every 20 minutes and cost 15¢.

SAN ANTONIO AGUAS CALIENTES

Stay on the bus about 10 minutes past Ciudad Vieja and you'll arrive at San Antonio Aguas Calientes, a well-known weaving community. Considering its proximity to tourist-infested Antigua Guatemala, this small pueblo sees relatively few outsiders. The 30-minute bus ride and a leisurely stroll around town will remind you that you really are in Guatemala. If you're interested in learning the art of backstrap weaving, ask one of the women in the plaza about a teacher and a price.

SAN ANDRES IZTAPA

Iztapa, about 45 minutes from Antigua Guatemala, is relatively unknown to tourists. Not so for many indígenas, who frequently visit to pay homage to **San Simón** (a.k.a. Maximón), the drinking and smoking

ALL IS FORGIVEN
BY SAN SIMÓN

Effigies of San Simón are found in villages all over the country. San Simón may be a saint, but he enjoys his vices: believers usually offer him a cigar and a stiff drink before asking for his help in personal matters. Because the church frowns on such practices, San Simón is kept under wraps, although in some places he's fairly accessible to (believing) travelers. Be respectful of those praying to San Simón, and remember that picture-taking is not recommended.

saint (*see* box, *below*). The color of the candle planted at the shrine reveals the worshiper's desire: red means love, green is luck in work, and black wards off enemies. Buses to Iztapa (50¢) leave hourly 6 AM–4 PM from behind Antigua Guatemala's central market. When you arrive, ask around for "la casa de San Simón." The idol is housed by a different family each year, and people are happy to help you find him.

You think you can come to Panajachel and avoid other travelers? The city is known to locals as "Gringo-tenango."

TECPAN AND THE IXIMCHE RUINS

A full morning's venture from Antigua Guatemala, the sleepy town of Tecpán and the nearby Iximché ruins have a bloody colonial history. The indigenous Cakchiquel tribe was ruling from Iximché when Pedro de Alvarado first arrived in the area in 1524. The Cakchiqueles allied themselves with the Spaniards to defeat the rival Quiché tribe and, true to form, the Spaniards later betrayed this confidence and the Cakchiqueles fled from Iximché. The Spaniards, thinking the area sufficiently pacified, tried to establish their very first capital at Tecpán. The Cakchiqueles spoiled these plans by attacking the Spanish settlement using guerrilla tactics. The Spaniards finally got the hint and closed shop. In 1530, they established their new capital out of the reach of the Cakchiqueles in Ciudad Vieja (*see above*). Hardly a trace remains of the Spanish influence. Today, Tecpán is small and quiet and hosts very few tourists—the biggest and perhaps only reason to visit. The ruins are about an hour's walk past Tecpán along a bumpy dirt road that few cars travel; look for the signs on the way. The site looks and feels sterile, with a freshly machete-mowed lawn, perfectly reconstructed ball courts, and tiny pyramidal structures. If you've seen a zillion ruins already, this place won't push your buttons. However, the isolated surroundings are a good place to relax under a shady tree and daydream about Iximché's glory days.

To get here from Antigua Guatemala (2 hrs, $1), take a bus to Chimaltenango, where you'll have to get on a bus headed to Los Encuentros—ask to be dropped off at Tecpán. From Guatemala City, buses leave directly to Tecpán (2¼ hrs, $1.50) hourly 6–6; you can also take buses headed to Quiché or Sololá and get off in Tecpán. The archaeological site is open daily 9–5, and admission is 25¢. A museum houses a few artifacts and a topographical layout of Iximché.

PANAJACHEL
AND LAGO ATITLÁN

Panajachel's setting is highly dramatic, bordered by three volcanoes that drop off into the crystalline waters of Lago Atitlán. A pleasant climate, spectacular scenery, and abundant tourist services make Pana an extremely popular destination for international travelers of all kinds, as well as a favorite weekend getaway for Guatemalans from the capital. Pana itself is tacky, although some travelers may find its slightly seedy hippie-oriented atmosphere comfortable. Still, Pana has some great budget restaurants and has tons of shops selling trinkets for the folks back home. You'll most likely tire of the touristy scene after a day or two, but don't leave without visiting one of the traditional pueblos nestled in the hills around the lake. These villages see much less tourism and have retained much of their unique tradi-

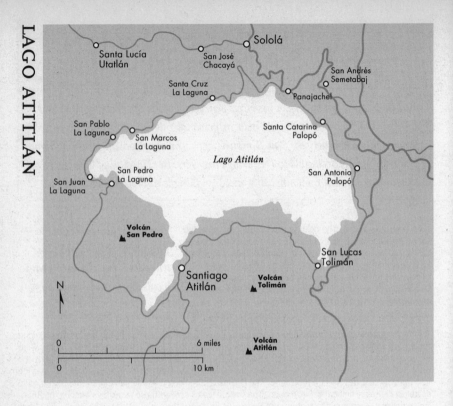

tional character; some travelers will prefer to stay here. Indígena in traditional dress commute to Pana by boat from the secluded pueblos to sell beautiful embroidered huipiles and handwoven sashes in shops that specialize in mass-produced Guatemalan "handicrafts," sold in bulk at wholesale prices. Although most visitors come to Panajachel for rest and relaxation, the Lago Atitlán area is an ideal place to go kayaking, mountain biking, or hiking. Kayak and bike rentals cost just a few dollars a day, and a number of mountain trails lead to breathtaking views of the lake.

BASICS

VISITOR INFORMATION • Open weekdays 8:30–5, Sunday 1:30–6:30, the **INGUAT** office (Calle Santander, in Rincón Saí complex, tel. 762–1392) has a nice map and bus and boat schedules posted on the window. If you're looking to explore the area or climb a volcano, Hector Solís is your man—he answers questions, addresses safety concerns, and is an all-around helpful guy. The message board at **Al Chisme,** a popular restaurant on Calle Los Arboles, is a good place to find all kinds of useful notices such as rooms for rent and airplane tickets for sale. If you're looking to extend your stay in Guatemala, **DHL Worldwide Express** (*see* Phones and Mail, *below*) processes visa extensions, saving you a trip to the capital. Drop your passport at the office in the morning and it'll be ready by the following afternoon.

MONEY • **Banco Industrial** (Calle Santander, across from Mario's Rooms; open weekdays 8:30–3, Sat. 8:30–12:30) has a 24-hour automated teller machine. It accepts ATM cards with the Plus system and does cash advances on Visa. **Atitlán Tourist Services** (Calle Santander, in front of Hotel Regis) also gives cash advances on Visa or MasterCard.

EMERGENCIES • The **police** station is near the end of Calle Principal next to the municipal building. **Panamedic Centro Clínico Familiar** (Calle Principal 0–72, tel. 762–2174) offers 24-hour medical attention—Dr. Francisco Ordoñez and his wife, Dra. Zulma Ordoñez, both speak English. **Farmacia Nueva Unión** (Calle Santander, 1 block below Calle Principal) is open daily 24 hours.

PHONES AND MAIL • TELGUA (Calle Santander, halfway between lake and Calle Principal) is open daily 7 AM–midnight. A number of businesses on Calle Santander offer "tourist services," including discounts on international phone calls and faxes; their signs are easy to spot. Rates are usually slightly (but not much) lower than you'd pay at TELGUA. The **post office,** open weekdays 8–4, is opposite the police station on a side street facing the church. For packages, it's safer to use one of the many businesses that specialize in shipping; try **Get Guated Out** (Calle Los Arboles, next to Galería Bookstore, tel. 762–2015) or **DHL Worldwide Express** (Calle Santander, in Rincón Saí complex, tel. 762–1474). In addition to international shipping, DHL has a courier service that runs to and from Guatemala City—the price ranges from $5 to $20, but it'll save you a trip. Next door, at **Maya Communications,** you can send or receive faxes and E-mail.

COMING AND GOING

The bus into Panajachel drops you off on Panajachel's main street, **Calle Principal,** which runs through downtown to the central market, church, post office, police, and city hall. Most of the budget hotels and cheaper restaurants are found along **Calle Santander,** which runs down to the lakeside boat dock. The bus into town drops you off near the intersection of these streets. **Calle Rancho Grande,** Pana's other semimajor street, runs parallel to Calle Santander. The road out of town leads to the villages of Santa Catarina Palopó and San Andrés Palopó, where it finally comes to a dead end.

BY BUS • Buses depart from just outside the Mayan Palace Hotel on Calle Principal. Rebuli buses leave daily for Guatemala City (3½ hrs, $2.50) every 45 minutes or so until 4 PM. One direct bus to Antigua Guatemala (3 hrs, $2.25) leaves daily at 11 AM, otherwise take a bus to Chimaltenango (2 hrs, $1.75) where you can transfer. There are direct buses to Chichicastenango (1½ hrs, $1.50) on market days (Sun. and Thurs.), other days take any bus to Los Encuentros (30 min, 50¢); and several direct buses to Quetzaltenango (2½ hrs, $2). To Huehuetenango (4 hrs, $2.50), take the bus to Quetzaltenango and ask to be let off at Cuatro Caminos; buses to Huehue pass this point hourly. If you miss your bus, you can always catch a bus to **Los Encuentros** (40 mins, 50¢) from where buses run later to all of these destinations. If you're willing to shell out the quetzales, a number of tourist agencies offer direct shuttles to Guatemala City, Antigua Guatemala, and Chichicastenango (on market days)—prices range between $8 and $20. Companies post departure times on sandwich boards lining Calle Santander.

If you're ready to pack up entirely and head for Mexico, the journey takes less than five hours and costs just $2.50. To La Mesilla or San Cristóbal, catch the Rebuli line to Los Encuentros, and then take the **El Condor** bus that leaves at 6 AM, 10 AM, and noon. If you're heading to El Carmen or Talismán, take any bus to Cocales, where you can connect with the **Galgos** bus heading for the Mexican border.

GETTING AROUND

BY BUS • Public buses run to the small towns around Lago Atitlán. Buses and minibuses leave every half hour for Sololá (20 min, 20¢). The bus to Santa Catarina Palopó (20 min, 15¢), San Antonio Palopó (40 min, 25¢), and San Lucas Tolimán (1½ hrs, 50¢) leaves Pana at 9 AM and at 5:30 PM. Private minibuses also circulate through these villages for about the same price as the public bus. Look for them at the corner of Calle Principal and Calle Santander.

BY BOAT • Boats leave from the public beach near the end of Calle Santander. The public ferries have set prices but the tourist prices are somewhat higher than the local rates. A trip between any two towns on the lake costs $1.50. Boat schedules change frequently, so check the schedule posted at INGUAT for current info. Six boats a day make the trip to Santiago Atitlán (1 hr)—the first leaves at 8:30 AM. Boats to San Pedro La Laguna (1½ hrs) leave daily every few hours starting at 8 AM, with stops in Santa Cruz La Laguna, Tzununá, San Marcos La Laguna, and San Pablo La Laguna. The last bus leaves San Pedro at 5 PM. Two boats leave daily at 9:30 AM and 2 PM for San Lucas Tolimán (1 hr) with stops in Santa Catarina Palopó, San Antonio Palopó, and other towns as requested. The boat returns at 1 PM and 4:30 PM. If you'd rather jet across the lake in a private motorboat, you'll have to bargain with the owner.

WHERE TO SLEEP

Panajachel has hundreds of simple rooms that cater to the thin-wallet set, but accommodations vary in size—always check before you pay to make sure you're not sleeping in a closet. Many small, informal hotels are on no-name side streets, but, with all the homemade signs that litter Calle Santander, you'll have no trouble finding them. If it's a little comfort you're after, Panajachel also has some moderately priced accommodations with most of the facilities you might need.

UNDER $15 • Hospedaje Rooms García. If you're willing to walk an extra block, this place is a great deal. Rooms upstairs are spacious, and the porch area is lighted at night so you can read in the fresh air. A laundromat next door is an added bonus. Doubles are $7. *4a Calle 2–24, tel. 762–2187. Take a left off Calle Santander on side street just before Mario's Rooms. 28 rooms, none with bath. Cash only.*

Mario's Rooms. One budget hotel always seems to be more popular with backpackers than the rest; in Panajachel, Mario's is the place. Rooms are bright and clean, and doubles cost $6 ($12 with private bath). A café in the front section of the hotel serves great food and has two shelves of mostly romance novels for sale. The central location (look for the vendor stalls across the street) adds to the place's appeal. *Calle Santander, just past TELGUA, tel. 762–1313. 18 rooms, 7 with bath. Cash only.*

Villa Martita Hotel. Tucked away behind a small grove of trees, this place has a charm that is severely lacking in most of Pana's hospedajes. Sunny doubles are $9 without bath, and two rooms with immaculate private bathrooms cost $25. Relax in the adorable garden or in the small café run out of the kitchen. Best of all, the showers are really, truly hot. *Calle Santander, 2 blocks from lake. 7 rooms, 2 with bath. Cash only.*

UNDER $20 • Hotel Galindo. Big, clean, comfortable rooms surround a huge blossoming garden, enticing hammocks hang strategically around the yard, and some rooms have brick fireplaces. Prices fluctuate wildly, but if you arrive during an off month or on a slow day, comfort can be yours for $12 a double. *Calle Principal, past Calle Los Arboles, on the right, tel. 762–1168. 14 rooms, 4 suites, all with bath. Cash only.*

Hotel Maya Kanek. On the main street at the edge of the old town, this place is in a quiet area with fewer foreigners than on the tourist side of Panajachel. Arranged like a miniature motel, rooms surround a secure parking area. Although the rooms are small and plain, they are clean and have good, firm mattresses. The owner is a friendly fellow, and he has assembled a thorough list of local boat and bus schedules in the lobby. Doubles cost $14 with private hot-water bath ($11 with shared bath). *Calle Principal, tel. 762–1104. 26 rooms with bath. Cash only.*

UNDER $45 • Rancho Grande. About halfway between the beach and the old town, the Rancho Grande is a series of bungalows that flanks the street of the same name. Every room in this bed-and-breakfast is unique, but all are spacious with excellent king-sized beds, wood ceilings, white stucco walls, tile floors, and locally woven rugs and bed covers. One of the best splurges in Guatemala, the $40 room price includes a lovely breakfast of German pastries. It's actually quite reasonable considering the quality. Some bungalows sleep five ($60), the suite has a fireplace and cable TV, and all units have porches and are separated by lawns and gardens. *Calle Rancho Grande, tel. 762–1554, fax 762–2247. 12 rooms with bath.*

CAMPING • Hotel Visión Azul runs a lovely private campground on the west side of town, 15 minutes up the hill toward Sololá. It's quiet and clean and offers a spectacular sunrise view of all three volcanoes, but don't be surprised if you're awakened by cows grazing in the wee morning hours. Sites are $5 per tent, plus $1.50 a person, and the place has a water faucet that occasionally works. Although you may be tempted, it is not wise camp on the public beach in town; it is neither comfortable nor safe.

FOOD

Pana's many gringo-owned cafés cater to the foreign palate, providing a welcome respite from comida típica. Also, a couple of snack shops on Calle Santander sell refreshing smoothies of papaya and pineapple. Lakefront comedores cater to weekend strollers and beer-guzzling tourists, serving decent food at reasonable prices; **Comedor Los Pumpos** often has terrific live marimba. If you're feeling creative, put together a sandwich—buy a loaf of bread from a local hippie and get vegetables from the **mercado central** on Calle Principal.

UNDER $5 • Mario's Restaurant. Right in front of Mario's Rooms (*see* Where to Sleep, *above*), this super-popular café has the largest servings for the cheapest prices in Pana. *Desayuno completo* ($2) includes two eggs, beans, freshly baked bread, fruit, and oatmeal and is served any time of day. If you think you're going to still be hungry, chow down on a crepe stuffed with fruit and yogurt ($2.25). *Calle Santander, just past TELGUA, across from Mario's Rooms, no phone.*

Sevananda. A vegetarian's delight and probably the best dinner deal in town—the owner serves up a different complete meal each night of the week ($2). The Saturday menu includes mint soup, excellent lasagna, beet salad, artichoke-and-carrot salad, and bread. *At the fork of Calle Santander and Los Arboles, on Los Arboles side, no phone.*

UNDER $10 • Al Chisme Restaurant. This popular restaurant owned by an American woman serves good food in a relaxed atmosphere. Seating is on a covered terrace or in the main dining room, where jazz or rock-and-roll entertains patrons. Many of the restaurant's regulars are a testament to the town's reputation as a hippie hangout. As a popular breakfast spot, Al Chisme serves homemade bagels and pastries, but lunch and dinner offerings are even tastier, ranging from chicken cordon bleu to shrimp curry crepes to three-cheese lasagna. *Av. de los Arboles, ½ block up from Calle Principal, no phone. Closed Wed.*

Circus Bar. Known mostly for its nightlife and occasional live bands, this place has also earned quite a reputation for its excellent pizzas ($4–$5) and perfectly seasoned pasta dishes ($3–$4). Puppets dangle from the ceiling and old circus posters decorate the walls. You may find yourself staying longer than you expect and spending more than you want. *Calle Los Arboles, next to Al Chisme, no phone.*

Restaurante Uruguayo. If you've had enough of Pana's hippie-dippy vegetarian-style restaurants, this is an excellent place to dine on Uruguayan cuisine, which revolves around the barbecue. The setup of this outdoor restaurant manages to provide an intimate, even romantic, environment right on the main drag—it's like you have box seats for the show that is Panajachel. Grilled dishes of beef, chicken, and excellent fresh fish are tasty, filling, and reasonably priced. *Calle Santander, no phone.*

Sunset Cafe. As its name suggests, this is a terrific spot to watch the sun set over the lake. Sip a drink or stay for dinner; the food's good but, at $5–$6 a plate, you're definitely paying for the view. *Bottom of Calle Santander, on left before beach entrance, no phone.*

AFTER DARK

With all the foreigners, Panajachel has a happening nightlife. **Circus Bar** (*see* Where to Eat, *above*) has a friendly atmosphere and, occasionally, decent live music, as does **El Aleph,** just across the street. If you're hankering for a game of Ping-Pong, try **The Last Resort,** a full-service bar with a mostly gringo clientele on the side street just before Mario's Rooms on Calle Santander. Local expatriates congregate at **Ubu's Cosmic Cantina** to veg in front of the TV, watching Simpsons repeats, cable TV movies and live CNN sports—no Spanish spoken here. If you'd rather join the local Guatemalans, head to the **cantinas** on Calle Rancho Grande or another small side street; by the time you finish a beer, you'll feel like a part of the family. **Al Chisme** (*see* Food, *above*) and **Bombay Café** on Calle Los Arboles are great digs for after-dinner coffee and dessert. If you want to catch a flick, the **Grapevine** on Calle Santander has a screening room with cushioned benches.

If you find the villagers in San Antonio to be camera shy, don't take it personally. Infants don't see the light of day for the first year of life: their faces are kept covered to ward off evil spirits.

OUTDOOR ACTIVITIES

BIKING • As Panajachel evolves from an isolated Guatemalan village into a booming lakeside resort, water sports are becoming more popular, giving Lago Atitlán a Club Med feel. That said, you might as well get involved. Rent a kayak or canoe at the public beach for $3 an hour or $10 a day. Better yet, rent a mountain bike at **Moto Servicio Quiché** (Calle de los Arboles, at Calle Principal) and pedal over to nearby villages. Rental rates are $1 per hour, $7 for 8 hours, or $9 for 24 hours. For a real challenge, take your rental bike on the ferry to San Pedro La Laguna. There, a hilly dirt road borders the lake on the northwest shore, bringing you through small, traditional towns that see few tourists. At **Tzununá,** a tiny village about 11 km (6¾ mi) from San Pedro, the road becomes a steep, narrow trail that continues on 5 km (3 mi) farther to **Santa Cruz La Laguna.** Since there's no trail from here through to Pana, catch a boat back (20 min, 20¢). Santa Cruz itself is an isolated mountainside village that sees few visitors. If you're too tuckered out to make it back to civilization, stay down by the shore at German-owned **Arco de Noe,** which is everything a traveler could want in a hotel.

HIKING • The bike route from San Pedro to Santa Cruz makes for an exhilarating hike as well. Start early, because the walk from San Pedro to Santa Cruz takes five to six hours even at a healthy pace. If you aren't up for the entire trek, you can catch the ferry back to Pana in towns along the way. Boat drivers can usually tell you what time the ferry passes through a particular town. Volcano lovers looking for a strenuous uphill climb to a fantastic panoramic view that few others have ever seen, should hike 11,500-ft Volcán Atitlán. For about $12, you can hire a guide in San Lucas Tolimán. Speak to Padre Gregorio, a local priest and social activist. You can usually find him at his office near the Catholic church. Padre Gregorio can also find you a place to stay the night, since it's best to get started on the six-hour climb around dawn. A slightly shorter and much easier volcano hike leads to the top of Volcán San Pedro, offering a view over of the entire Lago Atitlán area. Robberies have been reported, so it's safer to do the guide thing. Don't find them, they'll find you—as you get off the boat in San Pedro, guides will approach your boat offering foot and horse tours for $5–$10.

AROUND LAGO ATITLÁN

After you've had your fill of Pana, jump on one of the many small boats that ferry people and goods across the lake. If you're prone to motion sickness, take a boat ride in the morning while the water still smooth. By early afternoon, Xocomil—the biting wind that, according to the indígenas, burns out sin—begins to act up, making the boat trip feel like a roller-coaster ride. The lakeside villages are less commercial than Pana, radiating their own individual style through variations in dress, custom, and dialect. Unfortunately, most smaller villages don't have hospedajes or comedores, so you'll have to be sure to ask when the last ferry leaves for Pana, or be prepared to pay the private motorboat owners' emergency prices.

SANTA CATARINA PALOPO AND SAN ANTONIO PALOPO

These sister villages, just a short distance from Panajachel, are surprisingly traditional. The women wear traditional garb—in Santa Catarina they are decked out from head to toe in beautiful shades of teal, blue, and purple, while in San Antonio the costume is an intricately embroidered red huipil and a long, navy-blue skirt. Even more notable, this is one of only a handful of regions in Latin America where men still dress in traditional costume on a daily basis—their pants are designed with geometric motifs and calf-length woolen wraparounds fastened by leather belts or red sashes. In Santa Catarina, tourism has clearly affected the traditional lifestyle. Today, many people make their living by selling trinkets to tourists who stroll in from Panajachel. In San Antonio, however, village life still consists mainly of farming, weaving, and attending church services. An adobe colonial church marks the center of each town. The church steps are used as a social meeting ground, where all passersby are sure to stop for a while.

COMING AND GOING • Take Calle Principal toward the central market and look for the sign on a building wall indicating the road. Santa Catarina is an easy 4-km (2½-mi) walk from Panajachel. The 8-km (5-mi) walk to San Antonio is more daunting. A bus to San Antonio (20 min, 10¢) from the capital stops in Pana daily at around 9:15 AM. Minivans and pickups head in that direction throughout the day—they generally charge about 25¢. Ferries headed to San Lucas Tolimán stop in both villages en route. They leave Pana daily at 9:30 AM and 2 PM. The half-hour boat ride costs about 50¢. The last ferry leaves San Antonio at 4:30 PM.

SANTIAGO ATITLÁN

Nestled among three local volcanoes, Santiago Atitlán is only slightly less touristed than Panajachel itself. Like an aging diva, the lakeside town endures constant face-lifts to maintain its once-genuine traditional beauty. Ironically, the result is that it often looks run-down and dirty. A pathway leads from the lake shore up to the plaza and main church. The road is lined with shops selling artesanía—take a good look at the huipiles with elaborate embroidered depictions of fruits, birds, and Mayan gods. Many local women wear a "halo:" a 12-yard-long band wrapped around the head, while the men sport black-and-white striped calf-length pants with detailed embroidery below the knee. Santiago Atitlán is also a good place to pay a visit to San Simón, everyone's favorite smoking and drinking saint (see San Simón box, above). As you get off the boat, local children offer to lead the way to "Maximón" in exchange for a few quetzales. Otherwise, just ask around town—people are happy to tell you his current whereabouts. Every year, a different member of the local cofrade (religious society) houses the wooden idol and accommodates his many faithful followers. The ferry to Santiago Atitlán (1 hr, $1.25) leaves Pana at 8:30 AM and 10:30 AM, returning at 11:45 AM and 2 PM.

On a darker note, Santiago Atitlán has seen its share of political violence. The villagers are known for their spirited rebellions. The army first set up camp here in 1981, as a result of a so-called "guerrilla convention." Many villagers were murdered or "disappeared" in the years that followed. After a 1990 massacre in which 12 people were killed, the villagers protested the presence of the army in their town. To everyone's surprise, the army actually left, and Santiago Atitlán became a model for other highland towns working to replace the military and national police in their communities with local forms of authority.

WHERE TO SLEEP AND EAT

Hotel Tzutuhil (tel. 721–7174), the only five-story building in town, has doubles for $7, $9 with private bath. Rooms on the top floor have huge windows offering a great view of the lake and a peek into all the neighbors' yards. The rusty lounge chairs on the roof are more comfortable than they look. From the dock, walk four blocks up the main street; look for the hotel on the left corner. At $6 per person, **Hospedaje Chi Nim Ya** is a slightly cheaper option for solo travelers. It's on your first left as you walk up from the dock. Eat at one of the local comedores, or make a meal of piping hot tamales (15¢) from the market.

SOLOLA

Guarding the lake from on high, Sololá is culturally worlds away from Panajachel. Since few tourists stick around Sololá—they're all in hurry to get to the lake, 8 km (5 mi) below—its character and style haven't yet been totally co-opted to gringo purchasing power. Admittedly, there's nothing in particular to see here but the people themselves. Most of the men and women wear their traditional garb, the designs of which can be traced back to precolonial days. The streets around the central plaza are blocked off on Tuesdays and Fridays for the local market, when almost all the townspeople get decked out in all their splendor. Although it's a mainly a locals' scene where the indígena come to exchange goods, stalls catering to tourists have crept in around the perimeter. Buses headed to Panajachel (20 min, 20¢) pass through Sololá every half hour or so. Other buses go to Los Encuentros (25 min, 20¢), where you can catch buses to most other main towns (see Coming and Going, above). Minivans from Sololá also cart people to and from Los Encuentros and Panajachel.

CHICHICASTENANGO

Tourists love to shop, and Chichicastenango is one of Guatemala's *número uno* shopping stops. Empty for most of the week, on Thursdays and Sundays Chichi bumps and grinds with enthusiastic gringos and locals. Vendors set up shop while the dawn mist still lingers on the cobblestone streets. The result is proof that the joy of shopping is infectious. It's hard to resist temptation when you walk through aisle upon aisle of kaleidoscopic Guatemalan goodies for sale. The possibilities are endless: gorgeous huipiles from Nebaj, made-for-tourist "típico" clothing, wooden masks, wool blankets, woven bags, baskets, machetes, *metates* (a corn-grinding stone), jade, pottery, and everyday necessities from soap to cassette

In much of the world, men have lost traditional ways of dress. Not so in Sololá. Men here dress like Technicolor cowboys, with red pin-striped pants, an authentic, multicolored cowboy shirt, and a big ol' hat.

tapes to produce. Although the city tries to centralize the frenzied shopping activity around the plaza, surrounding streets are inevitably blocked off by the overflow. If it's any kind of reassurance, the town is famous for its ability to accommodate masses of people on market day. Try to come to Chichi early the day before market day: not only will you get better deals the evening before while the vendors are setting up, but part of the fun is to see the transformation of the lovely, sleepy town into a grand bazaar.

The local mix of Catholic and pagan practices adds a funky twist to this touristy locale. In 1540, the Spanish erected **La Iglesia de Santo Tomás** right on top of a Mayan altar. The indigenous people converted their pagan deities into Catholic saints without really changing their religious functions. Even many of the symbols overlapped, such as the Mayan cross and the Catholic crucifix. Chichi is still considered the Holy City of Quiché. The elaborate Catholic *dias santos* (saints' days) processions are followed by equally elaborate Mayan religious rituals, which unfold on the church steps. Believers kneel and pray quite vocally amid the smoke of sticky-sweet incense. At the base of the church steps, a small fire burns throughout the day and inside, pine needles cover the floor and corn husks, candles, and flower petals decorate the altars. When visiting, use the church's side entrance so you don't disrupt the rituals on the steps. Once inside, you'll have to etch the scene forever in your mind—picture-taking is taboo.

Chichi is an anomaly of sorts in that the Catholic Church openly accepts local pagan rituals, and an elected indígena council works hand-in-hand with the Church to administer the city. The council leaders, known as *cofrades* (loosely meaning brothers), are locally appointed. The cofradía is the most prestigious position in town, but like most good things, it comes at a heavy price. The cofrades have to pay for all of Chichi's holiday celebrations and fiestas out of their own pockets. This is especially costly during the town's grand **fiesta,** December 13–21, when the city explodes with parades and dances. During the festivities, the cofrades wear elegant silver costumes and carry staffs topped by a magnificent sun medallion. Unfortunately, the indígena are not totally free from Christian persecution. The shrine to the deity **Pascual Abaj,** on the hilltop outside of town, is often wrecked by zealous Christians. Each time, the elongated stone face is restored and believers continue their daily rituals. *Brujos,* the local shamen, preside over these ceremonies, and the villagers recite special prayers and offer candles, food, alcohol, and the occasional slaughtered chicken. To see the shrine, follow 9a Calle until you see the signs for the narrow footpath up the mountain. Boys hanging around the plaza will guide you to the shrine for a small fee and can tell you when the rituals take place.

BASICS

Banco del Ejército (6a Calle 5–40) is the only bank in town with hours to complement the weekend market. It's open Tuesday–Friday 9–noon and 2–4, Saturday 9–noon, Sunday 9–1. To get there from the plaza, walk north on 5a Avenida toward the Arco Gucumatz, and turn right on 6a Calle. For phone calls, go to **TELGUA** (7a Av. 8–24; open daily 7 AM–8 PM), two blocks behind La Iglesia de Santo Tomás. Two doors away, the **post office** is open weekdays 8–noon and 2–6.

COMING AND GOING

Buses headed in and out of Chichi stop by the **Arco Gucumatz,** a painted concrete arch two blocks north of the plaza, at the corner of 5a Avenida and 5a Calle. Several daily buses head to Guatemala City (4 hrs, $1.50) and Quetzaltenango (2½ hrs, $1). One bus leaves daily at 12:15 PM for Nebaj (3½ hrs, $1.25). A **Tres Estrellas del Norte** to the Mexican border town of Tapachula (6 hrs, $3.50) passes through Chichi daily at noon. The quickest route to towns in the Quiché Department is via Los Encuentros (25 min, 25¢), where you can get an onward connection. Buses zip back and forth between Chichi and Santa Cruz del Quiché (25 min, 25¢) all day long, stopping in the little villages along the way. On market days, shuttles also connect Chichi with Panajachel ($7) and Antigua Guatemala ($12).

GETTING AROUND

Chichi is laid out in the typical Guatemalan grid format, although it's a little tricky to figure out because of all the hills. But the town is small enough that you never feel truly lost (except, possibly, in the whirl of the market). Chichi's main strip is 5a Avenida, where you'll see the Santo Tomás church and the Arco Gucumatz. Most of the hotels, restaurants, and artesanía stores lie near the central plaza on 6a Avenida and 6a Calle.

WHERE TO SLEEP

Budget hotels tend to fill up quickly on Wednesday and Saturday nights, the days before the big market. If you're willing to spend a few extra dollars, you shouldn't have much trouble finding an available and even pleasant room. Another option is to head out to Santa Cruz del Quiché, 25 minutes away by bus; the budget hotels there don't fill up quite so quickly (*see* Where to Sleep in Santa Cruz del Quiché, *below*).

The cheap sleep standard here is the **Hospedaje Salvador** (3 blocks south of plaza, tel. 756–1329). Although rooms ($7, $10 with bath) are a bit musty, beds are a bit old, and hot water is available only for a couple of hours in the morning, what El Salvador lacks in comfort it compensates for with low rates and character. For about $10 a double, you can stay at **Posada Pascual Abaj** (5a Av., 1 block east of Arco Gucumatz, tel. 756–1055) or at **Posada El Arco** (4a Calle 4–36), a two-story building upstairs and to the left of Arco Gucumatz. Both are clean and have a relatively steady supply of hot water. For a little bit of affordable luxury, check out **Hospedaje Girón** (7a Calle, 1 block north of plaza, tel. 561–156), where a double with comfortable beds and a sparkling clean bathroom will cost you $15. Another step up, **Hotel Chugüilá** (5a Av. 5–24, tel. 756–1134) has a variety of elegant rooms around a lovely courtyard; those with shared bath cost just $15 per double, while a private bath will set you back $35.

FOOD

Chichi doesn't have the wide variety of foods available in Antigua Guatemala or Panajachel, but plenty of restaurants serve standard Guatemalan fare at good prices. Restaurants on the north side of the plaza offer sandwiches and *platos fuertes* (full meals) for $1–$3. **Restaurant Tzijolaj** has a second-floor balcony that overlooks the bustling market in the plaza below. Café Villa de los Cofrades, on the plaza, is a nice spot for a cold drink, but better food is available just a block north at **Restaurante Villa de los Cofrades** (5a Av. and 6a Calle, second floor). A tasty cheeseburger with fries goes for $1.25, and a big plate of steamed vegetables with soup and tortillas costs $2.25. But the best and cheapest food in town is at the market. Try a lunch of fried chicken, rice, beans, and salad served with a heaping stack of tortillas ($1.25) or a bag full of delicious steaming-hot tamales (50¢).

WORTH SEEING

Museo Regional. Although you're probably in town for the market, the Regional Museum is still worth a look. The one-room exhibit houses amazingly well-preserved Mayan pots with the original paint on the sides, huge jade beads, stone figurines, and two pieces of fine gold jewelry that somehow escaped the Spanish meltdown of precious metals. These priceless artifacts were all donated by villagers to Father Rossbach, the main priest in Chichi in the early 20th century. *In plaza, left of Santo Tomás church. Admission 20¢. Open daily 8–noon and 2–5.*

CHEAP THRILLS

The indoor vegetable market opposite the Museo Regional is an enthralling sight. Purely for locals doing their weekly grocery shopping, it's small enough for you to get a close look at how bargaining is really done. The upper-level balcony is a great place to take pictures without invading anyone's personal space. If you're into sunrises and the early morning mist that weaves in and out of the silent streets, climb the steps to the top of **Arco Gucumatz,** where you can gaze into the steep valley below.

SANTA CRUZ DEL QUICHÉ

The 25-minute ride from Chichi to Santa Cruz is filled with unnerving mountain switchbacks and a bird's-eye view of terraced farm plots. After the heart-stopping ride, however, the town itself is something of a disappointment, lacking the activity of Chichi and the vibrancy of nearby villages. The capital of the Quiché Department, Santa Cruz was a hotbed of indígena rebellion during the height of the guerrilla insurrection in the 1980s. One thing to see is the colonial church, made from the stones of the ruined Quiché capital of Utatlán. It houses a memorial to socially active priests killed in the area during the 1980s. Although the area is becoming more and more Ladinoized, the peace treaty provided for the education of children in indigenous areas with the goal of maintaining and fostering Guatemala's incredible diversity. Sadly, peace has not completely eradicated the danger of this countryside: in recent years, the isolated roads of this region have been the scene of numerous bus robberies and rapes. Never take night buses in the region, and carry few valuables. Despite the security problems, a general feeling of tranquillity prevails.

BASICS

Near the plaza, **Banco Industrial** (2a Av. and 3a Calle, Z1) changes traveler's checks and processes cash advances on Visa. They're open weekdays 8:30–5:30, Saturday 10–2. Make phone calls daily 7 AM–10 PM at **TELGUA** (1a Av., between 1a and 2a Calle, Z5). Also in Zona 5 is the post office (3a Calle, between "O" and 1a Avs.), which is open weekdays 8–4:30.

COMING AND GOING

Santa Cruz del Quiché is shortened to QUICHE on bus plaques. The **bus terminal** is on 1a Avenida, four blocks south of the central plaza on 6a Calle. Buses between Quiché and Guatemala City (4½ hrs, $1.50) pass through Chichicastenango, Los Encuentros, and Chimaltenango. Buses leave Quiché several times daily between 5 AM and 4 PM, with more buses on Thursday and Sunday. Direct buses to Quetzaltenango leave at 8:30 AM, 1 PM, and 2 PM, or you can go to Los Encuentros (1 hr, 75¢), where you won't have to wait long for a connection. Buses run between Quiché and Chichicastenango (25 min, 25¢) every 20 minutes or so daily from 6 AM to 6 PM.

WHERE TO SLEEP

Local efforts to bring potable water into surrounding pueblos occasionally cut off Quiché's water service temporarily. Be sure to ask if there is water before you agree on a price for a room. Two-story **Hotel San Pascual** (7a Calle 0–43, tel. 755–1107) is very large and very clean. A double with private bath goes for $11 ($7 without). To get here from the bus terminal, walk up 1a Avenida and turn left on 7a Calle. **Posada Calle Real** (2a Av. 7–36, two blocks below central plaza, no phone) has the best beds in Quiché. Although rooms themselves are average, the luxuriously soft mattresses with clean, starched, and pressed sheets will have you sleeping like a baby. As an added bonus, the posada has the only hot showers in town. A double room goes for $8.

CAMPING • You can camp for free 3 km (2 mi) outside town, at the Utatlán ruins (see Near Santa Cruz del Quiché, below). There's no designated campground, no water, and nothing nearby, so you're on your own. If the guard is around, it's best to let him know what you're doing to avoid any unfounded suspicions.

FOOD

Your options pretty much amount to meat dishes, hamburgers, french fries, and that old standby, rice and beans. **Cafetería Los Antojitos** (6a Calle and "O" Av.) has hamburgers for $1 and fried chicken plates for $2. An extension of Posada Calle Real, signless **Restaurante Calle Real** (2a Av. 7–36) serves a decent daily special of salad, pasta, meat, and tortillas for $2.50. Another good option is to join the locals at food stands on the plaza, next to the red-and-white municipal building. A Guatemalan "tostada" or grilled corn with lime cost less than 50¢.

NEAR SANTA CRUZ DEL QUICHE

RUINAS DE UTATLAN

The ruins of the ancient Quiché capital have a zillion names and spellings. Call 'em Cumarcaj, Gumar-caaj, Kumarcaaj, or by their Spanish name, Utatlán, and everybody will know what you're talking about. The city's fate was sealed in 1524, when Pedro de Alvarado killed the Quiché hero Tecún Umán. The Quiché leaders sought revenge, inviting the conquistador to Utatlán with plans to trap him. Unfortu-nately for the indígena, Alvarado was neither stupid nor naive enough to believe that the Quichés would welcome him with open arms. All it took was a few spies to confirm his suspicions. Alvarado agreed to enter Utatlán as long as the Quiché leaders visited his camp first. Sadly, the leaders fell into their own trap and were burned to death. Alvarado soon leveled Utatlán to further weaken the Quichés. Today, the ancient kingdom's glory days barely shine through in the few pint-size temples, grassy mounds, and intact ball court. What makes the site worth the half-hour walk are the signs that villagers still use the site for religious ceremonies. At one of the temples you'll see melted candles and ashes in the wall altar. A cave that once upon a time connected Utatlán to Quetzaltenango is the local brujos' favorite spot for carrying out pagan rituals, including chicken sacrifices. The floor is covered with pine needles, an occa-sional chicken feather, and charred fire circles.

COMING AND GOING • To get to the site, walk from the bus station toward the central plaza and turn left on 10a Calle. The cobblestone street turns into a dirt road leading straight to Utatalán. The walk through the countryside is sweat-free, lots of fun, and takes about 30 minutes. You can also hire a taxi at the plaza to drive you, wait while you look around, and bring you back. It shouldn't cost more than $7, and probably a lot less—don't be afraid to bargain hard.

IXIL TRIANGLE

A narrow weather-worn road winds its way into the Cuchumatanes mountain range, eventually stopping in the heart of the Ixil Triangle. This wild and untamed region is home to the Ixil people and the only place in the world where the Ixil language is spoken. The three principle villages—Nebaj, San Juan Cotzal, and Chejul—are set in a lush, green valley. The heavy fog and mist of the Ixil Triangle are roman-tic, but it's the people that give the area its haunting beauty. Some 95% of the population communicates solely in their native tongue, and only a handful of people in each town speak Spanish. The women wear colorful skirts, delicately embroidered huipiles, and an unusual headdress made from a long sash with big pom-poms on the ends. The Ixil remain a proud and traditional clan, clinging tightly to their indige-nous heritage.

The beauty of this mountainous region and its proud people was overshadowed by years of violent con-flict between the guerrillas and the Guatemalan army. A long history of land and labor conflicts made the Ixil Triangle an area ripe for rebellion. In 1975, the Ejército Guerrillero de los Pobres (Guerrilla Army of the Poor) was born with the organized killing of a local landowner. The guerrillas enlisted the support of entire families, who provided them with information, food, shelter, supplies, and helped to harass local army units. As the army moved in to occupy villages, indigenous villagers began to "disappear." Reports show that, within the first year, the tortured and dismembered bodies of 32 community leaders in Nebaj, 40 in Chajul, and 28 in San Juan Cotzal were discovered. This was only the beginning. Some estimates say that fully a third of the Ixil population was either killed or "disappeared" during the scorched-earth campaigns of the early 1980s, and thousands more fled to hide in the mountains. Some consider the human rights abuses in the Ixil Triangle to be the worst in Central America.

In the late '80s, the army shifted strategies, forming controversial "voluntary" civil patrols and forcing civilians to act as the first line of resistance against the guerrillas. With large-scale sweeps of even the most isolated areas, the army sought to capture dissidents and wipe out potential solidarity networks for the guerrillas. Simultaneously, the government established development programs and "model" villages to entice civilians to leave their mountain hiding places voluntarily and return to a more stable way of life. Since the 1996 peace treaty, solidarity groups are working with returning refugee populations to reestab-lish local agriculture and trade and make sure that promises are kept and human rights are respected so the population can begin to heal its wounds.

COMING AND GOING

Buses to Nebaj leave Santa Cruz del Quiché (4 hrs, $2) daily at 8 AM, 10 AM, 12:30 PM, 1 PM, and 3:30 PM. You can also get to Nebaj indirectly from Huehuetenango; take a bus via Aguacatán to Sacapulas.

From there, you can intercept a crowded bus headed to Nebaj from Quiché. The road from Huehue is crappy and becomes impassable during the rainy season, so ask at the bus terminal about conditions before heading out.

GETTING AROUND

Bus service in the Ixil Triangle is unpredictable, slow, and sometimes nonexistent. It is also notorious for testing the patience of the mellowest of travelers. Needless to say, all bus schedules are best guesses—check departure times and arrive early, especially if you want a seat. The one bus between Nebaj and Chajul is on Sundays, when a bus leaves Chajul at 5 AM for the market in Nebaj, returning to Chajul around noon. The bus to Nebaj from Chichicastenango is supposed to continue on to San Juan Cotzal (1½ hrs), but often doesn't. Other than that, travel beyond Nebaj is primarily by pickup or on foot. It's not too hard to hitch a ride on market days to Cotzal (Wednesday and Saturday), Chajul (Tuesday and Friday), or from these towns to Nebaj (Thursday and Sunday), but a ride back is never a sure thing so you should plan on spending the night. The most reliable form of transportation is your feet. It takes about four hours to walk from Nebaj to Cotzal, and another two hours from Cotzal to Chajul. The treks are interesting and scenic if you have the energy.

NEBAJ

Nebaj is the transportation hub for the region, so you'll have to come here before exploring the smaller villages. The Ixil Triangle's minimetropolis, Nebaj enjoys an economic prosperity unknown in the other towns. Don't get the wrong idea, it's not like it has a bank or anything, but at least the new hospital has almost modern facilities. Cobblestone streets lead to a central plaza with a large colonial church. On market days (Thursday and Sunday), the town swells with people who come from all across the northern region to sell goods including intricate and distinctive weaving.

Outside of town, plenty of short hikes will keep you busy. Two sets of gushing waterfalls are about an hour outside of town; take the road to Chajul and turn left before the bridge. Across the bridge, you can walk to Chajul, but the round-trip hike makes for a grueling day. Unless you catch a lift, you should plan to stay there or hope to find a bus back. If you're curious about the model villages, nearby Acul is one example. Acul was one of the first of these planned communities and is actually quite pretty, with lots of planted trees and a simple church. Follow the road past the cemetery and ask along the way for the path to Acul. It takes about an hour and a half on foot; the mountain trail is steep and tiring, but it's much shorter than the road and has the added bonus of great views of both towns.

WHERE TO SLEEP AND EAT

The moment you step off the bus, you will be surrounded by children hoping to guide you to a hospedaje for a quetzal. The hospedajes are all within a block or two of the central plaza. **Tres Hermanas** is the oldest in town; the $3 double rooms are popular with backpackers and Peace Corps volunteers. Two blocks down, both **Hospedaje Kauari** and **Hospedaje El Rinconcito** have brighter rooms with shared hot water bath for $3 and $4.75, respectively. If you're really willing to splurge—a whole $6 for a double—try the **Ixil Hotel**; it's the fanciest digs in town. You can eat at the Ixil's restaurant, have comida típica with the folks at Tres Hermanas, or try one of the comedores by the daily market.

SAN JUAN COTZAL

Nestled on a steep hillside about 20 km (12½ mi) from Nebaj, is the town of San Juan Cotzal. Although it seems close, it takes about two hours in a truck or four hours on foot to cover the curvy road between the two villages. Market days (Tuesday and Friday) see a colorful sea of local green-and-blue huipiles mixed with the costumes of other Ixil villages. Ask about rooms at the pharmacy on the corner of the plaza—if they don't have one available, they can point you in the right direction. Eat at the market or in one of the few comedores near the plaza.

CHAJUL

Another two hour's walk from Cotzal, Chajul is the most traditional of the Ixil Triangle towns. Very few villagers speak Spanish, and the women wear bold red huipiles and headbands woven with bright designs in yellow, white, blue and green. Travelers are still a rare sight here, so you'll probably feel more comfortable on market days (Tuesday and Friday). At least you can pretend to have a reason for being here,

DEVELOPMENT
OR DEPRESSION?

During the notorious scorched-earth campaigns of the early 1980s, entire villages were burned to the ground, crops were destroyed, and thousands of Ixil villagers were slaughtered. Survivors of the attacks fled to the mountains, rapidly forming a population of civilian refugees living with little food and no protection. It is estimated that, by 1987, as many as 30,000 civilians were living in what came to be called Communities of Population in Resistance. In the late '80s and early '90s, the military introduced development programs such as Fusiles y Frijoles (Bullets and Beans) and Techo, Trabajo, y Tortillas (Shelter, Work, and Tortillas) that were designed to entice civilians to return peacefully from their hiding places in the mountains in exchange for housing and food.

One integral part of these development programs was the establishment of dozens of "model villages." These experimental communities were designed to group indígena into small areas, enabling the state to monitor activities and discourage alliances with guerrilla groups. The model villages varied: some allowed villagers complete freedom of movement, while others were surrounded by barbed-wire fences with army watchtowers nearby.

The drastic transition to a structured and monitored lifestyle was not without its problems. Depression was common among the villagers, and the war-weary refugees often found it difficult to rebuild their lives after such massive changes. Also, a shortage of crop land close to town boundaries meant that most villagers had to trek long distances to reach the tiny plots they relied upon on for subsistence. For many, these model villages were comfortable prisons where the indígena of Guatemala were forced to give up their traditional lifestyles to become "model" Ladino citizens.

as you are bombarded by women and children selling their work at ridiculously low prices. On the second Friday of Lent (i.e., one month before Easter), pilgrims from all over the northern region come to the huge colonial church to pay their respects to the Christ of Golgotha. A few local families run makeshift pensions where you can get a bed and a meal for about $1.50. Ask at the post office, or check with people around the plaza.

QUETZALTENANGO

In the heart of the Western Highlands, Quetzaltenango is Guatemala's second-largest city. Just a few hours from Guatemala City, the Mexican border, and the Pacific coast, Quetzaltenango is a major transportation hub. Fortunately, Quetzaltenango doesn't have the traffic and scummy, crowded streets that make the capital an urban nightmare. Instead, it sits deep in a valley with a perfect view of the majestic

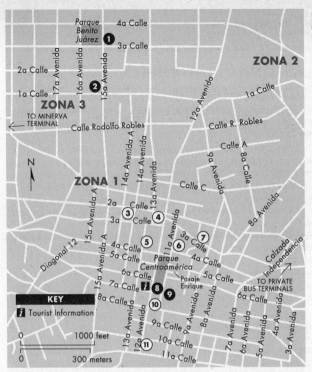

Sights ●
Catedral, 9
La Iglesia de San Nicolás, 1
Mercado La Democracia, 2
Museo de Historia Natural, 8

Lodging ○
Casa Kaehler, 5
Hotel Capri, 10
Hotel Colonial, 7
Hotel El Centro, 11
Hotel Modelo, 3
Hotel Río Azul, 4
Pensión Bonifaz, 6

QUETZALTENANGO

Volcán Santa María. The surrounding hills produce vegetables, corn, and, of course, coffee. That "eternal spring" that INGUAT raves about doesn't apply here—rainy days and cold nights are the norm. Travelers come to the area to relax by the luxurious hot springs before or after working themselves into a frenzy shopping. Tons of shops throughout the city sell woven goods, and local fabrics are known for their high quality. The first Sunday of each month is the main market day, and the Parque Centroamérica becomes a shopper's heaven. Even if the shopping thing isn't for you, you can watch the weaving process in many of the small villages in the area. Quetzaltenango is also a choice place to study Spanish, with several excellent programs that are widely considered more rigorous than those in Antigua Guatemala. Word spreads fast, however, and Quetzaltenango has recently become the most popular "alternative" site to study Spanish. The steady influx of foreign students has its advantages and can be a lot of fun, but Quetzaltenango is no longer the place to go if you really want to avoid speaking English. The city makes a great jumping-off point for excursions to villages in the surrounding valley that offer a variety of colorful markets, hot springs, and long nature walks.

Originally part of the Mayan Kingdom, the city was taken over in the 14th century by the Quiché, who called it Xelaju. It wasn't until later, when Pedro de Alvarado's troops renamed all the defeated Quiché cities, that the name Quetzaltenango, meaning Land of the Quetzal, was born. Today, the city is commonly referred to as Xela, in remembrance of its roots. By the early 19th century, Quetzaltenango had become as important as Guatemala City, and the city fathers attempted to form independent political ties with Mexico. Needless to say, this activity didn't please Guatemalan president Carrera, who pulled Quetzaltenango and the surrounding region into the Central American Federation in 1840. When the city made a second attempt at secession in 1848, cries of independence were silenced with brute force. During the coffee boom of the early 1900s, Xela climbed to new levels of wealth and prosperity. It was during this period that President Manuel Estrada Cabrera built the town's various neoclassical structures. Although it's hard to say if these monuments were a source of inspiration, Quetzaltenango does pride itself on being an intellectual center. In 1902, a disastrous earthquake shook the living daylights out of Xela. The city was eventually rebuilt, but it never again generated enough momentum to rival Guatemala City.

BASICS

VISITOR INFORMATION • INGUAT, next to the Casa de Cultura, gives out free maps and sells posters and videos, but don't expect any fascinating tidbits about the city—all you get is regurgitated brochure lines. *7a Calle, south end of Parque Centroamérica, Z1, tel. 762–4931. Open weekdays 8–noon and 2–6, Sat. 8–noon.*

MONEY • Nearly every Guatemalan bank has a branch on Parque Centroamérica. Two with longer hours are **Banco del Café** (12a Av., between. 5a and 6a calles, Z1; open Mon.–Thurs. 8:30–8, Fri. 8–8, Sat. 10–2) and **Banco Inmobiliario** (4a Calle and 12a Av., Z1; open weekdays 9–5:30, Sat. 9:30–2). Another money-changing option is the somewhat elusive **black market.** To find a dealer, ask in one of the appliance stores around the Mercado La Democracia (*see* Worth Seeing, *below*). You're sure to get a wink, a smile, and some helpful information, if not a transaction.

CONSULATES • Mexico. Getting a tourist card here will save you time and money at the border. Tourist cards are free, but be sure to bring a photocopy of your passport. If you're driving, you'll have to process your paperwork at the border; expect to pay a small fee ($1) if they decide to fumigate. *9a Av. 6–19, Z1, 2 blocks from Parque Centroamérica, tel. 763–1312. Open weekdays 8–11 and 2–3.*

LANGUAGE SCHOOLS • Quetzaltenango has more language schools than you can shake a stick at. For most you won't need to make advance reservations, although it's a good idea to call ahead during the tourist season (Dec.–Jan. and June–Aug.) Shop around, because some schools have accredited teachers and offer social and environmental weekend activities. Program prices range from $100 to $150 a week, including a home stay with a family. The following programs are very popular and come highly recommended by students.

Desarrollo del Pueblo. This nonprofit language school has an activist bent. Students are presented with opportunities to become directly involved in local community development projects and assist in coordinating long-term volunteer work if desired. *20a Av. 0-65, Z1, Quetzaltenango, Apdo. 41, tel. 762–2932, fax 761–6754.*

ICA. In addition to the excellent private Spanish-language classes, ICA also sponsors "ICAmigos" projects that include reforestation in water conservation zones, health education programs, and support for bilingual schools of indigenous languages and Spanish. *1a Calle 16–93, Z1, 09001, Quetzaltenango, tel. 761–6786. In the United States: 900 Frances St., Suite 351, Richardson, TX 75081, tel. and fax 214/699–0935.*

Proyecto Lingüístico Quetzalteco de Español has an intensive language program and organized activities. Funds raised through the school help support groups that promote and defend human rights. *5a Calle 2–40, Z1, tel. and fax 761–2620. In the United States: tel. and fax 502/961–2620.*

LAUNDRY • Drop off those dirty, smelly duds at **Lavandería El Centro** and come back an hour and a half later to find them washed, dried, and folded for less than $3. *15a Av. and 4a Calle, below TELGUA, Z1. Open Mon.–Sat. 8–12:30 and 2–7.*

PHONES AND MAIL • Xela has two **TELGUA** offices, both of which are open daily 7 AM–10 PM. The Zona 1 office is three blocks west of the Parque Centroamérica, on the corner of 15a Avenida and 4a Calle, on the second floor. The other office is in Zona 3 on 15a Avenida and 3a Calle, a block away from Parque Benito Juárez. The **post office** (15a Av. and 4a Calle; open weekdays 8–4) is just across the street from the Zona 1 TELGUA. The elegant but weathered neoclassical building has stone columns and decorative molding, and the inner terrace is now a basketball court.

COMING AND GOING

Both private and second-class buses service Quetzaltenango. The private buses cost a bit more, but you can make reservations in advance to guarantee a seat. All buses—even the ones marked DIRECTO—stop en route to pick up and drop off passengers, although the private do so slightly less frequently.

BY SECOND-CLASS BUS • Second-class buses use **Terminal Minerva** on 6a Calle in Zona 3. As you arrive, you'll be greeted by aggressive bus hustlers working among the hundreds of parked buses. As if that weren't hectic enough, the terminal also has a market. To transfer to a city bus, walk through the market alley and turn left on 4a Calle; keep going until you cross 25a Avenida. Buses marked PARQUE will bring you to Zona 1's Parque Centroamérica. Xela's banks, hotels, restaurants, and few tourist attractions are all within a few blocks. To get to Terminal Minerva from Zona 1, hop on any city bus marked TERMINAL.

Buses leave hourly to Guatemala City (4½ hrs, $4), Huehuetenango (2½ hrs, $1), Retalhuleu (2 hrs, $1), and San Andrés Xequl (15 min, 25¢). Buses also head hourly to Zunil (25 min, 25¢), San Francisco El Alto (1 hr, 60¢), and Momostenango (1½ hrs, 75¢) via Cuatro Caminos. To reach La Mesilla at the Mexican border, take a bus to Huehuetenango, where you can find a connecting bus. There are direct buses to Chichicastenango on Thursday and Sunday only. Otherwise, take Guatemala City bus to Los Encuentros (2 hrs, $1) and connect to a bus headed for either Chichi or Santa Cruz del Quiché. For Almolonga (15 min, 20¢) and Totonicapán (45 min, 50¢), it's best to avoid the chaotic Minerva Terminal and catch a bus from the rotunda on Calzada Independencia. The bus to Almolonga stops at the corner of 9a Avenida and 10a Calle, two blocks east and four blocks south of the Parque Centroamérica. Buses heading to Totonicapán start at 10a Avenida and 8a Calle.

BY PRIVATE BUS • Private buses sell tickets and leave from their own terminals. **Rutas Limas** (2a Calle and Calzada Independencia, Z2, tel. 761–2033) has service to Guatemala City (4 hrs, $5) daily at 5:15 AM, 7:15 AM, and 2:15 PM. You can also buy tickets from their office on 11a Avenida in Zona 1, a block above Parque Centroamérica, next to Pensión Bonifaz. **Lineas Américas** (Calzada Independencia, Z2, tel. 761–2063) runs between Quetzaltenango and Guatemala City (4 hrs, $5) five times daily from 5:15 AM to 8 PM. To get to the Lineas Américas Terminal from Parque Centroamérica, go three blocks east of 5a Calle, turn left on Diagonal 3, and left onto Calzada Independencia. **Galgos** (Calle Rodolfo Robles 17–43, Z1, tel. 761–2248) has the most destinations and departures of the private companies. Buses to Guatemala City (4 hrs, $5) leave six times daily between 3:30 AM and 4:45 PM. Buses leave from Guatemala City for Quetzaltenango seven times a day between 5:30 AM and 7 PM. Galgos is the only line that travels to the Mexican border at Talisman (7 hrs, $5), passing through Retalhuleu (1½ hrs, 75¢) and Tecún Umán (5 hrs, $4). To get to the Galgos Terminal from Parque Centroamérica, take 12a Avenida north and turn left on Calle Rodolfo Robles.

WHERE TO SLEEP

Hotels speckle every corner of the city, but the greatest variety of accommodations is around the park. The sophisticated and wealthy stay at the **Pensión Bonifaz** (4a Calle, north end of Parque Centroamérica, Z1, tel. 761–2182) for $60 a pop, but there are plenty of cheaper options.

UNDER $5 • Hotel Colonial. This rickety, run-down place has decent rooms with the usual setup: a bed, a chair, and a window. The shared bathrooms are primitive, bordering on unsanitary. A long porch on the second floor is nice for gazing out at the city's rooftops. Doubles are $4. Believe it or not, Hotel Colonial is a step up from most of Xela's cheapo spots. *3a Calle, behind Pensión Bonifaz and 1 block down, Z1, tel. 971–2488. 10 rooms, none with bath. Cash only.*

UNDER $10 • Casa Kaehler. This house has been around for more than 20 years. A favorite among budget travelers, it offers that extra bit of comfort everyone can appreciate. The colonial-style building has a courtyard, big private rooms, and clean bathrooms with hot water. Doubles with shared bath are $8; and if it's available, the hotel's one comfortable suite, with it's own bathroom, is worth the extra $2. *13 Av. 3–33, 1 block west and 1 block north of Parque Centroamérica, Z1, tel. 762–2091. 7 rooms, 1 with bath. Cash only.*

Hotel Capri. One of the nicest value sleeps, Hotel Capri is often filled with traveling Guatemalan families and the occasional backpacker. Rooms have clean private bathrooms; a double will set you back $5.50. A popular comedor with decent local eats occupies the front part of the hotel, facing the street. *8a Calle 11–39, 1 block below Parque Centroamérica, behind Casa de Cultura, Z1, tel. 761–4111. 20 rooms with bath. Cash only.*

UNDER $20 • Hotel El Centro. You'll get a hot bath, sunlit rooms, filtered water for brushing your teeth, and cable TV. The rooms are spotless, and the bathrooms have clean towels and soap. Doubles are $18. *10a Calle and 12a Av., 3 blocks south of Parque Centroamérica, Z1. 8 rooms with bath.*

Hotel Río Azul. For $12 a double, you'll get a great night's sleep in a very clean room with a private bathroom. Perfect. *2a Calle 2–51, Z1, tel. 763–0654. 16 rooms with bath. Cash only.*

UNDER $30 • Hotel Modelo. Founded in 1883, the Modelo is a small, family-run establishment that has maintained a distinguished appearance and a tradition of good service. Rooms face a couple of small courtyards with porticoes leading off the lobby, which also adjoins a fine little colonial-style restaurant. Much of the hotel's furniture is antique, and the rooms have wooden floors and stucco walls decorated with traditional weavings. Doubles with private bath and cable TV cost $25, but there's also a nearby annex, which has newer rooms that rent for $19. *14a Av. "A" 2–31, Z1, tel. 763–1376. 24 rooms with bath.*

FOOD

If the quickest way to you heart is through your stomach, then you'll fall in love with this town. Quetzaltenango's not big on comida típica, and restaurants cater to an international palate. At **Super Mercado La Selecta** (4a Calle, a block from Parque Centroamérica, Z1), you can find excellent cheese made by the local Xelac Cooperative. For delicate goodies like pastries and quiches, plant yourself at **Café Baviera** (5a Calle and 12a Av., 1 block west of Parque Centroamérica, Z1). **Café Berna** (16a Av., across from Parque Benito Juárez, Z3) has a similar menu, including exquisite freshly baked bread. Just before leaving town, be sure to stock up on the delicious chocolate-chip and coconut cookies from Bake Shop, near the Terminal Minerva on the other side of the street.

UNDER $5 • Blue Angel Video Cafe. A favorite hangout among foreign students, this place serves tasty soups and sandwiches for $1 and has a full coffee menu, including a café mocha for 60¢. The back of the menu lists more than 50 movies that you can watch for $1 a person in the back room, popcorn included. There's also a small collection of used books and magazines in English, which you can rent for 20¢ a day, or you can buy, sell, or trade your old novels. If the books and movies aren't enough to entertain you, they also have an impressive collection of board games available, including chess and backgammon. *7a Calle, between 15a and 16a Avs., Z1, no phone.*

Chicago Grill and Garden. This restaurant had a loyal clientele less than a week after its grand opening in 1995. Specialties include the tenderloin steak sandwich with melted mozzarella cheese ($3), a bacon cheeseburger with barbecue sauce ($3), and vegetable stir fry ($2.50). The servings are big, the food's tasty, and the waiters are probably the best in Guatemala. *13a Av. 5–38, Z1, no phone.*

Deli-Cafe. This cute, tavern-style restaurant has decent food at cheap prices. The menu isn't particularly original, but at 75¢ for a chicken sandwich, who's complaining? You can also get tacos for 50¢ and crepes (more like pancakes) with fruit for $2. Then wash down the whole shebang with a beer. *14 Av., between 3a and 4a calles, 1 block north and 1 block west of Parque Centroamérica, Z1, no phone.*

Pizza Ricca. If you're craving pizza with rich sauce, gooey cheese, a thin crust, and any topping you can think of, you're headed in the right direction. Pizzas are baked in clay ovens and take 15 minutes to be prepared—just long enough for you to salivate all over yourself. Cheese pizzas are $2, and salads with avocado and cucumber are $1. *14a Av., between 3a and 4a calles, 1 block north of Parque Centroamérica, Z1, tel. 761–8162.*

Restaurante Shanghai. Here, Guatemalan chefs do the Chinese thang. With red Chinese columns, painted dragons, and vinyl seats, the atmosphere is sort of like Denny's meets the Orient. You can get duck, shrimp and, of course, wonton soup for $2.50. Portions are huge. *4a Calle 12–22, west of Parque Centroamérica, Z1, tel. 761–4154.*

UNDER $10 • Café Restaurante Royal Paris. This eatery is by far the best place to dine in town. A menu of delicious salads, fish, and chicken is complemented by an artsy decor and old jazz tunes. Spaghetti carbonara ($3.50), fillet of fish ($4), and Caesar salad ($2.50) will all make your taste buds happy. A full-service bar and Latin guitar on the weekends make Royal Paris popular with the young professional crowd. *16 Av. 3–05, facing Parque Benito Juárez, Z3, no phone.*

El Kopetin. El Kopetin is comforting and familiar, with its wood paneling and long polished bar. The menu has a number of appetizers, like *queso fundido* (melted cheese served with condiments and tortillas), and a selection of meat and seafood dishes, often smothered in rich sauces. *14 Av. 3–51, Z1, tel. 761–8381.*

WORTH SEEING

For such a big city, Quetzaltenango doesn't really have much in the way of tourist attractions. You'll see lots of neoclassical architecture; look for the stone columns and intricate ceilings.

Parque Centroamérica. Much of that architecture stuff is represented in this central park, making it the most stunning plaza in Guatemala. As you walk through the park, you'll catch a glimpse of **Pasaje Enrique,** a crumbling old building with BEWARE OF FALLING GLASS signs posted on the inner passageway leading to 13a Avenida. It was planned as a shopping center for the rich and famous, but without a Robin Leach crowd, only a bar and an ice-cream shop could drum up enough business to survive. Also on the Parque Centroamérica is the recently refurbished **cathedral.** The old facade, which faces 11a Avenida, features life-size patron saints looking down upon the rest of us sinners. The Casa de la Cultura, on the south side of the park, houses the **Museo de Historia Natural** (open weekdays 9–6, Sat. 8–4), which displays some mildly interesting pre-Columbian pottery and historical information about the city. *Between 11a and 12a Avs., 4a and 7a calles, Z1.*

Parque Benito Juárez. The highlight of this secondary park is **La Iglesia de San Nicolás,** on the east side. This religious structure tries hard to be sophisticated, with flying buttresses and a baroque design. Ultimately, it looks out of place in Xela's mix of Greek and colonial structures. *15a and 16a Avs., 3a and 4a calles, Z3. From Parque Centroamérica, walk 3 blocks east to 15a Av., 8 blocks north.*

Mercado La Democracia. This four-block shopping area is lined with overstocked stores selling household goods, appliances, and produce. *Between 15a and 16a Avs., 1a and 2a calles, Z3. From Parque Centroamérica, 3 blocks east to 15a Av., 6 blocks north.*

AFTER DARK

Café Restaurante Royal Paris (*see* Food, *above*) will facilitate your caffeine buzz until midnight. **Salon Tecún** (Pasaje Enrique, off Parque Centroamérica), where the waitress doesn't speak any Spanish, is a cozy bar catering mostly to gringos and the Guatemalans who love them. On Friday and Saturday nights, nearby **El Garage** (Centro Commercial Ciani, on Blvd. Minerva, Z3) hosts a gay and hetero crowd. It's open from 9 PM to 2 AM, and the cover is a buck. In the same vein, check out **Music Center** (12a Av., below Calzada Minerva, Z3), where college students from San Carlos University hang out; beer is about $1.20. Finally, if all you're craving is chips and a dark tap beer, **Taberna de Don Rodrigo** (14 Av., near 1a Calle, Z1; open daily 10–10) should do the trick.

OUTDOOR ACTIVITIES

An hour's walk from town, the **El Baúl** lookout point offers one swell view of the surrounding valley. From Parque Centroamérica, take 5a Calle east for three blocks and turn left on Diagonal 3, then walk eight blocks and turn right at the EL BAUL sign.

About 3½ kms (1¼ mi) from central Quetzaltenango are the **Baños Los Vahos,** a series of natural saunas where you can sweat it out for a $1 fee. It makes a fun, cheap, and relaxing day trip from Xela. A smart indígena woman, who knows a tourist attraction when she sees one, runs a small hotel and comedor above the saunas. Rooms run about $5 per person, but you'll probably be more comfortable staying in Xela. Be sure to bring warm clothes for the walk back, because people have been known to faint from the drastic change in temperature from the steam baths to the cool mountain air. From Parque Centroamérica, walk south on 12a Avenida until it ends,

> *A believer explains, "San Simón cures people when doctors can't, he solves problems when lawyers can't; he's a good friend to have, especially when you're traveling, because even in the best of cars, the brakes can fail."*

turn left for two blocks, then right up the hill. Keep going until you see the sign for Los Vahos. Follow the dirt road up the mountainside and make the first right. It's near the top; when the road forks, veer left. The trip should take about an hour from the paved road. The bus to Almolonga will take you as far as Los Vahos.

The exhausting four-hour hike up **Volcán Santa María** rewards you with a spectacular view of the surrounding valley and the four other volcanoes to the east. It's a tough haul, but on a clear day the view is worth it. Bring plenty of food and water and something warm for the way down. To get to the base, take a bus from the Minerva Terminal to Llanes del Pinal (25 min, 20¢); they leave hourly 7–5. It's best to go with a group; ask around at the language schools to find willing companions or a guide.

NEAR QUETZALTENANGO

MOMOSTENANGO

After a rough 35-km (22-mi) bus ride from Quetzaltenango, you'll see Momostenango poking it's head out of a thick pine forest. This isolated town is the wool capital of Guatemala, and zillions of blankets and jackets are woven, dyed, and washed here before being sent to other markets. For quality goods at decent prices, check out the town cooperative, on the main street leading into town, just after the arch that says BIENVENIDOS A MOMOSTENANGO. It's open weekdays 8–12:30 and 2–5:30, Sunday 8–noon, and if you ask nicely, the friendly manager will show you around and explain the wool process. The town is much more happening on market days (Wednesday and Sunday), although the excitement is short-lived during the rainy season when folks head home early to beat the late-afternoon thunderstorms. Several hot springs lie within a few kilometers of the main plaza, and local children will happily lead the way to one (or all) of them for a few quetzales. The best place in town for shelter and sustenance is **Hospedaje Palcom** (1a Calle and 2a Av.). Rooms are $1.75 per person; try to get one upstairs. Palcom also has an excellent comedor—you'll eat especially well if you ask for the same meal the family is about to consume. Momostenango's water supply is sporadic, so don't count on running water—much less a hot shower—no matter where you stay. Direct buses leave for Momostenango (1½ hrs, 75¢) from Quetzaltenango's Terminal Minerva hourly from 9 to 4. Buses also leave from Cuatro Caminos until 2 PM. The last bus from Momostenango to Quetzaltenango leaves at 3 PM.

SAN ANDRES XEQUL

Fifteen km (9 mi) north of Quetzaltenango, San Andrés Xequl is home to what is likely the funkiest church in Central America. In the middle of a valley of cornfields, this neon-yellow church painted with bright blue angels, green vines, and a pair of menacing lions looks surreal. Although there's nothing to do in San Andrés, the church is worth a peek if you're passing by on your way somewhere else. To get here, hop on any bus heading to Cuatro Caminos and ask to be let off at San Andrés Xequl. The bus will drop you off less than a kilometer out of town.

SAN FRANCISCO EL ALTO

To round off your Guatemalan shopping spree, be sure to hit the Friday market in San Francisco El Alto. The market to end all markets, this one fills the central plaza to the bursting point, spilling onto a nearby field and into the surrounding streets. Enthusiastic vendors and equally enthusiastic shoppers from all over the highlands congregate to exchange goods and cash. You won't find anything different here, but the town's hilltop location makes it one of the more beautiful spots to shop. True to the town's name— El Alto means "the high one"—the streets seem to drop off into a 100-foot ravine carpeted with corn stalks. The ideal spot for all your Kodak memories is the church roof in the plaza. For 20¢ you can climb the bell tower and gaze dreamily down on the entire valley. If you feel like spending a few days here, try **Hotel Vista Hermosa** (3a Av., near the central plaza). Doubles are $5 and Rooms 6 through 11 offer stunning views of the volcanoes around the Quetzaltenango valley. Buses to San Francisco El Alto (30 min, 25¢) leave hourly from Quetzaltenango's Terminal Minerva.

TOTONICAPAN

Less than an hour from Quetzaltenango, Totonicapán is filled with *talleres* (workshops) where you can watch artisans make the clay pottery, wooden boxes, tin ornaments, and woven skirts that you see throughout the highlands. At the **Casa de la Cultura** (8a Av., between 2a and 3a calles) you can pick up a map that designates the locations of more than 60 talleres; most are within five or six blocks of the main plaza. Try to visit on a Tuesday or Saturday for the market, when an almost entirely indígena crowd livens up the streets. It's extremely colorful, very friendly, and cheaper than markets that draw lots of tourists. If you want to spend the night here, **Hotel San Miguel** (8a Av. between 2a and 3a calles) and **Hospedaje El Centro** (7a Calle between 7a and 8a Avs.) both have decent rooms for about $5 per person. **Comedor Lety** (8a Av. and 3a Calle) is the most popular comedor in town; full meals cost $1–$3. Buses leave Quetzaltenango for Totonicapán (45 min, 50¢) hourly from La Rotunda, a small bus terminal on Calzada Independencia at 2a Calle. The last bus out of Totonicapán leaves at 5 PM.

ZUNIL AND FUENTES GEORGINAS

Eight km (5 mi) south of Quetzaltenango, the little town of Zunil sits at the base of an extinct volcano. Zunil is a radiant highland village surrounded by the most fertile land in the valley. Mud and adobe houses are arranged around a whitewashed colonial church that marks the center of town. At the top of the hill on the outskirts of the village you'll find the local cemetery, which is lined with tombstones painted in soft, airy pinks and blues. Monday is market day, and women with flashy purple shawls crowd the indoor marketplace hawking fruits and vegetables that come straight from their own gardens. Zunil is another good place to pay your respects to San Simón. Here, the idol has become a tourist attraction, and gringos are charged 50¢ to see him. Everyone in town knows where he is, and almost everyone asks a favor of him at some time or another. Don't forget to bring a small gift. From Xela, buses to Zunil (25 min, 25¢) travel via Almolonga, leaving from the corner of 10a Calle and 9a Avenida in Zona 1.

Zunil's main claim to fame is the **Fuentes Georginas** hot springs, 10 km (6 mi) away. The springs are set against a natural stone wall, and lush tropical plants shield bathers from the sun's harsh rays. For $1, you can frolic in the water to your heart's content. There are two pools; the larger one has a rock and cement bottom, and the smaller, "natural" pool has a sand bottom. Weekends are busy, and the pools get a little murky. The larger pool is closed for cleaning on Mondays, and the smaller pool is closed on Wednesday, so the best day to come is on a Tuesday or Thursday. You can also spend the night in an adorable bungalow nearby; doubles are $10, with a fireplace and plenty of wood included. To get here, take a taxi from outside Zunil's church. It should cost about $3 a person round-trip, a little less if you're in a group. Be sure to agree on how long the taxi will wait at the hot springs before you go. Alternately, you can attempt the 2½ to 3 hours upward hike on foot. The hike is pleasant and walkable. Not far past the sheltered bus stop on the main road above Zunil you'll see the sign marking the dirt road to the hot springs. Don't count on hitching, because only the taxis use this road.

HUEHUETENANGO

Huehuetenango, just off the Pan-American Highway, was once part of the powerful Mam Maya Kingdom that dominated most of the highland area. It wasn't until much later that the Guatemalan Quiché came into the area to stir things up, pushing the Mam Maya up into the Cuchumatanes Mountains and as far north as Chiapas, Mexico. But you'd never really guess any of that in today's Huehue, a Ladinoized land of *ropa americana* and raunchy American "B" movies. For travelers, Huehue is a convenient stopover on the way to or from the Mexican border and a springboard for more isolated towns in the Cuchumatanes Mountains. Those just coming to Guatemala from Mexico might find it a decent intro to the highlands, but for the most part the city is friendly but boring with little to offer most travelers. Stay only as long as it takes you to get cash at the bank, call Mom from TELGUA, and pay a much-needed visit to a lavandería—more interesting places beckon.

Maybe the most interesting thing in Huehuetenango is the sluggish **plaza central** (between 4a and 5a Avs., 2a and 3a calles), which is hemmed in by an impressive old church, a cool clock tower, and a weird pink shell-shaped bandstand on the second floor of the Municipalidad. Just a few blocks east on 1a and 2a Avenida, is the considerably more active **indoor market,** filled with vendors selling everyday needs like chili peppers, hand-made sausages, and dish towels. There are also a few stands selling beautiful típico goods from remote highland villages. Nearby lie the tidy grounds of the ancient Mayan capital of **Zaculeu** (*see* Near Huehuetenango, *below*); the ruins are only 10 minutes away by bus and might be worth a visit if you've done all your errands and still have some time to kill.

BASICS

If you plan to visit the more isolated villages to the north, Huehuetenango is the last place to cash traveler's checks and take care of banking needs. **Banco del Agro** (2a Calle, north end of central plaza) is open weekdays 9–8, Saturday 9–2. The police station is at 5a Avenida and 6a Calle. **TELGUA** (open daily 7 AM–midnight) and the **post office** (open weekdays 8–4:30) are conveniently located side by side on 2a Calle, east of the central plaza. The post office is in the back of the building. The **Mexican Consulate** (5a Av. and 4a Calle; open daily 9–noon and 3–5), inside the Farmacia del Cid, issues tourist cards for $1 that will save you the hassle at the border.

COMING AND GOING

Huehuetenango is just off the Pan-American Highway, and buses from everywhere in the highlands pull in and out all day long. The easiest way to get to Huehue from just about anywhere is to get to Los Encuentros or Cuatro Caminos and catch a bus or passing truck from there. Buses into town leave you at the **terminal** on 6a Calle, 2 km (1 mi) from the central plaza. Minivans shuttle people from the terminal to the plaza for 10¢, leaving when they fill up. From the terminal, you can catch direct buses to La Mesilla (2½ hrs, $1.25) on the Mexican border, Quetzaltenango (2½ hrs, $1.25), or Guatemala City (5 hrs, $4.50). Buses leave daily from 5 AM to 5 PM. To Retalhuleu and the Pacific coast, take a bus headed to Guatemala City or Quetzaltenango and transfer at Cuatro Caminos. To Lake Atitlán and Chichicastenango, take a Guatemala City bus and transfer at Los Encuentros. To Antigua Guatemala, transfer at Chimaltenango.

If you're tired of sitting in contorted positions on "chicken buses" and want legroom for the five-hour trip between Huehuetenango and Guatemala City, take a first-class bus. Tickets are a little more expensive ($5.50), and you might have to buy them a day in advance. **Los Halcones** (7a Av. 3–62) has departures at 7 AM and 2 PM, **Rápidos Zaculeu** (3a Av. 5–25) leaves at 6 AM and 3 PM, and **Velazquez** (1a Av. near 2a Calle) shoves off at 2 AM and 10 AM.

WHERE TO SLEEP

Because it's a common pit stop on the way to and from Mexico, Huehuetenango has plenty of hotels from which to choose. What you get for your money varies quite a bit, so look around.

UNDER $5 • Pensión Astoria. This pension has dark doubles for $4.50, $7.50 with private bath. The main advantage is that the place is extremely secure: at night there is a guard, and the gates are securely locked. Sheets will be changed daily if you ask. Hot showers are lukewarm at best. The comedor inside serves breakfast only. *4a Av. 1–45. From plaza, a block east, and turn left. 18 rooms, 6 with bath. Cash only.*

UNDER $10 • Hotel Mary. Across from TELGUA and the post office, this hotel has spartan rooms with waxed floors. The rooftop terrace offers a view of Huehue, the surrounding mountains, and an excellent perspective of TELGUA's antennae and satellite dish. Doubles are $6.50, $11 with private bath. The comedor on the second floor has okay grub. *2a Calle 3–52, 1 block east of plaza, tel. 764–1618. 40 rooms, 22 with bath. Cash only.*

UNDER $25 • Hotel Zaculeu. If you want to "deluxe out" with color TV, an immaculate private bathroom, and filtered water in your room, head to this quasiluxury hotel with $21 doubles. There are several types of rooms to choose from: older rooms are cheaper and have more character, while newer rooms are bland but have cable TV and modern bathrooms. *5a Av. 1–14, tel. 764–1086. 29 rooms, 18 with bath.*

FOOD

Huehue is not going to win you over through your stomach. The town has its share of comedores, but few restaurants offer any variety. For breakfast, most hotels have their own comedores that serve up the standard oatmeal, eggs, frijoles, cheese, and tortillas for a buck. If you're craving real chocolate, Pringles chips, or even canned tuna fish at 2 AM, make a beeline for the 24-hour store at the corner of 1a Calle and 3a Avenida. Ice-cream lovers behold: the store carries Mars and Musketeer bars filled with rich vanilla ice cream, imported all the way from Illinois, USA.

Café Restaurante Jardín. This joint has one of the biggest menus around. Take your pick between Central American, Mexican, Huehuetenangoen, and *la casa comida* (home-cooked food). Try chicken pepín—a local dish of chicken prepared in an vaguely spicy sauce—for $3. Because it's open late, teenagers bring their dates here in the evening. *4a Calle at 6a Av., 1 block west of plaza, no phone.*

Comedor Hotel Central. On the first floor of Hotel Central, this place serves the best-value meals in town. A delicious lunch or dinner might include roasted chicken, carne asada, or chile relleno with soup, vegetable, rice, beans, salad, tortillas, and coffee for less than $2. Breakfast is *arroz con leche* (rice with milk and sugar), fruit, eggs, beans, cheese, tortillas, and coffee for $1.50. *5a Av. 1–33, no phone.*

Pizza Hogareña. With only six tables in the front room, this place is popular with folks who come here for that cozy hole-in-the-wall feel. The cheese on the pizza is excellent—quite unlike the typical Guatemalan cheese that's salty and crumbly. A large cheese pizza is only $3.50, and ice-cold fruit shakes are 50¢. *6a Av. between 4a and 5a calles, 1 block from plaza, no phone.*

Restaurante Bougamvillas. Popular with Huehue residents, this is one of the best comedores in town. For $2 they'll whip up a filling plate of chicken, beef, or chorizo (sausage), with soup or salad, frijoles, and tortillas. *5a Av. at 4a Calle, across from Banco de Guatemala, no phone.*

NEAR HUEHUETENANGO

ZACULEU

This ancient city was originally built around AD 600 by the Mam tribe of the ancient Maya. The site was chosen for its strategic location, with natural barriers on three sides. It's hard to imagine that two small ravines and a river could later act as a defense against 16th-century Spaniards, but unfortunately they worked all too well. The invading Spanish troops, led by Pedro de Alvarado's brother Gonzalo, realized they could not take Zaculeu by force and chose instead to cut them off and starve them out. Within two months, the city surrendered. Today, the ruins consist of a few pyramids, a ball court, a well-manicured lawn, and a skimpy two-room museum. If Zaculeu seems bare, it's because the Mam Indians didn't decorate their structures at all—this leaves little to marvel at except their size. If you've seen Mayan ruins before, you probably won't be impressed, but for the uninitiated, climbing around on the ancient pyramids will spark the urge to romanticize about the glory days of Mayan civilization. On a nice day, the grounds are a terrific spot for a picnic.

The site is open daily 8–noon and 2–6, and admission is 20¢. Buses to Zaculeu (15 min, 15¢) leave Huehue hourly from right in front of the school on 7a Avenida, between 2a and 3a calles. If you'd rather hoof it (45 min), several roads lead to the site; count on a full half-hour walk whichever way you go. One route is to follow 4a Calle west out of town until the road forks, take the dirt road to the right, then make another right at the next dirt road. Look for signs along the way.

CHIANTLA

Perched on the mountain above Huehuetenango, Chiantla is famous for its Virgen de Candelaria. Pilgrims—some crawling on their hands and knees—come from all over Guatemala to ask her divine intervention in healing the sick. On February 2, they arrive en masse to pray to her in the colonial church. The statue is beautifully capped in silver, and legend has it that a Spaniard, Señor Almengor, gave the Virgen to Chiantla as an offering after she saved his life in a mining accident. Buses to Chiantla (20 min, 10¢) leave Huehue every 20 minutes, 6 AM–7 PM, from the corner of 1a Avenida and 1a Calle. The bus stops near the town church.

TODOS SANTOS CUCHUMATAN

Although it takes three hours to cover the 40 km (24 mi) separating Huehuetenango and Todos Santos by bus, the bumpy, uphill ride is probably the best way to experience the tremendous height and mass of the Cuchumatanes Mountains. The winding dirt road is too narrow for oncoming buses to pass, and the ride can be especially gut-wrenching when one side of the road drops off into a 200-foot ravine. If heights scare you, grab a seat on the right side of the bus where you can stare at a solid, rocky mountain wall. The bus churns up the mountain in second gear, so you'll have plenty of time to memorize every last bit of vegetation. Be careful with weather exposure, the climate in the Cuchumatanes varies drastically—you'll get a sunburn during the day and freeze your ass off at night.

Todos Santos is a traditional town, and the villagers are decked out in vibrant garb. The men saunter around in candy-cane pants and pinstriped shirts with long embroidered collars. The women wear stunning red, pink, and purple huipiles with dark blue skirts. In the town cooperative, visitors can buy huipiles with old designs dirt cheap, because the village women refuse to be out of fashion. The town is quiet for most of the week, but on market day (Saturday), the streets hop with rhythm, people, and noise. The only time Todos Santos sees large swarms of visitors is during its rambunctious fiesta week, October 31– November 5, when highlanders come to the town to do some serious celebrating. A hot event is the annual horse race on November 1. All day long, the men ride from one side of town to the other, stopping briefly to wet their throats. But that ain't water, and by the end of the day, few riders remain in the competition and some only because they've roped themselves to their mounts.

Just outside the village are the Mayan ruins of Tojcunanchén, where traditional religious rituals still take place in accordance with the ancient Tzolkin calendar. To see the spot, follow the road past Comedor Katy and up the hill. The wooden crosses next to the mounds are memorials to the victims of the violence of the early '80s; they are scorched black from all the fires that have been lit around them. If you fall in love with Todos Santos—which you probably will—extend your visit to include a course at the language school. The **Proyecto Lingüístico de Español/Mam Todos Santos** (three blocks from plaza) offers courses in Spanish and Mam for $100 a week, including home stay with a local family. Remember that you'll have to pay in quetzales, since there are no banks in Todos Santos. Buses to Todos Santos leave Huehuetenango's terminal at 4 AM, 11:30 AM, and 12:30 PM. Arrive early to get a seat. Buses return from Todos Santos at 5 AM, 6 AM, 12:30 PM, and 1 PM. The ride takes just over three hours and costs $1.15.

WHERE TO SLEEP AND EAT

The best place to stay is **Hospedaje Casa Familiar,** where a clean, cozy double room costs $5. A hot shower or traditional sauna ($1); service of tea, coffee, and fresh-baked banana bread; and weaving lessons ($1/hr) are added bonuses. It's located just south of the bus stop, right above the Comedor Katy. For $2 a person, you can stay at **Hospedaje Tres Olguitas,** which also has a comedor with full meals for $1–$2. A local woman, **Nicolasa Geronimo Ramírez,** will rent you a room for $1.50, feed you, teach you weaving, and sell you beautiful handmade huipiles and purses made by members of a women's weaving cooperative. Her home is up the street past Comedor Katy on the right-hand side. **Comedor Katy** is a local haunt; you'll get the best service if you walk straight into the kitchen and ask what's for lunch. Full meals cost $1–$2.

NEAR TODOS SANTOS CUCHUMATAN

Several walking and hiking trails lead from Todos Santos through the surrounding countryside, offering great views of this beautiful region. Some trails are quite challenging, leading you over mountain passes and through streams, and most of the local villages are just, well, local villages. The point is to get out there and walk around, soaking up the beautiful countryside. **Mash** is a cute, traditional village 6 km (4 mi) from Todos Santos. Follow the road below the plaza and you should reach it within an hour. Tzunul is another small village two hours down the main road that goes past the cemetery and out of town toward Concepción. An hour and a half past Tzunul, you'll come to **San Martín,** a tranquil village with an interesting Friday-morning market. From there, buses headed back through Todos Santos and then on to Huehuetenango pass through San Martín daily at noon and 1 PM. Sit up on the roof for great views of the valley. A strenuous five-hour hike brings you to **San Juan Atitlán,** a traditional village where both men and women dress in styles that date back hundreds of years. You can make it there and back in a single day if you leave early. Pick up the trail at the Tojcunanchén ruins on the hill above Comedor Katy. Follow it to the top of the ridge and, instead of walking along the summit, take the tiny path straight down into the valley. You'll walk through a ranch and over two more hills before you reach the town.

THE PACIFIC COAST

If you're dreaming of a white, sandy coast, gentle waves, and kickin' back in a hammock and sipping a margarita, then the Pacific coast is the last place to look. La Costa Sur (as locals call it) is the armpit of Guatemala. Its black-sand beaches absorb the gross, sticky heat, and the ocean currents are swift and dangerous. The one exception is Monterrico, a nature reserve with inviting stretches of isolated coastline and less menacing waves where you can enjoy a refreshing swim.

This fertile region is the source of most of the country's agricultural production, both for domestic consumption and for export. Traveling along the coastal highway, you pass one enormous *finca* (farm) after another; each one employs hundreds of workers. Historically, finca owners relied on legal methods of forced labor to guarantee workers during key months of the year. Today, land shortages in the highlands ensure a steady supply of labor, as indígena migrate to the coast seasonally with no choice but to work for pitifully low wages and generally in substandard conditions.

The Guatemalan Pacific coast is actually quite short, and you can easily drive from Mexico to El Salvador in a day. Plenty of buses rumble down the route, too. There isn't much to detain you along the way other than a few archaeological sites near Retalhuleu and Santa Lucía Cotzumalguapa. The Mayan, Olmec, and Pipil artifacts are definitely worth a peek if you can muster up the energy to get to them in spite of the blazing heat. Needless to say, the coastal climate leaves a lot to be desired—it's hot, humid, and muggy as hell—and the mosquitoes sure love it. Malaria is not uncommon in these parts, so make sure you have plenty of protection. Any repellent that is 75% or more DEET should do the trick. Beware: the stuff is so potent it'll eat right through your leather or plastic watchband, etc. At night, try burning AUTAN, a type of incense made by Bayer (the aspirin people), that's supposed to ward off mosquitoes. You can buy it at most pharmacies in Pacific coast towns—at 20¢ a package, it's worth a shot.

RETALHULEU

Relatively clean and mellow, Retalhuleu is the prettiest city on the Pacific coast, but that's not saying much. The city—called "Reu" for short—is the capital and commercial center of the region and is home to the area's wealthy Ladino farmers. These *ricos* live in enormous Spanish-style estates and use the city as their playground. Most travelers stop in Reu on the way to or from the Mexican border. The Plaza Central (between 5a and 6a Avs., 5a and 6a calles) has a colossal colonial church with giant wooden doors framed by two fetching little fountains. A few of the main buildings surrounding the plaza are modeled after ancient Greek architecture, an effect that is as strange as it is eye-catching. The antiquated train station (5a Calle, 2 blocks west of plaza) is an interesting sight for train enthusiasts and one of the more picturesque spots in town. A few freight trains still pass run through Retalhuleu on occasion, but deteriorated tracks and damaged bridges mean that even these are dwindling to extinction.

BASICS

Banco Industrial (6a Calle, between 5a and 6a Avs.; open weekdays 8:30–7, Sat. 8:30–5:30) has a 24-hour ATM machine that uses the Plus system and processes cash advances on Visa. For phone calls, go to TELGUA (6a Calle, between 6a and 7a Avs.); they're open daily 7 AM–10 PM. The post office (open weekdays 8–4:30) is half a block away at the corner of 6a Calle and 6a Avenida. The Mexican consulate (5a Calle and 3a Av., 2 blocks east of plaza) is open to the public weekdays 4 PM–6 PM, and they refuse to answer any questions outside of those hours.

COMING AND GOING

A mere two hours from the Mexican border, Reu is the main pit stop for buses headed to the Tecún Umán and El Carmen crossings. Buses come and go from the Mercado San Nicolás (10a Calle, between 7a and 8a Avs., 3 blocks east of plaza). There is hourly service to Guatemala City (3½ hrs, $2.50), Tecún Umán (2½ hrs, $1.25), and Quetzaltenango (1½ hrs, $1). You can also catch buses en route at the bus terminal on 5a Calle, west of the plaza. To get here, follow 5a Calle west until you see the terminal's big parking lot, which is surrounded by fruit and vegetable stands.

WHERE TO SLEEP AND EAT

Accommodations are limited in Reu, so even the minimal comforts carry a high price tag. It's definitely worth paying extra to stay at **Hotel Modelo** (5a Calle, between 4a and 5a Avs., tel. 771–0256) or across the street at **Hotel Astor** (tel. 771–0475). Both have $15 doubles with clean rooms, bathrooms, TV, and—most importantly—ceiling fans that work. For a quick snack, try the **taco stands** on 5a Avenida just off the plaza. On the west side of the plaza, **Restaurante Fu-'Kuai** (5a Calle) serves decent, fresh seafood and vegetable dishes for about $4. Also on the plaza, **Cafetería La Luna** serves decent breakfasts, lunches, and dinners for $2–$3. **Pizza Rondinella** (5a Calle, 3 blocks north of plaza) has decently priced pizzas and burgers.

NEAR RETALHULEU

BORDER TOWNS

Even if you arrive late, there's no reason to linger overnight in either El Carmen or Tecún Umán. Both are nasty border towns, and you can always catch a bus heading to another spot—anywhere is better than staying here. The Tecún Umán crossing is the more popular, but border bureaucracy is rumored to be faster at El Carmen. If you don't already have a visa, you can get a tourist card from one of the official-looking chaps; it costs $5 and will last you 30 days. If you're driving, your car may have to be fumigated before you are allowed to cross the border, depending on the time of year and the mood of the official on duty. The charge for this service is $1–$2. Both borders are open daily 24 hours.

ABAJ TAKALIK

If you're a closet archaeologist in need of a little inspiration, the ruins of Abaj Takalik might do the trick. A team of archaeologists at work on the site have their hands full trying to reconstruct ceremonial temples and decipher the enormous stone stelae left by the Olmec tribe. Pottery shards and pieces of obsidian knives scattered throughout the ruins date back to AD 800. Not very much is known about this particular site except that a few of the stelae are older than the ones in Tikal. One of the Spanish-speaking field workers will show you around the ruins. If you're interested, ask him to show you the two stelae by the river 1 km (½ mi) away. One of these stelae is still a place of worship for locals; you'll see melted candles and incense ash from recent religious rituals. The site itself is spread out over 9 square km (3½ square mi), and artifacts are scattered on five separate sugar and coffee fincas, although four of these have refused to allow excavation. Much of the site is being lost to the plow. If you don't have your own wheels or $25 to spend on a taxi, it's a pain to get to Abaj Takalik. From Retalhuleu, jump on a bus going the Mexican border via Coatepeque and ask to be let off at El Asintal (30 min, 25¢). From there, it's a long way, so wave your thumb frantically for a lift into the town proper. The site is another 4 km (2½ mi) past El Asintal.

TULATE

Three hours from Retalhuleu by bus, Tulate has the only decent beaches in the area. The black sand gets scalding hot and the tide is a little rough for a casual swim, but it's clean and unpolluted. The one-street beach town is brimming with comedores ready to serve up fresh fish and cold drinks. Accommodation here is sketchy at best, with no screens and only a reed mat to sleep on—no different from the floor. Buses leave for Tulate (3 hrs, $1.25) daily at 5 AM, 8 AM, 11 AM, and 1PM. Return buses leave at 8 AM, noon, 3 PM and 5 PM.

SANTA LUCÍA COTZUMALGUAPA

The only reason to stop in Santa Lucía Cotzumalguapa, a boring town along the highway between Retalhuleu and the transportation hub of Esquintla, is to check out the stone carvings that have been found at nearby farms. Three sites—at Bilbao, Finca El Baúl, and Finca Las Ilusiones—have impressive carvings thought to date back as far as AD 400. The sites are close to town, but they aren't all easy to get to. If you plan to see them all on foot in one day, you'll need an abundance of motivation and patience. **Corpobanco** (open weekdays 8:30–8, weekends 8:30–12:30) is on the plaza, facing the church. TELGUA (open daily 7 AM–9 PM) is on Calzada 15 de Septiembre, halfway between the highway and the plaza.

COMING AND GOING

Buses from Guatemala City (2 hrs, $1) leave from the Treból Junction at Calle Bolívar daily every half hour until 5 PM, stopping at Santa Lucía's main plaza before arriving at the bus terminal (5a Av. and 6a Calle). Any bus heading along the coastal highway will drop you off 10 minutes outside of town—just follow Calzada 15 de Septiembre to the plaza. Buses leave the terminal every 20 minutes for Esquintla (30 min, 40¢), where you can find a bus to almost anywhere else in the country. To Guatemala City, take the direct bus, which leaves the terminal every half hour. If you're headed northwest toward Retalhuleu, you'll have to flag down a bus on the highway outside of town.

WHERE TO SLEEP AND EAT

Your best bet is to see the sites and get back on the road, but if you're stuck here overnight, you have two dismal budget options. **Pensión El Carmen** (5a Calle, half a block from the plaza) has suffocating, smelly rooms for $2 a person. **Pensión Reforma** (4a Av. 4–71, 1 block from plaza) has cleaner rooms for $3 a person, but the common bathrooms are disgusting and be forewarned that they won't tolerate "abnormal, dirty activities"—so none of that, kids. Outside of town, the **Caminotel Santiaguito** (highway km 90.5, tel. 884–5435) is worlds apart in both quality and price: $20 a night buys you a clean room with private bathroom, ceiling fan, and a swimming pool. **Comedor Lau,** half a block off the plaza next door to Farmacia Santa Lucía, has good Chinese food for $2–$4 a plate. A number of cheap comedores near the bus terminal serve standard Guatemalan fare.

NEAR SANTA LUCÍA COTZUMALGUAPA

BILBAO

A 15-minute walk from the plaza, this is the closest site to town and has the most well-preserved stones. The stones, carved by the Pipil around AD 600, have characteristics that suggest close relations with tribes in Mexico. There used to be more, but in 1880 nine of them were shipped to the Dahlem Museum in Berlin. To get here from the plaza, follow 3a Avenida up the hill and turn right after the El Calvario church; the site lies among the sugarcane fields on your left. If the cane is high, you probably won't be able to find the site without the help of one of the local kids who act as tour guides.

FINCA EL BAUL

About 4 km (1⅓ mi) beyond El Calvario Church, this site is still an active place of worship. Around two stone carvings atop a small hill you'll see the melted candles, incense ash, and makeshift altars left from recent religious rituals. To get here from El Calvario Church, follow 3a Avenida for about 4 km (2½ mi); after you cross a bridge, you'll get to a fork in the road with a sign that says LOS TARROS; follow the dirt road to the right for about 1 km (½ mi), until you see a small hill with trees on your right. A trail on the south side of the hill leads to the site at the top. The farm itself has a private collection of stone carvings, as well as some antiquated sugar-refining machinery. To get there, you'll have to go back to the fork in the road and this time go right; it's about 4 km (2½ mi) to the finca headquarters. Although the collection is open to the public, you're likely to be accompanied by one or more machine gun–toting private security guards. Don't let them intimidate you—if you've come this far, the collection is worth a look. There is a private bus that shuttles workers between the Tienda El Baúl, a few blocks above the plaza, and the finca a couple times a day. It's for workers only, but you may be able to negotiate a ride.

FINCA LAS ILUSIONES

Although slightly more out of the way, the collection at this site is extensive. Everything they've found on the farm—including hundreds of pottery shards, stone carvings both great and small, and a number of unique stelae—are conveniently kept together in one small, locked museum. If the guy with the key isn't around when you get there, you're just plain outta luck. It's worth the risk if you have the time and energy, and if you can't get into the museum, the collection of stone carvings outside is a decent consolation prize. To get here from the plaza, take Calzada 15 de Septiembre to the highway, head northeast until you pass a second Esso Station, and turn left onto a dirt road. The finca is just 10 minutes from the highway.

LA DEMOCRACIA

Tired of trudging from site to site in the sticky heat just to see more stone carvings? In the town of La Democracia, you don't have to. Huge stone heads, found at the nearby site of Monte Alto, have been transplanted to the town plaza, where they chill beneath the shade of a large ceiba tree. No one really knows how old they are, but some academics believe they predate any other finds in Guatemala. A museum (admission 50¢; open Tues.–Sun. 9–noon and 2–5) on the plaza has more stone carvings, pottery, and an impressive jade mask. Buses to La Democracia (30 min, 40¢) leave from Santa Lucía's terminal several times daily.

MONTERRICO

If you're looking to relax by the beach, forget the wanna-be resort towns and head straight to Monterrico. You'll be charmed by a beautiful coastline with warm, swimmable water and a friendly little town with good cheap places to eat fresh seafood. The town and its coastline are within the borders of the Biotopo Monterrico-Hawaii, a reserve for the protection of numerous species of birds and aquatic life that thrive in the coastal mangrove swamps. The most famous Monterrico residents are three endangered species of giant sea turtles that lay their eggs on these beaches. The turtles are not a tourist attraction; they come ashore only at night, hurrying back to the ocean to escape their predators, the worst of which are humans. The swamps are home to raccoons, opossums, green iguanas, and caimans (crocodiles), but don't count on seeing these elusive creatures in the wild. You can check out baby sea turtles, green iguanas, and caimans being raised in captivity at the administración, on the beach next to El Baule Beach Hotel (*see* Where to Sleep and Eat, *below*). The critters at the reserve headquarters are part of a project headed by CECON, an environmental organization tied to the University of San Carlos in Guatemala City.

Says Germán Magallán, a ruins guard, "In the city you have your stores, your hospitals. Life is rich here, too. We have everything: supermarket, pharmacy, all right next to us, growing from the ground."

The mangrove swamps are beautiful and well worth exploring, especially in the early morning or evening. You can explore on foot by following the trail that begins behind the headquarters; just look for the sign. It makes a circular route through the mangroves, entirely on land, and is excellent for bird-watching. The best way to explore the swamp is in a boat pushed along with a tall pole. This way you can navigate quietly through the network of small canals, upping your chances of seeing wildlife. Ask at the dock to hire a boat and guide; it's costs $2 an hour, or $10 an hour for a boat with an outboard motor.

The sticky heat that plagues the entire Pacific coast is made bearable at Monterrico by the ocean breeze. It can still get damn hot though. Don't even think about walking across the black sand without sandals. And bring plenty of mosquito repellent, especially in the rainy season—you'll need it. But more than anywhere else on the coast, the beauty of Monterrico overshadows both the humid heat *and* the mosquitoes. Unfortunately, this is no secret. Calm and quiet during the week, on weekends Monterrico is swarmed by Guatemalans escaping the city, and the posh hotels on the beach are filled to capacity.

COMING AND GOING

You can reach Monterrico two ways. The easiest is to take any bus heading east from Esquintla to Taxisco (45 min, 40¢). Buses leave Taxisco every half hour or so for La Avellana (30 min, 40¢). If you don't want to wait for a bus, it's pretty easy to hitch a ride. From La Avellana, a ferry takes you on a picturesque ride through the mangrove swamp to Monterrico. Ferries leave every half hour 4 AM–5 PM (20 min, 40¢). Buses from Guatemala City to Esquintla leave every half hour from the Trébol junction at Calle Bolívar (2 hrs, $1). Direct buses to La Avellana leave the Zona 4 terminal at 5 AM, 11 AM, and 1:30 PM (4 hrs, $2.25). A direct bus from La Avellana to Guatemala City leaves at 7 AM daily. The second route goes along the coast from the town of Iztapa; it takes longer, but it's an interesting bus ride. From Iztapa, walk down to the shore of the Canal de Chiquimulilla where boats wait around to ferry people across (5 min, 25¢–50¢). Ask to be dropped at Pueblo Viejo. From there, buses leave four times daily for Monterrico, at approximately 11:30 AM, 1 PM, 4:30 PM, and 6 PM. It takes two hours on a bumpy dirt road, stopping at nearly every house on the way, which gives you plenty of time to admire their bizarre-looking gardens. Buses return to Pueblo Viejo from Monterrico at 5:30 AM, 7 AM, and 11 AM (2 hrs, $1). A constant stream of buses goes between Iztapa and Puerto San José (20 min., 20¢), from where you can

BREWING UP HARDSHIP

Coffee is big business in Guatemala. The industry employs almost a quarter of the population and rakes in 40% of the country's import earnings. The ebb and flow of this giant is marked by the seasonal migration of hundreds of thousands of workers who descend from their highland villages to the enormous fincas of the southern coast. Working conditions on the coffee fincas leave much to be desired. Few workers are paid even the minimum daily wage of $2.25 a day. Efforts to organize to improve conditions are often met with intimidation and brutal repression by the finca owners' thugs, who are often backed by local officials.

A few years ago, frustrated by obstacles like these, the U.S./Guatemala Labor Education Project (US/GLEP) asked Starbucks, the leading gourmet coffee company and one of the largest coffee importers in the United States, to adopt a code of conduct that would require their Guatemalan suppliers to pay the minimum wage, ensure minimum health and safety standards, and respect the workers' right to organize. Starbucks declined, claiming that their suppliers already pay the minimum wage. While this may be true, you can't support a family on $2.25 a day—even in Guatemala.

Currently, workers are paid about 13¢ per pound of coffee that retails for $8.95 per pound; paying a more dignified wage would barely effect the multimillion dollar profits made by coffee retailers like Starbucks. Although small gains in living standards are being won by organized workers on some fincas, without the collaboration of major international buyers—and their consumers—it is unlikely that the situation will improve in the near future.

easily connect to Esquintla or Guatemala City. If you're headed to El Salvador, go through La Avellana to Taxisco. Buses pass through Taxisco every hour or so en route to the border at Ciudad Pedro de Alvarado.

WHERE TO SLEEP AND EAT

As Monterrico becomes more and more popular, prices are rising and more hotels are being built. To get to the hotels, walk down the main street to the beach and turn left; they're side by side right on the beach. The best deal is at **Hotel El Baule Beach** (tel. 873–6196), where simple doubles with private bathrooms and mosquito nets go for $10. It's always full on weekends, so reservations are recommended; call at 7:30 PM and ask for Lorena, a friend of the owner who will pass on the message. If you're with a group, **Johnny's Place** (tel. 633–0329) is fun; a private "bungalow" with two bedrooms (four beds), a bathroom, stove, refrigerator, and mosquito nets on all the windows, plus access to three small swimming pools, costs $50. During the week, you can stay for $10 a person. (Don't be scared if you hear gunshots—it's just the groundskeeper trying to scare away the birds.) If you're low on cash, you can usually rent a bed from a local for $2–$3 a night. Look for homemade signs along the main street. The beach itself is probably the nicest place to sleep—as long as you've got a bug-proof tent—and camping is free. Be sure you're above the high-water mark or you'll get a wet awakening. For food, all the hotels along the beach have their own overpriced restaurants; the one at Baule Beach is a better deal than the others ($4 a plate), and the food is pretty good. The main road is lined with restaurants specializing in seafood soup, fried fish, and fresh shrimp. Among them, **El Divino Maestro** is probably the best, with large portions and cheap prices. A big fish with tasty french fries and salad costs $3.50, $4 for shrimp. They also serve standard chicken or beef plates for $3.

TIKAL AND THE PETÉN

The flat, humid jungles, swampy *bajos* (lowlands), and tropical savannas of the Petén region constitute nearly a third of Guatemala's total area. Long ignored by the Guatemalan people, the isolated region only recently attracted the attention of government agencies interested in grooming the area for large-scale tourism. Once home to imperious Mayan rulers dripping with jade, today's Tikal is a full-blown tourist attraction with prices to match. Other Mayan ruins in the area are also hoping for their own piece of the international pie. Despite the adverse effects of this newest "gold fever" on the budget traveler's wallet, the awesome splendor of the Petén is a must-see on every wanderer's agenda, offering incredible opportunities for exploring lush tropical forests and majestic Mayan ruins.

The remoteness of the Petén region allowed the Maya city-state of Tayasal (buried under present-day Flores) to evade Spanish conquest until the late 17th century. With no gold to plunder, few natives to exploit, and a hot, sticky climate, the Petén had little to hold Spanish interest. For nearly two centuries, the few inhabitants of this isolated frontier scratched out a meager existence with little help or interference from officials in the far-off mountains to the west. In the late 1800s, the discovery of chicle (the natural resin base for chewing gum) suddenly made the previously untapped forest flow with "white gold." From the tile streets of Flores to the brothels of San Benito, chicleros (gum workers) brought new life into the Petén. Ultimately, however, the chicle camps never amounted to more than semi-isolated outposts, and it wasn't until 1970 that a dirt road linking the region to the rest of the country finally appeared. Even today, the road remains largely impassable at the height of the rainy season. Peténeros remain independent folks who pride themselves on their tenacity, self-reliance, and knowledge of the jungle. The people of the Petén continue to make their living from chicle and other gifts of the forest. Here, the *plato del dia* (meal of the day) is jungle fowl, venison, armadillo, or *tepisquintle* (a jungle rodent).

The Petén is the largest forest reserve in Central America, and most towns are nothing more than a collection of thatched huts sprouting from the forest. However, dusty cement towns such as Sayaxché, San Benito, and Santa Elena are growing at a frightening pace, and as each new dirt road emerges, its sides are quickly lined with ramshackle huts and piles of fresh garbage. A more serious threat is the continued exploitation of the Petén's natural resources for timber, tourism, and agricultural uses. It seems that the ecological destruction that may have hastened the downfall of the Classic Maya has once again begun to tear at the green shields of Petén. However, environmentalists are engaged in progressive efforts to save what some have dubbed "the lungs of the Americas."

A pilgrimage to the Petén is not without its problems: hellish heat and humidity, numerous bugs, and miserable roads can be demoralizing. Those prone to motion sickness should take that Dramamine before heading down the highway from hell. Buses are often stopped by the police at document checkpoints, so be sure to carry your passport on you. Roadside bandits have always been a problem along the road into the Petén, so use common sense: don't travel at night and don't carry more cash than you must. Another potentially serious problem is malaria. It is endemic to the region, so consider taking a chloroquinine treatment, such as Aralen, especially if you will be spending some time in and around the Sayaxché area. Bring lots of repellent, a mosquito net (a must for camping), citronella candles or coils, voodoo spells, and anything else that will ward off these little vampires. Cholera and giardia are also problems in the area. *Agua purificada* (purified water) is available in most towns, but it's a good idea to bring iodine or a portable water purifier—especially if you plan to going off the beaten track. When confronted by the sumptuous rugged beauty of the Petén and its people, minor travel irritations are a small price to pay.

FLORES AND SANTA ELENA

Bastions of civilization against the deep-green jungle that spills into Lago Petén Itzá, Flores and Santa Elena are sister cities tenuously connected by single causeway. With dusty, cement-tile streets, grille windows, and orderly stucco houses, Flores offers a sense of relative calm and tranquillity not seen in the other towns of this frontier zone. Old and quite established by Petén standards, Flores has had a chance to settle. It can't grow anymore; in fact, it's shrinking—the tiny island is slowly being reclaimed by the rising waters of the lake.

Flores dates back to 1221, when an Itzá Mayan ruler from the Yucatán stole the bride of one of the lords of the neighboring city of Izamal. Hunac Ceel, the offended neighbor, invaded the area and drove the Itzás southward. They finally settled on the shores of the lake and built the city of Tayasal on the island. Cortés visited once in 1525, stopping just long enough to drop off a sick horse. Story goes that this strange new beast was venerated like a god and when the horse bit the dust, the Itzá built a stone effigy in its likeness. Locals say that on a clear day you can still the statue at the bottom of the lake, where it was dropped centuries ago. Long a last outpost of Mayan independence, Tayasal was finally conquered by the forces of Martín de Ursua, in 1697. The conquest took a single day—probably due to the fact that within the Mayan calendar, 1697 marked the beginning of a new cycle and was prophesied to be bring momentous changes. Ursua spent the next day destroying all the idols; supposedly there were so many that it took an entire day to smash them all. After the drama of conquest, the town was largely left to itself, until this newest infiltration of tourists.

The relative peace of Flores is broken before you even get halfway across the causeway connecting it to Santa Elena on the mainland. Santa Elena displays the bustling action of a true frontier town in all its energetic, unabashed, and obnoxious glory. You can feel Santa Elena growing: from the noisy airport to the grimy market, it buzzes with new construction and fortune seekers. Nearby San Benito is a sleazy collection of bars, drunks, and brothels, but the smaller, laid-back communities of San Andrés, San José, and San Miguel are relatively untouched by tourism, and the people are warm and hospitable.

BASICS

VISITOR INFORMATION • Dozens of hotels, restaurants, and travel agencies offer "free visitor information," but they're just trying to sell you something. **INGUAT** (tel. 926–0533; open Mon.–Sat. 7:30–11 and 3–6:30), in Santa Elena's airport, has information in English.

ProPetén is an ecological organization that sponsors **CINCAP**, an ecological and cultural information center about the Petén. Browse through binders filled with information in English about all the hotels, restaurants, and travel agencies in the Petén, or peruse the library of books on Mayan history and culture, birds and wildlife, or traveling. ProPetén also runs an language school in San Andrés and arranges ecotours to the jungle, El Mirador, and the Scarlet Macaw Trail. *In main plaza, next to church, Flores, tel. 926–1370. Open Tues.–Sat. 9–1 and 2–8, Sun. 4–8 PM.*

MONEY • In Santa Elena, **Banco Industrial** (Calle Principal, tel. 926–0281; open weekdays 8–5:30, Sat. 8–2:30) is next to the bus stop, near the main market. They change cash and traveler's checks and can help process cash advances on Visa. Upscale hotels and restaurants also change cash, but they offer poor rates.

LAUNDRY • Most hotels have a *pila* (laundry sink) that you can use to wash your clothing. In Flores, **Flores Lavandería** (open Mon.–Sat. 8–8, Sun. 8–2) will wash your clothes for $3 a load. Look for it on Calle Centroamérica, next to Restaurante La Canoa.

MEDICAL AID • **Dr. Umberto Azurdia** (Calle Central 3–95, tel. 926–0045) is a local physician with an excellent reputation. He sees patients at his office near the bus station weekdays 7:30–noon and 3–5, weekends 8–11. **Farmacia Universal** (open Mon.–Sat. 7–1 and 3–8, Sun. 7–1) is within stumbling distance across the street.

PHONES AND MAIL • Flores's **post and telegram office** (open weekdays 8–4) is just off an alleyway to the right of the main church. You can have mail sent care of Lista de Correos, Flores, Petén. In Flores, you can reach an AT&T or MCI operator from the public phone in front of Hotel La Casona de la Isla. Make collect or credit-card calls and receive incoming calls at Flores's **Cahui International Phone** (Calle 30 de Junio, tel. 926–0494), in front of Hotel Santa Rita. Make national and international calls in air-conditioned bliss at Santa Elena's busy **TELGUA** (7a Av.), which is open daily 7 AM–9 PM.

KEY

i Tourist Information

Lago de
Petén Itzá

Lodging ○
Casona de La Isla, **3**
Hotel La Canoa, **6**
Hotel Peregrino, **4**
Hotel Las Rosas de
San Miguel, **2**
Hotel El Tucan, **5**
Sabana Hotel, **1**

Calle Unión

Parque
Central

Calle 15 de Septiembre
Calle 10 de Septiembre
Calle 30 de Junio
Av. Barrios
Centroamérica
Calle 15 de Septiembre

Calle

Calle de La Playa Sur

0   600 feet
0   150 meters

Causeway

TO SANTA ELENA
AND BUS TERMINAL

TRAVEL AGENCIES • Even if you're usually not hip to agency-sponsored tours, you might want to reconsider in the Petén. While you should probably cruise to Tikal on your own, tours to more remote sites such as El Ceibal and El Mirador are often cheaper and less frustrating than going by yourself.

Asociación de Rescate y Conservación de Vida Silvestre (ARCAS) offers way-off-the-beaten-track tours with experienced guides to remote archaeological sites. It's that no-guilt ecotourism thang—ARCAS is committed to protecting the environment, and their proceeds generate income for local Petén communities—so tell all your friends. *Trips to El Mirador, Uaxactún, El Zots, Nakabe, and Naranjo run about $35 a day. Santa Elena, tel. 926–0077. Open weekdays 8–noon and 2–6.*

Explore arranges expeditions to El Ceibal ($30 for one day), El Ceibal and Aguateca ($120 for two days), Dos Pilas ($150 for three days), and Yaxchilán ($125 for one day). Believe it or not, these trips are actually good deals. *Calle Centroamérica, Flores, tel. 926–0655. Open weekdays 8–noon and 2–6.*

San Juan Travel is the oldest travel gig in town. They run minibuses to Tikal ($3 each way), Belize City ($20), and Chetumal ($30), and arrange one-day tours of El Ceibal, Lago Petén Itzá, and Santa Elena's Aktun Kan Cave, Tikal, and Uaxactún for $30–$40. *In Hotel San Juan, just over the causeway, Santa Elena, tel. 926–0042. Open daily 8–noon and 2–6.*

Total Petén Tours also arranges tours throughout the Petén area and have minibuses to Tikal, Sayax-ché, Quiriguá, Belize City, and Chetumal. With competitive rates, they're giving old-boy San Juan Travel real run for their money. For the best deals, try to get a big group together. *Flores, tel. 926–0662. Open daily 7–noon and 2–6.*

COMING AND GOING

BY BUS • Buses come and go from bus terminals smack-dab in the middle of Santa Elena's central market, across from the Hotel El Diplomático. In this region, high "gringo" fares are sanctioned by INGUAT; we list them here, but if you can finagle the local price, more power to you. With frequent daily service, **Fuentes del Norte,** just west of the bus terminal, and **Maya Express** (Calle Principal, Santa

Elena, tel. 926–0157) will bump and jostle you to or from Guatemala City for $12–$15, although most people opt to stop overnight in Poptún (see South from Flores, below) to break up the journey. The grueling trip takes anywhere from 12 to 20 hours, depending on how many stops the bus makes. In high tourist season, try to buy your ticket at least a day in advance. Daily **La Pinita** buses (Calle Principal, Santa Elena, tel. 926–0726) head to Sayaxché (1½ hrs, $3) at 6 AM, 8 AM, 4 PM; to Uaxctún (2½ hrs, $2) at 1 PM; and to Tikal (1½ hrs, $2) at 6 AM, 8 AM, and 1 PM. If you're heading to Poptún (4 hrs, $5) or Río Dulce (8 hrs, $8), take a bus bound for Guatemala City and get off on the way. Four buses leave daily before 1 PM for El Naranjo (7 hrs, $5), where you can catch a boat to the Mexican border. La Pinita buses also travel to Melchor de Mencos at the Belizean border (3 hrs, $4). Most buses list all their destinations on the sign, but you may have to ask around until you find the one you want.

BY MINIBUS • Private minivans are by far the best way to travel to Belize City (5 hrs, $20) or Chetumal (8 hrs, $30), at the Belize–Mexico border. Rather than packing onto a crowded bus, switching bus lines, and reloading at each border, you can take a minibus that will whisk you straight to your destination in relative comfort and style. Buses leave daily at 5 AM. From Belize City, you can connect with a boat to the cays, and from Chetumal connect with a bus to Mérida or Cancún. Contact Total Petén Tours or San Juan Travel for tickets (see Travel Agencies, above), which also have minibuses to Petén destinations.

HITCHING • That thumb of yours can really help you get around this sparsely populated frontier, but only during the daytime. Plan ahead so you won't be trying to hitch after dark or you may end up stranded in the middle of nowhere. Outside Flores, Santa Elena, and Tikal, visitors are rare and most drivers are happy to pick up a needy stranger. Also, you can usually flag down a taxi pickup truck (look for the metal racks). All roads in the Petén lead to Flores, so you should have no trouble finding a ride here. When you get out, say thank you and ask *¿Cuanto cuesta?* (How much?). Between Santa Elena and Tikal, only a minibus or a regular bus is likely to pick you up, and the driver will charge you just the same.

BY PLANE • The Santa Elena **airport** is 1 km (½ mi) east of the causeway. At the airport, you can rent a four-wheel-drive jeep for $50 a day at **Los Jades** (tel. 926–0734). **Aerovías** (tel. 926–1477), **Aviateca** (tel. 926–1238), and **Tapsa** (tel. 926–4860) have flights to and from Guatemala City, Belize City, Cancún, and Chetumal (Mexico). In recent years, fares from Guatemala City have dropped considerably and usually hover around $35 each way. The comfortable half-hour flight is well worth the cash for at least one way—your other option is a long, bumpy bus ride over unpaved roads. Fares to Mexico and Belize run between $125 and $175 each way. To catch a bus to the airport (30¢), wait at the corner of 8a Avenida and Calle Principal in Santa Elena. Look for the yellow school buses or buses marked URBANO. Alternatively, taxis and shuttles will get you to or from the airport for about $10.

GETTING AROUND

One street goes around the island, while cross streets radiate out from the circular central plaza. On the south side is the *relleno* (causeway), a dusty path that connects the city to the mainland. In Santa Elena, the causeway becomes 7a Avenida, the main north–south street. About three blocks south of the causeway, 7a Avenida crosses the main east–west street, Calle Principal de Santa Elena. This street leads west into San Benito, where it becomes Calle Principal de San Benito. Local buses run between the three towns about every half hour.

BY CAYUCA • Before the causeway was built in 1970, these small boats were the only way to get on and off the island. Today, cayucas continue to ferry people—mostly tourists—to and from San Benito and small communities on the lakeshore like San Andrés and San José. Expect to pay $4–$15 (depending on the size of the group) for a tour of the lake. In Santa Elena, cayucas usually leave from behind Hotel San Juan II; follow the lakeside road west of the causeway until you see boats on the far side of the hotel to your right. In Flores, any of the hotels can arrange a trip for you. You can also rent a cayuca from Hotel El Tucan (see Where to Sleep, below) for a couple of dollars.

WHERE TO SLEEP

Yep, you're in the tropics now for sure. Which means that you'll have to get used to lots of bugs and a powdery brown dirt that coats everything. Worse yet, those nasty mosquitoes are rather clever creatures, and they've discovered a great spot to congregate: the bathroom. In general, hotels in Flores are cleaner and more luxurious but more expensive than those in Santa Elena. The budget digs in Santa Elena tend to be scummy and not very secure. One good alternative for campers and those who would prefer to stay closer to nature is the town of El Remate, 30 km (18½ mi) outside Santa Elena (see below). To get to El Remate (1 hr), take any bus heading toward Tikal.

UNDER $10 • **Hotel El Tucan.** Right on the lakeshore, it offers simple rooms with fans, clean sheets, and shared cold-water bath. It is sort of grungy, so definitely wear the shower shoes. *Calle Cen-*

troamérica, Flores, tel. 926–00577. From causeway, right through first alleyway, then turn right. 4 rooms, none with bath.

Hotel La Canoa. The rooms at this family-run joint have clean sheets, a fan, and a private bathroom for $9 a double. There's no sign out front, so just ask at Restaurante La Canoa (see Food, below) if they have a room. Most places in town charge a lot more for similar stuff. First bldg. after causeway, Flores, no phone. 8 rooms with bath.

Hotel Las Rosas de San Miguel. Right on the water, this small, charming bright pink hotel has cheap and immaculate rooms for $4 a bed, or $6 for a private room. You'll feel right at home in this warm family atmosphere as you relax in a hammock and sip an ice-cold limonada straight from the tree. Marta cooks up a storm and will do your laundry for a small fee. Her husband, Oscar, offers boat excursions at the fairest prices in town. If you need to leave Oscar and Marta a telephone message, call the community phone (tel. 926–0269) between 7 and 5. Go to Tienda y Restaurant La Unión (see below) and ask for the flag to signal for the free boat to pick you up, no phone. 4 rooms, none with bath.

Hotel y Restaurant Peregrino. This is a great hidden deal. It's known as "Comedor Luci," and you'd never know they have rooms for rent. The clean, private bathrooms have hot water, and each room has a fan and crisp, freshly ironed sheets. The staff is really friendly, and the food at the comedor is good and reasonably priced as well. All that for $9 a double—now, aren't you lucky? Av. Reforma, Flores, tel. 926–0477. From causeway, right through the first alleyway, left on Calle Centroamérica, then right onto Av. Reforma. 4 rooms with bath.

UNDER $30 • Casona de La Isla. This upscale three-story hotel is a welcome escape from the heat, the dust, and the bugs. It's true, the clean $25 doubles are (amazingly) insect-free, and each one has a private bath with hot water. You can sunbathe on one of the chaise longues by the pool, or just vegetate in front of the TV (cable) in air-conditioned luxury. Calle de la Playa Sur, Flores, tel. 926–0523. From causeway, left past 4 alleyways, turn right and walk 3 blocks. 27 rooms with bath. Laundry.

Sabana Hotel. One of the best hotels on the island, the Sabana has a sundeck, a restaurant, and simple rooms with views of Lago Petén Itzá. Bright doubles will set you back $25. Calle La Union, north side of island, tel. 926–1248. 23 rooms with bath.

FOOD

The food scene in Flores is dominated by flashy, trendy, and expensive restaurants. **El Jacal** and **Mesa de los Mayas** both serve exotic jungle creatures like armadillo, wild turkey, or tepisquintle (an endangered jungle rodent), all in a Tarzan-style decor. Santa Elena is characterized by foul comedores filled with grime, dogs, bugs, and who-knows-what-else. There is, however, a happy medium. In Santa Elena, **Comedor Ceiba** has good food; you can get chicken with tortillas, rice, and salad for $2, or pancakes for $1.75. If you resign yourself to paying more than you want to, Flores will pamper your palate with a slew of different culinary styles. If you plan to camp, stock up on food at Santa Elena's central market, and don't forget the agua pura. After hours, most everyone just hangs out in the main plazas of Flores and Santa Elena, but there are free marimba concerts on Thursday and Sunday evenings from 8 to 10 in Flores's parque municipal

UNDER $5 • Chal Tun Ha. This little waterfront restaurant is a pleasant addition to the rustic eateries that abound on the isle. The structure itself is hardly inspiring—a cement building planted on gravel— but its many windows take advantage of the view. The limited menu offers simple but well-prepared items from the lake or stuffed peppers. Southwest corner of the Flores, no phone.

Tienda y Restaurant La Unión. Chow down a hearty spaghetti meal ($2.50), or enjoy fresh fish with rice and salad ($3.50). The cafeteria is connected to a store that has a chummy family atmosphere. Adorable kids buy candy and play jacks while you enjoy a great view of the lake. Calle de la Unión, across from Posada Tayasal, Flores, no phone. From causeway, turn right on Calle de la Playa Sur until it ends, then left, and immediate right. Look for yellow sign.

UNDER $10 • Café Bar Las Puertas. With its splattered paint decor, this is the place to get a really good cup of coffee and recharge your batteries in a relaxed, cultured environment. During the day, peruse piles of magazines while listening to anything from Vivaldi to Bob Marley to Stevie Ray Vaughn to Sade. Kick back and enjoy live music at night while feasting on one of the scrumptious vegetarian dishes. They also serve the best pasta in Flores for about $5. Carnivores can enjoy a delicious steak for $8. Flores, no phone. From causeway, 2 blocks down first alleyway.

Restaurant Don Quixote. Chow down on some killer paella ($5), right on the water in this boat-turned-restaurant. They have a full bar, cool breezes, classical music, and a wonderful view of the lake. Just past the causeway on lake, Flores, no phone.

Restaurante El Tucan. Inside Hotel El Tucan, this restaurant offers a chance to come face to face with local wildlife. As you sit watching the lake, you're likely to be approached by one of the hotel's parrots, an oversized turkey, or the resident toucans, who hop from table to table looking for handouts. Try the Mexican combo plate ($6) or the *enchiladas suizas* (enchiladas with cheese and green salsa; $5) or get a drink at the full bar. The fruit drinks ($1) are as heavenly as their food. *Calle Centroamérica, Flores, tel. 926–0577. From causeway, right through first alleyway, turn right.*

Restaurant La Canoa. This place is always busy serving hungry travelers. Portions are big, and prices are reasonable. Fish dinners come with salad and rice ($3.50), and the fried chicken ($3) is decent. Some nights you'll have trouble finding a seat among the travelers watching sports on the cable TV. *Calle Centroamérica, across from Helados Gemines, Flores, no phone. From causeway, turn right through first alleyway past, left on Calle Centroamérica.*

CHEAP THRILLS

On a small island just east of Flores, **El Petencito** is a small zoo and conservation project where animals and plant life are on display to educate the public and finance Petén conservation efforts. That's nice, but it's not why you're here. Your $1 entrance fee brings you to the most killer **water slides** (*resbaladeros*) in Central America. These three cement chutes were designed with pure excitement (not safety) in mind and will give even the most avid thrill-seeker the adrenaline rush of a lifetime. Although you may wind up filtering half the lake through your sinuses, nothing beats the feeling of shooting down at breakneck speeds, only to get tossed through the air into the tropical water and emerge to the vision of pure jungle surrounding you. The 200-ft slide on the left is particularly dangerous (and exciting) because it hurls you around a hairpin curve before sending you flying over the water. If they aren't running already, look for the two taps on the ground by to the right of the slides. You can only divert water to one slide at a time, so pick your poison and go for it. You're taking an extra risk if you go at the height of the dry season (late April or early May), so you should probably walk down the steps to check the depth of the water before jumping in. To get here, take a cayuca from Santa Elena or Flores for $5–$8 (*see* Getting Around, *above*).

NEAR FLORES AND SANTA ELENA

BIOTOPO CERRO CAHUI

On a small peninsula on the north shore of Lago Petén Itzá, this parcel of relatively untouched forest was established as a haven for the Petén turkey, a regal bird that looks like a peacock. Closer to human settlement, the wildlife here is shyer than at Tikal, where the same beautiful turkeys strut nonchalantly through the open fields. A long trail circles the park and climbs to the top of a hill, where an A-frame shelter offers a magnificent view of the lake. It's worth the hike if you want to camp, are a serious botanist, or just want a nice walk. To get here by cayuca, be prepared to shell out $50–$60 for the long, beautiful ride across the lake—if you can get a group together it's worth the cash. A quicker and considerably cheaper option is to catch a Tikal-bound bus (30¢) or minivan ($3) from the central market in Santa Elena and get off halfway there in the camper's-heaven town of El Remate (*see* Where to Sleep, *below*). The Biotopo is about 3 km (2 mi) from the main road along the lakeshore.

WHERE TO SLEEP • El Gringo Perdido. If you've been waiting all your life to live in the jungle, here's your big chance. You can either camp under a palapa hut next to the small banana plantation for $3 a person, or pay $6 to stay in a hammock in a bungalow. Following a fire in January 1997, the owner built a series of rustic but comfortable bungalows, each with its own cold-water bathroom (the new outdoor shower has glorious hot water and an amazing view of the lake). Bungalows vary in size, and most have three beds. You'll be asked to share ($14 a person) if the place fills up, but the location compensates for any minor discomforts. Everything is designed for minimal environmental impact: incredible vegetarian meals are cooked in a solar-powered kitchen, food is grown on the organic farm, and all structures are built with material from the jungle itself. The meditation hut has great views overlooking the water, and the peaceful stillness is accompanied by the sounds of the jungle's wildlife. There are also dormitory-style beds for $14, and private bungalows with their own bathrooms. *El Remate, 3 km (1½ mi) down the road to Biotopo Cerro Cahui, tel. 236–3683 in Guatemala City. 40 beds.*

El Mirador del Duende. Doubtless one of the most intriguing campsites in Central America. The site's owners have created this spot as a lifelong experiment in adopting ancient Mayan techniques to build shelter and grow organic food. Built in the Mayan style and using local materials, eight individual bungalows sit atop ancient platforms overlooking Lago Petén Itzá. Hammocks and mosquito nets are provided, and for $5 a person you get a lake view. Hiking, relaxing, and getting in touch with your spiritual self are optional. They cook three organic vegetarian meals a day. *El Remate, tel. 926–0269. On the right-hand side of road across from the lake, 1 km (½ mi) south of road to Biotopo Cerro Cahui.*

EL MIRADOR

Way, way north of Flores, vast El Mirador rises from the swampy lowlands just 7 km (4 mi) from the Mexican border. Before Tikal, this was the largest center of the Preclassic Mayan world. The sight is mostly unexcavated, but it's hard to miss it; the temples are taller than the ones in Tikal, and the highest building is a towering 18 stories high. The long trek to El Mirador begins across the lake from Flores in the town of San Andrés. From there, frequent pickup trucks will take you 60 km (20 mi) north to Carmelita for around $5. In Carmelita, you can arrange the five-day mule expedition by contacting the local Tourism Committee. Get all supplies in Santa Elena before heading into the jungle. Bring some goodies to share with the guards at the site and with the chicleros you'll camp with along the way. Check with INGUAT (*see* Visitor Information, *above*) in Santa Elena to see if you'll need a special permit for the site. You can also arrange a tour with ARCAS in Santa Elena (*see* Travel Agencies, *above*), or find a guide in Uaxactún (*see below*).

TIKAL

Every Maya enthusiast (and average Joe) the world over must make a pilgrimage to Tikal, the greatest Mayan site yet discovered. This is the most-visited tourist attraction in the Petén—and for good reason. Smack in the middle of 575-square-km (222-square-mi) **Parque Nacional Tikal,** the towering temples are ringed on all sides by miles of virgin rain forest. The area around the ruins is great for checking out birds, butterflies, plants, monkeys, and flowers that spend their entire lives hundreds of feet above the forest floor in the dense canopy of trees.

Way back in 600 BC, the first Maya settled on a patch of high, dry ground surrounded by soggy Petén swampland. Not only was this prime piece of real estate spared the floods of the bajos, but it was also rich in obsidian, a volcanic glass used for chipping into razor-sharp tools. The population grew, and by 200 BC some major works of architecture—including a version of the North Acropolis—began to take shape. By AD 100, the Great Plaza had been built, but Tikal was still dominated by the northern city of El Mirador. It wasn't until the arrival of a powerful dynasty around AD 300 that the area swelled to full power. King Great Jaguar Paw sired a lineage that would build Tikal into a city rivaling any of its time. By AD 500, it's estimated that the city covered over 47 square km (18 square mi) and had an estimated population of 90,000.

By the sixth century, Tikal maintained jurisdiction over a large part of the Mayan world, probably thanks to a ruler called Caan Chac ("Stormy Sky"), who took the throne around AD 426. Under Caan Chac, Tikal became an aggressive military and commercial center that dominated the surrounding centers with a power never before seen in Mesoamerica. The swamps protected the elevated city from attack and allowed the leaders to spot any approaching enemy miles before they reached the city center. Intensive agriculture in the bajos provided food for the huge population. A valuable obsidian trade sprang from the city's strategic trading position near two rivers, and Tikal formed strong ties with two powerful centers: Kaminal Juyu in the Guatemalan highlands, and Teotihuacán, near present-day Mexico City.

Tikal suffered a major setback in AD 553, when Lord Water, a ruler of Caracol to west, mounted an invasion of the Petén. By AD 562, Water had reached Tikal, where he captured and sacrificed the king. The city didn't recover until the ascension of Ah-Cacao ("Lord Chocolate") in AD 682. It was Ah-Cacao and his successors who commissioned the construction of most of the city's great temples. Continuing the tradition of great structures, Ah-Cacao's son commissioned Temple I, which he dedicated to his dear old dad, whom he buried right beneath it. He also ordered the construction of Temple IV, the tallest temple at Tikal. By the time of his death in AD 768, Tikal was at the zenith of its power and would remain so until its mysterious abandonment around AD 900.

For almost 1,000 years, Tikal remained engulfed by the humid, green tropical mass. The conquistadors must have passed right by the overgrown ruins, mistaking them for tall, rocky hills. The native Peténeros certainly knew of its existence, but no Westerner meddled officially until 1848. The site started to receive archaeological attention in 1877, when Dr. Gustav Bernoulli commissioned locals to remove the carved wooden lintels from across the doorways of Temples I and IV. These items headed to a museum in Basel, Switzerland. In 1881 and 1882, English archaeologist Alfred Percival Maudslay made the first

MAYAN
CHRONOLOGY 101

Traditionally, Western anthropologists have divided Mayan history into three main periods: the Preclassic, Classic, and Postclassic. Although academics question the validity of such a uniform chronology, the traditional labels are still in use.

The Preclassic (2,000 BC–AD 250) period is characterized by the influence of the Olmec, a civilization centered on the Gulf coast of present-day Mexico. During this period, cities began to grow, especially in the southern highlands of Guatemala and El Salvador. By the Late Preclassic (300 BC–AD 250), the Maya had developed an advanced mathematical system, a impressively precise calendar, and one of the world's five original writing systems.

During the Classic (250 BC–AD 900) period, Mayan artistic, intellectual, and architectural achievements literally reached for the stars. Vast city-states were crisscrossed by a vast number of paved roadways, some of which still exist today. The great cities of Palenque (Mexico), Uaxactún (Guatemala), and Quiriguá (Guatemala), were just a few of the powerful centers that controlled the Classic Mayan world. But none matched the majesty and power of Tikal.

The single largest unsolved mystery about the Maya is their rapid decline during the Terminal Classic (AD 800–AD 900) period. The current theory is that siege warfare caused rural people to seek shelter in the cities. The growing urban populations drained the agricultural potential of the land around the cities. As crops failed, famine ensued, causing a mass exodus out of the cities and into smaller, sustainable population centers.

The Maya of the Postclassic Period (AD 900–AD 1511) were heavily affected by growing powers in central Mexico. Architecture, ceramics, and carvings from this period show considerable outside influence. Although still dramatic, Postclassic cities such as Mayapán, Chichén Itzá, and Uxmal pale in comparison to their Classic predecessors. By the time the Spanish conquest reached the Yucatán, the Maya were scattered, feuding, and easy to conquer.

---

map showing the architectural features of this vast city. As he began to unearth the major temples, he recorded his work in dramatic photographs—you can see copies in Tikal. His work was continued by Teobert Maler, who came in 1895 and 1904. Both Maler and Maudsley have causeways named in their honor. In 1951, the Guatemalan Air Force cleared an airstrip near the ruins to improve access for large-scale archaeological work. Today, Tikal is known to include some 3,000 unique buildings.

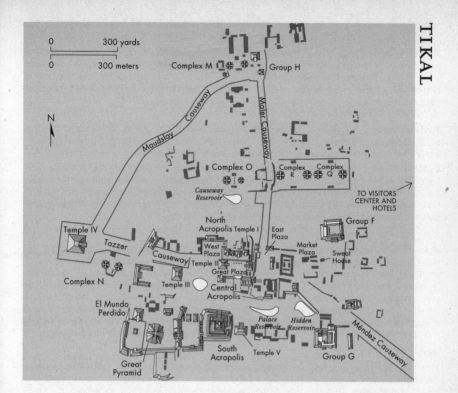

BASICS

Although you'll get better rates in Flores and Santa Elena, you can change cash and traveler's checks at lousy rates at hotels and at Comedor Tikal. The visitor's center has a **phone** and a **post office** (open weekdays 9–5, weekends 9–4). They also have a good map of the park and will arrange a guided tour. Go with Miguel Marín, a veteran guide who has conducted tours for the likes of the BBC and the Smithsonian. His six-hour bilingual tour takes you to places you'd miss on your own. The tour costs $25. You can find Sr. Marín at the visitor's center, or get hold of him through San Miguel's community phone (tel. 926–0265).

COMING AND GOING

Bring your passport. If the police or army stops your bus for a document check and you don't have your passport, they will fine you. There are also occasional reports of buses along this route being stopped by guerrillas and robbers. The good news is that the stretch of asphalt between the airport in Santa Elena and Tikal is the only paved road in the Petén, specially designed to whisk tourists through the jungle as quickly and comfortably as possible.

From Santa Elena, three **La Pinita** buses (Calle Principal, tel. 926–0562) to Tikal (2 hrs, $3.50) leave from the bus terminal in the center of the main market daily at 6 AM, 8 AM, and 1 PM. Buses returning from Tikal have the same schedule. Minibuses are a less crowded, more dependable, and quicker way to Tikal. The schedules vary, and you can buy tickets from **San Juan Travel** (Santa Elena, tel. 926–0142) and **Total Petén Tours** (Flores, tel. 926–0662), or at any of the nicer hotels in Flores. Tickets are sold for $6 round-trip, but you can get an open return if you plan to spend several days in Tikal or head north to Uaxactún and Río Azul.

WHERE TO SLEEP

Tikal is a ways from the nearest civilization and, since it takes at least two days to really see the ruins, camping is your best option. If that's out of the question, your other option is to stay in one of the overpriced hotels. Across from the museum, the **Jaguar Inn** has bungalows for $52 and tents for $10—either way it's pretty scummy. The electricity in the whole area shuts off at 9 PM.

Jungle Lodge. The largest hotel in the park, the lodge offers rooms with private or shared baths, a restaurant, and a pool, all of which are surrounded by jungle and only a short walk from the ruins. Keep your eyes open for surprises on the grounds, like ocellated turkeys or scarlet macaws. The restaurant is best avoided in favor of the nearby cantinas. Most doubles are $60, but they have a handful of less attractive rooms with shared bath for $25. *Tikal park headquarters, tel. 477–0574; for reservations, fax 476–0294 in Guatemala City. 46 rooms, 34 with bath.*

Tikal Inn. Rooms are big, clean, and secured with padlocks on the doors. The pool is a good place for a soothing swim after a hard day at the ruins. Doubles are $55 a night, and meals are extra. *The lodging farthest from park entrance, just off parking lot close to the runway. 22 rooms with bath.*

CAMPING • Tikal's official campground is a few thatched-roof shelters on a field just opposite the main parking lot. Nothing fancy, but the majestic Petén turkeys seem to like it, and this is the rare bird's main hangout. The site has a 24-hour guard, but the water supply isn't dependable, so your best bet is to bring water and groceries from Santa Elena. Unfortunately, the camping isn't free—a whopping $6 a person is charged to sling a hammock or pitch a tent.

FOOD

At any one of the lodgings listed above, you'll pay $6 for a meal that you could buy at a comedor for $3. The comedores are clean and slop on huge portions. **Comedor Imperio Maya** serves a complete breakfast ($2) and will make sandwiches ($1.50) for a Tikal jungle picnic. You can also buy water, fruits and vegetables, and some supplies, but their selection is limited. They also have free luggage storage for customers ($1 for noncustomers). **Comedor Piramide** is a favorite with the local guides—the food is yummy, reasonable, and served in big portions. **Comedor Tikal,** closest to the park entrance, is a pleasant place for dinner ($5) and changes cash and traveler's checks. All the restaurants are near the park entrance, which is at least 20 minutes from the closest ruin, so it's best to bring a lunch instead of traipsing to and from the temples.

WORTH SEEING

First things first. When you fork over the $8 entrance fee, make sure to get your pass stamped so you can stay in the park an extra two hours (until 8 PM) and watch the glorious sunset. It takes two days to really see all the sites, although the fleet-footed athlete can easily visit all the major temples in a single day. Bring a sack lunch to tide you over and tote a flashlight—it'll help you find your way back after dark and is good for exploring the eerie dark temple passageways, where you'll stumble upon awesome masks and painted carvings.

Great Plaza. Just after the guardhouse, you'll stumble upon the well-kept lawn of the immense Great Plaza, surrounded by four tremendous structures. This is the very heart of Tikal. It would be no exaggeration to say that the city began in this very place more than 2,000 years ago, although the present-day site is the result of successive plazas built on top of earlier ruins. To the east is Temple I; closing off the plaza to the west is Temple II. To the north you'll see the temples of the North Acropolis, and to the south is the Central Acropolis.

Temple I. Also known as the Temple of the Great Jaguar for a symbol on one of the carved lintels, this temple was built in honor of Ah-Cacao by his son in about AD 700. Temple I is considered the best example of traditional Mayan temple construction, with a pyramid structure, wide stairs leading to the top, a sturdy platform, an elevated roof, and nine terraces (nine was a sacred number to the Maya). The stairs are known as a "construction stairway," because they were built first and used by workers to transport blocks and mortar to construct the rest of the pyramid. The beautiful wood lintels throughout Temple I are built from the rot-resistant zapote tree. Deep underneath the temple is the tomb of Ah-Cacao himself—you can see a reconstruction of it in the museum.

Temple II. Right across the plaza is a slightly smaller but equally spectacular structure. A three-tier pyramid sits on a platform; inside, three rooms are connected by narrow hallways. As you climb the steps on the outside of the pyramid, you'll notice a wonderful echo—a testament to Mayan architectural genius. The acoustics were supposedly so precise that rulers could whisper to each other from the tops of the two temples unheard by anyone in the plaza below. The back of Temple II is one of the best places to watch flocks of parrots, toucans, and trogans (green relatives of the quetzal).

The North Acropolis. This group of small temples, stelae, and masks is perhaps the most complex structure in the Mayan world. Its foundation dates back to 100 BC, but successive layers were built upon layers until it became the massive structure it is today. This is a fantastic spot to flick on that flashlight and descend into a series of tunnels that hide two unusual 10-ft-tall masks, still sporting some of their original paint. The North Acropolis housed a number of bizarre archaeological treats, including a red stela that you can see in the museum and the tomb of a priest who went gently into that good night accompanied by no fewer than nine servants.

The Central Acropolis. On the other side of the Great Plaza lies a maze of courtyards, temples, and palaces. **Temple III** lies west beyond Temple II. Climb to the top and check out the cool restored wood lintels over the doorways. South from Temple III is **El Mundo Perdido** ("The Lost World"), a complex of some 38 buildings. In the center, ringed by low palaces, rises the **Great Pyramid,** the oldest Mayan structure at Tikal. Huge, eroded masks on the north side are shaded by palapas; climb the wide stairs to a dusty platform at the top. The top of the pyramid is different from those of the other pyramids, most of which have a little room rather than just a flat platform. This is a wonderful place to watch hawks soaring above the forest canopy.

Temple IV. At 212 ft tall, this temple the largest structure ever built by an ancient people of the New World; look for it northwest of El Mundo Perdido. The humongous structure is still largely covered in jungle, and the ascent takes you scrambling over roots and up wooden ladders to the main platform. A metal ladder brings you to the roof comb. When get to top, you'll be rewarded with an inspiring view of the green expanse of jungle that seems to stretch forever.

Temple of the Inscriptions. If you have more time to spend at Tikal, head for this building (Temple VI) at the far southeast end of the city center. Although a beautifully carved stela lies at the bottom, the temple itself is run-down, so it doesn't have as many clear inscriptions as the name would suggest. The real attraction of this temple is its distance from the crowds. Lively monkeys like to feed in the large zapote trees surrounding it.

As the former mayor will proudly tell you, "Uaxactún is closer to heaven, for it is here that the Maya chose to watch the movements of their sacred stars."

Silvanus G. Morley Museum. Visit this museum to check out the many goodies that were found inside the temples at Tikal. Exhibits include exquisitely carved pieces of bone and jade, as well as beautiful pottery and a replica of the tomb of Ah-Cacao. The real one is under Temple I. *Inside visitor's center, across from the comedores. Admission $2. Open weekdays 9–5, weekends 9–4.*

UAXACTÚN

The ruins of an ancient city, once Tikal's cross-town rival, lie next to the thatched-roof huts of today's Uaxaxtún, a small and friendly frontier town. The locals are true Peténeros who continue to make a living in partnership with the surrounding forest. It's the kind of place where everyone is amazed that there are people who don't cook over a fire or wash clothes by hand in hollowed-out logs like they do. Anyone with more than a passing interest in the northern frontier should head in this direction.

The temple ruins are among the most impressive in the Petén, outside of Tikal. Behind the huts south of the runway you'll find Group E, the Maya observatory. As you climb the large temple near the gate, stop to see if you can tell which giant masks are bats and which are jaguars. To the east, you'll see three small temples; each was carefully placed so the sun rises over the one farthest south at the winter solstice (December 21), over the one farthest north at the summer solstice (June 21), and over the middle temple and its two stelae at the spring and fall equinoxes. Groups A and B, on the north side of the runway, include several large temples and palaces to explore. To the west you'll find where the Mayas carved out the building materials for their temples and stelae. It looks strangely abandoned, as if the workers suddenly dropped their saws in midslice and never returned.

Unstoppable adventurers should continue on to **Río Azul,** in the far northeastern corner of Petén, where Belize, Mexico, and Guatemala meet. From there, you can continue into Mexico. The ruins here are very large but still unrestored. Río Azul is connected to Uaxactún by a barely passable dirt road: you may be able to hitch a ride here, or at least to where the road splits in Dos Lagunas. You can arrange trips in Uaxactún at El Chiclero or EcoCamping (*see* Where to Sleep and Eat, *below*) for around $30 a day.

COMING AND GOING

La Pinita buses to Uaxactún leave from Santa Elena at around 12:30 PM and from Tikal at around 2 PM. Buses out of Uaxactún leave at around 6 AM. You can try hitching a ride early in the morning from Tikal, or arrange a tour from Flores or Santa Elena (*see* Travel Agencies in Flores and Santa Elena, *above*). The dirt road beyond Tikal becomes impassable in the rainy season, but the really gung-ho can make the 6-hour, 24-km (16-mi) walk from Tikal. The road is well marked and easy to follow.

WHERE TO SLEEP AND EAT

Once you get into the town of Uaxactún, you'll see one or two small stores and a bar—basically bamboo huts with small signs. **Comedor Imperial, El Esfuerzo,** and **Comedor y Refresquería Ady** all offer comida típica for $2–$4. The town's only hotel, **El Chiclero,** has a restaurant, garden, and a small zoo. Small, adequate rooms and a pour-the-water-over-your-head shower run $8 a double. You can hang your hammock and mosquito net at **EcoCamping** for $3. They have a night watchman, showers, and a laundry sink.

SAYAXCHÉ

An hour and a half west of Santa Elena over a stomach-turning bumpy road, the bus suddenly comes to a screeching halt and the road sinks into the waters of a wide river. Look across and you'll see the tiny town of Sayaxché, the political and commercial center of the southwestern Petén. Boats come here to pick up fuel and supplies for the small towns deep in the swampy interior. This is the most convenient base for visiting the ruins in this part of the Petén, most of which are only accessible by boat. Although none have been restored to their former glory, the sites of Aguateca, El Ceibal, and Dos Pilas all offer any aspiring Indiana Jones an incredible adventure within wet, mosquito-filled forests that are even deeper and darker than those around Tikal. Beware: this is a malaria hot spot—cover yourself with repellent, use the mosquito net, take the chloroquinine, do anything you can to stay healthy. Buses leave from Santa Elena (1½ hrs, $3) daily at 6 AM, 8 AM, and 4 PM. Once here, hunt around for a supply boat on the river to take you to Río Usumacinta, Yaxchilán, or the Mexican border. Halfway between Santa Elena and Sayaxché is **La Libertad,** a one-comedor town with a gas station. Here, the road splits off to the Mexican border, and it's a great place to hitch or find a truck driver willing to take you with him on the long road to Alta Verapaz.

The town's one and only bank, **Corpobanco** (tel. 926–6137), can sometimes change cash and traveler's checks and dollars. Stores will change cash at lousy rates, but you should try to bring enough quetzales to hold you over. You can pick up a good map with all the tourist information you need from **Restaurant Yaxkin** (tel. 926–6101). The bilingual owner, Rosendo Girón, can help you arrange trips to any of the local sites. Sr. Girón also runs a campsite where you can pitch a tent for $3; from the river, go up the street and look for his place on the right-hand side. **Hotel Guayacan** (tel. 926–6011) is the most expensive lodging in town ($8.50 for a double without bath), but it's also the cleanest and least basic, with a patio overlooking the river. It's the first building on the left-hand side across the river. Another spot is friendly, family-run **Casa Kilkan,** where basic but immaculate rooms cost $4. It's about five minutes from the main part of town—ask for directions. Besides really good, cheap food, **Restaurante La Montaña** (1 block from Hotel Guayacan, tel. 926–6114) has a tourist agency that runs regular trips to El Ceibal, Aguateca, and Dos Pilas. They can also arrange lodging at **Posada Caribe** ($50 per person, with meals), a hotel on the Río Petexbatún that is within walking distance of Dos Pilas.

NEAR SAYAXCHE

EL CEIBAL

Pull out the insect spray and lather up: the ancient site of El Ceibal lies deep within a humid stretch of jungle swimming with blood-sucking pests. The extremely well-preserved stelae depict rulers with mustaches and straight noses jamming on carved, guitar-like scepters in a style that is definitely not Mayan. Some archaeologists think that the sight was actually ruled by the Toltec of Mexico. You can camp in the thatched shelters near the park entrance for free; as usual, bring some extra food and drink to share with the guards. The cheapest way to get to El Ceibal is to ask in Sayaxché for any vehicle bound for El Paraíso. For less than 50¢, the driver will drop you at the head of the trail; from there, it's an hour's walk to the ruins. You can easily hitch back that afternoon. For a more comfortable ride, you can rent a boat in Sayaxché for about $50 for a six-person group. The boat will ferry you down the Río de La Pasión and drop you off by a narrow path; it's just 30 minutes through the jungle to the ruins. Although you'll hear howler monkeys and birds, it's difficult to see any animals through the thick vegetation. You can also arrange guided tours in Sayaxché or Santa Elena; they're a little more expensive, but they'll save you a lot of time and hassle.

DOS PILAS

At its height around AD 700, Dos Pilas was one of the most important Mayan centers in the Petén. One of the site's most interesting features is a staircase with hieroglyphics that record the capture of a Dos Pilas ruler in AD 643. Dos Pilas is accessible only by boat. After traveling an hour up the Arroyo Petexbatún ($40 round-trip), you'll be dropped at Paso Caribe, where you can hire a guide to take you the 12 km (7 mi) to the site, where you can rap with the archaeologists and pitch your tent for free. Guides usually charge $10–$15 a day. If you are really passionate about ruins, and have the time and money to spare, look into Aguateca and Yaxchilán. It's not often that you get a really good opportunity to scrounge around in the jungle.

SOUTH FROM FLORES

Two routes head south from Flores to Guatemala City. One is a grueling three-part journey from Flores to Chisec (6 hrs, $4), Chisec to Cobán (5 hrs, $3.50), and finally to Guatemala City (5 hrs, $3). The other is a grueling two-part journey from Flores to Río Dulce (8 hrs, $4), and from Río Dulce to the capital (5½ hrs, $5). This is one of the most remote and poorly kept stretches of road in Guatemala, so buckle down, cushion yourself with a few chickens, and prepare for the ride of your life. About an hour and a half south of Flores, the bus enters the foothills of the Maya Mountains and the fun really begins. The kamikaze bus driver barrels through the largely uninhabited jungle, tackling hairpin turns and monster potholes at full speed. If you're really in a rush, your best option is to take an overnight express bus, where you can get a real seat. The road is slowly being improved, so not far in the future you (and your behind) may be able to enjoy the miles of jungle and grass huts without the horrific bounce. For now, your best bet is to stop and relax in Finca Ixobel, a bustling gringo resort spot outside of Poptún.

El Ceibal takes its name from the ceiba trees, which were sacred to the ancient Maya, who believed they held up the heavens.

WHERE TO SLEEP AND EAT

Before reaching Finca Ixobel, you pass Poptún, a cute Petén town where you can see about staying at the finca at **Restaurante Fonda Ixobel** (tel. 926–7363). Definitely make a point to eat here, too—they serve up some of the most delicious food in Guatemala. If you arrive before dark, you can get a ride from the restaurant to the finca for $1.

In the cool pine forests just south of Poptún lies a gringo paradise. Treat yourself to a tossed green salad made with vegetables and herbs straight from the gardens of the working farm. Play volleyball, shoot some hoops, or take a dip in the sumptuous swimming hole. You can camp under a thatched palapa or in one of the treehouses for $3; a coed dorm has beds for $4. The latrines are the deepest in the country, and the shower water is wonderfully hot. The finca runs an incredible river cave expedition ($2.50) that travels over a mountain and into an cavern with an underground river. With candles in hand, you plunge into the water and wade through to a waterfall where you can jump over stalagmites into a deep pool far below. They also run inner-tubing ($10) expeditions, jungle treks, or horseback riding ($8) tours of the area. Nearby is **Naj Tunich,** a cave with Mayan paintings. Some of these beautiful paintings depict erotic scenes. They are closed on and off because of looting; ask for details at the finca. To get here, take one of the **Fuentes del Norte** buses that run between Guatemala City and Flores; ask to be dropped off at Finca Ixobel. It costs $6 from Río Dulce and $3 from Flores. The farm is about a 1-km (½-mi) walk back from the main road.

CENTRAL AND EASTERN GUATEMALA

While scads of tourists stream to the artsy boutiques of Antigua Guatemala, the market at Chichicastenango, and the gringo-drenched shores of Lago Atitlán, few visitors head east of the capital to the central and Caribbean regions of Guatemala. They don't know what they're missing. These highlands pack in so many different worlds that you may suffer culture shock at each bus stop. From the reggae beat and Creole seafood of the Caribbean coast to the mariachi bands and cacti of the dry cattle-ranching hills of Zacapa; from the mist-covered forests and waterfalls of Alta Verapaz to the blasting nightclubs and brothels of Puerto Barrios, this region is a perfect example of multifaceted Guatemala. Speak a few halting words of Kekchí in the main market of Cobán, tap on an African drum in Puerto Barrios, or light

CENTRAL AND EASTERN GUATEMALA

EL QUICHE

Chimaltenango

ATLANTIC HWY.

★ Guatemala City

Uspantán

Parque Nacional Las Victorias
Santa Cruz
Verapaz

Cobán
San Pedro
Carchá

BAJA VERAPAZ

Rabinal

Salamá

Tactic

Purulhá

La Cumbre

Biotopo del
Quetzal
Mario Dary Rivera

San Juan
Chamelco

Yiquiche

Xucizul

ALTA VERAPAZ

Chisec

Sebol

Lanquín

Semuc
Champey

Grutas de
Lanquín

Río Cahabón

Panzós

Chimeniá

Tuilá

Jalapa

El Progreso

El Jícaro

Río Hondo

Estanzuela

Zacapa

Gualán

El Estor

IZABAL

Modesto Méndez

TO POPTÚN
AND EL PETÉN

CHIQUIMULA

Chiquimula

TO
EL SALVADOR

El Florido

Copán

Esquipulas

Agua Caliente

Quiriguá

Río Motagua

Mariscos

Lago Izabal

Morales

La Ruidosa

El Relleno
Fronteras

Castillo de
San Felipe

Biotopo de
Manatí

El
Golfete

P.N. RÍO
DULCE

Río Dulce

Las Siete
Altares

Livingston

BELIZE

Bahía de
Amatique

Punta
de Manabique

Puerto Barrios

HONDURAS

N

KEY

Ferry

0   20 miles
0   30 km

154

a candle at the shrine of the Black Christ in Esquipulas—such actions are sure to bring out the hospitality and curiosity of locals who talk to few foreigners.

If you're hankering to get off the gringo trail and do some exploring, central and eastern Guatemala is a great place to start. Outdoor buffs will find that the region offers unmatched natural spectacles. Among the most beautiful are the dramatic cliffs that line the Río Dulce; the natural wonders outside Lanquín, where the river alternately gushes through underground caverns in a white fury and produces the turquoise pools of at Semuc Champey; and the spectacular scenery between Chiquimula and Esquipulas.

COBÁN

Set in a cool, misty valley, Cobán is a quiet, laid-back place in which to unwind. The city's population is almost completely indigenous, and although the traditional dress looks as close to European clothing as it can get, local Kekchí and Pokom cultures continue to run strong. Cobán is usually pretty sleepy, but things really get pumping in July and August, when the town's two major festivals fill the streets and colonial plazas with tourists, street vendors, and a big artisans' market with crafts from all over Guatemala. Other times of the year travelers use Cobán as the gateway to the innumerable indígena villages nearby, each with its own ruin, cave, or colonial church to explore. The *monja blanca* (the "white nun," Guatemala's national flower) grows everywhere in the misty surrounding forest, and the *quetzal* (the national bird) lives in the moss-covered trees.

Beware of the bird! Ixobel—scarlet macaw attack bird and finca resident—must be practicing for the tropical remake of "The Birds." It particularly enjoys dive-bomb attacks of horseback riders.

The demure nature of modern cobaneros offers few clues about their fervid ancestry—the local Rabinal Maya were one of the most feared and ruthless tribes of the Americas. When the Spanish arrived in the early 1500s, the Rabinal were involved in a century-old conflict with their bitter enemies, the Quiché. When the conquistadores finished with the Quichés, they expected to do the same to the Rabinal. Nope. Fierce Rabinal warriors sent the Spanish packing and the area became known as Tezulutlán, "The Land of War." Although the Spaniards failed to overcome the Rabinal with brute force, they finally succeeded with ideology, ultimately managing to secure the area by converting the native tribe to Christianity. In 1537, Fray Bartolome de Las Casas, a Jesuit priest known as a crusader against the maltreatment of the indígena by the Spanish crown, struck an unusual bargain with his compatriots: if Spain would keep its military forces out of the area for five years, Las Casas and his boys would work on the heathen souls of the Rabinal; if the project was successful, the Spanish would get their land and no one would get hurt. Las Casas began his mission by translating religious hymns into local languages. The wise chief realized that the Spanish weren't just going to go away, and agreed to be baptized as a political means to help his people. The Rabinals followed suit, and the "conquest" of the region was a massive diplomatic accomplishment. By the end of the allotted five years, the area was dotted with orderly Spanish-style villages, earning the land the new name of Verapaces, "the Lands of True Peace."

The indígena continued to live more or less unmolested until the 1880s, when German immigrants flooded in to establish the vast coffee fincas that still cover the surrounding hillsides. They transformed the city of Cobán from a mostly indígena outpost into an isolated and wealthy enclave having little contact with the rest of Guatemala. This period of European high society was short-lived, however. With the onset of World War II, the U.S. government pressured Guatemala to expel the Germans, many of whom were outspoken proponents of Hitler. In the late '70s and early 1980s, political unrest further shattered the "land of true peace." On May 29, 1978, in the Alta Verapaz town of Panzós, soldiers opened fire on a group gathered to protest the army's expropriation of their lands. More than 100 unarmed men, women, and children were killed that day, their bodies dumped into two mass graves that had already been prepared outside of town. The massacre is often considered a turning point in Guatemala's political history, marking the nation's entrance into the period of severe military brutality that reached its peak in the 1980s. Today Cobán is again peaceful, a bastion of civilization kept forever green by the *mus mus hab* (also called *chipi chipi*), an on-and-off drizzle that forces the town to adopt a calm, slow tempo.

BASICS

VISITOR INFORMATION • The **visitor information office** (open Mon.–Sat. 9–12:30 and 2:30–6) is right off the main plaza, behind a tiny playground next to TELGUA. Besides a map and a couple of brochures, you can get a humongous list of all the things to see and do in Alta Verapaz as well as information in English about hotels and restaurants. They also organize one-day tours to the Lanquín Caves and Semuc Champey (*see* Near Cobán, *below*) for about $20 per person in a group of six people.

The Proyecto Ecológico Quetzal (2a Calle 14–36, tel. 952–1047) is a nonprofit organization run by Peace Corp volunteers that offers trips into the Quetzal Reserve. A two-day trip costs $20 and includes a Kekchí guide and an overnight stay with a Kekchí family.

CHANGING MONEY • Banco del Agro (1a Calle and Av. 5, Z2, tel. 952–1273) changes cash and traveler's checks weekdays 9–8, Saturday 9–1. Right next door, **Banco del Ejército** (tel. 952–2387; open weekdays 8:30–8, Sat. 9–2) has longer hours and a Western Union wire service.

EMERGENCIES • The **police** (tel. 952–1225) are in Zona 2 on 1a Calle, at 5a Avenida. The **Red Cross** (3a Calle 2–13, Z3, tel. 952–1459) has ambulance service to the regional hospital (8a Calle 1–24, Z4, tel. 9521–315). **Farmacia Carvi** (1a Calle 4–53, Z4, tel. 952–3094) is the only 24-hour pharmacy in town. It's down the hill behind the cathedral, on the main road toward San Pedro Carchá.

LAUNDRY • Lavendería La Providencia (Diagonal 4, Z2, right off main plaza) will wash and dry a load for $3 or less. They're open Monday–Saturday 8–noon and 2–5.

PHONES AND MAIL • TELGUA (1a Calle and 3a Av., Z1, tel. 952–1498) is open daily 7 AM–midnight; look for the huge white-and-blue sign right off the main square. The **post and telegraph office** (3a Calle 2–02, Z3, tel. 952–1140) is in an unmarked building with brick-framed windows. It's behind the main market, across the street from Pollo Campero—let your nose do the walking and then look above the glass doors for the fading CORREOS & TELEGRAFOS sign. The post office is open weekdays 8–4, but there is 24-hour telegram service.

TRAVEL AGENCIES • Epiphyte Adventures will take you on a real adventure for reasonable prices. Friendly English-speaking guides run tours to the Petén and throughout Alta Verapaz. One-day tours to Lanquín and Semuc Champey start at $20. The company has an ecological bent, and works in cooperation with ProPetén, an ecological organization committed to conservation and sustainable development activities. *1 block north and 1 block east of TELGUA, tel. 952–2169.*

COMING AND GOING

BY BUS • Cobán is served by **Escobar/Monja Blanca** (4a Av. and 2a Calle, Z4, tel. 952–1952), right near the public bus terminal. They go to Guatemala City (5 hrs, $4) every half hour from 2:30 AM to 7 AM and then hourly until 4 PM. These are first-class Pullman buses with assigned seats, so buy your ticket in advance. Second-class buses to Uspantán in the Quiché Region (5–6 hrs, $4) stop in front of Tienda Cobán (2a Av., at 1a Calle). The northbound bus to Sebol (7 hrs, $2) leaves daily at 5:45 AM and 10 AM from in front of Cine del Norte (1a Calle and 2a Av.). Buses to El Estor, near Lago Izabal (9 hrs, $4), leave twice daily from Cobán's main **bus terminal.** The terminal, a dusty lot in front of the gymnasium, is just down the hill to the left of the church. If you're headed to the Petén from Cobán, take the 1 AM bus to Chisec (5 hrs, $4) from in front of the Tienda Cobán, or try to catch a ride in one of the pickup trucks that leave around 5 or 6 AM. In Chisec, catch the noon bus to Sayaxché (4 hrs, $4), but plan on spending the night there—the last bus to Flores/Santa Elena (1½ hrs, $3) leaves at 3 PM. Buses leave the terminal every 20 minutes for San Pedro Carchá, San Juan Chamelco, and other small nearby villages for under 20¢.

HITCHING • Hitching south of Cobán is fairly easy. A good place to scout a ride is La Cumbre, a major junction connecting the roads to Alta Verapaz, Baja Verapaz, and Guatemala City. Another safe bet is the junction near Tactic, where the road from El Estor meets the road to Cobán. The visitor information office discourages hitching at night or outside of these areas, mostly due to a recent increase in the number of robberies and rapes.

GETTING AROUND

Cobán is so small that finding your way around is *no problema*. The main plaza is a triangular park set on top of a ridge with a strange concrete pavilion in the center. The main street, 1a Calle, runs east–west through town, leading out to San Pedro Carchá, 6 km (4 mi) away. The cathedral is on the east side of the main plaza. Behind the cathedral is 2a Avenida, which runs south to the post office, the main market, and Pollo Campero; to the north, the street drops steeply down to the gymnasium, the main bus terminal, and another market. You'll find most of the hotels, shops, and restaurants within a few blocks of the main plaza and the cathedral, especially on 1a Calle. You can also pick up a great map at Epiphyte Adventures (*see above*).

WHERE TO SLEEP

It can be difficult to find an available room in Cobán during the August fiestas. **Hotel Nuevo Monterey** (6a Av. 1–12, Z1, tel. 952–1131) has clean, simple rooms with windows and fresh linens for $7 a double. Although the rooms off the street are noisy, **Hotel La Provedencia** (Diagonal 14 2–43, Z2, tel. 952–1209) has clean doubles with private bath, crisp sheets, and the usual chilly showers for $5. It's located right off the main plaza. The hotels listed below all have friendly service and display their INGUAT-approved rates so you'll avoid the illegal "gringo prices."

Don Jerominos. Just outside of nearby San Juan Chamelco, this is a great place to really get away from it all. There's nothing to do all day long except go inner-tubing, swimming, hiking . . . or just relax with a book from Jerry's vast collection. The view is great, the environment is quiet, and all meals served are vegetarian. Single rooms ($15) are located in the wooden front house, while doubles ($25) are in simple self-contained bungalows with private bathrooms. *Aldea Chajando, no phone. From Cobán terminal, take bus to Chamelco (15 min, 20¢). From Chamelco, hitch or take Chamil bus (10 min., 20¢) and ask to be dropped off at Don Jerominos. Look for small sign in front of cornfield, near last powerline pole. Cash only.*

Hotel Central. The medieval shields that decorate the patio of this quiet hotel recall the town's German roots. Unfortunately, the patches of fungus that decorate most of the rooms are more reminiscent of an old, damp bathroom. Unless you suffer from asthma or allergies, it shouldn't be too much of a problem, however, and the place is quiet and otherwise spotless, with fast and friendly service. Doubles are $9, including private baths with hot water. *1a Av. 1–79, Z4, tel. 952–1442. Next to Café San Jorge, left of cathedral (no sign). 14 rooms with bath. Cash only.*

Hotel de Acuña. This place has everything you could ask for—comfortable and clean rooms, sparkling shared bathrooms, and a pleasant courtyard garden. Plus the showers are wonderfully hot and there's a laundry service. The owners, Ashley and Marcio Acuña, know the area well and can arrange local excursions. There's a bulletin board with travel information, as well as a small café. Rooms are $4.20 per person. *4a Calle 3–11, Z2, tel. 952–1547. From main plaza, 2 blocks down from Cine Turía. Cash only.*

Hotel Don Juan Montalbatz. Named for the indigenous Kekchí chief, this hotel traditionally hosts the contestants for the Rabin Ajau beauty contest (*see* Festivals, *below*). The enormous rooms have cable TV, huge comfortable beds, chunky pillows, and sparkling private bathrooms—all for $8.35 per person. They also have a small artesanía store, a book exchange, and a travel-information center where they arrange tours to the area's attractions for $18–$32. Relax over a cappuccino or an imported beer in the garden while enjoying classical, marimba, or jazz music. Three nights a week they show movies with popcorn for all. *3a Calle 1–46, Z1, tel. 952–0033. From 1a Calle, walk left, head downhill to 3a Calle, and turn right. 15 rooms, 13 with bath. Laundry. Cash only.*

Hotel La Posada. This traditional old inn near the central plaza is a tasteful, comfortable spot—definitely the classiest place to stay in Cobán. Rooms have wood floors and beamed ceilings, and they are furnished with antiques and decorated with Guatemalan handicrafts, as are the porticoes and hallways. The hotel has a beautiful little garden and a cozy restaurant with a fireplace that serves mostly local food. For entertainment, a TV lounge and Ping-Pong table suffice. Doubles cost $32. *1 Calle 4–12, tel. 652–1495. 14 rooms with bath.*

CAMPING • Campers are in for a real treat: the villages surrounding Cobán offer tons of parks where you can camp for free. Just eight blocks southeast of the main plaza, the 203 acres of **Parque Nacional Las Victorias** (*see* Outdoor Activities, *below*) are yours to stake out. Go to the **park administration** (open weekdays 8–4), near the automobile access road, to get permission to use the official camping area next door. If the office is closed when you arrive, just go ahead and pitch your tent, but check in with them when they open in the morning. If the official campground bores you, countless picnic shelters and palapas beckon the creative camper. Bring water and supplies from town. You'll definitely need mosquito repellent and a net, and be sure to have something warm to sleep in—Cobán is not in a state of "eternal spring" like the tourist guide claims. Outside of town, San Pedro Carchá, Lanquín, and Tactic all have palapa-covered campgrounds (*see* Near Cobán, *below*), and you can find similar camping possibilities throughout the Alta Verapaz region.

FOOD

Cobán has a number of regional specialties of which residents are (rightly) proud. The most famous is *Kak'ik* (also spelled *Cacic* or called *Caldo de Chunto* or *Caldo de Chompipe),* a delicious turkey soup packed with a leg, a wing, a breast, and tons of delicious internal goodies. Kak'ik is usually accompanied by another regional specialty, tamales. These hot, corn-dough treats wrapped in banana leaves can be found almost anytime at the market or bus stop for pennies apiece. Local drinks reflect the crops grown in the region: cacao, coffee, cardamom, and sugarcane.

DEVIL'S JUICE

Boj is a local liquor with an interesting legend behind it: once upon a time, a demon was wooing a harp player and brought her sugarcane juice to help her to play. Before giving her the drink, the demon pricked his finger and a drop of blood fell into the sweet liquid, creating the first cup of boj. Even today it's said that drunken men are given to fighting because they are filled with the "blood of the devil."

Just off the central park are a number of delicious and squeaky-clean food stands; try a *churrasco* (grilled steak taco with avocado and onions) for $1.25. One of the best stands is **Empanadas Argentinas,** right in front of TELGUA, where you'll find hot chicken or beef *empanadas* (turnovers) for 50¢ apiece. There are also a number of cheap comedores, where you can get a filling meal for less than $2. At **Café Marito** (1a Calle, next door to Hotel La Posada, no sign) you can eat breakfast, lunch, or dinner for a buck. **Tacos Pique** (1a Calle 4–11, Z1, tel. 962–3503) serves up delicious Mexican-style tacos ($1.50), good soups ($1), and yummy fruit drinks (75¢). Campers and day-trippers can stock up on fruits and vegetables at the main market, or at the little shops along 2a Avenida that sell pan dulce, sandwich meat, and cheeses.

Cafetería San Jorge. This place offers stupendous Guatemalan food at low prices and is one of the most popular spots among locals. Come at lunchtime for an extra-special menú del dia; you get chicken ($3) or beef ($3.50) with corn, vegetables, avocado, rice, and delicious soup. If you're lucky, you might be able to chow down on the best Kak'ik in town for $3.50 a bowl. They serve it Saturdays only and you have to come early because they often run out. *1a Calle 1–79, Z4, no phone. Across from cathedral, on left-hand side. Closed Sun.*

Cafetería Santa Rita. This small comedor is very popular with the locals—and no wonder, considering the rock-bottom prices. You get chicken or beef, rice, salad, and a cool drink for less than $2. They also brew up a decent cup of coffee. The service is friendly and efficient. *2a Calle, Z2, just off main plaza, no phone.*

Restaurante El Refugio. As the staff rush to open the door to the bathroom, to pull out your chair, or to refill your glass every three sips, you may ask yourself: is this good manners, annoying, or just plain entertaining? Whatever your perception, this is the place to find elegant dishes at reasonable prices. Try pavesa, a hearty bowl of soup ($1.50) that tastes suspiciously like French onion. At lunchtime, you can fill up on their menú del dia for less than $2. Try some turtle soup ($4), lasagna ($5), or asparagus salad ($3.50), and wash it all down with a cocktail from the bar. *2a Calle 1–34, Z2, tel. 952–1338. Follow la Calle behind cathedral, turn left on first street downhill toward bus terminal. Look for large wooden building on first corner to your left.*

DESSERT/COFFEEHOUSES • Cobán is the coffee capital of Guatemala and is home to a handful of places where you can sit and sample a cup of one of the local blends while you watch the chipi-chipi. At **Café La Posada** (1a Calle 4–12, Z1, tel. 952–1495) you can enjoy some coffee and eat your cake, too—all on their patio overlooking the main plaza. The café at the Hotel de Acuña (*see above*) offers a relaxing atmosphere in which to contemplate your reality. The rose-garden courtyard at Hotel Don Juan Montalbatz (*see above*) is a stately place to get caffeinated on the local blends. If you've developed an addiction at this point, you can also buy some of the region's famous beans at *Dieseldorff* (3a Calle 4–12, Z2, tel. 952–1286), one of Cobán's oldest coffee fincas.

Café El Tirol. At last! A real café where you can get that Guatemalan coffee everyone talks about—in more than 37 different flavors. Take your pick from an espresso with chocolate and caramel, or one with vanilla ice cream, each for 85¢. Or try Krupnik ($1.25), with honey, lemon, and vodka to counteract the caffeine. *1a Calle 3–13, Z1, across from Posada Hotel, no phone. Look for small sign and turn into driveway; café is to your right.*

WORTH SEEING

The **El Calvario Church** is a short walk from the prosperous modern markets of central Cobán, but as you zigzag up the hill toward the church you'll enter a world far away in both time and culture. The cobblestone path to the top is bordered by a series of small shrines, each hiding a cross darkened with ash. The offerings inside include feathers, hair, and coins stuck to the crosses and walls with gobs of wax. If you sit a while, you might see families muttering prayers in Kekchí. The view from the top of the hill is one of the best in the city. The church itself offers another chance to see bloody sculptures of Christ and devoted worshippers kneeling in the flicker of candles. You can look around during the daytime from 7 to 7, or attend a Sunday mass in Kekchí at 7 AM or 10 AM. Just next to El Calvario is **La Ermita de Santo Domingo de Guzmán,** the clubhouse for Cobán's *cofradía* (elected religious officials). From TELGUA, walk three blocks west, turn right, walk two blocks, and then turn left. Look for the stairs to the church on your right.

The **cathedral** in the center of town is interesting not for its architecture but for some weird tidbits inside. Near the altar is an Englishman's account of his travels to Cobán at the beginning of the century. To the right of the cathedral is the **convent.** Built in the late 1500s, it is one of Cobán's oldest surviving buildings. More recently, it was used as a shelter for hundreds of Kekchí indígenas who fled from their war-torn villages in the early 1980s. At festival time, arts and crafts from the surrounding communities are on display inside.

FESTIVALS

The **National Folklore Festival** annually draws people from all over Guatemala and features folkloric dances and typical foods from every part of the country. One of the most important parts of this festival is the election of the **Rabin Ajau** ("daughter of the king"), the winner of a beauty pageant that involves a parade of traditional costumes from the villages of Guatemala. The festival usually takes place in the last week of July and takes place in the national gymnasium behind the main bus terminal. Buy tickets ($3–$4) at the **municipalidad** on 1a Calle, next to Banco de Occidente. Cobán continues the party with its own town fiesta in honor of the patron saint of Cobán, Santo Domingo de Guzmán. Throughout the first week of August, the town holds parades, fireworks, marimba concerts, and fascinating folkloric dances depicting the perseverance of the indigenous population in the face of Spanish aggression.

AFTER DARK

Nighttime brings out those friendly drunks who want to take you to the "disco," but aside from the lecherous comments, Cobán is reasonably safe. **Le Bon Discoteca** (3a Calle 3–38, Z3, tel. 952–1673) is across the street and down a block from Pollo Campero. They open at 8, but the boogie-ing begins around 10 PM and the party goes on until 3 AM. Although the red light and stream of scantily clad women wandering down from upstairs suggests this is more than just a disco, cobaneros also come here in couples and the atmosphere remains pretty classy for a disco. Cover charge is $1 on Friday and $2 on Saturday.

OUTDOOR ACTIVITIES

For hiking, jogging, camping, or picnicking, head to **Parque Nacional Las Victorias.** Once a German coffee finca, this huge city park is now an ecological reserve for the native plant life of Altz Verapaz. One tiny corner of the park is accessible by car, but a web of trails extends far into the mountains above Cobán. You could easily spend a couple of days wandering around this reserve, and it's close enough to the center of town to make a great place to camp (*see above*). To get here, walk past the El Calvario Church and the park entrance will be on your right. A large sign with a map of the extensive trails greets you as you enter.

In the **Vivero Verapaz** orchid nursery you can see a variety of the gorgeous flower, including the *monja blanca,* Guatemala's national flower. The best time to visit is from October through February when most of the flowers are in bloom. The nursery lies 1 km (½ mi) southwest of Cobán on the old road to Guatemala City. After you cross the bridge, take the second dirt road to your right. Look for a small artificial pond and giant tree ferns to your right. The Mittlestaets will happily guide you through their prized plants for $2 Monday–Saturday 9–noon and 2:30–5. On Sunday, it's open only in the morning.

NEAR COBAN

SAN PEDRO CARCHA

Just 6 km (4 mi) from Cobán, this midsized town is famous for its silver work. The **Platería Típica Carchá** (9a Calle 2–31) is a family-owned and -operated store where you can pick up lovely handmade jewelry and colorfully embroidered blouses; it's the small turquoise building on your left just as you come into town. The town church sits in a flower-filled main square, and next door is a small **regional museum** (open weekends 9–noon and 2–5). A 15-minute walk from the center of town, **Las Islas** has free camping and a great swimming hole. Follow Diagonal 2 to the end, take the right fork, and walk up the dirt road to the park entrance. The palapa shelters are perfect for hanging a hammock and a mosquito net;

a small store sells sodas and snacks, but bring food and water from town. Buses to Carchá run every 15 minutes, 6 AM–7 PM, from the main bus terminal in Cobán for a mere 5¢.

BIOTOPO DEL QUETZAL "MARIO DARY RIVERA"

As the road winds up into the mountains north of Baja Verapaz, the climate takes a turn as dramatic as those in the twisting road. These cool slopes are home to Guatemala's national bird, *Pharomacrus moccinno,* or, in lay terms, the quetzal. This brilliant green creature has been revered since ancient times, when it was incorporated into one of the most important religious cults of Mesoamerica, *Kulkulcán,* which means the feathered serpent. Today, this bird continues to be the most important of national symbols. You'll see its image plastered everywhere—from effigies hanging in bus windows to the design on the national currency. To native Mesoamericans, killing a quetzal was an offense punishable by death, and the bird still remains under legal protection. Unfortunately, the habitat it depends on for survival is quickly falling to the ax. The Biotopo del Quetzal, which stretches up and over a steep hillside, is intended to give the bird a permanent home. Two meticulously cleared trails—one 2 km (1 mi) long, one 3½ km (2¼ mi) long—lead through the reserve. Beautiful waterfalls are scattered throughout the reserve; the one near the park entrance feeds a small bathing pool. The quetzales themselves are reluctant hosts, but your chances of seeing one are best in the early morning or late afternoon. In the February–May breeding season, you have a better chance of catching a glimpse of the green bird. The park is open daily 6 AM–4 PM. You can camp for free on one of five small, grassy camping plots, each with a picnic table and a barbecue pit. There are plenty of places to hang a hammock and mosquito net, and as usual, bring supplies in from town. **Hospedaje Los Ranchitos,** right next to the reserve, charges $9 a double for a room with shared bath—which is too much for what you get. They have simple comedor-type meals for $2.

COMING AND GOING • The reserve is at Kilometer 161 of the Carretera del Atlántico, 4 km (2½ mi) from the town of Purulhá. From Guatemala City, take an **Escobar/Monja Blanca** (8a Av. 15–16, Z1, tel. 652–4869) bus headed to Cobán and ask the driver to let you off at the park entrance. The 3½-hour ride costs about $2.50. From Cobán (45 min, 60¢), take a bus toward Guatemala City from the Monja Blanca Terminal. It is also quite easy to hitch in either direction from the reserve.

LANQUIN

Lanquín's claim to fame is a pair of nearby natural wonders. The town itself is a small community of Kekchí Indians whose three churches reflect the heavy indigenous influence—they have no pews, and altars are covered with candles and offerings of flowers, food, and incense. **La Divina Providencia** is Lanquín's one-stop shopping experience, with a hotel, comedor, pharmacy, and tienda all under one roof. Simple rooms with a clean shared bath go for $1.50 a person, and hearty meals are served in the adjoining comedor for $2 each. The town generator starts up at 6 PM and winds down just three hours later at 9. Another lodging option is the **Hotel El Recreo,** where immaculate bungalows, a pool, and even a small zoo are yours for $4 a person. It's located 1½ km (1 mi) past the cave. Buses to Lanquín (3½ hrs, $3) leave Cobán's main terminal at 6 AM, 12:30 PM, 1 PM, and 3 PM. Return buses leave the main plaza at 5 AM, 1 PM, and 3 PM. Come early to get a seat.

About 1 km (½ mi) outside town, the Lanquín River appears aboveground, gushing out of huge dark caverns in a spectacular white roar. These caverns are the **Grutas de Lanquín.** An established trail with iron railings will help you keep your footing among the huge stalactites and stalagmites. To play it safe, officials have recently covered the cave with a closed gate. If you ask at the policía nacional in the municipalidad in Lanquín, someone will open it and switch on the lights ($2 per person). Bring a good flashlight for exploring. Even if you don't want to go inside, one of the best times to visit the caves is in the evening, when thousands upon thousands of bats spill out of the caverns. Bring something to cover your head. You can camp for free under two large palapas at the site. The caves are just off the main road, 1 km (½ mi) before you reach Lanquín.

Reputed to be the most beautiful spot in Guatemala, **Semuc Champey** is a must-see. Set on a natural limestone bridge, a series of crystal-clear turquoise bathing pools are fed by tiny rivulets of water trickling through the forest. Upstream, the calm is broken in a turbulent white fury as the Río Cahabón plunges into the dark caverns below the pools. Local guides warn, "Don't fall in, it'll take 40 days for the body to come out the other side." Downstream, the waters emerge in an equally forceful rush, plunging on through the valley below. If you can't bear to leave, you'll find a few benches and an area to pitch a tent. To get here, follow the main road through Lanquín, past the plaza and municipalidad, and begin winding your way through the hills. Ten steep km (6 mi) and about three hours later you'll reach a bridge crossing the Río Cahabón. Follow the small footpath to the right, where you pay the 40¢

THE LIVING WELL

One of Tactic's weirdest attractions is El Pozo Vivo (the Living Well). At first, the well looks like a big zero—just a small, boring pond off the highway. But look closely and you'll see the mud at the bottom oozing and bubbling. As you watch, leaves and rocks move, disappear, and reappear.

Legend has it that a young Indian princess was bathing in a pool when a band of invading Spaniards came upon her. The leader and the princess stared deeply into each other's eyes. They immediately knew that they were soul mates, and ardently consummated their love in the bushes. The Spaniard then had to fight off all his men to keep them from ravishing her, but he was slain in the process. When the princess's father found her crying over her dead lover, he proclaimed that, according to their laws, she must be stoned to death unless a man would marry her in her fallen state. Although a man from the village offered to save her, the princess chose to die. They say that the pond is disturbed by human voices because she walks there to this day. Just by the pond is a liquid amber tree, and in the split of it, you can see two lovers kissing.

entrance fee. If that three-hour hike doesn't agree with you, you might be able to catch a ride with one of the infrequent tourist-transport pickups ($4). Another option is to get a group together in Cobán for an organized tour (*see* Visitor Information, *above*). Bring a bathing suit, a camera, and good shoes. Be aware that if you leave stuff unattended, you may have a lighter pack to tote around, since finders keepers is the current rule.

TACTIC

Just 45 minutes away from Cobán by bus, Tactic is something of a cultural island. The people here are of Pokom Maya descent, and they dress and speak differently than the larger surrounding Kekchí population. The town is set on a hill, and above it, at the top of a dirt path, is the Church of Chi-Ixim. The path is crowded with women balancing full baskets of corn on their heads and men carrying loads of firewood strapped to their backs. Behind the church are the ruins of the fortified city of Chicán, the Pokoms' former hangout. If you're up for a swim, check out the waterfall-fed pools at a picnic spot called **Chancé.** You can camp at the Pozo Vivo (*see* box, *below*) for $1 per person or rent a hammock for 40¢; the entrance fee is 20¢. Look for the sign on the main road. Buses leave for Tactic (30 min, 40¢) every half hour between 6 AM and 6 PM from Cobán's main terminal.

LIVINGSTON

Situated on the Gulf of Honduras at the mouth of the Río Dulce, Livingston might as well be it's own Caribbean island—the only way to get to or from the town is by boat, and the culture is closer to that of Jamaica than the rest of Guatemala. Livingston is home to the Garifuna people. They are descendants of Arawak Indians and Africans, who came originally from St. Vincent, an island in the Lesser Antilles. After 20 years of resisting British encroachment, the Garifuna were forcibly removed from their homeland and dumped on Roatán, Honduras. The Garifuna migrated to the mainland, settling all along the Caribbean coast from Belize to Nicaragua. Each year on November 15, Livingston hosts a festival to celebrate the arrival of the Garifuna on the coast of Guatemala. A number of sailboats reenact the original voyage from Roatán, and the town rejoices with traditional music and dancing.

Livingston's single paved street is the only evidence left of its heyday as a large port for the Guatemalan coffee exporting boom of the late 19th century. Today, Livingston's residents make their living mostly from fishing or the tourist industry. Once you arrive, lay down your worries and settle down under a coconut palm. Reggae, ganja (not a good idea for tourists; you might end up doing time in an infamous Guatemalan prison), and the soft lick of waves measure out the slow pace that draws visitors to this small laid-back community. At night, roving bands of Garifuna musicians and dancers perform for crowds of tourists. The Garifuna are famous for their punta dancing—they may grab you out from the crowd and teach you some moves you didn't know your body could make.

BASICS

Livingston has just one bank, **Banco de Comercio** (tel. 948–1568; open weekdays 8:30–4), where you can cash traveler's checks, exchange dollars, or receive cash through Western Union. From the pier, make your first left and walk up the hill about 100 yards. The **Almacén Koo Wong** (uphill from pier, on right) will change U.S. and Belizean dollars, cash traveler's checks, and might even make a deal in other currencies, judging from his collection of foreign bills. Their 5% commission is the best rate in town. **TELGUA** (open daily 7 AM–9 PM) and the **post office** (open weekdays 8–noon and 2–4) are right next to each other, halfway up the hill from the pier, on the right. The **medical clinic** (open weekdays 8–noon and 2–8) is just past the TELGUA, on the right.

COMING AND GOING

The only way to get to or from Livingston is by boat, which you can take from either Río Dulce (Fronteras) or Puerto Barrios. The trip from Puerto Barrios is the cheaper and easier of the two. Boats leave Puerto Barrios daily 10:30 AM and 5 PM, except on Sunday when the first boat leaves at 10 AM sharp. A mere $1.50, this 1½-hour trip may be the cheapest boat ride in Guatemala. Arrive well in advance to stake a spot on the boat because when it gets full, they start to kick people off at random. The boats that return to Puerto Barrios from Livingston leave at 5 AM and 2 PM and are equally popular and crowded. A more flexible option is a to take a collective boat to and from Puerto Barrios (30 min, $3), which will bring you on your fast and wet way, but only until 3 PM.

From Río Dulce, the "mail boat"—which has nothing to do with mail—leaves on Tuesday and Friday at 6 AM, returning from Livingston at 9:30 AM. The trip takes three hours and costs $6. On the return trip from Livingston to Río Dulce, the boat makes a stop at the Aguas Calientes (*see* Near Livingston, *below*). If you have a little time, you can work a boat tour of the area into your return trip. For $9–$15, you'll hit all the sights along the way. Just ask the boat operators in Livingston, by the dock. **Exotic Travel Agency** (from the pier, uphill to left, inside the Bahía Azul Restaurant) can also arrange the tours.

GETTING AROUND

In tiny Livingston, each street is more or less its own neighborhood. As you walk toward town from the pier, the first street to your left is Barrio Marco Sanchez Díaz, where you'll find the most budget hotels. As you continue up the hill along Calle El Centro, you'll reach the center of town, which is bursting with *almacenes* (department stores), comedores, and restaurants. If you turn left on Calle de la Iglesia, you'll pass still more eateries until you hit the conspicuous African Place. Keep walking straight past Cafetín Lili, and you'll end up on the beach.

WHERE TO SLEEP

Livingston has every type of lodging, from ridiculously overpriced **Hotel Tucan Dugu** ($80 and up) to cheap, stuffy, cell-like rooms. Luckily, there's a decent middle range, where you'll find a little bit of affordable comfort. It's harder to find affordable lodging during the weekends and festivals, when prices double and everything fills up. If you can't get into one of the hotels listed below, **Hotel Vista Del Lago** has clean but hot and stuffy rooms with thin mattresses for $6 a double. The owner also rents bikes and canoes by the hour. To get here, make a left on Barrio Marco Sanchez Díaz, walk east toward the Casa Rosada, and look for the little white hotel on the right. At quiet and neat **Hospedaje Lebeneri,** you'll pay $4.60 for a small double with a fan. From the pier, walk up Calle El Centro, turn left onto Calle de la Iglesia. At the church, turn right past the electronics store and look for the sign on the left-hand side.

UNDER $5 • Hotel Caribe. Caribe's $3 doubles lure scads of budget travelers. Rooms are small, hot, and basic, and the general bathrooms long for a good scrubbing. Still, there's a Ping-Pong table, and you can lock your room with your own padlock. Make sure you make the midnight curfew—otherwise you may have to get better acquainted with the sidewalk than you'd planned. *Barrio Marco Sanchez Díaz, next to Hotel Henry Berringsford, no phone. 27 rooms, 6 with bath. Cash only.*

CREOLE COOKING IS GREAT WHEN TORTILLAS LEAVE YOU FLAT

Creole cooking on the Caribbean coast is like nothing else in the country. Coconuts, bananas, and mounds of fresh seafood will tantalize even the most tortilla-jaded taste buds. If you play your cards right, you may be able to escape tortillas entirely, because meals often come with small bland rolls called pan de coco (bread made with coconut milk). Here's a diner's guide to Creole cuisine:

- *Tapado is a bouillabaisse of vegetables, shrimp, crab, boiled green plantains, and fish.*

- *Rice and beans (in Creole, "Rays an' Beenz") are not your typical rice and beans. You'll be wowed instead by a mix of red beans and rice cooked in coconut milk with vegetables and spices.*

- *Jujuto (pronounced Hu Hu Tu) is a fish soup cooked with coconut milk. You eat it not with a spoon, but by scooping it up with fried balls of mashed plantains.*

- *Sopa de caracol is a soup made with conch meat. It's supposed to be great for lower back muscles, which need to be loose and wiggly for salsa dancing and any other sweaty activities that involve tons of hip action.*

Hotel El Viajero. Right on the water, this hotel has a pretty garden, comfortable beds, and a helpful and friendly staff. Large, bright doubles have fans and cost just $4. *Barrio Marco Sanchez Díaz, third hotel on left, no phone. 12 rooms, 8 with bath. Cash only.*

UNDER $10 • The African Place. Modeled along the lines of a Moorish palace, with tile floors, Islamic archways, grilled windows, and even an Arabian stallion, this big white castle has doubles for $6. Despite the gaudy decor, the rooms are clean and spacious. *Calle de la Iglesia, no phone. From pier, follow Calle El Centro as it makes a sharp left before Cafetín Lili. 23 rooms, 6 with bath. Cash only.*

Bungalows Salvador Gaviota. Talk about getting away from it all—this place is a 10-minute boat ride from Livingston pier. Right on Quehueche Beach, the self-contained bungalows come with a hot plate, sink, little table, private bathroom, and foam mattresses—all for $9. You can buy comida típica or choose from the limited supplies at the little store. The only downside is that you are *really* isolated. There have been frequent reports of thefts along the beach path to Quehueche Beach, so you shouldn't walk. You're dependent on the local boats that make the trip daily from Livingston to the Siete Altares (*see* Near Livingston, *below*). *Quehueche beach, no phone. 5 bungalows with bath. Cash only.*

UNDER $20 • Hotel Henry Berringsford. This incongruous-looking white slab of a building is the only place in Livingston where you can get a double room with private bath, air-conditioning, and cable TV for just under $20. There's a small swimming pool to cool off in, and they rent boats and jet-skis to zip around the ocean. The room rate includes breakfast, and you might be able to haggle down the price. *Down the street to the left of the public dock, no phone. 40 rooms with bath.*

La Casa Rosada. This waterfront bungalow hotel can best be described as the most luxurious way to "rough it" in Guatemala. Each of the 10 basic bungalows is furnished with bright highlands furniture and a pair of twin beds covered with mosquito nets. The shared bathrooms are clean and comfortable, and the shower inside the main building has hot water. That building also houses a restaurant that serves excellent meals and snacks and has a fine patio overlooking the water. Cathey Lopez, the friendly owner, also arranges river trips from the Casa's private dock. The Casa fills up quickly, so make reservations if possible, or arrive early. Doubles with shared bath are $16, but if you're alone, tell Cathey you're willing to share. *Down the street to the left of the public dock, no phone. 10 rooms, 6 with bath.*

CAMPING • Biotopo de Manatí (*see* Near Livingston, *below*) has palapas where you can sling a hammock or pitch a tent for $1 per person. The skeeters here are vicious, so come equipped with a mosquito net and repellent. To get here, hire a boat in Livingston and ask the boat's owner to leave you at the reserve (it should cost less than $9 per person with a group). Either arrange to have the driver pick you up at a later date or hook up with a group of day visitors.

FOOD

Not only is Livingston one of the very best places to eat fresh seafood, it's also a bastion of Creole cooking (*see* box). And once you get some, you'll be rushing back for more. **Cafetería Coni** (Barrio San Francisco, across from the African Place) is the best place to munch on Creole eats; try the jujuto for $5. Be sure to place any special requests early—as much as a day in advance—because many of the dishes take hours to prepare. **Cafetín Lili** (Barrio Barrique, on main road toward the beach) serves good seafood and vegetarian dishes on a patio overlooking the street. They have a $5 tapado and other similarly priced specialties. If your sweet tooth has got you in a frenzy, the women on the street sell snacks like *dulce de coco* (a sticky coconut goodie) or *dulce de leche* (a light brown fudge) for 20¢.

Cafetería UBAFU. Bob Marley is still alive and well here at this Rastafarian shrine, and he's eating well, too. Chicken, rice and beans with coconut milk all go for $2.50, or order specialty items a few hours in advance. The musical group UBAFU can be seen here nightly—keep an eye out for Estrella, who can move in ways that are astounding. *Calle de la Iglesia, no phone. Just past Restaurant Margoth, on the right.*

Restaurant Margoth. This place has a rustic decor with hanging shark teeth, tortoise shells, plants, and wood carvings. Wrestle through a sea of other ravenous diners to one of the many wooden tables with green-checkered tablecloths. Once you're seated, feast on some of the best Garifuna cuisine around. The tapado ($5) is a seafood lover's dream come true. They also have succulent steak ($5) and shrimp ($6) dinners. Don't miss out on Margoth's famous banana bread—ask her to bake you a loaf of your own ($6) to bring camping or on a picnic. They also have a full bar. *Calle de la Iglesia, across from Church of Nasarene, tel. 948–1069.*

AFTER DARK

Cool down, mellow out, and let your soul drift to the throbbing beat of reggae and punta that turns Livingston into one big party every weekend. In a palapa hut just off the beach, **Barique Place** is having a big party and everyone's here—Garifuna, German, Canadian, Guatemalan, Argentine . . . you get the picture. On Fridays and Saturdays after 8 PM, pay 40¢ to get in with the masses and just start dancing. Groups of musicians and punta dancers perform at locations all over town. **Banana Republic** (just off Calle El Centro, across from Mr. Coffee) has music nightly, as do **Restaurant Margoth** and **Cafetería UBAFU** (*see above*).

NEAR LIVINGSTON

Livingston is the best base from which to see all the sights of the Río Dulce, Guatemala's widest river. To explore, however, you'll have to rent a boat from the pier. A group of eight people should be able to go to the Biotopo, Aguas Calientes, Río Dulce, and the Castillo San Felipe for $9–$12 each.

LOS SIETE ALTARES

Just north of Livingston, these cool falls trickle into a series of tiered aquamarine pools, forming the *Siete Altares* (Seven Altars) in a brilliant green cathedral of towering rain forest. As you climb over the slippery rocks, each waterfall seems more beautiful than the last. You haven't reached the top until you get to rocks set over a deep pool; from there you can leap into the water. Fifteen minutes by boat from Livingston, it's not the cheapest excursion ($6–$8 a person) around, but it's really worth it; the pools are a slice of heaven. Don't walk the hour-long beach route, because there have a number of machete-point robberies along the way.

BIOTOPO DE MANATI AND AGUAS CALIENTES

When your boat turns inland to the river, brace yourself for some spectacular tropical scenery. As the river narrows, the land around you rises to limestone cliffs covered in jungle. Keep an eye out for dolphins and white herons. At the base of one of the cliffs, a sulfur spring emerges. **Aguas Calientes** is a warm spot in the water where you can soak comfortably. At first the sulfuric rotten-egg smell might seem unappealing, but after a couple of minutes of hot-water heaven, you'll forget all about it. As you continue up the river, the cliffs slowly open into a large gulf, where flocks of egrets race beside your boat. At the north end is the **Biotopo de Manatí** (open daily 7–4). The reserve's lagoons are the hideout for elusive manatees, who are unlikely to make an appearance. The Biotopo runs a small nature center (complete with mounted wildlife) and maintains a short trail thorough the park. You can also camp for $1 (*see* Where to Sleep, *above*). Tour boats pass through frequently, so you won't have trouble finding your way back to civilization.

RÍO DULCE

This settlement is actually two towns, El Relleno and Fronteras, located on opposite sides of an obnoxious concrete bridge arching over the Río Dulce. Just beneath this expensive monstrosity, the abjectly poor do their washing and bathing just yards from filthy rich Guatemalans in their opulent yachts. The towns are overrun by garishly painted prostitutes and their drunken clients, while the rich—including boat-sailing gringos—run off to their playgrounds along the banks of the river. Still, Río Dulce has become a popular access point for the breathtaking boat ride to Livingston, which takes you through awesome tropical scenery.

It is said that sailors mistook the manatees in the area for mermaids.

BASICS

Everything you'll need is found south of the bridge, along Fronteras's main road. **Banco Del Agro** (½ km south of Librería Ribani) changes cash weekdays 9–4, Saturdays 9–1. There are two community **phones** that you can use daily 7–7; one is below the Hospedaje Marilu, and the other is behind Librería Ribani. The **post and telegraph office** (open weekdays 8–noon and 2–6) is next to La Cabaña de Don Diego, a seedy disco. English-speaking doctors staff the **Ak' Tenamit Medical Clinic** (open daily 7–4), which is only accessible by boat. They can be hailed on Channel 88 over the radio system that serves as a substitute telephone service for local residents.

COMING AND GOING

BY BUS • The **Litegua** office is just before the bridge in Fronteras. Buses to Guatemala City (5½ hrs, $5) leave at 3 AM, 5:30 AM, 7:45 AM, and midnight. To get to Puerto Barrios, take any El Relleno bus to the first crossroads (45 min, 60¢) and hail a bus marked PUERTO BARRIOS (1½ hrs, 60¢).

BY BOAT • You can arrange a boat ride to Livingston at Hollymar's Restaurant (*see below*) for $9–$13 per person with a group. A cheaper and slower option to Livingston is the "mail boat" (3 hrs, $7) that leaves Tuesday and Friday at 6 AM and returns at 9:30 AM. If you can afford it, take the six-day boat trip to Belize on the 46-foot **Catamaran Las Sirenas** ($289 per person, double occupancy). The ship is docked at El Tortugal's marina; call over the radio.

WHERE TO SLEEP AND EAT

Río Dulce caters mainly to the yacht-club crowd, but you'll find a few places that are more moderately priced. **Hotel Rio Dulce** has small, clean basic rooms for $5.35 a double. It's just before the bridge on the road that veers to the right. A 15-minute walk from Fronteras, in the small town of San Felipe, **Rancho Escondido** (VHF 10) has rustic, tidy, and welcoming rooms, and breakfast or dinner is included for $5.50 per person. Take a pickup truck there from in front of Librería Ribani, or call over the radio for a ride. **Hollymar's Restaurant and Bar** has a laid-back atmosphere and groovin' music. It's a good place to meet fellow voyagers, get together a tour group, or just enjoy some choice grub. They serve crepes, omelets, calzones, and sandwiches for $3–$5. It's a block down from the bridge, on the water to the left. Two other places are accessible by boat only. Walk down the road leading to the river to **Cafetería Emy,** where you can use the radio. **El Tortugal** charges $3 for a night in a hammock, tent, or cot, and towels and sheets cost $1 extra. They rent kayaks and Windsurfers, show movies at night, and have a restaurant and bar where you fill up on a delicious meal for $3–$5. **Hacienda Tijax** (VHF 09) has a "backpackers special"—$9 per person in a dormitory cabin, breakfast included. They have their own nature reserve, jungle trail, and volleyball courts.

NEAR RIO DULCE

LAGO IZABAL

Ringed with forest and green mountains, this is the largest lake in Guatemala and a a hideaway for wealthy Guatemalans. The Spanish established the port of Bodegas, now called **Mariscos,** to ship out all their Guatemalan booty to Europe. English pirates, greedy for their own piece of the pie, sailed the Río Dulce to raid the galleons. The Spanish built **Castillo de San Felipe** ($1), the awesome stone fortress complete with a moat, drawbridge, dungeons, turrets, and rusty chains and cannons. The castle adjoins a park where you can swim or picnic among the Guatemalan families. Hire a boat in Fronteras ($3 round-trip) for the five-minute ride.

PUERTO BARRIOS

Puerto Barrios is the capital and the largest city in the department. The town was once a thriving port, but the commercial boom is long since over, leaving behind the rusting railroad cars, dilapidated warehouses, and paint-chipped wood buildings that give this town a run-down, comfy feel. The few blocks of sleaze near the market and bus station give way to simple wood shacks, green lots, and old stilt houses. In this section of town the people are as warm as the tropical air, and a simple "buenas noches" will almost unfailingly make even the most hard-faced ship worker smile. Other than a quick look around, though, there's little reason to spend much time in Puerto Barrios. The thriving nightlife might lure you out for an evening before your morning bus to Livingston or Guatemala City, but it gets awfully coarse at night, when the sleazier elements take over the streets. Luckily, there are numerous taxis around to hail—if you are planning on being out.

BASICS

Lloyds Bank (7a Calle and 2a Av., tel. 948–0165) changes cash and traveler's checks and does advances on Visa. **Banco del Café** (13a Calle and 7a Av., tel. 948–0588) changes dollars, sells and cashes traveler's checks, and has the American Express Moneygram Service. The **national hospital** (tel. 948–3071) is outside town on the north side, toward Santo Tomás. The **Red Cross** (tel. 948–0315) runs ambulances, and the **police** (tel. 948–0305) are always handy in a jam. **TELGUA** (8a Av. and 10a Calle, near main church) is open daily 7 AM–midnight; look for the cement tower with a cross on top. The **post and telegraph office** (6a Calle and 6a Av.) is in the center of town. The post office is open weekdays 8–4:30, and the telegraph office is open daily 24 hours.

COMING AND GOING

BY BUS • The **bus station** (6a Av., between 9a and 10a calles) has luggage storage for 20¢ a bag. Litegua buses (tel. 948–1172) shuttle to and from Guatemala City daily 1 AM–4 PM. You can choose between the hourly corriente service (6 hrs, $5), which makes a whole lot of stops along the way, or *especial service* (5 hrs, $6), which leaves seven times a day and makes fewer stops. To the Petén, you'll have to go to La Ruidosa (50 min, 60¢) and change to a **Fuentes del Norte** bus. Don't get confused with another bus company called Fuente del Norte (not Fuentes), which runs luxury buses to Esquipulas and Chiquimula. To Chiquimula (5 hrs, $3), second-class **Transportes Vargas** buses leave hourly 3:45 AM–3:45 PM daily from just outside the Litegua station. To get to El Estor, take a bus to the Cruce Rinchera (2½ hrs, $1), and take a pickup truck to Mariscos (45 min, 60¢). From Mariscos, take the 1 PM boat to El Estor (2½ hrs, $1.20).

BY BOAT • The main *muelle* (pier) is at the end of 12a Calle, on the edge of town, where you can catch boats to Livingston. Regular boat service also heads to **Punta Gorda,** in Belize (2½ hrs, $6.50). Buy tickets in advance from **Agencias Líneas Marítimas** (open weekdays 7–noon and 2–5), near the pier. Boats leave Tuesday and Friday at 7:30 AM. Try asking around at the pier for a cheaper option; a large freighter or supply boat may be able to take you along.

GETTING AROUND

The bus into town plunks you down in the center of town, across from the main market. Follow the blasting music to the center of Puerto Barrios around 6a and 7a calles, 6a and 7a avenidas. Slimy bars, one cool dance club (*see* After Dark, *below*), and a number of 24-hour restaurants fill the area. If you get in from the pier, walk inland down 12a Calle and turn left at the railroad tracks on 6a Avenida. All travelers should consider taking a **taxi** through the less reputable downtown streets and the main shipping area. Taxis hang out by the main market and bus station and charge about $1–$2 to go to the pier, Hotel Del Norte, or the motels.

WHERE TO SLEEP

Two types of lodging dominate Puerto Barrios. Close to the bus station and market are the real cheapos, where simple, grimy rooms come complete with drunken sailors, painted women, and plenty of late-night noise. Your best option is the moderate hotels that cater to the ships' staff, a few blocks away from the "action." **Hotel Victoria** (4a Av. and 10a Calle, tel. 948–0453) has relatively quiet and affordable box-like rooms for $3.50 a person. It's a little musty and dusty, but the ceiling fan helps make it bearable. The hotels listed below tend to be quiet and a better value than most.

Hotel Del Norte. This building once catered to the banana bigwigs in the early 1900s, and it retains its old-fashioned charm. The $15 double rooms are quiet, tidy, and quaint. Warped wooden porches overlook the best park in town and offer a view of the huge ships as they leave the nearby main dock. Take a relaxing swim in one of the two swimming pools, both of which offer an ocean view. *7a Calle at 1a Av., near ocean, tel. 948–0087. 34 rooms, 15 with bath. Laundry.*

Hotel y Restaurante La Caribeña. This hotel has a reception desk, a cafeteria, maids in pink uniforms, and rooms that are quiet and safe—but the atmosphere is sterile and motellike. Doubles with bath are $9. *4a Av., between 10a and 11a calles, tel. 948–0384. From pier, head toward town and turn left on 4a Av.; it's 2 blocks down on the left side. 42 rooms, 33 with bath. Cash only.*

FOOD

By a long shot, the best place in town to chow down on seafood is the crowded **Embajada de los Pescadores** (3a Calle and 4a Av., tel. 948–0341–8). Order the *sopa de mariscos* ($6) and prepare to get wet as you plunge into this huge bowl of seafood soup. To get here from the center of town, walk down 7a Avenida toward the ocean, turn right down the vacant lot a block before reaching the Hotel del Norte, and follow the street with the wood shacks. The Embajada is on your left in a two-story concrete building. **Cafetería Amy** (6a Av. between 8a and 9a calles, tel. 948–0982) is a cute comedor where you can get a hearty meal for $3. At **Pizzeria y Pastelería Salinas** (7a Calle and 7a Av., tel. 948–0593) you can get a medium pizza for $6. **Pepin Burger** (17a Calle between 8a and 9a Avs., tel. 948–0515) is an incredibly friendly, low-priced, and popular eatery, with good chile rellenos (75¢), tacos ($1), and a great grilled steak and onion sandwich ($1.40). Try the *vaca negra* (10¢), a chilly Coke-and-ice cream shake.

In 1840, John Lloyd Stephens, an American, was so taken with the ruins of Quiriguá that he wanted to dismantle it and ship it home to the United States as a souvenir. Luckily, the asking price for Quiriguá was too high, and the site stayed put.

AFTER DARK

Puerto Barrios's nightlife is bustling, if somewhat unsavory. The sleaziness is centered around the bars and nightclubs near 6a and 7a calles, at 6a and 7a avenidas. Here, as in Livingston, the sounds of reggae and punta dominate, but salsa, merengue, and American rock are thrown in to mix it up a bit. A slightly older, mostly Garifuna crowd enjoys the sound of punta music at **La Canoa** (5a Av. between 1a and 2a calles, toward ocean). The club is small, but its tiny dance floor stays bouncing Friday–Sunday after 8PM. Walking down dark 5a Avenida late at night can be scary, so you may want to take a taxi. On the weekends **La Colonia** (23a Calle and 7a Av., tel. 948–0285) is jam-packed with gay and straight couples working up a sweat under flashing lights. The action starts after 8 PM and goes on till dawn. It's a ways from the center of town, so you'll probably want to hop in a cab. Cover $1–$2.

CHIQUIMULA

Yee-haw! Y'all made it to the ropin', ridin', ranchin' center of the Eastern Highlands. Chiquimula is a large city, set in a dry, wide-open plain where cactus sprout up among large cattle ranches. The people here are Ladino, the language spoken is Spanish, and the fashion of the day is leather boots, blue jeans, and, of course, cowboy hats. In fact, as you watch someone ride a burro down the tiled streets of town, you might be fooled into thinking you've been shipped north to Central Mexico. Chiquimula is Ladino Guatemala in all its macho, proud, and festive glory. If you're not in too much of a hurry, stick around long enough to explore the nearby ruins of Quiriguá.

COMING AND GOING

The **bus terminal** (1a Calle between 10a and 11a Avs.) is in a dusty plaza surrounded by a ramshackle market. Chiquimula is the transportation center of the Eastern Highlands, so buses come and go all day long. **Rutas Orientales** travels to Guatemala City (3 hrs, $2) and Esquipulas (45 min, 80¢) every half hour from 4:30 AM to 7 PM. **Transportes María Elena** (tel. 842–0812) leaves for the Petén (11 hrs, $8) at 6 AM and at 3 PM, stopping along the way at Zacapa (30 min, 20¢), Río Dulce (3½ hrs, $2) and Poptún (8 hrs, $6). **Transportes Vilma** (tel. 842–2069) goes to El Florido (2½ hrs, $1) every hour and a half from 5:30 AM to 3:30 PM. **Transportes Vargas** heads to Puerto Barrios (5 hrs, $2) hourly from 5 AM to 3 PM. Minibuses (around 75¢) zip to nearby Zacapa and Esquipulas as soon as they fill up.

WHERE TO SLEEP AND EAT

If you're breezing through and don't want to stray into the center of town, there are plenty of cheap comedores and rough, grimy places to crash around the bus terminal. If you're utterly destitute, you can stay in a hammock at **Hotel Cabrera** for $1—at least you'll be off the ground. But, hey, why suffer when you don't have to? The better budget places lie along 3a Calle, two blocks south of the terminal. As you cruise uphill toward Chiquimula's **central plaza** (between 6a and 7a Avs., 3a and 4a calles) you'll pass plenty of cheap food and lodging options. **Hotel Río Jordan** (3a Calle 8–91, tel. 842-0997) has clean $4 doubles and a TV lounge to hang out in. Just before the plaza, **Hotel Hernández** (3a Calle 7–41, tel. 842-0708) is the best budget choice in town. The $5 doubles with shared bath are immaculate, and there's even a small swimming pool. If you've had it up to your gills with comida típica, **Restaurante y Cafetería El Tesoro** (3a Calle 6–51, across from central plaza, tel. 842-0026) serves up good cheap Chinese food. Popular with the younger set, **Deli Pizza** (3a Calle and 8a Av., above Esso gas station, tel. 0/420–271) will charm you with cheesy garlic bread ($1) and pizza ($5–$8). **Restaurant Guayacan** (3a Calle 8–11) has a full bar, live music on weekends, and a $3 lunch special that is to die for.

NEAR CHIQUIMULA

QUIRIGUÁ

Set in the midst of a banana plantation, Quiriguá may not be the largest Mayan site you'll visit, but it's certainly the most bizarre. In the main plaza, huge monoliths covered with thatched palapas rise out of a neatly trimmed lawn. Quiriguá was established in the 3rd century AD as a satellite center to Copán, 50 km (31 mi) to the south. It remained secondary to it's larger neighbor until AD 737, when the Quiriguá ruler Cauc Sky captured and beheaded the ruler of Copán. Cauc Sky was awfully proud of himself, it seems, because he began erecting the enormous monoliths as a testament to his own glory. You can still see his worn and nose-chipped image on most of the monuments. Quiriguá reached its greatest heights around AD 800, but like other Classic Maya centers it was mysteriously abandoned around AD 900.

Admission to the site is 20¢, and it's open daily 8–6. You can camp for free under one of the two palapa shelters in the parking lot and use the bathrooms just inside the park entrance. There are a couple of small comedores where you can get a modest meal for about $3. Even so, consider bringing food and water from town. Buses traveling between Guatemala City and Puerto Barrios, Chiquimula, and Esquipulas pass the site. From Puerto Barrios, the trip takes 3½ hours and costs $1.50. From Chuquimula, it takes 2½ hours and costs $1.25. The bus will drop you off at the dirt road leading to the site; ask to store your pack in the back room of the large store on the main highway. From the highway, it's less than an hour's walk, but you can usually find a truck going your way—give the driver a quetzal for his troubles. There is also a bus (20¢) to the site, but be sure to get the one to the ruins and not the one to El Progreso or you'll get stuck in the middle of the banana plantation.

ZACAPA

Admittedly, Zacapa's not the kind of place you go to hear a bunch of feel-good stories about the Guatemalan wild, wild east. The town is mostly an early chapter in the bloody history of Guatemala. It was here that General Carlos Arana, who rose to the presidency in 1970, earned the nickname "Butcher of Zacapa." The old colonel is quoted as saying, "If it is necessary to turn this country into a graveyard in order to pacify it, I will not hesitate to do so." Well, he did. Under the pretext of an effort to eliminate several hundred guerrillas, he massacred more than 10,000 rural Guatemalans in the provinces of Zacapa and Chiquimula during the late '60s and early '70s. But the majority of the bloodshed has long since moved to other parts, leaving Zacapa to dry in the cactus-dotted plains. Other than their rodeo-like fiesta in the first week of December, the only thing worth visiting in Zacapa is **Los Baños de Santa María** (open daily 8–6), a set of natural hot springs. For $4, you can rent a private room with a deep, steamy, tiled tub; a nice cool bed; and your own bathroom. It's an utterly peaceful way to soothe your aching body. To get to the baños, walk the 4 km (2½ mi) north of town. You can try to hitch, though few vehicles pass this way, or you can take a taxi for $10 round-trip. To get to Zacapa from Chiquimula, take the second-class bus (30 min, 20¢) heading toward the Petén, or hop on one of the slightly faster minibuses. They leave as fast as they can fill 'em up.

ESQUIPULAS

The road from Chiquimula twists through pine forests and cliffs, emerging on a high ridge overlooking a wide valley below. From above, you instantly feel the aura of peace and spiritual power that has drawn pilgrims to Esquipulas since pre-Columbian days. Before the conquest, this was the sight of a Mayan shrine. Apparently, the peaceful vibes that this shrine brought to the valley were so strong that the indígena chose to surrender to the Spaniards without spilling a single drop of blood. The Spanish called it Esquipulas, "the place where the flowers abound." Today, flowers still abound, but now they lie at the feet of a new shrine—**the Black Christ**—that draws believers from all over the Americas. In 1595, sculptor Quirio Cataño carved the image from dark mahogany wood. Right from the beginning, the image was accorded miraculous powers. But it wasn't until 1737, when Guatemalan bishop Pardo de Figueroa was cured of a chronic illness, that the image emerged as one of the most powerful Christian shrines in the Americas. Figueroa himself ordered the construction of a huge white basilica, and his body is buried beneath its beautiful silver altar.

Up close, the Black Christ looks cold and twisted, hung on a round silver crucifix and surrounded by hundreds of flickering candles. But the devout kiss the small statues, which sit at the bottom of the Christ, with passion.

The moment you get to town, you'll realize that the Black Christ is not only just the spiritual but also the economic heart of this community. The photographers clamoring to sell you a picture of yourself by the basilica and all those ratty pensions are mere introductions to the souvenir-filled **central market.** This is where the bus drivers get those gearshift handles that have an image of Christ encased in plastic (and you thought you'd never find one for yourself!). Cotton-candy and hot-dog stands are scattered among stalls packed with cheap plastic rosary beads, bumper stickers, pennants, and baskets of *pan del señor* (a nasty bread said to have miraculous powers). The best and least expensive selection of medals, crucifixes, rosaries, and postcards is just to the right of the church in the basilica's own store (open daily 8–6).

BASICS
Banco del Ejército (2a Av. 11–56, under Hotel Payaqui, tel. 843–1217) is open weekdays 8 AM–8:30 PM. They change cash and traveler's checks and have a Western Union service. **TELGUA** (open daily 8–8) is on Boulevard Centroamérica, near the end of Doble Vía.

COMING AND GOING
Esquipulas is served by **Rutas Orientales** (Doble Vía, tel. 843–1366), just to the right of the basilica. Service to and from Guatemala City (4 hrs, $4) runs every half hour, 3:30 AM–5:30 PM. Microbuses and second-class buses run to and from Chiquimula (45 min, 75¢–80¢) regularly throughout the day. The official border fees come to about $6 if you don't have a visa, and $1 if you do, but there could be some "extra" fees to pay, depending upon the whims of the border staff.

GETTING AROUND
Calle Real, also called Calle Principal or 3a Avenida, connects the churches at either end of town. Right in front of the basilica is a large, two-way street called Doble Vía, which connects the main highway with the dusty bus terminal below the Cine Galaxia.

WHERE TO SLEEP
The good news is that there are dozens upon dozens of lodgings in Esquipulas at ridiculously low prices. The bad news is they are mostly pretty wretched. Insects crawl through holes in the grimy sheets and straw mattresses, the rooms are small, and dark and unmentionable horrors lurk in the murky waters of the *servicios generales* (shared bathrooms). But there are exceptions. **Hotel Villa Real** (3a Av. 8–58, tel. 0/431–431) has a garden courtyard and clean, cheery double rooms for $8. The four rooms at **Casa Norman** (3a Av. 9–20, tel. 943–1503) fill up fast; the spacious and immaculate $12 doubles come with private bath.

Hotel Esquipulas, across from the basilica, has clean doubles and privileges to Hotel Payaqui's pool for $9. Expect all prices to at least double during Semana Santa and the first two weeks of January, when even the innkeeper at the rattiest pensión may have to turn you away like Mary and Joseph.

FOOD

Numerous clean street carts sell tacos (60¢), french fries (20¢), and tamales (40¢) to snack on. The no-name comedor across the street from Hotel Legendario serves terrific grilled steak and onion sandwiches for $1; it's open from 7 PM to 1 AM. Grab a bar stool at popular **Cafetería La Rotonda** (Doble Vía; open daily 9 AM–10 PM), a huge round soda fountain just off the road that comes in from the main highway. Munch on some juicy chicken, salad, and fries ($2.50) or order a burger ($1–$2) through one of the glass take-out windows. Upscale **Restaurante Los Arcos** (Doble Vía, in front of basilica, tel. 943–1124) is invariably cited as the best restaurant in town. The atmosphere is a little sterile, but its tasty seafood might be what you need. Ten minutes out of town, **Comedor Lorena** (open daily 6 AM–9 PM) is worth the trip even if it's not on your way. Here you'll find some of the best comedor food ever spread on a tortilla. They also have a huge fish with a hearty green salad, potato salad, beans, rice, tortillas, and *fresh* cheese for $4. Take one of the minivans toward the Aguas Calientes border, and ask the driver to let you off. On the way back, you can easily hitch.

WORTH SEEING

Masses in the **basilica** rank among the most spectacular in the country—it's hard not to be impressed by the Gregorian chants that end the evening mass just as the sun sets outside. Masses take place Monday–Saturday at 6:30 AM, 11 AM, and 5 PM, and on Sunday and religious holidays throughout the morning and at 5 PM. The actual residents of Esquipulas steer clear of the basilica, choosing instead to worship at the **Church of Santiago Apostól.** This is the town's true cultural heart. Look inside for some interesting statues. At the back of the church is one of Christ entombed.

FESTIVALS • The Black Christ is said to be at its most powerful in the week of **January 15.** During this time, the town swells with tens of thousands who crowd the hotels and choke the streets with cars and buses. Even the poorest villages scrape together enough funds to send at least one representative to pray for their well-being. On **March 9,** Esquipulas celebrates the day Quirio Cantaño brought his blessed sculpture to their city. The other town fiesta, for its patron saint Santiago Apostól, is held **July 21–28.** The event is celebrated Ladino-style, with parades, salsa dancing, and crazy contests like relay races where grown men push cars around town with balloons in their mouths and potato sacks on their feet.

OUTDOOR ACTIVITIES

For a bird's-eye view of Esquipulas and the surrounding valley, climb about 10 minutes to the top of **Cerrito de Morola,** a hill that rises up out of the center of town. To get to here, make a left in front of the Church of Santiago Apostól. Follow the road to the end and make a right; a cobblestone street zigzags uphill, passing shrines depicting the passion of Jesus. Keep going until you get to the final shrine, the crucifixion, where the cobblestone ends. Up the steep steps to the left is a candle-filled walk-in shrine dedicated to Our Lady of Fátima, and a tremendous view of the valley below.

Villagers mined stones from the **Cueva de las Minas** (Cavern of Las Minas) to build the inner sanctum of the basilica. The faithful come to leave candles and other offerings. To get here, walk down 2a Avenida behind the basilica (and past the huge and cool-looking graveyard). Go up the side of the mountain, and the path will lead you down to the caves right on the other side.

The **Piedra de los Compadres** (the Stones of the Godparents) has an interesting, if lurid, story attached to it. More than 200 years ago, a group of young people and their godparents began the long pilgrimage to Esquipulas on foot. As the journey continued, they got to know each other better and better, and, just before they reached town, their relationship got just a bit too close. In the middle of their sin, they were turned to stone, and here they sit to this day. It's basically just one rock set on top of another but pilgrims come and light candles to ponder those carnal temptations. The rocks are in Aldea Belén, outside town on the road that goes straight past Santiago Apostól.

SALVADOR EL

BY CARLOS PINEDA

UPDATED BY MELISSE GELULA

Most people's knowledge of El Salvador doesn't extend far beyond what they've seen in newspapers about the country's 15-year civil war, which finally ended in 1992. The umbrella organization of revolutionaries, the Farabundo Martí Front for National Liberation (FMLN), traded guerrilla tactics for political strategies to participate in El Salvador's democratic electoral system. Today, peace does reign, and the Salvadoran *pueblo* (people) are committed to making it a lasting one. Yet a culture that has seen remarkable violence does not readily put away its arms, and overt political violence has given way to a dramatic increase in both street and organized crime. As a result, it is not uncommon to see rifle-toting "policemen"—who might be better described as uniformed adolescents—standing outside the big hotels and banks, or walking with purpose through tourist areas in small groups of three or four. While travelers should clearly take commonsense precautions, especially in the urban jungle that is San Salvador, the potential danger should not deter you from getting to know El Salvador.

Whether the country's violent history and ample social strife turn you on or off, El Salvador does present distinct advantages and disadvantages as a travel destination. Despite efforts to bolster tourism, most of the country is still unaccustomed to travelers, and you'll find very little that is geared specifically toward tourists' needs, appetites, and interests, especially outside the capital. There are few fluent English speakers, and even basics like electricity and water are never fully reliable. It is also one of the most densely populated countries in the New World, with almost 6 million people coexisting in an area about the size of Massachusetts. If you're looking for an easy vacation, you're better off heading back to tourist-ready Guatemala, Costa Rica, or Belize, because El Salvador's complicated beauty is somewhat hard-won. The complex history and genuinely friendly people, not to mention the inexpensive prices and utter lack of foreigners, will win over the hearts of travelers who are strong of will and long on patience. For those who honestly want to see, feel, touch, and taste a Central American country, El Salvador is the real McCoy.

One appealing aspect of El Salvador is its small size. The country is only 200 km (124 mi) long from end to end, and major roads are well paved and reasonably maintained, so bus rides between cities never take more than four hours. This means that El Salvador's wonderful diversity of people, places, landscapes, and climates is more accessible than one might guess. Although the country suffered almost complete deforestation, this age of eco-awareness—and its eco-tourist potentials—has not been lost upon the powers that be, who struggle to make conservation pay for itself. The national parks of the

171

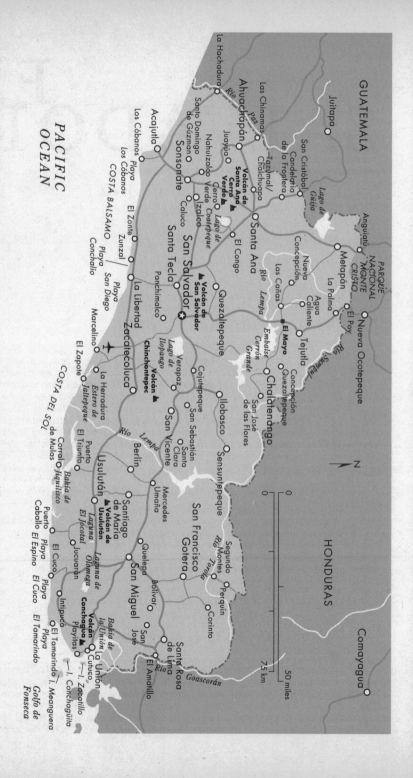

EL SALVADOR

PACIFIC
OCEAN

GUATEMALA

HONDURAS

northwest, several impressive volcanoes (some still marginally active), and a few sizable lakes offer a wealth of natural beauty. The rich volcanic soil produces huge quantities of coffee, sugar, cotton, and fruit for export. On long stretches of pasture in the north and west, cattle and sheep graze behind endless miles of barbed wire. The climate is hot and humid in most places, although the higher elevations are refreshingly cool, and hundreds of narrow rivers provide places to splash around.

San Salvador, the mammoth capital city, offers the usual urban mélange of good and bad. It's wretched to the eyes and often to the heart, but it has plenty of rockin' nightlife and bountiful day trips to volcanoes, lakes, beaches, waterfalls, and artisan villages. Devastated by the civil war, the north and northeastern departments of El Salvador are the least populated and most impoverished areas in the nation. A strong sense of community within the villages has been necessary to the repopulation and regeneration of this weathered countryside, and as a result heavy stares with "what are you doing here?" connotations are not uncommon. Ultimately, though, people are surprisingly friendly and hospitable as long as you make an effort to be both respectful and accessible. The rugged grandeur of the thinly populated northwest is largely ignored by Salvadorans, including the beautiful Montecristo cloud forest and the stunning Lago de Güija. Although the west saw its share of bloodshed during insurrections earlier this century, it remained relatively calm during the civil war. Coffee-covered mountains provide the backdrop for some of the country's best hiking and camping, and the Sonsonate region is home to several indigenous communities. Two beautiful, central lakes, Lago de Coatepeque and Lago de Ilopango, lure visitors with swimming, boating, and scuba diving for volcanic rock. The Pacific coast is a long and relaxing string of good beaches ranging from the surfing mecca of La Libertad to the ritzy resorts along the Costa del Sol to the quaint fishing village of Las Playitas. East of San Salvador stretches a mountain chain where volcanic lakes, sulfuric baths, and some serious off-the-beaten-track camping and hiking await. Farther to the east lies the minimetropolis of San Miguel, the last major stop before the Honduran border towns to the northeast.

By some estimates, U.S. aid doubled El Salvador's gross national product during the height of military "cooperation."

El Salvador's variety of natural beauty makes its history of conflict seem that much more tragic. Its grisly past mocks the hopeful name passed down by the Spanish: "The Savior." You'll meet few people in this country whose lives haven't been affected by one of the longest and bloodiest civil wars of this century. It will never be known how many men, women, and children lost their lives in resistance movements dating back to the Great Depression, although the figure is estimated to be well over 100,000. How El Salvador became the violent, terrorized nation that shocked the world during the 1980s is a story of uninterrupted greed, corruption, and exploitation that began five centuries ago. The original peoples were part of several different tribes related to the Maya and the Toltecs, including the Pok'omames, Lencas, Chortis, and later the Uluas and Pipiles. They numbered perhaps 100,000 in the 16th century, but without the large population seen in Guatemala, the area's indigenous communities were easily conquered by the Spanish. The long nightmare that has since crept across the Americas stemmed rather unceremoniously from this conquest, beginning a legacy of disease, slavery, and destruction of customs, economies, culture, and religion. By the 19th century, wealthy Spanish settlers began to seize the land in renewed earnest, consolidating large plots into huge *haciendas* (estates) and exploiting the land for the production of luxury crops for European consumption. The first claim to independence came from national hero Padre José Matías Delgado in 1811. After independence was finally achieved in 1821, the new country embarked on two more decades of civil war in which the wealthy fought each other over retaining if not increasing property and labor rights.

At the same time, Europe developed a taste for a stimulating new product: coffee. As Spanish settlers and other fortune seekers immigrated to exploit the lucrative bean, subsistence farmers and their modest plots were quickly swallowed up by increasingly powerful coffee interests. It worked out wonderfully for the new coffee magnates: the *campesinos* (peasants) no longer had their own land to work and, conveniently, the plantations needed sowing and harvesting. Inhuman working conditions and slave-like treatment were de rigeur in the Americas at the time, and El Salvador's overwhelmingly white elite had an entire colonial ideology to back them up in their racially motivated division of labor. Unrest among the workers was quickly squelched, however, as national oligarchs used force to keep the social structure intact, first with private armies and later with national armed forces. The oligarchy's immense economic power enabled them to retain firm control of both the state and the military.

As time passed the economic gap between the tiny Salvadoran elite and the underclass majority increased rapidly. In 1881, the government put an end to common lands, the legal basis for the sovereignty of traditional villages. From then on, even as the fertility of Salvadoran lands increased the country's income, the larger part of the population sank deeper into the poverty of tenant agriculture. The political legacy of a landless multitude has perpetuated the remarkably violent history of El Salvador: even today, the most heated political debates in this densely populated country center around the use and ownership of the limited amount of arable land. Inevitably, both the destruction of indigenous farming and the growing population of impoverished *Ladino* (people of mixed indígena and European descent) campesinos led to protest. Generally small and unorganized, peasant insurrections in the late 19th century were put down with ease, but nothing lasts forever.

The Great Depression brought plummeting coffee prices and increasing tensions to El Salvador. Backed by a coalition of urban progressives, workers, and peasants, a reformist landowner named Arturo Araujo was elected president in 1931. From the beginning, Araujo was sandwiched between the growing demands of desperate peasants—who were losing even subsistence work as plantations remained idle—and the growing intolerance of the oligarchs, who sensed real change in the political climate. Increasing tensions still further, a political activist named Farabundo Martí entered the scene. Martí's Marxist ideology and commonsense mobilization tactics attracted thousands of impoverished farmers, workers, and students. The Latin American elites were terrified.

In January 1932, a series of municipal elections won by Communist candidates was voided by a new, indignant leader, General Maximiliano Hernández Martínez. The general's army smashed an ill-fated Communist insurrection in the coffee center of Sonsonate with unprecedented brutality. The event, known simply as *la matanza* (the massacre), was a bloodbath that left 30,000 dead and set the tone for other government-sanctioned human rights abuses. In the town of Izalco, groups of 50 men were tied together by the thumbs and led to the wall of the Church of the Assumption, where they were shot. Victims were forced to dig mass graves for themselves before being dropped into the hole by machine gun. The roadways were littered with bodies killed indiscriminately by the National Guard. Campesinos learned a harsh lesson about the dangers of pressing for social change.

In the mid-20th century, the Cold War turned hot in Central America. President Kennedy's Alliance for Progress sought to bring stability to the region by diminishing communist appeal through direct-aid programs. Although these millions of dollars stimulated economic growth in the country, the wealth remained concentrated in the hands of those best able to manipulate political resources. Even as agricultural exports multiplied tenfold in the 1960s, the Salvadoran people ranked within the top five most malnourished populations in the world. The number of peasants thrown off their land rose steadily from this time on.

During this period, new economic groups within the cities, especially the growing professional and working classes, began to press for liberalization. José Napoleón Duarte's Christian Democratic Party allied with the National Revolutionary Movement to challenge the oligarchy in 1972; but Duarte's electoral victory still didn't stop the military from declaring victory for their own candidate. Popular protest, ranging from civil disobedience to armed insurrection, came soon after. The military met these movements with counterinsurgency units, often under the tutelage of U.S. intelligence. The most infamous was ORDEN (a Spanish acronym meaning "order") whose members drifted in and out of El Salvador's renowned right-wing death squads.

The 1979 Sandinista victory over the dictatorship of Anastasio Somoza in Nicaragua only increased the panic among El Salvador's embattled elite. Although a military coup by reform-seeking, low-level officers succeeded in 1979, it eventually failed to produce the desperately needed changes. Peasants, workers, students, and intellectuals were targets of right-wing violence, but a particularly gruesome war was waged against the Catholic clergy, who openly criticized the government's treatment of the poor. As a result of this major shift in ideology on the part of the Church, priests and nuns were found shot, raped, and mutilated. In March 1980, Archbishop Oscar Romero, a leading human-rights advocate, was gunned down while delivering a sermon in an annex to La Iglesia Divina Providencia. The judge placed in charge of the investigation narrowly escaped assassination himself. No killer was found, but many say the government and judicial system didn't look too hard.

Soon after the Romero assassination, four guerrilla organizations and the Communist Party united under the leadership of the FMLN. The FMLN's armed insurgency was backed politically by the Democratic Revolutionary Front (FDR), a coalition of reformers demanding an end to military repression. In the 1980s, Christian Democrat José Napoleón Duarte returned to the political scene backed by tremendous U.S. support. Touted as a moderate, a national hero, and a voice for democracy, Duarte proved himself incapable of controlling the army, the death squads, and the "Fourteen Families," who have constituted the country's oligarchy since the mid-19th century. Colonel Roberto d'Aubisson, founder of the ultra-rightist ARENA party and suspected death-squad director, criticized Duarte's "weakness" in dealing with the communists, and conducted covert military operations against guerrilla supporters. Caught between the military's might and inflexibility and the surprising resilience and popular support of the FMLN, Duarte presided over an agonizing civil war in which he could do nothing more than pay lip service to democracy while soliciting further U.S. funding.

In the early 1980s, President Reagan brought joy to the oligarchy in the form of unprecedented levels of U.S. aid. This economic assistance failed to address the needs of the rural populations, and by many reports actually funded a redoubling of military repression, evidenced in part by the growth of the military from 10,000 to more than 80,000 by the end of the decade. One of the most gruesome and tragic examples occurred in December 1981 when the military's Atlacatl Battalion, led by the infamous Colonel Mantras, marched into the northeastern village of Mazote and massacred more than 1,000 villagers and nearby residents. In a typical example of U.S. tunnel vision, the Reagan Administration proclaimed El Salvador one of the Central American battlegrounds against Communism in the Western Hemisphere. Aid to the Duarte government continued at remarkably high levels, despite growing concern about human-rights abuses committed with U.S. money, and even periodic rumblings within Congress. Guns, helicopter gunships, rocket launchers, and special counterinsurgency training programs were poured into El Salvador's military. The Salvadoran army "disappeared" people, decimated popular organizations, created an atmosphere of fear, and sent thousands fleeing the country for safer ground.

In Catholic "liberation theology," poverty is no longer seen as the will of God, but rather as the design of rich people who want an unfair piece of the pie.

In the late '80s, the conflict seemed endless. In November 1989, six Jesuit educators, their housekeeper, and her daughter were brutally murdered in their homes at the national university. Later that month the FMLN shocked the Salvadoran government and army with its "final offensive," which involved pitched battles in the heart of the capital. For nearly a month, the army and air force indiscriminately attacked areas of FMLN support, dropping bombs over several densely populated, poor neighborhoods. After untold thousands of casualties, the FMLN had to withdraw. Both sides claimed victory in the battle, but the stalemate was painfully obvious. Beginning in 1990, perhaps as a unique case of diplomacy through mutual exhaustion and frustration, rebel-government negotiations started making unprecedented progress. A truce and peace accord, both mediated by the United Nations, officially ended 12 cruel years of civil war in February of 1992.

The accord's major achievement was the termination of the armed conflict, including a demobilization of the FMLN and a downsizing of the military. The infamous and repressive Policía Nacional (PN) has been replaced by the Policía Nacional Civil (PNC), comprised mostly of new members, but also a portion of ex-military officers and ex-guerrillas. Judicial and electoral reforms were initiated, and the March 1994 elections heralded FMLN participation at regional and parliamentary levels. The former guerrilla group did not post its own candidate but supported Rubén Zamora, a social democrat. Calderón Sol, the rightist Asociación Republicana Nacional (ARENA) candidate, won the presidential race, but the right failed to gain an outright majority in the legislature.

National and municipal assembly elections in 1997 saw an increase in the FMLN vote, and they now hold one third of the seats in the National Assembly. New presidential elections will be held in 1999. These elections, though a vast improvement over past days when machine-gun bunkers and clear plastic ballot bags decorated polling stations, were still plagued by corrupt procedures such as the "participation" of dead voters. Efforts to bring human-rights offenders to justice have also moved agonizingly slowly. Nearly half of the ex-guerrillas, soldiers, and campesinos who were slated for land-reform transfers have not received them, and most of the successful land transfers have involved marginally productive land far removed from the recipient's original home. Many ex-combatants on both sides are unemployed, feeding an already chronic national problem. All of this does nothing to alleviate rapidly increasing levels of crime and poverty. Some called the 1992 peace accord the world's first "negotiated revolution," but the uneven distribution of wealth and land that spurred the revolution has not changed significantly, and most of the country's basic social ills remain the same.

THE BUS CIRCUS

What to expect on a Salvadoran bus: the ubiquitous static-filled radio blaring Top 40 circa 1978; aisles jampacked with passengers who couldn't get a seat; hordes of chattering vendors simultaneously scrambling in through the back door (yes, that's the emergency exit), forcing their (polite but determined) way up the aisle with newspapers, snacks, and a cornucopia of usless trinkets for sale, then leaping off before the fare is collected at the end of the trip. Claustrophobia is the extra price you pay on these otherwise affordable and entertaining jaunts.

BASICS

MONEY

The Salvadoran *colón* is occasionally referred to as the *peso*. It's worth approximately 12¢, so 8.7 colones equal U.S.$1. The coins are confusing to use because some denominations are the same size; a one-colón piece looks like a 10-*centavos* (Salvadoran version of pennies) coin, a five-centavo piece is the same size as 25 centavos, and so forth—so look carefully. Because the buying power of local currency is quite low, it is also possible that you can spend two weeks in El Salvador and never see a centavo.

CHANGING MONEY • Changing money in El Salvador can be a pain. U.S. cash is generally accepted at restaurants, hotels, banks, borders, and anywhere you change money—this is not the case with other foreign or Central American currencies—so it's a good idea to carry some U.S. dollars with you. Only banks and the bigger, luxury hotels change traveler's checks; American Express checks are the most widely accepted. You should also carry your *ficha de compra* (original receipt of purchase) since many banks will want to see it before changing traveler's checks. Most banks can process cash advances on your Visa or MasterCard, but it can take a while and you'll be charged extra for commission, interest, and exchange. American Express members will find that the easiest way to get money is from the AmEx office (tel. 279–3844) in San Salvador's Centro Comercial La Mascota (*see below*), where you can write personal checks from your bank account at home. Major banks, like **Banco Hipotecario** and **Banco Cuscatlán,** have branches even in small cities, although bank policies may vary slightly at each locale. El Salvador's bank machines are not wired to read your hometown bank's card, so don't count on getting money this way. Finally, don't bother with the black market street exchange unless you have no other options.

COMING AND GOING

BY BUS • **Terminal Puerto Bus** (Alameda Juan Pablo II, at 19a Av. Norte, San Salvador, tel. 222–3224, fax 222–2138) is an international terminal for several bus lines comparable to U.S. buses, with air-conditioning and toilets, including **King Quality, Comfort Lines, Ticabus,** and others. Routes include Guatemala City (5 hrs, $6.50, about every hour 3:30 AM–4:30 PM), Tegucigalpa, Honduras (7 hrs, $16, 6 AM and 1 PM), and Managua, Nicaragua (11 hrs, $35, 5:30 AM). **Pullmantours** operate international routes from the Hotel Presidente (Av. La Revolución, near the Zona Rosa, San Salvador, tel. 243–2044). First-class service is available on all routes; call for specific departure times and prices. Buses also depart here for Costa Rica and Panama via Managua, but brace yourself for a long journey.

BY PLANE • The Salvadoran national airline, **TACA** (Edificio Caribe, Plaza Las Américas, San Salvador, tel. 298–5055 or 298–5066, fax 279–3223 or 223–3757), has a very good reputation. They fly between San Salvador's airport (tel. 339–9155) and all other Central American capitals like Guatemala City ($99) and San José, Costa Rica ($202). Most other Central American airlines also have daily flights to San Salvador. TACA runs flights from the United States (tel. 800/535–8780), as do several U.S. airlines, such as Continental, American, and United. There are no direct flights to and from Europe or the South Pacific; visitors from these places should transfer in Miami or Houston. Depending on the time of year, it may be cheaper to fly into Guatemala City and then take a bus (*see below*) to San Salvador. For airline phone numbers in the United States, *see* Air Travel *in* Chapter 1.

GETTING AROUND

There are no civilian train lines in El Salvador, so buses or rental cars are your best bet for domestic travel.

BY BUS • Salvadoran buses are of the school-bus variety (but decidedly more colorful) and are numbered according to what route they travel, but you can also clearly read their destination on the windshield. Bus travel is cheap: most trips cost about 50¢ per hour, with rates increasing 20% on weekends. Service is frequent with departures several times an hour from a bustling, somewhat gritty bus terminal, although certain destinations have only a few buses a day. Intercity buses rarely travel at night and last departures are usually between 4 and 6 PM. Leave early in the morning and plan ahead so you don't get stuck in a small town without lodging. Don't plan to arrive by bus "just in time" for anything. Times listed in the chapter are estimates, and delays are common. Mastering the *desvío* (highway junction) is an important skill in Salvadoran bus travel. On many journeys, you'll take one bus to a desvío, get off at a junction of some kind, and then pick up another bus heading to your destination.

BY CAR • El Salvador has top-quality highways, especially between the major cities. The CA-1, or Pan-American Highway, runs right through the middle of the country. Some smaller roads are more primitive, but generally passable. You can rent cars—at rates approaching those of the United States—in the capital and some other cities. Most secondary roads stay open all though the rainy season, but cautious drivers can rent a four-wheel-drive vehicle or a pickup truck. To drive, all you need is a valid U.S. or international driver's license. You should bring proof of your rightful possession of the car; proof of insurance isn't necessary, although it's good to have.

Women who want to sip a few beers may sometimes get a few questioning glances. Go ahead, smack machismo in the face and do what you want, but in some places you may need to smack a few borrachos (drunks) who think they have license to join you.

BY BIKE • Although few travelers take advantage of it, biking is actually a pretty good way to get around El Salvador. The country's small size and network of secondary roads lend themselves to the sport, and bicycle repair shops can be found even in smaller towns. The terrain is far less mountainous than that of Guatemala or Costa Rica, but there are still plenty, maybe too many, hills, and you won't find lots of single tracks. Western El Salvador and the serpentine coast are managable places to bike because they are less mountainous, although biking in the north and northeast may be most rewarding, allowing access to otherwise inaccessible areas. **Boscaino** (333 2a Av. Sur, at 6a Calle Poniente, tel. 222–2573) in the capital is a decent place to buy equipment and ask questions.

WHERE TO SLEEP

Most towns have decent, clean rooms with private bath for $10–$20 per person. Hotels hail by many different names—*hospedaje, posada, cabaña, casa de huespedes,* and *hotel*—but the name doesn't tell you a thing about quality or price. There are only a few sanctioned camping areas in the country, mostly in the west. More expensive and luxurious hotels can be found in the capital and some tourist areas.

TAX • Most goods and services are levied with a 13% value-added tax. Big hotels charge an additional 10% tax to the cost of your room.

FOOD

Comedores (typical restaurants) blanket the country, serving up decent-sized meals with meat for about $2–$3 per plate. These are often very informal, unlicensed establishments that, in some areas, are actually the front room of someone's home or hostel. Meals in comedores are typically quite tasty and carefully made, and they will likely be closer to what the locales are eating than elsewhere, so you needn't be shy about pulling up a chair. In most places, the food situation is simple: pay more, get more. Middle-class restaurants run $3–$8, and fancy places can set you back $8–$15. Meals in popular beach towns will cost more. Not surprisingly, many nicer places, especially in San Salvador, cater to an aspiring North American palate, so you may find unwanted inflections of the everyday in your meals far away.

The most typical of the *comida típica* (typical plate) is the *pupusa*, a tasty fried tortilla filled with beans, cheese, or *chicharón* (pork skin). Pupusas are traditionally served with pickled cabbage and are the

CLUB MED IT'S NOT, BUT, AT LEAST IT'S FREE

El Salvador's best lodging deal is a triad of free Centros Obreros, found near La Libertad, Playa Tamarindo, and Lago de Coatepeque. They are designed for anyone in the country who wishes to take advantage of them, and they offer usually clean, basic cabañas on large, shaded grounds. Lodging is free (yes, free) for up to two weeks, but you'll need to bring your own sheets and permission from the **Ministerio de Trabajo** *(400 15a Calle Poniente, Edificio Urrutia Abrego, Centro de Gobierno, tel. 222–8151), in the capital.*

specialty of the house in *pupuserías*. Quick, tasty, and safe, they're a good way to fill up on the cheap (15¢–25¢ apiece). A Salvadoran breakfast is usually eggs, beans, sour cream or cheese, tortillas, a plantain, and coffee. *Juevos picados* are scrambled eggs with a few veggies mixed in. For lunch, expect beef, chicken, or fish with rice, beans, tortillas, and sometimes a small salad. *Mariscada* is a delicious seafood soup.

DRINKS • *Minutas* are icy, slushy drinks sweetened with honey—truly a godsend on hot afternoons, but they're often made with unpurified water. The most common drinks are *gaseosas* (sodas), *refrescos* (fruit drinks with tons of sugar), and *cerveza* (beer). Two omnipresent varieties of good, locally made brew are Pilsner, with the ace of hearts on its label, and the richer Suprema, in the green bottle. Both are manufactured by the Meza family–owned Cervecería La Constancia S.A., who also run a sports bar in the capital called Soccer City (Blvd. de Los Héroes).

TIPPING • There seem to be two common scenarios regarding restaurant service in El Salvador: the food server will treat you like either royalty or the invisible man. In a sense, this makes tipping easy, but you should be prepared to leave a *propina* of 10%–15%. Also, don't confuse the amount of time it takes to prepare food here with poor service; food preparation can take an incredibly long time, so avert the possibly of becoming hostilely impatient and head out for dinner when you're *about* to be hungry. Hotel and upscale restaurants usually add a 10% gratuity, so scrutinize the check closely.

OUTDOOR ACTIVITIES

El Salvador has a series of recreational parks called *turicentros* all over the country. They usually have swimming pools, ball fields, basketball courts, and grassy areas for picnicking or lounging, and they are sometimes the only places to see tall, tropical tree species. The upper slopes of El Salvador's many impressive volcanoes and mountain peaks are among the few natural and unpopulated areas in the country. Since the peaks are fairly low—Cerro El Pital is the country's highest peak at 8,950 ft—day hikes will bring you to breathtaking views. Hot springs and cool lakes offer relaxation and water sports. Parque Nacional Cerro Verde in the west and Parque Nacional Montecristo in the northwest are the places to go for serious camping and nature hiking. Water lovers will appreciate several jammin' lakes in the northern and western regions of the country. Hiking or camping in the Chalatenango of Morazán region will bring you through rural countryside dotted with small villages. If the ocean is your game, head to the Pacific Coast for tanning, surfing, and some boating. **Ríos Tropicales** (4620 Calle El Mirador, Colonia Escalón, tel./fax 223–2351), in San Salvador, specializes in rafting and sea-kayaking excursions; trips cost about $45–$50 a day. They also sell a limited supply of quality camping gear at first-world prices.

VISITOR INFORMATION

The **El Salvador Embassy** in Washington, DC (tel. 202/331–4032, fax 202/331–4036), and its additional consular offices in the United States have some literature about traveling in the country, so look in a phone book for the one nearest you and give them a call when planning your trip. The recently established national tourist board, **Corporación Salvadoreña de Turismo (Corsatur)** (508 Blvd Hípodromo, Colonia San Benito, San Salvador, tel. 243–0427), open weekdays 8–noon and 1–5:30, has replaced the Instituto Salvadoreño de Turismo (ISTU), which is now only responsible for the Turicentros and national parks. If you arrive at San Salvador international airport between 10 AM and 5:30 PM, stop by the Corsatur booth and pick up a few quite-basic brochures available in English. Some of the larger hotels, such as the Hotel El Salvador, have their own travel offices on premises.

Good maps of El Salvador are not easily found, so always keep your eyes peeled for one. Get a good one in a travel store before you depart if you can, or try car-rental offices, airport travel counters, and the bigger hotels when you arrive. You may be surprised to find that when requesting an official map of the country you are handed something akin to the map of Disney's Magic Kingdom, replete with thick, black lines that look like they were made with crayon. The **Instituto Geográfico Nacional** (Calle Poniente and 43 Av. Norte, tel. 260–6417 or 260–7920) in San Salvador sells decent maps at American prices; a helpful country map and an equally good map of the capital may prove extremely useful.

You can find most other Salvadoran government organizations in the Centro de Gobierno, off of Alameda Juan Pablo II, just up from the Parque Infantil. **Concultura** (tel. and fax 224–3679) is the organization that manages archaeological sites and the *casas de cultura* (cultural centers) throughout El Salvador. Their main office in San Salvador, on Avenida de La Revolución in front of the Feria Internacional, can give you information on sites and events. Most towns throughout the country will have a **Casa de Cultura**; designed to promote community education and awareness of cultural heritage, these places are also good at orienting travelers. They are usually open weekdays 8–noon and 2–5, Saturday 8–noon.

Don't visit San Salvador's immigration office looking "loose," i.e., wearing shorts, a T-shirt, or sandals. Officials may decide they don't want to let a scruffy person through the door, and then where will you be?

TOUR OPERATORS

Because much of El Salvador is always already off the beaten path, you may want some help planning and navigating your journey. **Jolly Tours** (Centro Comercial Feria Rosa, Santa Tecla, tel. 243–4600, fax 243–2514) offers airport pickup and arranges tours to the coastal beaches, volcanoes, and archaeological sites. **Amor Tours** (73 Av. Sur and Olimpica, San Salvador, tel. 223–5130 or 224–2529, fax 279–0363) is a Mundo Maya agent, which means they cover the Mayan sites and arts as well as sightseeing and adventure destinations. **SET Tours** (3597 Av. Olimpica, San Salvador, tel. 279–3236, fax 279–3235) can arrange ecological excursions in the form of bird-watching, fishing, trekking, volcano climbing, and rafting in El Salvador and Honduras. **El Salvador Divers** (5020 3a Calle Poniente, San Salvador, tel. 264–0961, fax 264–1842) will give you a scuba lesson before taking you diving in a lake which was once a volcano crater.

VISAS AND TOURIST CARDS

American, Canadian, Central American, and most European citizens *do not* need visas to enter El Salvador for stays of less than 90 days as a tourist. If you think you might need one, call your country's embassy, or bring your passport and two passport-size photos to any Salvadoran consulate or embassy and they will issue you a visa; there is no fee. When you arrive in El Salvador by land or by air you will be charged $10 for a tourist card, good for 30 days. If you need an extension, go to the **immigration office** (tel. 221–2111; open weekdays 8–noon and 1:30–4) on the second floor of the Centro de Gobierno in San Salvador. You'll have to spend $3 on photos (which you can get outside the building) and another $1.50 for "paperwork," but you can do it all in one or two hours depending on the crowd. There are also a lot of little fees for coming and going. To cross the border, for example, you'll pay anywhere from $9 to $17 by car or bus, less if you're on foot. For foreigners, this fee is usually requested in U.S. dollars, so bring some along. The mandatory airport departure tax is $20.

HEALTH

You can defeat many ailments by watching what you eat and drink. Traveler's diarrhea, amoebas, giardia, and cholera occur in about that order of frequency. As usual, don't drink unpurified water or eat food that isn't fresh or prepared upon request, and those with very sensitive stomachs may want to eat only cooked, peel-it-yourself, or pickled produce. You should ask if the food has been washed with *agua purificada o hervida* (purified or boiled water), and be particularly careful in areas that don't have running water. Good hotels and restaurants are typically quite careful. When not in the lap of luxury, remember that ice served in your otherwise safe drink may not be purified, so in not-so-nice environments ask for your beverage *sin hielo.* Prepare in advance for the possibility of becoming sick by bringing Pepto-Bismol (the chewable tablets are convenient), Immodium, and a prescription of ciprofloxacin (which helps with travelers' diarrhea when you can no longer take the over-the-counter products) with you.

The sun is mighty strong here, even during the rainy season, so a high SPF sunscreen and the consumption of plenty of fluids to avoid heatstroke are required. As for mosquito-borne diseases, dengue fever is much more common in El Salvador than malaria. Bring bug repellent—the higher the DEET content the better—which can usually be found in camping equipment stores. You can get just about any medication without a prescription from a pharmacy, but never rely on pharmacists for detailed medical advice because they have no formal training.

PHONES AND MAIL

Phones are becoming more prevalent in El Salvador, but many places still do without them. **Antel,** the national phone company, has an office in virtually every Salvadoran city, town, and *pueblito,* from which operators can connect your international and domestic calls. Domestic calls are cheap, and since you pay after the call is made, you don't need a pocketful of centavos as with public telephones. Also, you can reach an **AT&T USA Direct** operator by calling 190 (or 800–1767) from almost any phone in the country. For **Sprint,** call 191 (or 800–1776), and for **MCI,** dial 195 (or 800–1767). El Salvador's country code is 503.

The regular *correo* (mail) is cheap, very slow, and often unreliable. Do not send money, objects, or anything you really want to arrive home. Letters usually arrive in two or three weeks. Letters to the United States cost about $1, and slightly more to Europe and Australia. The best way to send important stuff to the United States is through one of the many express services. **UPS** (tel. 245–3845), **Jetex** (tel. 263–3845), **Urgente Express,** and **Gigante Express** are safe, reliable, and usually deliver the goods within three to six days. They have small branches and larger offices throughout the country. It costs about $5 to send a regular letter, about $10 for a one-pound package. **DHL Worldwide Express** (104 47 Av. Norte, tel. 260–4466 or 260–7722) in San Salvador is the fastest and most professional shipping company. They cost more, but they can have a package to the States in two working days. With a major credit card, the larger hotels can mail packages for you, if you're staying with them. To receive mail at post offices around the country, have it addressed to you at Lista de Correos, name of city, name of department, El Salvador, Centroamérica.

DOS AND DON'TS

When meeting with government officials, army, or police, try to dress more formally, and always explain your business or needs calmly. Avoid taking close-up pictures of individuals or official structures unless you have permission. In rural areas, most people won't mind if you cross their land or pasture, but try to get permission; this becomes mandatory if you're camping. On buses, always give up your seat for elderly people or women carrying small children.

WHEN TO GO

The country sees more vacationers during the November–April dry season, and hotel prices are accordingly somewhat higher. The May–October wet season is cheaper and greener, but you'll see quite a bit of rain—expect daily downpours and some days may get completely washed out. For the most part, though, rain is predictable, and once you've figured out that it pours every evening from about 6 to 9, it won't infere with your plans. Ponchos are okay, but unless you're planning mountain treks, a sturdy umbrella will do fine. Although the rainy season cools things down a bit, El Salvador is *hot* year-round. However, bank on it getting chilly at night when you're hiking and camping at higher elevations.

HOLIDAYS AND FESTIVALS • In addition to the standard Central American holidays (*see* Holidays and Festivals in Chapter 1), El Salvador's most important public holiday is **Día de Independencia** on September 15. You get your standard revelry as well as lots of military pomp and circumstance. Events around Holy Thursday, Good Friday, and Easter Sunday comprise Semana Santa (Holy Week) in March or April. August 3–6 sees the arrival of the **El Salvador del Mundo** festival, which consumes the country and the capital, and then by the sixth virtually empties it as residents head out on vacation; expect mass partying, dancing in plazas, impromtu and grand parades, floats, clowns, and music. At Corsatur (*see* Visitor Information, *above*), you can request the *Calendario de Fiestas Patronales de El Salvador,* which provides information on more than 200 **patron saint festivals** held annually in communities throughout the country. The Day of the Dead, or All Soul's Day, is celebrated November 1–2 with parades.

FURTHER READING

Revolutionary Movements in Latin America: El Salvador's FMLN and Peru's Shining Path, by Cynthia McClintock (U.S. Inst. of Peace, 1998); *Coffee and Power: Revolution and the Rise of Democracy in Central America,* by Jeffery M. Paige (Harvard, 1997); *Bitter Grounds,* by Sandra Benitez (Hyperion, 1997); *The Massacre at El Mozote,* by Mark Danner (Vintage, 1989); *Salvador,* by Joan Didion (Vintage, 1983); *In the Mountains of Morazán: Portrait of a Returned Refugee Community in El Salvador,* by Mandy MacDonald and Mike Gatehouse (LAM Bureau, 1995); *El Salvador* (photographs), by Larry Towell (W.W. Norton, 1997).

SAN SALVADOR

Some travelers give El Salvador's capital about 15 minutes before writing the city off as a hellish urban monstrosity. It's true that you'll never be more than 10 ft from someone trying to sell you something and that you'll sweat buckets, and if you think you can taste the pollution in New York, in San Salvador you can eat it with a fork. But give the place a chance, if for no other reason than necessity. The capital has services and resources that you cannot find elsewhere in the country and is the only logical jumping-off point for most longer trips. You'll probably pass through several times during your travels in the country, and you may end up staying for a while and even enjoying it. Make your peace with it early and accept San Salvador for what it is: an aspiring modern city in a developing country.

One important piece of advice: stay away from large military installations. Consider it a mutual bargain—you leave them alone, and they leave you alone.

San Salvador is easily the densest major city in Central America. The official population is about 1 million, but that figure increases by at least half when you include outlying suburbs, shantytowns, migrant populations, and the city's homeless. This mass of humanity lives about 6,600 ft above sea level in a smog-trapping basin called Valle de las Hamacas (Valley of Hammocks), so named for the region's swinging history of earthquakes. The city has been destroyed and rebuilt several times since its founding in 1525 and consequently bears hardly a trace of its colonial heritage. In October 1986, much of the capital was leveled by an earthquake that left more than 1,000 dead. The foundations of the capital shook in a different way in November 1989, when the FMLN's ferocious "Final Offensive" claimed an untold number of lives through urban gun battles and aerial bombings of poor residential neighborhoods by the government air force. Today, the city still struggles to rebuild and improve itself, and the burdensome financial realities of a developing nation can still be seen in the ghostly skeletons of buildings, the "temporary" locations for government services, and in the endless shanties around the city's edge.

In general San Salvador is a lot safer than it used to be, and the people are delighted to see foreigners enjoying their town. But like any other inner city, parts of the capital have their street crime, gang activity, and organized crime. Travelers stand out and can be singled out by the omnipresent street beggars, while cramped sidewalks make backpackers easy targets for pickpockets and backpack-slashers. The situation is made worse by frequent power failures—always carry a good flashlight. Water shortages, especially during the dry season, can prove another serious hassle. Although the situation is improving, the tap water still shuts off sometimes, usually when your hair is full of shampoo. If you travel like a Boy Scout, you could keep a small basin of water ready for your basic morning grooming, just in case. Despite San Salvador's sprawling and frantic appearance, getting around the city isn't too difficult. Buses are cheap, run frequently, and go everywhere. Explore the city, take commonsense precautions, and head out to the lakes or the coast as soon as you're done.

BASICS

VISITOR INFORMATION

Corporacion Salvadoreña de Turismo (CORSATUR). Two locations, one at the airport that is open irregularly and another in the Zona Rosa, dole out bus schedules, tour information, pamphlets on sites worth seeing—not all of which are current, however, or in English—and maps. The people at the tourist office are friendly and will go out of their way to help you, especially if you're patient with them and try to use

SAN SALVADOR

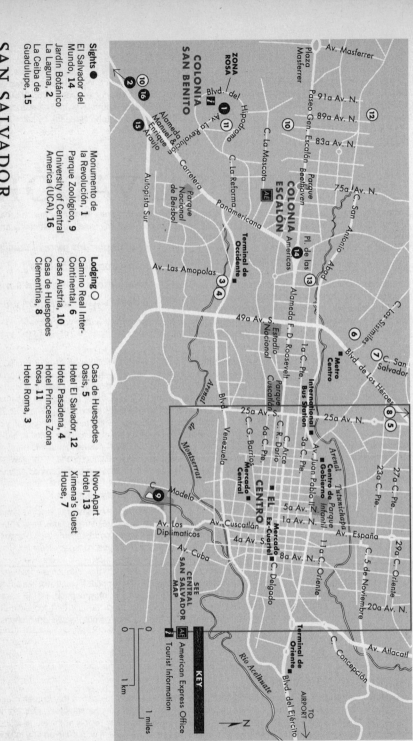

Sights ●

El Salvador del
Mundo, **14**
Jardín Botánico
La Laguna, **2**
La Ceiba de
Guadalupe, **15**

Monumento de
la Revolución, **1**
Parque Zoológico, **9**
University of Central
America (UCA), **16**

Lodging ○

Camino Real Inter-
Continental, **6**
Casa Austria, **10**
Casa de Huespedes
Clementina, **8**

Casa de Huespedes
Oásis, **5**
Hotel El Salvador, **12**
Hotel Pasadena, **4**
Hotel Princess Zona
Rosa, **11**
Hotel Roma, **3**

Novo-Apart
Hotel, **13**
Ximena's Guest
House, **7**

KEY
Ⓐ American Express Office
ⓘ Tourist Information

a little Spanish. Or, after consulting the official El Salvador Web site (www.virtualnet.com.sv/tourism/index.htm), fax or E-mail CORSATUR for information before you go. *508 Blvd. del Hipódromo, tel. 243–7835, 243–7836, or 243–7837, fax 243–0427, e-mail mturismo@ejje.com. Open weekdays 8–noon and 1–5:30.*

The former tourism office, **ISTU**, now solely deals with Touricentros and national parks. *619 Calle Rubén Darío, between 9a Av. Sur and 11a Av. Sur, tel. 222–8000, 222–0960, or 222–4044, fax 222–1208. Open weekdays 8–5:30.*

A fairly new organization, the **Salvadoran Chamber of Tourism** (Centro Comercial Feria Rosa, Santa Tecla, tel. 243–2458) is helping businesses become tourist destinations and may have some recommendations or information.

AMERICAN EXPRESS

AmEx will replace lost or stolen cards and traveler's checks. For members, they'll hold mail, let you receive faxes for free, or send them for a fee. *Centro Comercial La Mascota, first office on lower level, tel. 279–3844. Open weekdays 8–noon and 2–5.*

CHANGING MONEY

Although changing cash is easy, many banks won't change traveler's checks without the original receipt—begging, screaming, and crying generally won't help. One way around this is the American Express office, but only if you have *their* checks. The best strategy is to try your hotel first—consider the few colóns you lose in a mediocre exchange rate due payment for sparing yourself the hassle of bank-hopping. Alternatively, most branches of **Banco Hipotecario** and **Banco Cuscatlán** also change traveler's checks without the original receipt. Hipotecario's main office is on Avenida Cuscatlán at 4a Calle Poniente, near the domed Catedral Metropolitana; Cuscatlán's main office is just a block away, on Avenida Cuscatlán at 6a Calle Poniente. Other banks will change cash and traveler's checks (with the original receipt) at any of their dozens of branches or smaller *casas de cambio* (money-exchange houses) throughout the city. In El Centro, the biggies line Avenida Cuscatlán, while casas de cambio can be found along Av. Juan Pablo II opposite Parque Infantil. Banks and casas de cambio keep similar hours—usually weekdays 9–5, Saturday 9–noon—but go early to avoid lines. The MetroCenter Sur on Boulevard de los Héroes has a cash machine that processes advances to Diner's Card.

EMBASSIES AND CONSULATES

Embassies are generally open 8–5. Some close their doors for lunch breaks, but it's a willy-nilly kind of thing.

Canada. *111 Av. Las Palmas, tel. 224–1648 or 298–3292, fax 279–0765.*

Costa Rica. *Centroamericana Bldg., Alameda Roosevelt 3107, tel. 279–0303 or 223–0273, fax 223–7975.*

Guatemala. *15a Av. Norte 135, near Calle Arce, tel. 222–2903 or 271–2225, fax 221–3019.*

Panamá. *2838 55a Av. Norte, tel. 298–0884 or 298–0773, fax 298–0773.*

United Kingdom. *4828 Paseo General Escalón, tel. 298–1763 or 298–1769, fax 298–3328.*

United States. *Blvd. Santa Elena, in Antiguo Cuscatlán, tel. 278–4444, or 263–0003, fax 278–6011.*

EMERGENCIES

For **police** or **ambulance,** dial 123 or 121.

MEDICAL AID

Many doctors in San Salvador have been trained in North America and speak fluent or at least functional English. Unless you've bought traveler's insurance that is accepted in El Salvador, you might be required to pay on the spot with cash or credit cards. West of the center, **Hospital Rosales** (25a Av. Norte and Calle Arce, tel. 222–5866 or 222–5800, fax 222–4968) will attend to your needs. Also west of the center, in Colonia Escalón, **Hospital de la Mujer** (81a Av. Sur and Calle Juan José Cañas, tel. 263–5111 or 263–5182, fax 263–5187) provides specialized medical attention for women. If your problem isn't severe, or if you just need some specific medication, try a pharmacy; **Farmacia Internacional** (Blvd. de los Héroes and Av. Juan Pablo II) is open 24 hours daily. If you have other specific questions or concerns, call the **Red Cross** (Av. Henry Durant and 17a Calle Poniente, Centro de Gobierno, tel/fax. 222–7743 or 222–5155 in emergencies).

PHONES AND MAIL

Antel charges about 50¢ to make a collect call. Their main office is in El Centro, on the corner of Calle Rubén Darío and 5a Avenida Sur, opposite a McDonald's. It's open daily 6 AM–10 PM. A smaller, less hectic branch is in the Torre Roble in the Metrocentro on Boulevard Los Héroes. Don't be fooled by the huge Antel sign at Calle Rubén Darío and 23a Avenida Sur—it's just an administration building.

The central **post office** is just north of the Centro de Gobierno, east of Parque Infantil. They'll hold mail sent under your name to Lista de Correos, Correos Centro Gobierno, San Salvador, El Salvador, Centroamérica; you'll need your passport to pick it up. A smaller branch is in the Metrocentro on Boulevard Los Héroes. *Tel. 271–1922. Open weekdays 8–5, Sat. 8–noon.*

COMING AND GOING

BY BUS

El Salvador's bus system is efficient and extremely cheap, but buses are usually crowded. Most longer rides leave from one of the two main terminals: **Terminal de Occidente** (49a Av. Sur and Blvd. Venezuela, tel. 223–3784) serves destinations more or less west of the capital, and buses from **Terminal de Oriente** (where Av. Peralta turns into Blvd. Ejército Nacional, tel. 222–0315 or 222–7578) go north and east. Bus 34 runs between the two terminals and passes through the city center on the way.

TERMINAL DE ORIENTE • Buses to San Vicente (1½ hrs, $1) leave about every 10 minutes. Service to San Miguel (3 hrs, $3) runs every 15 minutes. Buses to Usulután (4½ hrs, $2) leave at 7 AM, 8 AM, and 9 AM. Chalatenango (2½ hrs, $1) and San Miguel (3 hrs, $2.50) both have bus service every 15 minutes. Buses leave every 40 minutes for El Poy, at the Honduran border (4 hrs, $2). To the Honduran border at El Amatillo (5 hrs, $4), service is hourly.

TERMINAL DE OCCIDENTE • Buses leave for Sonsonate (1½ hrs, 50¢) about every 10 minutes. Service to Santa Ana (1¼ hrs, 50¢) runs about every eight minutes; ask for the bus going *via Calle Nueva*—it's faster.

BY CAR

A number of international rental agencies have offices at the airport, which is convenient since getting to San Salvador can be a real drag without a car. Expect to pay $45 a day or $225 a week for a basic car with air-conditioning and unlimited mileage. For better rates, check out **Sure Rent** (Blvd. de los Héroes, at 23a Calle Poniente, tel. 225–1810), which has Toyota compacts starting at $30 a day and brand-new Korean models with air-conditioning at $40, both with unlimited mileage. Ask for Robert, who speaks immaculate English. Other options with toll-free reservation numbers include **Avis** (137 43a Av. Sur, tel. 224–2623, fax 298–6272), **Bargain** (6 79a Av. Sur, tel. 279–2811 or 223–1668, fax 224–4674), or **Dollar** (2226 Prolongación Calle Arce, tel. 224–4385, 279–2069 or 223–3108, fax279–2138). All these international outfits have desks at the Hotel El Salvador. For sturdier four-wheel-drive vehicles and cellular phone rental, try **Tropic** (3579 Av. Olimpica, tel. 223–3236 or 223–7947, fax 279–3235).

BY PLANE

The **Aeropuerto Internacional Comalapa** (tel. 330–0455), 44 km (27 mi) south of San Salvador, has a post office, bank, and a sometimes-open tourist office. The national airline, **TACA** (Plaza de las Américas, Caribe Bldg., tel. 298–5055 or 298–5077, fax 223–2757), serves only foreign destinations. A number of other airlines also fly between San Salvador, North America, and other Central American capitals. Domestic flights use **Aeropuerto Ilopango**, 13 km (8 mi) east of San Salvador.

AIRPORT TRANSPORTATION • The international airport is a 45-minute drive from the capital. A taxi ride in with one of the drivers waiting for tourists at curbside will cost $20 or so, but be on the lookout for price gougers. The minibus *colectivo* is a better option at $2. You can also walk through the parking lot to the bus stop on the highway immediately in front of the airport and look for Bus 138B, which passes several times an hour. Another option is **Taxis Acacya** (tel. 239–9271); their colectivo service costs about $4 and leaves a few times a day. Call for times. Of course, if you're planning to stay with one of the swanky hotels, when making your reservation ask if they'll send a car for you.

GETTING AROUND

Central American capitals are notorious for their navigational nightmares, and San Salvador ranks among the most chaotic. Look at a map to familiarize yourself with the layout before taking off, so you

ROLLING OVER
THE SCARS OF WAR

One visitor couldn't believe his eyes. While cruising the streets of San Salvador, he had seen plenty of pedestrians crazy enough to jump out into rush-hour traffic to cut a few seconds out of the commute home, but these two guys were in wheelchairs! They ran through stoplights ahead of the cars in souped-up trikes with numbers on the back. It's was truly incredible. El Salvador today is filled with ex-soldiers, ex-guerrillas, and civilians who were severely crippled by land mines during the war. These so-called "inválidos" bravely participate in the rituals of daily life: farmers, community leaders, and businessfolks go about finding ways to do what they need to do. And don't believe for a second that they live without their national obsession: El Salvador's amputee soccer team won Boeing's international amputee's soccer tournament three times in a row. By all counts, El Salvador gives new meaning to the concept of "wheelchair access."

can rely on memory when the street name is omitted from the curb on which it should be painted. The chaos and sheer density of the place will probably overwhelm you at first, but it gets easier as you go. Every Salvadoran city is laid out the same way: avenidas run north–south and calles run east–west, forming a big grid. Addresses are often given as the intersection of a calle and an avenida. Street names can be confusing. There is more than one Calle Poniente, and a numerical prefix before each one distinguishes it from the others: for example, 1a Calle Poniente is a block south of 2a Calle Poniente. **El Centro** is the neighborhood downtown, around the intersection of the central avenida and the central calles. The central avenida is called **Avenida Cuscatlán** south of the central calle, **Avenida España** to the north. Similarly, the central calle is **Calle Delgado** east of the central avenida and **Calle Arce** to the west. Numbered avenidas are labeled *norte* (north) or *sur* (south), while numbered calles are called *oriente* (east) or *poniente* (west). One of the capital's main thoroughfares is undergoing a serious identity crisis: east from El Centro, 2a Calle Poniente becomes Calle Rubén Darío, then Alameda F. Delano Roosevelt, and finally Paseo General Escalón.

Given the layout of the city, navigating in a car is quite simple, but you must be prepared for distractions in the form of monster-size potholes; window-tapping vendors, begging children, and fire-eaters at stoplights; and labyrinthine detours around enormous construction sites. At press time, Alameda Roosevelt at Boulevard de Los Héroes was a veritable quarry, and a section of Boulevard Venezuela was also impassable because of construction.

If you're in El Centro and need to go anywhere within about 10 blocks, go on foot—traffic is so congested that a leisurely walking pace will probably beat anything on wheels. For longer trips, buses run faithfully from dawn until about 8 PM. Bus fare is about 25¢ before 6 PM and 35¢ after, but some minibus lines charge more. From El Centro, **Bus 29** goes to Terminal de Oriente, **Bus 34** runs between the two bus terminals and along Avenida de la Revolución to the ritzy Colonia San Benito and its Zona Rosa southwest of El Centro. **Bus 101** travels westward via Calle de la Mascota on its way to Santa Tecla, and **Bus 52** goes west to the Colonia Escalón, ending in Plaza Masferrer. Taxis are cheap and plentiful, but you should always settle on a price before taking a ride, because there are no meters. A five-minute trip (without traffic) runs about $3.

WHERE TO SLEEP

There's almost no such thing as a middle-of-the-range hotel here. Spartans who can stand grime will find some good deals, or, on the other hand, if you're willing to splurge, you'll buy yourself a good portion of sanity. Power and water occasionally go out, especially in the rainy season, so have a flashlight, maybe some candles, and a full water bottle handy. However, many hotels pride themselves on having their own generators for such instances. For stays at cheaper places, you also might want to bring a towel along. If you're a fussy or squeamish traveler, spend your money on a good, albeit somewhat familiar, hotel room in the capital; you'll find cheaper lodging with a Salvadoran flavor elsewhere in the country to be more comfortable, funkier, and just as clean.

Budget travelers usually stay in El Centro, the center, where a surprising number of low-grade options exist. Also centrally located but less nerve-racking are the areas around the bus terminals, which are safer and quieter, although still a little grimy, and have the obvious advantage of proximity to transportation. For a bit more money and lots more comfort, head a few blocks northwest of El Centro to the burgeoning, funky area off Boulevard de los Héroes, somewhat behind the Camino Real. This area is safe, quiet, and a real relief after a day downtown. Women alone should definitely stay west of El Centro or in one of the better hotels. Luxury hotels congregate around the Zona Rosa, but they can also be found in pleasant neighborhoods elsewhere. And by the way, if you came to San Salvador with the idea of camping, think again. You absolutely cannot camp in or near the city—even the turicentros are patrolled for after hours-trespassers.

EL CENTRO

El Centro is for those who can handle dark, rough streets at night and chaos during the day. Stay here only if you have early morning business downtown.

UNDER $10 • Hotel Internacional Custodio. The manager's cheery welcome assures you that your stay at Hotel Custodio will be more pleasant than your experience in the neighborhood surrounding it. Dreary but functional rooms are $7 with a clean, but compact communal bathroom; rooms with private baths are $9. Make some friends, grab some brews, and head up to the fourth-floor patio to check out the panoramic view of San Salvador. *109 10a Av. Sur and Calle Delgado, tel. 222–5698. 32 rooms, 20 with bath.*

Hotel León. Just around the corner from Hotel Custodio, León's courtyard and large size help to alleviate much of the street noise. A third-floor grungy but workable room with private bath costs $5, but the water pressure doesn't always reach that high, so rooms on the first floor are more expensive; fans are extra. *621 Calle Delgado, tel. 222–0951. 35 rooms with bath. Luggage storage, parking. Cash only.*

UNDER $20 • Hotel Centro. If you're staying in El Centro, it might as well be at Hotel Centro. It's clean and orderly, and the staff is courteous. Rooms are small and windowless, but immaculate, and they have TVs, phones, and private baths. The immediate neighborhood gets tough at night, but for $17, consider it a trade-off. *410 9a Av. Sur, tel. 271–5045. 15 rooms with bath. Laundry. Cash only.*

NEAR TERMINAL DE OCCIDENTE

The industrial area around Terminal Occidente is ugly but relatively safe, and it has budget lodging. **Hotel Pasadena** (3093 Blvd. Venezuela, tel. 223–7905) lacks most amenities, but this 16-room hotel does have decent hammocks—swinging in them is a fun way to keep cool. The $7 doubles are clean but shabby, but the private bathrooms could use an introduction to Ajax. Another tidy-cheapy is **Hotel Roma** (3145 Blvd. Venezuela, tel. 224–0256), whose cheerful interior contrasts with the *Amityville Horror* facade. A large, clean double with fan and private bath costs about $7. The management is friendly, and the small restaurant serves cheap soft drinks and good simple meals.

NEAR TERMINAL DE ORIENTE

Calle Concepción has good prices in a bearable neighborhood. To get to the lodging area from Terminal Oriente, walk west along Boulevard del Ejército, turn right onto 24a Avenida at the second traffic circle, walk three blocks, and turn left onto Calle Concepción at the third traffic circle.

UNDER $15 • Hotel Cuscatlán. Cuscatlán is a good deal—for $10 you'll get a fairly neat room with tv and private bath. Some rooms are dark and possibly damp, so ask to see several rooms until you find the one you like best. *675 Calle concepción, tel. 222–3298. 35 rooms with bath. Cash only.*

Hotel Izalco. Izalco is clean and more comfy than the other hotels in the area. The beds are big and firm, rooms come with tvs, and the bathrooms give you that rare sensation of hygiene and privacy. Doubles with ceiling fan are $12. *666 Calle concepción, tel. 222–2613. 40 rooms with bath. Cash only.*

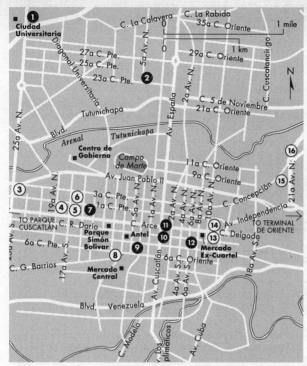

Sights ●

Basílica del
Sagrado Corazón, **7**

Centro Monseñor
Romero, **1**

Catedral
Metropolitana, **10**

El Calvario, **9**

Don Rua, **2**

El Rosario, **12**

Teatro Nacional, **11**

Lodging ○

Azaleas Guest
House, **3**

Family Guest
Home, **6**

Hotel American
Guest House, **4**

Hotel Centro, **8**

Hotel Cuscatlán, **17**

Hotel Fénix, **5**

Hotel Internacional
Custodio, **13**

Hotel Izalco, **15**

Hotel León, **14**

NEAR BOULEVARD DE LOS HÉROES

In the safer, quieter area west of Boulevard de Los Héroes, you'll find a series of residential guest houses that offer clean rooms with that just-like-home feel. Other than the posh hotels, this is definitely the place to stay in San Salvador—women in particular will be a lot happier and safer here than in other parts of the capital. Two good options are **Hotel Fénix** (953 17a Av. Norte, tel. and fax 271–1269) and **Family Guest Home** (925 1a Calle Poniente bis, tel. 222–1902, fax 221–2349), where pleasant doubles with fan, private bath, and hot water go for $18. Generally, places of this kind are run by a single family with the help of a few employees, but in Colonia Centroamérica, you'll find a series of guest houses owned by popular movement organizations that cost the same or less than the family-owned variety. **Casa de Huéspedes Clementina** (34a Av. Morazán and Calle Washington, tel. and fax 225–5962), **Casa de Huéspedes Oasis** (1 Pasaje Sta. Marta, at Pasaje Guillén, tel. 226–5983), and **Azaleas Guest House** (1302 23a Av. Norte, tel. 225–7616) all have management and clientele invested in social issues such as women's rights, rural development, education, and health care.

UNDER $20 • Hotel American Guest House. Homey $14 doubles with private bath, hot water, and fans are found at this guest house near the international bus station. A defunct fountain and an enclosed patio café overlooking the street are both conducive to lengthy discussion or solitary mental perambulation. *119a Av. Norte, btw 1a Calle Poniente and Calle Arce, tel. 271–0224, fax 271–3367. 9 rooms, 4 with bath.*

Ximena's Guest House. This is a good place to meet other travelers of the backpacking or bohemian set. The two-story hotel encircles a small courtyard good for socializing or reading. Doubles cost around $14, and there's a suite for about $35. *202a Calle San Salvador and Colonia Centroamérica, tel. 226–9268, fax 225–2638. 13 rooms, 6 with bath. Restaurant.*

Camino Real Inter-Continental. This hotel has everything you'd expect in a good, international hotel—including spotless rooms with lots of amenities—without an iota of attitude. Unfortunately the prices are also up to international standards. It's a few minutes walk to several good restaurants and bars, and right across the street from Metrocentro, a huge shopping mall, but from the palm tree–dotted, yellow-brick terrace or the gardens at poolside, you'd never know it. The staff is helpful and multilingual. *Blvd. de Los Héroes and Av. Simimiles, tel. 260–1333 or 260–3888, fax 260–5660. 228 rooms with bath. Restaurants, bar, air-conditioning, in-room safes.*

ZONA ROSA

This is the center for upscale living and nightlife, so you might find hotels, as well as shops, restaurants, and clubs, on the expensive side here.

UNDER $100 • Hotel Princess Zona Rosa. The newest hotel in San Salvador (opened in 1997), the Princess is jumping on the bolster-the-economy-with-tourism bandwagon. You'll get a very skewed idea of the city if you stay here in fairly standard rooms among the elite, overlooking the expensive discos, restaurants, and outfits of Zona Rosa, but you'll be treated well, enjoy modern amenities, and will want for nothing. *Av. Magnolias and Hipodromo, tel. 298–4545, 263–8547, or 263–8554, fax 298-4500. 210 rooms with bath. Restaurant, bar, air-conditioning, in-room safe.*

ON THE OUTSKIRTS

Colonia Escalón is a developing commercial and residential neighborhood in the northwest corner of the city near the volcano and the many red-roofed, white-stucco homes on the verdant hills surrounding it. The newly monied are building houses here, and although the strip along Paseo General Escalón is bustling with restaurants, the Galerías shopping center, movie theaters, and bars, quiet pockets can still be found.

UNDER $65 • Casa Austria. These guest-house rooms cater to anyone looking for a little privacy and space. The four rooms in Colonia Escalón are near the Galerias, a shopping complex, and share a computer with Internet access. Rooms are clean and quiet but otherwise unremarkable; think B&B with a corporate twist. Doubles are $60 and include breakfast. *Calle Jucuarán and Poligono G, tel. 278–3610, fax 278–3105; 601 Calle Padres Aguilar and 87 Av. Sur, tel. 263–6989, 264–5869, fax 264–5870. 16 rooms with bath. Restaurant.*

Novo Apart-Hotel. Another hybrid hostel in which rooms are more like self-inclusive studio apartments. Come here if you'll be staying a while or if cooking for yourself is important to you. Rooms face gardens with sculptures and a pool; there are also hammocks for swinging and dozing. It's almost equidistant from the nightlife in Colonia Escalón and Boulevard de Los Héroes. *At the end of 61 Av. Norte, north of 1a Calle Pointe, tel. 260–2288, or 279–0099, fax 260–5053. 50 rooms with bath. Air-conditioning.*

UNDER $100 • Hotel El Salvador. Exorbitant renovations have kept this sprawling place at the center of international travel—you get the feeling that you're among statesmen and journalists. In 1998, two of El Salvador's wealthiest families were joined here by way of a wedding with a guest list of nearly 1,000. Rooms are carpeted, modern, and appointed with all possible amenities. Some have original artwork by local artists and exceptional views of the city and volcano. *89 Av. Norte and 11 Calle Poniente, tel. 263–5444, 263–2643, or 800/817–4822 in the U.S.,fax 263–2583. 240 rooms with bath. Restaurants, bar, air-conditioning, laundry.*

FOOD

Restaurants in the capital are generally casual, save for a few upmarket exceptions, and are typically closed between lunch and dinner from 3 to 6. Although a lot of them serve rather dull, "international" menus, there are enough exceptions to make eating out an adventure. Do not assume that credit cards or traveler's checks will be accepted. If you enjoy *platos típicos,* you'll have no problem keeping your stomach happy in San Salvador—almost every block has a restaurant, comedor, or pupusa stand with cheap and decent eats. Vegetarians can always fill up on rice, beans, and vegetables. Pupusa fanatics should head to the stands along 9a Avenida Sur, between 4a Calle Poniente and Calle Vasconcelos. In the city's markets you'll see lots of cheap and tasty food, but use common sense to avoid a case of the unutterables. For groceries, **Supertienda Tapachulteca** (Calle Rubén Darío and 5a Av. Norte, near Antel), a sort of department and food store combo, is a good choice for travelers in need of all sorts of supplies. Another grocery is **Super Selectos**; you'll find one in MetroCentro shopping center on Boulevard de Los Héroes. Tap water in the capital is treated and relatively safe, but that's no guarantee it won't make you feel ill.

EL PASEO GENERAL ESCALÓN

This busy, blossoming neighborhood near the Hotel El Salvador contains several good, upmarket restaurants and a variety of nightlife possibilities.

UNDER $10 • Sports Bar & Grill. Although it's somewhat of a novelty here, you might think you're at home when you see the menu offering buffalo wings, burgers, pasta, and salads. *Paseo Escalón and 99a Av. Norte, tel. 263–6201.*

UNDER $15 • El Bodegón. This Spanish restaurant is one of the more upscale choices for lunch and dinner. Look sharp and have something grilled, such as fish or chicken ($12–14), or try the seafood paella ($9). *Paseo Escalón and 77a Av. Norte, tel. 263–5283. Closed Sun.*

UNDER $20 • Hunan. Attentive service, posh decor, and entrées such as spicy Szechuan chicken and saucey lo mein noodles made with "imported ingredients" distinguish this place from other more moderately priced Chinese eateries. *Paseo Escalón and 99a Av. Norte, tel. 263–9911.*

Kamakura. Yes, you can get hand-rolled, fresh sushi in El Salvador. The tempura is light and flaky and sometimes comes with a pinwheel of battered lotus root. *Paseo Escalón and 93a Av. Norte. tel. 263–2401.*

EL CENTRO

UNDER $5 • Cafe Bella Napoles. This busy local watering hole is an excellent place to escape the frantic streets of El Centro. They have a huge menu, with everything from tamales to salads. Two vegetarians can split a mushroom pizza ($3), and down-home folks will snork up the roast chicken with potatoes ($2.30). They also have a large bakery that sells scrumptious goodies. *113 4a Av. Sur, tel. 222–6879.*

Koradi. Vegetarians, rejoice! Koradi has various Latin American and international dishes with a no-meat twist. Try a soy burger ($1) or a whole-wheat pizza with soy ham (whew!) or veggies ($1). Wonderful fresh pineapple, tomato, or carrot juices are 75¢, and healthy breads and pastries are baked fresh daily. Also on the premises is a terrific natural products store where you can find many a vitamin and a variety of medicinal plants. *225 9a Av. Sur, near 4a Calle Poniente. Closed Sun.*

Quinto Sol. Indígena-style murals and poetry celebrating reflection, discovery, and change adorn the walls of this colorful restaurant, creating a peña-like atmosphere. Weekday lunch specials served from 11:30 AM until 2 PM are a good deal—for $1.25 you can choose from a number of platos típicos like *pollo asado* (grilled chicken) or *bistec encebollado* (steak with grilled onions). Come on a Friday or Saturday night for live Latin dance rhythms and arguably the best night life in El Centro. *15a Av. Norte and 1a Calle Poniente. Closed Sun.*

Restaurante El Pulpo. The name means "the octopus," and it's one of the few decent restaurants with seafood that won't cost you a week's rent. It's in a working-class neighborhood near a university, so the clientele is diverse and laid-back. You'll get large portions of fresh seafood for reasonable prices; for $3–$4.50 choose from shrimp with rice, fried fish, or an excellent *sopa de mariscos* (seafood soup). Wash it down with a draft beer at 80¢ a glass. *Calle Arce and 15a Av. Norte.*

Restaurant Oriental. This local favorite offers a wide variety of no-nonsense food at no-nonsense prices. The place is clean and spacious, with seating inside or outside. Don't let the name confuse you—there's nothing particularly "oriental" about the menu. You'll find a green salad for less than $1; spaghetti with cream sauce for $1.50; chicken, beef, or seafood dinners for about $3; or a steamy and vegetable-laden dish of shrimp chow mein for $2.50 (ask for it without the bologna strips). *711 1a Calle Poniente, at 11a Av. Norte.*

NEAR TERMINAL DE ORIENTE

Calle Concepción won't dazzle you with it's culinary excellence, but it does boast some good, simple comedores close to budget lodging: **Comedor Doris** (678 Calle Concepción, tel. 221–0306) serves basic rice, beans, vegetables, and cheese for $1.50; carnivores pay an extra dollar. Across the street, below Hospedaje Emperador, **Comedor Rosita** (665 Calle Concepción, tel. 222–7572) serves a meal of rice, beans, and salad for $1.25; the same with chicken is $2.

NEAR BOULEVARD DE LOS HÉROES

North on the boulevard toward Calle San Antonio Abad you'll see a slew of fast-food burger and chicken places. Turn left onto Calle Sisimiles behind the Camino Real and find a range of restaurants from Chinese to steak house. Other medium-priced, good-quality restaurants and bars cluster along Calle San Antonio Abad near Comercial San Luis and Boulevard Universitario.

UNDER $5 • La Ventana. Theoretically you could eat here every day (except Monday when they're closed), for every meal. Try the crepes for breakfast ($3), a sandwich for lunch ($4), and the pasta special for dinner ($5). There are good choices for vegetarians, too. *Calle San Antonio Abad at Calle Principal, tel. 226–5129. Closed Mon.*

Metrocentro Sur. This shopping mall has an open-air food court with dozens of small restaurants. It's all here: almost-like-California taquerías, fish-and-chips, crepes, and Chinese. An average meal costs $2–$3, but prices can go much higher. *Take Bus 52 from Alameda Juan Pablo II to Blvd. de los Héroes.*

Restaurante Queco's Tacos. At the beginning of posh Paseo General Escalón, this wannabe-Mexican joint serves terrific food at the best prices in the area. It also makes a good springboard for the Escalón nightlife. The tacos (two for $2) are awesome, as are the quesadillas ($1.50). *3952 Paseo General Escalón, ½ block west of Parque Beethoven, no phone. Take Bus 52 from Alameda Juan Pablo II.*

Vegetarians should head to Boulevard Universitario, where you'll find **Sol y Luna** (at Av. C, lunch and dinner) and **Todo Natural** (at 39a Av. Norte, lunch only). Meals at both places are are inexpensive ($2) and satisfyingly simple, usually involving fruit, cheese, tortillas, and beans. You've got to have a stack of pupusas under a thatched roof before you can say you've experienced El Salvador. To meet this requirement in the capital, visit **Pupusería Margoth** (Blvd. de Los Héroes, south of Calle San Antonio Abad).

DESSERT/COFFEEHOUSES

Café Don Pepe. If you spend more than a couple of hours touring El Centro, give yourself a break and drop in here for a cold drink, pastry, or sundae (it ain't Häagen-Dazs, but it's cold, sweet, and only $1). They also serve food, but it's marginal and overpriced. Oh yeah—it's *air-conditioned,* so bring all those postcards you've been meaning to write and chill, so to speak. *4a Calle Poniente and 9a Av. Sur, no phone.*

Cafetería Jaicel. Students and locals get okay pastries and small meals in this clean, unpretentious café. The best reason to come is for the wonderful fresh-fruit *licuados* (smoothies)—you get a mongo glass for 70¢. Beware: the crushed ice they use is from tap water. *904 15a Av. Sur, between Calles Rubén Darío and Arce, tel. 221–4814.*

Cyber Café. Although the servers crash and phone lines go down a lot, El Salvador is slowly getting on-line. This is a good place to check your E-mail (about $4 per hour), slurp coffee, and listen to music among the wired UCA students. *Av. Rio Lempa and Calle Marmara, tel. 243–0056.*

WORTH SEEING

CENTRO MONSENOR ROMERO

This memorial, at the Universidad Centroamericano José Simeon Cañas (UCA), will sober any visitor. It was here that the six Jesuit educators, their housekeeper, and her daughter were gunned down in 1989. Outside, you'll find a monument and a small rose garden in their memory; inside you can purchase books, pick up information and newsletters, and see graphic photos of the victims as they were found the following morning. *Interamericana and Autopista Sur. Take Bus 44 from Boulevard de los Héroes south to the University.*

CHURCHES

In El Centro, a huge, crippled gray dome is almost all that's left of the **Catedral Metropolitana** (2a Calle Oriente, between Av. Cuscatlán and 2a Av. Sur), where Archbishop Oscar Romero was buried after being gunned down in 1980 by the military in Colonia Miramonte. It's pretty impressive even from a distance, which is good because repairs and seismic reinforcement keep all onlookers outside, although occasionally travelers can talk their way in to see the tomb. In much better condition is **Iglesia Calvario** (end of 6a Calle Oriente, at 3a Av. Norte). Its haunting, almost Gothic appearance makes it seem much older than it is. The double steeple of **La Basílica del Sagrado Corazón de Jesús** (Calle Arce, at 13a Av. Norte) is also under repair, but you can still enter through the east door daily 8–6 to see the spectacular interior or attend mass. **El Rosario** (6a Av. Norte, between Calles 2a and 4a Poniente) is the burial site of Father José Matías Delgado, a major figure in Central American independence movements. A trek from the Centro, **Iglesia Don Rua** (3a Av. Norte and 23a Calle Poniente) has a distinctive clock tower and stunning stained-glass windows. Check local schedules for mass times, but most churches hold services several times per day, usually at 6 AM, 8 AM, 9 AM, and 5 PM.

JARDIN BOTANICO LA LAGUNA

Located in an extinct volcanic crater more than 2,500 ft above sea level, La Laguna has a huge collection of plants and flowers from around the world. The garden is a welcome respite from the city's unceasing gray, offering one of the city's few long, shady walks. *Take Bus 101C from Calle Rubén Darío and 13a Av. Sur, get off at Antiguo Cuscatlán. Admission $1.25. Open Tues.–Fri. 10–5, weekends 10–6.*

MONUMENTO DE LA REVOLUCION

Straight from an Orwell novel, this monument to the creation of the Salvadoran constitution is in San Benito, at the entrance to the wealthiest, most exclusive neighborhood in San Salvador. The irony of the placement of the statue is inescapable, given years of repression and undemocratic practices by the elite. *Take Bus 34 to the end of Av. de la Revolución.*

PARQUE ZOOLOGICO

With more than 600 animals in residence, this zoo is pretty snazzy. The tourist office calls it the "most modern zoo in Central America," and the inhabitants seem to live in a relatively tolerable environment. *From El Centro, take Bus 2 MODELO from near cathedral, or Bus 17 PANCHIMALCO from 12a Calle Poniente's central market bldg.; ask to be left at zoo. Admission 60¢. Open Wed.–Sun. 9:30–5.*

TEATRO NACIONAL

The national theater is an inescapable El Centro landmark. Huge columns line the entryway, making the steps and area in between a favorite place for jewelry vendors to sell their goods and passersby to take a break. Check inside or at ISTU for a schedule of plays and cultural events. *2a Av. Sur and Calle Delgado.*

SHOPPING

City dwellers get all their daily staples at the huge **mercado central**—it's no tourist market and a good place to pick up basic stuff for cheap. Open dawn to dusk, it begins at the Iglesia El Calvario and ends at the huge enclosed market near 12a Calle Poniente. **Mercado Ex-Cuartel de Artesanía** (8a Av. Sur, between Calle Delgado and 1a Calle Oriente), open daily 7:30–5:30, is the most interesting shopping area in the capital. Bargain for handwoven textiles, ceramics, and other crafts, and you'll usually get decent prices.

Should you venture into one of the capital's 500 tougher-than-nails dive bars, be ready to leave should someone not like the way you look, dress, or smell. This is not your turf.

AFTER DARK

After dark it's really *dark*. Keep in mind that when you go out on the town at night, many streets are lighted sparsely, if at all, and many buses stop running at 8 PM. It's no fun to get caught on a long, dark stretch of street: bring a flashlight, have a pretty good idea of where you're going, and be prepared to pay for a taxi back to your hotel. Do not accept rides from strangers. Travelers should think twice about going into the hundreds of small dive bars in the city unless they can handle themselves—and their Spanish—in tough situations. You can easily detect these boozy joints, because they often have that universal someone's-about-to-get-killed ambience. Women should be especially careful, even in groups. Also, men traveling alone should definitely watch out for the activities of the *dormilonas*. These are mostly young women who just love to be your friend—all the way up to when they drug your drink, and your last waking memory of your new girlfriend is her frisking you for all you've got.

That said, you can and should have a good time in San Salvador—there's plenty of dancing and live music to keep you up and going into the wee hours. You'll find a less glitzy, more rough-and-tumble scene downtown; for a genuine strobe-light, disco-ball, bop-till-you-drop nightclub scene, cruise west of downtown.

EL CENTRO

Although considered a bit seedy and rumored to be filled with dormilonas, the wide Avenida Juan Pablo II has several locales that throw great fiestas on weekends, when scads of middle- and working-class folks come to party down. **Restaurant El Farolito** (143 Av. Juan Pablo II) has cheap drinks, live bands, and weird karaoke shows. The best and most artistic spot is **Quinto Sol** (*see* Food, *above*), where you can shake that body (well, hips more than upper body) to salsa, cumbia, merengue, and other Latin grooves on a wide dance patio.

BOULEVARD DE LOS HÉROES

Boulevard de los Héroes offers mass quantities of lively, if expensive, nightlife and is fairly convenient to most lodging. A series of restaurant bars across from MetroCentro Sur offers plenty of seating and moderately priced drinks. On a side street off the boulevard, **La Luna** (228 Calle Berlín) could easily be in San Francisco, New York, or Paris. You'll pay a $2–$4 cover but won't be disappointed by the patio setting and postmodern mix of surreal and indigenous imagery. Check the schedule of cultural events, which include art flicks, theater, and every genre of live music. **El Corral Steak House** (1 block south of Hospital Bloom) is open till 1 AM with superb live salsa and a lively crowd. San Salvador isn't exactly bursting with that groovin' feel, which is why phunksters will love **Kairos Discotec,** where techno and hip-hop will leave your ears a-ringing. Alternative rockers and metal-heads should definitely blaze left at the end of the boulevard and saunter over to **Sanzibar** (2137 Calle San Antonio Abad), San Salvador's only hard-core rock club, where the tragically hip play pool and listen to live local bands Thursday–Sunday. To get to Boulevard de los Héroes from El Centro, take Bus 52 to **El Mundo Feliz,** a big kiddie amusement park at the beginning of the boulevard; a taxi back should cost about $3. Bus 44 runs along the boulevard, if you don't want to walk.

At night **La Ventana** (*see* Food, *above*) fills up with gringos, expats, and locals for drinks, food, or dancing, which spontaneously breaks out in the lobby. If you can, sit at the bar and watch the friendly bartenders crank out all kinds of amazing concoctions. And who's that on the wall behind the bar? Could it be Virginia Woolf? Next door to La Ventana is **Tre Diablos,** another fun spot for drinks. Also near Commercial San Luis is **L'Harpa** (one block west and north), El Salvador's only Irish pub, which was opened by volunteers from Ireland who stayed.

PASEO GENERAL ESCALÓN

West of El Centro, Colonia Escalón also boasts a rockin' upper-crust nightlife. Most of the movin' and shakin' is centered around Paseo General Escalón—groove with the crowds at **Lapsus** (5454 Paseo General Escalón, tel. 298–6778) or look for live music and hip folk at the bar **Chantilli.** To get here, take Bus 52 from El Centro toward Plaza Masferrer.

ZONA ROSA

In ritzy (and a little cheesey) Colonia San Benito, along Boulevard del Hipodromo and Boulevard San Benito, the Zona Rosa is home to San Salvador's most exclusive and expensive nightclubs. The action starts around 9 PM and some spots stay pumping all night long, but be aware that nonmembers are often turned away from clubs in this area. If you want to rub shoulders with San Salvador's beautiful people, come to **Mario's** (Blvd. San Benito); wear something decent and be ready to spend some colones. Look for mellow **Reggae Bar** or less crowded and less expensive **Le Club.** Flashy **K-Oz** (open Thurs.–Sat.) on the third floor of the Plaza Suiza shopping mall, should satisfy your discotheque needs. To get here from El Centro, take Bus 34 to the Monumento de la Revolución.

CHEAP THRILLS

If you need a break from EL Centro's most intense neighborhoods, cruise down to **Parque Simón Bolívar** (13a Av. Sur and Calle Rubén Diario). The atmosphere here is calm by San Salvadoran standards— you'll see people hanging out on benches and in the gazebo. If lounging isn't your speed, the basketball court is always a central attraction and you might be able to muscle in on a pickup game.

NEAR SAN SALVADOR

LOS CHORROS

Los Chorros is *the* spot for San Salvador residents with the money and the time to get away. Six kilometers (4 miles) north of Santa Tecla, this beautiful natural gorge helps you forget the visual brutality of the capital. Freshwater springs and small waterfalls lie below volcanic cliffs—spend the day walking and swimming to your heart's content. Several nameless restaurants serve basic platos típicos for $2–$3; the ones by the entrance are cheaper, but the places down by the pools sell mongo bottles of Cerveza Regia for $1.60. The rooms at **Hotel Monteverde,** across from the entrance, are nice enough and reasonable at $15 for a double. Bus 79 to Los Chorros (45 min, 25¢) leaves the capital every 10 minutes from 11a Avenida Sur and Calle Rubén Darío. You can also catch the same bus en route in Santa Tecla (*see below*). Los Chorros admission is just under $1 and it is open daily 7–5.

LAGO DE ILOPANGO

Filling a giant volcanic crater 15 km (9 mi) east of the capital, Ilopango is the country's largest and deepest lake, with an area of over 120 square km (46 square mi). Swimming is fine, but be careful because the water gets deep fast. If you forgot your skivvies, you can rent a bathing suit at the ceviche stands for

50¢ with a $1 deposit. At about $4 per half hour, boat rides are expensive, though it's not bad if you share the ride. As you zip around, check out the ostentatious homes of El Salvador's rich and famous along the private shores, or go visit the island of Puntún. About $12 will get you all the way to **Cerros Quemados** ("Burned Hills"), an island created by an 1880 volcanic eruption. The island holds an annual **festival** on December 15. Smack-dab on a prime lakeside beach is the **Apulo turicentro** (admission 90¢; open daily 7–6:30). Of Apulo's hotels, both **Hotel Familiar** and **Hotel Malvinas** have $10 doubles. Neither is particularly clean, but they do have beach access, so you won't have to pay at the turicentro. Small restaurants dot the shore, where fresh fish costs about $3 per plate. At the stands by the water, seafood thrill-seekers should try the mussel ceviche ($3), scraped right out of the shell before your eyes. Toss in some of their nuclear chile, and wash it down with a beer. But beware, even though many people eat them, there is no guarantee *you* won't get sick. Bus 15 for Apulo (1 hr, 20¢) leaves from Avenida España and 3a Calle Poniente in San Salvador every half hour. For a quicker route, try taking Microbus 140, leaving from behind Iglesia Rosario. Ask to be let off at the road leading to the lake; it's a 4-km (2½-mi) walk downhill.

PANCHIMALCO

About 15 km (9 mi) south of the capital, the peaceful village of Panchimalco is probably the most beautiful town within an hour of San Salvador. Here, descendants of the indigenous Pipil live a surprisingly traditional life surrounded by lush green mountains and dramatic jutting boulders. It's hard to believe the urban sprawl is so close—but it's a good thing it is, since Panchimalco doesn't have any lodging. The town's tranquil, cobblestoned streets and simple buildings surround a plain but elegant colonial church. Around the corner from the bus stop is the **Casa de la Cultura** (open weekdays 8–5, Sat. 8–1), where you can learn about the town's pre-Columbian heritage. The surrounding area is ideal for hiking, and if you haul yourself to one of the summits, you'll be rewarded with spectacular views. The town's yearly **festival,** on the first Sunday of March, features a parade called the "Procession of Palms and Flowers." Panchimalco is a good side trip if you're going to Parque Balboa (*see below*), because it's only about 10 minutes from the park entrance. To get to Panchimalco (50 min, 15¢), take Bus 17 from 12a Calle Poniente in San Salvador's central market; it leaves several times an hour.

PARQUE BALBOA

This nearby turicentro is pleasant and green—a great place for a picnic, but the area's big attraction is **Puerta del Diablo,** a 45-minute walk from the entrance of the park. "The Devil's Gate" is a pair of enormous boulders that you can climb for a spectacular view of Lago de Ilopango. The climb looks intimidating, but the stairs going up the rock are solid—be sure to wear decent shoes and be extra careful when it's wet. Locals warn about theft and recommend that you leave your passport at your hotel, carry little money, and go with a group. If you forgot your picnic basket, pick up some food at one of several good pupuserías just outside Parque Balboa. To get to the park, hop on Bus 12, marked MIL CUMBRES (40 min, 15¢), at the corner of Calle 29 de Agosto and 12a Calle Poniente in San Salvador; it leaves frequently and is sardine-city. Bus 12 also continues on to the Puerta del Diablo if you're not up for the walk.

RUINAS DE SAN ANDRÉS

Halfway between San Salvador and Santa Ana, San Andrés makes an easy day trip from either city. These are the ruins of a regional indigenous capital that flourished between AD 600 and AD 900. You can climb upon the small pyramid and its two temples, frolic in the grassy courtyard, or just rest and absorb the panoramic vista of green farms melting into cloud-covered mountains. Admission is free, and there is a small but informative museum. To get to the ruins, first go to Santa Tecla (*see below*). From there, Bus 201 (30 min, 25¢) leaves from Parque San Martín in Santa Tecla every 10–15 minutes and lets you off 1 km (½ mi) from the entrance.

SANTA TECLA

Santa Tecla, 13 km (8 mi) west of the capital, was founded immediately after the catastrophic earthquake of 1854 as El Salvador's new seat of authority. Although it only held that honor for about a year, many people still call it Nueva (new) San Salvador. Today, this middle-class suburb is the departure point for trips to nearby volcanoes and makes a mellow getaway in itself. Santa Tecla's two central parks are right next to each other. The pretty one, **Parque San Martín,** houses the **Casa de la Cultura** (open weekdays 9–noon and 2–5, Sat. 8–noon), where you can discuss the state of latino culture with the dedicated and friendly director or participate in an art class. Nearby **Parque Daniel Hernandez** is the one surrounded by the **mercado** where you can find excellent meals for less than $1. Meanwhile, local musicians provide the ambience with rancheras and other traditional folk songs. For more active entertainment, a large park near the entrance to the city has several basketball courts and soccer fields. Overnighters should head to signless **Hospedaje Guerrero** (Calle Daniel Hernandez 4–3, 3½ blocks from Parque Daniel Hernandez), where small, safe, and tidy doubles go for $4. To get to Santa Tecla, take Bus 101 (30 min, 25¢) from 11a Avenida Sur in El Centro; it bus leaves every 10 minutes or so.

VOLCAN DE SAN SALVADOR

This volcano is definitely visible from town (there it is, looming over there!). It makes a great day hike, and you'll get some cool views of the Puerta del Diablo (*see above*) and the whole Valle de las Hamacas. The crater of the lower peak is nicknamed **El Boquerón** ("The Big Mouth"), and the higher one is called **Pichacho.** Circling the volcano takes a good two hours, but if you've still got it in you, circumnavigate El Boquerón's crater. Getting to the volcano is a chore: take Bus 101 from 11a Avenida Sur in the capital to Santa Tecla (30 min, 25¢). From there, Bus 103 leaves once an hour for Boquerón, stopping just over 2 km (1 mi) from the crater.

NORTHERN EL SALVADOR

Northern El Salvador is beautiful, mountainous territory. It is also the poorest region in the country and was most devastated by the conflict; virtually every community north of Colima was visited by the army and guerrillas. The region welcomes the relative stability brought by the end of the war, but opinions about the current state of affairs vary. Overt repression has decreased, but poverty, brought about by a stunning inequity of land ownership, remains a central issue of debate. The United Nations, European Community, and USAID are all here to hasten post-war development and spend a lot of money on fancy land cruisers with cute logos stuck to the doors. On the positive side, life here is changing. Agriculture is being redeveloped—the area's primary crop is corn, the country's staple food and the main component of all those tortillas and pupusas you've been eating. Small communities are slowly repopulating with returning refugees from Honduras. As a foreigner, you may be greeted with an initial frigidity, but patience usually has its rewards—most everyone here has a wealth of fascinating, if horrifying, stories.

In the northwest, your best bet for outdoor fun is hiking and camping. The mountains north of Tejutla are gorgeous and rugged places for communion with friends and nature. Parque Nacional Montecristo is the best-known nature reserve in the country, providing a beautiful setting for camping and hiking. In more remote areas, the risk of running into thieves or armed groups is relatively low but must be accounted for before you head out. Clearly, don't camp next to main towns, army barracks, or other people's property. Bring a good tent, because sudden downpours can be quite brutal.

The **Troncal del Norte** is the paved highway that runs from the capital to the Honduran border at El Poy. Most bus transportation in this region centers around a highway junction called **El Desvío de Mayo,** or simply El Mayo, about 1½ hours due north of the capital (75¢) and about two hours south of El Poy (75¢). From El Mayo, you can travel east to Chalatenango, west to Nueva Concepción, or north to El Poy. Although buses pass frequently, you should be ready to wait up to an hour for the one you want. Then be prepared for crowds: you may wind up with your face shoved up against a basket of angry hens. Metapán and the nature areas to the northwest are most easily reached through Santa Ana in the west. You can try hitching, but only do so away from a bus stop, and you'll probably wait longer than you would for a bus.

CHALATENANGO

About 55 km (34 mi) from the capital lies Chalatenango. With a population of 30,000, it is the largest city in the region and the commercial center of the area. Strong local support by the FMLN made the town a center of conflict—a large garrison of troops still resides here, and their morning exercises and marches may be your daily alarm clock. Despite this, the town manages to retain a tranquillity and charm characteristic of the northern communities. Although the people of Chalatenango are definitely poor, the place escapes the seething urban squalor of the capital. Poverty, resistance, pride, and a recovering happiness amid the scars of violence make Chalatenango a worthwhile place to visit. A particularly good time to be here is around June 24 for the **patron saint festival.** Otherwise, check out the **mercado central** (Calle José María San Martín and Av. Libertad) in the middle of town, where you can grab some lunch and watch the goings-on. Or, cool off at the **Aguas Frías** turicentro; it's open daily 8–6 and admission is 90¢. Just a block from the central park, **Antel** (Calle José María San Martín and 5a Av. Sur) will handle your phone needs daily 6 AM–10 PM. To get to Chalatenango from the capital (2½ hrs, 60¢), take Bus 125 from Terminal de Oriente; it leaves every 15 minutes until 6:15 PM.

WHERE TO SLEEP AND EAT

East of the central bus stop, eat at **Comedor El Portalito** (3 4a Calle Poniente), where breakfast, lunch, or dinner will set you back about $2. The food is standard, but the patio overlooking the street is great for people-watching. If you're planning to stay the night, funky **Hospedaje Nuevo Amanecer** (9 1a Calle Oriente, at Av. Fajarda) has acceptable rooms for $3 per person, although the 6 AM checkout is a traveler's nightmare. **Hospedaje La Inez** (19a Calle San Martin, across from Antel, no sign) is a better choice, despite thin, mushy mattresses. Señora Inez charges $3 a person and will make you feel like part of the family if you're sociable and respectful.

NEAR CHALATENANGO

CONCEPCION QUETZALTEPEQUE

Here, daily activity stubbornly braves the passage of time—a hammer building a house matches a slow heartbeat.

This charming village is just 10 km (6 mi) west of Chalatenango. Civil war ravaged this place, but today the atmosphere is quite different from that of its larger neighbors' because hardly a soldier is on the street. Although recent changes—such as the paving of cobblestoned streets to accommodate transit—threaten to destroy the charm of the village, its reputation as "Hammock Capital" of El Salvador is an appropriate testament to the town's mellow character. The best reason to visit may be to purchase one of these swinging masterpieces; check out the **Hammock Cooperative** (tel. 335–2666, fax 325–2520) near the central bus stop. Reyna Martinez, María Escobar, or Concepción Cayax will display any of a variety of beautiful hammocks that range in price from $20 to $60. Visit the **Casa de Cultura,** up the hill behind the church, to hear more about how the hammock craft came to Concepción Quetzalpeque and about the town's **patron saint festival** the first weekend of November. To get here, try Bus 300B, which runs infrequently from Chalatenango's bus terminal (20 min, 15¢). Alternatively, Bus 125 passes through Chalatenango on its way from the Terminal de Oriente in the capital—it will take you as far as the intersection for Concepción, where you can wait for one of the pickup trucks that run frequently to town.

Near Concepción Quetzaltepeque are some excellent places to enjoy the great outdoors in virtual solitude. Several rivers have wonderful swimming, and a multitude of beautiful, low mountains lie within easy walking distance. Ask in Concepción or in Chalatenango about hikes to **Montañona** or **Cerro de Cielo.** For a commanding view of the mongo **Cerrón Grande** mountain, ask around about pickups that leave for the pueblito of **Llano Grande,** about 8 km (5 mi) from town.

VILLAGES

Since 1992 there has been a movement of people back into towns that were devastated and evacuated during the civil war. Known as repopulated communities, these small towns are worth the effort required to get there. **San José de Las Flores** is home to an amazing *taller* (artisan's workshop) where women welcome you to watch quietly as they work. The village's decrepit church is still in use; look for silhouettes of Romero painted upon pillars surrounded by crumbling walls. Other villages to visit include **Guarjila** and **San Antonio Los Ranchos.** Ask around for rides and buses leaving east out of Chalatenango; it's better to leave early in the morning, because the already infrequent bus transit slows after midafternoon.

LA PALMA

The last city of any size before you reach the Honduran border is La Palma, 8 km (5 mi) south of the border. This small town is notable as the home of dozens of workshops where artisans craft ceramic, cloth, and wooden goods to sell in the capital. You can watch the artists at work and buy directly from them in their shops. Check with the **Casa de la Cultura** (open weekdays 9–noon and 2–5), on 1a Calle Poniente just below the main square, for info on which workshops welcome visitors. La Palma also makes a good departure point for a number of nearby activities. Journeys from La Palma include **Rio**

Nunuapa, 4 km (2½ mi) away; **Miramundo** and **La Peidra Cayaguanca,** both 10 km (6¼ mi) away; and Las Pilas, 15 km (9½ mi) away. The truly macho might be up to the challenge of **El Pital,** El Salvador's highest peak at 8,900 ft; it's about 13 km (8 mi) from La Palma. All these distances are approximate, and anyone attempting the longer hikes and climbs should come fully equipped. Call home to brag about your adventures from **Antel** (open daily 6 AM–8 PM), a block from the park, near the bus stop. From San Salvador's Terminal de Oriente, Bus 119 leaves for La Palma (4 hrs, $1.10) and the Honduran border town of El Poy (*see* Near La Palma, *below*) hourly from dawn until 3 PM. In La Palma you can catch buses to Tejutla (1 hr, 75¢), the El Mayo desvío (1½ hrs, $1), and El Poy (20 min, 25¢).

WHERE TO SLEEP AND EAT

The only lodging in La Palma is **Hotel La Palma** (tel.335–9464), near the town's entrance; fortunately its red-tile walkways, exposed-beam overhanging porches, and tropical foliage make it an enchanting place to stay. Good beds, modern quality, and rustic style go for about $20 per room. Ask here about nearby outdoor adventures. Twenty minutes down the road to El Poy, **Hotel Cayahuanca** is a good place to stay while preparing for hikes. It has a dozen clean, comfortable rooms for $7 ($11 with private bath). The owner, Juan, will talk with you for hours about his experiences with wine, women, the government, and the guerrillas. The little restaurant serves huge plates of good food for around $4, and there is a laundry sink where you can wash your clothes.

NEAR LA PALMA

EL POY (TO HONDURAS)

El Poy is a classic border town: filthy, tiny, and full of fast-talking money changers. In short, don't plan on spending much time here. Immigration is open daily 6–6, but it's best to get there early so you'll be sure to catch a bus to **Nueva Ocotepeque** on the Honduras side. Be prepared to pay exit fees (around $10) and don't try to enter Honduras without a visa if you need one (*see* Visas and Tourist Cards, in chapter Basics, *above*) because you'll be turned away.

METAPÁN

Although this northwestern town near the Guatemalan border offers little in itself, it serves as the only solid base from which to visit the beautiful Lago Güija or Parque Nacional Montecristo. **Antel** (open daily 6 AM–9 PM) is on 2a Calle Oriente and 2a Avenida Sur, and the **post office** (open weekdays 8–noon and 2–5, Sat. 8–noon, Sun. 8–11) is 2 blocks uphill and around the corner on Calle Luna.

Metapán's **bus terminal** is on the dusty, muddy main highway near the closed-down movie theater. From the capital, Bus 201A (3½ hrs, 70¢) leaves leaves from the Terminal de Occidente several times daily; it's actually quicker to take Bus 201 DIRECTÓ to Santa Ana and connect to Bus 235 (1½ hrs, 40¢), which leaves every 15 minutes. If you're headed out of the country, Bus 211 and Bus 235 (in transit from Santa Ana) leave for Angüiatú at the Guatemalan border (20 min, 25¢) every 15 minutes or so. Keep in mind that from the border, it's an hour to Esquipulas and another four to Guatemala City, not including waiting around. Plan ahead.

WHERE TO SLEEP

Welcome to the **Hotel California** (left side of main highway, 5 blocks north of bus terminal, tel. 442–0561), one true bright spot in Metapán. It's not exactly life in the fast lane, but it does have seven very clean rooms with keen bathrooms and fans. You'll pay $6 for one big bed. The friendly owner will gladly let you use the laundry sink. If California's full or if you're economizing, go to **Hospedaje Central** (2a Av. Norte and Calle 15 de Septiembre). It's a good deal: $3 for a room with one big bed, but the best rooms, in the newer part of the building, come with private bath for $4. Although the building is rundown and dark, the management does keep the place really clean.

FOOD

For quality eats, try the large, open-air **Multidelicias** (2a Calle Oriente, tel. 442–0226), a block down from the mercado municipal on the main highway. A decent medium pizza with one topping costs $4.75, and they serve sandwiches, burgers, standard meat dishes, pastries, and ice cream. The *galletas rellenas* (filled cookies) are a treat for 20¢ each. Down the street, near Antel, **Sorbetería Polar** is popular with local workers and offers cafeteria-style service for $2. Enjoy the zillion flavors of icy, sweet *minutas* (snowcone) for 70¢ at **Kiki Minutas** (2 Calle Oriente, between 4a and 6a Av. Sur).

PARQUE NACIONAL MONTECRISTO

Montecristo National Park has the most pristine natural beauty in El Salvador. It's part of **Parque Internacional El Trifinio,** a forested international park jointly operated by El Salvador, Guatemala, and Honduras. The range of animal and plant life is amazing, and a number of endangered species, such *quetzales* (a bright green tropical bird) and spider monkeys, have made Montecristo their home. The highlight of the preserve is the super-humid cloud forest, which starts at around 7,000 ft. A journey here is a dark, wet odyssey amid huge trees and mysterious forest life. It rains more in the cloud forest than anywhere else in the country—over 6½ ft annually—and the mists that cover the mountain, especially at night, mean that nothing ever dries out. This is the closest you'll find to a fairy forest, with a mystical, almost surreal ambience. In addition to 7,600-ft **Cerro Montecristo,** two other peaks, 7,900-ft **Cerro Miramundo** and 7,100-ft **Cerro El Brujo** lie nearby. With altitudes like these, it can get cold despite the humidity, so bring a jacket.

The cloud-forest portion of the park is closed April–September to ensure undisturbed animal breeding; the rest of the year both visiting and camping are permitted. During the closed season, you can still explore the other forested areas of the park, relax in the picnic area, and visit the small flower garden. The **Administración del Parque Nacional Montecristo** (tel. 442–0119) at the park entrance issues permits to visitors.

COMING AND GOING

Getting to Montecristo is quite laborious—a 14-km (9-mi), four-wheel-drive vehicle-only road heads from just past the bus terminal in Metapán to the entrance of the preserve. There's some talk of an organized transportation service in the future, but for now you'll have to ask around to hire a private vehicle. It's not cheap—expect to pay about $25. Bus drivers and their helpers often have good info or talk to Carlos Humberto, the friendly owner of **Tienda La Esperanza** (1 block from bus terminal, open daily 7 AM–8 PM), a store where you can find sliced bread, tuna, peanut butter, canned vegetables and other food for camping. Sr. Humberto keeps a good eye on what's passing toward the park because his store rests right on the turnoff to Montecristo. You can also try planting yourself on the store's steps at around 6 AM and waiting to see if any passing four-wheelers will give you a lift. Weekdays, park service vehicles tend to go by at around 7 AM. Tried and true hikers should go ahead and walk the distance. Unless you make it a day trip, you'll have to camp, since the park has no lodging.

LAGO DE GÜIJA

Arguably the most beautiful lake in the country, Lago de Güija lies in both Salvadoran and Guatemalan territory. It was a site of great religious importance to Toltec and Pipil tribes. Local legend has it that the lake was formed after several nearby volcanoes erupted and the lava flows altered the directions of several rivers, which, in turn, flooded and destroyed a couple of nearby towns, Zacualpa and Güijar. Lost-city tales and rumors of sunken treasure abound. To get here, take Bus 235 (20 min, 25¢) from Metapán toward Santa Ana and get off at the village of **Desagüe,** near a store called **Chalet López.** Make sure to ask the bus driver tell you where to get off because it's easy to miss. From there, it's about a half-hour walk to the lake. Follow the road a short distance until you come to a fork, bear right, follow the train tracks over a bridge, and bear right again. From there, ask someone where the boats are; the shore is pretty close, but it's hard to find. Buses run along the main highway by Desagüe from early morning until late afternoon, so the lake makes an easy day or half-day trip. Camping is very good along the pastured lakeshore, but mostly disappears when the water levels are high.

Lago de Güija has a number of curious sights, and a local fisherman will take you on a good two-hour tour for $11–$20. This should get you to and from the island of **Tipa,** which offers great views of **Volcán Chingo** and **Volcán Ipala,** both near the Guatemalan border. Nearby **Cerro Negro,** on the island of Tipa is not really a hill, but rather a cluster of volcanic boulders that form something akin to a cave. Fishermen use it for protection during dangerous storms or just to chill and have lunch. The arm of land that extends on the left from where the boats take off is Las Figuras, so named for the hieroglyphics carved into boulders here. ISTU came several years ago and hauled away a bunch of the stone-carved drawings to the national museum (thanks, folks), but you can still see at least a dozen interesting carvings in varying degrees of discernability—use your imagination and you might find Jerry Garcia among the animal and human shapes. During dry times, Las Figuras becomes part of the shore and you can walk right there. Follow the road near the boats until you begin to round the tip—you won't have to look too hard, just keep walking and you'll know 'em when you see 'em. You can also rent a canoe from a local fisherman for not more than a couple of bucks per day. You can swim in the lake, although it gets pretty brown from mountain runoff.

WESTERN EL SALVADOR

The west is popular with both tourists and nationals for its dramatic natural beauty, the most famous examples of which are Cerro Verde and Lago de Coatepeque, south of Santa Ana. Small rivers and scenic waterfalls abound, too, especially near Sonsonate. Campers and hikers will certainly want to spend some time exploring this region; the heavy rains during July to October make it rough going but more beautiful. The rural areas here are also home to the few indigenous communities that have survived in El Salvador. Their distinctive dress, language, and customs are dying out fast as urbanization and "progress" spread.

Although the FMLN was active all over the country, the west saw much less violence than did other parts of El Salvador. Most of the west is better off economically than the war-scarred northern and eastern departments. Its mild climate and fertile hills make it the coffee-growing center of the country and the source of a great deal of export-generated wealth. While the bucks certainly aren't distributed equally, agriculture does provide subsistence work for thousands of campesinos and helps to dissipate some of the class-based social strife.

SANTA ANA

Salvadoreños call Santa Ana *la segunda ciudad,* the most important and largest city after San Salvador. With less than a quarter-million people, this "second city" isn't particularly large, but it is the center for commerce and agriculture in this prosperous region. The generally placid city comes alive during the annual **festival,** July 17–26, when music, beauty pageants, dances, fireworks, and mechanical rides all become part of the party. Unless you're in town for the festival, however, you probably won't find much reason to stick around. Most of the residents go indoors by 9 PM, and although Santa Ana is a quarter the size of the capital, the people here are just as tense and even more insular—don't be surprised if you feel like you have the word GRINGO stamped on your forehead. Use Santa Ana as a convenient hub for the natural beauty of the outlying areas.

BASICS

Major banks are clustered around 2a Avenida and Calle Libertad, just a block from the cathedral. **Banco Salvadoreño** (2a Av. Sur and 1a Calle Poniente) changes traveler's checks and does credit-card advances. Like most banks in town, it's open weekdays 9–5 and Saturday 9–noon. A 10-minute walk from the town center, the **Hospital San Juan de Díos** (1a Calle Oriente and 13a Av. Sur, tel. 447–1555) provides 24-hour emergency treatment and specialized medical attention. The **police** station (tel. 440–7827) is at 4a Avenida Independencia. Just behind the cathedral on the corner of 5a Avenida Norte and Calle Libertad Oriente, **Antel** is open daily 6 AM–10 PM. The central **post office** (2a Av. Sur and 7a Calle Poniente) is open weekdays 7:30–5, Saturday 8–noon, and Sunday 8–11.

COMING AND GOING

From the capital, take Bus 201 from Terminal de Occidente. Take one marked DIRECTO, which travels via Calle Nueva (1 hr, 70¢), or you'll trudge through a dozen podunk towns for more than two hours before reaching Santa Ana. Buses run every 15 minutes or so from early morning until about 6:30 PM. Bus 236 goes to San Cristóbal at the Guatemalan border (1¼ hrs, 50¢), leaving every 15 minutes between 5:45

AM and 5 PM. Bus 235 goes to Metapán (1½ hrs, 60¢), with some continuing to Angüiatú at the Honduran border; it leaves every 15 minutes between 4:30 AM and 6 PM. Bus 216 leaves for Sonsonate (1¼ hrs, 50¢) every 15 minutes between 5 AM and 5:30 PM.

GETTING AROUND

Santa Ana's **bus terminal** (10a Av. Sur and 15a Calle Poniente) is at least 15 minutes from Santa Ana's center, which is bordered on the north by the **cathedral** (between 1a and 5a Avs. Norte, near Calle Libertad Oriente). From the bus terminal, walk north on 10a Avenida Sur, and you'll pass a cluster of small businesses ending at **Parque Menéndez** (Calle Libertad and 10a Av. Sur); from there, hang a right on 2a Calle Poniente to get to the heart of the action. Near the cathedral, you'll find the **mercado central** (1a Calle Poniente, between and 8a Avs. Sur), an enormous covered building selling everything from fresh vegetables to Walkman radios, and the **Teatro de Santa Ana** (Av. Independencia, between 2a and 4a Calles Poniente). If you're in a hurry, or you have lots of luggage, local Bus 51 (10¢) runs between the bus terminal and the center frequently until around 7:30 PM.

WHERE TO SLEEP

Lodging in Santa Ana is not as plentiful as you might expect from a city that ranks second only to the capital. And, in most cases, rooms are more pricey than they should be for what you get.

If you complain that your hotel room is too noisy, don't expect to be moved; the desk clerk might just bring you a bigger TV!

UNDER $20 • Hospedaje Livingston. Livingston offers large, clean double rooms with functioning private baths for $15 (less with shared bath). The rooms are rather dark, and each room has only one big bed, but all the essentials for a decent night's sleep are here. *17 10a Av. Sur, between 7a and 9a Calles Poniente, tel. 441–1801. 30 rooms, 20 some with bath.*

Hotel Internacional. The staff is really nice and you'll enjoy pleasant $15 rooms with clean beds, cable TV, and fans; the hotel has purified water and a second-floor patio (overlooking the gated parking lot). Bathrooms are kinda cramped and not necessarily divided from the rest of the room. Since the hotel is situated on a busy corner with several bus stops, be sure to ask up front for a *quiet* room in the main building. *25 Calle Poniente and 10a Av. Sur, 5 blocks south of bus terminal, tel. 440–0804 or 440–0810. 15 rooms with bath. Laundry. Cash only.*

Hotel Libertad. Although one of the better hotels in Santa Ana, Hotel Libertad is still nothing to write home about. The rooms are large, clean, well kept, and all have good fans. It's just that everything's a tad run-down here. However, it's a block from the cathedral and a mere $15 a night. *1a Av. Norte and 4a Calle Oriente, tel. 441–2358. 1 block from cathedral. 11 rooms with bath. Cash only.*

UNDER $60 • Hotel Sahara. Certainly the nicest place to stay in Santa Ana. Air-conditioned rooms with private baths and cable TV cost $49–$59 for two, or $69 for three people. *10a Av. Sur and 3a Calle Poniente, tel. 447–8832 or 447–0458, fax 447–8865. 18 rooms with bath. Laundry.*

FOOD

Santa Ana is brimming with good restaurants and cheap and basic comedores, and most serve decent food. Comedores that sell pupusas and cheap platos típicos are everywhere.

UNDER $5 • At **Café Cappuccino** (Independencia Sur, between Calle Libertad and 1a Calle Poniente), espresso drinks and as-you-like-them omelets ($2) are the way to go for a cheap and tasty breakfast. **Los Horcones** (1a Av., between the cathedral and Calle Libertad) is a funky and convenient place right near the plaza to stop for a fresh-fruit smoothie ($1) in their jungle-inspired setting or on the terrace. Inexpensive meals (including those for the vegetarian) are also available here. Tasty vegetarian fare, homemade whole-wheat rolls, herbal remedies, and assorted good-for-you groceries are available at **Restaurant Talitunál** (5a Av. Sur, between Calle Libertad and 1a Calle) at low prices. The menu changes daily, but offerings are sure to be fresh.

UNDER $10 • Toto's Pizza (1a Calle Poneiente and 1a Av. Sur, no phone) serves $8 pizzas that feed two or three and has a large, safe (we think), mostly fresh salad bar for $3 for a large bowl. **Regis Restaurant** (9a Calle Poniente and 6 Av. Sur, no phone) is somewhat of an all-meals cafetería that accommodates a wide range of appetites and budgets; you can spend a few dollars on a light lunch of soup and salad or closer to $10 on seafood specials. **Lover's Steak House** (4a Av. Sur and 17a Calle Poniente, no phone), with an indoor open-roof terrace, serves casual, medium-priced, nothing-special fare, but they have a TV. Beware the gritty, tasteless mariscara called the "Sinfonia Lover's."The rice dishes, such as the *arroces con camaron* (seafood with rice, $6), is kind of like stir-fried Chinese take-out. For excellent service in a pretty building with rose-washed walls, hardwood floors, and potted plants, visit **El Tucán Gourmet** (33 Av. Independencia and 9a Calle Oriente, tel. 441–1071), one of Santa Ana's finest restaurants. Salvadoran artwork adorns the walls, including a lovely painting of a Spanish dancer done in red hues. For lunch or dinner, have a glass of wine and try the *filete de pescado al ajillo* (fish with fresh herbs) for $8 or *pollo al limó* (lemon chicken) with vegetables and rice for $6. For simple and quick food, **Manlito,** next door, sells burritos. Go to classy **Restaurant Los Patios** (21a Calle Poniente between Independencia and 4a Av. Sur, tel 440–4221) for the beautiful open-air courtyard and stone garden as well as the food. Grilled steak, chicken, and seafood cost around $10 here, but there are less expensive choices—and you can charge it.

WORTH SEEING

The gothic **cathedral** is impressive both inside and out, even in its current state of disrepair. Next to the cathedral is the baroque **Teatro de Santa Ana,** whose beautiful and well-maintained exterior belies the years of neglect inside. Completed around 1910, the building was converted into a movie theater during the Martinez dictatorship of the 1930s and remained so until 1979. By then, customer abuse, water damage, and lack of maintenance had destroyed much of the exquisitely detailed work. The Mexican government is now funding a restoration project that should be finished by the year 2000. Nonetheless, you can still appreciate much of the original work, and the technical process of restoration is interesting in itself. Occasionally, the theater hosts artistic and cultural events—ask at the front desk. Both of these structures face crowded **Parque Libertad,** where you can check out a city map that highlights businesses, government buildings, and other places of interest. Nearby, at **Cine Novedades** (Calle Libertad and 3a Av. Sur), you can watch six-month-old movies for a couple of bucks.

NEAR SANTA ANA

CHALCHUAPA AND THE TAZUMAL RUINS

The Mayan ruins of Tazumal ("Place of the Burned" in the Quiché language) are El Salvador's most important and best-preserved pre-Columbian site. If you're coming from ruin-rich Guatemala or Belize, you may find the site somewhat underwhelming; nevertheless, it makes a good half-day trip from Santa Ana. The site provides a glimpse into the lives of several indigenous civilizations dating from at least 3,000 years ago. Archaeological evidence suggests that the residents had trading partners in other parts of Central America and even Mexico. Unfortunately, only a small part of the 10-square-km (6¼-square-mi) area has been excavated, although excavation continues on and off. Until more structures are uncovered, Tazumal's main attractions are the large pyramid and ball court. The pyramid, most likely a religious temple, can be climbed from several sides and offers an inspiring view of the town of Chalchuapa and the surrounding countryside. The small museum at the site displays a number of relics found at Tazumal, although many of the best ones have been taken to the national museum in the capital. The photos and bilingual descriptions of the site's history and the restoration process describe many of the problems archaeologists encounter when trying to maintain the structural integrity of a stone building that is several thousand years old. *Admission $3. Open Tues.–Sun. 9–5.*

COMING AND GOING • From Santa Ana, Bus 218 leaves every 10 minutes for Chalchuapa (30 min, 20¢). Buses 202 and 210 will also get you here. You can get off the bus in town or just outside town by the cemetery. The ruins are a two-minute walk from there. If you're on your way out of the country, you can take a private bus that leaves for Guatemala City (3½ hrs, $6) from outside **Hotel Córdoba,** just outside town on the Santa Ana–Chalchuapa highway. The schedule says it leaves hourly, but in reality it's more like every two hours. If you are driving in from Santa Ana, head for Ahuachapán. In Chalchuapa, make a left at the Texaco station and continue to the road's end where you'll find the ruins.

WHERE TO SLEEP AND EAT • The town of Chalchuapa is pleasant enough and has places to stay, if you're in no rush or don't mind being 30 minutes away from major bus connections in Santa Ana. The centrally located **Hotel Gloria** (Av. 2 de Abril and Calle General Ramón Flores, tel. 444–0131) has eight large, clean rooms with private baths for the unbelievable price of $4 per person. The management, however, can be rather surly. Grab a chicken plate ($2–$3) or a hamburger ($2.50) at **Deli Pollo** (7a Av. Norte, at Calle General Ramón Flores), or satisfy your sweet tooth with a shake or ice cream. Near the **market** (3a Av. Norte, between 2a and 4a Calles Oriente) are a number of mom-and-daughter eateries that serve very tasty platos típicos to a local clientele for about $1.

SOUTH FROM SANTA ANA

The best-known natural wonders of western El Salvador lie in the mountainous area between Santa Ana and Sonsonante, farther to the south. Make Lago de Coatepeque your base and you won't be disappointed. The solace of its quiet waters and its low-key surroundings close to Cerro Verde (and Santa Ana) rank it among the prettiest places to visit. This is the place to spend some time swimming in Lago de Coatepeque or do some serious volcano hiking in Parque Nacional Cerro Verde. Any bus traveling south of Santa Ana along the Pan-American Highway will bring you with in a few hundred meters of town.

LAGO DE COATEPEQUE

Set high in the mountains, Lago de Coatepeque is one of the most dramatic and beautiful sites in El Salvador. The enormous crater lake has an area of 26 square km (16 square mi) and a depth of 390 ft, offering some of the best swimming, sightseeing, food, and lodging in the country. The climate is cool and fresh, and volcanic springs keep the water temperature remarkably comfortable. Sit back and gaze at the enchanting Cerro Verde or the looming Santa Ana and Izalco volcanoes. The lake hasn't been polluted by reckless commerce or development—in fact, the only things that mar the lovely atmosphere are the dozens of fancy homes that line the shore, making some of this natural wonderland private property.

During your visit, look for the crab hunters using snorkeling gear in the shallow parts: a smile or a cold beer might borrow you some time gazing at the amazing variety of creatures and plants just beneath the surface. During the week you'll practically have the lake to yourself, although during the crowded weekends you have a better chance of sharing the cost of a boat ride around the lake. Local passenger boats give half-hour rides for around 75¢—if you can muster up at least 12 people. A ride to **Agua Caliente Island** is 1½ hours round-trip and can't be done for much less than $20 round-trip, unless you politely offer to rent a rowboat from one of the locals. Although it looks close, it'll take a good while to get out there by oars alone. As the name (Hot Water) suggests, volcanic springs beneath the surface keep a small pocket of water at hot-tub temperature. Make sure to yell like Tarzan and fling yourself off the trapeze-like swing into the water.

COMING AND GOING

If you are traveling by car, take the CA-1 Pan-American Highway to the Lago de Coatepeque/Cerro Verde exit (about 124 km or 77 mi west of San Salvador) where you'll find lots of fruit stands and tortilla vendors. Continue straight down this road (billboards will confirm that you're headed in the right direction), slowing or stopping to take in a view of the lake before the road winds its way down. There are roadside vendors along the way selling sodas and seats to those who want to contemplate the view under a canvas tarp. When the pavement turns to dirt, you know you've reached the road to the hotels. The horrible condition of the road should slow you down considerably, but don't let it stop you from finding your lakeside retreat. It's a good way down to the hotels, but you won't get lost, since the road ends just past them. To get to the lake from Santa Ana, take Bus 220 (1½ hrs, 30¢), which leaves every 25 minutes from the bus terminal. From the capital, take Bus 201 ORDINARIO and get off at El Congo, where you can catch Bus 220. To get to Cerro Verde, take Bus 220 back to the El Congo junction, where you can pick up Bus 248 en route from Santa Ana. It leaves three times daily. The bus will let you off in the main town; everything's within a few hundred feet on the main road.

WHERE TO SLEEP AND EAT

Camping is available at the **Centro Obrero,** a free government workers' resort 4 km (2½ mi) before the main town. It has basic accommodations and an affordable restaurant. Technically, you need to get prior permission from the **Ministerio de Trabajo** (400 15a Calle Poniente, Edificio Urritia Abrego, Centro de Gobeirno, tel. 222–8151) in the capital—if you didn't, it's still worth a try, especially during the week. You can eat cheaply at one of the simple comedores near the lake, but if you want to sample any of Coatepeque's delicacies—most notably *guapote* (bass) and freshwater crab—you'll have to spend some real money at one of the hotel restaurants. Also, for a small fee, the hotels allow nonguests to use their pool and terrace to lounge for the day. Inquire at the door. As far as formal lodging goes, the least expensive, most relaxing, and most intriguing deal on the lake is **Amacuilco Guest House** (tel. 441–0608). Your host, Sandra Salinas, loves to work with foreign travelers and will show you around the number of outdoor decks with hammocks, nooks, and crannies. The murals, artesanía, and colorful walls and decks add flavor to this hip joint. If you're staying for at least five nights, you can also sign up for Spanish or Nahuat language classes. You can take your carefully prepared, reasonably priced meals right on the water, or climb down the ladder into the lake for a swim. Simple rooms for two or three people with adjoining clean baths run $11–$20. Just down the road, **Hotel Torremolino** (tel. 446–9437) offers luxury accommodations in colonial style for about $30 with private bath. Torremolino has a small, clean swimming pool in case you're hankering for chlorine instead of the freshwater lake. The chichi restaurant on the premises is tastefully decorated and has a large, covered dock where you can eat right on the water. Breakfast is the best value: juice, eggs, plantains, and coffee for $3.50 will start your day off right. Continue the good feeling throughout the afternoon with a magnificent shrimp-stuffed avocado for $4. On Sunday afternoon, you can dance to *cumbia* (cousin to salsa) and romantic live music performed by the Orquesta Maya Club from Santa Ana; check with the hotel for the exact schedule. You can also hear music on weekends at the **Hotel del Lago** (tel. 446–9511), El Salvador's oldest hotel, long popular with the country's vacationing presidents. Today the gorgeous ceramic tile floors remain along with some of the original wooden beams, shutters, and doors. Guests have a choice of the older Spanish-style or newly renovated rooms, which are about $30 and $50, respectively. Unlike the other hotels, there is a small stretch of beach here as well as a terrace and a swimming pool. A visit to the high-ceilinged restaurant is worthwhile whether you stay here as a guest or not; they serve fresh-caught fish and seafood daily. In the evening, if you're lucky, you may cross the path of a strolling mariachi band. There are several simple **tiendas** and **comedores** along the road that sell soda, foodstuffs, supplies, and, if you're lucky and diligent, a choco-banana (banana dipped in chocolate). Hidden between the Amacuilco and Torremolinos right on the water is a tiny, really informal **pupusería,** where they will crack open a coconut for you to drink; look for the smoke coming off the grill and head down for a snack.

PARQUE NACIONAL CERRO VERDE

The name means green hill but, at 6,500 ft above sea level, "hill" is something of an understatement. Cerro Verde offers spectacular views of the Santa Ana and Izalco volcanoes and of Lago de Coatepeque, while the thickly forested mountains make for awesome hikes. Cerro Verde is an extinct volcano, home to one of the most diverse communities of plants, trees, and wildlife in the country—there are supposedly 127 varieties of birds. From the parking lot, you can choose between several clearly marked trails. Some take you through thick pine forest, some to the top of volcanoes, and others to breathtaking panoramas. Speak with the rangers at the station for information on current trail conditions. The mild 30-minute "Nature Walk" is especially good for those who want a taste of the outdoors, with good views of both Lago de Coatepeque and El Volcán de Santa Ana, without a strenuous hike. The air here is clean and crisp year-round, and the high altitude can bring a serious chill, so bring a jacket. *Admission $2. Open daily 8–5.*

A more serious hike is up the Volcán de Santa Ana, which at 7,800 feet is the highest volcano in El Salvador. Also known as Lamatepec ("Father Hill"), this big daddy is technically still active, although it hasn't erupted in quite some time. A walk to its crater and back takes about four hours, starting from the Cerro Verde parking lot via the "Nature Walk" trail. Prepare for that strong rotten-egg smell, since you'll surely get a whiff of the sulfuric lagoon in the crater. From the rim of the volcano you also get a good view of Cerro Verde and Volcán Izalco, a comparative speck of a volcano at 6,000 ft. The only place to buy food along this hike is at the store in **Finca San Blas,** so you may want to bring some provisions in your backpack.

Other hard-core hikers will want to take on Volcán Izalco, one of the world's youngest volcanoes. This geological rarity was born in 1770, when a small hole near Cerro Verde shot up thousands of feet in less than a month, spewing out molten rock and flames with such violence that sailors dubbed it El Faro del Pacifico (Lighthouse of the Pacific). It's now almost 1,900 m (6,000 ft) high. After almost two centuries of continuous activity, Izalco suddenly went to sleep in 1957, but it may still have some serious fireworks left. Geologists say that so many layers of lava poured down the volcano during its active phase that the cone's surface is almost entirely dead—it takes a mean weed to grow on those gray-black slopes. The climb to the Izalco crater is not as daunting as it appears from the hotel lookout, but it takes about three hours of hard hiking round-trip. Because it's not an often-trodden path, only the adventurous or experienced hiker should attempt it. Head down the main road 494 ft until you see a clear entrance to the forest to your right. Zigzag down to the base of the volcano through the forest, and then pick your best way up. There are a few flat spots to camp among the trees, but those with true grit will want to set up camp on the fine-sand camping spots within the cone itself. Lace up them boots, and be careful of your ankles and the folks below you as you descend this slippery slope. The hardest part of the trip is the hike back up through the forest.

COMING AND GOING • If you are traveling by car, take the CA-1 Pan-American Highway to the Lago de Coatepeque/Cerro Verde exit where you'll find lots of fruit stands and tortilla vendors. Sample some fresh fruit here and then continue on, keeping your eyes peeled for the split in the road. The road to Cerro Verde is off to the left; aggravatingly, it is not marked. Continuing straight will bring you down a winding road lined with tall grass and billboards to a scenic spot from which to view the lake under a canvas tarp, ending at the dirt road to the Lago de Coatepeque hotels. Getting to Cerro Verde without a car can be frustrating, mostly because you may not get enough time here unless you spend the night. The only direct route to Cerro Verde in the country is from Santa Ana, and it takes at least two hours. From Santa Ana, buses that read EL LAGO on them or those that are numbered 348 or 220 leave hourly for Cerro Verde. If you're coming from the capital, you'll have to change buses in El Congo. From San Salvador, take a bus toward Santa Ana and ask to get off in El Congo, near the Cerro Verde exit off the Pan-American Highway. Buses heading to the park pass through El Congo. Any vehicle, including Bus 248, traveling westbound from CA-1 Pan-American Highway and passing through El Congo follows the so-called Carretera Panorámica, which circles Lago de Coatepeque and offers great views of lake, mountain, and volcano. The road also makes it easy to proceed directly to Cerro Verde from the lake, without returning to Santa Ana—simply catch Bus 248 at El Congo. From Sonsonate, take Bus 209 via Cerro Verde, which leaves you at the desvío 14 km (9 mi) from the top; it leaves more or less hourly. Thumbing a ride from the desvío is possible but no sure thing, especially if you're in a group. Also watch out for thieves: robberies are on the rise, especially on the weekends.

WHERE TO SLEEP AND EAT • Hotel de La Montaña is the only game in town, with luxurious rooms for about $30 during the week (the price almost doubles on weekends). It also has a spiffy and expensive restaurant on the premises. The hotel has a somewhat unfortunate history. It was built in the 1950s to have a bird's-eye view of the active Izalco cone. Unfortunately, when construction was finished in 1957, so was the volcano's activity. Park rangers ask that you keep your tent near the parking lot for safety reasons. As for food, you'll find a low-cost comedor along the trail to the *mirador* (lookout) of the Santa Ana volcano, although they don't seem accustomed to serving tourists. Your best bet is to bring a picnic lunch from the city.

SONSONATE

Founded in 1552, Sonsonate is one of the oldest cities in El Salvador. Today, it's a major center for the coffee and cattle industries. It is also just 8 km (5 mi) south of the town of Nahuizalco, where a large population of Pipil has resided for centuries, even prior to Spanish occupation. Indígena from outlying pueblos come to Sonsonate to sell their produce on Calle San Antonio—meander west from the plaza to find some cheap comedores and informal market flavor. Sonsonate is long and narrow, with the bus terminal at one end and the **Plaza Central** and market at the other. **Paseo 15 de Septiembre** is the long street that runs through the middle of town. The large, green Plaza Central merits a few sedentary moments—it's below street level. Other than a visit to some fine colonial churches, you won't find much to see or do in the town proper. Although its beautiful environs are hilly and green, the city itself is run-down and grungy. It's best visited briefly on the way to or from the coast.

BASICS

Sonsonate's banks are open weekdays 9–5, Saturday 9–noon, but you might have trouble changing money after 4 PM. An exception is **Bancasa** (1 Calle Poniente, on Plaza Central), where they will change cash and traveler's checks and process credit card advances any time during open hours. Just off the plaza, **Antel** (Av. Rafael Campo and 2a Calle Oriente) is open daily 7 AM–10 PM. A fine **post office** (4–2 1a Av. Norte) is in a fancy building 2 blocks up from the plaza; it's open weekdays 8–noon and 2–5, Saturday 8–noon, Sunday 8–11.

COMING AND GOING

Sonsonate's **bus terminal** (Calle 15 de Setiembre, between 14a and 16a Avs.) is a 15-minute walk south of the center. Bus 205 leaves every five minutes for San Salvador (1½ hrs, 60¢). To Santa Ana, take Bus 216 (1 hr, 50¢), which leaves every 15 minutes. Bus 259 (2 hrs, 60¢) leaves for La Hachadura at the Guatemalan border every 15 minutes. Your other choice is Bus 249, which leaves every 15 minutes for Ahuachapán (2 hrs, 60¢). From there, it's another 30 minutes to the border crossing at Las Chinamas.

WHERE TO SLEEP

Near the bus terminal, **Hotel Florida** (1–2 18a Av. Sur, tel. 451–0967) rents grungy but livable doubles with fan and shared bath for $7. All the other hotels near the bus terminal rent in 12-hour increments, so they aren't really deals unless you're a latecomer and an early riser. Or, perhaps you should simply head straight for **Hotel Orbe** (2a Av. Sur and 4a Calle Oriente, downhill from plaza, tel. 451–1416 or 451–1517), the best hotel in town. It has 32 clean rooms with great beds and clean, private bathrooms, and it costs $8 for a room with one big bed or $12.50 for a room with two beds; chronic lack of water is thrown in for free.

FOOD

The popular and friendly **Sabor Club** (tel. 451–1751), on the central plaza, serves great licuados, shakes, and cheap lunches, and they even bake their own cakes. Half a block from Antel is **Hilay** (1–3 Av. Rafael Campo, tel. 451–0116), a wannabe Chinese restaurant. The food, although not particularly authentic, isn't bad—the wonton soup is a good effort for $2, and chow mein or chop suey plates with meat cost only $3. Clean, plastic, and air-conditioned **Pizza Atto's** (tel. 451–3878) hosts Sonsonate yuppies in a modern mall next to the bus terminal. Loaded pizzas ($6–$7), including a great veggie combo, are big enough for two modest appetites or one large one. Smaller appetites (or wallets) should try the melted mozzarella sandwich ($1.25) or cruise the salad bar ($2.75). In the late afternoon and early evening, look for señoras selling *pan relleno,* a scrumptious concoction of bread, chicken, salad, and onions that costs 60¢. The women usually set up underneath the BANCO AGRÍCOLA COMERCIAL sign at the central plaza.

NEAR SONSONATE

ATECOZOL TURICENTRO

One of the best-known turicentros in El Salvador, Atecozol is pretty enough to be on a postcard (and it is). It's got basketball and soccer courts, forested trails, mazes of terraced pools, pre-Columbian-style architecture, and an impressive statue of **Atonatl,** an indigenous hero who scored one for the home team by lancing an arrow into the conquistador Pedro de Alvarado in 1524. To get here, take Bus 53a from the plaza or the bus terminal to the town of Izalco (20 min, 10¢). If you tell the bus driver you're going to the turicentro, he'll drop you off and point you in the right direction—it's less than a kilometer from the stop and you'll know you're getting close when you cross a stinky stream.

JUAYUA

Amid the coffee fields and rolling hills north of Sonsonate rests the mild town of Juayúa. This clean community is a place to escape the bustle of commercial centers and (surprise) explore the countryside. One of the local sights is **Los Chorros,** a series of natural waterfalls that, with the help of El Salvador's hydroelectric company ANDA, has become a maze of terraced pools for bathing. The pools are a half-hour walk from the town center: from the cental plaza, walk uphill along 1a Avenida Sur and make your first right on Calle Merceditas Caceres. Continue to the edge of town, bearing right at the fork, and walk another kilometer along the dirt path. Follow one of the narrow paths downhill to your right to an impressive view of the first falls and a good place for a shower. Warning: do not swim back through the tunnels at this waterfall. You may end up with a one-way ticket through the center of the hillside and down to some nasty turbines. Once you finish bathing, head back to the main trail and continue on to explore the remaining terraced falls. There's no lodging in Juayúa, so it's a day trip unless you camp. If you want to sleep over, continue almost to the end of the trail and take the stone steps up to a flat area overlooking the hydroelectric facility. It's a potentially transcendent spot, but bring a bag to clean up the trash left behind by others—it'll improve your stay significantly. Try in the hills or ask to pitch a tent in someone's coffee field. **La Cocina de Lupita** (Calle Merceditas Caceras, near 1a Av. Sur) offers quality food for cheap. You eat whatever's cooking that day—a large meal usually goes for around $1.25. To get to Juayúa (50 min, 25¢), take Bus 249; it leaves every 15 minutes from the Sonsonate terminal.

SALTO LAS VICTORIAS

Two km (1 mi) past the tiny town of **Caluco** are the Las Victorias Waterfalls. The falls themselves are low, wide, and brown—certainly not the epitome of natural beauty. All the same, the walk here takes you through a slew of glorious crop fields and tiny villages, and the waterfall will certainly cool you down. Bus 432 leaves for Caluco (1 hr, 35¢) every couple of hours starting at 6 AM. From there, follow the main trail past the soccer field about 2 kilometers (1 mi). You'll cross railroad tracks and pass through a small village. It's hard to find the falls through all the thick vegetation, but listen for the sound of rushing water and don't give up. If you're coming from the turicentro, just walk back to the main highway, turn right and walk 1,640 ft to the desvío. There you can wait for a bus or a pickup truck heading toward Caluco, or walk the 2 km (1 mi) to town.

SANTO DOMINGO DE GUZMÁN

Santo Domingo de Guzmán was originally an ancient Pipil Indian village called *Toponomia* ("River of Thorns" in the Nahuat language). Today, this small town remembers its indígena heritage much more than other parts of the country, and a few people continue to speak Nahuat exclusively. Talk to the owner of the small kiosk at the town center or the director of the **Casa de Cultura**—both are lively and knowledgeable people who will answer all your burning questions. The Casa de Cultura is on your left across from Antel on your way to the falls. If you read Spanish, ask to see the *Monografía de Santo Domingo de Guzmán,* a document that outlines cultural, economic, and historical information on the community. Many of the townswomen are excellent sculptors. Elizabeth García and her daughters run a workshop where you can admire or purchase a variety of sculptures and vases for $2–$4. Look for it behind Antel, around the corner from the Casa de Cultura. Unfortunately, Santo Domingo de Guzmán does not have any hospedajes, and the hilly, rocky area is not especially tent-friendly. Ask at the alcaldía or at the police, both near the center of town, about sleeping on the hard floor of the **Casa Comunal**—there shouldn't be a problem and it's free. There are a few nameless comedores around town; one is yellow and near the town center and another is green and located at the entrance to town. Ask early to make sure they will be serving that day. From Sonsonate, take Bus 246 from Calle San Antonio (*not* from the terminal); it leaves every 45 minutes beginning at 7:15 AM. The trip takes at least 40 minutes over a crude road. Unless you plan to stay the night, go early—the last bus out of Santo Domingo Guzmán leaves at 3:30 PM, and passing pickup trucks become infrequent around the same time.

The reason that most travelers come to Santo Domingo Guzmán is to experience the dramatic and isolated natural beauty of the nearby **waterfalls.** A word of warning: the journey to these falls is not just a stroll through the forest. You'll have to stone-step across a river several times, and, depending on path conditions, you may have to walk in it for some distance. But don't miss the opportunity because of the difficulties—just come prepared. About a half-hour walk from town, **Salto El Escuco,** also called *El Saltillo* (the little waterfall), is the nearer of the two falls. From the bus stop, follow the main drag to its end and bear right across the footbridge. After about 1,640 ft, the road narrows into a trail along the right side of the river. Cross the river by hopping those slippery rocks, and continue around a small pasture— you might have to open a barbed-wire gate, but it's there to keep cattle in, not you out. From here, listen for the falls and be ready to traverse plenty of wet boulders and a couple of short but hair-raising ledges. The falls are an awesome sight. The river plummets more than 150 ft into a small pond at the bottom, which is prime for bathing. If you don't mind the wispy wet air, there may be some sand here on which to pitch a tent. The truly adventurous should return to the main part of the river and follow it to the 300-ft **Salto La Tepechapa,** also called *El Saltón* (the big waterfall). Getting here depends upon your dexterity and stamina. The trails along the river are only about a foot wide, and you'll end up using the riverbank and even the river itself as you go. A competent hiker can make the trip in about two hours. Since there aren't any signs marking the way, ask passersby if you're heading in the right direction. You can also hire a competent guide in Santo Domingo for about $3, or flash that winning smile and make some friends—you may find someone to accompany you for free. Politely recompense with food and drink. If your trip to the falls left you thirsting for more, or if you don't feel like making the trip, visit **Los Arcos,** a natural arch-shaped bridge 2 km (1 mi) south of town.

PACIFIC COAST

The Pacific coast of El Salvador is truly a vacation destination. The 320-km (200-mi) coast is dotted with beautiful bays, tropical lagoons, and marshy areas that are home to an amazing variety of birds and other wildlife. Don't expect to find a secluded tropical paradise—towns take up the nicer stretches of sandy coast, and elsewhere rocky cliffs drop straight down into the crashing surf. A top-quality highway, Central America 2, runs the length of the coast, making for a beautiful drive as far east as Acajutla. About midway along the highway is the big, boring town of **Zacatecoluca** (rhymes with "pack a Czech bazooka"), 60 km (37 mi) southeast of the capital. The city itself is completely forgettable, but it's one of the best departure points for the elite and exquisite Costa del Sol. The Pacific coast is *the* vacation spot for anyone in the country who can afford to vacation, so it can get crowded; time your visit right (i.e., come during the week) or accept the company gracefully, and your visit here will be quite relaxing.

LA LIBERTAD AND
THE COSTA BÁLSAMO

Costa Bálsamo runs from Acajutla east to the main vacation town of La Libertad. The region is named for the indigenous but now-scarce balsam trees that once were the world's richest source of the medicinal resin. Nowadays the 75-km (46-mi) stretch is a vacation area where you can expect to share the sand, especially on weekends when it fills up like a fat pupusa. Although Libertad is by far the most popular spot, the beach here isn't as good as lesser-known gems nearby. Unlike most other beaches in El Salvador, these have surfers in abundance. The point just west of town sports a world-class wave, while venerable Playa Zunzal is the most famous beach on the Costa Bálsamo. It's considered by many to offer the best surfing in Central America.

Once El Salvador's premier shipping port, La Libertad has a new raison d'être—it's a growing and worthwhile fun-in-the-sun hot spot. The black volcanic sand tends toward the mucky, but the water and waves are awesome. Less experienced swimmers should watch out for the undertow, and all should keep their ears open for shark (*tiburón*) warnings. One of the more interesting events of the day is the return of the fishing boats to the pier, where they're hoisted up with a winch in a procedure that is sometimes scary and always entertaining. The pier itself is the site of the **mercado,** with oodles of fresh fish and shellfish. The big trawlers come in on Sundays and hold a colorful fish and crustacean auction. The **Complejo Turístico de La Libertad** (admission $1; open daily 7–5) lies just east of the pier and has the usual restaurants, tiendas, swimming pools, and basketball courts. Those thirsting for *el ritmo latino* should stop by the **Casa Comunal** (Av. Bolívar, between Calle Calvario and 1a Calle Poniente) to see when the next dance party will happen; usually it's on a Friday, Saturday, or Sunday.

The only way to rent surfboards is from Yepi, a local fellow who also shapes them. He lives on 4a Calle Poniente, next to Hotel Amor y Paz and across from Sandra's Restaurant. Yepi doesn't always have rental boards available, but when he does he rents them for about $2 per hour, or make him an offer for the whole day. Check early for availability and you might not even have to leave a big deposit. **Antel** (open 6 AM–8 PM) is on 2a Calle Oriente, at 2a Avenida Sur; the **post office** (open weekdays 8–noon and 1:30–5, Sat. 8–noon, Sun. 8–11) is around the corner on 2a Avenida Sur. Most of the hotels, restaurants, and action lie along 5a Avenida Sur, which stretches south to the water, and along 4a Calle Poniente, along the coast to the east. **Playa Conchalío** offers decent swimming just a kilometer west of town; head west on 2a Calle Poniente, cross the bridge, and make your first left.

COMING AND GOING

La Libertad doesn't have a bus terminal. Buses generally pass through on Calle Calvario heading west, or on 2a Calle Poniente heading east. From the capital (1 hr, 30¢), Bus 102 leaves every 15 minutes from Parque Bolívar at 4a Calle Poniente and 13a Avenida Sur. From Zacatecoluca, Bus 540 leaves only a few times per day before noon. Buses 80 and 192 go to nearby beaches (15¢–20¢), leaving frequently from 4a Avenida Sur and Calle Calvario.

WHERE TO SLEEP

Fancy, expensive hotels abound in La Libertad, frequented by wealthy *capitalinos* taking long weekends. On the east end of town, elegant **Hotel El Malecón de Don Lito** (east of the turicentro, tel. 335–3201) has $40 air-conditioned rooms with private baths, a restaurant with reasonably priced seafood, and a swimming pool right on the ocean. (If you look around, you'll invariably notice quite a Don Lito monopoly around town. All his hotels offer about the same accommodations at basically the same price.) A good budget bet is **La Posada Familiar** (5a Av. Sur and 4a Calle Poniente, tel. 335–3252), where basic, clean rooms with private baths go for $15, but try to make a deal with the friendly manager, especially if you're staying more than one night. **Hotel Rick** (4a Calle Poniente and 5 Av. Norte, tel. 335-3033) is where the surfers stay (and eat) in simple, clean rooms with private baths that cost somewhere between $12 and $18. Just outside of town, about 5 km (3 mi) west of La Libertad on the Coastal Highway, is the pleasurable **Hotel Los Arcos** (tel. 335–3490), where spare, large, air-conditioned rooms with particularly hard beds surround a courtyard, fountain, and—believe it or not—heated pool. While here you've got to try the seafood, particularly the fried fish stuffed with shrimp and slathered in onions—the medium-size order will be larger than your plate. Rooms ($30–$40) can be a little noisy.

FOOD

In Libertad, you're in for mostly seafood at expensive-to-moderate prices. There are a few budget joints, though. At **Comedor Carnitas Lucy** (2a Calle Oriente and 2a Av. Sur, across from Antel), standard prepared foods and great scrambled-egg breakfasts reign supreme—just about anything you'd want costs $1.50–$3. West of the center, **Pupusería El Viajero** (2a Calle Poniente, across bridge) is rumored to have the best pupusas in town, but unfortunately it's often closed. Even vegans can find a home at **Fuente de Salud Naturista Emmanuel** (Calle Calvario and 3a Av. Norte). See what's cookin' in the kitchen—the vegetable soups are sublime and cost only about $1. Soy-milk licuados are also available for 60¢. More expensive seafood restaurants line 4a Calle Poniente, west of Avenida Bolívar, continuing around the curve down 5a Avenida Sur getting ritzier as you go. **Restaurante El Viejo Alta Mar** (Calle 4a Poniente) satisfies seafood cravings for modest prices. Try a $8 fish plate, or the $7 *mariscada* (seafood soup). **Restaurant Punta Roca** (Calle 4a Poniente) and **El Delfín** (Calle 4a Poniente and 5a Av. Norte) are two tasty choices for medium-to-high priced lunch, dinner, or drinks along the water. A similar strip lies just east of town on Playa Obispo. These restaurants also host the majority of Libertad's nightlife, with folks gathering to drink and listen to music. Solo stragglers should avoid Rancho Irraman on 4a Calle Poniente; it's a lively youth gang hangout.

NEAR LA LIBERTAD

COSTA BÁLSALMO BEACHES

Beaches here tend to be either good for swimming and sunbathing or good for surfing, but usually not both. Several great surf beaches lie west of La Libertad, including **Playa Zunzal** and **Playa El Zonte.** Both have rocky shores and fairly consistent breaks. Zunzal has a good, safe right-point break, which is not as intense as the break in town. El Salvador's biggest swells are to be found June through November. Official lodging is available in La Libertad, but an unnamed comedor is available where you can eat a great fish dinner for less than $1. East of Libertad, **Playa San Diego** has relatively clean sand and moderate waves. Be careful of riptides: they might not look that bad, but drownings are not unheard-of. The bus will drop you off by an area dotted with restaurants and prison-style one-bed cabañas that go for about $4.50 per night. If you're not looking for food or lodging, get off earlier on the dirt road and cross on a path through the houses to the beach. Bus 80 travels east–west, passing any given point every half hour. From Libertad, it's 30 minutes west to Zunzal, and 45 minutes to Zonte. Playa San Diego is 30 minutes east of Libertad.

THE COSTA DEL SOL

The "Coast of the Sun" stretches southeast from La Libertad to El Zapote (due south of Zacatecoluca). Salvadorans come from every corner of the country to enjoy the beaches here, so don't expect an untouched tropical getaway replete with your own coconut grove. The most developed area lies along a thin strip of land separating the **Jalatepeque estuary** from the ocean; these beaches are all beautiful and clean, with strong waves and fine sand. These 15 km (9 mi) are also among the richest in El Salvador—fabulous homes (easily mistaken for large hotels), lots of Mercedes Benzes, and sky-high price tags adorn the beaches. Be careful not to wander onto someone's private property: many homes have private guards or attack dogs.

El Zapote is an entertaining, often crowded, beach town. Tons of day-trippers come to swim at the beach and hang out at the multitude of thatch-roofed eateries. If you've got some time, visit one of the nearby estuary islands and their cool beaches. Hire a boat at the Jaltapeque estuary by El Zapote; it'll cost you anywhere from $5 to $10 per boatload each way. A little haggling is okay. Solo travelers should try water-hitching—just offer a few bucks to tag along on a boat that's already been hired out. Watch out for the unpredictable currents by the mouth of the estuary. The town of **Los Blancos,** 7 km (4½ mi) west of El Zapote, is the only comparatively "budget" spot in the area, although it's actually little more than a beachside cluster of restaurants and hospedajes that don't overcharge.

COMING AND GOING

A single road runs east to El Zapote, at the end of the peninsula. From Terminal de Occidente in San Salvador, Bus 495 leaves for El Zapote (2½ hrs, 60¢) about every half hour. If you're already in El Zapote, it might be much faster and easier to hitch a ride with a microbus—ask around at the vans; you shouldn't pay much more than $2. If you're coming east from La Libertad or Zacatecoluca, ask to be let off at the **Los Arcos** desvío and wait for a bus the rest of the way to the beach.

WHERE TO SLEEP

Luxury accommodations dominate the region. The nicest of the bunch is **Izalco Cabaña Club** (next to turicentro, tel. 334–0614 or 263–0044, fax 264–1170), where air-conditioned rooms with private baths facing the beach run about $85. Another ritzy hotel is the **Costa del Sol Club** (25a Av. Sur and 4a Calle Pte., tel. 222-6764 or 222-8249 for reservations, 334–0630 for the hotel), where overnight rates (around $100) often include meals. Access to sports facilities, including minigolf and pools, is also standard. Small **Kennymar** (no phone) in Playa San Marcelino is a budget option on the beach at about $15. In Playa Los Blancos, the **Hotel Pacific Paradise** (on the Playa El Zapote strip, tel. 260–6256 or 271–2606) is a little dilapidated but has private bungalows ($100) and less expensive singles ($60), all with private bath, TV, and air-conditioning. Lovely gazebos, hammocks, and beachfront property compensate for the lack of decor. Truly cheap, possibly grungy additional places can be found in Los Blancos.

FOOD

The quality of the food, especially the seafood, in the area is good, but you might find yourself paying New York City prices at the hotel and resort restaurants. Alternatively, you could visit a tienda for picnic items or try one of the stands outside the turicentro. Another option is **Restaurante El Gran Chema**, less than a kilometer east of the turicentro in Los Blancos. Seafood at this big and busy eatery is good, if not spectacular, and you can fill up for around $3. The outdoor restaurants in El Zapote charge about the same for decent *típica* food.

USULUTÁN

Lying 30 km (19 mi) southwest of San Miguel, this former center of the pre-Pibil Lenca civilization shows virtually no memory, opinion, or appreciation of its pre-Columbian past. Today, Usulután is a big, drab city of 70,000 that makes a good jumping-off point for a number of coastal destinations, including Laguna El Jocotál, a protected reserve for migratory birds. The architectural centerpiece of Usulután is a camouflaged tower (8a Calle and 8a Av.), a local legacy of the civil war when guerrillas attacked the garrison to interrupt peace talks. Almost everything you'll need or want can be found in or near the **plaza central.** Just a block from the municipal building on Calle Grimeldi, **Antel** is open daily 6 AM–9 PM. The **Casa de Cultura,** attached to the municipal building on Calle Malera, is worth a visit if you're planning to stay in the area. A stroll through the market areas will reveal the city's dependence upon shrimp, as huge baskets overflow with the tasty little critters. Death aficionados can visit the very colorful **cemetery** just outside the city; to get there take any westbound bus and ask to be let off at *el cementerio*. At night you shouldn't stray far from the center: the streets empty by early evening, and the surrounding area is only marginally safe.

COMING AND GOING

The **bus terminal** lies about a 10-minute walk east, down the main highway. The following buses leave every 10–15 minutes, with service starting around 4 AM and ending around 4:30 PM to 6 PM: Bus 373 to San Miguel (1½ hrs, 60¢), Bus 302 to Zacatecoluca (1¼ hrs, 60¢), Bus 349 to Santiago de María (1 hr, 45¢), Bus 363 to Puerto El Triunfo (1 hr, 30¢).

WHERE TO SLEEP

If Costa del Sol hotels are beyond your means, you may want to base yourself here. Comfy, clean rooms with private baths and air-conditioning are about $15 at **Hotel Palmera** (5 mi east of town on Costal Hwy., tel. 662–0161), which, with a pool and restaurant, is an especially resourceful choice unless you don't want to be on the outskirts of town. Simply put, **Hotel España** (Calle Grimeldi, just off Parque Central, tel. 662–0378) is a good, cheap place to spend the night. Big, clean, bug-free double rooms are $12 with private bath, $10 without—the general baths are actually clean and work fine. The patio is covered with large plants, giving the place a pleasant, healthy aura. The in-house restaurant has a long table where guests eat or watch the tube; the cooks make whatever they have, and plates average $3. You get clean rooms with puny bathrooms at **Hotel Florida** (26 4a Calle Oriente, tel. 662–0540) for next to nothing. The outdoor hammocks are a pleasant touch, but the 10 PM curfew here may cramp your style. Florida's little restaurant serves soft drinks, beer, and basic meals at moderate prices. Follow 4a Calle Oriente up from the plaza or down from the bus terminal and look for the big green door (no sign).

Another option is the **Posada del Viajero** (6a Calle Ote, between 2a and 4a Av. Norte, tel. 662–0217), where there's a local vibe and a cute courtyard and doubles cost less than $10.

FOOD

Simple outdoor stands line the park and are good places to stop and enjoy cheap eats or a drink. Let's face it, pizza in Central America is no great shakes. That said, **Family Pizza** (4 Av. Guandique, near plaza, tel. 662–0272) actually makes a pretty decent pie with a lot of cheese, good veggies, golden crust, but virtually no tomato sauce. A medium-sized meat or veggie pizza ($6–$7) should be plenty for two people. The rather upscale **Lathyno's Restaurant** (2 Av. Guandique, near plaza, tel. 662–0674) has a relaxing patio, fountain, bar, and good food. The house specialty is a high-grade steak dinner, which costs around $9. Vegetarians will enjoy the *espagueti a la primavera* (pasta and veggies in white sauce) with salad and garlic bread for $4—politely ask them to go easy on the salt. Big salads and a variety of specialty omelets cost around $3, while chicken dishes run around $5. **Café Terraza** (4a Calle Ote, between Av. Dr. Guandiquil and 2a Av. Norte, no phone) serves inexpensive light fare, snacks, and beverages to its youthful clientele. **Restaurant Don Rancho** (1a Calle Ote, no phone) also has cheap sandwiches, fries, and salads among other snack-like foods presented buffet-style. Next door you'll find a **Pollo Campero,** the ubiquitous El Salvadoran chicken-in-a-bucket joint.

NEAR USULUTÁN

PUERTO EL TRIUNFO

The best reason to visit Usulután is its proximity to this little harbor and the delightful cluster of islands in the **Bahía de Jiquilisco,** an estuary for mangrove trees and seabirds. Passenger boats travel regularly to Isla Coral de Mula, but to others you'll have to carefully negotiate your own travel arrangements. Puerto El Triunfo itself is just another large fishing village; you don't want to swim here—ships dump their garbage wherever they want, and the water smells of the town's refuse. In a big red-and-white building 1½ blocks from the park where the buses line up, **Hotel Jardín** (1a Av. Sur) has a dozen shabby but okay rooms if you've got to stay here; a double with bath goes for $6. The big restaurant inside serves standard seafood and meat dishes for $2–$4; it also doubles as a bar where local fishermen and drivers gather for some serious drinking and roughhousing. Near the park are a number of small stands and pupuserías. If you're not squeamish about drinking unpurified water, try an iced *fresco de arrayan,* a light, sweet, fruit drink that makes life worth living in the heat. To get to Puerto El Triunfo, take Bus 363, which leaves from Usulután's bus terminal (1 hr, 30¢) every 15 minutes. If you're traveling west to Zacatecoluca or the capital, get off at the desvío, where you can flag down a passing bus.

From the port, catch a boat to the nearby bay islands. None of the island villages have lodging, but camping is a good option, if you've come equipped for it. **Corral de Mulas** is one of the larger bayside communities—it is often referred to as another island, even though it actually rests on a peninsula. A walk across the peninsula will bring you to a magnificent clean fine-sand beach, one of the finest in El Salvador. You'll probably be the only one dodging coconuts and playing Robinson Crusoe. Put your tent near the palm trees (beware of falling coconuts); a hearty ocean breeze keeps the bugs at bay. Alternatively, rent $2 hammocks and eat cheap, decent home-cooking at the home of **María Luisa Anaya,** next to the short pier. You can also check out several bay islands, including **Isla Madresal,** where cool beaches and clean, mellow surf are the norm. Best of all, it's possible to visit them on the cheap because local passenger boats charge just $1–$2 per person. If you're not planning to spend the night, you'll have to get an early start (6 or 7 AM) and make sure your boat makes a return trip in the afternoon. Otherwise, you'll have to shell out $10–$15 to hire a private boat to bring you back. If you can find a willing boat-lender, try renting by the day.

LAGUNA EL JOCOTAL

This small marsh between Usulután and San Miguel is an unofficial sanctuary for migratory birds. You can view herons, egrets, and other waterbirds feeding on fish among the mangroves and tall marsh grasses. Getting here is no simple task, however, and is only worth it if you're an avid bird-watcher and have mud-proof boots. From the Coastal Highway, take the Cantón Borabollón exit, which degenerates into mud after a mile. Local fishermen can be approached for a lift to the lagoon for a few dollars.

ISLA DE SAN SEBASTIÁN

This beautiful bay island merits a visit—for now. For some years now it's been targeted as the area with the most potential for tourist development in El Salvador. Visit *before* the island's tranquil fishing hamlets become Club Med-landia. To get here from Usulután, take Bus 298 to Puerto Parada (1 hr, 35¢); it leaves every hour and a half starting at 5 AM. From there, catch a boat to San Sebastián.

VOLCAN DE USULUTÁN

It's a serious trek to the summit of this 4,800-ft volcano. The bus to the pueblo of **Gualache** passes the bus terminal infrequently. From there, it's at least two hours of good hiking to the top; ask in town for a guide or for directions to the correct trail. For an even longer hike, walk toward the volcano up 9a Avenida Norte, which becomes Calle La Peña and enters a small village; just keep walking straight. At the top, good views of the countryside await.

LA UNIÓN

On the Golfo de Fonseca, about 45 km (28 mi) southeast of San Miguel, this nondescript port town offers access to nearby volcano trekking, beaches, and the Islas Salvadoreñas (*see below*). The beaches in town are bunk—don't even bother. La Unión itself is slow, hot, and easygoing. Use it as a way station rather than a destination. This is the country's second-largest port, and shipping is the livelihood for many residents, while others are dependent on the large fishing industry. For visitors, there is a bit of dining and dancing nightlife here worth checking out. **Calle General Menéndez** is the main drag, dividing numbered avenidas into north (toward the sea) and south. Numbered calles run parallel to Calle Menéndez and the waterfront. A well-maintained and attractive **church** (Calle General Menéndez and 1a Av. Norte) faces the large **plaza central.** The **mercado** spans the block between 1a and 3a avenidas Norte along Calle Menéndez; it goes steadily from a little after sunrise until late afternoon and (big surprise) is a great place to find cheap tasty grub. Many banks and casas de cambio will change dollars, but **Banco Cuscatlán** (Av. General Cabañas, next to plaza) will also change traveler's checks if you have the original receipt. It's open weekdays 8:30–4:30, Saturday 8:30–noon. **Antel** (1a Calle Oriente and 5a Av. Norte) is open daily 7 AM–9 PM.

COMING AND GOING

The **bus station** is in the north end of town on 3a Calle Poniente, 1 block from the waterfront. Bus 301 runs from San Salvador's Terminal de Oriente (3 hrs, $1.50). Bus 324 from San Miguel, Bus 342 from Santa Rosa de Lima, and Bus 383 from El Tamarindo all take about 1½ hours, and cost 60¢. If you're catching a boat out of town, note that the docks are actually a couple of kilometers outside the city in **Cutuco.** Cargo ships leave for Nicaragua several times per week and will take you on the three-hour ride for around $18 (definitely bargain). Although you should by no means count on this, you also may be able to find a sea ride to Honduras.

WHERE TO SLEEP

Stay away from the grimy hotels near the market, except **Casa de Huéspedes El Dorado** (2a Av. Norte and Calle San Carlos, tel. 664–4724)—not to be confused with the grungy *Hospedaje* El Dorado—where for $6 you get a large double with private bathroom, clean towels, a hammock, and a fan. The beds are big, the private baths are scrupulously clean, and everything works. The **Hotel Portobello La Union** (4a Av. between 1a Calle and Calle San Carlos, tel. 664–4113) is a relatively new, clean, and family-run place that has cheap $5–$10 rooms with private baths, hammocks, and on-site parking. The **Hotel Centroamericano** (4a Calle Oriente, between 1a and 3a Avs. Sur, tel. and fax. 664–4029) has $15 rooms that are large but somewhat institutional. You'll probably share a bathroom with another room, but the hotel often plays host to various cool organizations, so you might meet some interesting folks. Call ahead for reservations. **Hotel San Francisco** (Calle General Menéndez, between 9a and 11a Avs. Sur, tel. 664–4159) covers all the basics in decent fashion: big rooms, big comfy beds, fans, private baths, towels, water, and laundry sinks. A big plus is the second-floor balcony, perfect for chillin' with your sweetie or a beer (or both). The $6 rooms all have one double bed and one hammock; if you want air-conditioning, fork over $15. Rooms away from the street are quieter.

FOOD

Comedor y Pupusería Marya (Calle General Menéndez, at 11a Av. Norte) is a decent, family-run dive serving basic meat and chicken plates for about $2. Near the church, **Pastelería y Batijugos Claudita** (Calle General Menéndez and 3a Av. Norte) serves stellar licuados ($1.50) and has a small bakery; the large mushroom pizza ($8) will feed two or more.

Specializing in Mexican food and seafood, **Gallo's Restaurante** (3a Av. Sur and 4a Calle Oriente, tel. 664–4282) serves good chicken fajitas ($4.50) and an even better fish fillet prepared in garlic butter and white wine ($5). Vegetarians will enjoy the enchilada Santa Rosa ($3.50), made with with melted cheese, guacamole, rice, and beans. This is also the entertainment spot of La Unión, where strolling mariachi bands drop by after dark to play all night, so put on your boogie shoes. The well-stocked bar makes this the place to tie one on, although you'll have to walk through a poorly lighted and somewhat freaky area to get back to the main drag; seriously consider taking a taxi home.

AFTER DARK

La Unión's nightlife isn't exactly booming. However, there's potential here and you do have a few choices. At the end of 11a Avenida, **Miramar** and **Amanacer Marino** are expensive seafood restaurants, but budget diners can afford the *bocas* (appetizers) and the ocean view is free. If you're feeling frisky, you can usually rent a four-piece mariachi band for just under $2 a song. Near the water, **Discotec Amigos** (end of 3a Av. Norte) is your typical disco scene favored by a young crowd. On Wednesdays at 7 PM they show movies for 60¢, and Thursday–Saturday from 7 PM to 2 AM you can dance to various Latin and rock grooves. Lastly, don't forget about **Gallo's** (*see above*), where it's always a party. You'll appreciate a local gesture shared by all of these eateries: a truly brilliant mind decided that complementary bocas are to be served with their beer.

NEAR LA UNION

VOLCAN DE CONCHAGUA

If you're up for a day-long volcano trek, head over to the nearby town of **Conchagua,** where you can climb the volcano of the same name. The hike to the 4,100-ft summit is only about 4 km (2½ mi), but the uphill grind through pine trees and a cooler microclimate will take at least two hours. The fabulous views of the bay and surrounding islands are worth the work. If you squint into the distance, you may be able to spot Honduras. Buses to Conchagua (15¢) pass the bus station several times an hour starting at 6 AM.

PLAYITAS

Traveling the few miles to the simple fishing village of Playitas or one of the nearby islands (*see below*) will make your visit to La Unión much more pleasurable. Playitas is just what the name advertises: a little black-sand beach—you can walk its length in a couple of minutes. At one side the land curves and juts out a bit toward Islas Conchagüita and Meanguera. Explorers can follow this around; but beware, many of the seaside rocks are unstable and a briar patch of *chichicates* (stinging nettles) that would daunt even Peter Rabbit claims the vegetated area above the rocks. **Tienda y Mariscos Marleny** is the best restaurant in town, with an outstanding whole fried-fish lunch for less than $2. It's also a hospedaje, where a double with a good bed, fan, and private bath will set you back $3.50. From La Unión, Bus 418 to Playitas (40¢) leaves from the defunct railway station at 3a Avenida Sur and 4a Calle Oriente several times per day, starting at 9 AM. Although a direct ride would take little more than a half-hour, you should count on double that because the bus stops every few hundred feet to drop off passengers and their week's shopping. Infrequent pickup trucks also make the trip.

ISLANDS

If you want to get to one or more of the nearby gulf islands, you'll have to go with a fisherman—there isn't a tourist boat in sight. Prices vary according to how good the boat owner's catch has been lately, his first impression of you, and your ability to haggle effectively in Spanish. Most of these salty sea captains talk a very fast, mumbled, and slang-filled Spanish: make *sure* you've got a mutual understanding before you get into the boat, and that the price is *ida y vuelta* (round-trip). Your best bet is to cut a half-now-half-later deal with someone who'll drop you off and pick you up. The best time to get a boat is early in the morning around 5 or 6. That means catching a pickup from La Unión at 4 AM or spending the night in Playitas. Most boats leave the islands around 4 PM; if you're not ready to return when they are, you'll have to camp for the night. Local authorities don't seem to mind the spontaneous camping, and the islands all have plenty of lush vegetation, beautiful palm trees waving in the wind, and deserted beaches. **Zacatillo** and **Conchagüita** are the closest islands to Playitas. Both are great for hikers and solitary sun-worshipers. Trips to these should run $7–$13. **Isla Meanguera,** about 40 minutes away by boat, has a small fishing village with a hospedaje. Meanguera has been the object of a bitter territorial dispute with Honduras, and Salvadorans are mighty proud that their neighbor hasn't been able to take possession. On weekends, you might be able to catch a ride on one of the cargo boats leaving

Meanguera for the scenic trip to La Unión. If you're coming here from Honduras, make *sure* you have an El Salvador visa and proper entry documentation. If found without, you'll have plenty of trouble and probably a stiff fine. In Meanguera you might also find a boat to Honduras, but no guarantees.

EL TAMARINDO

On a sheltered bay 19 km (12 mi) south of La Unión, this fishing village is delightful, if a bit smelly. It has minimal tourist facilities and more character than some of the highly frequented spots up the coast. Thousands of fish lie drying under the sun, destined for kitchens far and wide, and thatched houses line paths that wind their way helter-skelter to the ocean. The beach itself is inviting, with timid waves, fine sand, clean water, and great views of the islands. Visit for the day or part of one. Keep north or south of the village to avoid its litter problem and on weekdays you'll practically have this beach wonderland to yourself. Camping is possible but the strip is narrow—your tent will practically be in the water—and local hospedajes are not recommended. Spend the night in Playa Negra (*see below*). For cheap eats, however, check out **Comedor Viajero** down the road toward town, where good, whatever's-in-the-pot meals go for $1–$2. Not far from Tamarindo is **Las Tunas,** another beach of similar character, although with a wealthier, more developed hotel strip a few kilometers away from the main village. Several buses, including Bus 383, come here directly from La Unión's bus station (1½ hrs, 35¢). Beware of opportunistic drivers inviting you aboard the bus for Intipucá: it's faster but drops you off on the wrong side of the inlet of El Tamarindo, so you'll have to walk more than a kilometer and catch a ferry (25¢) to the other side. Hitching is quite common in these parts.

PLAYA NEGRA

If your travels have you jaded, stop at this beach area for comfy lodging options and decent sit-down restaurants. **The Hotel Playa Negra** (on the road to El Tamarindo, tel. 661–1726) is an affordable choice with air-conditioned doubles and triples with baths ($35–$45), a pool, and, lo-and-behold, a 24-hour restaurant. **Torolo Cabāna Club** (Playa El Tamarindo, La Unión, tel. 263–0044) is new, stylish, and has $85 rooms with beach views (about $70 without). You can take in the ocean scene from the pricey restaurant, too. A good, medium-priced seafood joint nearby is **Restaurant La Mariscada,** where you dine under brightly colored umbrellas from 7 AM until 10 PM.

EASTERN EL SALVADOR

Many towns in the east are basic El Salvador, and some have interesting artisan traditions, but the hub of the east, San Miguel, is your textbook large third-world city. The region also has a couple of enjoyable, little-known surprises; south of the main east–west highway near Santiago de María is a rugged mountain chain where volcanic lakes, sulfuric baths, and great off-the-beaten track camping and hiking await. In many areas rolling hills, cattle pastures, pigs, chickens and the hard-working, insular, but warm and welcoming culture of the campesino predominate. For many, the Morazán department north of San Miguel is a discomforting surprise; as one of the most war-torn, impoverished, least populated, and hottest areas in the nation, it is rough traveling but scenic and eye-opening.

COJUTEPEQUE

Cojutepeque, 45 minutes east of San Salvador, is a happening city well worth visiting. The town's main attraction is the **Cerro De Pavas** ("Hill of Turkeys"—although there are no turkeys in sight, unless you count the soldiers lurking around the site). To get here from the **parque central,** walk through the long, narrow **mercado** along Avenida Raul Contreras; you'll find **Antel** (open 6 AM–10 PM) on your right. From there, several roads lead straight up to the top and make for a leisurely half-hour walk or a heart-starting jog. For an inkling of what El Salvador was like before it was largely deforested, scurry up the lushly vegetated middle route where you're likely to see a few interesting animal species, such as the grand fluttering blue morpho butterfly and the usual populations of fiery *parejas* (couples) smooching away. Don't go alone unless you're truly undaunted by the constant warnings about thieves on remote hills. At the summit you'll find beautiful views of Lago de Ilopango and the countryside, as well as the shrine of the **Virgen de Fátima.** The statue was brought here in 1949 from Portugal, where the Virgin was first sighted in 1917—the sighting was eventually declared a miracle by the Vatican. Be on your best behavior—it is a holy place for the pilgrims who come here. Not surprisingly, the army has made its presence felt on this strategic hilltop—the best views are from the soldiers' posts at the summit. They will let you visit; just relax and don't act suspicious. The Virgin's **festival** day is May 13, a particularly popular day for visitors. To get to Cohutepeque (45 min, 25¢) from San Salvador, take Bus 113 from across from Terminal de Oriente; it leaves every half hour until 6:30 PM.

WHERE TO SLEEP AND EAT

At **Motel Villalobo** you'll get a relatively decent room with shared bath for $5–$7, depending on whether you leave by the evil 7 AM checkout time. Villalobo is in a sort of minisuburb—from the church, head down Avenida Santa Ana until you reach the highway, then turn right and walk less than a kilometer until you pass the soccer field. From there, go downhill to your left and take the first right onto Calle Principal, the first left onto Avenida Los Dinámicos; you'll see it on your right. **Panadería Fátima** (317 2a Av. Sur, 1 block from the church) is possibly the best bakery in the country, with wonderful, fresh-baked cookies, cakes, and breads. At **BBQ Barbacoa** (Calle J. Francisco López, 1 block downhill from church, below Leo's Pizzeria), you'll find a variety of Salvadoran, Mexican, American, and Italian dishes for $2–$4. The cheeseburger with avocado will rock your world, and baked potatoes with broccoli are a find; both set you back less than $2. For your Saturday night fever, ask what's going down at **Los Pichardos Restaurant and Disco** (Av. Santa Ana at 7a Calle, near the ice-cream shop) or at **Restaurant Kativos** (2 km, or 1 mi, back by highway), where on weekends there are often live bands.

SAN VICENTE

The city of San Vicente, 50 km (31 mi) east of San Salvador, is something of a mixed blessing. The town is charming and tranquil with a flair of colonial elegance, but a military compound with black-booted, machine gun–toting soldiers interrupts the grace of the city. In the 1830s, San Vicente was the country's temporary capital. Today it is an unpretentious middle-class city that serves as a base for several interesting day trips. Unless you have particular reason to fear the military, get used to them—most of the soldiers are just kids anyway and will not mind directing confused travelers.

The town doesn't offer much by way of architecture, and even the church is ho-hum. The one obvious exception is the unusual **clock tower** right in the middle of the **parque central**—the top offers a terrific view of the city; find the park attendant to open the gate so you can climb up the stairs. He claims the lock is to prevent high-dive suicides, but it's probably a military precaution. The enormous military compound stretches from the park a full block to 1a Avenida; you only wish you could miss it. Just a little way outside town is the **Amapulapa turicentro** (admission 90¢, open daily 7:30–5:30), where folks come to picnic and swim in a huge concrete pool with a high dive. There are kids everywhere, and the green water is *a la natural*. To get to the turicentro, catch a pickup headed left down the road at the T-fork before Hospedaje Diamento (*see* Where to Sleep, *below*). Rumor has it that there's a trail leading to nearby Volcán Chichontepec (*see* Near San Vicente, *below*), but you'll have to ask around.

BASICS

On the side of the park opposite the military base, you'll find **Antel** (open daily 6:30 AM–9:30 PM) a half-block from the church. Down a bit farther is the **post office** (Calle 1 de Julio and 2a Av. Norte), open weekdays 8–noon and 2–5, Saturday 8–noon, Sunday 8–11. The local branch of **Banco Hipotecario** faces the main square and is open weekdays 9–6, Saturday 9–noon.

COMING AND GOING

To get to San Vicente from the capital (1½ hrs, 50¢), take Bus 116 from Terminal de Oriente; it leaves every 15 minutes until 6:30 PM. Bus 301 travels to and from San Miguel; it stops on the main highway a few kilometers outside town. From the center of town, you can take a local bus to get to the desvío where you can flag down other buses as they pass through. You could also walk to the junction—it's long but scenic.

WHERE TO SLEEP

The best spot in town is the **Hotel Villa Españolas** (Av. JM Cornejo, between Calles Antonio Cañas and Domingo Santos, tel. 333–0322) in a modern, Spanish-style building, which has rooms with TV and private bath for $15. **Hotel Central Park** (9 Av. José María Cornejo, tel. 633–0383) is, surprise, surprise, right next to the central plaza. The bright and narrow inner courtyard offers an escape from the street. A double room with private bath, fan, and telephone will cost you $7. At **Casa de Huéspedes El Turista** (4a Calle Poniente and 1a Av. Sur, tel. 633–0323) you get a room with towels, clean water, comfy hammocks, fans, and nice bathrooms for about $12. Getting here is tricky: from the church, walk 1 block past the barracks, turn left, and walk 2 blocks down Av. María de Los Ángeles Miranda, which becomes 1a Avenida.

FOOD

Cafeteria-style **Comedor Rivoly** (15 1a Av. Sur, tel. 333–0492) is about as close as you're likely to come to dorm food; It's fast, rude, and cheap; and has long hours (daily 6 AM–8 PM). Chicken tamales are a good bet at a buck each; vegetarians will have to resign themselves to the usual rice and beans, although sometimes they serve creative vegetable concoctions. If you want to treat yourself right, **Restaurante Casa Blanca** (11 2a Calle Oriente, tel. 333–0549) is the place to do it. It's a pleasant, quiet spot frequented by a fairly upscale local crowd, and the outdoor tables lend an easy, laid-back atmosphere. The house specialty is delectable grilled shrimp or steak, but it will set you back $8. If that seems steep, you could (a) share a dish, (b) order the chicken for $4, (c) request the $3 vegetarian chop suey, or (d) drink a lot of beer and eat the comlimentary bocas. **Chentino's Pizza** (Calle Alvaro Quinonez, no phone) is a cheap and tasty pizza place and juice bar rolled into one.

NEAR SAN VICENTE

LAGUNA DE APASTAPEQUE

This medium-size crater lake is reasonably attractive and clean and is ideal for serious swimmers. No lifeguard is around to save you if you're flailing, and it gets deep fast—over 300 ft in the middle. On weekdays you'll have the lake practically to yourself, so if you don't want to pay the $1 admission fee to use the turicentro facilities, simply swim in another part of the lake. Open daily 8–5, the turicentro buildings and gardens are well-maintained, and a thatch-roofed restaurant sells chicken ($2) and fish ($3). If you're interested in smaller, less touristed lakes nearby, ask the person at the gate about **Laguna Bruja** or **Laguna Crenaga**. Apastapeque turicentro is on the opposite side of the main highway from town, about 7 km (4 mi) from the desvío. From San Vicente, the Bus 156 marked SANTA CLARA (only!) goes directly to the park, leaving infrequently from the corner opposite the military base. Alternatively, take any bus headed back to San Salvador, get off at the desvío, and catch Bus 301 for San Miguel; ask to be let off near "la laguna," and walk or hitch the last 1½ km (1 mi) to the park.

VOLCAN CHICHONTEPEC

It's hard to miss this 7,200-ft work of nature. There are several paths, but the best trail leaves from San Emigdio (near Verapáz) and takes about four hours to the top. No matter which route you take, however, allow yourself four to six hours to get up. Be realistic about your endurance, especially because you'll need to tote *at least* 3 liters of water per person. You'll pass through kilometers of coffee fields, which eventually give way to natural vegetation and a riveting view of the surrounding countryside. Bus 18 for San Emigdio (1 hr, 30¢) leaves from the San Vicente's church at 5 AM, 8:45 AM, and 11:30 AM; the last return bus leaves San Emigdio at 4 PM.

INFIERNILLO

Approaching the base of Volcán Chichontepec from south of Verapáz you come to this beautiful, natural hot spring. Strong sulfuric fumes have made the affectionately named Infiernillo ("Little Hell") a popular medicinal retreat. Slip into the water and think about the happy distance between you and your workplace. Buses to Verapáz (45 min, 30¢) leave hourly from Farmacia San José, near the mercado central.

SANTIAGO DE MARÍA

Santiago is possibly the most scenically located town in eastern El Salvador, and that's saying a lot in this beautiful and serene part of the country. The region, south of the main highway that runs from San Vicente to San Miguel, is rustic and poor coffee-growing country—you'll see the crop all over the beautiful mountains around town. The lively and attractive city was spared the ravages of the war—save for a brief occupation by rebels in which the then-president Cristiani's private coffee crop was looted—and today you won't find a military presence to mar the fierce pride of the inhabitants. When visiting Santiago, give yourself at least a day to explore the surrounding countryside. **Cerro Tigre,** to the east, offers several good hiking paths. One leads to a higher peak, another to a lower peak, but both take about two hours and provide commanding views of the town and the valley below. To the west, **Volcán de Alegría** has a crater lake known as the **Laguna de Alegría,** which is known more for its medicinal properties than its recreation; the sulfur (rotten-egg-like) fumes emanating from the volcanic rock are said to have therapeutic value when inhaled. To get here, you'll have to take the bus halfway to Berlín (see Coming and Going, below) and ask to be let off in Alegría. From there, it should take about an hour to get to the lagoon, and at least another hour to the top of the volcano.

COMING AND GOING

Bus trips in this part of El Salvador are rough but very beautiful. Always try to get a seat facing northward to enjoy breathtaking views of the Río Lempa and Honduras in the distance. Bus 301 travels the main east–west highway, passing about every 15 minutes; take it to the El Truinfo junction and then cram into one of the Speedy Gonzalez microbuses headed toward Santiago (20 min, 20¢). They leave several times an hour. From Santiago de María the microbuses returning to the highway junction leave from 1 Avenida Norte and Calle Bolívar, two blocks from the park. Bus 348 travels between Santiago and Berlín (see Near Santiago de María, below) (40 min, 30¢) hourly until 5 PM.

WHERE TO SLEEP AND EAT

Complete with a terrace and pleasant garden patio, **Hotel Villahermosa** (4 3a Av. Norte, tel. 663–0146) is the friendly pride-of-the-town hotel. Clean and well-maintained doubles go for $15 with private bath. Next door, **Hospedaje El Quetzal** is an option if Villahermosa is full, but the atmosphere is a little creepy and they lock the doors at 8 PM. Tolerably clean doubles with shared bath are just $5. The clean, simple **Restaurante El Único** (2 2a Av. Sur, right on the park) serves seafood and meat dishes for $2–$3, and **Carnes y Mariscos Tony** (2a Sur, across from the park) serves—guess what?—meat and seafood, mostly shrimp, until midnight.

> The outside wall of Berlín's church has a mural commemorating the late Archbishop Romero with his unheeded words: "The only peace that God wants is based on truth and justice."

NEAR SANTIAGO DE MARIA

BERLÍN

You won't find much to do in this little town 20 minutes west of Santiago de María but wander around nearby forested mountains. Because of its location on prime coffee-growing soil, Berlín was coveted by both sides during the war. You can still see bullet holes in the church tower and in places along the plaza. Today local schools are named after U.S. congressmen who sponsored bills for aid to the region. When in town, ask about excursions to nearby **Cerro Pelón,** or hike to the massive geothermal power plant, **El Tronador** (The Thunderer), just over 5 km (3 mi) from town. To get to El Tronador, head to **Canton de Zapotilla,** a village just northeast of Berlín, and look for the signs. Stay overnight at **Hospedaje Berlines** (4a Calle Oriente and 2a Av. Sur), a very simple, clean hotel where $4 doubles have TVs and private bathrooms. Two blocks away, on Calle Dr. Antonio Guandique across from the church and park, are an **Antel** and cheap **comedores.** The road between Berlín and Santiago de María has been hailed as one of the most beautiful stretches of highway in the country; Bus 348 (20¢) makes the 20-minute trek. From anywhere else it's not too shabby either; take Bus 301 (which travels the main east–west highway) to the Mercedes Umaña desvío, then take Bus 354 to town (30 min, 25¢), which leaves every half hour or so.

SAN MIGUEL

With almost 200,000 residents, San Miguel is the third-largest city in the country and a major commercial center. Industrial goods, household products, and consumer electronics are sold all over the place, giving the city a warehouse feel. Big and busy, San Miguel escapes the hellish frenzy of the capital but lacks the charm of many smaller cities. Come here to get your bearings, buy something major, or even to relax—but don't expect much adventure or diversion, except maybe during the November 17–21 **festival** of the Virgen de la Paz.

For a city of this size, sightseeing possibilities are pretty limited. The **cathedral** is large and imposing, but rather artless for an important religious building. A block behind it sits the **Antiguo Teatro Nacional,** a more elegant building where you might be lucky enough to see an event. The theater season heats up around mid-August and continues through the November festival. Check around the plaza for announcements or ask at the theater to get the scoop on shows and times—you can usually get into private events if you dress decently and smile a lot at the entrance. For nightlife, meander along **El Triángulo,** a fairly meager strip of clubs and restaurants near the exit to San Salvador. There you can join locals with cash at **Restaurante El Alazán,** which charges a $3–$4 cover for super-loud karaoke and live music shows. On weekends, you might catch a soccer game at the **Estadio Municipal**; look for the tall lights at the end of 4a Calle Oriente. Check the paper or ask around for game times. If you're burning (almost literally) for a swim, cruise over to the **Altos de la Cueva** turicentro—the pool lays no claim to magnificence, but it's there and open daily 8–5. Bus 94 passes the plaza often, heading west on 4a Calle Oriente. A short trip from town are the **Ruinas de Quelapa.** Although most everything has yet to be unearthed, the ruins make a good escape from the city. To reach Quelapa (45 min, 20¢), take Bus 90 from 2a Avenida Norte by the central plaza. The ruins are about a 20-minute walk out of town.

BASICS

Antel (open daily 6 AM–9 PM) is right on the plaza central. Just a few blocks away, the **post office** (4a Av. Sur, at 3a Calle Poniente) is open weekdays 7:30–noon and 1:30–5, Saturday 7:30–noon, Sunday 8–11. A number of **banks** and **casas de cambio** lie along 2a and 4a calles Poniente, opposite the cathedral; you can change dollars weekdays 8–5 and on Saturday mornings. The large and relatively well-equipped city **hospital** has a limited English-speaking staff. It's a good way west of the town center; to get here, either take a taxi or hop on the bus marked HOSPITAL, which leaves from 4a Calle Poniente.

COMING AND GOING

Bus 301 leaves every 15 minutes for San Miguel (3 hrs, $1.50) from the capital's Terminal de Oriente. You can go virtually everywhere in the east from San Miguel's **bus terminal** (6a Calle Oriente and 10a Av. Norte). The following are all 1- to 1½-hour trips that cost around 60¢, with buses leaving several times per hour: Bus 373 to Usulután, 324 to La Unión, 328 to San Francisco Gotera, 330 to Santa Rosa de Lima, and 320 to El Cuco. Other buses go to smaller cities; ask for more info at the station.

GETTING AROUND

Finding your way around town isn't very hard, as long as you're amenable to change. Avenidas run north–south; the main one is called **Avenida G. Barrios** in the north end of town and **Avenida E. Gavidla** in the south. Smaller, numbered avenidas are labeled *norte* (north) and *sur* (south). Calles run east–west; the main one is **Calle Chaparrastique** to the west and **Calle Sirama** to the east of the town center. Smaller, numbered calles are *poniente* (west) and *oriente* (east). The **plaza central** sits between 2a and 4a calles on 4a Avenida Norte. The **mercado central** is always a zoo and is a maze of pure mud after a good rain; it begins in earnest near the cathedral at Calle Chaparristique, extending south for several blocks. You'll find everything necessary to sustain the travelin' life within just a few blocks of the town center.

WHERE TO SLEEP

Crash near the bus terminal if you don't mind a bit more dirt and noise for your dollar. Or head about 15 blocks southwest of the town center to a quieter but more expensive residential neighborhood.

NEAR THE BUS TERMINAL • These hotels are decent, popular with backpackers and bus travelers, and close to the city center, but the area around the bus station is a little seedier than a wary foreigner might like. At family-run **Mini Hotel Novel** (102 10a Av. Norte, behind bus terminal), windowless, dimly lighted doubles with fan and hammock go for $6 ($7 with a TV). Just one block from the bus station, **Hotel San Rafael** (704 6a Calle Oriente, tel 661–4113) is another option. This pleasant three-floor building has a *comedor* and will let you a simple, clean double with private bath and air-conditioning for $15 (cheaper rooms available). San Rafael has a 9:30 PM curfew. **Hotel La Terminal** (6a Calle Oriente, tel. 661–1086) is just across the street from the bus terminal and feels potentially safer than the others. Cramped rooms with amenities such as air-conditioning and a TV are about $20; those without get a fan and pay $5 less. **Hotel Migueleño** (610 4a Calle Oriente, tel. 660–2737), just a block from the bus station, has plenty of clean rooms with great bathrooms, fans, and a courtyard that shuts out street noise. Best of all is the price—just under $6 per double. Mind the 10 PM curfew.

SOUTH OF THE CENTER • South of the town center is more residential, quieter, and probably safer than most other parts of town. Unless you have lots of baggage, you can still walk here from the bus station. If you're arriving late (after 6 PM) and leaving early (before 8 AM) in the morning, head directly to

Hotel Modelo (208 17a Calle Poniente, tel. 661–3122). Their spotless and relaxing $8 doubles would be a superb deal if not for the 12-hour rate and lack of screens on the windows, which invites bugs to join you for the night.

Hotel El Mandarin. The most comfortable accommodations in town are to be had here, where you can also get tasty Chinese food. Both the hotel and restaurant are reasonably priced, and you feel you're in the hands of a carefully managed place. Rooms are simple, clean, and are equipped with cable TV and air-conditioning for $30–$35. *Off the Pan-American Hwy, just south of Calle 8a, across from Pops Ice Cream, tel. 669–6969. 32 rooms with bath. Restaurant.*

Trópico Inn. This old yet reputable place was the site of a peculiar moment in El Salvadoran history. In 1989, a local beauty pagent attended by the vice president was interrupted by a guerrilla attack on the city. Ten years later, you'll pay mostly for the caché of the hotel's name and fame, but you'll have TV, air-conditioning, and phones in your otherwise run-down $40 room. *303 Av. Roosevelt Sur, tel. 661–1800 or 661–0748. 105 rooms with bath. Restaurant, laundry.*

FOOD

Comedor Buen Gusto (6a Calle, between Avs. 4a and 6a) is really an oyster bar hole-in-the-wall. If you've had your shots and they're open for business, order them by the dozen. **Comedor Carolina** (Av. José Simeon Cañas and 3a Calle Oriente) is one of the best spots around, with enough variety to please many a herbivore or carnivore. They start serving lunch before the breakfast platters are all finished, so you'll end up with the Salvadoran version of brunch for about $3. Pastries for pennies are yours when you visit **Pasteria Lorena** or **Pasteria Francesa,** which, like Burger King and McDonald's, are neighbors competing on the same

> *Cuco means ghost in Spanish, but it can also mean "the sly one"— an apt description of the owners who actually charge money for the hovels that pass for lodging.*

block of 1a Avenida between 4a and 6a calles. Eateries of all manner flank 4a Calle, including a fast-food **Pollo Campero,** a medium-priced sit-down place with animal skins on the wall called **Restaurant Gran Tejano,** a chic little place for broiled chicken and seafood called **Baty Carnitas,** a juice bar, and an ice-cream shop. Two upscale choices are **Restaurant La Pampa Argentina** (Av. Roosevelt at 5a Calle Poniente, no phone), where steak, chicken or seafood entrees with all the fixings fill you up for less than $10, and **Restaurant La Pradera** (Av. Roosevelt, just south of La Pampa Argentina, no phone), which offers similar fare but is slightly more expensive and atmospheric.

NEAR SAN MIGUEL

EL CUCO

About 37 km (16 mi) south of San Miguel on the Pacific Coast, El Cuco may be the most popular beach in El Salvador. The beach is huge, with clean, fine sand, but during the week it's virtually barren of vacationers. Even the drive over the coastal mountains to El Cuco is beautiful, and it includes a good view of the Volcan de San Miguel. Many private homes line the beach, so some innocuous trespassing may be required. Smile, and hold up your pail and shovel as signs of your good faith if you're caught, or, if possible, simply ask permission to cut through. If you're staying the night, you can pitch a tent on the beach, or pay to stay in one of the seaside cabañas, which are nothing but open-air huts with hammocks and usually without locks. If you want something more than that, local hotel rooms cost more than they're worth—there are also number of hospedajes where you can pay $3.50–$6 for a miserable little shack you'd be loath to let your dog sleep in. The best "budget" place in town is the **Hotel Los Leones Marinos** (tel. 661–2870), down the fancy hotel strip on your left as you enter town. Decent, clean double rooms go for $12–$18, depending on whether you want a fan and hammock, but here's the clincher—you don't get a mattress! A thin bedspread is graciously draped over the hard fiber-woven bed board. Alternatively, you can pay $32–$65 for a breezy, palm-tree setting and a room with a thatched roof and brick floors at **El Tropiclub Cabañas** (2 km [1.5 mi] from El Cuco along beachside road, fax 661–1399). The food scene here is also a little depressing, but as long as you're a seafood fan you should find something to ward off hunger. Look for the outdoor stands and comedores selling cheap, fresh fish concoctions along the road leading to the beach; **Tienda y Comedor Sofy** has an attractive array of comida a la vista, including a huge fried-fish plate for only $2. To get here, Bus 320 leaves San Miguel for El Cuco (1½ hrs, 60¢) every 90 minutes until about 4 PM. From anywhere else, get a bus to the desvío outside of San Miguel, where you can intercept the packed bus to El Cuco.

LAGUNA DE OLOMEGA

Like many spots of interest in El Salvador, this is an off-the-beaten-path adventure for the carefree traveler. Before you head out, know that the area has no hospedaje or real restaurants. That said, the best
time to visit the lagoon is August through October, when heavy rains bring up the water level. The rest
of the year it's more like a large navigable swamp brimming with fish. Although fish populations are
dropping because of overharvest, the lagoon is still the lifeblood for fishermen in the waterside villages,
and fish is the main grub for miles around. Locals favor the tasty *guapote* and the sturgeon-sized *tilapia*.
Small villages nestle in the serene hills on the other side of the lagoon; you can cross in passenger boats
(35¢) that leave at 8 AM, return at 3 PM, and leave again at 4 PM. **Olomegita** and **La Estrachura** are two
of the larger communities nearby, and you can stop by **Los Cerritos,** a little island where locals like to
swim and sunbathe. If you miss the regular ferry, make a deal with an independent boat owner or rent
a canoe to do your own exploring. The hour-long canoe ride to Los Cerritos should cost less than $5,
guide included. Motorboat travel costs about $6 an hour; a trip to the pueblos on the opposite lake shore
will cost around $15. The dearth of formal lodging means that locals open their homes to travelers, and
camping is possible in some spots across the water, but beware of serious rains putting a damper on
your plans. Bus 384 will take you to the lagoon from San Miguel (1½ hrs, 50¢). From La Unión, take the
bus toward San Miguel to the desvío in **Carmen** (30 min, 35¢), where you can catch one of the infrequent buses or frequent pickups to Olomega (30 min, 25¢).

VOLCAN CHAPARRASTIQUE

Standing 7,000 ft high, this lava monster is one serious climb. The volcano has been quite active during the past 100 years; the last time it blew its top was 1976. Take the bus to **La Placita** (45 min, 60¢)
from the Farmacia San Miguel in the marketplace. Pickup trucks also make trips from the market for
about the same price. From La Placita you're in for about two intense hours of cardiovascular action to
the summit.

MORAZÁN

There are good reasons to travel in the northeastern department of Morazán, but none of them have to
do with luxury, convenience, or fast-paced excitement. Morazán is sparsely populated, impoverished,
and underdeveloped, even for El Salvador. This is the land of the Salvadoran campesino, a land rich in
tradition and pride, with a history of repression, defiance, and popular movements. Despite their smiles
and warmth, many here still bear deep scars from the 15 years of active conflict between the FMLN and
the FAES (*Fuerzas Armadas de El Salvador*). Come if you are ready to smile humbly yet confidently, converse when the opportunity arises, traverse hilltops and mountains, and perhaps scratch the surface of
understanding the region's complex past, present, and future. One piece of advice—always carry water,
because dry spells are common and sponge baths often necessary.

SAN FRANCISCO GOTERA

The capital of the Morazán department, 30 km (19 mi) north of San Miguel, feels like a child stifled by
authoritarian parents. The government army never managed to hold its own in the region, much less
control it, so the powers-that-be did the next best thing—they turned Gotera into a virtual military bunker
with more soldiers than you can shake a stick at. During the '80s, Gotera became a de facto refugee
camp housing thousands of people, particularly those from the north, who were pushed out of their
homes. Luckily, the military presence has been reduced nowadays, confining itself mostly to the
grandiose bunker near the movie theater. Mostly, Gotera serves as a gateway to the towns farther
north—it's worth taking a look, but you'll probably want to move on rather quickly. The only exciting time
to stick around is November 7–16, during the **festival** of San Francisco. If you're passing through town
on a Sunday, check out the weekly **mercado,** where you'll find colorful hammocks in every size and
material at some of the best prices anywhere. Every evening at 6 PM (or whenever the power comes on),
the town plays the *lotería* (lottery) in the center of the market area. At **Cine Morazán** (3a Av. Sur and 4a
Calle Poniente, across from church) catch up on all those movies you wanted to see last year for the low,
low price of $1; shows start at 7 PM. For phone calls, **Antel** (Av. Norberto Cruz and Calle José Simeon
Cañas) is open daily 6 AM–10 PM. To get to San Francisco Gotera, take Bus 328 from San Miguel's bus
station; it leaves every 20 minutes until 5:30 PM.

WHERE TO SLEEP

The lodging situation is pretty bleak. **Hotel Arco Iris** (25 Av. Morazán, tel. 664–0492) is the better of the two hotels on the main drag. Clean doubles with private bath, fan, hammock, and a decent bed go for $5. The manager is quite attentive and seems concerned about guests' comfort. **Hospedaje San Francisco** (23 Av. Morazán, tel. 664–0066) is less attractive than its next-door neighbor. Doubles go for $9 with private bath, or $3.50 without, but it all depends on how business is going, so bargain away. Both places do the curfew thing—10 PM.

FOOD

Just around the corner from the budget hotels, **Restaurant El Bonanza** (3a Calle Poniente, at Av. Morazán, tel. 664–0306) is the place to go for a serious meal. With air-conditioning and cable (HBO ¡Olé!), Bonanza definitely caters to the few well-to-do of Gotera, and as a result it's rather pricey. That said, you'll get a huge fried fillet of fish for $4, and the fried chicken is a bargain at $2. The house specialties are grilled shrimp and cream of seafood soup; both cost $6. Across the street, **Comedor Melita** is much cheaper and offers a beautiful selection of comida a la vista. It's cafeteria-style dining with the usual meaty choices, although vegetarians can enjoy the veggies. Prices are about 50¢–$2.50 per plate.

For a light breakfast of coffee and sweet breakfast breads just a block from the main bus stop, go to **Cafetería Yaneth** (4a Calle Ote, between 2a and 4a Avs.), where until 9 PM you can also get a humble burger and fries for next to nothing.

Early evenings in Gotera, hang out with local kids on the side streets. Little girls play hopscotch and boys play street soccer, hardly noticing the heavily armed soldiers who are their neighbors; kids play their games while the grownups play theirs.

SEGUNDO MONTES

Around 1990, refugees of the civil war began to filter back into the north from Honduras. With the aid of a number of national and international organizations, a group of refugees founded the "repopulated" community of **Segundo Montes,** 20 km (12 mi) north of San Francisco Gotera. Named after one of the six Jesuit educators killed by the military in 1989, Segundo Montes incorporates several organized settlements that advocates hail as "model" repopulated communities. The generation of children that is now in primary school may be the first to have the opportunity of attending university. Although health care and education are well above national rural standards, it remains to be seen whether the peoples' post-war economic needs can be met in this fashion. San Luís is Segundo Montes's main settlement, where you can catch buses heading to other villages and northern towns. At the bus stop, grab a meal at **Comedor La Guacamaya Subversiva,** named after a comedy show on the FMLN's *Radio Venceremos* (Radio "We Will Overcome"). The comedor serves basic platos típicos for $1–$2. Uphill from the village center, you'll find **Antel** (open daily 6–6). Turn left at Antel to find the **Centro Cultural.** The comedor here offers good food at budget prices and offers a vista of the countryside that inspires deep gulps of fresh air. To get to Segundo Montes, take Bus 332 from San Miguel (2¼ hrs, 50¢); it leaves every 1½–2 hours, passing though San Francisco Gotera on the way.

PERQUÍN

About 11 km (7 mi) north of Segundo Montes, near the Honduran border, lies **Perquín,** the only town of any size in the area. The town was once known as the capital of the FMLN; today sleepy Perquín is home to the eye-opening **Museo de la Revolución Salvadoreña** (admission $1.20; open Tues.–Sun. 9– noon and 1–5), where you can see documents, accounts, photos, posters, equipment, and weapons of the revolutionary movement. If you've come to El Salvador in part for its recent revolutionary history, a stop here should be on your itinerary. Three buildings are divided into thematic rooms such as Room of Heros and Martyrs, and the Origins of War Room. Furthermore, the museum should provoke plenty of conversation with the friendly ex-guerillas who give the tours and the local residents who saw their fair share of guerrilla activities. The hills around Perquín are great for short to medium-length hikes; the **Cerro Pelón trail** starts opposite the museum and continues along the hillside ridge past the trenches where revolutionaries literally dug in for battle. The **Cerro Gigante trail** begins just past the hospedaje. Both are 15- to 30-minute hikes ideal for picnics, camping, and general panorama appreciation. For longer treks, continue along the ridges into the countryside. **Comedor PADECOMSM** (8a Av. Sur, 1 block north from the church) is a popular, makeshift food place where you select from daily prepared offerings. Ask about other food options at the museum. Just outside town, **Casa Huéspedes El Gigante** has clean dormitory-style rooms with incredibly nice communal bathrooms for $3 per person in what used to be a lumber mill. It's the only lodging around. Go down the road leading south out of town, and make your first right. To get to Perquín, take Bus 332, which passes through Segundo Montes and San Francisco Gotera on it's way from San Miguel (3 hrs, $1.50). Return trips to San Miguel leave every couple of hours just until 1 PM or so.

NEAR PERQUÍN

Near Perquín lies the tiny village of **El Mazote,** site of the infamous massacre that left more than 1,000 dead. On December 11, 1981, the Atlacatl batallion of the Salvadoran government army systematically gunned down the town's entire population, later dumping the bodies in mass graves or burning the bodies in their homes. The lone survivor is Rufina Amaya, an older woman who has dedicated her life to recounting the incident to as many people as possible so it might not be forgotten. In the village is a monument to the slain victims, about a dozen houses, and a small store. To get here, take Bus 332C, which leaves from San Miguel at 5:30 AM; it will drop you off 20 minutes outside the village. From Perquín, you'll need to take a bus heading south to the main desvío (10 min). From there, you can catch the Bus 332C when it passes through at about 8 AM or walk the rest of the way (about 1½ hrs). The walk is particularly beautiful after the village of Arambala, taking you through rolling hills and fields of maize. There are several stores along the way where you can buy drinks (bring water anyway) and make inquiries. Although many visitors find their way here, drivers of rental cars beware: the road is crummy. From Perquín, take a right at the fork in the road to Arambala. Follow this road, keeping left, for 11 km (7 mi).

SANTA ROSA DE LIMA

Aside from hot and wet, Santa Rosa is everything that Gotera is not: the military is practically absent and the people are laid-back, open, and relaxed. Because the town is close to the border town of El Amatillo, locals are used to strange faces—you won't get that look from people that asks "What are you DOING here?" Santa Rosa really gets going August 25–31 during the **Festival de Agosto,** when bullfights, carnival rides, and general hell-raising abound. Aside from the festival, there's not much to do but coast around the nearby hills and rest up before pushing on to Honduras. Change cash only at **banks** and **casas de cambio** along 4a Calle Oriente; they're usually open weekdays 8–5. **Antel** (Calle Girón and 4a Av. Norte) is open 6 AM–9 PM daily. A number of **jewelry shops** on Calle Giron across from Antel may interest you. Prices start at around $10 for basic 10-karat gold earrings. To get to Santa Rosa from San Francisco de Gotera (1½ hrs, 60¢), take any bus heading south and ask to be let off at the Kilometer 18 desvío. From here, buses pass several times an hour to Santa Rosa. Shuttling between El Amatillo (½ hr) and San Miguel (1½ hrs), Bus 330 passes through town about every 30–40 minutes. Catch them at the bus station between 4a and 6a calles Oriente.

WHERE TO SLEEP

Santa Rosa is the last major Salvadoran town before Honduras, and one would think a good place to stop for the night if you're running late. Desperados can get bargain-basement prices but not much in the way of quality. **Hotel El Tejano** (Calle Giron, near 6a Norte, tel. 664–2459) is a nearly bearable choice. Almost-clean $5 doubles come with fan, hammock, and dusty floor. Beware of the 9 PM curfew and 7 AM check-out. A better choice (apply your lesser-of-two-evils philosophy here) is **Hotel El Recréo** (Calle Giron and 4a Av. Norte, next to Antel, tel. 664–2126), where you get big, clean rooms with firm double beds, boomin' overhead fans, and window screens to keep the bugs out—all for $3.50 a person. The only drawback is the dreadful communal bathrooms, but those are unavoidable in these parts.

FOOD

La Pema (tel. 667–6055, closed Mon.) is definitely the best restaurant around. In fact, it's famous in eastern El Salvador, garnering the attention of the nation's elite. There's nothing ostentatious about the place though, and diners choose from a few daily offerings, usually one seafood and one meat or poultry dish. You might have to ask for directions to find this place, in an unmarked red and white building next to BanCo on 4a Calle. In Salvadoran style, this is definitely a lunch place, so go before 4 PM when they close. The large **mercado** next to the main plaza has dozens of stands for quick and cheap eats. **Comedor Nuevo** (6a Calle Poniente, between Av. General Larios and 2a Av. Sur, near bus terminal) hosts a crowd of regulars who bump elbows at the close-set tables; it's a good place to meet people because it's awfully hard to ignore the folks around you. Basic meals of steak, fish, or chicken cost $2. Right near the budget hotels, **Comedor Servi-Amigos** (Calle Giron, ½ block downhill from 4a Av. Norte) is much the same; a friendly staff serves standard breakfast, lunch, or dinner for around $2. Also nearby is **Pollo Campestre** (Calle Girón, next to Antel), an upscale Kentucky Fried Chicken. A full chicken dinner costs $3, but ask them to substitute a *licuado con leche* (ice-cream shake) for the coffee and soda. With the air-conditioning and good lighting, this makes an ideal spot to sit and slurp with a good book.

COSTA RICA

BY MICHELE BACK AND OLIVIA BARRY, UPDATED BY DAVID DUDENHOEFER

osta Rica grabs the attention of travelers from around the world for good reason. Very few places on Earth offer everything that this tiny country about the size of West Virginia does; you'll find blue morpho butterflies the size of your hand, enchanting beaches, sulfur springs, and vistas verging on orgasmic. Costa Rica is the easiest Central American country to travel in: it has an amazingly stable social and political environment, and its economy has been transformed by North American capitalist culture. Not surprisingly, travelers who expect to find something like the rich indigenous culture of Guatemala are often disappointed. But if you look past the fast-food outlets that dominate San José's Plaza de la Cultura, you'll discover the cultural heritage of Guanacaste cowboys, Meseta Central coffee farmers, and Caribbean fishermen.

The vast majority of Costa Rica's population is of Spanish descent, although in the past century, the country has received immigrants from Germany, Italy, England, and many other European nations. There are hundreds of thousands of Nicaraguans and Salvadoreans living in Costa Rica—some arrived as refugees when armed conflicts wracked their countries, others came in search of work—and tens of thousands of South Americans. About 40,000 people of African descent live on the Caribbean coast and lowlands. Their ancestors came from Jamaica or elsewhere to work on railroad construction or banana plantations. The cities also have plenty of citizens of Chinese ancestry. The indigenous population of Costa Rica numbers around 30,000—approximately 1% of the population—divided into eight ethnic groups. Most Indians live near or in the Talamanca Mountains, where the largest of the nation's 22 reservations are located. Despite Costa Rica's legacy of "social justice," racism is an ingrained element of the country's value system, with blacks and Indians predictably perched on the lowest rungs of the social ladder. Thankfully, though, Costa Rica lacks the kind of racial tensions that plague the United States, and on the whole, is much more integrated.

The human rainbow that Costa Rica is today began forming in 1502, when Christopher Columbus landed where the city of Limón sits today, and encountered Indians who traded their glittering gold pendants for Euro-trinkets. Believing that the area was filled with gold, he named the region Costa Rica (Rich Coast). Subsequent Spanish subjugators searched for golden fortunes, but they were largely unsuccessful, and the few who hung around turned to agriculture. The local indigenous nations resisted the Spanish colonists, but disease and warfare decimated the native population, which never really recovered. Because there weren't enough Indians to create the kind of slave states that developed in the Andean and Meso-American regions, colonial Costa Rica was a land of poor farmers who worked their own land, a circumstance that some historians consider responsible for the country's democratic tradition. Geographically isolated from the colonial centers in Mexico and South America, Costa Rica developed much more slowly than the greater Spanish Empire. Several attempts to settle the Caribbean and southern Pacific coasts failed, leaving the Spaniards and their mestizo (mixed-descent) offspring to populate the temperate Meseta Central, which to this day remains the home of the majority of the country's population.

Costa Rica became an independent nation in 1821, and, except for a couple of short-lived dictatorships, it stands as one of the oldest democratic republics in Latin America. The country has no standing army; the 1949 Constitution dismantled the armed forces, and people are very proud of this fact. But don't get the wrong impression—it's not exactly proletarian rule. The country now relies on more than 7,000 civil and rural guardsmen (and a very few guards*women*) to maintain public order. The *guardia* carry guns, wear green uniforms, and according to most locals, they aren't to be trusted. They're everywhere, but they're definitely more like cops than soldiers. If attacked, Costa Rica would seek assistance from the Organization of American States, and Uncle Sam, no doubt.

The country has devoted a hell of a lot of time, money, and work toward the preservation of its biggest resources: its varied flora and fauna. In a region rife with deforestation and other forms of environmental destruction, Costa Rica has managed to set aside 13% of its land as national parks or reserves. Those protected areas hold an amazing array of plants and animals, including more than 1,000 species of orchids and more species of birds than are found in all of the United States and Canada combined. The country's forests are the natural equivalent of the Louvre, with their massive kapok trees, colorful heliconias, howler monkeys, toucans, tapirs, dinosaurian iguanas, and delicate hummingbirds.

Although Costa Rica may tout itself as an environmental paradise, virgin forests are still being logged, and, in the Central Valley, the air and water are under siege from polluters.

Everything's relative, though. In the past 50 years, more than two-thirds of the rain forest has been burned away or chopped down to make room for cattle pasture, banana plantations, and other agricultural activities. Only during the past two decades has conservation become a prime concern. Today, Costa Rica's 21 national parks and wildlife refuges are heavily visited—more than 600,000 tourists each year—and the dollars those nature-loving visitors leave in the country have won more Costa Ricans over to conservation than any treatise on deep ecology ever could. Now, some environmentalists are calling for stricter limits on the number of visitors allowed in any area, to make sure the ecotourists don't love that tropical nature to death.

Now for even more bad news. The single largest threat to *tico* (Costa Rican) national identity is you, dear traveler. Many Costa Ricans have forfeited their land and traditions only to wind up in dead-end service-industry jobs. But people in depressed regions still pray for the god of tourism to resurrect their local economy. In a country so saturated with tourism, it's not at all clear whether the industry will find its second wind.

Costa Rica's high standard of living and history of stability make it an oasis of peace in a region characterized by poverty and political turmoil. As one of the most important outposts on the international gringo trail, it is quite feasible to travel here without speaking a word of Spanish. Don't be scared away by all the tourists, though—you'll miss out on some of the world's most incredible beaches, tropical forests, and wildlife. In fact, the sheer diversity of natural beauty is reason enough to come here, and there are tons of ways to enjoy it. Costa Rica's popularity means that you'll be welcomed over and over into a friendly subculture of international travelers, with all the resulting privileges and obligations. Even permanent residents from the United States are usually mellow, open-minded people committed to preserving all that Costa Rica has to offer. Also, despite the fact that Costa Ricans see gringos on an almost daily basis, they're still generous with a smile and a greeting for everyone they meet. You'll be rapidly engaged in conversation and, in rural areas, even invited to people's homes. Ticos are also extremely polite; *con mucho gusto* (with pleasure) is the disarming common response to *gracias* (thank you), and most of the time you can believe them.

BASICS

MONEY

Except in San José, where all banks are full-service, the two major banks handle different transactions. **Banco Nacional de Costa Rica** accepts traveler's checks, money orders, and Canadian dollars, and

NICARAGUA

Peñas
Blancas

Lago de Nicaragua

Los Chiles

La Cruz

*Golfo de
Santa
Elena*

P. N.
GUANACASTE

Caño
Negro

Upala

R.N. DE
VIDA SILVESTRE
CAÑO NEGRO

ALAJUELA

P. N.
SANTA ROSA

P. N.
RINCON
DE LA VIEJA

Liberia

GUANACASTE

Nuevo
Arenal

Lago
Arenal

Arenal

**Arenal
Volcano**

La Fortuna

El Coco

Comunidad

Bagaces

Tilarán

Ciudad Quesada
(San Carlos)

So

Migu

*RESERVA
BIOLÓGICA
LOMAS
BARBUDAL*

Cañas

Santa Elena

Filadelfia

Belén

Monteverde

*RESERVA
BIOLÓGICA
MONTEVERDE*

Zarcero

Flamingo

Huacas

Tempisque

P. N.
PALO VERDE

San Ramón

Nara

A

Tamarindo

Sta.
Cruz

P. N.
BARRA
HONDA

Atenas

Nicoya

Isla
Chira

*Golfo de
Nicoya*

Puntarenas

*R. N. DE FAUNA
SILVESTRE
OSTIONAL*

*Península
de
Nicoya*

Caldera

PUNTARENAS

Nosara

Samara

Paquera

*RESERVA
BIOLÓGICA
CURÚ*

Tárcoles

*RESERVA
BIOLÓGICA
CARARA*

Tambor

Jacó

Cóbano

Mal Pais

Montezuma

*RESERVA NATURAL
ABSOLUTA CABO BLANCO*

Cabo Blanco

Parrita

N

PACIFIC OCEAN

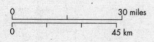

0   30 miles

0   45 km

Caribbean
Sea

Río San Juan

Río Sarapiquí

Río Colorado

R.N. DE
FAUNA SILVESTRE
BARRA DEL
COLORADO

HEREDIA

Puerto Viejo

Cariari

Tortuguero

PARQUE
NACIONAL
TORTUGUERO

LIMÓN

La
Virgen

ZONA
PROTECTORA
LA SELVA

Guápiles

Parismina

Cinchona

P. N.
BRAULIO
CARRILLO

Río Reventazón

Siquirres

Puerto
Limón

uela

Heredia

San José

MONUMENTO
NACIONAL
GUAYABO

Río

Turrialba

PARQUE
NACIONAL
CAHUITA

Cahuita

Puerto Viejo
de Talamanca

Manzanillo

Cartago

CARTAGO

Bribrí

Sixaola

CORDILLERA DE TALAMANCA

PARQUE
NACIONAL
CHIRRIPÓ

n Marcos

Santa
María

SAN JOSE

San Isidro
de El General

PARQUE INTERNACIONAL
LA AMISTAD

Quepos

P. N.
MANUEL
ANTONIO

Ujarrás

Salitre

Buenos
Aires

PANAMA

Dominical

Palmar
Norte

Cortés

Palmar
Sur

INTERAMERICAN HWY.

San
Vito

Río
Claro

Neily

Drake
Bay

Uvita

Golfito

*Golfo
Dulce*

Península
de Osa

Pto.
Jiménez

Zancudo

Paso
Canoas

PARQUE
NACIONAL
CORCOVADO

Carate

Cabo
Matapalo

gives cash advances on Visa cards. **Banco de Costa Rica** usually deals only with U.S. dollars in cash and traveler's checks. Both are open 8:30–3:30. It's always quicker to change money in San José, where the smaller, private banks are the best bet. Tourist hotels usually give lousy exchange rates. The money changers who work on the streets in San José are rip-off artists, and should be avoided; the ones in the airport are a bit less shifty. ATMs are found all over San José and in other major cities—check the **Banco Popular**—but you may have to get your card authorized for use abroad.

HOW MUCH IT WILL COST • If you're expecting the big bargains of Guatemala in Costa Rica, think again. Although food and transportation are still fairly reasonable, lodging will take the bulk of your budget. Expect to pay at *least* $15–$30 a night for a decent double room, unless you're into roughing it. Meal prices run from $2 for breakfast to $5–$8 for dinner, but in San José you can still find hearty lunch specials for $3–$4. A beer will run you 70¢ to $1.50, and a cup of coffee, two bits to a buck. Most bus fares range from $3 to $6, and most domestic flights cost around $50. You can get by on less if you camp or stay at lodges where you can cook your own food.

CURRENCY • The *colón* is the basic monetary unit, which was once broken into 100 *centimos,* but is now worth a mere fraction of a penny. Coins range from 1 to 100 colones, whereas bills get as big as 10,000 and 20,000. Restaurants, hotels, and merchants usually round up. Prices quoted in this book are based on an exchang rate of 270 colones to the U.S. dollar. All banks offer the same government-set rate.

COMING AND GOING

BY PLANE • Major airlines serving the Juan Santamaría Airport in San José (tel. 443–2942) include **American** (tel. 257–1266), **Continental** (tel. 296–4911), **Delta** (tel. 257–4141), and **United** (tel. 220–4844), as well as the Central American **Grupo TACA** (tel. 296–0909), which has daily flights from several U.S. cities. Travelers from Canada usually need to fly to the United States and connect to San José, unless they catch a charter flight. From Europe, travelers hop aboard **British Airways** (tel. 223–5648) or **Iberia** (tel. 257–8266). From Australia and New Zealand, travelers should fly to the United States and then continue to San José. *See* Chapter 1 for more info on flying into Central America. **Aeroperlas** (tel. 440–0093) has five direct flights a week between the Panamanian city of David to San José, with connections to Bocas del Toro and Panama City.

BY BUS • **Tica Bus** (Calle 9 at Av. 4, tel. 221–8954) and **Panaline** (Calle 16 at Av. 3, tel. 255–1205) express buses dash daily between San José and Panama City (17 hrs, $20). Tica Bus departs San José at 10 PM and Panama City at 11 AM, while Panaline departs both cities at 2 PM. If you're in the northern Panamanian town of David, take a **Tracopa** (Calle 14, Av. 5, tel. 221–4214) bus to San José; those buses depart San José at 7:30 AM.

Tica Bus departs for Managua (11 hrs, $9) daily at 6 and 7 AM, leaving Managua at the same time. Buses depart Managua the following day for Tegucigalpa (2 days, $20), San Salvador (2 days, $18) and Guatemala City (2½ days, $35). Overnight stays aren't included in ticket prices, but the bus stops at reasonable hotels in Managua and San Salvador.

GETTING AROUND

BY BUS • Buses are the cheapest and most popular transportation in Costa Rica. They're reliable for the most part, but flat tires, late departures, mechanical difficulties, and overcrowding do occur. There are two types of buses: *directo* (direct), which run frequently between the main towns, and *corriente* (indirect), which serve the main towns as well as more remote villages. Besides price (directo buses charge a third to twice as much) and the security of an assigned seat (corriente seats are available on a first-come, first-served basis), there's not too much difference between the two types. Both take about the same amount of time, stopping every few miles, its seems, to pick up passengers on the road. Also, you'll only get an assigned seat if you start your trip at the terminal of origin. If you board somewhere between point A and point B, you'll often have to squeeze on and ride standing up.

Sunday buses are always jam-packed with families and howling babies. Depending on the driver and the company, tickets should be purchased at the terminal or on the bus when you board. Some drivers will wait to charge you when you get off. Sometimes buses are mismarked, so ask the destination before you board. None of the buses have much room for luggage—leave what you can in San José. You might be asked to put your luggage under the bus, but most people stick their stuff in overhead compartments or hold it on their laps. Bus trips to the southwest are particularly long; consider flying if you have the cash.

BY CAR • Many people rent cars while in Costa Rica, which can be an expensive but convenient way to explore the country. Surfers usually rent four-wheel-drive vehicles, but unless you plan on straying from the beaten path, they're not really necessary and are considerably more expensive than standard vehicles. There are dozens of car-rental companies in San José, including the big U.S. outfits and lots of local ones. Rates vary considerably through the course of the year, so you're best off looking under *Rent* in the yellow pages and calling a number of places. Look for specials advertised in the *Tico Times*. Minimum rental age is 25, and you'll need a valid passport, credit card, and driver's license (not international). For info on specific car-rental companies, *see* Basics in San José, *below*.

If you made it all the way down to Costa Rica in your own car, congratulations. Theft is common (mostly of stuff out of your car rather than the car itself) so always park in a secure area—there are dozens of parking lots in downtown San José—or hire someone on the street to watch your car. If you're staying for a long time, you'll be charged an import tax, which is often the value of the car itself, but you can avoid the tax by taking the car out of the country for 72 hours every 90 days. There are gas and service ⸢st⸣ations in practically every town and scattered along the highways, but gas costs at least 50% more ⸢than⸣ it does in the United States.

⸢BIK⸣E • It's possible and it's beautiful, but it's difficult. Costa Rican roads weren't designed for bikes ⸢(they⸣ weren't designed for cars). Don't ride along the Pan-American Highway: cars and buses whiz ⸢by you⸣, and they're not going to stop to ponder who has the right of way. A mountain bike is prob⸢ably best⸣, especially in the wet season; most of the scenic roads are steep and poor. Biking is more ⸢popular on the fl⸣at Caribbean Coast and in the southwest. You ⸢can rent bikes for⸣ $6–$20 a day, but the rental bikes usually ⸢aren't great. Bring you⸣n if you can, but be aware that the climate ⸢is hard o⸣n bikes. Bike theft in the major cities is com⸢mon, so lock up⸣ with discretion.

Ticos give directions in meters; cien metros (100 meters) usually equals one city block.

HITC⸢HING⸣ ⸢• Hitchin⸣g isn't illegal in Costa Rica, but, as everywh⸢ere, you should be⸣ careful. On major bus routes, like the Pan-⸢American Highway,⸣ hitching is a bitch because locals assume that if you're a decent, responsible travele⸢r, you've got e⸣nough money to pay for a bus ride. People most willing to pick up hitchhikers are t⸢hose driving truck⸣s or other cargo vehicles; they'll generally let you hop in the back. The more gringo-hippie parts of Montezuma and Puerto Viejo de Talamanca see more hitching, and the general rule is that the more remote a location, the easier it is to get a ride. Sometimes you'll be asked to pay for gas or for the service—if they don't quote you a specific price, usually slipping the driver $1–$2 is appreciated. This is probably the safest place in Central America for women to hitch, but you really shouldn't do it alone. If you do, take the usual precautions and beware of the usual suspects.

BY BOAT • Ferries regularly shuttle punters from the mainland to the Osa and Nicoya peninsulas. A ferry to Puerto Jiménez from Golfito will cost $3; from Puntarenas to Paquera is also $3. Ferries do *not* run from one peninsula to the other. Private charter boats are often the only way to reach isolated beaches, islands, and scuba-diving spots.

BY PLANE • **SANSA** (tel. 221–9414) has a fleet of small planes that make daily flights from San José's Juan Santamaría Airport to nearly two dozen destinations within the country. Most flights are all under an hour, and tickets are $30–$50 each way. **Travelair** (tel. 220–3054) flies out of the domestic airport in Pavas, close to San José. They have more flights and tend to be more punctual, but they charge $50–$80 for one-way tickets. Some locations in the southwest, such as Puerto Jiménez and Golfito, are best reached by plane—a 1-hour flight as opposed to an 8-hour bus ride.

WHERE TO SLEEP

Costa Rica's popularity among travelers has caused hotel prices to rise a bit, and the gap between the decent places and the dives to widen. Lodging prices in all but the cheapest hotels drop between 20% and 40% during the low season. Credit cards are accepted by most midpriced and higher-end hotels, which often offer such services as laundry, tour booking, and luggage storage.

HOTELS • Costa Rica may not have the kind of accommodation bargains you'll find in the countries to the north, but it's got plenty of unique, good-value, quality digs. Major towns have pensions or hotels with basic rooms and *baños colectivos* (shared baths) for about $6–$10 per person. Beds range from hard to hammocks, but more important than the bed is a working fan. Hot water is usually available in the central part of the country, but only sparingly on the coasts. Always make sure that your room has a good lock; some hotels only have a padlock on the door. If you leave valuables in your room, lock them with a luggage lock. Larger hotels should feel comfortable, especially if you have been traveling elsewhere in Central America. They usually have a security guard in the lobby at night, and you can often leave valuables with someone at the front desk.

HOSTELS • Costa Rica has 13 HI youth hostels, and it should be getting more as lodge and hotel owners glom on to the international-backpacker thang. The main hostel, **Toruma** (*see* Where to Sleep in San

José, *below*), is the information and reservations center for the hostels and provides good info on budget travel. Each hostel has its own rates, which depend on how remote the area is. Rate lists are available at Toruma. About half the hostels have communal dorms and bunk beds (you don't need a sleep sheet); the other half are set up like hotels. HI members get a 20% discount, and if you're not a member, you can only join at Toruma. Nonstudents are welcome.

CAMPING • Most campgrounds are close to the beach or in national parks, and they charge around $3 per person per night for use of showers, toilets, and laundry basins. Campgrounds are fairly basic, and some don't let you have fires, so a portable stove may be a worthy investment if you plan to camp extensively. Some of the best camping facilities are found in national parks, but they are also the most expensive places, because you have to pay almost $7 a day.

Major transportation hubs don't have campgrounds. It isn't safe to sleep at bus terminals or in city parks because you could get robbed. You're legally allowed to camp or just crash on any beach in the country, but theft is pretty common in Costa Rica, which makes leaving a tent full of valuables unattended while you go for a hike or swim a dangerous proposition. Stock up on food and supplies at *pulperías* (corner stores) in beach towns, and bring plenty of insect repellent.

FOOD

Nobody travels to Costa Rica for haute cuisine, which keeps both the cost and the variety of food at a minimum. Although the variety of restaurants has improved in recent years, learn to love rice and beans if you don't want to spend too much money. In the morning, ticos eat *gallo pinto* ("two-toned rooster"), a mixture of leftover rice and black beans. In the afternoon and evening they eat *casados* ("married people"): rice, beans, salad, and a cooked vegetable with chicken, meat, or fish. All this runs about $3–$5, according to the restaurant. Food on the Caribbean coast is a lot more interesting, including such treats as rice and beans in coconut milk and *rondon* (fish and tuber stew).

The cheapest restaurants, called *sodas,* look like little diners and are really the most interesting and authentic places to chow down. They are common in the city center, at bus terminals, in the municipal market, along the highway, and inside budget hotels. They're generally open daily 6 AM–10 PM. They often don't bother writing up a bill, so just ask how much you owe. Chinese restaurants, found in any major town, are also a good bet for plentiful plates, including lots of vegetables. When you order drinks at almost any bar, they'll give you free or cheap ($1) appetizers called *bocas* ("mouthfuls"). *Ceviche* (fish or seafood cooked by the citric acid in lime juice) is a popular appetizer, especially on the coast. If you want to splurge, there are numerous restaurants in the cities and larger tourist destinations that serve what is best described as an "international menu." Unfortunately this often means a rather drab, unoriginal imitation of European and American cuisine. There are exceptions, of course.

DRINKS • In Costa Rica, 97% of the water is potable, but in rural areas, especially on the coast, you may want to stick to the bottled stuff. Bottled water and club soda are readily available. *Refrescos* are fruit shakes if ordered with milk, smoothies if ordered with water. Make sure you try *cas,* a tart regional fruit, or *maracuyá* (passion fruit), *carambola* (star fruit), and *guanabana* (soursop). Costa Rican coffee is wonderful, but unfortunately the best beans are exported. *Café con leche* (coffee with milk) is very rich, and ticos ritually take it with breakfast. As for the adult beverages, Costa Ricans like to drink as much as the next person—you'll notice that the seriousness of the drinking generally falls in inverse proportion to the size of the town. Serious drinkers will be seen downing large quantities of *guaro,* a dirt-cheap, heavy-duty pale rum served everywhere. *Café Rica* is a Kahlua-type coffee liqueur usually consumed only by tourists.

TIPPING • A 13% sales tax and 10% service charge are automatically added to the bill in most restaurants. Needless to say, you shouldn't feel pressed to tip any more unless the service was outstanding, you have a big crush on the waitperson, or you plan on coming back regularly. Tipping taxi drivers is not necessary.

OUTDOOR ACTIVITIES

Costa Rica is a mecca for outdoor activities of every ilk. Whether it's rock climbing in Chirripó National Park or surfing in Pavones, outdoor enthusiasts are almost certain to find what they're looking for here. The country is famous for its whitewater rivers, with several international competitions to date, and Olympic kayaking teams using them as a winter training ground, but there are plenty of rafting trips that are perfect for neophytes. Horseback riding is available just about everywhere, and trips range from a 2-hour jaunt into the forest to a waterfall to an all-day trek through the mountains to Arenal and Monteverde. Some of the best windsurfing in the world is available on the western end of Lago Arenal, and wave rippers have dozens of surf breaks to choose from on two coasts. Pavones, in the southwest corner of the country, has one of the world's longest left-breaking waves. There is also good skin diving off both coasts, ranging from the mellow coral reef of Cahuita to the deep-water rock reefs in the Playa del Coco and Drake Bay areas of the Pacific coast, where divers often spot giant schools of fish, several species of sharks, and manta rays. Mellower outdoor activities include the numerous wildlife-viewing opportunities afforded by hikes or trips in motorized dugout canoes in the country's extensive system of national parks and other protected areas.

VISITOR INFORMATION

The English-speaking **Toruma Hostel** (*see* Where to Sleep in San José, *below*) has a small tourist-info center offering discounted tours for students and current information about the budget scene in Costa Rica. The *Costa Rican Outlook* is put out bimonthly by Away From It All Press (Box 5573, Chula Vista, CA 91912–5573, tel. 800/365–2342) and has some good general information on travel in the country.

GOVERNMENT TOURIST OFFICES • Instituto Costarricense de Turismo (ICT), or Costa Rica Tourist Board, has an office beneath San José's Plaza de la Cultura, where English-speaking staff will answer questions but refrain from giving subjective advice. Invaluable maps and comprehensive bus schedules are available free of charge. Lodging lists are available for some regions as well as pamphlets and brochures for tour companies, hotels, etc. They also have some information about the country's national parks. *San José: Plaza de la Cultura, Calle 5, between Avs. Central and 2, tel. 222–1090, 223–1733 ext. 277, or 800/343–6332. At underground Museo de Oro entrance. Mailing address: Apartado Postal 777–1000, San José. Open weekdays 9–5.*

The **ICT** also has an information center in Juan Santamaría Airport (tel. 443–2883), outside San José, but their hours are more sporadic. Other branches are located at the Paso Canoas and Peñas Blancas border crossings, but they are even less reliable. Few towns have an official information center, but you can always get your questions answered at hotels and restaurants that cater to tourists.

Most showers in Costa Rica are electrically heated (not to mention ineffective). All those wires coming out of the shower head may make you paranoid about electrocution, but it's perfectly safe; just leave those heavy metal tools out of the bathroom.

BUDGET TRAVEL ORGANIZATIONS • The OTEC office in San José offers general information and reserves tours, rental cars, and plane flights worldwide. *Calle 3 at Av. 3, in Edificio Ferencz, 275 m north of Teatro Nacional, tel. 256–0633.*

VISAS AND TOURIST CARDS

If you're from the United States, the United Kingdom, or Canada and have a valid passport, you will be given a 90-day visa upon arrival in Costa Rica; citizens of Australia and New Zealand are given 30-day visas upon entering the country, but can extend them to 90 days at the **Migración** office outside San José (La Uruca, on highway to airport) open weekdays 8:30–3:30. If you want to stay even longer in Costa Rica, follow the lead of other gringo "residents" and take a 72-hour trip out of the country (most go to Panama) and you will be granted another 90 days upon your return. If you fly out of Juan Santamaría Airport, you'll have to pay a departure tax of $17.

HEALTH

Costa Rica doesn't pose as many health risks as most other countries in Central America. In fact, most visitors don't take any special percautions. Malaria pills may be a good idea if you're going to spend a lot of time on the Caribbean coast, but the best policy is to use insect repellent diligently, because there are several other mosquito-carried diseases present in the country, such as dengue, which is rarely fatal, but always a drag. The country has about two dozen species of poisonous snakes, none of which are agressive, but you'd be wise to avoid stepping on one—watch where you put feet and hands, and don't walk in a jungly area at night without a flashlight.

The worst health hazard to a traveler in Costa Rica is acually the beautiful ocean; rip currents drown dozens of people every year. Riptides are common on both coasts any time the surf is up. If there are big waves, and you don't have a lot of experience swimming in the ocean, don't go in deeper than your waist. If you are ever caught in a current, swim parallel to the shore till you're well out of it, then swim back to the beach riding the waves in.

Pharmacies fill every prescription imaginable, but prices are often high. Contact lenses and solutions are available at prices similar to those in the United States and usually come with a free eye exam. Women should bring an adequate supply of birth-control devices, though condoms are readily available.

Costa Rica is a fairly safe place to travel. Nonviolent crimes, such as petty theft, are the most common. Always keep your money on your person and be aware of your surroundings. Thefts occur mainly in the sleazier areas of San José such as the Coca-Cola terminal, but have also been reported in Cahuita, Manuel Antonio, Montezuma, and Jacó. Also women should watch out on the Caribbean Coast, where *atorcaguas* local sentiments tend to take things way too far. If you get into a bad situation, however, the *guardia rural* (police) are probably not the first people to go to—most locals don't trust them. A call to your embassy or consulate is a better option.

Alcohol is probably too present in Costa Rica, but drunks of all sorts are frowned upon—be respectful when you party. Pot is all over the country—pretty easy to come by but still illegal—and you could get into serious trouble if you're caught rolling, though you may just end up paying a hefty bribe.

RESOURCES FOR GAYS AND LESBIANS

ILPES, a private organization that promotes the rights of gays and lesbians, has a bilingual hotline operating weekday afternoons (tel. 283–3374 or 283–2532; 1–6 PM). The **Associacion Triangulo Rosa** is a gay organization with an English information number (tel. 234–2411). **ALUDIS,** another gay/lesbian group, answers the phone in Spanish (tel. 223–3758). The best places to meet *gente del ambiente* (gays) in San José are the two most popular gay nightspots, Deja Vu and La Avispa (*see* After Dark in San José, *below*). Gay-friendly regions include San José and Manuel Antonio; a general rule of thumb is if tolerant expats inhabit the area, it's mellower for gays and lesbians.

¡Pura Vida! A Travel Guide to Gay and Lesbian Costa Rica (Orchid House, 1993) doesn't win any awards for exquisite prose, but it does have a good list of gay and lesbian bars, cruising spots, and organizations in San José. Look for it at specialty bookstores in your country.

WORKING ABROAD

The most popular work-abroad program, **Council for International Exchange and Education** (*see* Chapter 1), provides a three-month work permit for $160, but but you'll have to find your own job and housing once you arrive in Costa Rica. There are actually plenty of jobs available *without* a permit, though some beach towns have hard-ass immigration who are on the lookout for "dry-backs," as illegal workers who have flown in from the north are known. Your greatest asset is speaking English—a dozen or so language institutes in San José hire foreigners pretty regularly, and though the pay is lousy, they demand neither experience nor work permit. Bilingual elementary and high schools hire most of their teachers in Febraury, but you should contact them in November or early December; they're tougher to get into, but they pay much better than the language institutes. Other skills, such as massage therapy or computer programming, open other doors. Some hotels, restaurants, and tour offices hire foreigners, but those are tougher jobs to score without a work permit. In San José, the bulletin board at the **Toruma Youth Hostel** posts current volunteer and paid work opportunities for foreigners ranging from vegetarian cooking to building latrines in national parks.

VOLUNTEER PROGRAMS • Biology nuts, especially, will find a lot to do in Costa Rica. Volunteer programs abound; if you're interested in doing something green, you're in luck. **La Asociación de Voluntarios para el Servicio en Areas Protegidas (ASVO)** is a conservation organization that works within the country's Environment Ministry, placing volunteers in national parks and protected areas. Volunteers need to be over 18, have some kind of insurance, be willing to work a minimum of 15 days, and pay $10 a day to cover the cost of room and board. Their San José office is in the MINAE Building, on Calle 25 between Avenidas 8 and 10 (Apdo 11384-1000, San José, tel. 233–4533, fax 233-4989); you'll have to provide them with a photocopy of your passport, a photograph, and two letters of recommendation. **Ecole Travel** (Calle 7, between Avs. Central and 1, tel. 223–2240) helps students hook up with internships though their "Ecole Experience" program. The **Cooperative Santa Elena** (tel. 645–5006) often has volunteer positions for its projects in the Monteverde area. **Jardin Gaia** (tel. 777–0535) is an animal rescue center in Manuel Antonio that sometimes accepts volunteers. The **Kukula Foundation** (Limón, tel. 758–1454) and **Vecinos** (San José, tel. 227–3868) both work with kids. **Earthwatch** recruits volunteers aged 16 and older for two- to four-week expeditions. Projects vary from archaeological expeditions to biological surveys. For more information, call 800/776–0188.

The **Humanitarian Tour Foundation** is run by Gail Nystrom. The multifaceted organization supports self-sustaining, reciprocal development programs around Costa Rica. Possible projects to donate money or time to include work with women prisoners and a children's project in Limón. For more information, call 506/282–9862, or write to Apartado 458, Santa Ana Centro, Costa Rica.

STUDYING ABROAD

Language programs are available all over San José and the surrounding area, as well as at a few of the beach towns. It is considerably more expensve to study Spanish in Costa Rica than in most other Central American countries—you'll pay several times what you would in Guatemala—but the professors tend to be more professional. San José offers the widest variety of programs: **ICADS** (Curridabat, tel. 255–0508), **ICAI** (Av. 11 bis at Calle 13, tel. 233–8571), **ILISA** (San Pedro, tel. 225–2495) **Intensa** (Calle 33 at Av. 5, tel. 225–6009), and **Mesoamerica** (San Pedro, tel. 234–7682) all have good reputations. There are at least two dozen other schools in the city, so shop around. If you'd rather study at the beach, check out the **Escuela D'Amore** (tel. 777–1143) in Manuel Antonio, which ain't cheap, but has a great location. **La Escuelita Dominical** (tel. 787–0012), in the beach town of the same name, is cheaper. **ISLS** (tel. 800/765–0025) and **Amigos Travel Services** (tel. 888/310–1064) are U.S. companies that have information about and can set you up with Spanish courses in Costa Rica.

PHONES AND MAIL

You can call anywhere in Costa Rica from a pay phone using 5-, 10-, or 20-colón coins or calling cards, according to the phone. All numbers are seven digits long. You can make international calls from any phone, collect or with a phone card, by dialing the long-distance operator of your choice: **AT&T** (tel. 0800–011–4114), **MCI** (tel. 0800–012–2222), or **Sprint** (tel. 0800–013–0123). The country code, which must precede any number listed in this book if you're calling from abroad, is 506.

If you're wondering why all four Costa Rican beers—Imperial, Bavaria, Pilsen, and Tropical—taste suspiciously similar, it's because they're all produced by the same company. Where's a good microbrewery when you need one?

The central post office in San José is the fastest and most reliable post office in the country; postcards to the United States are 30¢ and 45¢ to the United Kingdom, letters are 45¢ and 60¢ respectively. Regular postal service is slow (two weeks to a month, according to destination) unless you send it from San José, in which case it should take only about eight days. The American Express affiliate in San José (*see* Basics in San José, *below*) is the most reliable place to receive mail. You can also receive mail through the *Lista de Correo* at any local post office. Have it addressed to: name on your passport, Lista de Correo, town, province, Costa Rica. The post office will hold it for one month, but letters are often filed incorrectly and postal workers have difficulty reading foreign handwriting. Make sure they check under your *last,* not second (or middle) name. Discourage loved ones from sending presents, cash or money orders, or checks—they often get ripped off.

DOS AND DON'TS

The overwhelming presence of gringos in Costa Rica gives many the idea that this is their turf. Well, it ain't. Ticos are much more courteous than you might be used to, and you should take that into account before you bark out an order. At least smile and say "*Buenos días*" (Good morning) before asking for what you want in restaurants and hotels. Take time to converse a little bit with the people providing services, and chances are they'll warm up to you more. Fairly traditional undercurrents still exist, and just because ticos are used to seeing sunburned, topless gringos in shorts doesn't mean they like it, especially in the more remote areas. Be modest and discreet with your habits wherever possible. When camping or otherwise exploring national parks and beaches, always leave the area as you found it. Although many ticos litter indiscriminately, this is not where you should follow the locals' lead.

WHEN TO GO

The two-season rule (*see* Chapter 1) is in effect here, except on the Caribbean coast, which gets rain almost year-round. Accommodations are more expensive and harder to come by in the dry season (December–April), which is far more touristed. If you don't mind the rain, the "green" season (May–November) is the best time to visit. July and August are actually very nice on the Pacific side of the country, whereas September and October tend to be sunnier along the southern Caribbean coast. Temperatures range from 60° to 70° in the Central Valley and 70° to 80° on the coasts year-round. Semana Santa (Easter Week) and the week between Christmas and New Year are the worst times to visit—all the ticos are traveling, so you won't be able to find a hotel room anywhere outside San José. Schoolchildren are on vacation from mid-December till March, and during these months families crowd the beaches on weekends. During the final weekend in February, the last before school starts, the beaches are always jam-packed.

HOLIDAYS AND FESTIVALS • Semana Santa, the week leading up to Easter Sunday, takes place in late March or early April. Other holidays are **June 15,** Corpus Christi Festival, with morning floral processions in smaller villages; **July 25,** Guanacaste Annexation Day, with a huge festival in Liberia; **August 2,** Día de la Negrita, celebrated with a massive procession to Cartago; **September 15,** Independence Day; and **October 12,** Día de la Raza, celebrated with a raging party in Limón.

FURTHER READING

A Traveler's Literary Companion, edited by Barbara Ras (Whereabouts Press, 1994). *The Costa Rica Reader,* edited by Marc Edelman and Joanne Kenen (Grove Weidenfield, 1989). *The Costa Ricans,* by Richard Biesanz (Waveland Press, 1988). *Life Above the Jungle Floor,* by Don Perry and Sarah Lara (Simon & Schuster, 1986).

SAN JOSÉ

"A cien los mamones, ricos mamones. . . pipa fría, bien fría," ring out the calls of street vendors in the area around the Mercado Central, where the smells of stale beer and ripe mango mingle with odors much less agreeable. Hot salsa rhythms blast from clothing stores, while citizens shuffle slowly down the crowded sidewalk and men unload fresh seafood from nearby trucks. The Central Market scene is just one of many in this city of contrasts, where lush parks, charming museums, fancy shops, and cheap "Tico" lunch specials served at funky little eateries compete with the overwhelming influence of North American capitalism and fast-food joints.

San José is the capital of the province of the same name and of the nation. The busy metropolis is the center of governmental, economic, and cultural activity. *Josefinos,* as the residents of the city are called, number about 400,000; at least 600,000 more live in the suburbs. Josefinos are generally progressive folks interested in political activism: you might meet a taxi driver who doubles as a teacher for underprivileged kids, or a hotel owner campaigning to reduce the noise in her neighborhood. Most residents of the city are proud of their country's democratic heritage and confident that they can continue to make improvements upon it. One of the economic means to this end is, obviously, tourism, and it may seem like everyone you meet is involved in the industry in one way or another. Another result of the emphasis on tourism is that you'll almost always be greeted with a smile in San José. Of course the relationship between native and visitor has its other side—don't be surprised if you hear a few gripes about the *norteamericanos,* although these are few and far between.

Most travelers are a little ambivalent about "San Chepe," as ticos refer to the city. San José is a cool place to hang out, but not for an extended length of time. The city has all the activity an urban prowler could desire—funky nightlife, for example—but the congestion, pollution, and stress of city life become wearing. In comparison to other major cities of Central America, San José is more relaxed, easier to navigate, and very friendly, but problems of theft and drugs are on the rise. Most travelers limit their stay in San José, using it as a transportation hub to other destinations, but the city also makes a good base for exploring the surrounding Central Valley.

BASICS

VISITOR INFORMATION

The **visitor information center,** run by the Instituto Costarricense de Turismo (ICT), has an office next to the Museo de Oro, underneath the Plaza de la Cultura. The brochures and pamphlets scattered about are aimed at tourists with money to burn; ask at the counter for the most recent bus schedule, a road map, and the annual *Costa Rica Tourist Information Guide.* Although they're not allowed to make recommendations, the multilingual staff will gladly answer your questions. *Calle 5, between Avs. Central and 2, tel. 222–1090. Open weekdays 9–5.*

Fundacion de Parques Nacionales. This nonprofit organization in a residential neighborhood on the northeast end of San José, near the Santa Teresita Church, provides practical information about the country's national parks and can even reserve cabin or camping space for you at Chirripó or Corcovado national parks. *San José; 300 m north and 175 m east of Iglesia de Santa Teresita, tel. 257–2239. Open weekdays 8–5.*

SAN JOSÉ

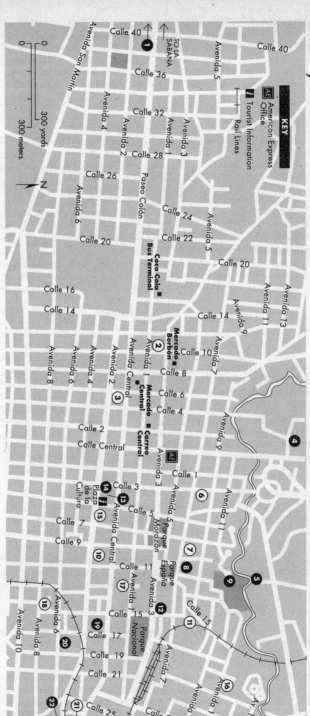

KEY

AE American Express Office

i Tourist Information

Rail Lines

0 ————— 300 yards
0 ————— 300 meters

Sights ●

Centro Costarricense de La Ciencia y La Cultura, **4**
Jardín de Mariposas Spirogyra, **5**
Museo Crimonológico, **20**
Museo de Arte Costarricense, **1**
Museo de Arte y Diseño Contemporáneo, **13**
Museo del Jade, **9**
Museo de Oro, **14**
Museo Nacional, **19**
Parque Zoológico Simón Bolívar, **10**
Teatro Nacional, **15**
Universidad de Costa Rica, **22**

Lodging ○

Casa Ridgway, **18**
Cinco Hormigas Rojas, **12**
Hotel Aranjuez, **10**
Hotel Astoria, **8**
Hotel Avenida Segunda, **10**
Hotel Bienvenido, **2**
Hotel Diplomat, **3**
Hotel Loy-Loy, **6**
Pensión de la Cuesta, **17**
Tica Linda, **16**
Toruma Hostel, **21**

AMERICAN EXPRESS

The downtown American Express office sells traveler's checks, cashes personal checks, holds mail, and replaces lost or stolen credit cards. Note that it roves back and forth between two locations: weekdays 8:30 AM–4 PM the office is on the third floor of the **Banco de San José**; the office moves across the street to **Credomatic** weekdays 4–7 PM and Saturday 9–1. You can change traveler's checks at the Banco de San José. *Calle Central, between Avs. 3 and 5, tel. 256–9911 or 257-1793. Mailing address: c/o American Express Mail Service, Apartado Postal 5445–1000, San José, Costa Rica. Open weekdays 8:30–4*

MONEY

The state-run **Banco Nacional** and **Banco de Costa Rica** can be a pain in the neck, with hellish lines, especially around the middle and end of every month. You're better off changing money and cashing traveler's checks at one of the smaller private banks or a casa de cambio. The **Banco Metropolitano** (Av. 2 at Calle Central, tel. 257–3030; open weekdays 8:15–4) across Avenida 2 from the Catedral, is a quick, centrally located place to get your colónes. **Banco Lyon** (Calle 2, between Avs. Central and 1, tel. 257–9511; open weekdays 8–4) is similarly convenient. The **Casa de Cambio G.A.B** (Las Arcadas, 2nd Floor, tel. 223–7221; open Mon.–Sat. 9–5) is located next door to the Gran Hotel Costa Rica and opens some days the banks don't. If you're staying at the hostel, you can hit the **Banco de San José** (Av. Central at Calle 31, tel. 222–933 or 253–5257; open weekdays 8–4) across the street.

BLACK MARKET • Black-market exchanges aren't illegal, but they're not advantageous and are often dangerous: street rates for traveler's checks are actually worse than what you'll get at the bank, and most money changers who work on the streets are quick change artists with pockets full of counterfeit bills. You can usually find them around Calles 2 and 4 and Avenidas Central and 2, muttering "*Dólares, cambio dólares.*"

BUDGET TRAVEL AGENCIES

Ecotourism is booming in Costa Rica, as are fly-by-night companies whose "green" agendas have more to do with American dollars than forest preservation. **Costa Rica Expeditions** (Av. 3 and Calle Central, tel. 222–0333), among the more reliable operators, offers a 15% student discount on several tours. HI members who'd rather see the country on their own can make reservations for hostels throughout Costa Rica at the **Toruma Hostel** (*see* Where to Sleep, *below*). It's not a travel agency, but the staff happily help make travel arrangements for members and give advice to all weekdays 8–4, Saturday 8–2.

OTEC has an excellent reputation for its tours, work-exchange program, and cheap international flights. They're the only travel agency in San José that offers student discounts, but you must have an ISIC or youth card to be eligible. They issue cards at the office for $15; bring two passport photos and proof of age or current school enrollment if you plan on getting one there. *Edificio Ferencz, Av. 3 and Calle 3, 275 m north of Teatro Nacional, tel. 256–0633. Open weekdays 8–5, Sat. 8–2.*

EMBASSIES

Canada. *Sabana Sur, next to the Tennis Club, tel. 296–4146. Open Mon.–Thurs. 8–noon and 1–5, Fri. 8–1. In an emergency, leave name and number and they'll call you back.*

Great Britain. *Paseo Colón, between Calles 38 and 40, tel. 221–5566 or 221–5816 for recorded information. Open weekdays 8–noon and 12:30–1:30. Closed weekends, but an emergency number is on the recording.*

United States. FYI: The folks at the embassy won't pretend they're psyched to see to you. *In Pavas (west of the city), tel. 220–3939. For lost passport information, tel. 220–3050 daily 8 AM–11:30 PM. Take a Lomas or Zona 2 bus from the Coca-Cola market to the front gate of the embassy. Open weekdays 8–4:30 (lunch hour varies).*

EMERGENCIES

For any emergency, you can dial 911. **Ambulance** and **Red Cross** (tel. 128), **traffic police** (tel. 222–9330), **fire** (tel. 118).

LAUNDRY

Getting your laundry done in Costa Rica is relatively expensive. Hotels with laundry service usually wash by the piece, and the bill adds up fast. If you've got a lot to wash, you'd be wise to look into one of San José's many *lavanderías* (laundromats). **Lavandería Costa Rica** (Av. 3 at Calle 21, tel. 233–0489; open Mon.–Sat. 9–7), across from the old Atlantic train station, is one of the city's least expensive. There you can wash and dry a 5-kilo (11-pound) load of clothes for about $4; or if you can't be bothered to wait around, they'll wash and fold your things for about $1.80 a kilo.

MEDICAL AID

Costa Rica's health-care system is one of the best in Latin America. In fact, costs and waiting times are very reasonable. **Clínica Bíblica** (Av. 14, between Calles Central and 1, tel. 257–0466) has 24-hour emergency care, a 24-hour pharmacy, and, during the day, doctors that speak English. **Clinica Católica** (Guadelupe, tel. 225–5055) offers pretty much the same services. **Farmacia Fischel** (Av. 3 and Calle 2, tel. 257–7979) is open Monday–Saturday 8–7 and has free delivery. In San Pedro, **Farmacia del Este** (Av. Central and Calle 9, tel. 253–5121) is open daily 24 hours.

PHONES AND MAIL

The **correo central** is a huge light-green building behind the Banco Nacional's main branch. Enter the south door to receive mail (bring your passport), send packages weighing over two kilos, send telegrams, or send and pay for faxes at window 18. Each letter received costs about 10¢, faxes are 50¢ a page to receive and $2.50–$4 to send. Enter the central door to buy stamps or to send letters or small packages. Upstairs, visit the **Museo Telegráfico y Filatélico** (tel. 223–9766, ext. 204), open weekdays 8–4. Also on the top floor is the **Oficina Filatélica** (tel. 223–9766, ext. 251), where stamp collectors can shop weekdays 8–4. *Calle 2, between Avs. 1 and 3, tel. 223–9766. North entrance open weekdays 7:30 AM–9 PM, Sat. 8–noon. South entrance open weekdays 7:30–5. Mailing address: Lista de Correos, Correos Central, San José, Costa Rica.*

If you find yourself being accused of an minor offense like speeding, you may be able to get out of hot water by paying a "multa" (fine, but essentially a bribe) directly to the offended officer.

ICE (Av. 2 and Calle 1, tel. 255–0444) is open daily 7 AM–10 PM. They sell local long-distance calling cards and have half a dozen phones available for calling. **Radiográfica Costarricense** (Av. 5 and Calle 1, tel. 287–0515) will let you call collect for free to anywhere except Europe, for which they charge 75¢. They also have fax and E-mail services; Internet navigation and E-mail costs $3 per hour. They're open weekdays 8 AM–10 PM, weekends 8–8.

COMING AND GOING

BY BUS

Buses run from San José to almost everywhere in the country (*see* individual destinations for bus info). Less frequented towns have fewer direct buses, and isolated areas may require several connections. To make your trip more challenging, bus terminals and stops (some unmarked!) are scattered throughout the city. The tourist office (*see* Visitor Information, *above*) puts out a well-updated free list of bus services and terminals; it'll be your personal Costa Rican bus bible.

The former Coca-Cola bottling plant is the closest thing San José has to a main bus terminal. Bordered by Avenidas 1 and 3 and Calles 16 and 18, to the west of downtown, the **Coca-Cola bus terminal** serves mostly western and northern destinations. Watch yourself and your belongings around here, because the area is a favorite for groups of young pickpockets. The best way out of the terminal is to head south toward the **Coca-Cola market,** turn east at the hospital, and walk up Avenida Central about 6 blocks toward the center of town. If you're too tired to walk, there are always taxis waiting outside the bus station, and **Sabana Cementerio** buses stop a few blocks away on Paseo Colón.

BY PLANE

Costa Rica's international airport and main domestic terminal is **Juán Santamaría Airport** (tel. 443–2942), about 16 km (10 mi) northwest of San José and 3 km (2 mi) south of Alajuela. In the airport, a branch of **Banco de Costa Rica** changes money weekdays 8–4. If the bank is closed, the black-market boys who hang out by the taxis will gleefully change U.S. dollars, but not much else. There is no luggage storage available in the airport. The visitor-information booths are open daily 8–5, but you can grab brochures anytime. Several gift shops, a restaurant, a chapel, a post office, phones, rest rooms, and a bar can help you kill time while you're waiting for your flight.

AIRPORT TRANSPORTATION • If you have a pack that you can rest on your lap, the cheapest way into San José from the airport is to take the bus from Alajuela, which passes by the airport. Buses run every 5–10 minutes 4:30 AM–midnight (50¢). The bus will drop you off on the west end of downtown, across from La Merced Church (Av. 2, between Calles 10 and 12). The buses don't have much room for luggage, so most people hop in a taxi and pay $10 for the ride to San José. Get two or three people together for a central destination and split the fare or your driver will fill the cab and charge each person separately.

BY CAR

A car guarantees you freedom from the often strict schedules of tours and buses, but renting is pricey (see Coming and Going by Car in Costa Rica Basics, above). Many of San José's numerous rental agencies have offices at the airport and along Paseo Colón. **Ada** (tel. 233–7733), **Budget** (tel. 223–2384), and **Hertz** (tel. 221–5959) are some of the more competetive, but take the time to shop around.

Welcome to the world of superdefensive driving and baffling Central American car etiquette. Speed limits and seat-belt laws are enforced, though you'd never know it from the crazy, high-speed manner in which ticos drive. Read the traffic rules that the rental agency gives you and rely on a good map rather than verbal directions. You can buy maps at car-rental agencies or pick one up (free) from the tourist office (see Visitor Information, above). Also, if you park your car on the street, someone may volunteer to watch it for you; tip them about 50¢ per hour.

GETTING AROUND

While wandering around San José, do yourself a favor and keep your eyes on the street signs—otherwise the proliferation of similar-looking buildings and Pizza Huts may have your head spinning. The streets form a simple grid, but there are a few twists. Avenidas run east–west, increasing by odd numbers north of **Avenida Central** and by even ones to the south. Calles run north–south, increasing by evens to the west of **Calle Central** and by odds to the east. Streets are generally marked, but most josefinos don't give directions according to street address. Instead they will tell you how many meters away a place is from a particular landmark, often **Parque Central,** the **Catedral,** or **Teatro Nacional.** Getting around will be easier if you keep track of which way is north, and remember that 100 meters equals one city block.

The main thoroughfares downtown are Avenidas Central and 2 and Calle Central. Most areas of interest to the traveler are in the heart of the city, north of Avenida 2. Eight blocks of Avenida Central, between Calles 9 and 6, are closed to street traffic, forming a consumer corridor of vendors and pedestrians. At Calle 14, near Hospital San Juan de Dios, Avenida Central becomes **Paseo Colón,** a ritzy strip of restaurants and car-rental agencies that dead-ends in **Parque La Sábana.** West of Calle 6, around the mercados (markets) and the Coca-Cola bus terminal, the neighborhood gets quite iffy, growing worse as you move north. Avoid walking in this area at night; stick to the well-lighted Avenidas Central and 2 instead. South of Avenida 2 also merits a nighttime warning. Generally you will be safe if you walk in groups at night. Be warned that all women, even in groups, will be verbally harassed by men near downtown bars.

BY BUS

Public transit in San José is cheap and extensive, but within city limits it's usually faster and less hassle to walk. Buses to outlying neighborhoods are more useful. Fares, usually 15¢–30¢, are prominently posted on the front window and inside the bus. Marked and unmarked paradas·(bus stops) are scattered throughout the city, and most residents can direct you to the right piece of sidewalk. Usually you can use the buzzer to signal when you want to get off; when these are broken or missing, tico men whistle, while ticas call out, "¡Parada, por favor!" (Stop, please). Most buses run till 10 or 11 PM.

Take the **Sábana/Cementerio** bus to get to Paseo Colón if you don't feel like walking several long blocks from the center of town. Frequent **San Pedro** buses depart from Avenida Central between Calles 9 and 11. To get back to San José from San Pedro proper, hop on any of the buses waiting next to the church. The tourist office (see Visitor Information, above) has information on other specific bus routes throughout the San José area.

BY TAXI

All those little red-hots you see zipping around San José are official taxis. The drivers are required by law to use the meter, and they add 20% to the fare after 10 PM. If the meter isn't on and running, ask the driver to "ponga la maría, por favor." If you've flagged a pirate taxi, or one without a working meter, agree on a price beforehand. Many taxis will try to scam the innocent gringo by saying the meter doesn't work. Don't be afraid to refuse the ride if this happens, but don't slam the door or you'll get yelled at. A ride across the city or to the nightspots in San Pedro should cost $2–$3.

WHERE TO SLEEP

Many of the city's cheaper hotels are *de paso* (places for a quick horizontal mambo), but there still enough budget spots for those who actually want to sleep, where the indiscriminate traveler can crash for less than $10. You're better off dropping $20–$30, however, so you can get a truly comfortable, pleasant room, preferably in the the delightful historic barios of Amon, Otoya, and Aranjuez. If you're on a tight budget, you can get the most for your money by staying at one of the hostels, which have extra services such as laundry, kitchen privileges, or breakfast. Two more pieces of advice—don't stay near the Coca-Cola bus terminal unless you're willing to shut yourself in your room by 6 PM, and call ahead, because hostels and the more popular hotels fill up quickly.

AVENIDA SEGUNDA

There are several simple hotels on the busy Avenida 2 that are relatively safe and near the Plaza de la Cultura and its nightlife. Most popular among shoestring travelers is the **Tica Linda** (Av. 2, between Calles 5 and 7, next to Bar La Esmerelda), long a popular hangout for hippie burnouts from around the world. A dingy double here costs $9 (singles are $4.50), and a bed in the cramped dormitory is $3.50. The communal bathrooms have hot water, and on weekends, you get to enjoy live ranchero music blasting into the wee hours from the bar next door.

Hotel Avenida Segunda. For a bit of peace and cleanliness, head up to this place, where second-floor rooms let in lots of light and air during the day, although the streetfront rooms get noisy. The communal bathrooms are clean and have hot water. A room for two is $11, while a single goes for $7.50. *On Av. 2, between Calles 9 and 11, tel. 222–0260. 250 m east of Teatro Nacional. 17 rooms, none with bath. Laundry. Cash only.*

You too could be a lucky winner! Buy a lottery ticket just outside the post office—they're only about 25¢. Results are broadcast nightly at 7 PM on Channel 7 and in the daily papers. Ask your friendly ticket vendor for more details.

NEAR THE COCA-COLA BUS TERMINAL

Hotel Bienvenido. If you absolutely must be near the Coca-Cola bus terminal or the market, try the Bienvenido, a huge former movie theater that was remodeled and divided into small, spotless rooms with private hot-water baths. Generic but comfortable doubles are $16. If you can get a group of four together, they'll let you stay in the downstairs dorm rooms for $5 a person. The friendly management is very concerned with safety and recommends staying away from the area north of the hotel. *Calle 10, between Avs. 1 and 3, tel. 233–2161. 300 m east and 50 m north of the Coca-Cola bus terminal. 44 rooms, 39 with bath. Restaurant.*

Hotel Diplomat. A five-minute walk from the Coca-Cola, and half a block from the Mercado Central, this clean, colorless place is in a considerably safer neighborhood, between the Avenida Central pedestrian mall and busy Avendia 2. Small but spotless rooms have hot-water baths, telephones, and decent beds, while the fancy second-floor restaurant serves three meals at decent prices. *Calle 6 between Avs. Central and 2, tel. 221–8133. 50 m south of Mercado Central. 30 rooms with bath. Restaurant, bar.*

BARRIOS AMON, OTOYA, AND ARANJUEZ

These historic neighborhoods cover San José's most pleasant corner, where tranquil side streets hold stately old buildings, well-kept parks, and some of the city's nicest B&Bs. Hotels here are close to most of San José's major sights, as well as a good selection of restaurants and bars.

Cinco Hormigas Rojas. This bed-and-breakfast is run by a woman artist whose colorful paintings are on display throughout the house. A beautiful double room in a quiet neighborhood, a huge breakfast, and that groovy, feeling-pampered mood can all be yours for $39 ($29 for a single). Breakfast is served in the lobby or in the tiny garden out front. Bathrooms are communal, though extremely clean. *Calle 15, between Avs. 7 and 11, tel. 257–8581. 7 rooms, 1 with bath. Laundry.*

Hotel Aranjuez. It's no accident that this out-of-the-way B&B spends most of the year full—it's one of San José's lodging treats. Occupying several former homes in the quiet residential neighborhood of Barrio Aranjuez, this friendly, family-run hotel has a variety of spotless, tasteful rooms surrounding garden patios and quiet sitting areas. A $35 double ($28 single) with bath includes cable TV, free phone calls and E-mail service, a hearty breakfast buffet, and discounts on tours. Every room is different, and some are nicer than others, so you may want to look at a few before you check in. *Calle 19 between Avs. 11* and 13, tel. 256–1825. 200 m east and 200 m north of emergencias, Hospital Calderon Guardia. 30 rooms, 22 with bath. Laundry.

Hotel Astoria. Slightly dingy, sparsely furnished $12 doubles and communal hot-water baths draw an interesting mix of budget travelers and strange locals to this funky old inn near the Parque España. Huts in the backyard, far from the bathrooms, are available for $8 a double. The bright lobby has some comfy chairs and a TV set. Proximity to the Limón buses and most major sights is another plus. *Av. 7, between Calles 7 and 9, tel: 221–2174. 50 m west of the INS Bldg. 19 rooms, 3 with bath. Cash only.*

Hotel Loy-Loy. Head straight for the second-floor rooms in this hotel, which are light, airy, and clean. The Loy-Loy also has that rare commodity in San José's low-budget lodging—yes, folks, private hot-water bathrooms. Shower for hours in reclusive bliss and you won't even care about the basic furnishings or peeling paint on the ceiling. Doubles are $14, singles $10. *Calle 3, between Avs. 7 and 9, tel. 223–8803. 450 m north of Plaza de la Cultura. 9 rooms with bath. Luggage storage. Cash only.*

Pensión de la Cuesta. This friendly, colorful B&B has long been a favorite with travelers. Located in an old wooden building on historic Cuesta Nuñez, down the hill from the Parque Nacional, the pensión charges $30 a double for simple rooms with communal baths surrounding a bright, sunken sitting room where complimentary breakfast is served, and where guests gather to chat or read. You are welcome to use the kitchen, and the receptionist can help with travel arrangements. *Av. 1, between Calles 11 and 15, tel. 255–2896. 50 m west of Assamblea Nacional. 9 rooms, none with bath.*

HOSTELS

Casa Ridgway. This quiet hostel is associated with the Quaker Peace Center next door. The local Quakers are actively involved in human rights and environmental issues in Costa Rica, and this hostel is an excellent source of information for those interested in political activism. It's located on a quiet dead-end street near the massive court and judicial police buildings and a short walk from good eats, bars, movie theaters, and museums. Private doubles are $20 (singles $10), and a bed in the dorm room is $8. The fee includes use of a newly remodeled well-equipped kitchen and a small library of English books and magazines. The communal bathrooms are large, clean, and have hot water. Alcohol, drugs, and smoking are prohibited, and quiet time is 10 PM–7 AM. *Av. 6 and Calle 15, tel. 233–6168 (ask for Casa Ridgway). Near the Tribunales de Justicia in a small, discreetly marked house. 20 beds. Kitchen, laundry. Cash only.*

Toruma Youth Hostel. Costa Rica's main youth hostel is the hip hangout for budget travelers. As a matter of fact, you might be tempted to move on after days of speaking English with other travelers, but it makes a good first stop. HI members pay $10 ($12 for nonmember students, $13 for nonstudents) for a bunk with sheets in a single-sex room, breakfast, and use of huge hot-water showers. As the *albergue llave* (key hostel), Toruma offers travel advice and makes reservations for the rest of Costa Rica's growing hostel network. It's also the place to join HI. Your $15 membership means discounts in all of Costa Rica's hostels; in some, you'll make up the cost of membership in one night's stay. Reserve three months in advance during the busy season (Dec., Jan., and May–Aug.). *Av. Central, between Calles 29 and 31, Barrio La California, tel. 253–6588 or 224–4085. Across street from Kentucky Fried Chicken. 123 beds. Reception open daily 6 AM–10 PM. Cash only.*

FOOD

There are hundreds of places to eat in San José. The cheapest, and most interesting, are roasted-chicken joints, Chinese restaurants, or *típica* restaurants (places who specialize in simple dishes like rice and beans) called *sodas*. The best deals are daily lunch specials ($3–$4 including a fruit drink), or the standard *casado*, which includes rice, beans, a simple salad, vegetables, and some sort of meat or fish. The quality of food served by most sodas is fine but no cause for gastronomic orgasm, but the places often have unique, individual characters. Unfortunately, the massive influx of American and American-influenced fast-food joints is beginning to eat away (no pun intended) at the smaller, privately owned restaurants.

That said, **Pizza Hut** is actually good here, and it's one of the only places where you can get a sanitary salad bar for less than $4. There's one on Avenida 1 between Calles 3 and 5, and another on Avenida Central between Calles Central and 1. **Rosti Pollos** (Calle 5 between Avs. Central and 1, tel. 256–2626), half a block north of the Gold Museum, is the local answer to fast food, serving a quarter chicken roasted over coffee wood, mashed black beans, a simple salad, a fresh tortilla, and refreshment for about $4, as well as an array of other entrées and great desserts. Paseo Colón and the neighborhoods just outside San José are the districts to head to for more upmarket eating, including some interesting ethnic options.

To buy supplies or munchies, check out the supermarkets downtown, such as **La Gran Vía** (Av. Central, between Calles 1 and 3; open Mon.–Sat 8–7:30), or the blue-and-white **Mas X Menos** (Av. Central, between Calles 9 and 11; open Sun.–Thurs. 8–8, Fri. and Sat. until 9). *Panaderías* (bakeries) and *reposterías* (pastry shops) abound, and good produce is sold in or near the **Mercado Central** (between Avs. Central and 1 and Calles 6 and 8). At night, most 24-hour restaurants become barlike, and even the plainest bars serve *bocas* (hors d'oeuvres), usually spicy and salty to keep you drinking, for about $1–$2 an item.

DOWNTOWN

Most restaurants in downtown San José may not be the place for a calm, elegant meal, but the multitude of budget eateries will satisfy your hunger economically. There are, however, a few spots where a few more bucks not only buy better food, but a bit of ambience as well.

UNDER $5 • Pipos. Located on the busy Avenida Central, across from the San Pedro bus stop, this narrow eatery is a popular lunch spot, thanks to its $3 specials, which include soup, a fruit drink, and, sometimes, desert. The menu also includes such tico standards as *arroz con pollo* (rice with chicken) and *olla de carne* (a soupy beef stew with cassava, carrots, and potatoes). The *plato vegetariano* combines an excellent salad with a fish filet for just over $3. They also have a tempting selection of home-baked cakes and pastries. *Av. Central between Calles 9 and 11, tel. 223–4623. Closed Sun.*

San José is small enough to walk around easily, assuming you don't pass out from diesel fumes or get plowed down by a car. Watch out for killer potholes—even in the sidewalks—and caños (ditches) that are deep enough to get lost in.

Restaurant Fulusu. This easy-to-miss place stands apart from most of the city's abundant Chinese eateries because of the authenticity of its vittles. At times, all the patrons are Chinese. Steer clear of the cheap plates near the front and order one of the dishes like the spicy chicken with cashew nuts or Szechuan beef, which easily satisfy two people. Start off with a dozen *empanadas chinas* (pot stickers). *Calle 7, between Avs. Central and 2, tel. 223–7568. Closed Sun.*

Soda Bar y Restaurant Paris. This 1950s-style diner, replete with Formica tables and cranky waitresses, serves tasty, typical Costa Rican fare at very palatable prices. Vegetarians on a tight budget will be happy with the *casado corriente*, a full meal for about $3, whereas the $2 gallo pinto with an egg will do in a pinch. *Av. 3, between Calles 3 and 5, tel. 222–2818. Closed Sun.*

Vishnu. Pink Formica tabletops and giant tropical landscapes papered onto the walls are all the decor this popular vegetarian restaurant offers, but then, it's the inexpensive, tasty food that keeps it packed with locals. The best deal is always the daily special—a full meal with drink and desert for $3—but they also offer veggie burgers and big fruit salads topped with ice cream. *Av. 1, between Calles 1 and 3, tel. 222–2549.*

UNDER $10 • El Balcón de Europa. Amid a sea of balding heads, glistening wood panels, and reactionary quotes, you'll find a cluster of travelers. Munch on the free cheese and bread while the kitchen crew whips up an amazing $5 *pasta arrabiata* (bacon, mushrooms, and basil). The risottos aren't bad, and the *plato mixto* (pasta sampler) is a good bet for $6. The house wine is good, and you can finish off the meal with a potent espresso and grappa-drenched fruit. *Calle 9, between Avs. Central and 1, tel. 221–4841. Closed Sat.*

ALONG PASEO COLON

Paseo Colón is a ritzy area with some great (spicy!) seafood options.

Macchu Picchu. This small Peruvian restaurant packs 'em in. The entrées, like the *picante de mariscos* (spicy seafood) or *pulpo al ajillo* (garlic octopus), both $6.50, are excellent. If you come with a group, your best bet is to order several appetizers and share them. Typical Peruvian potato dishes are all under $4, and the ceviche ($4) is the best in the city, according to resident Peruvians. Be forewarned—the hot sauce is *hot! Calle 32, between Avs. 1 and 3, tel. 222–7384. 225 m north of Kentucky Fried Chicken on Paseo Colón. Closed Sun.*

NEAR SAN JOSÉ

The neighborhoods outside of San José are good for a culinary change of pace. Ask around for local favorites or try one of our picks below.

THE MULTIPURPOSE GUAVA

If you're in Costa Rica at the end of the dry season, be sure to try a guava. It looks like a big, flat plantain. The thick peel is cracked open to get to the sweet fruit surrounding the seeds inside. Once you're done eating, the peel makes a great weapon. The expression "dar un guavazo" means to hit someone really hard, presumably with a guava peel.

UNDER $10 • Il Pomodoro. "The Tomato" dishes out inexpensive Italian food near the university. Hipsters, university types, and families order up pizzas made with a pungent but tasty local cheese and a variety of toppings: *chile dulce* (red bell pepper), *hongos* (mushrooms), and many, many meats. Small pizzas range from less than $3 to about $5. The pasta is reasonable at $3–$6 a dish, and a decent glass of red wine is available for $1.50. *San Pedro, on Av. 1, 100 m north of the church, tel. 224–0966.*

Restaurante Marisquerías. One of the best seafood places in San José, it's well worth the $1.50 taxi ride to Guadalupe to chow down on quality seafood in a shiver-me-timbers atmosphere. House specialties include the ceviche cocktail for less than $4. The lip-smackin' mixed plate of *bocas variadas* includes fish tacos, fried yucca, fried fish, and shrimp for under $5. *West of Parque Central de Guadalupe, tel. 224–8830. Tell taxi driver, "Frente al Palacio Municipal Guadalupe."*

CAFÉS

Costa Rican coffee is strong, and a few places still serve it the old-fashioned way: hot milk in one pitcher and hot coffee in the other. Coffee is not generally taken alone but with bread or a sweet. Glistening, flaky carbo treats lurk behind many a glass counter, but most are as tasty as cardboard. For the authentic sugar-and-caffeine high, combine **Churreria Manolo**'s (Av. Central, between Calles 2 and Central) killer greasy, sugary churros (50¢) and a cappuccino ($1). The places listed below have good eatin' *and* good coffee. Whatta deal.

La Esquina del Café. Okay, so it looks a little like a tourist trap, but this is the place for cappuccinos and lattes made with *frothed* milk—you won't get that anywhere else in San José. The coffee, roasted fresh daily from six different coffee zones of the country, can also be bought in bean form for $10 a kilo. The coffee here is the smoothest you'll drink. Coffee drinks and pastries are about $1 each. *Av. 9 and Calle 3, tel. 257–9868.*

Café Ruiseñor. This café, located in Teatro Nacional (*see* Worth Seeing, *below*), wins the prize for most relaxed atmosphere. Have a cup of tea and rest your weary head against cool marble while gazing at the frescoes on the ceiling. Atmosphere doesn't come cheap—coffees run anywhere from $1 to $9, depending on how much alcohol or ice cream is added. Try the *sinfonia vienesa,* a delicious concoction of espresso, chocolate, vanilla ice cream, and whipped cream ($3). Cakes are about $1.75. This is a great place for single women to sit without getting hissed to death. *Tel. 233–4488. In Teatro Nacional, on Plaza de la Cultura.*

ICE CREAM • Ice cream is an art in this country, and after a long, dusty bus ride, it may just save your sanity. The crème de la cream is dished out by two prolific chains, **Pop's** and **Mönpik.** There is a Mönpik on Avenida Central at Calle 6 and another on Avenida Central at Calle Central. You'll also find a Pop's on Avenida Central, between Calles 11 and 13.

WORTH SEEING

Most of San José's major sights are downtown and easily reached on foot. Notable exceptions are the sprawling Parque La Sábana (*see* Outdoor Activities, *below*), which contains the Museo de Arte Costarricense, the University of Costa Rica in San Pedro, and the Jardín de Mariposas Spirogyra. These can be easily reached by bus or taxi from downtown. No matter how you plan your sightseeing, you'll inevitably pass by the **Plaza de la Cultura** (between Avs. Central and 2 and Calles 1 and 3). Home to the Museo de Oro and Teatro Nacional, the plaza is also a good place to hang out, listen to the same

Andean flute bands that seem to be everywhere in the world now, flirt, people-watch, and just let the day develop.

CENTRO COSTARRICENSE DE LA CIENCIA Y LA CULTURA

The most entertaining exhibit at this former prison is the **Museo del Niños** (Children's Museum), with 38 rooms of historical and anthropological exhibits as well as short videos and games that demonstrate scientific principles. Also part of the center is the **Museo Histórico Penitenciario** (Penitentiary History Museum), which contains original prison cells and a number of astonishing murals done by prisoners, often in their own blood. Multimedia works by contemporary Latin American artists grace the walls of the **Sala de Exhibición.** If you see just one thing in San José, make this the one. *North end of Calle 4, tel. 257–8595. Admission $3. Open Tues.–Fri. 8–3, weekends 10–4.*

JARDIN DE MARIPOSAS SPYROGYRA

One of the nicest, least expensive, and easiest to visit of the country's butterfly gardens, Spyrogyra is hidden at the end of a dead-end street near the Centro Commercial El Pueblo. The garden is perched over the nothern edge of the Parque Zoológico Simón Bolivar, in a forested ravine that belies its urban location. The self-guided tour begins with a video about the ecology of these flying jewels, and ends in a screened flyway inhabited by about 30 different species, each of which has its different brilliant coloration. You'll definitely want to visit this place when the sun is shining—morning during the rainy season—because that's when the butterflies are most active. *Barrio Tournón, 50 m west and 150 m south of brick San Francisco church, tel. 222–2937. Admission $6. Open daily 8–3.*

Everyone loves Pop's mango ice cream, and Mönpik has a weird blue ice cream called "pitufo" (smurf), but the ice-cream treat that can't be missed is called "trits": a chocolate-swirl sandwich with a crumbly cookie crust found all over the city.

MUSEO DE ARTE COSTARRICENSE

The work of Costa Rican artists from the past 200 years is displayed inside a quiet, colonial-style building that was formerly the terminal for Costa Rica's first international airport. Exhibitions change every few months, but most represent *lo tico* through local landscapes and portraits or the use of local materials such as wood and stone. Take a peek upstairs, where the golden relief mural lining the walls of the **Salón Dorado** depicts the history, culture, and nature of Costa Rica. *East end of Parque La Sábana, 50 m south of Paseo Colón, tel. 222–7155. Take Sábana/Cementerio bus from Av. 3 downtown and get off at first Sábana stop. Admission $2 (free on Sun.) Open Tues.–Sun. 10–4.*

MUSEO DE ARTE Y DISENO CONTEMPORANEO

Work from all over Latin America is shown at this small gallery. Several artists are featured each month, and some of the exhibits are mind-altering. Ask Carlos the curator what exhibits are coming to town. *Av. 3 and Calle 15, tel. 223–0528. In the Centro Nacional de la Cultura, northwest of Parque Nacional. Admission $4. Open Tues.–Sun. 10–4.*

MUSEO CRIMINOLOGICO

Body parts and aborted fetuses float around in formaldehyde as object lessons for leading a clean, legal life. Foren*sick* exhibitions and a display of more than 8,500 weapons confiscated by the police department draw large groups of voyeurs. This museum is extremely popular among ticos, so take a Tums and come on down. This museum is also good for the quote of the decade: "Accepting an invitation from strangers of a doubtful reputation can have its risks." (Hmm . . .) *In the Organismo de Investigación Judicial (the police department); Av. 6, between Calles 17 and 19, tel. 257–0666, ext. 2180. South of the Museo Nacional, across from the Tribunales de Justicia. Admission free. Open Mon., Wed., and Fri. 1–4.*

MUSEO DE JADE

The Jade (pronounced "hah-day" in Spanish) Museum, along with the Museo de Oro (*see below*), definitely rates high on the "ooh, aah" scale in more ways than one. The darkened, environmentally controlled labyrinth is crammed with an amazing array of indigenous artifacts, including the largest collection of American jade in the world. Check out the jade tubes used as bras by the wives of important chiefs. They fastened the tube underneath their breasts—the original underwire. Then there's the famous room devoted entirely to fertility symbols, from colossal penises to female figurines with stylized genitalia. The 11th-floor view of San José is astounding, even on an overcast day; an adjacent room to the Jade Museum exhibits the work of contemporary Central American artists. *Instituto*

Nacional de Seguros, 11th Floor; Calle 9 and Av. 7, tel. 223–5800, ext. 2587. Admission $2. Open weekdays 8:30–4:30.

MUSEO NACIONAL

During the 19th century, the castle-like National Museum was a cultural center known as the Cuartel Bellavista. Displays span archaeology, botany, colonial history, and culture. Look for the enormous round stones left by the *Diquí* tribe, some of which are 8 ft in diameter and weigh up to 3 tons. It seems they were used for religious or meteorological purposes, but no one quite knows how the *Diquís* managed to make the stones perfectly spherical. They're considered national treasures, and it's forbidden to transport them out of the country. *Calle 17, between Avs. Central and 2, east side of Plaza de la Democracía, tel. 257–1433. Admission $1.25. Open Tues.–Sat. 8:30–4:30, Sun. 9–4:30.*

MUSEO DE ORO

Part of the **Centro del Banco Central de Costa Rica,** the Gold Museum houses a huge and compelling display of adornments from Costa Rica's indigenous cultures in an actual vault below the Plaza de la Cultura. The collection stands in striking contrast to the simple glass beads the Spaniards traded for such treasures. Explanations in English and Spanish guide you through the various ways indigenous tribes turned raw gold into ornamental objects. Also under the Plaza de la Cultura, on the first level, is the **Museo Numismática** (Coin Museum), only of interest to collectors or historians. The **Exhibición de Arte,** on the second level, gives an excellent overview of the country's art history. The guards are extremely anal about searching you for any bombs you might toss into the galleries, but they're not as concerned about checking student IDs—claiming to be a student has been enough for many a young traveler to get the big-time discount. *Calle 5, between Avs. Central and 2, tel. 223–0528. Under Plaza de la Cultura. Admission $5. Open Tues.–Sun. 10–4:30.*

TEATRO NACIONAL

The delicate frescoes, gilded trim, and subtle stonework of the National Theater drip neoclassic Eurolust. The center of Costa Rican fine arts for more than 100 years, the theater is worth a look if you're into architecture, history, or culture. For an even more baroque experience, go during an actual performance; a cheap ticket to a concert of the National Symphony costs just a bit more than the admission charge. Check the posters at the door or call the box office for current performances. *Av. 2 and Calle 3, tel. 221–1329. Admission $2.50. Open Mon.–Sat. 9–5, Sun. 10–5.*

UNIVERSIDAD DE COSTA RICA

The University of Costa Rica, in San Pedro just east of San José, is a great place to hang out and meet people, especially if your Spanish is pretty good. The open-air gallery at the **Facultad de Bellas Artes** (College of Fine Arts), on the east side of campus, hosts music recitals on Monday nights. If the Museo Criminológico didn't satisfy your thirst for the yucky, scurry on over to the **Museo de Insectos** (tel. 207–5318; open weekdays 1–4:45) in the basement of the Artes Musicales Building, just north of Bellas Artes. A $2 admission fee buys you a good look at dead insects in re-created habitats and information in English and Spanish on everything from insect sex to the diseases these little buggers cause. Readers of Spanish literature should browse around the many off-campus bookstores. Anyone who eats cheap (you know who you are) will enjoy the vast selection of inexpensive lunch places in the neighborhood around the university. Weeknights at the university are mellow, but nearby bars are packed with students and intellectuals on weekends. To get to San Pedro, walk a few miles east along Avenida Central's strip of yuppie shops and bars, or take a $2 taxi ride from downtown, or hop on a bus on Avenida Central between Calles 9 and 11, and get off at the first stop after the "rotonda" with the fountain in the middle of it. *In San Pedro, 250 m north of church.*

PARKS

Parque Central. This is a seedier but more authentic take on the plaza scene. The Catedral Metropolitana, to the east of the plaza, recently underwent extensive restoration to repair damage from several earthquakes. The massive kiosk that dominates the park was donated to the city by Nicaraguan dictator Anastasio Somoza in the 1960s. Supposedly, the Declaration of Independence of Central America was received and confirmed on this site, which puts the cruising, money-changing, and selling of lottery tickets into an entertaining context. It's life, liberty, and the pursuit of booty nowadays, so women probably won't want to stay too long. *Between Avs. 2 and 4, Calles Central and 2.*

Parque Morazán. By day, this park is home to hundreds of screeching kids from the elementary school across the street, as well as the most intolerant tourists in San José from the obnoxious gringo hangouts nearby. On weekends, families stop by on their way to the nearby Parque Zoológico Simón Bolivar (*see below*). At night, the park turns into the prime make-out spot for sexually frustrated young ticos. Immediately to the east is **Parque España,** a shady, plant-filled haven that lost its claim to hanky-panky fame when bright street lamps were installed around the park. North of Parque España is the **Casa Amarilla,** Costa Rica's Ministry of Foreign Affairs, a yellow building that once belonged to Andrew Carnegie, and the ugly concrete **Instituto Nacional de Seguros,** the nation's social-service building, which houses the Museo de Jade (*see above*). To the east stands the **CENAC,** a walled complex that holds the offices of the Ministry of Culture, two theaters, and the Museo de Diseño y Arte Contemporaneo (*see above*). *Between Avs. 5 and 3, Calles 5 and 9.*

Plaza de la Democracia. This plaza behind the Museo Nacional was constructed in 1989 to commemorate the centennial of democracy in Costa Rica. The large cement monument topped with a few sculpted figures was created later and is dedicated to "Pepe" Figueres, the three-time president who led the 1948 revolution and abolished the nation's army with a ceremony in the former fortress that now houses the Museo Nacional. At the bottom, a bustling souvenir market sells folk art, jewelry, and T-shirts—be careful of thieves there. *Between Avs. Central and 2, Calles 17 and 13b.*

PARQUE ZOOLÓGICO SIMÓN BOLIVAR

This zoo and botanical garden offers a lush and shady exposure to Costa Rica's flora and fauna—and there's a moon walk for the kiddies. The token (and nonnative) tiger restlessly pacing in its small cage is depressing, but the majority of the other animals have enough space to breathe. Tons of tico families come here on the weekend to torment the monkeys and feed the occasional escaped parrot. Placards posted around the zoo emphasize the necessity of preserving native wildlife—let's hope at least a few people are reading them. *North of Museo de Jade, tel. 233–6701. From Parque España, take Calle 7 north to Av. 11 and look for sign to the zoo. Admission $1.25. Open weekdays 8–3:30, weekends 9–4:30.*

CHEAP THRILLS

Get cultured! Or at least down a few free glases of wine. In any given week, there are invariably a few **openings** of art exhibits at San José galleries or cultural centers. Most are open to the public, so put on your best outfit and head over. Monday is probably the most popular night, but there are a fair amount of openings from Tuesday to Thursday—check the "Viva" sections of the daily *La Nación* for an ad announcing an *inauguración,* then ask a local or look in the phonebook for the location of the indicated "*galleria*" or "*centro cultural.*"

Do you ever reminisce about those elementary-school field trips to the roller rink? If so, head on over to San Pedro, where you can strap on those skates once again at **Salón de Patines Music.** *Av. Central, just past the rotunda, tel. 224–6821. Admission Sun.–Thurs. $2, Fri. and Sat. $2.50 (includes skate rental). Open daily 7 PM–10 PM.*

FESTIVALS

The week between Christmas and New Year's features two parades down Avenida 2: a noisy marching affair on December 26, and *El Tope* (a horse parade) on December 27. The nearby town of Zapote hosts a carnival midway, bull fighting, and heavy drinking for that entire week. During **Semana Universitaria** (University Week), beginning about April 20, students at the Universidad de Costa Rica cast off academics to spend the week drinking and dancing. Each *facultad* (school) throws its own party and builds a float for the parade. Every other year, San José hosts the **Festival Internacional del Arte (FIA)** (International Art Festival): two weeks of theater, music, and dance performed at venues scattered around the city. Although some acts are a bit expensive, others may be quite affordable or even free. Also on the expensive side, but of high quality, are the acts that arrive in July and August for the **International Music Festival,** which includes concerts in the National Theater and fancy hotels around the country. Early December is marked by **the Festival de Coreógrafos,** a week of modern dance performances by local troupes.

MARKETS

Leave your sense of time and direction behind and wander around the narrow aisles of the **Mercado Central** (between Avs. Central and 1, Calles 6 and 8). The enclosed, block-long market is stifling and stuffed with veggies, fruits, tropical flowers, rows of meat and fish stands, shoes, fragrant herbs, even housewares and souvenirs. Hunker down among locals and other travelers at a food stand for one of the cheapest meals anywhere. A few blocks away is the seamier **Mercado Borbón** (Av. 3 and Calle 8), a damp cave of produce sellers that is not nearly as interesting. The area in and around both these markets can be a hands-on experience in more ways than one: watch your back, your front, your money, and your manners. Do not bring your passport, wads of money, gold Rolex, or other valuables on this field trip. Borbón, in particular, may not be much fun for women alone or even in pairs. If you're staying in an outlying neighborhood, ask for the time and location of the local *fería*, a weekly open-air market held in each neighborhood.

AFTER DARK

San José's varied nightlife ranges from seedy, smoke-filled bars to fancy dance clubs where the Latin rythms of salsa and merengue alternate with pop hits from the great north. Check local papers—the *Tico Times* or *La Nación*—for information on cultural events, movies, plays, gallery openings, and concerts. If you just want the night to happen to you, wander up the **Avenida Central** to the east end of the pedestrian zone, where a number of bars and restaurants lie within a radius of a few blocks. A livelier, though younger, spot is the university area of **San Pedro,** where a dozen bars and restaurants offer varied ambience and lots of cheap pizza. A more expensive and touristy option is **El Pueblo**—a shopping center that looks like a colonial village north of town, with an array of bars, restaurants, and discotheques, many of which stay open till the birds start singing. Wherever you end up, take a taxi back to your hotel if you stay out late. Most of the gay and lesbian bars are south of Avenida 2, in some not-too-safe neighborhoods. San Pedro also offers some cool alternative hangouts. If you're a woman, try to get a group together to go out—tico men tend to think single gringas are more than fair game.

CINEMAS AND THEATERS

Movie theaters scattered around downtown San José usually show American films with Spanish subtitles, although the selection often leaves a bit to be desired. A nexus of cultural activity, **Sala Garbo** (Av. 2 and Calle 28, tel. 222–1024) shows great international films (check *La Nación*). The concrete cave of its basement **Bar Shakespeare** occasionally offers live jazz. **Cine Variedades** (Calle 5 between Avs. Central and 1), the city's oldest movie house, shows more artsy films, as does the University of Costa Rica (*see* Worth Seeing, *above*) at the **Abelardo Bonilla auditorium** in the Estudios Generales Building. Check the billboard posted outside for times and prices.

The abundance of *teatros* is testament to the ticos' love of theater, from ridiculous farce to biting satire. If you understand enough Spanish to follow a play, look for the announcements in *La Nación*. Companies from around the world come to perform at the two largest theaters, the **Melico Salazar** (Av. 2 and Calle Central, tel. 233–5172 or 233–5424) and **Teatro Nacional** (*see* Worth Seeing, *above*). Schedules are posted outside both theaters, and shows are advertised in *La Nación*; tickets range from $4 to $20, according to the act. If you're not quite fluent enough to enjoy Spanish-language theater, the expat **Little Theater Group** regularly offers plays in English; check the *Tico Times* to see if and where they're performing.

BARS

El Cuartel de la Boca del Monte. Popularly known as "El Cuartel," this bar gets packed on Wednesday nights, when most the of the city's best lookers and gawkers crowd together to see, be seen, listen to live music, and basically enjoy the thrill of crowding together. On any other night, it's a mellow, tasteful place, perfect for a pleasant conversation and a good meal. Be sure to check out their menu of fancy cocktails. *Av. 1, between Calles 21 and 23, 200 m east of Parque Nacional, tel. 221–0327.*

La Esmeralda. It's not exactly an expression of indigenous Costa Rican culture, but the Mexican *ranchera* music that people head to La Esmeralda for has been popular here since the early part of this century. Dozens of bands hang out in and in front of this massive bar—Costa Ricans head there to hire them for parties—so you need merely snap your fingers for a tune, but be forewarned that each song costs money, and they don't play cheap. The best deal is to show up late on a week night, when it's usally packed, and enjoy the music other tables pay for. *Av. 2 between Calles 5 and 7, tel. 233–7386.*

Beatles Bar. This dimly lighted, Canadian-owned bar a few blocks from La Esmeralda specializes in another type of music imported from the north: good ol' rock and roll. They usually have '60s and '70s rock blasting from the sound system—including regular doses of the Liverpool Four—but you may sometimes hear something from the '80s or '90s. They also ocassionally get a live band for the weekend, and on Wednesday night it's karaoke; blow the crowd away with your "Bohemian Raphsody!" *Calle 9, between Avs. Central and 1, tel. 222–8060.*

SAN PEDRO

The bars in and around the university town of San Pedro, just to the east of San José, tend to be more affordable than many of the city's watering holes, and there's a decent selection. Head two blocks east of the church and turn left to reach the main party drag, and as you walk toward the university, you'll pass at least a dozen bars. The music blasting from those establishments ranges from the more traditional Latin American sounds of salsa or nueva trova folk music to pop and rock of all denominations.

MUSIC AND DANCING

Like any good Latin American people, Costa Ricans love to dance, and dozens of popular clubs scattered around the city are bound to be packed on any given weekend night as the locals shuffle and swing to the irresistable rhythms of slasa, merengue, rock, reggae, cumbia, boleros, rap, techno, and anything else that's got a beat. Some clubs play only Latin music, but most play a good mix of tropical and northern sounds. Keep in mind that most discotheques charge covers of $5 to $10 on weekends, and have basic dress codes—save the T-shirt and grubby jeans for San Pedro.

An upbeat combination of Latin music with some northern pop sounds keeps the sweaty, enthusiastic crowd of working-class ticos dancing at **Salsa 54** (Av. 10 and Calle 21, tel. 222–6806), one of the only discos left downtown. **Kontiki Point** (Av. Central at Calle 42, tel. 257–6049) is a large, modern dance club inside the Centro Colón, at the western end of Paseo Colón, that plays more pop than most places and hosts occasional raves. On the opposite end of town is **Coyote** (Av. Central at Rotonda San Pedro, tel. 257–0035), a trendy discotheque in the basement of the Mall San Pedro. **Plaza** (tel. 222–5143), across the street from El Pueblo, is another popular spot that attracts a crowd similar to that of Coyote. The Centro Commercial has two discotheques: **Coco Loco**, which almost exclusively plays Latin music, and **Infinito**, which has two dance floors—one for Latin music, and one for more northern sounds—and is where people who can't stop partying gather during the wee hours.

You might need your cédula (photo ID) to get into Costa Rica's discos. The drinking age is 18.

GAY NIGHTLIFE

San José is internationally renowned for its thriving gay scene. **Cafe Mundo** (Calle 15 at Av. 9, tel. 222–6190), a lovely old house in Barrio Otoya, is frequented by gays and straights, who head there for great food and ambience. Look for the garishly painted unicorn outside **Bar Unicornio** (Av. 8, between Calles 1 and 3, tel. 221–5552). This classy, mostly lesbian bar plays mariachi and salsa music nightly 7 PM–midnight. Other underground clubs dot the city, but they're impossible to find without a local; even the most established hangouts are usually signless and have totally nondescript exteriors.

Déjà Vu. Make no mistake, boys and girls, this is *the* bar for gays, lesbians, open-minded straight folks, and people of any other orientation you can think of. Loud techno music bumps you into the wee hours as beautiful boys in skirts and G-strings sweat and grind together. The male strip show can get pretty raunchy, so have a drink or five on open-bar nights (Wed. and Fri.) to cool down. Take a taxi because the area is pretty sketchy. *Calle 2, between Avs. 14 and 16, tel. 223–3758. Cover $3 (Wed. and Fri. $5). Open Tues.–Sat. 8 PM until everyone's done.*

La Avispa. Christmas trees and pool tables crowd the back of the club, but up front there's plenty of room to dance to technopop and romantic Latin tunes. The clientele is mostly women, except on nights of "shows," when some of the cutest things in skirts are men. *On Calle 1, between Avs. 8 and 10, tel. 223–5343. Cover $2 Thurs.–Mon., free Tues. and Wed. Open Tues.–Sat. 8 PM–2 AM.*

OUTDOOR ACTIVITIES

Parque La Sábana is a gigantic recreation center that includes soccer fields, a baseball diamond, an Olympic-size swimming pool, tennis courts, volleyball nets, and jungle gyms. Be on the lookout for a gigantic cement cross, a 50-meter fountain on an artificial lake, militant Boy Scouts, and jogging high-school boys spouting every English vulgarity they know. *End of Paseo Colón. Take Sábana/Cementerio or Sábana/Estadio bus from cathedral.*

WHITE-WATER RAFTING

Costa Rica boasts some of the world's best rafting. **Aventuras Naturales** (San Pedro, behind the Banco Nacional, tel. 225–3939), **Costa Rica Expeditions** (Calle Central and Av. 3, tel. 257–0766), and **Ríos Tropicales** (Calle 32, between Paseo Colón and Av. 2, tel. 233–6455 or 800/272–6654 in the U.S.) offer similar trip prices. A one-day beginner's excursion on the Reventazón River costs around $70, while a more advanced trip on the spectacular Pacuare River will run you around $90. The price includes breakfast and lunch, transportation to and from San José, all the necessary equipment, and guides.

SWIMMING

Most places in Central America don't have good places to swim—you're stuck dealing with either murk, brine, or pollution—but the area around San José has been blessed. The waters of **Ojo de Agua,** a recreational complex near Alajuela, are chilly but clean and unchlorinated—and underpopulated if you go on a weekday. Buses from San José leave about once an hour from Calle 18 and Avenida 3. The area around Cartago abounds with nice little *balnearios* (pools): **Ujarrás, Charrara,** and **Orosí** (*see* Near Cartago, *below*) are the best in the province.

THE MESETA CENTRAL

If the crowds and smog of San José have you gasping for air, you're in luck—space and tranquillity are less than an hour away. Surrounding the capital are the cities and villages of the Meseta Central, an elevated valley bordered by mountain ranges to the north, east, and south. This rich agricultural region has been touted for centuries as the be-all and end-all of Costa Rica, much to the resentment of the outlying provinces. Still, the Meseta Central is the place to be if you're looking to venture from the capital without leaving it behind entirely. Hike deep into the cloud forest to the lakes atop Volcán Barva, take a refreshing river dip in Tapantí National Park, or browse through colonial churches in Orosí, Ujarrás, and Cartago—the things to do here are as varied as the vegetation and climate.

The provincial capitals of Alajuela, Heredia, and Cartago can be used as hubs to explore outlying villages, but generally don't merit much time in themselves if you're just passing through. To guarantee yourself a seat on the bus, you'll often find it easier to start your journey from San José instead of another city. If you're thinking of hanging out for a while, look for a friendly reception in towns such as Turrialba and Alajuela—both have hosted gringo residents who arrived "just passing through" and wound up staying for years.

ALAJUELA

At first glance Alajuela is nothing special, just a midsize city filled with kitschy stores selling shoes, underwear, and hair clips. Most travelers simply use Alajuela, about 22 km (16 mi) northwest of the capital, as a transportation hub to Volcán Poás or the highland towns of Sarchí and Zarcero, or as a last-night stopover close to the airport. You might be missing out. *Alajuelenses* are extremely open and outgoing people. Take a walk through the **mercado** (between Avs. Central and 1, Calles 4 and 6), or hang out in one of the city's parks. **Parque Central** (between Avs. Central and 1, Calles Central and 1) is pleasant, green, and shaded by massive mango trees. The free **Museo Histórico Cultural Juan Santamaría** (Av. 3, between Calles Central and 2, tel. 441–4775) is worth checking out if you want to know how Costa Rica kicked some greedy Americans' butts in 1856. The museum is open Tuesday–Saturday 10–6.

COMING AND GOING

Tuasa (tel. 222–4650) buses to Alajuela (30 min, 40¢) leave from Avenida 2, between Calles 10 and 12, in San José and stop at the **Juan Santamaría International Airport.** Buses run in both directions daily every five minutes, 5 AM–8 PM, and then every 10 minutes 8 PM–midnight. The two blocks between Avenidas Central and 2 and Calles 8 and 10 function as Alajuela's **bus terminal.** Catch buses here to the Butterfly Farm (40 min, 50¢), Sarchí (1½ hrs, 50¢), and Poásito (1½ hrs, 75¢), where you can get a taxi to Volcán Poás (*see* Near Alajuela, *below*).

GETTING AROUND

Alajuela is no booming metropolis, but you might get confused if you stray too far from downtown, because streets aren't marked once you get off the main drags. Avenidas run east–west, calles north–south. Orient yourself at Parque Central (between Avs. Central and 1, Calles Central and 1)—odd

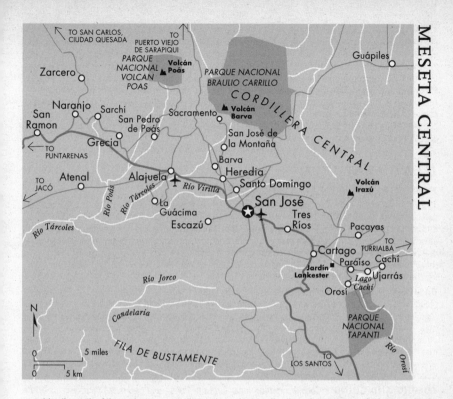

avenidas lie north of the park, even ones lie south, and odd calles lie to the east, even to the west. Marking the edges of the city are the **cemetery** (east), **La Agonía Church** (west), the **courthouse** (north), and the very conspicuous **McDonald's** (south).

WHERE TO SLEEP

Alajuela has more than its fair share of visitors, which means you'll generally pay a lot and get a little. **Villa Hostel Real** (Av. 3 and Calle 11, tel. 441–4022), 100 meters north and 100 meters west of Parque Central, is no deal at $20 for a double without a bath, but it is a great source of information about the surrounding area, and travelers flock here in droves. If you're totally strapped for cash, both **Hotel Rex** (Av. 1, between Calles 6 and 8, tel. 441–6778) and **Hotel El Real** (Calle 8, between Avs. Central and 1, tel. 441–2048) are near the bus terminal and offer fairly depressing doubles with cold-water communal bath for $11 and $6 a night, respectively. The cheapest and perhaps most pleasant option is to camp on the grounds of the Tuetal Lodge (*see below*).

Mango Verde Hostel. The Green Mango is close to Parque Central and the museum. Rodolfo, the affable owner, offers hot-water doubles with full kitchen privileges for $26. Chill out with other travelers in the TV lounge. *Av. 3, between Calles 2 and 4, tel. 441–6330. 25 m west of the museum. 10 rooms with bath. Laundry.*

Pensión Alajuela. SAVE MONEY says the sign on the outside this intimate pensión, and indeed you will. Bright doubles with private hot-water bath are $20 a night ($15 with a shared bath)—about as low as you can go in Alajuela without sacrificing cleanliness or sanity. On a quiet street on the north side of town, the pensión is popular with U.S. retirees. *Av. 9, between Calles Central and 1, across from the courthouse, tel. 441–6251. 10 rooms, 6 with bath. Bar, laundry. Cash only.*

Tuetal Lodge. Perched in the hills north of town, this friendly place has rustic cabins and camping spots scattered around a 7-acre coffee farm near the tiny community of Tuetal Norte. Cabins cost $40 for two ($45 with kitchenette), or you can pitch a tent for $7 ($10 for two people). *3½ km (2¼ mi) north of Alajuela's center, tel. 442–1804. 6 cabins with bath. Restaurant, laundry.*

FOOD

For the best-value eats in town, head to the **mercado** (between Avs. Central and 1, Calles 4 and 6, 100 m east of the bus terminal). You'll find several inexpensive restaurants of the roasted-chicken variety around the terminal. Surrounding Parque Central are a handful of burger joints where the food is tasty, but you'll be charged gringo prices for the cool view. One block west of Villa Hostel Real, the popular **Pizza Ovis** (Av. 3 and Calle Central, tel. 441–4328) serves up tasty thin-crust pies for $2 (small) and $4 (medium). At the northwest corner of Juan Santamaría Park, relax with a beer ($1) on one of the balconies at **Restaurante La Jarra** (Calle 2, between Avs. Central and 2, tel. 441–6708). Try tasty arroz con pollo (rice with chicken, $5) or *corvina* (sea bass) prepared a number of ways ($6–$7). The place jumps after 8 PM on weekends.

NEAR ALAJUELA

PARQUE NACIONAL VOLCAN POAS

Just 37 km (23 mi) north of Alajuela, massive, active Volcán Poás is one of the most accessible and visited volcanoes in Costa Rica. The banded, brown-gray crater is 1½ km (1 mi) wide and 1,000 ft deep, and at the bottom of it lies a pale blue-green lake that is usually boiling and belching plumes of sulfuric steam. Poás entered a more active phase in 1989, and now sporadically emits geyserlike eruptions; at one point acid rain caused by its sufluric gas damaged local crops, and toxic fumes forced the government to close the park for a while. The most popular park in Costa Rica, Poás is packed with visitors during the dry season, especially on weekends.

BASICS • The best time to see the crater is in the dry season, or early in the morning, before afternoon clouds and drizzle descend. Hiking into the crater itself is prohibited, but a 10-minute walk up a paved road leads you to a breathtaking—and very popular—view of the crater, its lake, and the surrounding hills. There are also two 30-minute hikes: one leads to a view of the blue-green **Laguna Botos,** while the other winds through the surrounding dwarf cloud forest. Look for the lines of poetry (in Spanish) posted intermittently on placards. Dress in layers and be prepared for rain and intense sunshine. Temperatures change dramatically, and the top of the volcano at 8,900 ft can get cold and windy but is sometimes quite hot. *Admission $6. Open daily 8–3:30.*

COMING AND GOING • Consider renting a car to get to Poás—you can make your own schedule and arrive early, before clouds ruin the view. From San José, take the General Canas Highway to Alajuela, drive through the center of town and continue north up the slopes of Poás, following the signs. If you're limited to public transportation, a packed **Tuasa** (tel. 222–4650) bus goes directly from San José to the volcano once daily. It leaves from the Parque de la Merced (Avenida 2 and Calle 12) at 8:30 AM, stopping at the Alajuela bus station at 9 AM. The bus stops once in Alajuela, where they collect the $4 fare, and again at a restaurant where you can buy sandwiches and drinks ($1–$2), before finally arriving 10:30 AM. You'll have about four hours to explore before the bus leaves again at 2:30 PM. Another option is to take a bus from Alajuela to Poásito (1½ hrs, 75¢), 16 km (10 mi) from the park. From there, hitchhike or take a taxi the rest of the way. Or take a taxi from Alajuela right to the park—it costs about $30 round-trip, and you'll need to tell the driver when to come back for you.

WHERE TO SLEEP AND EAT • There's a small cafeteria inside the park where you can pick up snacks, but it's cheaper to bring your own lunch. If you want to stay overnight, make reservations at **Albergue Ecológico La Providencia** (tel. 380–6315, fax 290–0289), which has elegantly simple cabins with gas-stove kitchenettes at $37 ($29 students) for a double with bath; breakfast is included and the tranquillity and view are something special. The proprietors offer a three-hour horseback tour through primary-growth forest, reforested areas, and up the back side of Poás for $20. The *albergue* (lodging house) is a short drive or a long walk from the park entrance. Follow the highway to a green gate, about 1½ km (1 mi) outside the park. From there it's maybe 2 km (1¼ miles) up the hill on a red-gravel road.

FINCA DE MARIPOSAS

Brilliant blues, vibrant greens, rich reds, and majestic purples flutter by at the Butterfly Farm. Forty minutes southwest of Alajuela, in the town of La Guácima, the farm spreads over 4 acres. The $14 admission includes a bilingual video and tour with enthusiastic guides who encourage you to handle caterpillars and pupae. The last tour begins at 3, but go early in the day, before the rain makes the butterflies hide. The'll also pick you up from and return you to downtown San José for $6. From San José, buses to La Guácima (1 hr, 50¢) leave from Avenida 1, between Calles 20 and 22, daily (except Sunday) at 11 and 2, returning at 12:15 and 3:15. You'll have more time to explore the farm if you take a bus from Alajuela (40 min, 50¢). From Calle 8, between Avenidas 2 and 4, take a Ciruelas/Guácima Abajo bus at 6:20, 9, 11, or 1 and ask the driver to let you off at the Finca de Mariposas. Buses to Alajuela pass the farm at 9:45, 11:45, 3:45, 5:15, and 5:45. Buses to San José pass at 12:15 and 3:15. *Tel. 438–0115. Open 9:30–4:30.*

SARCHI AND GRECIA

Sarchí, a pleasant village 32 km (20 mi) north of Alajuela, is known for delicate woodwork, brilliantly painted ox carts, and comfy, collapsible leather rocking chairs. Most of the souvenir shops are south and north of the town's center—look for them on the highway and ask the bus driver to let you off when you see one. The hungry visitor can chose from many cheap sodas; **Super Mariscos** (100 m north and 50 m east of main plaza, tel. 454–4330) has great ceviche ($4) and atmosphere. **Tuan** (tel. 441–3781) buses leave for Sarchí (1½ hrs, 50¢) from Calle 8 at Avenida Central in Alajuela every half hour 5 AM–10 PM. Alternatively, travel to Sarchí via the small town of Grecia, famous for its bright red, metal church, which was made in Belgium more than a century ago and shipped to Costa Rica. The area's wealthy coffee farmers thought a metal church would better withstand earthquakes, and they were apparently right. If you're interested in insects, check out **Joyas del Bosque Húmedo** (Jewels of the Rainforest), a small museum half a block north of the park's western edge (tel. 494–5620). **Balneario Tropical** (3 blocks down the hill to the left of church) is a natural pool where you can swim Tuesday–Saturday 9:30–5 and Sunday 9–5 for $1.50. Buses go to Grecia (75¢) every hour from the Coca-Cola bus terminal in San José. From Grecia, buses to Sarchí leave about every half hour from the west side of the terminal.

The following are considered pejorative unless used by other members of the ambiente (gay community): "tortilleras" (dykes), "militar" or "tractor" (butch), "las locas" (queers).

ZARCERO

Ninety minutes northwest of San José, the small town of Zarcero looks like it was designed by Dr. Seuss, but the cypress shrubs trimmed in bizarre animal shapes that decorate the park in front of the church are the work of another man—Evangelista Blanco. You're almost certain to spot Evangelista trimming a shrub or hanging out in his modern office as you explore the fanciful park; he works seven days a week. The interior of the church, which is more than a century old, is covered with elaborate pastel stencils and detailed religious paintings by Misael Solis, who completed the paintings more than 50 years ago. Zarcero is renowned for its cheese and peach preserves, both of which are sold in stores around town and just out of town on the highway. Stop at **El Tiesto Souvenir Shop** (across from the park, tel. 463–3196) and talk politics with the owner, Rafael, a native tico who lived in New Jersey for a while. He knows everything about the area and will arrange day trips to nearby waterfalls for $17 a person, lunch included.

COMING AND GOING • Zarcero's mountain climate and friendly atmosphere make it a good day trip from San José. **Autos Transportes Ciudad Quesada** (tel. 255–4318) has buses from the Coca-Cola bus terminal. You want one marked SAN CARLOS; they leave once an hour 5 AM–7:30 PM daily. A SAN CARLOS DIRECTO bus will cost $2 and take 1½ hours. Other San Carlos buses cost just $1 but take a longer, more indirect route and are more crowded. Be sure to ask the driver to let you off in Zarcero. You'll find return buses, which pass through Zarcero every hour on the hour, at the red bus stop across the street from where you get off. On weekends and in the late afternoon, you may have to wait for a bus that's not packed.

WHERE TO SLEEP AND EAT • If you're staying a while, **Hotel Don Beto** (to your left as you face the church, tel. 463–3137) has comfy doubles for $15–$25, according to the room. **Restaurant Zarcero,** across from where the bus stops, has tasty casados and *batidos* (milkshakes)—a full meal costs less than $3.

HEREDIA

Just a half-hour bus ride north from San José is Heredia, capital of the province of the same name and a bustling university town. Tucked in the hills of a rich coffee-growing region, Heredia is a city that feels like a neighborhood—people are chatty and mellower than in the capital. Heredia's main point of interest is palm-lined **Parque Central** and the surrounding historical buildings. The historic **Iglesia de la Immaculada Concepción,** on the east side of the park, has a small, peaceful garden and an impressive stained-glass window depicting the Virgin. It was completed more than 200 years ago, and such structural details as thick walls, small windows and stout buttresses have helped it survive a number of big earthquakes. On the northeast corner of the park is **Casa de la Cultura.** Once a presidential residence, it now serves as an art gallery. Admission is free, and it's open daily 8 AM–10 PM. Next door is **El Fortín,** a stout, circular tower. The tower is closed to the public, but they usually let gringos climb the condemned turret (at their own risk) to see the city and surrounding mountains. From Parque Central, walk east down Avenida Central to the rambling, green campus of the **Universidad Nacional.** The UNA has the reputation of being the country's most radical university; you'll find neorevolutionaries swilling beer at nearby bars (see Food, below). The **Centro de Arte** (east side of campus, where Av. Central ends) shows student plays—check the billboard for show times and dates.

COMING AND GOING

Microbuses Rápidos Heredianos (tel. 233–8392) has frequent service to Heredia (30 min, 30¢) from Calle 1, between Avenidas 7 and 9, in San José. Buses in either direction leave daily every 10 minutes 5 AM –10 PM, with stops in Tibas and Santo Domingo. Get off at the last Heredia stop—you'll be close to Parque Central, the market, and cheap lodging. Catch a return bus nearby, across from **Mönpik** ice-cream parlor (Av. 4, between Calles Central and 1). Buses leave Heredia for the nearby towns of Barva and San José de la Montaña (to Braulio Carrillo).

GETTING AROUND

Heredia is a compact city, centered around Parque Central, between Avenidas Central and 2 and Calles Central and 2. Odd streets lie to the east, even to the west; odd avenues lie to the north, even to the south. If you forgot your compass, just remember: facing the church entrance in the plaza, your nose is pointing east. Major landmarks are the **post office,** on the northwest corner of Parque Central; **Casa de la Cultura,** on the northeast corner; the **Red Cross,** on Calle Central, between Avenidas 1 and 3; and the **Mercado Viejo** (old market—don't bother looking for the new market), between Avenidas 6 and 8 and Calles 2 and 4.

WHERE TO SLEEP

For some weird reason, the hotels in Heredia are always full, so reservations are a must. **Pensión Herediana** (Calle Central, between Avs. 4 and 6, no phone) charges $12 a double and has hot water, but the rooms are dank and dumpy. The wood-paneled rooms at **Hotel Ramble** (Av. 8, between Calles 10 and 12, 350 m from the market, tel. 238–3829) are just about luxurious, with private, hot-water baths, for $25 for a double.

Hotel Heredia. This family establishment crawls with Central American kitsch—lots of red vinyl, turquoise paint, flowers, and signs that proclaim NO SE AQUILA POR RATOS (i.e., This is not a nooky-nook). Doubles with hot-water baths are about $25. The neighborhood, Barrio Fatima, is safe and quiet, because it's a little outside the city center. Make reservations a few days in advance. Calle 6, between Avs. 3 and 5, tel. 238–0880. 200 m west and 250 m north of post office. 10 rooms with bath. Cash only.

FOOD

Heredia is peppered with cheap sodas, and the most inexpensive tico food is in the Mercado Viejo. For cheap rice dishes and the most lightbulb fixtures you've ever seen on a single ceiling, try the Chinese restaurant **Ho Wah** (Av. 4, between Calles 2 and 4, tel. 237–3636), open daily 5 PM–11 PM. Restaurant/bar **Chaparral** (next to the Casa de la Cultura, tel. 237–1010) is open daily 11–11 and serves good meat dishes and Chinese food for $4–$6 a plate; just don't eat by the never-cleaned aquarium or you'll lose your appetite. Near the university, students munch desserts at **Fresas** (Calle 7 and Av. 1, tel. 237–3915) daily from 8 until midnight, or plan revolutions and term papers over beers and bocas at **La Choza** (Av. Central, between Calles 5 and 7, tel. 237–4166), open weekdays 5 PM–10 PM, Saturdays 10–10.

NEAR HEREDIA

CAFE BRITT FARM

Ever wonder how your cup of joe went from bean to brown liquid? The folks up at Café Britt, about 2 km (1 mi) north of Heredia, are more than happy to show you. Their popular Coffee Tour includes a walk through the fields and roasting plant, a play about the history of coffee and, of course, lots of time for you to buy coffee and everything related to it. Tours cost $20 including round-trip transportation from San José. Call 260–2748 for reservations; tours begin daily at 9 and 11 AM (also at 3 PM during the dry season) and last about 2 hours. The farm is a 10-minute ($2) taxi ride from downtown Heredia, or you can take the bus to Barva, which leaves from the Red Cross in Heredia (Calle Central, between Avs. 3

and 1), and get off when you see the "COFFEETOUR" CAFE BRITT sign on your right; walk 5 minutes west and you're there. If you have time to burn after the tour, visit **Barva.** Head over on the same bus, or you can hoof it—it's less than 2 km (1 mi) north of the farm. Barva is an old colonial town that has been declared an historical monument. Viewing the preserved adobe buildings hemmed in by coffee fields provides a picturesque diversion.

PARQUE NACIONAL BRAULIO CARRILLO

This immense national park begins 20 km (13 mi) northeast of San José, extending 113,000 acres toward the Caribbean coast. Braulio Carrillo protects the virgin rain forest on either side of the highway to Guápiles and Puerto Limón. You can get some idea of it as you pass through on the highway, but inside is another world. Everywhere you look, green things sprout, twist, and bloom. Bromeliads and orchids cling to arching trees. Moss, lichens, and fungi ooze from every nook and cranny. The resident fauna, including white-faced monkeys, paca (a large rodent), and brilliant blue morpho butterflies, creep, crawl, and flutter amid more than 6,000 species of plant life.

BASICS • Temperature and rainfall are unpredictable and change according to the elevation, and the terrain varies from flatlands to the 2,900-meter- (9,500-ft-) high Volcán Barva. Wear sturdy hiking shoes and carry rain gear. The December–April dry season is the best time to visit, although "dry" is never exactly the word for this park because the area gets almost 15 feet of rain annually. You can enter Braulio Carrillo through three points along the highway. The **Zurquí** station is most convenient to San José and the other Meseta Central towns. Here you'll find the **administration and visitor center** on the highway about 2 km (1 mi) into the park, 500 meters before the Zurquí tunnel.

"Ah, she's complaining today," says Sra. Rodríguez as Poás rumbles in the distance. "There must be a lot of visitors."

From the station, a half-mile trail leads to a *mirador* (lookout). The beginning of the trail is difficult—recommended by the park service for the "physically fit"—but the rest is fairly easy. Another 22 km (14 mi) down the highway toward Limón is the **Quebrada Gonzales** (or Carrillo) station, which has an information center, bathrooms, and potable water. The park's third entrance, and easist area to visit from Heredia, is the **Volcán Barva Sector,** 4 km (2½ mi) northeast from **Sacramento,** a small town about 18 km (11 mi) north of Heredia. The Volcán Barva sector of Braulio Carrillo is less visited than the other two areas and consists of wonderful cloud-forest flora. A 6½-km (4-mi) hike passes the three freshwater lagoons that nestle in the craters of the now-extinct volcano. You can camp in the park for $8 per person per night, but you must bring your own tent, cooking stove, and sleeping bag. The folks at the **Area de Conservación Cordillera Central** (tel. 256–2717) can answer specific questions about the park. *Admission $6. Open 8–4.*

COMING AND GOING • To reach the Zurquí station or Quebrada Gonzales (Carrillo sector), take a **Coopetraga** (tel. 223–1276) bus toward **Guapiles** from Calle 12, between Avenidas 7 and 9, in San José. Service runs about every half hour daily 5:30 AM–7 PM and costs $1. When you board, let the driver know which station you want. To get back, you'll have to flag down a bus along the highway—this can be difficult on weekends, when buses are crowded. Getting to the Volcán Barva sector is something of an ordeal. You'll want to spend the night in Heredia and catch a morning bus. Buses leave from the Mercado Viejo, at 6:30 AM, 11 AM, and 4 PM every day except Sunday, when there is no early bus. The bus passes through **San José de la Montaña** to drop you at **Paso Llano.** From Paso Llano, hike 4 km (2½ mi) up a paved road to Sacramento, then another 4 km up a hellish, clay- and cow dung–covered road to the park entrance. The last return bus to Heredia is supposed to pass through Paso Llano at 5 PM. You'll need a four-wheel-drive vehicle to drive to the park entrance, although any car will make it as far as San José de la Montaña.

CARTAGO

Forty-minutes southeast of San José lies the capital's conservative, Catholic sibling. Originally the center of Costa Rican culture and the country's capital for 300 years, Cartago was devastated by earthquakes in 1824 and 1910. Although several funky turn-of-the-century houses still line the main streets, many historical landmarks were destroyed—including the original **cathedral** (between Avs. 1 and 2, Calles 2 and 4), which has been transformed into a pretty garden. On the east side of town, the elaborate Byzantine structure of the **Basilica de Los Angeles** (Calle 16, between Avs. 2 and 4) houses the shrine of the Virgen de Los Angeles, Costa Rica's patron saint (*see* Our Lady of Interracial Harmony,

THE ROCK
OF THE CHURCH

Costa Rica's patron saint, the Virgin of Los Angeles, is popularly known as "La Negrita" (the little black one). To an atheist or skeptic, she may look like a little black rock surrounded by gold and jewels, but to a believer, she is a manifestation of the Virgin Mary's ubiquitous influence and the vehicle of countless miracles. On August 2, 1635, La Negrita was discovered on the outskirts of Cartago by a peasant girl who took her home. Her miraculous reappearance in the same spot every time she was removed was interpreted as a divine order to build a basilica on that very spot. Each year on August 2, hundreds of ticos walk from San José (and farther) to the shrine, which is now surrounded by promises, trophies, letters of thanks, and tiny metal "milagros," images of everything from heads and hands to airplanes and eyeglasses.

below). The basilica's soaring angels contrast sharply with the macabre air of nearby Volcán Irazú and rumors of ghosts in the cathedral ruins. Cartago is the transportation hub for the nearby towns of Paraíso, Orosí and Ujarras.

COMING AND GOING

Buses run between San José and Cartago round the clock, but service is less frequent in the early morning. **SACSA** (tel. 233–5350) buses run to Cartago (45 min, 40¢) from Calle 5 at Avenida 18 in San José. This is a sketchy area, so take a taxi. San José buses stop in front of the cathedral ruins, but they leave from Cartago's **terminal** (Av. 4, between Calles 2 and 4, 100 m north of the cathedral ruins). Service to nearby towns departs from the south side of the ruins on Avenida 1 between Calles 2 and 4.

WHERE TO SLEEP

Just north of the market, the good folks at brand-new **Hotel Dinastia** (Calle 3, between Avs. 6 and 8, tel. 551–7057) charge $20 for a clean double with hot-water bath ($16 if you share a bath). If you're not into staying near the market, cruise over to **Los Angeles Lodge** (Av. 4, between Calles 14 and 16, tel. 591–4169), a bed-and-breakfast across the street from the basilica. Clean, cheery doubles ($35) have private hot-water bathrooms and cute little glass vanity tables (break out that lipstick, girls!). In the May–November off-season, call in advance so someone can open the place up.

FOOD

Cartago isn't exactly an overwhelming culinary experience, but then neither is Costa Rica. Several cheap places are downtown along Avenidas 2 and 4. Near the basilica, **Restaurant La Cabañita** (Av. 2 at Calle 16, tel. 551–4546) has reasonably priced seafood and steak dishes. *Filet al ajillo* (fillet in garlic sauce) goes for $5, while refreshing batidos made with fruit are under $1. Across from the basilica, below the Los Angeles Lodge, **La Puerta del Sol** (Av. 4, between Calles 14 and 16, tel. 551–0615) serves your basic Costa Rican fare. Across from Parque Central, **Restaurante Apolo** (Calle 1 and Av. 2) has good sandwiches, soups, and rice dishes for about $3. **Ambientes** (Av. 1, across from the ruins, tel. 552–0151), a good roasted-chicken place, is also a popular nightspot.

NEAR CARTAGO

JARDIN BOTANICO LANKESTER

About 6 km (4 mi) east of Cartago, the Lankester Gardens (tel. 552–3151) sprawl over 25 acres. Although the gardens are most spectacular February–May, when more than 80 species of orchids bloom, the greenery is pretty cool any time of year. They're open daily 8:30–3:30 and admission is about $2.50. Bring a discreet snack, because no restaurants are nearby and picnicking is discouraged. To get to the gardens, take a Paraíso bus from the south side of Cartago's ruined cathedral and ask the driver to let you off at Jardin Lankester; the gardens are a 10-minute walk from the main road. If you drive, head east on the road two blocks south of the basilica and watch for the entrance on the right.

OROSI VALLEY

The Orosi Valley, one of the first parts of Costa Rica to be settled by the Spanish, is known for its spectacular views, colonial edifices, and the national park nestled at one end of it. If you're looking for a small-town experience away from the bustle of San José and nearby cities, consider spending a night in **Orosi**, or enjoy the view from Paraíso, or the tropical nature of **Tapantí National Park.**

OROSI • The main attraction of this small colonial town is a low, adobe **church** dating from the mid-1700s, where you're welcome to enter quietly and check out the intricate religious paintings and altars. The **Museo Franciscano San José de Orosi** (tel. 533–3051), adjacent to the church, houses religious artifacts from the colonial era, many of which were brought down from Mexico and Guatemala. Admission is 50¢, and it's open daily 9–noon and 1–5. If you feel like a swim, head for **the Balneario de Orosi** (300 m south and 200 m west of church), which has two pools (the big one is filled only on weekends) fed by a lukewarm mineral spring. Admission is $1.50; open Wednesday–Monday. One km (½ mi) south of Orosi, in the tiny town of Palomo, is **Los Patios,** a thermal bath complex with much hotter water than the Balneario. Admission is $1.50; open Tuesday–Sunday. Stay at **Montaña Linda Orosi** (tel. 533–3640), where you'll find a warm bed, breakfast, hot showers, bikes for rent, and a whirlpool. Dorm-style beds go for $5.50 ($7 with breakfast), while private rooms are $8 (doubles $12); pitch your tent for $2. They serve good, cheap meals and also have a kitchen that guests can use. They can also arrange a variety of affordable tours to area attractions. Aside from **Montaña Linda,** the nicest place to eat in Orosi is **Restaurante Coto** (tel. 533-3032), which has a porch with a thatched roof overlooking the soccer field; it's the perfect spot to enjoy a $2.50 plate of arroz con pollo (chicken with rice) or a whole-fried snapper with fries and salad ($4–$5). To get to Orosi (30 min, 25¢), take a bus from 25 meters southeast of Cartago's cathedral ruin. Buses run hourly, more or less on the hour, weekdays 6 AM–10 PM and make the last return to Cartago at 6:30 PM. The bus will drop you off in front of the soccer field by the church; you can catch a bus back to Cartago across the street. If you drive, head east on the road two blocks south of Cartago's basilica, and turn right at Paraíso's central park.

UJARRAS • About 10 km (6 mi) southeast of Paraíso stand the ruins of Costa Rica's oldest church, built in the late 1600s and abandoned 150 years later. The ruins are surrounded by lovely gardens, and several short walking paths head into the nearby coffee plantations. About 1½ km (1 mi) to the west of the ruins is the balneario and recreation area of **Charrarra** (tel. 574–7557), which overlooks the Cachí Reservoir. A popular spot with ticos on weekends, Charrarra includes a swimming pool, basketball courts, a soccer field, and lots of covered picnic areas. Admission is $1.25; open Tuesday–Sunday 8–6. To get here, catch a **Cachí** bus from Cartago or from **Paraíso,** a small town 4 km (2½ mi) toward Cartago from Orosí.

PARQUE NACIONAL TAPANTI

Tapantí National Park, about 13 km (8 mi) southeast of Orosí, protects a vast and verdant valley drained by the boulder-strewn Orosi River. More than 200 species of birds have been identified in the park, including the rare resplendant quetzal. A gravel road heads deep into the park, from which several trails wind their ways into the surounding cloud forest. Two good bird-watching trails are **Arboles Caídos** (Fallen Trees) Trail and the steep **La Pava** Trail, which starts about 4 km (2½ mi) down the main road from the park entrance. Near the La Pava Trail, make a short, steep hike to a *mirador* (lookout) over the valley. Tapantí's rugged terrain is also home to a variety of mammals, insects, amphibians, and reptiles. Look for the electric-blue morpho butterfly, and, in June, July, and early August, for the metallic golden beatle. Beginning about 2 km (1 mi) from the entrance, the 45-minute **Oropéndola** and **Patanoso** trails lead to swimming holes off the river.

Unless you're driving, Tapantí is accessible only by taxi. Find one in Orosí, on the east side of the soccer field by the church. The ride is about $6 each way, and drivers will happily return to pick you up later. Bring rain gear and weatherproof walking shoes; the reserve is damp even in the dry season, with 254 in. of rain annually. The park and the **information center** at the entrance are open daily 8–4. The entrance fee is $6. The park has bathrooms, picnic areas, and potable water, but no camping facilities. For further information, call **Amistad Atlántico** (tel. 758–3996), a regional branch of the National Park Service. If you can afford it, it's well worthwhile to stay at the **Kiri Lodge** (1 km [½ mi] before Tapantí, tel.

284–2024), which has comfortable rooms with nice views, a private forest reserve with 12 km (7 mi) of trails, and horseback tours. A double with private hot-water bath is $30, breakfast included.

PARQUE NACIONAL VOLCAN IRAZÚ

The weird moonscape around Volcán Irazú conjures up visions of UFO landings or Earth's primordial past. About 32 km (20 mi) north of Cartago, the volcano's barren gray craters are surrounded by sparse, shrubby vegetation and thick clouds. A bilious green lake and a number of gaseous fumaroles (volcanic vents) steam away at the bottom of the principle crater, which is 1,000 ft deep. Irazú has been pretty mellow since its last eruption on March 19, 1963, which happens to be the day John F. Kennedy visited Costa Rica—coincidence or conspiracy? Eruptions and avalanches killed people and livestock, but the ash that fell on the agricultural region of **Tierra Blanca** enriched the soil for years to come. Rangers warn that the volcano is entering another active phase, so pay attention to their advice—several curious spectators were killed in the '63 eruptions. On a clear day, you can see all the way to the Pacific or Caribbean coasts, Lago Nicaragua, the banana lands of Guapiles and the Río Frío, and Cachí and the Orosí Valley.

BASICS • Try to get a car and get here early, before the clouds roll in. The small trails that wind around the craters and through the surrounding vegetation are technically off-limits, but the prohibition is rarely enforced. The park is open daily 8–3:30 and costs $6. You can't camp in the park, but there are a couple of restaurants and hotels in and around the nearby town of San Juan de Chichuá. Bring a jacket—at 11,200 ft, it gets damn cold up there.

COMING AND GOING • **Buses Metropoli** (tel. 551–9795 or 272–0651) has a bus to Irazú (2 hrs, $4 round-trip) that leaves from in front of San José's **Gran Hotel Costa Rica** (Av. 2, between Calles 1 and 3) weekends at 8 AM. The bus stops in Cartago, on the north side of the cathedral ruins, at about 8:30 to pick up more people. Fare from Cartago is $3. The return bus leaves the park at 12:15 PM, stopping at a restaurant for a 30-minute lunch.

TURRIALBA

Lying among sloping fields of sugarcane, coffee, and bananas on the Caribbean side of the Cordillera Central mountain range, Turrialba is a remarkably friendly, warm town with a farming-community feel. The climate in this region, 64 km (40 mi) east of San José, is much warmer and more humid than the central valley highlands, but nights can get chilly, and it often rains during the dry season.

Although tourism has noticeably decreased since the completion of the highway through Guapiles and the termination of rail service, Turrialba still draws river enthusiasts for rafting and kayaking on the nearby **Ríos Reventazón and Pacuare** (see Outdoor Activities in San José, above). Hotels listed below can hook you up with local outfitters for trips on those rivers. About 2½ km (1½ mi) southeast of town is the impressive, tropical-agriculture investigation center **CATIE.** The grounds are open to the public daily 8–4, and it's a good place for a short bike ride or stroll. To the northeast lies Costa Rica's most significant archaeological site, the **Monumento Nacional Guayabo** (see Near Turrialba, below), which sits on the lower slopes of the massive **Volcán Turrialba.** There's not much to do in town but hang out. The trees of the pleasant **Parque Central** are thick with hissing, shirtless teenage boys. At night, the bars swell with drunken men, and the one discotheque, **Faro,** just southwest of the Guayabo/Santa Teresita bus terminal, pumps out the jams.

COMING AND GOING

Transtusa (tel. 556–0073) has hourly buses to Turrialba from a small terminal at Calle 13 between Avenidas 6 and 8 in San José. Directo (1½ hrs, $1.50) and corriente (2 hrs, 75¢) buses run daily 5:30 AM–10 PM. You can catch the corriente bus as it passes through Cartago, but then you'll make the sweaty trip standing, so it's best to leave from San José. Turrialba's terminal, 100 meters west of Parque Central, offers frequent service to Siquirres with connections to Puerto Limón. One hundred meters south of the San José/Siquirres terminal is another terminal with service to local towns, including Guayabo and Santa Teresita.

GETTING AROUND

You might notice that Turrialba's streets aren't aligned exactly along a north-south-east-west grid ("west" is actually closer to southwest, for example). Ask a local to point out their version of cardinal directions or you'll get confused. Take heart: the town is fairly small, and people point and gesture broadly when giving directions. Major landmarks are the abandoned train station at the southeast corner of town and

RIDE THOSE RAPIDS WHILE YOU CAN

Each year, hundreds of rafters and kayakers from all over the world flock to Costa Rica's wildest rivers, the Pacuare and the Reventazón. They all wax enthusiastic about the rivers' raging rapids and the delicate natural beauty on the banks. But all those rafting excursions aren't pulling enough profits for the powers that be, so in 1999, Costa Rica's electric company, ICE, is damming the lower Reventazón, which already has a dam at Cachí. Similar plans to dam the Pacuare are in the initial stages. Whether tourism or luz (electricity) wins out remains to be seen.

the white cement tower of the church in Parque Central. Unlike most Central American churches, this one is on the south side of the park. Río Turrialba borders the town to the north.

WHERE TO SLEEP

You're not looking at too many options here. The clean and cheery **Hotel Interamericano** (tel. 556–0142) is located behind the Bodega del Ferrocarril—walk south from the San José/Siquirres terminal, cross the railroad tracks, and follow the road to the left. Proprietors Edgar Francisco and Blanca Rosa Vasquez offer spotless, airy doubles with shared cold-water baths for $12 ($14 with a private bath). They serve breakfasts and can help you plan your stay in the area or hook you up for rafting and kayaking. The **Hotel Turrialba** (100 m west of the gas station, above Super Dirasa, tel. 556-6654) lacks the personality of the Interamericano, but it does have such amenities as hot water, TV, and a self-service laundry room. A double with a private bath costs $18 (single, $12). For more luxurious lodging, head for the hills outside of town.

Pochotel. It's a $6 taxi ride out of town, but these rustic cabins have huge windows that open out to Turrialba and the surrounding mountains. On a clear day you can see the Caribbean from here. Doubles with hot water go for $35. Oscar, the mellow owner, is a progressive guy committed to recycling and other proenvironment activities. *In the hills south of Turrialba, tel. 556–0111. 8 cabins with bath. Laundry.*

FOOD

Turrialba is sprinkled with greasy-spoon sodas as well as standard fried-chicken joints with palatable casados or chicken-fries-drink combos for less than $3. If you're sick of that scene, try **Restaurante La Garza** (Parque Central, tel. 556–1073), where locals whoop it up at the bar or take it easy over lunch or dinner daily 10 AM–11 PM. The filling *plato del día* ($3.50) is a good choice. For Chinese food, including *pollo en agridulce* (sweet-and-sour chicken, $3.50) and stir-fry ($4), go to **Nuevo Hong Kong** (Parque Central, tel. 556–0593). Sit down to eat, or get takeout like the locals; it's open daily 11–11. Stock up on fruits, vegetables, and cheese Fridays and Saturdays at the weekly **market** held on the south side of town right in front of the railroad tracks. Favorite hangout restaurants at night include **Soda Burbujas** (Parque Central) and **Pizzería Pan y Vino** (50 m south and 25 m east of San José bus terminal), which is closed Tuesday.

NEAR TURRIALBA

MONUMENTO NACIONAL GUAYABO

On the slopes of Volcán Turrialba, wrapped in a misty rain forest, lies Costa Rica's most important archaeological site. It's no Tikal, but hey, this ain't Guatemala. Which is to say that while the area is rumored to be filled with pre-Columbian ruins and artifacts, the powers that be in Costa Rica have been pretty lax about excavating the area. Of 49 acres set aside as an archaeological site, only two have been excavated. The uncovered results include stone foundations, an elaborate system of roads, still-functioning aqueducts and water-storage tanks, and some petroglyphs (engraved stones). All this was constructed between 800 BC and AD 1400, when archaeologists believe the area was an important religious and political center and home for 15,000–20,000 people.

BASICS • Several paths lead through the archaeological site and the surrounding rain forest. A cheesy brochure, in English or Spanish, outlines the interpretive trail through the site. Pick one up at the information booth as you go in. Beautiful bromeliads and orchids sprout from every possible inch, and the liquid, gurgling calls of the *oropéndola* birds can be heard frequently on the two-hour hike. The best time to visit is during the January–May drier season. The entrance fee is $6, and the monument is open daily 8–3:30.

COMING AND GOING • The last stretch of road is so bad that you need four-wheel-drive to reach Guayabo. Without a car, it is conservatively a two-day trip, unless you want to pay a taxi at least $12 each way from Turrialba. All buses to Guayabo leave from Turrialba's local terminal (100 m south of the San José/Siquirres terminal). Ignore the painted schedule; it's been wrong for years. Buses marked GUAYABO leave Turrialba Monday–Saturday at 11 AM and 5 PM, arriving at the monument about an hour later. Buses marked SANTA TERESITA depart Turrialba's local terminal daily at 10:30 AM, 1:30 PM, and 6:30 PM. This bus drops you at a crossroads 2½ km (1½ mi) from the monument; hike the rest of the way up the hill. Catch a return bus from Guayabo Monday–Saturday at 12:30 PM or 6 PM, or at the Santa Teresita crossroads daily at 1:15 PM or weekdays at 4:15 PM.

WHERE TO SLEEP AND EAT • Camping in the park is encouraged. Currently eight sites are open, all with access to flush toilets, cold-water showers, and barbecue pits. The cost is about $1 per person. Eat at one of the family-run **sodas** along the road to the monument.

GUANACASTE AND THE NORTHERN LOWLANDS

Guanacaste is without question the weirdest region in Costa Rica. Imagine a typical shit-kicking, tobacco-spitting, Marlboro-smoking kinda place full of cattle and cowboys, then shift it to the land of tropical rain forests—you're beginning to get the picture. The driest province in the country, Guanacaste is famous for its cattle, and much of the land is used for grazing, even the highland areas. Guanacaste used to be an autonomous region but citizens opted to annex themselves on July 25, 1824. Costa Rica barely edged out Nicaragua, which lies just north of the province, as the country of choice, and *guanacastecos* are usually more patriotic to their region than to their country. Guanacaste is also the center of Costa Rican folklore, and you can sometimes hear typical songs wailed in the canteens of smaller towns.

Most of Guanacaste used to be dry forest. It's sad to ride a bus through the rural areas knowing that two-thirds of all Costa Rican forest has been cut down, and that much of the deforestation occurred here. The most-visited areas in the region are the beach towns and resorts of the Nicoya Peninsula (*see* Península de Nicoya, *below*) and the cloud forest of mountainous Monteverde, both of which look more typically Costa Rican than the rest of Guanacaste. Other than that, it's flat, dry, barren, and hot.

LIBERIA

Founded in 1769, Liberia is the capital of Guanacaste and the region's largest city. It is also the only city in Costa Rica with its own flag. Liberia has glorified the role played by the *sabanero* (cowboy)—the town even has a museum (in the visitor's center) and monument dedicated to him on Avenida Central. Most travelers pass through Liberia on their way to the famous beaches and national parks of Guanacaste. If you enter Costa Rica overland from Nicaragua, Liberia is a convenient jumping-off point, and with the opening of an international airport nearby, the city is becoming a major transportation hub. If you're in the area around July 25, don't miss the varied celebrations that surround the anniversary of the annexation of Guanacaste. Liberia celebrates that week with a raucous rodeo, complete with bucking broncos, parades, free concerts, folk dancing, and other events. Liberia also celebrates *fiestas cívicas* in February, around the time of the full moon.

BASICS

Banco de Costa Rica (Av. 1 and Calle Central, tel. 666–1267; open weekdays 9–3), **Banco Lyon** (Av. Central at Calle 7, tel. 666–2974; open weekdays 7:30–5, Sat. 8–noon), **Banco Nacional** (Av. Central at Calle 8, tel. 666–0996; open weekdays 8:30–3:45), and **Banco de San José** (Av. Central, between Calles 10 and 11, tel. 666–2020) all change traveler's checks and give cash advances on Visa. If the banks are closed, and you're in dire need of moolah, seek out **Mr. Beto Acón** at Restaurante Chung San (*see* Food, *below*). The **hospital** (tel. 666–0011) is on the northeast edge of town; for an ambulance, call **Red Cross** (tel. 666–0994); for **guardia,** dial 666–0409. **Lavandería Egaliz** (tel. 666–0267) is located 525 meters east of the church. The **post office** (Calle 8, between Avs. 1 and 3), 200 meters north of Banco Anglo Costarricense, is open weekdays 7:30–5:30 and offers fax service. Make international calls and send faxes at **ICE** (Calle 8, between Avs. Central and 2), open weekdays 7:30–5 and Saturday 8 AM–11:30 AM. The **information center** (300 m south and 100 m east of municipalidad, tel. 666–1606) houses the sabanero museum and dispenses free maps, brochures, and a bounty of info about the national parks in the area. It's open Monday–Saturday 8–noon and 1–4.

COMING AND GOING

El Pulmitán de Liberia (tel. 666–0458 in Liberia or 222–1650 in San José) has 10 buses a day from San José to Liberia, starting at 6 AM and ending at 8 PM (4 hrs, $3.50). San José-bound buses depart from the a small terminal 2 blocks south of the main bus terminal (Liberia, 200 m east of Pan-American Hwy.). **Empresa Arata** (tel. 666–0138) has five buses to Puntarenas from Liberia. Beach-bound buses to **Playas del Coco** (six daily) and **Playas Hermosa** and Panama (five daily) leave from the main terminal. Buses run eight times a day to La Cruz and the Nicaraguan border; southbound buses to **Nicoya** leave every hour. Buses to Cañas (1 hr, 75¢), a transfer point for **Lago/Volcán Arenal** (*see below*), leave daily at 5:45 AM, 1:30 PM, 3 PM, and 4:30 PM, although both Cañas and the turnoff for Monteverde can be reached by taking any bus headed for San José or Puntarenas.

The international **Aeropuerto Daniel Oduber** (6 km [4 mi] west of town, tel. 666–0695) is serviced by all buses (20 min, 50¢) headed for Playas del Coco, Hermosa, Santa Cruz, and Nicoya, but the simplest way to get there is by taxi (tel. 666–0274) for $4.

WHERE TO SLEEP

Liberia has an abundance of fleabag hotels that you'll want to avoid. One of the best bets for those on a tight budget is the **Posada El Tope** (Calle Central, between Avs. 2 and 3, tel. 666–3876), which has basic rooms in two old houses that share baths and include the use of a simple kitchen. Rooms in the Casa Real, across the street, are nicer than those in El Tope itself. You'll have to get to the **Hospedaje Casona** (Calle Central at Av. 6, tel. 666–2971) early, or call ahead, to be the lucky occupant of a giant, airy room for $5 a person, with communal bath. It's one of the few places in Liberia that doesn't accept credit cards. **Hotel Liberia** (75 m south of park on Calle Central, tel. 666–0161) has stuffy but clean rooms with communal baths for $5 per person, while a double with bath costs $12–$17. The **Hotel Guanacaste** (Av. 1 at Calle 12, tel. 666–0085) has slightly overpriced rooms with baths for $12 per person. They also have a grassy camping area ($6 per person). If you can afford a bit more comfort, try **El Bramadero** (Pan-American Hwy. at Av. Central, tel. 666–0371), where air-conditioned rooms with private hot-water baths surround a swimming pool ($36 a double).

FOOD

Cattle (and beef) are king in local eateries, but there's also plenty of fresh seafood available, thanks to the proximity of a large fishing fleet at Playas del Coco. A consistent, though slightly expensive place for surf or turf is **El Bramadero** (Pan-American Hwy., tel. 666–0371). **Pizza Pronto** (Av. 4 and Calle 1, tel. 666–2098), located in a lovely old former home, offers 23 different pizzas baked in stone ovens, as well as pastas, meat dishes, and sandwiches. For the cheapest eats, hit the sodas and food stands that dot the streets surrounding the central park, or the municipal market (Av. 3, between Calles Central and 2, 100 m north of park). Liberia also has a veritable buffet of cheap Chinese restaurants, such as **Restaurante Chung San** (Av. 1 and Calle 3, 328 100 m east of church, tel. 666–2906), and **Restaurante Cuatro Mares** (Av. Central, between Calles 3 and 5, tel. 666–0988). **Supermercado Palí** (Av. 3, between Calles Central and 2) is where do-it-yourselfers can get supplies.

HELADERIAS • To jive with the snail's pace of the town, spend a lazy afternoon at **Cafetería Donde Marco** (Av. 1, between Calles 3 and 5, tel. 666–2080) and drool over a frothy papaya and banana milkshake ($1). The evening dessert spot for locals and tourists is the parkside **Las Tinajas** (Calle 2, between Avs. Central and 1). Or grab an ice-cream cone from **Pop's** (Calle 2, between Avs. Central and 1) or **Mönpik** (Av. 3, between Calles 2 and 4).

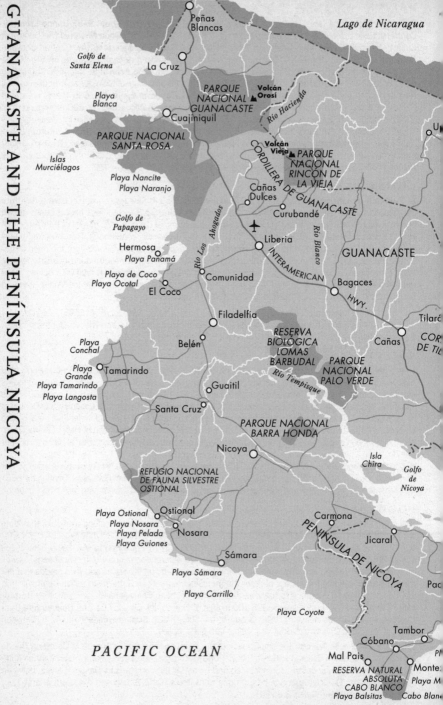

Lago de Nicaragua

Peñas
Blancas

*Golfo de
Santa Elena*

La Cruz

*Playa
Blanca*

**PARQUE
NACIONAL
GUANACASTE**

**Volcán
Orosí**

Río Hacienda

Cuajiniquil

**PARQUE NACIONAL
SANTA ROSA**

**Volcán
Vieja**

**PARQUE
NACIONAL
RINCÓN DE
LA VIEJA**

*Islas
Murciélagos*

Playa Nancite
Playa Naranjo

Cañas
Dulces

Curubandé

*Golfo de
Papagayo*

Río Los Ahogados

Liberia

Río Blanco

GUANACASTE

Hermosa
Playa Panamá

INTERAMERICAN

Bagaces

Playa de Coco
Playa Ocotal

Comunidad

HWY.

El Coco

Tilará

Filadelfia

**RESERVA
BIOLÓGICA
LOMAS
BARBUDAL**

Cañas

COR
DE TIL

*Playa
Conchal*

Belén

**PARQUE
NACIONAL
PALO VERDE**

*Playa
Grande*
Playa Tamarindo
Playa Langosta

Tamarindo

Guaitil

Río Tempisque

Santa Cruz

**PARQUE NACIONAL
BARRA HONDA**

Nicoya

*Isla
Chira*

*Golfo
de
Nicoya*

**REFUGIO NACIONAL
DE FAUNA SILVESTRE
OSTIONAL**

Playa Ostional
Playa Nosara
Playa Pelada
Playa Guiones

Ostional

Nosara

Carmona

PENÍNSULA DE NICOYA

Jicaral

Pac

Sámara

Playa Sámara

Playa Carrillo

Playa Coyote

Tambor

Cóbano

Mal País

**RESERVA NATURAL
ABSOLUTA
CABO BLANCO**

Playa Balsitas

Monte

Playa M

Cabo Blan

PACIFIC OCEAN

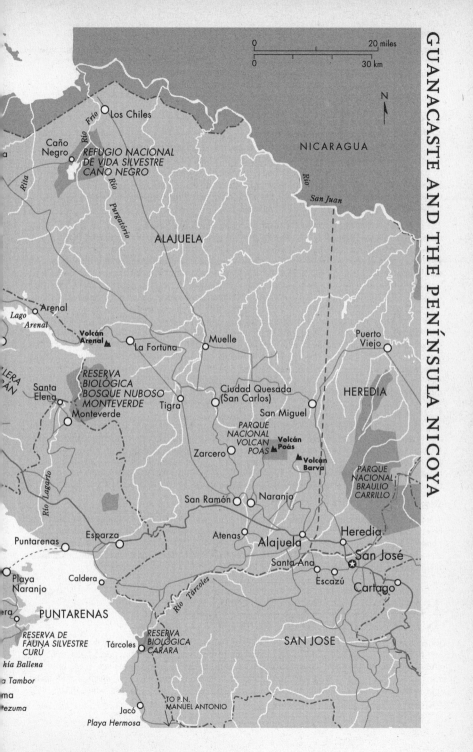

20 miles
30 km

N

Los Chiles

Caño Negro

Rio Frío

Rio

Rita

REFUGIO NACIONAL
DE VIDA SILVESTRE
CAÑO NEGRO

Rio Purgatorio

NICARAGUA

Rio San Juan

ALAJUELA

Arenal

Lago Arenal

Volcán Arenal

La Fortuna

Muelle

Puerto Viejo

RESERVA
BIOLÓGICA
BOSQUE NUBOSO
MONTEVERDE

Santa Elena

Tigra

Ciudad Quesada
(San Carlos)

San Miguel

HEREDIA

Monteverde

Rio Lagarto

Zarcero

PARQUE
NACIONAL
VOLCÁN
POAS

Volcán
Poás

Volcán
Barva

PARQUE
NACIONAL
BRAULIO
CARRILLO

San Ramón

Naranjo

CORDILLERA ...ÁN

Esparza

Atenas

Alajuela

Heredia

San José

Puntarenas

Santa Ana

Caldera

Playa Naranjo

Escazú

Cartago

Rio Tárcoles

PUNTARENAS

RESERVA DE
FAUNA SILVESTRE
CURÚ

Tárcoles

RESERVA
BIOLÓGICA
CARARA

SAN JOSE

hía Ballena

a Tambor

ma

ezuma

Jacó

TO P.N.
MANUEL ANTONIO

Playa Hermosa

259

AFTER DARK

Cine Olympia (Calle Central, between Avs. 3 and 5, tel. 666–1504) shows long-forgotten blockbusters from the Unite States. The disco at **Bar Kurú** (Av. Central, 200 m east of Pan-American Hwy., tel. 666–1036) plays salsa, merengue, and enough disco to bring John Travolta back onto the floor.

PARQUE NACIONAL SANTA ROSA

About 48 km (30 mi) from the Nicaraguan border is the much-visited Santa Rosa National Park. The 9,169-acre park was once an enormous cattle estate, but Santa Rosa is best known for the decisive battle fought here on March 20, 1856. Patriotic Costa Ricans took arms against U.S. filibusters under the leadership of U.S. mercenary William Walker, who wanted to make Costa Rica a slave state. **La Casona,** the restored colonial ranch house where the battle took place, now holds museum displays about the battle and the park's ecology.

The park itself is divided into two sections: the more popular **Santa Rosa** sector, and the northern **Murciélago** (bat) sector. During the rainy season, the park gets 31–94 inches of rainfall, and from January to March, strong winds gust through the area. Beyond the entrance gate (open daily 7:30–4:30), where you get a free map and brochures with the entrance fee ($6), hitch the 7 km (4½ mi) to the Casona and **administración** (tel. 695–5598). Guides are sometimes available, or you can explore the five trails on your own—keep and eye out for white-tailed deer, spider monkeys, magpie jays, and coatis (long-nosed racoon cousins). Hike an hour (3½ km [2½ mi]) to **Sendero Los Patos** for a view of a forest-filled canyon. Two hours (6 km [4 mi]) gets you up to the **Mirador Valle Naranjo,** where you can take in the whole Pacific coast. In the dry season, you can walk or drive (four-wheel-drive only) 12 km (7 mi) to the beautiful **Playa Naranjo,** which has excellent surf (it's usually a dangerous place to swim) and camping sites, but no potable water. During holidays and the dry season, there are enough cars making the trip that you can often hitch to Playa Naranjo. **Playa El Hachal** (16 km [10 mi] from the station) and **Playa Blanca** (8 km [5 mi] from the station) are the best beaches in the Murciélago sector, but you'll need a four-wheel-drive vehicle to visit them. During the quarter moon from December to February, leatherback turtles sometimes visit those beachs.

COMING AND GOING

To get to Santa Rosa from Liberia, drive north on the Pan-American Highway, or board any of the eight buses leaving the main terminal for La Cruz (45 min, 65¢) or Penas Blancas (the border) between 5:30 AM and 8 PM. The driver will let you off by a paved road that leads to La Casona and camping area, 7 km (4 mi) away; you can usually hitch a ride for that stretch. To get to Murciélago, take a bus from Liberia to the town of **Cuajiniquil,** 10 km (6 mi) north and 10 km (6 mi) west of the main park entrance. From there, you'll have to walk 8 km (5 mi) to the Murciélago station.

WHERE TO SLEEP AND EAT

The park's campgrounds are good and, at $1.75 a person, the price is right. The Santa Rosa sector has one full-service camping area near La Casona and simpler campsites on Playa Naranjo that don't have potable water. Meals (breakfast is $2.50, lunch and dinner, $3.50) can sometimes be arranged at the dining hall (call ahead). The Murciélago sector camping area is next to the ranger station, but if you bring food and supplies, you can overnight at the beaches.

PARQUE NACIONAL RINCON DE LA VIEJA

Rincón de la Vieja is an active volcano that last erupted in 1997. Scientists classify it as active in the sense that it produces sulfuric fumaroles. There are strange volcano-related wonders such as boiling creeks, stinking streams and lagoons, bubbling mud pools, and vaporing steam jets. Look, but don't touch or you'll burn the skin off your hands, and don't get too close to the edge, which is often brittle and unsafe. But the park itself also protects vast expanses of tropical forest, where hikers may encounter an array of interesting critters.

On the east side of the **Las Pailas** sector of the park, you can cool off in the icy lakes beneath the roar of cascading waterfalls. Trek 5 km (3 mi) to the giant **La Cangreja** waterfall and swim in its crystal-clear **Blue Lake**. A bit closer are the smaller **Escondidas** waterfalls (45 min). Or explore the **Poza Río Blanco** pools just 600 meters from the park entrance. West of the entrance is a small camping area followed by a circular 3-km (2-mi) adventure that leads to a waterfall (often dry, even in the wet season), hot lava rocks, boiling mud pots, and a minivolcano with boiling pools and a warm, thermal stream. Dry, steaming, and sulfur-smelling, this little inferno is reminiscent of witches' brews and the enchanted forests of Lothlorien.

If you want to hoof it up to the top of the volcano, you should start the 6,225-ft ascent at 6 AM to avoid the afternoon clouds and rains that entirely wipe out the view. Hike a tough 8 km (5 mi) west of the entrance gate to the thermal baths and you may encounter toucans, white-face monkeys, or collared pecarries. One km (½mi) farther is the **Santa María** sector of the park, where there's a small camping area, a small museum, and a number of hiking trails and lookout points.

COMING AND GOING

There are two routes to the park, neither of which are serviced by public transportation and both of which are rough. The road to the Santa María sector heads due west from Liberia. The road to the Las Pailas sector heads east from the Pan-American Highway, 5 km (3 mi) north of Liberia. The park is located about 22 km (13 mi) down either of these gravel roads. The entrance fee is $6. If you don't have a four-wheel-drive vehicle, check with the Hotel Guanacaste (*see above*) in Liberia, from where a minivan heads to the park every day at 7 AM (if they have at least three passengers) and returns from the park at 5 PM ($10 each way). Call one day before to reserve. A taxi from Liberia should charge about $25.

Much of the beef raised in Guanacaste is used for fast-food hamburgers.

WHERE TO SLEEP AND EAT

Camping is available inside the park at **Las Pailas** for $1.75 per person, plus the $6 daily admission fee. You'll want to bring plenty of sustenance from Liberia. Camping is also allowed in the **Santa María** sector, but it's 7 km (4 mi) from the main Rincón wonders. **Hacienda Lodge Guachipelín** (6 km [4 mi] east of Curubandé, tel. 284–2049), near Las Pailas, has rustic rooms with private baths for $34–$38. Family-style meals cost $5–$8; horseback and hiking tours run $17–$25. The nearby **Rincón de la Vieja Mountain Lodge** (27 km [17 mi] northeast of Liberia, tel. 256–8206 or 695–5553) is the place to head if you've got a IYHF card. That hostel offers members dorm-style accommodations for $18 per person and family-style meals for $6 a shot. The also have $25 horseback and hiking tours of the park and surroundings. They even provide transportation from Liberia for up to six people for $25 each way.

PLAYAS DEL COCO

Playas del Coco is the closest beach to Liberia, and for many a traveler, one of the most convenient places to catch a bit of the old surf, sand, and sun. Set deep in tranquil bay, this long beach of dark grey sand was one of the country's first resorts, and it continues to be a predominantly tico vacation town. Behind the northern half of the beach stand the vacation homes of wealthy San José residents, whereas the southern half is backed by the humbler homes of local fishermen; whose boats are moored offshore. Although hardly the country's prettiest beach, El Coco, as it is popularly known, offers safe swimming waters, fresh seafood, and access to some of the country's best skin diving.

COMING AND GOING

It takes about 30 minutes to drive to Playas del Coco from Liberia—turn left at the light, and follow the signs. There are also six buses daily from Liberia between 5:30 AM and 6:15 PM.

WHERE TO SLEEP AND EAT

Being a predominantly tico beach, El Coco has some of the best deals on the Pacific coast. **Cabinas El Coco** (tel. 670–0110), to the right at the end of the road, has 80 rooms, about half of which are right on the beach, a waterfront restaurant, and a disco, which can be a problem for light sleepers on weekends. A simple, clean single with a fan and private, cold-water bath costs $12 (doubles $20–$25). The **Luna Tica** (tel. 670–0127), two blocks to the south, has similar rooms on the beach, or across the street in the Anexo, for $12 a single and $18 a double. The nearby **Coco Palm** has spacious, spotless rooms, hot water, and a pool for $25 a single ($45 doubles), breakfast included. For peace and quiet, head 1 km (½ mi) north of town to the secluded **Villa del Sol** (tel. 670–0085), a family-run B&B with a swimming pool and excellent dinners. Doubles are $35–$40. The cheapest food in town is served at the sodas on the main road just before the little seaside park. For fresh seafood and an ocean view, head to **La Guajira** (50 m south of park, no phone) where either a fish fillet or rice with shrimp costs less than $6. For something different, head for **Le Bistrot,** where the French owner serves such delicacies as *corvina* (sea bass) in a macadamia sauce ($7.50), or **San Francisco Treats,** where you can top off a vegetarian lasagna ($5) with a killer brownie sundae ($2.50).

OUTDOOR ACTIVITIES

SKIN DIVING • Several dive operators offer trips to at least half a dozen sites in the Bahia Culebra, around the Islas Murciélagos (Bat Islands), where divers can see big schools of fish and often manta rays and several species of sharks. **Bill Beard's Diving Safaris** (tel. 672–0012) is one of the oldest dive operators in the area.

NEAR PLAYAS DEL COCO

PLAYA HERMOSA

Hermosa, a swath of pale sand north of Playas del Coco washed by calm waters and backed by tropical foliage, is definitely more attractive than El Coco, but at the same time, it lacks the variety, nightlife, and bargains you'll find in the fishing port. The cheapest place to stay on Hermosa is **Cabinas El Cenizero** (first entrance, tel. 672–0186), where simple rooms a shell's toss from the beach cost $13 a single and $27 a double. The nearby **Cabinas Playa Hermosa** (tel. 672–0046) have slightly nicer rooms and lots of spots to relax under the palm trees for $40 a double ($25 single).

MONTEVERDE

Monteverde is one of Costa Rica's top tourist spots, which may have resulted in some overpriced rooms and overtraveled trails, but all you have to do is see the place to realize what all the fuss is about. It not only has gorgeous scenery and unforgettable sunsets, it can also be a great place to see wildlife, if you take the time and make the effort to escape the binocular-toting crowd. The ride to the town, about 160 km (100 mi) northwest of San José, takes you from the Pan-American Highway up to a twisty, narrow highway past breathtaking views—for those with enough confidence in the bus driver to take their eyes off the road—of Puntarenas and the Gulf of Nicoya. Once you arrive, you can't help but be wowed by the stupendous landscape. At an elevation of 5,000 ft, the Monteverde Cloud Forest Preserve is continually bathed in mist. You can explore a natural mosaic of forests within the 26,000 acres of protected wilderness, home to everything from howler monkeys to emerald toucans and resplendent quetzals. Unlike the government-owned national parks, the trails in this private reserve are incredibly well maintained. Temperatures range from 55°F–75°F, and precipitation is the norm, so bring warm clothes and rain gear.

Monteverde is not your typical Costa Rican town. It was founded in the early '40s by five Costa Rican families who raised cattle and produced cheese, for which the region is still famous. In 1951, 11 Quaker families arrived here from Alabama, having escaped the U.S. draft, and settled in armyless Costa Rica. They chose Monteverde because its remoteness would enable them to live and practice their religious beliefs in peace. The Quakers left much of the area's forest as it was. In 1972, George Powell, a U.S. conservationist, combated local loggers to create what is now the cloud-forest preserve. The Quaker community has declined in numbers because of emigration and intermarriage, but the Quaker influence can still be felt in religion, business, and culture. They're not how they appear on the oatmeal box, but they're definitely not your typical tico—they look like farmers from Kansas.

BASICS

To take care of business, go to **Santa Elena,** on the highway about 5 km (3 mi) before Monteverde. Santa Elena has a **Banco Nacional** (tel. 645–5027), which is open weekdays 8:30–3:45 and changes traveler's checks and grants Visa cash advances, but the lines could test a Quaker's patience. The post office **Cortel** (50 m SW of church, tel. 253–1901) is understaffed and rarely open, so save those postcards for San José. The espresso café **Chunches** (50 m SE of Banco Nacional, tel. 645–5147; open Mon.–Sat. 9–6) sells used English books, newspapers, and maps and has a laundromat. The **health** clinic (200 m down road to Monteverde, tel. 645–5076) is open weekdays 7–4 and weekends for emergencies only. Public phones are located at the supermarket and **Cooperativa La Esperanza** (across from post office) in Santa Elena. Toward Monteverde, find phones at the **Abastescador Cerro Plano** (1 km [½ mi] from Santa Elena), the grocery store by CASEM (*see* Worth Seeing, *below*), and at the visitor info center in the preserve.

COMING AND GOING

Transportes Tilarán (tel. 645–5159 or 222–3854 in San José) express buses from San José to Santa Elena and Monteverde (4 hrs, $5) leave from the Auto Transportes Tilarán station (Calle 12, between Avs. 9 and 11). Buses leave San José daily at 6:30 AM and 2:30 PM and return to San José at the same times. If you're coming from Puntarenas, take the 2:15 PM bus to Santa Elena (3 hrs, $2) or any bus that stops at the Santa Elena turnoff before 4 PM. Buses from Santa Elena to Puntarenas depart daily at 6 AM. Buy your tickets in advance during the high season at the Transportes Marza office (across from Banco Nacional, tel. 645–5159) daily 6 AM–noon and 1–3. Depending on road conditions, **Auto Transportes Soto Mena** (tel. 661–1255) runs a bus from Tilarán to Monteverde at 12:30 PM and back at 7 AM.

GETTING AROUND

The town of Santa Elena is a small triangle with roads branching off at each corner. Travel southwest to the Pan-American Highway and San José. The northwest road branches off at Banco Nacional, passes the soccer field, and then forks left to Tilarán and right to the Santa Elena preserve. The southwest road, beginning at Hotel El Tucan (*see below*), ends at the Monteverde preserve. The 6-km (4-mi) road winds its way up the mountain and past Cerro Plano (Montegringo in local parlance) and most of the Monteverde area hotels and restaurants, which tend to be pretty spread out.

About the mud—all the miraculous cosmetic effects are a commercial hoax, according to park officials. The sulfur and other acids harshly dry your skin, so use at your own risk. Also, taking anything, including the mud, from the park is prohibited.

There is very limited bus service between Santa Elena and the preserve, which means you can expect to hoof it a bit if you don't have a car. Walking takes about 90 minutes. Alternatively, cars pass constantly so hitching is a good bet, or taxis charge $5.50 each way. A minibus leaves Santa Elena for the preserve (20 min, 80¢) at 6:30 AM and 1 PM, returning at noon and 4 PM; they pick up passengers along the route. San José–Monteverde buses (60¢) will pick up passengers in Santa Elena at approximately 10:30 AM and 6:30 PM, and take them as far as the cheese factory (about half-way to the preserve), but they don't always pick up passengers en route; buses leave the cheese factory at 6:30 AM and 2:30 PM.

WHERE TO SLEEP

With advance reservations, you can stay inside the **Monteverde preserve** (call 645–5122). Bunks are secreted away above the info center at the entrance. It'll cost you $3 per night and an additional $18 for three hearty meals in pretty simple accommodations. To get deep into the cloud forest, stay in a *refugio* (*see* Worth Seeing, *below*). The **Hotel El Bosque** has a small camping area ($4 per person). Most of Monteverde's hotels are scattered along the road that connects Santa Elena to the preserve, many of them near patches of forest or nice views. Unfortunately, most of them don't cater to the budget traveler. You'll pay less for accommodations in Santa Elena, but you'll be in a town and a long way from the Monteverde preserve.

MONTEVERDE • Hospedaje Mariposa. Secluded on a hill and surrounded by forest, this tiny, family-run inn is just a 15-minute walk from the Monteverde preserve. The rooms are large and clean, and each is equipped with two beds and a bathroom. Doubles are $30 in the high season, $25 in the low season, breakfast included. Outside your door, hummingbirds party it up. *On left side as you walk toward preserve, just before Hotel Villa Verde, tel. 645–5013. 3 rooms with bath. Cash only.*

Hotel El Bosque The name means "The Forest," which no doubt refers to the patch of woods that lies between the restaurant and the rooms. The restaurant overlooks that sylvan scene, whereas the rooms are in an open area planted with flower gardens. Although low on personality, rooms are clean, comfortable, and not too dear at $40 a double ($30 a single). *On the right just before CASEM and Stella's Bakery, tel. 645–5158. 21 rooms with bath. Restaurant.*

Hotel Villa Verde. The closest place to the preserve, Villa Verde is nice, especially its spacious restaurant and lounge, complete with fireplace and lots of windows—the pefect place to watch the sunset.

Expect to pay $49 for a double with bath, breakfast included. Their tours are great—wherever you want to go, they'll take you there. *On left side as you walk toward preserve, tel. 645–5025. 22 rooms with bath. Restaurant, laundry.*

Pensión Manakin. This place is simple on the outside, but cozy on the inside. The Villegas family has opened their house and their hearts to international travelers—you'll feel like you live here. Three-course meals ($4), served with wine and coffee, are phenomenal. Doubles with bath are $20. Rooms with shared bath are $6 per person. If the pensión isn't full, students get a 10% discount for group or multi-night stays. *30 m before Hotel de Montaña, 50 m off main street, tel. 645–5080. 12 rooms, 5 with bath. Cash only.*

Pensión Monteverde. It may be a long trek down the hill, but the quiet, friendly Pensión Monteverde enjoys a great view and is situated next to a private, 28-acre forest reserve. Rooms cost $8 a person, or $24 including all three meals. *1 km (½ mi) down the hill from Cerro Plano (follow signs to the butterfly garden), tel. 645–5156. 10 rooms, all with bath. Cash only.*

SANTA ELENA • Albergue Santa Elena. The bright dining area of this HI-affiliated hostel often bristles with groups of student travelers. So-so rooms with private bath are $10 per person ($15 for non-members in summer); those without bath cost $5. The hostel allows guests to use the kitchen, arranges tours, and provides access to the Internet. *50 m east of bank, tel. 645–5051. 14 rooms, 11 with bath. Laundry. Cash only.*

Arco Iris Ecolodge. The laid-back German owners of this small, attractive lodge are sure to befriend you and provide good advice about how to spend your time in the area. Your conscience will be put at ease by the composting and waste-water filtering, while your palate will be thrilled with the gourmet dinners and amazing breakfast buffet ($5). They have a small nature library and can arrange horseback riding and other excursions. Rooms are surrounded by patches of forest; every one is different, and prices vary, but a standard double costs $45. *50 m east of bank and up the hill, tel. 645–5067. 9 cabins with bath. Restaurant, laundry.*

Hotel El Tucan. Simple wooden rooms with common areas and wholesome tico food served in the restaurant downstairs are what this pension has to offer. The two-story, family-run hotel charges $7 per person without bath ($10 with bath). All rooms and bathrooms are clean and remodeled. *100 m east of bank, tel. 645–5017. 14 rooms, 7 with bath. Restaurant, laundry. Cash only.*

Pensión Colibrí. Macha, the owner, is the woman-of-the-year, according to beaming customers of "The Hummingbird Hotel," usually student travelers. The rooms with communal bath are small and the thin walls let in the noise of the charismatic family, but at $6 a person, you won't find anything cheaper in the area. The hotel also has two doubles with private bath for $20, and the owner sometimes prepares meals for her guests. *50 m east of bank. 8 rooms, 2 with bath. Laundry.*

SAN GERARDO • Monteverde Conservation Field Station. If you want to stray from the crowd and stay at the edge of the cloud forest, check out this spectacular, isolated spot north of the Santa Elena Preserve. A large lodge with a spectacular view of Volcán Arenal and lots of forest to explore, the field station is open to the public when not being used for a course or seminar. Dorm-style lodging costs $15 per person, or $30 including three meals, but you can bring food from Santa Elena and cook for yourself. If there are less than five people, they charge an additional $13 per day for the field station, so you're best off getting a small group together, especailly if you have to take a taxi there. *Contact Shirley at the Monteverde Conservation League, across from the gas station in Monteverde, tel. 645–5003. 26 beds. Cash only.*

FOOD

The restaurants in Monteverde are (surprise) more expensive than those in Santa Elena. **Restaurant Daquiri** (across from Santa Elena church, tel. 645–5133) has good, cheap food in large portions: try the casados ($3.75). The **Restaurant El Tucán** (in Hotel El Tucán) also serves wholesome, inexpensive tico food. The **Hotel Arco Iris,** near the center of Santa Elena, serves excellent dinners for $5–$8 and is open to non-guests if you call (tel. 645–5067) and order before 4 PM. **Pizzería de Johnny** (Cerro Plano, tel. 645–5066) bakes up killer pizzas in a wood-burning oven and also serves an array of other delicious culinary creations for a little bit less than Arco Iris. **Restaurant El Bosque** (in Hotel El Bosque) serves a predictable selection of tasty meat and seafood dishes at reasonable prices. **Stella's Bakery** (across from CASEM, tel. 645–5560) offers some excellent sugar highs and light lunches, but it is also a bit pricey. The cheapest place to have lunch in Monteverde is actually the soda at the preserve. **La Cascada** (½ km [¼ mi] past CASEM, no phone) is best known for its nightlife, and it hosts an international dance scene on weekends. For a beer and loud Latin music in Santa Elena, swing by **Taberna Valverdes** near the church.

WORTH SEEING

Reserva Biológica Bosque Nuboso Monteverde. The Monteverde Cloud Forest Preserve is private, so the directors of the governing Tropical Science Center can do whatever they want. That's why they charge an exorbitant fee of $8 for international visitors (students with international ID card pay $4). The preserve is a moist cloud forest spanning both sides of the Continental Divide, which you can explore on various trails. The 2-km- (1-mi-) long **Sendero Bosque Eterno** (Eternal Forest Trail) passes a small waterfall. The 5-km (3-mi) **Sendero Bosque Nuboso** (Cloud Forest Trail) takes you to the Continental Divide, where you can admire the forest of the preserve's Caribbean side. There are many hiking variations: You'll receive a map at the entrance, and $1.75 gets you a self-guide booklet describing the plants and animals in the area and five self-guided tours. They also offer guided tours ($15) bright and early every morning that last 3½ hours and provide an excellent introduction to the local flora and fauna, increasing your chances of seeing such rare birds like the quetzal (tel. 645–5112 to reserve). If you aren't in a rush and want to explore deep regions of the 16,055 acres, spend the night for $3 at one of the rustic *refugios* inside the preserve: **El Valle** and **El Alemán** are only a 3-hour walk from the entrance. **Refugio Eladios** is about 6 hours away. Each refugio has a kitchenette, good drinking water, and bunk beds. Bring your own food and bedding. Direct all questions and reservation requests to the visitors center (tel. 645–5112 or 645–5122). The entrance booth is open daily 7–4, but the preserve remains open until 5:30.

Bosque Lluvioso de Santa Elena. If you thought Monteverde was something special, you ain't seen nothing yet. The community of Santa Elena, with the help of Canadian youth volunteers, transformed a government-granted rain forest into this private preserve, the profits from which support the local high school. There are a number of trails of various lengths covering 10 km (6 mi) of primary and secondary forest, one of which passes a spot from which you can see Volcán Arenal. You'll receive a map at the entrance (tel. 645–501), where there's an info display area, gift shop, restaurant, bathroom, and some feeders attracting beautiful hummingbirds. You're best off taking a taxi here and walking (hitching) back; get here are as early as possible. *5 km (3 mi) north of Santa Elena, tel. 645–5014. Admission $5. Open daily 7–4.*

Sky Walk. Down the hill from the Santa Elena preserve is this novel attraction that lets you tiptoe through the treetops on a series of suspension bridges, providing a monkey's-eye view of the luxuriant, aerial garden of the cloud-forest canopy. Get here early if you're into bird-watching. *5 km (3 mi) north of Santa Elena, tel. 645–5796. Admission $5. Open daily 7–4.*

CASEM (Cooperativa Comité de Artesanas Santa Elena y Monteverde). This cooperative of 137 women and three men sells handicrafts such as hand-painted T-shirts and embroidered dresses and aprons at "bargain prices." *Monteverde, tel. 645–5190. Open weekdays 8–5, Sat. 10–4.*

Jardín de Mariposas Monteverde. Local species of butterfly are hand-raised in the three enclosed gardens at this butterfly farm. This is a great option anytime, even when it's raining. *Mariposas* (butterflies) flutter around, especially in the morning. Admission includes a 45-minute bilingual guided tour and all the time you want to spend in the screened-in flyway. *½ km (¼ mi) down the hill from Cerro Plano (follow signs). Admission $6. Open daily 9:30–4.*

Orchid Garden. More than 400 different species of orchids are on display at this small garden and research project, including the world's smallest flower. Gabriel, the fellow who runs it, is a font of knowledge on the delicate and complex plants. At press time, the garden was located next to the Pizzería Johnny (*see above*) but was going to move to spot near the CASEM. *Monteverde, tel. 645–5510. Open daily 8–5.*

OUTDOOR ACTIVITIES

CANOPY TOURS • If you not only want to *see* monkeys in Costa Rica but act like one too, take a canopy tour. Using climbing equipment, you slide down cables strung between treetops in the cloud forest. Scary maybe, exhilarating, definitely, but don't worry—the 2½-hour, $40 adventure includes trusty bilingual guides. When it's time to come back to earth, they teach you to repel down a tree trunk (The Canopy Tour, next to Restaurante Daquiri, tel. 645–5243). Sky Walk (*see above*) also has a canopy tour that includes suspension bridges, cable flights across valleys, and a hilltop tower from which you can see about a quarter of the country.

HIKING • Apart from the fabulous trails in the Santa Elena and Monteverde preserves, there are a number of cheaper, less-traveled paths in the area. Because those trails are at a slightly lower elevation than the cloud forests, the climate is drier and some of the flora and fauna are different. The **Finca Ecologí** has four different trails leading through patches of forest to waterfalls and views. Until two years ago, the owner farmed corn, beans, coffee, and bananas on part of his land, but today he devotes it entirely to preservation. *Down the hill from Cerro Plano (follow signs), tel 645–5363. Admission $5. Open daily 7–4.*

HORSEBACK RIDING • Horses are a big deal in Monteverde, and they're used by locals for transportation and by tourists for sightseeing. They aren't allowed into the preserves, but you can trot into the surrounding scenic valleys. **Meg's Stables** (Monteverde, tel. 645–5560) has healthy, able-bodied horses and offers bilingual tours. **Arco Iris** (*see* Where to Sleep, *above*) offers horseback tours on a private farm. **Albergue Santa Elena** (*see* Where to Sleep, *above*) and **Desafio** (next to Restaurante Daquiri, tel. 645–5874) can arrange a full-day horseback adventure over the mountains to the Volcán Arenal area.

VOLCÁN ARENAL

Go to Volcán Arenal at night: if you're lucky, you'll see spectacular, bright orange lava shooting into the sky and flowing down the bare mountainside. Don't even think about hiking the volcano without an experienced guide! One of the most active in the Western Hemisphere, this volcano about 128 km (80 mi) northwest of San José sometimes explodes as often as every half hour, although it also has its quiet spells. It actually wasn't even considered a volcano until July 29, 1968, when it came back to lfe with an explosion that destroyed two villages and killed 80 people. The volcano is picture-perfect when it's not shrouded in rain clouds. During the day, smoke and gas clouds spew into the air every time the volcano erupts. Nearby are the hot springs of Tabacón, an amazing waterfall, and **Lago de Arenal,** an artificial lake and a prime place for windsurfing. At the foot of the volcano is the town of La Fortuna, also known as La Fortuna de San Carlos or just plain Fortuna, which offers plenty of lodging and dining options, as well as tours to the volcano, hot springs, waterfall, caves, Caño Negro (*see below*), and whitewater rafting on the Sarapiquí River.

COMING AND GOING

Because its attractions are so spread out, the Arenal is one area where it really comes in handy to have a car. If you drive here from San José, you have three routes to choose from: the quickest heads north from San Ramón, past lots of rain forest; the second-quickest is via Naranjo and Cuidad Carlos, which takes you through the lovely town of Zarcero; the third route, via Alajuela and Vara Blanca, takes you past the beautiful La Paz Waterfall. If you get here by bus, the most popular route is via Ciudad Quesada (San Carlos) to La Fortuna. **Garaje Barquero** (Calle 12 at Av. 9, tel. 232–5660 or 255–4318) has direct buses (4½ hrs) for La Fortuna that leave San José mornings at 6:15, 8:40, and 11:30 and return from La Fortuna at 12:40 PM and 2:45 PM. Or you can take an **Auto Transportes Ciudad Quesada** (tel. 255–4318) bus from San José to Ciudad Quesada (3 hrs) departing from the Coca-Cola bus station hourly 5 AM–7 PM and then catch the bus 6 from Ciudad Quesada to La Fortuna (1 hr, $1) at 10:30 AM, 1 PM, 3:30 PM, 5:15 PM, or 6 PM). From Tilarán, **Auto Transportes Tilarán** (Calle 12 at Av. 9, tel. 222–3854 in San José or 695–5611 or 695–5324 in Tilarán) operates buses daily at 7:30, 9:30, 12:45 PM, 3:45, and 6:30 from San José to Tilarán (4 hrs, $3); they return to San José at 7 AM, 7:45 AM, 2 PM, and 5 PM. **Transportes Tilarán-San Carlos** (tel. 465–5010) runs buses daily at 7 AM and 12:30 PM from Tilarán to La Fortuna (3 hrs, $2). They return to Tilarán around 8 AM and 5:30 PM. From northwest Costa Rica, buses travel regularly between Tilarán and Cañas, which is on the Pan-American Highway and thus serviced by regular buses from **Transportes La Cañera** (Calle 16 at Av. 3, tel. 221–0953), as well as **Pulmitán** buses to Liberia (*see above*).

WHERE TO SLEEP AND EAT

La Fortuna is overflowing with restaurants, hotels, and tour operators. The competition is stiff, and you'll probably be bombarded with special offers from kids on bikes when you come into town. Steer clear of these hucksters and head for the **Hotel La Fortuna** (1 block east and 1 block south of soccer field, tel. 479–9197), where a single is $8 and a doubles are $16 for a private bath and complimentary breakfast. There's a large, covered deck upstairs with a perfect view of the volcano. Other good hotels include the cozy **Hotel Las Colinas** (150 m south of the Banco Nacional, tel. 479–9107), which has nice rooms with private baths. Ask for one on the third floor for a volcano view. **Cabinas Mayol** (tel. 479–9110), a couple of blocks south of the soccer field, has comfortable doubles for $18. Rooms and cabins at **Cabinas Jessy** (1 block south and 3 blocks west of soccer field, tel. 479–9076) go for $4 a single ($6 with bath) and $8 a double ($12 with bath).

You can camp at **Los Lagos** (tel. 479–9126), on the forested lower slopes of the volcano, for $5. You'll want to hire a four-wheel-drive taxi to reach this isolated spot, high above town, but once you're there, you'll have plenty to keep you busy: trails for hiking through the forest, horseback riding, and lakes with canoes and swimming.

The best restaurant in town is **Rancho La Cascada** (soccer field, tel. 479–9145). Overhead is an architecturally amazing thatched roof lined with flags from around the world. If you've got a car, head toward the volcano to **La Vaca Muca** (tel. 479–9186), about 1 km (½ mi) west of town; it's famous for serving big portions of typical Costa Rican cuisine. You can also get cheap, wholesome food at **El Jardín** (1 block east of soccer field, tel. 479–9072). Off the main road a bit, look for **Nene's** (tel. 479–9192), the locals' favorite steakhouse.

OUTDOOR ACTIVITIES

Because most activity is on the other side of the volcano from La Fortuna, a night tour is the best way to see it if you don't have a car. **Aventuras Arenal** (east side of ICE, tel. 479–9133), **Desafío** (across from Restaurante La Cascada, tel. 479–9464), and **Sunset Tours** (½ block north of west side of soccer field, tel. 479–9099) offer three-hour evening tours ($20–$25) to the volcano's active side, where you might be able to witness a full-fledged lava eruption. On the way back they stop at Tabacón Hot Springs (*see below*), but admission usually isn't included in the price of the tour.

The same operators also offer tours to the Caño Negro Refuge (*see below*) for around $40; it's much easier, faster, and cheaper than busing up north to Los Chiles and hiring a boat on your own. Other excursion options include spelunking in Venado Caverns, the horseback trip up to the Catarata de la Fortuna (*see below*), and rain-forest hikes on the volcano's lower slopes. Desafío also offers white-water rafting trips on either the Toro or the Sarapiquí rivers ($80), as well as horseback trips up to Monteverde ($70).

NEAR VOLCÁN ARENAL

TABACON HOT SPRINGS

The volcano-heated Tabacón River flows down Arenal's northern slope, filling a series of pools that have themselves become tourist attractions. About 12 km (7 mi) northwest of La Fortuna, where the river passes under the road, are two very different hot-spring experiences. On the left you'll find the fancy **Tabacón Resort** (tel. 222–1072), which has a swimming pool with a swim-up bar and waterslide, a soothing waterfall, and secluded pools in the river with front-row volcano views for $14. On the right side of the road is a quieter, more natural spot with a few shallow pools and rustic changing rooms; use of the facilities costs only $4, but unfortunately, you can't see the volcano erupt from here.

CATARATA DE LA FORTUNA

Set at the back of a lush valley 6-km (3½-mi) southwest of La Fortuna, the 50-meter-high Fortuna Waterfall is one of Costa Rica's great sights. The pool the waterfall pours into is a popular swimming hole, but there are quieter pools downstream that are surrounded by boulders perfect for flaking out. The whole scene is surrounded by rain forest protected within a reserve managed by the local community (admission $2). It takes a couple of hours to walk from La Fortuna, which is why folks without wheels usually either take a horseback tour or hire a taxi to get them close.

TILARÁN AND NUEVO ARENAL

Tilarán and Nuevo Arenal are situated on the opposite end of Lago de Arenal from the volcano, 2–3 hours by car. The reason most people visit these small, untouristed towns is to windsurf on the the western end of the lake, where the trade winds whip down a valley creating similar conditions to those of the Columbia River Gorge. Between Tilarán and Nuevo Arenal lies the main windsurfing area, where equipment can be rented at several places. **Hotel Tilawa Viento Surf** (8 km [4 mi] from Tilarán, tel. 695–5050) offers equipment rentals, instruction, and nice rooms ($65 double with bath). Older rooms at the nearby Rock River Lodge (10 km [6 mi] from Tilarán, tel. 695–5644) cost just $45 for a double with bath; they also rent equipment.

Situated 6 km (4 mi) from the southwest end of the lake, Tilarán has an upbeat, youthful air. In the large central park, school kids shoot hoops and drench each other in water fights. One of the cheapest places to stay is **Hotel Central** (1 block east and ½ block south of the southwest end of park, tel. 695–5363), where singles start at $4 and a double with a private bath is $12. The **Hotel Tilarán** (west side of park, tel. 695–5043) charges $6 a person for a room with bath. Feast on good, cheap tico food at **Restaurante Nixon** (2 blocks north of park, tel. 695–5724) or **Restaurante Mary** (south side of park, tel. 695–5724).

Nuevo Arenal, on the northwest end of the lake, is farther than Tilarán from the windsurfing hub, but just 1 km (½ mi) from the water. It's quieter and smaller than Tilarán, hosting only a traveler or two a day. Four km (2½ mi) east of town are the **Arenal Botanical Gardens** (tel. 694–4273), which are devoted to the preservation of plants and flowers from around the world. It's open daily 9–5 and costs $4. Two km (1¼ mi) west of town, is the **Gordo Stable** (tel. 694–4092), where you can saddle up for a ride through the forests. They charge $25 for a half day or a full day of guided tours. **Hotel Tajas** (1 block east of park, tel. 694–4169) charges $6 a person for a room with private bath, and you can use their washing machine. The attached restaurant is ritzy (for Costa Rica, anyway) but is reasonable at around $4 a meal. For great German food, eat across the street at **Soda Picante** (tel. 694–4132), or for equally impressive pizza, pasta, and scrumptious desserts, trek down to **Pizzeria and Restaurant Tramonti** (near the lake, tel. 694–4280).

REFUGIO NACIONAL DE VIDA SILVESTRE CANO NEGRO

During the wet season the Río Frío floods the *llanura* (plains) south of Los Chiles, turning the remote, swampy Caño Negro Wildlife Refuge into a large lake that is home to myriad birds and other earth-bound wildlife. During the dry season it dries out entirely, and most of that wildlife moves onto the nearby Río Frío. Boat tours leaving from the town of **Los Chiles**, 3 km (2 mi) south of the Nicaraguan border, are the best way to see the river and seasonal swamp. If you have a small group, it can be worth-while to hire your own boat and driver ($60 for 3 hrs) from **Doña Julia's** restaurant, across from the park in Los Chiles (tel. 471–1032); if not, it's cheaper to go on a tour from La Fortuna. It is also possible to explore the reserves forests on horseback (summer only) from the town of Caño Negro.

The town of **Caño Negro,** located inside the refuge, is a small agricultural community where you can find basic accommodations and horses and guides for exploring what's left of the area's forests. The area has been the site of some conflict over land distribution over the years, but it is a good place for travelers who want to experience rural Central American life and support grass-roots ecotourism.

COMING AND GOING

Buses to Los Chiles (5 hrs) leave from San José's Coca-Cola terminal daily at 5:30 AM and 3:30 PM, returning at the same hours. From Ciudad Quesada (San Carlos), nine buses make the trip to Los Chiles every day. To reach the pueblo of Caño Negro, you must first travel to Upala. **Autotransportes Upala** (tel. 470–0061) buses run daily from San José (6 hrs, $4.25) at 3:15 PM and 3:45 PM. From Liberia, take a bus to Cañas (*see* Coming and Going in Liberia, *above*) and transfer to one of five daily Upala buses. From Upala, **Transportes Salas** (tel. 470–0053) runs buses to Caño Negro (2 hrs, $1.75) from the bus station at 11:15 AM and 3:45 PM and from the bridge at 4:30 PM. Return buses leave Caño Negro daily at 5:30 AM and 1:30 PM. Return buses from Upala to Liberia leave daily at 5 AM, 9 AM, and 3:30 PM.

WHERE TO SLEEP AND EAT

Cabinas El Querque, on the left-hand side right off the lagoon as you enter town, has rickety double cabins for $8.50, with bedding and netting included. They also offer camping for $1.75 a person, and you can use their bathrooms and showers. The **reserve administration office** (tel. 460–1301) has lodg-ing for 10 people, with preference given to researchers and student groups. The cozy bunks are $5.50 a night if you bring your own bedding—if not, bedding costs a whopping $11 extra per night. Don't for-get the mosquito net or you'll be eaten alive. There are two decent restaurants in town: **Restaurante Machon** (town square) and **Soda La Amistad** (across from Cabinas El Querque), which houses the only phone in town (tel. 460–4164). The food is basic but fresh.

PUERTO VIEJO DE SARAPIQUI

By day the area is greener than the Emerald City. At night, yellow-green fireflies glow and cast a south-ern bayou spell. Scoop up a cup of the steamy air and drink a taste of Puerto Viejo, a town in the northern lowlands of Heredia. Once an important post on the Río Sarapiquí, Puerto Viejo has been rediscovered by workers from the surrounding *bananeros* (banana plantations) who come to town to party on paydays (the 15th and the last day of the month) and by naturalists on their way to nearby reserves. For travelers, Puerto Viejo's big attractions are the nearby **La Selva Biological Station** and boat trips down the **Rio Sarapiquí,** where you're likely to see crocodiles, iguanas, and all kinds of birds. Locals with motorized canoes offer river tours for about $20 an hour, which isn't bad if you can get a small group together. Call **Edwin Alemán Martínez** (tel. 766–6095), or simply head down to the dock, where there are always boats available. **El Gavilán Lodge** (tel. 234–9507), near La Selva, also offers boat and horseback tours.

BASICS • If you plan to explore the Puerto Viejo region, check with the **Toruma Youth Hostel** in San José (tel. 253–6598 or 224–4085) before you come. They offer good trips and significant discounts to HI members and have connections with **El Plástico,** a hostel in the **Rara Avis** rain-forest preserve near **Horquetas** (18 km [11 mi] west of Puerto Viejo). Day trips to **La Selva** (tel. 776–6565) are not only more affordable, but also much better for seeing wildlife. La Selva is a biological station run by the Organization for Tropical Studies (OTS) that has 420 species of birds, 1,200 howler monkeys, poison dart frogs, and large rodents called agoutis, among other animals. It is primarily a research center for biologists from around the world, but they offer one of the country's best nature tours for $20 a person. Wear sturdy shoes and bring a rain poncho and insect repellent. The four-hour tours start at 8 AM and 1:30 PM; if you take the morning tour, it's worthwhile to pay an extra $5 for lunch. You'll see even more wildlife if you spend the night; dorm-style accommodations cost $60 per person ($75 single) and include one guided hike and three meals. The entrance to La Selva is on the west side of the road, about 7 km (4 mi) south of Puerto Viejo; a taxi should cost $3.

COMING AND GOING • Buses to Puerto Viejo take two different routes, both of which head past remarkable scenery. The express buses (2 hrs, $2) take the Atlantic Highway through Braulio Carrillo National Park. Less frequent buses head through Vara Blanca (4 hrs, $2.50) passing **Volcán Poás** and the **Cascada de la Paz** (Peace Waterfall). All buses leave from Calle 14 at Avenida 9 (tel. 259–8571). Express buses, which pass through **Río Frío,** depart at 8 AM, 10, 11:30, 1:30 PM, 3:30 and 4:30. Buses that go via Vara Blanca leave San José at 8 AM, noon, and 3 PM.

WHERE TO SLEEP AND EAT • If you can't afford to stay at La Selva, Puerto Viejo has a small selection of hotels, but you should make a reservation, especially during the high season, or you'll get stuck paying by the hour in one of the town's love lairs. **Hotel Bambú** (across from soccer field, tel. 766–6005) has nice but pricey modern rooms with private baths, TV, and big windows for $45, double or single. The restaurant downstairs seerves decent Chinese food. The friendly family at **Mi Lindo Sarapiquí** (50 m from Seguro Social Bldg., tel. 766–7074) charges just over $15 for a double with private bath and ceiling fan. The restaurant is also a favorite spot for late drinks and dinners; entrées run about $5. **Cabinas y Restaurant Monteverde** (across from the soccer field, tel. 766–6236) has musty rooms with private baths for just under $8 a double ($6 a single), and the popular restaurant serves basic tico food. **Pollos al Pastor** (50 m from the dance hall) serves up awesome chicken dinners ($2) with homemade tortillas, pickled plantains (try 'em), and all the jalapeños you can stand.

PENÍNSULA DE NICOYA

The Nicoya Peninsula has a split personality. While the coast is beachy and gringo-laden, the dry and rural inland region is devoted to cattle raisin' and slow livin'. As if that weren't schizo enough, it's divided further: the Guanacaste section, to the north, is far more developed than the scenic and fairly uncrowded beach towns to the south, around Puntarenas. **Playa Tamarindo** is overdeveloped, but other beaches such as **Sámara** and **Carrillo** are just days old in Costa Rica's tourism boom. And **Playa Montezuma,** while exhibiting a particular strain of gringo culture—think a wee bit of Berkeley in Costa Rica— has its own offbeat charm. Virtually tourist-free, proud **Nicoya** offers the comforts of a commercial city without losing the quiet pace so dear to the region. The peninsula's national parks are well preserved and undervisited; come here to explore caves, waterfalls, and pristine forest.

Bus service connects the larger cities to each other and to the more popular beaches, but forget about catching a bus from beach to beach; you'll have to backtrack to the inland hubs of Nicoya or Santa Cruz.

Consider renting a jeep, especially for Nosara and the southern Montezuma area. If you use public transportation, you'll find that the Montezuma area is practically a separate region from the rest of the peninsula, reached via ferry from Puntarenas. Hitching is common all over the peninsula, as is unauthorized camping on the beaches.

PLAYA MONTEZUMA

This is about as close as you'll get to a Costa Rican version of Berkeley. Long-haired hippies, ultravegetarian ecologists, drug-happy Deadheads, and tan beach bums all find their way to the small but mighty gringo colony of Montezuma (also called Moctezuma), near the southern tip of the peninsula. Once nasty and drug-infested, Montezuma has cleaned up its act and ranks high as one of the hot spots for young American and European vacationers. The town is so small you can see almost everything from where the bus drops you off, but the party-loving population doesn't let it sleep, and bars belt out reggae and rock all day long. The beautiful beaches to the north of town offer great camping but are too rocky for swimming or surfing. The **Cabo Blanco Reserve** (*see* Near Montezuma, *below*) has an enchanting forest, but Montezuma's main attraction is a number of waterfalls and freshwater swimming holes ideal for skinny-dipping. Hike 20 minutes up the little road that curves around the beach, cross the river, and follow the path marked CATARATA (waterfall). If you're in for a real challenge, walk two hours north on the beach to a larger fall that cascades into a deep pool of turquoise water.

BASICS

Make international phone calls at the ICE phone at **Chicos Tienda** (next to Hotel Moctezuma, tel. 642–0258). **Florry,** next to Pensión Jenny (*see* Where to Sleep, *below*), does laundry in a day. The **visitor information center** (open daily 8–10:30 and 4–8) at the main intersection in town offers snorkeling tours, bike rentals, and info about Cabo Blanco. Rent horses at the no-name bread store at the north end of town.

COMING AND GOING

If you're using public transportation, you have to reach Montezuma via Puntarenas. Take the **Asociación Paquereña** ferry (in Puntarenas, tel. 661–2830) to Paquera (1 hr, $1.50), then a **Rafael Angel Rodriguez** bus (tel. 272–0770) the rest of the way to Montezuma (2 hrs, $2.50). Ferries depart from behind the Puntarenas Market at 6 AM, 11 AM, and 3:15 PM and are met by buses to Montezuma. Return buses leave Montezuma at 5:30 AM, 10 AM, and 2 PM, connecting with return ferries. This is the only bus service on the southern part of the Nicoya Peninsula. To go anywhere else, you'll have to backtrack to Puntarenas and catch a ferry to Playa Naranjo (*see* Coming and Going in Puntarenas, *below*).

WHERE TO SLEEP

If you stay right in town, you'll be in the middle of things, but that generally means loud bar music and street noise. **Hotel Moctezuma** (tel. 642–0058) reverberates between the two bars in town. A sturdy double with an ocean view and a so-so bathroom goes for $15, a single with communal bath is $7. Next door, the popular, beachside **Cabinas Mar y Cielo** (tel. 642–0261) has doubles that open onto a balcony with a hammock for $25. For relative peace and quiet, check into the hotels and cabins that line the road to Cabo Blanco Reserve. **Pensión Jenny** (250 m down road to Cabo Blanco) offers the cheapest doubles in town—$6 per room—if you can put up with roosters crowing at 4 AM. More expensive doubles ($20)—you're paying for the secluded hillside swimming pool—are at **Cabinas La Cascada** (500 m down the road to Cabo Blanco, tel. 642–0057). The blue ribbon, however, goes to resort-style **Hotel Amor del Mar** (down the road to Cabo Blanco, across from waterfall entrance, tel. 642–0262), where $30 buys a double with collective bath and breathtaking ocean views (doubles with private bath start at $35).

CAMPING • Camping is legal anywhere on the beach as long as you stay 50 meters away from the shore. This turns out fine because this is where the palms are, ideal for hanging your hammock. **El Rincón de los Monos** (15 min north of town, enter by some shacklike homes, tel. 642–0048) has ample facilities: bathrooms, lockers, showers, washing machines, and a restaurant (open May–Nov.). Camp in the small shady area for $3 per person, or just pay $1 to use the facilities.

FOOD

Restaurants abound in Montezuma, but most are overpriced. Whole-wheat bread and low-fat smoothies have overtaken good ol' rice and beans. To take part in this organic, multigrain, fro-yo extravaganza, stop by tico-owned El Sano Banano (*see below*) or the more expensive gringo-owned **Restaurant El Jardín** (15 m down road to Cabo Blanco). Thankfully, traditional food hasn't been completely wiped out—join the locals at **Las Gemelas** (100 m north of Hotel Moctezuma). Grab a slice of pizza at **Pizzeria del Sol** (next to Hotel Moctezuma, tel. 642–0059; open daily 3–9) and, for dessert, a slice of banana bread at the hole in the wall (literally) around the corner from the pizzeria.

El Caracol. Popular with local ticos, this place is sure to give you heaps of tasty food for a good price. Hiding behind trees, this three-table restaurant operates out of the kitchen of the family that runs it. *250 m down road to Cabo Blanco; look for the sign to Pensión Jenny, no phone.*

El Sano Banano. The service sucks, but even locals make a daily stop here for the hippest and cheapest health food in town. Come in at 7:30 PM (a little earlier to get a good seat) when U.S. and Latin blockbusters air on a huge, outdoor movie screen. Spend the required purchase of $1.50 on pumpkin muffins, banana-yogurt shakes, or a scrumptious veggie burger. A meal averages $5. *50 m uphill from visitor center, tel. 642–0272.*

AFTER DARK

This town may be young and fun-spirited, but it goes to bed early: restaurants close at 9 PM, bars at 11 PM. **Bar El Chico's** (next to Hotel Moctezuma, tel. 642–0261) is younger and louder than the bar at the hotel itself. If you're willing to head out of town, the party spirit doesn't fizzle until dawn at **Kaliolin Disco,** which pumps out techno, salsa, merengue, and reggae on Wednesdays, Fridays, and Saturdays. It's 2 km (1¼ mi) away, but free taxis run there and back, leaving every half-hour from town.

NEAR MONTEZUMA

REFUGIO DE FAUNA SILVESTRE CURÚ

Director Adelina Schutt welcomes students and scientists to her wildlife refuge on the southeastern tip of the peninsula. A maximum of 30 visitors a day can choose from 17 well-marked trails—one difficult 2-km- (1-mi-) long uphill hike through the deciduous forest leads to a white-sand beach. The lowland sections of the refuge are used as an experiment in sustainable agriculture; the ocean forest and highlands are untouched, open to scientific research. Currently, the folks at Curú are experimenting with organically grown mangoes, melons, and papayas, and breeding cattle by artificial insemination. The endangered spider monkey is being bred at the refuge and released in groups back in the wild—in 1993, the first baby spider monkey was born in the wild, without refuge care. The $5 you pay gets you a guided all-day tour from a knowledgeable local for $10. You can't camp in the refuge, but you can stay in one of the six cabins or in the main house. It costs $25, which includes all meals, but availability depends on whether there's a rush of student researchers filling up the place. Call ahead to see (tel. 661–2392). To get here, take the Paquera–Montezuma bus from either Paquera or Montezuma (*see* Coming and Going, *above*). Ask the driver to drop you off at the road to the refuge, which is 7 km (4½ mi) south of Paquera. From here it's another 2½ km (1½ mi) to the entrance; the director will arrange to pick you up or, if she's busy, she'll leave the gate open and you can walk. A taxi from the Paquera dock costs $10—scads of 'em will solicit you as you get off the boat.

RESERVA NATURAL ABSOLUTA CABO BLANCO

Cabo Blanco, a huge stretch of land on the southern tip of the peninsula, became Costa Rica's first declared conservation area in 1963. As an "absolute" nature reserve, it must be preserved in its pristine state, resulting in very strict guidelines for visitors. One example: rangers will check your bags as you leave to make sure you don't take any shells or rocks. A single trail, **Sendero Sueco,** is open to the public—and it's a doozy. Starring howler and white-faced monkeys, coatimundi, anteaters, agouti, and snakes, the 5-km (3-mi) trail starts at the administration building and goes up, down, around, and through an evergreen forest until you hit the beach. Swimming is technically prohibited, but some cool off after the hike with a little skinny-dipping. Camping isn't allowed, but $10 gets you room and board nearby at **Doña Lila**'s country-style home. It's ½ km (¼ mi) before the park entrance, the last house on the left. *Open Wed.–Sun. 8–4. Admission $6.*

**COMING AND GOING • ** The bus to Cabo Blanco (40 min, $2.50) leaves Montezuma at 9 AM and returns from the park at 4 PM. If you have spare time, walk back to Montezuma on the rocks along the shore. It takes about three hours and there's no marked trail—just follow the coastline. Taxis parked near the Montezuma bus stop will usually take groups to the reserve for $5 a head.

NICOYA

Although it's a commercial and political center for the northern peninsula and a transportation hub for outlying beaches, Nicoya maintains a tranquil attitude and prides itself on being the "heart and spirit" of the rural Guanacaste Province. Nicoyans are remarkably friendly and the small-town atmosphere is homey, probably due in part to its isolation in the peninsula's interior, far from any crowds. If you happen to stumble into town a few days before July 18, you'll have a good ol' time celebrating the annual **rodeo and festival.** Otherwise, check out the 300-year-old colonial church next to the plaza or spend some time people-watching in peaceful Parque Central, soaking up some of the Guanacastecan pride that adds a spark to the hypnotic easygoingness of the town. For nighttime fun, **Discotheque Chicago Patinroll,** next to the bus terminal, is open Friday–Sunday.

BASICS

Change cash or traveler's checks or get a cash advance on your Visa at **Banco de Costa Rica** (in front of Parque Central, tel. 685–5010; open weekdays 9–5) or **Banco Nacional de Costa Rica** (on main road out to San José, tel. 685–5366; open weekdays 8:30–3:45). Do the postal thing at **Cortel** (Parque Central, tel. and fax 685–6402) weekdays 7:30–5:30. The **public health clinic** (100 m east of post office, tel. 685–5021) serves ticos and travelers free of charge weekdays 7–3. The **Red Cross** (tel. 685–5458) will bring you to the nearby **hospital** (near highway, north of center, tel. 685–5066) in an emergency. **Bar El Molino** (next to hospital, tel. 685–5001) serves as the local visitor information center.

COMING AND GOING

Empresa Alfaro (tel. 222–2750) runs buses from San José to Nicoya (5 hrs, $4.50) seven times daily 6:30 AM–5 PM. Buses return to San José seven times daily 5 AM–5:20 PM, leaving from Nicoya's **main terminal** (100 m east and 200 m south of Parque Central, tel. 685–5032). Alfaro also runs service to Playa Naranjo that connects with the **Coonatramor** ferry (tel. 661–1069) to Puntarenas and then another bus to San José. This option takes about four hours and costs $4.50. Buses also depart from the main terminal to Nosara at 9:30 AM or 1 PM (returning at 6 AM and 12:45 PM) and to Samara at 8 AM, 10 AM, noon, 3 PM, and 5 PM (returning at 4 AM, 5:30, 6:30, 7:30, 1:30 PM, and 4:30). From Nicoya's other, smaller **bus station** (4 blocks north of the main terminal, across from Hotel Las Tinajas), **Transportes La Pampa** (tel. 685–0111) has service to and from Liberia, with stops in Santa Cruz and Filadelfia, every hour or so 5 AM–7 PM.

WHERE TO SLEEP

Hotels in Nicoya serve more businesspeople than tourists, so cheapies with any character to speak of get busy during the week. The best deal for your money is probably the **Hotel Chorotega** (200 m south of Banco de Costa Rica, tel. 685–5245), where $10 gets you a double room with private bath and a view of the garden patio (a single with bath is $7). At **Hotel Las Tinajas,** present your student ID and you'll be charged only $13 for a nice double room with bath and fan ($16 for nonstudents). **Pensión Venecia** is the place to go for super-cheap digs; a single with communal bath is just $3.50 ($7 a double), although their rooms are short on space and privacy.

FOOD

The town's lack of attractions means you don't have to pay through the nose to get good food. Join the locals at popular **Soda El Colonial** (Parque Central; closed Sun), housed in an old adobe building; it's *the* place for breakfast and cheap casados. Nicoya's large Chinese population means almost every other restaurant on or near the main street specializes in *comida china*. **Restaurante Teyet** (50 m south of Parque Central, in front of Hotel Jenny) is one of the better Chinese restaurants, with 75 dishes on the menu. Although also Chinese-owned, **Cafe Daniela** (main street, 75 m south of supermarket, tel. 686–6148), another breakfast option, serves tico food, pizza, and good pastries. Next door at the **Restaurant Nicoya** (main street, 75 m south of supermarket, tel. 685–5113) you'll feel like you just stepped into China, thanks to hanging lanterns, bright red tablecloths, and an ample menu of Asian taste treats.

NEAR NICOYA

PLAYA SAMARA

When you reach Sámara, 29 km (18 mi) south of Nicoya, you'll see a sign proclaiming it the "best beach in America." Okay, maybe that's overstating it, but just a little. Two forest-covered hills jut out on either side of a clean, white-sand beach, forming one giant cove ideal for swimming. The coral reef offshore offers excellent skin diving, although you'll need a boat to get there. Although it is packed during the big holidays, Sámara is pretty quiet most of the year and is not nearly as developed as Tamarindo and other beaches farther north.

For snorkeling and scuba excursions, head to the **Vaca Loca** (*see below*) or **Hotel Giada** (150 m from beach on main road). Public phones are located by the soccer field and at **Pulpería Mileth** (where main road meets the beach, tel. 680–0445). The **post office** and **police station** are across the street. Fifteen minutes away by bus, Playa Carrillo is a miniature, semisecluded version of her big sister. Beware of the water, which gets deep close to shore. A taxi between the two beaches costs $4; flag down the red jeep circling through the area, or, if you're really motivated, walk 90 minutes along the beach.

COMING AND GOING • **Empresa Alfaro** (tel. 222–2750 or 223–8361) has direct bus service daily to and from San José (6 hrs, $5.50). The bus leaves from Playa Carrillo at 4 AM, stopping in Sámara at 4:15, except on Sundays, when they leave Carrillo at 1 PM. Buses leave San José at 12:30 PM from Calle 14, between Avenidas 3 and 5, and pass through Sámara just before arriving in Carrillo. **Empresa Rojas** (tel. 685–5352) runs buses between Sámara/Carrillo and Nicoya (2 hrs, $1.50). Buses leave from Carrillo at 5:30 AM, 6:30, 7:30, 1:30 PM and 4:30 daily, stopping by Sámara 15 minutes later. Return buses leave Nicoya at 8 AM, 10, noon, 3 PM, and 5.

WHERE TO SLEEP AND EAT • In Sámara, you can camp on the beach at **Camping Cocos** (200 m down street that runs parallel to the beach) for $3 per person, or stay at any of a number of hotels. **Cabinas La Arena** (300 m before beach on the main road, tel. 656–0320) has simple but clean rooms with fans and small baths for $10 a person. The nearby **Pensión Magaly** (25 m north of Cabinas La Arena, tel. 656–0052) has more basic rooms with private baths for $6 a person ($4 a person for communal bath) and dry-season tent sites for $2.

Casa del Mar. A mere 75 meters from the beach, Casa del Mar has an array of sleeping options. Bright rooms upstairs that share baths cost $35 for a double ($30 a single), whereas larger rooms with private baths are $50. Breakfast is included in the price of the room, and the restaurant serves good Italian food. *100 m down street that runs parallel to beach, tel. 656–0264. 15 rooms, 10 with bath. Restaurant.*

La Vaca Loca. These bright and spacious rooms with hot-water baths, porches, and one double bed in each are a bargain for a couple at $30 or $25 for a single guest. The restaurant in front serves good tico food, and the owners arrange scuba diving and snorkeling trips. *200 m down street that runs parallel to beach, on left, tel. 656–0265. 4 rooms with bath. Restaurant.*

NOSARA AND BEACHES

Set a bit inland, the small town of Nosara is a good base for exploring area beaches. Seven kilometers (4¼ mi) to the north is **Playa Ostional,** where on almost any given night June–December you can see at least one turtle lay her eggs. The real spectacle, however, is the *arribada* (arrival by sea), when as many as 2,000 olive ridley turtles waddle out of the ocean on the same night—this tends to happen during a three-quarter moon. While turtle-watching, stay at the **Guacamayo** (down road from entrance to beach), where a double is $8.50, or across the street at one of **Cabinas Ostional**'s $6.50 doubles. Find cheap eats around the corner at a small nameless soda. South from Nosara are **Playa Pelada,** a good swimming beach, and **Playa Guiones,** with the best surf turf in the area. In town, **Cortel** (100 m from soccer field, tel. 680–0857) serves as post office and police station.

COMING AND GOING • **Empresa Alfaro** (tel. 222–2666) has service from San José to Nosara (6 hrs, $6.25) daily at 6 AM, stopping in Nicoya on the way. The return bus leaves from Nosara's soccer field daily at 12:45 PM. An **Empresa Rojas** bus (tel. 685–5352) bound for Nicoya (2 hrs, $1.50) leaves Nosara daily at 6 AM. The return bus leaves Nicoya's main terminal at 1 PM. Unless you've rented a car, getting from beach to beach can be expensive and slow. Hitchhiking is common, or call **Taxi Nosara** (tel. 680–0857).

WHERE TO SLEEP AND EAT • **Hotel Chorotega** (3 km [1½ mi] down road to Nicoya) has a restaurant and comfortable doubles with shared bath for $12, but it's so far from the beach you'd better have a car. The shabbier **Cabinas Agnel** (500 m down road to Nicoya) has doubles with private bath for the same price. **Almost Paradise** (on hill above Playa Pelada, tel. 685–5004) charges $40 for its doubles with ocean views. The French-owned **Café de Paris** (tel. 380–0271) serves good food and baked goods and has a few rooms that rent for $25 a double. A popular spot for cheap seafood is **Doña Olga's** (Playa Pelada). For lunch, dinner, or a ranch-style Sunday brunch step into **El Ranchito** (across from soccer field).

PARQUE NACIONAL BARRA HONDA

Barra Honda is the place to be if you're into spelunking; the park's 42 caves are 70 million years old and have gorgeous stalactites and stalagmites. Unfortunately, the general public is allowed into just one—60-ft **La Terciopelo.** Park officials require that anyone exploring the cave be accompanied by local guides, who charge $34 for one person, $40 for two, and $46 for three to eight, so try to get a group together. Rent equipment from the park office for an additional $11 per person. Thankfully, Barra Honda has a lot more to offer than the caves—the tropical dry forest that covers that hill is home for hawks, monkeys, deer, parrots, and countless other creatures, and the trails that traverse it pass some spectacular views.

BASICS • Barra Honda is open daily 8–3, and park admission is $6. From Nicoya, take a taxi ($8) or catch the 12:30 PM bus to Santa Ana and walk the last 3 km (1¾ mi). Stay just outside the park at **Complejo Ecoturístico Las Delicias** (tel. 685–5580). Campsites with bath and shower facilities go for $3 a person, while $8.50 gets you a bed in one of three seven-person cabins. Check in and get tourist info at their restaurant.

PLAYA TAMARINDO

Tamarindo, 29 km (18 mi) west of Santa Cruz, is the most touristed beach in Guanacaste. The beach itself isn't notably clean or beautiful, and the main reasons to come here are to surf, people-watch, or sunbathe. The past few years have brought an influx of expensive, European-owned hotels and restaurants, and nowadays you're just as likely to meet an American surfer or Italian restaurateur as a tico. This international mix offers a diversity of attitudes and lifestyles; the downside is a definite tension between foreign hotel and restaurant owners and the local ticos who watch them snatch profits from the tourist economy. Tamarindo's made-for-tourist shops distribute visitor info and rent anything that moves: snorkeling equipment, boogie boards, surfboards, bikes, kayaks, and mopeds. Try **Tamarindo Rentals** (main road, tel. 654–4078), the **Palm Shop** (white shack on main road, tel. 654–4223), or **Iguana Surf** (200 m down right-hand fork off side street).

COMING AND GOING

From San José, **Empresa Alfaro** (tel. 222–2750 or 222–2666) runs an express bus to Tamarindo (5½ hrs, $4.50) daily at 3:30 PM. Return buses leave daily at 6 AM, with an additional run at 1 PM on Sunday. To ensure a seat, buy your ticket a day in advance at **Hotel Tamarindo Diría,** the huge peach-colored complex on the main road; it's open for ticket sales Monday–Saturday 8–6. **Folklórico** buses run to and from Santa Cruz (2 hrs, $1.50) four times daily 4:30 AM–3:30 PM. In Santa Cruz, transfer to buses for other destinations.

WHERE TO SLEEP AND EAT

Cabinas Rodamar (main road, on left entering town, tel. 653–0109) offer some of the cheapest and most basic digs in town: a small double room with a window, a bath, and a fan costs $15 ($9 a single). They'll also let you camp for $2 a person. Farther down on the right is the beachfront **Hotel Dolly** (tel. 653–0017), where $8.50 per person gets a room with shared bath on a garden patio and tight security. **Pozo Azul** (main road, across from Banco Nacional, tel. 653–0208) has big rooms with private bath, hot plate, refrigerator, and several beds for $25–35; they're a good deal for three people. **Cabinas Marielos** (across the street from the beach, tel. 653–0141) has nice little rooms with private baths that open onto a colorful garden for $30 a double. **Hotel Zullymar,** down the street (tel. 653–0140), has big, bright, modern rooms surrounding a swimming pool for $50 a double, and nearby Cabinas Zullymar are smaller, dimmer, and older, but cost only $28 a double. **Tito's** (600 m down right-hand fork of side street) has a good típica restaurant and beachside campsites for $2 per person. The spacious rooms with private baths at **Cabinas 14 de Febrero** (across the street from Tito's, tel. 653–0238) are quite a deal for $22 a double ($18 a single), and they even add a kitchen and dining area for guest use. The Italians who own the four beautifully decorated cabins (doubles $40–$50) at **Arco Iris** (300 m up left-hand fork of main road and 200 m uphill to right, no phone) also give massages and do tattoos. They have a common cooking area for guests, although you'll be tempted to eat at their great vegetarian restaurant. In town, you can munch on fresh seafood while watching the waves roll in at the open-air **Restaurante Zullymar,** where a fish fillet costs about $7. You'll get better food for less money if you forfeit the view and cross the street to **Fiesta del Mar** (tel. 653–0139), where they have cheap daily specials of typical tico dishes with lots of fresh seafood, and they give you free appetizers and rice pudding for dessert.

THE CENTRAL PACIFIC COAST

A haven to both visitors from *el norte* and city-dwelling ticos, Costa Rica's central Pacific coast is a quick jaunt from San José. The bathwater-warm water is ideal for swimming, surfing, and boogie boarding, and the beaches have relatively little trash despite heavy tourism. The surfer colony of **Jacó** sees hordes of Canadian and U.S. tourists, as does the beautiful beach town of **Manuel Antonio.** The tropical forests and pristine beaches of **Parque Nacional Manuel Antonio,** inhabited by monkeys, sloths, and iguanas, will convert the most confirmed city-snob into a nature lover—for the day, at least. Quality restaurants, unique hotels, and a thriving bar scene mark nearby **Quepos,** home to many older foreigners who came to visit and couldn't bear to leave. Only **Puntarenas** is the ugly duckling: polluted and dull, it's only worth a stop long enough to catch a ferry to the Península de Nicoya. Travel is generally inexpensive on the Pacific coast, especially during the rainy season, but expect to pay more when things dry out and the tourists start reappearing.

PUNTARENAS

Puntarenas, 112 km (70 mi) west of San José, is a poor, funky port town built on a long, sandy peninsula that stretches out into the Golfo de Nicoya. Once popular with tico tourists, the town's pervasive stench of pollution has all but driven them away and squelched any dreams of it becoming Club Med—the rancid sewage smell makes it impossible to hang out on the beach. Along the town's polluted southern edge is the developed but deserted **Paseo de los Turistas,** lined with terrace restaurants and expensive hotels. The north shore, with shipyards, ferry docks, and a market, is equally polluted. Most people stop in Puntarenas just long enough to catch the ferry to the Península de Nicoya, but surfers (who don't worry about niceties like clean water) often hang around, since the rivermouth left of Boca Barranca, just south of town, is the country's second longest wave after Pavones. Puntarenas celebrates two annual festivals. The last three days of November are devoted to **La Fería del Marisco,** a seafood festival that includes beach sports, dances, and, of course, the fruit of the sea. During the week of July 16, **La Fiesta de la Virgen del Mar** (Festival of the Sea Virgin) is a giant week-long party.

BASICS

You can change traveler's checks or get a credit-card advance at **Banco Nacional** (Av. 3 and Calle 1, tel. 661–0233) weekdays 9–3. **Banco de San José** (Av. 3 and Calle 3, tel. 661–2838) has similar services and is open weekdays 9–5. Change cash weekends or after hours for a lower rate at Supermercado Pali (*see* Food, *below*), sit-down restaurants, and nicer hotels like the **Tioga** (Av. 4, between Calles 17 and 19, tel. 661–0271). The **Hospital Roble de la Puntarenas** (8 km [5 mi] east of town, tel. 661–0033) is a better choice for medical attention than Hospital Monseñor Sanabria, on the north shore. Make international calls at the visitor center or **ICE** (Av. Central, between Calles 2 and 4, tel. 661–0166). The **post office** (50 m south and 50 m west of Casa de la Cultura) copes with faxes in addition to its regular services. The **visitor information center** (Av. Central and Calle 3, in the Casa de la Cultura, tel. 661–1169) has a direct AT&T phone to the United States, as well as tourist info. It's open weekdays 9–4. The nearby **Marine Museum** (tel. 666–1606) has some neat old photos of Puntarenas, as well as information about Cocos Island, a national park 480 km (300 mi) to the southwest.

COMING AND GOING

BY BUS • Buses for San José leave from the main **terminal** (Calle 2, between Av. 2 and Paseo de los Turistas) on the south shore. **Empresarios Unidos de Puntarenas** (Av. 4, between Calles 2 and 4, tel. 661–2158; in San José, Calle 16, between Avs. 10 and 12, tel. 221–5749) runs a direct shuttle to and from San José (2 hrs, $2) every 30 minutes 6 AM–7 PM daily. Indirect buses (2½ hrs, $2) leave daily every two hours 4:15 AM–8 PM. Buses to all other destinations leave from a nearby bus stop on Paseo de los Turistas, between Calles 2 and 4. This is where you can catch the bus to Jacó and Quepos (3 hrs, $2.50); five departures daily between 5 AM and 3 PM. From the same spot, **Empresa Avata** (in Liberia, tel. 666–0138) has five daily buses to Liberia (2½ hrs, $2.50). One bus leaves daily for Santa Elena, near Monteverde, ($2.50) at 2:15 PM, while buses to Tilarán ($2) leave every day at 11:30 AM and 4:15 PM.

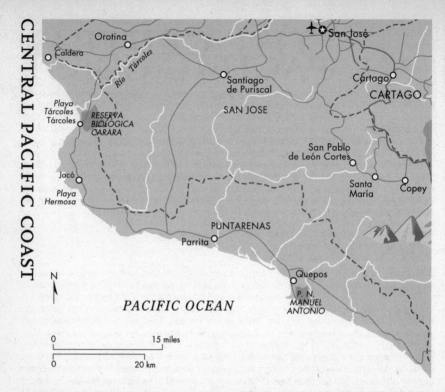

CENTRAL PACIFIC COAST

RESERVA BIOLÓGICA CARARA

PACIFIC OCEAN

```
0          15 miles
0          20 km
```

BY BOAT • From a dock behind the central market, about six blocks north of the bus station, a boat operated by **Asociación Paquereña** (between Calles Central and 1, tel. 661–2830) will transport you ($1.25), your bike (80¢), or your motorcycle ($1) to Paquera (1 hr) on the Península de Nicoya. The boat, which runs three times daily, at 6 AM, 11 AM, and 3:15 PM, connects to a bus that heads to Montezuma. The office, open daily 6–6, stores luggage for day trips only (50¢). If you're traveling by car, go to the peach-colored **Naviera Tambor** office (Av. 3 and Calle 31, tel. 220–2034), at Puntarenas's northeast dock, to catch a ferry to Paquera (1 hr). They charge $1.50 per person and about $9.50 per car. The ferry makes four trips daily each way 4:15 AM–7:15 PM. Across the street, **Coonatramor** (Av. 3, between Calles 31 and 33, tel. 661–1069) runs a ferry back and forth to Playa Naranjo (1 hr, $1.50), on the Península de Nicoya, five times daily 3:15 AM–7 PM.

GETTING AROUND

Because it is located on a peninsula, Puntarenas has two coastlines, referred to as the north and south shores, which are at some points no more than 100 ft apart. To the west, the city ends in a small, rocky point. Five avenidas run east–west, and 60-odd calles run north–south. Banks, shops, hotels, and the tourist-information office are all in the center of town, and the **central market** is on the north shore on Calle 3 at Avenida 2. You can walk to most places, but to reach the northeast dock it's easier to take a bus down Avenida 1; taxis are easy to find on the main avenidas. Avoid the red-light district around Las Playitas, which stretches from Calle 6 eastward; it's wretched and druggy.

WHERE TO SLEEP

The handful of hotels in town that aren't love shacks are close to the market and the Asociación Paquereña ferry office, just a few blocks north of the bus station. During the day the area is bustling with port activity, but at night you're a wee bit close to the red-light district—keep a firm hold on your bags, walk briskly, and consider taking a taxi. You get the most for your money at the three-story **Gran Hotel Choroteg,** (Calle 1, between Avs. 1 and 3, tel. 661–09980), located catercorner to Banco Nacional, where rooms and bathrooms are spotless and you don't need to bother with a private bath, because each bathroom is shared by only two rooms. Singles start at $9, doubles at $14.50. The **Hotel Ayi-Con**

(Calle 2, between Avs. 1 and 3, 50 m south of market, tel. 661–0164 or 661–1477) has a night watchman posted at the entrance, so it's safer and quieter than the rock-bottom hotels. Private and collective bathrooms are both fairly clean, and singles start at $6.50 ($9 with bath). The local HI hostel, **Cabinas San Isidro** (1 block south of hospital, tel. 253–9625 or 663–5261), has two swimming pools and a bar and is on the beach, which makes the $12 they charge members quite the deal.

FOOD

Restaurante Aloha (Av. 4 Bis, between Calles 19 and 21, tel. 661–0773) is one of the best, though not the cheapest, places for seafood. Because it's located on the Paseo de los Turistas, it's also a nice spot to sit and watch the world go by. The locals pack the **Kaite Blanco**, on the north shore west of the docks (take a taxi), which not only has cheap dinners, but also serves copious seafood *bocas* free if you drink. The central market is the cheapest option, but choose carefully—some stands are noticeably more skanky than others. You can get a whole pie for $4 at **Pizzeria Veletta** (Av. 4 Bis, at Calle 17, tel. 661–0369), open daily 11–11. **La Taberna Cervecera Bierstube** (Av. 4 Bis, between Calles 21 and 23, tel. 661–0330) serves expensive seafood but, thanks to the south shore breeze, is a nice place for a beer. You can buy groceries at the gigantic, food-filled **Supermercado Pali** (Calle 1, near Banco Nacional, tel. 661–1962).

JACÓ

Most side streets in tiny Jacó lead straight to the beach, where a few restaurants serve cocktails with fine ocean views. Tough life.

Jacó, 2½ hours southwest of San José, is a year-round tourist magnet, although the type of tourist varies with the season. During the wet months, Jacó is transformed into a Southern California surfer colony, with drunken revelers packing the discos. The dry season brings a calmer, older, mostly Canadian crowd who've tucked away their sweaters and come to bask in the sun. The beach itself is kind of skanky, but it's still a great place to ride horses, swim, boogie board, and surf. Away from the beach, rent bikes and motorcycles to tour the mountains and countryside (*see* Outdoor Activities, *below*).

BASICS

Change cash weekdays 9–2 at **Banco de Costa Rica** (across from Cabinas Supertica, tel. 643–3695) or weekdays 8:30–3 at **Banco Nacional** (across from Rayo Azul supermarket, tel. 643–3072). After hours, change cash and traveler's checks (at worse rates) at hotels and nicer restaurants. You can make international phone calls, send a fax, and get tourist info—not to mention maps and stamps—at the **visitor-information center** (near Macho hardware store, tel. 643–3248) in the center of Jacó. Wash your clothes for about $3 at the adjacent **laundromat** (tel. 643–3000) or at **Roxanna** (next to Cabinas Supertica, tel. 643–3478), which is open daily 24 hours. **Tropix Int'l** (center of town, tel. 643–3654) does money transfers weekdays 9–5. The **Farmacia Jacó** (in front of Rayo Azul supermarket, tel. 643–3205) is open Monday–Saturday 8–8 and, super conveniently, a full 24 hours on Sunday.

COMING AND GOING

Buy tickets to San José from the small, pink **bus terminal** (tel. 643–3135; open daily 7–noon and 1–4) at the north end of Jacó's lone main street, 125 meters north of Best Western Hotel. Express buses leave from the Coca-Cola bus terminal in San José (tel. 223–1109) at 7:30 AM, 10 AM, and 3:30 PM daily for Jacó (2½ hrs, $2.25); buses make the return trip daily at 5 AM, 11 AM, and 3 PM. Buy tickets for San José in advance or you might end up standing the whole way. Buses to Quepos also stop at Jacó; direct buses depart San José daily at 6 AM, noon, and 6 PM (2 hrs, $4). Buses between Quepos and Puntarenas run five times daily from 5 AM to 3 PM ($1.25), stopping at Jacó on the coastal highway outside town.

WHERE TO SLEEP

Jacó is not cheap, but during the rainy season the rates listed here drop between 20% and 40%. Surfers who are trying to stretch their last dollars out for a few more waves often end up at **Chuck's** (around the corner from Restaurante La Hacienda), where a few small rooms share a bath. If you get stuck, a cheap fallback ($3 per person) is **El Hicaco** (tel. 643–3004), a campground with showers, toilets, laundry basins, and electricity; look for it behind the owner's house across from the Red Cross at the south end of Jacó's main drag. Although you can't make reservations, in the high season call before you arrive, because in the past, they've had to turn people away.

Cabinas Alice. Spread along a narrow beachfront lot, these small rooms are a bit dark, but clean, with tile floors and and tiny porches, for $35 double or single. The hotel has a tiny pool, and its restaurant is one of the best places for fresh seafood and typical Costa Rican cooking. *End of first street south of the Red Cross, tel. 643–3061. 22 rooms with bath. Restaurant, laundry.*

Cabinas Jacó Colonial. This brand-new two-story hotel—with spacious rooms, hot water, and a pool—is popular with young ticos. You'll have to walk about 20 minutes from the center of town, but at least the rooms are cheaper than most in these parts: a double with private bath is $32 in the high season (singles are $16). *Tel. 663-5261. Walk south on main road past Red Cross; hotel is in front of church. 10 rooms with bath. Cash only.*

El Jardin. Located on the north end of town, this small, French-owned hotel has simple but comfortable rooms with private baths and fans for $22 a double. Rooms surround a decent-sized swimming pool, and the hotel is just a shell's toss from the beach. *North end of town, on road leading to beach, tel. 643–3050. 7 rooms with bath.*

Los Ranchos Bungalows. This is a hopping place where travelers congregate and suntan by a teardrop-shaped pool. Chat with the friendly North American owner, or tune into a surf report given by one of the poolside gringos. All rooms have hot water and huge beds. Triples are $25, six-person cabins $50. *Down street from Cabinas Supertica, tel. and fax 643-3070. 12 rooms with bath.*

FOOD

The best value and most interesting restaurants line the main street in the center of Jacó; try **Soda Chaca** (open daily 6 AM–10 PM), across from Cabinas Supertica, where for just $1 you get a chicken, beef, or fish dinner with rice, beans, salad, and juice. Surfers dine in the center of town at **Wishbone Eatery** (tel. 643–3036; open daily 11–3:30 and 5–9:30), where the portions are small but the pizza is great. If your cabin has a kitchen, stock up on the basics at **Supermercado Rayo Azul** (across from Banco Nacional, tel. 643–3027), which takes traveler's checks, Visa, MasterCard, and U.S. dollars. If you're a film buff, the hole-in-the-wall **Picnic Inn** (in front of Disco La Central, tel. 643–3388) mixes not-so-recent movies with dirt-cheap tico specialties.

Chatty Cathy's. This friendly, second-floor restaurant is the place for a hearty breakfast. By the time you finish sampling the breakfast pitas, cinnamon rolls, and banana pancakes you'll probably be swearing off lunch, but come noon, you may well get the urge to wander by and see what Cathy's offering for the midday meal. *30 m south of El Recreo, no phone. Closed Mon. and Tues.*

El Recreo. If it swims in the sea, you're likely to find it on El Recreo's extensive menu, and you can bet it's fresh. Everything—from the ceviche (marinated fish) to the *camarones al ajillo* (shrimp scampi)—is tasty and reasonably priced. It's located on the main drag, under a giant thatched roof. *Across from the Rayo Azul supermarket, tel. 643–1172.*

Killer Munchies. It's hard to decide which is more entertaining: the gringo surfer-stoners or the wait-people who flip your pizza before shoving it into a wood stove. The Killer Munchies pizza, with three kinds of meat, is mouth-watering, unless of course you're a vegetarian. *200 m north of Cabinas Supertica, tel. 643–3364. Closed Tues.*

AFTER DARK

Young locals and tourists pair up and cut loose to techno, salsa, reggae, merengue, and rock on the dance floor at **La Central** (near Red Cross, tel. 643–3076). The pickup scene here is a serious affair, so be prepared. Beers are two-for-one on Sundays, and there's no cover except on Saturday (when it's $2.25). The crowd at **Los Tucanes** (tel. 743–3226; open Tues.–Sun. 7:30–1), across the road, is older, tamer, and more local. After sweating it out at the disco, follow the crowds and drink until 5 AM at the open-air **Pancho Villa** (opposite Red Cross, tel. 643–3571).

OUTDOOR ACTIVITIES

Every year, surfers make the pilgrimage to Jacó. If you've come to surf or swim, watch out for the currents. Another thing to keep on eye on is your belongings: theft is a problem, so don't leave anything unattended on the beach. In the center of town, **Fun Rentals** (tel. 643–3242; open daily 8:30–5:30) rents motorcycles ($20 for 4 hrs) and bicycles ($6 for 4 hrs); look for flags hanging out front. **Alcides** (200 m south of Red Cross, tel. 643–3203) offers guided horseback tours for $20.

MANUEL ANTONIO

Known for the national park of the same name, the coastal enclave of Manuel Antonio boasts some of the country's most impressive scenery: pale beaches, washed tuquoise sea, steep hillsides draped with exuberant foliage, rugged offshore islands, and vast Pacifc views. It is also one of the spots in Costa Rica that offer travelers the best selection of things to do, with an array of outdoor diversions from sea kayaking to horseback trips into the rain forest.

The park itself is one of Costa Rica's smallest and most popular, which means that it can get crowded, especially during the peak tourist season. The National Park Service limits the number of visitors that can enter in one day, and the park is closed Mondays. You should try to visit the park as early in the day as possible to increase your chances of seeing wildlife. Manuel Antonio is an excellent place to see animals, such as capuchin monkeys, white ibises, iguanas, sloths, and the tiny squirrel monkey, which is only found here and in Corcovado. The park's beaches, however, are probably its main attraction—white sand backed by thick foliage—and Playa Manuel Antonio, the second beach inside the park, is the best for swimming and snorkeling. There is also a short trail that winds its way through the forest that covers Punta Catedral, past a spectacular ocean view, which you'll definitely want to hike. Admission is $6.

The small beach town of **Manuel Antonio,** just outside (and the gateway to) the park, is brimming with hotels. While you'll never forget it's a tourist spot, at least the crowd includes some interesting characters: a few surfers, a lot of college students, and a surprisingly large number of gay men who have made this place a gay-friendly vacation mecca. For cheap restaurants and hotels, head a half hour north to the small fishing town of **Quepos**—by day, it's a lazy home to many foreigners, ages 40 and up, who came to visit and never left; by night, it's a prime spot for residents and tourists to mingle over *bocas* (appetizers) and beer, or dance the night away.

BASICS

MANUEL ANTONIO • Most services are in Quepos, but you can change money at lousy rates in some hotels and bars in Manuel Antonio. Phones are located at the north end of town by Restaurant Mar y Sombra, at the south end by the park entrance, and in the center at Soda Marlin. If you're craving an international newspaper or magazine or a used English-language book, stop by **La Buena Nota** (in Manuel Antonio, by bridge at north end, tel. 777–1002; in Quepos, Calle 2 at Av. 1, tel. 777–0345). Manuel Antonio's **Laundry Service Daisy** will wash your pants and shirts for less than $1.

QUEPOS • **Lynch Tourist Service** (Calle Central, between Avs. Central and 1, tel. 777–1170) has an English-speaking staff and is open Monday–Saturday 8–6, Sunday 9–12:30. Change money weekdays 8:30–3 at **Banco Nacional** (Av. 3 and Calle Central, tel. 777–0113). If you need to change money or process money transfers, stop by **Western Union** (Av. Central, between Calles Central and 2, tel. 777–1312 or 777–1150) Monday–Saturday between 9 and 6. **ICE** (Calle Central, between Avs. 3 and 5, tel. 777–0166) handles faxes and international calls weekdays 8–3:30. **Cortel** (tel. 777–1471) has fax, telex, and postal services and is open weekdays 6:30–5:30; look for it at the north end of the soccer field, 4 blocks east of the bus station. In a medical emergency, call the local **Red Cross** (tel. 777–0116).

COMING AND GOING

From San José, direct buses to Manuel Antonio (3½ hrs, $5) all stop at Quepos's **bus station** (Av. Central, between Calles Central and 1, tel. 777–0318), open Monday–Saturday 6–11 and 1–5, Sunday 6 AM–2 PM. These buses leave San José daily at 6 AM, noon, and 6 PM; return buses leave Manuel Antonio's only bus stop at 6 AM, noon, and 5 PM, with an additional 3 PM bus on Sunday. Area bus service is handled by **Transportes Morales** (tel. 777–0318); call 'em for the latest schedule and fare info.

Indirect buses to Quepos from San José run five times daily 7–6, with five return trips daily between 5 and 4; the five-hour trek costs around $3. Between Quepos and Puntarenas's main bus station there are five buses a day 4:30 AM–3 PM; you'll pay $3 for this 3½-hour ride. **Transportes Blanco** (tel. 777–2550) has four buses daily from Quepos to Dominical and San Isidro, leaving Quepos at 9 AM, 1:30, 4:30, and 6:30 PM.

GETTING AROUND

Local buses run between Quepos and Manuel Antonio (30 min, 30¢) every half hour from sunup to sundown, with a few night buses. You can also take a taxi between Quepos and Manuel Antonio for $3; hail one at the Quepos bus terminal or call **Taxis Unidos** (tel. 777–0425). Taxis on their way back from Manuel Antonio will usually pick up people along the way and take them to Quepos for 70¢. To reach the park itself, walk south down the main road in Manuel Antonio. At high tide you'll have to wade through the estuaries that define the park's northern border; don't spend too long in that water; it's got raw sewage in it. Better still, cross at low tide. At the entrance to the park you'll find the info center and a map of the trails.

WHERE TO SLEEP

Unfortunately, you can't camp in the park itself, but you can set up a tent next to the **Restaurant Manuel Antonio** (tel. 777–1237), on the circle at the end of the road to the park, which charges $2 per person and has a simple bathroom and shower.

MANUEL ANTONIO • In a pinch, try the dark and dank **Cabinas Ramirez** (next to Mar y Sombra, tel. 777–0003), popular because of their beachfront location and because the owner, Hernán, is a swell guy. A room with a bath costs $20, double or single, but on weekends, you'll be dangerously close to the local discotheque. **Restaurant Manuel Antonio** (end of the road, tel. 777–1237) has a few rooms upstairs with private bath and fan that cost $20 a double, and one cheaper room downstairs that shares the outdoor bath with campers. The following hotels are located off the main road, on side streets that begin next to Soda Marlin.

Albergue Costa Linda. Popular with international travelers on tight budgets, this updated hotel with outdated prices is the cheapest in town. Cramped singles go for $6, and doubles start at $12. Rooms surround a garden patio, in the corner of which are the large communal bathrooms. *100 m north of Soda Marlin, tel. 777–0304. 20 rooms, none with bath. Cash only.*

Cabinas Irarosa. Okay, so it's a little farther from the beach and the main part of town, but it's well worth the walk. For just $7 per person, you get a private two-bedroom cabin with fans, a beautiful garden, and plenty of peace and quiet. On the downside, the cabins are small and a bit run-down. *400 m from Soda Marlin, tel. 777–1089. 6 cabins with bath. Laundry. Cash only.*

Hotel Vela Bar. The cheapest single is $25, and doubles start at $35, but this place is actually underpriced for what you get. The rooms try for a Swiss chalet look, while the exterior strives for Mediterranean—a strange juxtaposition, but it works in a trippy sort of way. The restaurant in front, under a thatched roof, serves an interesting selection of saucey dishes. The cheaper rooms fill quickly, so call ahead. *200 m down road that starts at Soda Marlin, tel. 777–1071. 10 rooms with bath. Laundry.*

QUEPOS • The cheapest sleeps—$3.50 for a bed in a ramshackle open-air hotel—are in the main part of town, between the bus terminal and ocean. Slightly more expensive cabinas are really just large rooms with private bathrooms, fans, and a lot of character.

Hotel Majestic. What distinguishes this hotel from the town's other cheap digs are the turquoise and pink walls and sunny balcony. It's a block west of the bus terminal, with box beds ($4 per person), sanitized white sheets, and clean communal bathrooms. *Av. Central, between Calles 2 and Central, tel. 777–1045. 12 rooms, none with bath. Cash only.*

Hotel Malinche. If you'd like a little more privacy and quiet, head for this small hotel a block west of the bus station. The rooms are bigger and brighter than the other places, and the hotel has a parking area; double rooms cost $16 with a fan, and twice that for air-conditioning. *Av. Central, between Calles 2 and Central, tel. 777–0394. 29 rooms with bath.*

Hotel Ramus. This place is so tacky it's cool. Red-vinyl furniture, wooden paneling, plastic flowers, and ornate drapery somehow combine to make a funky fashion statement. Each room (most with three beds) has two fans, a large bathroom, and worn-out mattresses and springs that make entertaining, sometimes incriminating, squeaky noises. A single with private bath costs $7 (double $10). *Av. Central Bis, between Calles 2 and Central, tel. 777–0245. 17 rooms with bath. Cash only.*

FOOD

MANUEL ANTONIO • Look for funky restaurants along the main street about 1 km (½ mi) from the park entrance. **Mar y Sombra** (tel. 777–0510), next to Cabinas Ramirez at the north end of the main road, has tables under the palm trees overlooking Playa Espadilla (otherwise known as Beach 1). Although you can't beat the ambience, you'll get a comparable meal for less money at **Soda Marlin** (main intersection, tel. 777–1120) or **Restaurante Perla** (main intersection, tel. 777–1891). The latter has a menu that's positively Shakespearean: choose from "Shrimp As You Like Them" or "Chicken As You Like It."

QUEPOS • Happy hour lasts all day in Quepos, reflecting the easy attitude of this quiet town. And if you like seafood, you're in serious luck, because restaurants along the shore on Calle 2 serve whole fried fish for about $3. Take in the gentle sea breezes over *café con leche* (coffee with milk) or an ice-cold beer. For the cheapest, fastest tico food, take a bar seat at Soda Marciela or Soda La Coquita in the bus terminal's **Mercado Municipal de Aguirre** (Av. Central, between Calles Central and 1).

El Kiosko. Although it's near a fairly busy section of Calle 2, El Kiosko is actually quiet and even slightly romantic. Sip a daiquiri ($2.25) or feast on a fruit plate ($1.60) under the hanging garden of ferns and tropical flowers. Meals average $5. *Calle 2 and Av. 2, 50 m south of park, tel. 777–0185.*

Restaurante Isabel. Located across main drag from the ocean, this popular corner establishment serves fresh seafood at great prices. A grilled filet of *dorado* (mahimahi) or tuna with a nice salad and fries costs less than $4. They also offer a bit of atmosphere to complement the cuisine, with potted palms, ceiling fans, and wicker chairs in the corners where you can relax and enjoy a cocktail before your meal. *Calle principal, next to Hotel Kamuk, tel. 777–0137. Closed Wed. during low season.*

AFTER DARK

Manuel Antonio by day, Quepos by night. Bar-hopping and meeting people are big in Quepos, where folks of all sorts mix in an open-minded, friendly atmosphere. You'll hear waves of cheers from the popular sports bar **El Banco** (Av. Central, 25 m east of Calle 2, tel. 777–0478; closed Wed.). If you want to chill out in a darker and mellower environment, head over to **Mar y Blues** (Av. Central, between Calles Central and 2), open daily 5–midnight. Drink in class at the new **Nueva Boca** (north end of Calle 2, 75 m past Av. 3, tel. 777–0279) or just sweat it out at **Discotheque Arco Iris** (tel. 777–0449), just past the bridge at the north end of Quepos. By the time you hit the ritzy after-bar **Kamuk** (Av. Central, near Calle 2, tel. 777–0379), open daily until 2 AM, you're bound to have already shared a few chugs with most everyone here. If you don't mind a seedier scene, shoot pool and make some bets with the local guys at **Pooles Soda El Pueblo** (Av. 1 and Calle 2).

OUTDOOR ACTIVITIES

BEACHES • Manuel Antonio's four incredible beaches are often referred to by number. **Playa Espadilla** (Beach 1) is the only one outside the park, extending alongside the city of Manuel Antonio. **Playa Espadilla Sur** (Beach 2) is the first beach you come to inside the park. Both of these are swimmable, but be *very careful* of the riptides—several people drown each year. The best beach for swimming is **Playa Manuel Antonio** (Beach 3), the second beach you'll hit inside the park, where the waves are small and the water bath-like. The deep cove this beach is set in is one of the best snorkeling spots in this area. **Puerto Escondido** (Beach 4) is more scenic than accessible; you'll reach it at the end of Puerto Escondido Trail (*see below*). Beaches 2 and 3 have bathrooms and showers, but remember not to use soap or shampoo—you'll murder the water critters. There are two nude beaches in Manuel Antonio: inside the park, **Playitas Gemelas** is marked by a sign halfway through Puerto Escondido Trail. It's small and inaccessible at high tide. Outside the park, north of Playa Espadilla, is a nude gay beach, simply called **Playitas.** You have to cross some treacherous rocks to get here.

HIKING • The park has five trails, all of which are marked on a map that's sold at the info center at the park entrance (there are also a few signs along the way). Bring bug spray, sunscreen, and water bottles (which you can refill with potable water from fountains). All trails begin at the park entrance; follow the road just right of the entrance for the 3-km (2-mi) **Punta Catedral** loop; it takes about an hour and offers breathtaking views. On the left, the 1-km (½ mi) **El Perezoso** (Sloth Trail) offers a good chance of encountering slow-moving sloths. Short but steep **El Mirador** (.6 km [¼ mi]) is the place to spot monkeys—but don't feed them, even if they ask nicely. Watch out for hanging "vines"—really snakes—and for actual vines with nasty cactus-like spurs on the 4-km (2½-mi) **Puerto Escondido Trail,** which is a little rough at the end; you'll want go when the tides are low so you're not wading through water—look for the blow hole as you emerge from the forest onto the rocky beach.

NEAR MANUEL ANTONIO

LONDRES

Set in the hills 40 km (24 mi) east of Quepos, the little agricultural community of Londres is lovely pastoral spot, but most travelers head there specifically to visit the **Cerro Narra Reserve** (tel. 382–5344), a 2,000-acre private nature preserve that offers a more challenging and less trodden alternative to the hiking trails in the national park. The reserve's crown jewel is the 200-ft **waterfall** located deep inside it, but its trails wind through some impressive tropical forest, where you're likely to see all kinds of wildlife. reserve offers day tours, camping, and sometimes has volunteer positions available. Six bus travel to Londres from the bus station in Quepos.

THE CARIBBEAN COAST

The steamy lowlands of eastern Costa Rica stretch to the warm, clear waters of the Caribbean Sea. Welcome to an entirely different country, a land of mangrove swamps and coral reefs, where weary travelers can recharge under the potent sun on glittering white- or black-sand beaches. South of the provincial capital of Puerto Limón you'll discover the awesome surf of Puerto Viejo de Talamanca, and in Cahuita and the Gandoca-Manzanillo Wildlife Reserve you can snorkel and dive. North from Limón stretch the verdant canals of Tortuguero, lush humid jungles, and protected turtle-nesting sites. Almost half the coast is protected by national parks. Remember your *capa* (rain gear), though; there is no such thing as a dry season here.

More than a third of the province's population is of Afro-Caribbean descent, and at least 5,000 Talamanca (Bribri) Indians live in reservations near the Panamanian border. Blacks were subject to legal discrimination until the constitution of 1949; the area's population remains socially, politically, and economically marginalized. The northern regions are isolated and difficult to access, while the more populated areas of Limón and the south struggle against crime and crack, although these problems are not as bad as the San José tourism industry would have you believe. Today, residents continue to bear a strong resentment against the central power of San José, proudly declaring their cultural and linguistic differences.

The Caribbean isn't as big a money-maker as the Pacific coast; accordingly, prices are a bit lower and tourism isn't as entrenched. English is widely spoken by many *limónenses*. The dialect is a little challenging, but understandable. "Okay" means "good-bye," and "all right" is used as a passing greeting. The traditional greeting, "wha' happen," is less heard but still used. Another cultural difference enjoyed by most travelers is the food. Rondon (rundown) is a succulent stew of local tubers and meat or fish. On Sunday, the traditional dish is rice and red beans cooked in coconut milk, a welcome variation on good old beans and rice. The fresh-baked fruitcake, *pan bon,* is also coconutty. Seafood is fresh, plentiful, well cooked, and less expensive than inland. However, during the *temporada* (busy season), December–May, lodgings are crowded. The famed jungle train traversing the region bit the dust (big bummer), but the ride from San José to the transporation hub of Limón takes only about two hours on a slick highway. Enjoy the trip 'cause it's the fastest you'll get anywhere in this area. Road conditions are subject to the whims of nature, and you'll quickly learn to hate **AutoTransportes MEPE,** the only bus company that serves the area. To avoid the sticky, dusty, and rarely prompt bus, many travelers hitch between the beach towns of Cahuita, Puerto Viejo, Punta Uva, and Manzanillo. People in the area are fairly mellow about picking up hitchers, but as usual, keep your sixth sense on the alert.

PUERTO LIMÓN

The biggest town on the Caribbean coast is densely populated and undertouristed. Faded paint and intricate moldings on a few buildings intimate a more happening past, but the April 1991 earthquake left the city in a state of slow, steamy decay. Limón, as the city is more commonly known, is an essential travel stop if you're continuing north to the canals of Tortuguero or south to the beaches of Cahuita and Puerto Viejo. The town attracts tourists during the annual *Día de la Raza* (Columbus Day) celebrations around October 12. A tidal wave of ticos and tourists floods the streets for Carnaval, a week of street parades, Caribbean music, and nonstop partying. Otherwise, most travelers get out of Limón as fast as they can, frightened off by warnings of theft, assault, and drug problems. Some ticos call the city *Piedropolis* (Crack City). The city's evils are exaggerated, but do exist; approach the area with open eyes. Don't wander around Limón by yourself at night—nighttime areas to avoid completely include the *malecón* (seaside jetty) and Parque Vargas.

Limón has long been excluded from the Costa Rican mainstream; racism and resentment are strong on both sides. The population of Limón, mainly of African descent, justifiably feels marginalized. After the 1991 earthquake, help was ridiculously slow in arriving; as one local put it, "Women were having babies on the football field and people were dying of malaria." The situation was so grave that the city took out a two-page ad in *La Nación,* one of Costa Rica's daily newspapers, condemning the government author-

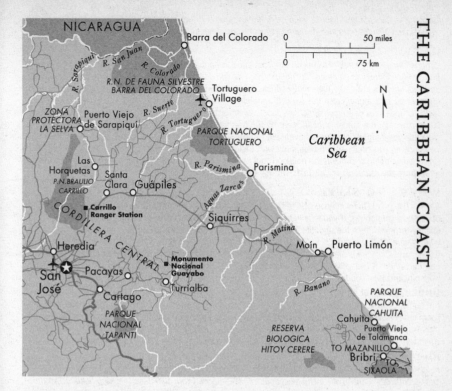

NICARAGUA

Barra del Colorado

0   50 miles

0   75 km

R. Sarapiquí

R. San Juan

R. Colorado

R.N. DE FAUNA SILVESTRE
BARRA DEL COLORADO

Tortuguero
Village

N

ZONA
PROTECTORA
LA SELVA

Puerto Viejo
de Sarapiquí

R. Suerte

R. Tortuguero

PARQUE NACIONAL
TORTUGUERO

Caribbean
Sea

Las
Horquetas

P.N. BRAULIO
CARRILLO

Santa
Clara

Guápiles

R. Parismina

Parismina

Aguas Zarcas

Carrillo
Ranger Station

Siquirres

R. Matina

CORDILLERA CENTRAL

Heredia

San
José

Pacayas

Monumento
Nacional
Guayabo

Turrialba

Moín   Puerto Limón

R. Banano

Cartago

PARQUE
NACIONAL
TAPANTI

RESERVA
BIOLOGICA
HITOY CERERE

PARQUE
NACIONAL
CAHUITA

Cahuita
Puerto Viejo
de Talamanca

TO MAZANILLO

Bribri

TO
SIXAOLA

ities for their oblivion. Ruins from the quake can still be seen, and under- and unemployment are all too present. Developing Limón is just not on the top of the government's list of priorities.

BASICS

You can change money at banks around Avenida 2, 50 meters north of the San José bus stop. **Banco Nacional** (Calle 3 and Av. 2, tel. 758–0094) is across from the southeast corner of the mercado and open weekdays 8:30–3:45. For slightly longer hours, try **Banco de San José** (Av. 4, between Calles 2 and 3, tel. 795–0155), 75 meters east of the bus stop for Cahuita and Puerto Viejo: they're open weekdays 8–noon and 1–5. On weekends you're out of luck unless the management of your hotel can help you out. **Hospital Dr. Tony Facio Castro** (tel. 758–2222), in a big blue-and-white building at the north end of the malecón, has English-speaking doctors in the emergency room. The **Red Cross** (Calle 3, between Avs. 1 and 2, tel. 758–0125), 50 meters south of the southeast corner of the mercado, offers ambulance service only. The **post office** (Av. 3 and Calle 3, across from northeast corner of mercado, tel. 758–1543) is open weekdays 7:30–5:30. Make international calls at **ICE** (open Mon.–Thurs. 8–5, Fri. 8–4) or use your phone card at the pay phones on the south side of the mercado.

COMING AND GOING

You don't have many options. The San José–Limón train is a thing of the past, Limón's airstrip is for charter flights only, and hitching is impractical, dangerous, and discouraged. Unless you rent a car, you're going to have to hop on the bus, Gus. **Auto Transportes Caribeños** (tel. 221–2596 or 257–0895) has hourly buses 5 AM–6:30 PM to Puerto Limón departing from the big Terminal del Caribe (Calle Central, between Avs. 15 and 17), in the northern neighborhood of Barrio Tournón; the 2½-hour trip costs $3. **Coopelimón** (tel. 223–7811) has six buses daily 6 AM–4 PM, leaving from near the old Atlantic train station (Av. 3, between Calles 19 and 21) east of Parque Nacional. Return buses to San José leave from Limón's main bus station (Calle 2, between Avs. 1 and 2), 100 meters east of the mercado. **Empresarios Guapileños** (tel. 223–1276, 710–7780) runs buses every half hour 6 AM–9 PM to Siquirres and Guápiles that can drop you off inside Braulio Carrillo National Park. They leave from the Terminal del Caribe, as does **Transportes MEPE** (tel. 758–3522 or 257–8129), which has four buses daily to Sixaola, stopping in Cahuita and Puerto Viejo de Talamanca, and direct buses to Puerto Viejo and Manzanillo departing at 10 AM and 4 PM. The fare to any of these destinations is less than $5.

GETTING AROUND

Limón crawls over a beak of land pointing east into the Caribbean. There are no street signs, so you may find Limón difficult to navigate for the first hour or so. Use the following landmarks to orient yourself. South of Limón's center lie the **muelle** (dock) and the railroad tracks. **Parque Vargas** occupies the easternmost tip of the city. From the park, the **malecón** (seaside jetty) winds north along the coast toward Moín. Limónenses often give directions as *abajo,* toward the malecón, and *arriba,* away from it. **Avenida 2** runs through the center of town, passing the north edge of Parque Vargas and the south edge of the **mercado municipal.** Numbered avenidas run east–west, starting parallel to the railroad tracks; numbered calles run north–south, beginning with Calle 1 at the western edge of Parque Vargas. The occasional bus zips up and down the malecón, but most everything is within walking distance. You can take a taxi from the mercado or call **Taxis-Unidos de Limón** (tel. 758–2483).

WHERE TO SLEEP

Most of the hotels in town have ceiling fans, but mosquito nets are few—bring your own or enjoy a night of restless scratching. If you're a light sleeper, opt for the hotels along the malecón, because they're slightly removed from the nightlife around the mercado. Few hotels have hot water, but why would you want it here? Call ahead for reservations on weekends, especially during high season (December–April, Easter, and Carnaval). Sleeping on the beach or in the park is downright *dangerous,* and there are no campgrounds. If you're totally stuck, head for the **Red Cross** (Calle 3, between Avs. 1 and 2); they may take pity and loan you the floor.

UNDER $10 • El Cano. This family-run establishment is very respectable: "no drunks, no women of the night," states Doña Naomi. The dark, simple rooms are humble but safe, and the communal bathroom is *very* basic. It's definitely the cheapest place available without the accompanying riff-raff—doubles with bath are $9. *Av. 3, between Calles 4 and 5, tel. 758–0894. 50 m west of the NW cnr of mercado, above Tienda El Regalón. 17 rooms, 4 with bath.*

Hotel Linda Vista. Turquoise neoclassic columns and thin white particle board separate you from your neighbors and the bar below. The clean but boxy doubles with communal baths go for about $8. *Av. 2, between Calles 4 and 5, near the mercado, tel. 758–3359. From San José bus stop, walk 50 m north and 250 m west (away from the malecón)), make a left on the first street. 35 rooms, none with bath. Cash only.*

UNDER $20 • Hotel Ancón. Long a Puerto Limón favorite, the Ancon offers cleanliness and comfort at reasonable prices. Spacious, air-conditioned rooms with tiled baths cost $24 a double ($18 a single). Another plus is the fact that the hotel's restaurant is one of the city's best. *Av. 3 and Calle 3, tel. 758–1010. 250 m north of the San José bus stop. 39 rooms with bath. Restaurnt, laundry.*

Hotel Internacional. This hotel north of downtown is a pleasant, plant-filled respite from the heat outside. Super-clean doubles with desks, private baths, and fans are $11; air-conditioning is available for an extra $6. The location is quiet and near the local swimming beach. *Av. 4, between Calles 2 and 3, tel. 758–0434. 20 rooms with bath. Cash only.*

Hotel Palace. A short crawl from the San José bus stop, this budget hotel sprawls through the second story of a large building, overlooking a mellow stretch of Calle 2. What the Palace lacks in cleanliness, it makes up for in character. Fairly quiet doubles with communal bath are $13, while $19 gets you a pleasant room near the balcony and a private bath. Ask to see more than one room (some are dark cells). One guest reports he gave a free peep show. *Calle 2, between Avs. 2 and 3, tel. 758–0419. 75 m north of the San José bus stop. 20 rooms, 7 with bath.*

FOOD

Good-value grub and basic provisions are easily found in the simple, but unique sodas surrounding the mercado, or in the supermarket across from the southeast corner of the mercado. The sodas dish up very economical meals, but sit inside and keep an eye out for drugged-out hustlers; proprietors are usually adept at settling nasty situations. **Doña Toda,** at the southeast corner of the mercado, serves up tasty $2 casados (a full dinner). Check out the spacious, sea-wrapped restaurant on the ground floor of the **Park Hotel** (intersection of Av. 3, Calle 1, and the malecón, tel. 758–3476); it's one of the city's best.

Soda Palón. The rickety wooden stools on the street have an invisible sign that reads LOCALS ONLY—but feel welcome to crowd the fluorescent plastic booths inside, where Spanish-dubbed TV overwhelms the clinking cutlery of tired old men and gossiping teens. The patient waitress purses glowing pink lips and hands you a filling *medio casado* ($1.50). If you're in town on Sunday, be sure to stop in for the rice and beans special. *Northwest corner of mercado, in red building, no phone.*

Springfield. North of the center near the hospital, this popular restaurant is worth the walk for excellent Caribbean food in an ample, almost elegant dining room (it has tablecloths). Rice and beans, traditionally a Sunday dish, is available here every day. The $4 plate includes your choice of meat, from fresh fish to the politically incorrect turtle fin. On Tuesdays, the house special is a tasty rondon. *Across from hospital, tel. 758–1203. Take a taxi, or walk in a group down malecón toward hospital.*

WORTH SEEING

The thick, sweaty cement walls of the **mercado municipal** form niches for vendors of turtle meat, plastic shoes, and medicinal herbs. A hub of commercial and social activity, the mercado is a good place to become acquainted with local smells, exchange a few smiles with limónenses, and pick up a snack of fresh fruit for a stroll through **Parque Vargas,** at the eastern tip of the city. The park is no place to relax at night, but during the day it's a peaceful, humid haven of damp grassy squares and shady corners, where hummingbirds play tag around hibiscus flowers. Weekend mornings find groups of young men and women gossiping and covertly checking each other out, while oblivious little kids pick at the wide gravel walkway. Here starts the winding cement malecón with a view of the little island, **Uvita,** which Columbus visited 500 years ago.

OUTDOOR ACTIVITIES

Puerto Limón isn't exactly famous for its natural beauty. The local swimming hole, *los baños,* is near the malecón at the end of Avenida 5, but the water is polluted, so you might have more fun getting in on a game of basketball at the nearby courts. Beach lovers, don't despair: just 3 km (2 mi) north is **Playa Bonita,** a clean white-sand beach that seems light years away from Limón's crumbling buildings. To get there, catch one of the semifrequent buses to Moín that leave Limón from Calle 4, between Avenidas 4 and 5, about 100 meters north of the mercado.

Take a dip (clothing optional) in the ocean at night and see your body light up as phosphorescent plankton attach to your skin and glow like stars. Ask a local if they're out or watch for them glowing in the crests of waves.

TORTUGUERO

The **Parque Nacional Tortuguero,** 83 km (52 mi) northwest of Limón, is the largest nesting site in the Western Hemisphere for the green turtle, which lays its eggs between July and October (peak time is late August). One of the most diverse biological areas of the country, the 35-km- (22-mi-) long park is home to sloths, manatees, monkeys, toucans, and fishing bats, among hundreds of other furry, feathered, and scaly creatures. Although San José bursts with tour agencies running trips here, the park is totally accessible to the independent traveler as long as you're willing to go over your budget for a couple of days. If you prefer to visit Tortuguero on a tour out of San José, you'll find the cheapest packages at Ecole Travel or through the Hotel Aranjuez (*see* San José, *above.*) **Tortuguero Village,** just north of the park, is a peaceful, developing community that provides the basic necessities and a lot of friendly, honest conversation.

BASICS

The kiosk in the middle of the village is crammed with information about the history of the area and the development of the turtles. Way on the north side of the village is the new **Tortuguero Natural History Visitors Center** (tel. 710–0547; open Tues.–Sun. 1–6), with bilingual exhibits, maps, reference books, and a short video on the history of turtle conservation. The **Administración de Tortuguero,** the park's central headquarters, at the south end of the village, is staffed daily 8–6. They sell tickets to the park and will respond to **emergencies.** You can mail from the **Cortel** (open weekdays 7:30–5), on the main path in the middle of the village, but your postcard will reach its destination much quicker if you post it from San José. There are public phones at the general store and at Miss Junie's (*see* Food, *below*).

COMING AND GOING

Alternatives to the expensive tours do exist, but getting to Tortuguero isn't cheap no matter how you do it. If you're in a real hurry and don't mind spending, you could fly. **SANSA** (tel. 233–0397) flies to Tortuguero Village for $50 each way. Flights leave from San José's Juan Santamaría Airport. You can get tickets at the Grupo TACA office in San José (across from the northeast corner of La Sabana Park).

BY BOAT • Tortuguero is becoming more of a tourist run, so you're likely to be offered a boat to the park while you're in Limón; boats leave from the dock in nearby Moín. The going rate is $60 per person round-trip, but you can usually get boat owners to lower the fare to at least $50 for a group, and possibly $40 for groups of six or more. Watch out for misinformed middlemen at the Limón bus station—they'll tell you the trip is $40 a person just to get you and your bags to Moín, then slap you with an extra $10–$20. To avoid this, talk directly to tour boat operators. **Victor Camacho** (beeper 297–1010) runs three boats to Tortuguero. Call him a day in advance to arrange a trip and he'll pick you up at your hotel in Limón and take you to the dock in Moín. Or try **Laura's Tropical Tours** (tel. 758–2410), also in Limón—they charge $50 round-trip for a minimum of two people and may offer discounts for groups of four or more. Agree on a return date beforehand or ask if you can phone for pickup a day in advance. The 4-hour boat ride is spectacular—sloths and howler monkeys hang out in the trees by the canal, and the marshes are filled with cranes, herons, and bright orange butterflies—definitely worth eating beans and rice for a week.

GETTING AROUND

Tortuguero Village is fairly cozy. A maze of dirt paths sprouts off one main footpath, which runs north–south through the village. At the far south end is the **park administration.** More or less in the center of town, right across from where the boats dock, is the **information kiosk.** Another good landmark is the **general store,** north of the headquarters on the main path. The canals lie to the west, the Caribbean to the east. If you're still getting lost, the kiosk has a good map permanently printed on plastic.

WHERE TO SLEEP

Tortuguero Village has an abundance of reasonably priced lodges; wander along its narrow footpaths and you'll see plenty of signs that say CABINAS. The nicest rooms in town are at **Cabinas Miss Junie** (tel. 710–0523), in the bottom floor of a long cement building overlooking the lagoon. Rooms are fairly new and clean, with tile floors, decent beds, and fans; a double with bath costs $30. **Cabinas Meryscar,** just off the beach to the southeast of the general store, charges $8 a person for basic rooms with large, clean, communal bathroom in a slightly moldy, but homey atmosphere. East of the information kiosk, on the Caribbean coast, **Cabinas Sabina** charges $4.50 a person but is kind of grim and has outdoor showers. Both places have a 10 AM checkout. If you prefer a quieter, more natural setting, head across the lagoon from town to the **Manati Lodge** (2 km [1 mi] north of town, tel. 383–0330), where spacious rooms set between tropical gardens and the rain forest cost $30 for a double. The friendly owners can arrange trips on the canals. Your credit cards won't do you any good in these parts.

CAMPING • With a waterproof tent and mosquito net, you can happily camp in the park, although it will cost you a bit of money to get there. **Estación Jalova,** the formal campsite at the southernmost entrance of the park, is accessible only by boat. Have your captain drop you off and arrange to continue on to Tortuguero Village another day. It costs $2 per person plus the park entrance fee—you're welcome to use the rangers' basic bathroom facilities, but bring your own food. Currently, there are no campgrounds in Tortuguero Village or near the north side of the park, but ask around when you get there—you might be able to camp on the grass near the beach.

FOOD

The best restaurants are local residences with the front patio converted to a dining room. Get a group together and enjoy family-style dining (i.e., you pass massive platters of food around) at **Miss Junie's,** at the far north end of the main path. Talk to her in advance to see if she can cook that day. She'll size you up and charge accordingly—about $5 for dinner, a little less for lunch. You may be served rice and beans, tender *chayote* (a local veggie), fish, or chicken. Miss Junie also makes an awesome pan bon—order it in advance along with your meal. Cabinas Meryscar (*see* Where to Sleep, *above*) also has tasty food for about $3–$5 a meal, and Doña María may even make a late-night omelet for starving jungle explorers. In front of Cabinas Meryscar, **Restaurant Pancana** (a.k.a. Edna and Jacob's) serves excellent but more expensive meals and some of the best baked goods in Costa Rica.

WORTH SEEING

The most popular activity is the night beach tour to see the *deshove* (laying of the eggs). Yes, it's cool to watch a herd of turtles storm the beach and squeeze out their progeny in the moonlight, but park officials are tightening visitor regulations in reaction to an alarming decrease in successful deshoves. You can see egg-laying along the beach both in and out of the park, but either way you must have a guide—

beach tours are $6 a person, and you'll usually only be allowed to see a single deshove. Wear lots of mosquito repellent and dark clothing and don't bring flashlights or cameras.

You can explore the park on your own or with a guide. Two self-guided trails start at the park administracion, or you can canoe in on you own along the canal. Unless you're Tarzan's great-grandchild, however, you'll see more wildlife with a sharp-eyed guide. A couple of the guides in Tortuguero are slightly shady types out to make a fast buck—stick with the folks listed below. **Rubén Aragón** charges about $3 per person per hour for guided park tours, but if you assemble a group, you might be able to strike a deal. One of his tours climbs the Cerro de Tortuguero, the highest point on the coast—wear your mud gear. He also rents canoes for less than $2 an hour. Look for his house 50 meters north of the park entrance. Two other highly recommended guides are **Mr. Dama** and **Chico Torres.** Both are seasoned, well-informed, and highly committed to educating travelers about the wildlife in the area. Their canal tours will bring you close to toucans, monkeys, and Jesus Christ lizards (so named because they walk on water). Dama and Chico will even cut you some water-bearing vines or sap from the *chicle* (gum) tree. Early morning tours are $3 per person per hour; night tours are a little more. If you go with the same guide for the turtle tour and a jungle tour, you might be able to get a deal on both the guide price and the park entrance fee—find your guide when you get into Tortuguero and have him accompany you when you buy your park ticket. Dama lives on the coast just east of Cabinas Meryscar, and Chico can be found north of Cabinas Sabina; ask someone in the village if you're having problems tracking them down.

NEAR TORTUGUERO

BARRA DEL COLORADO

This remote village about 65 km (40 mi) north of Tortuguero is popular for sportfishing, but another reason for coming is to explore the 230,000-acre **Refugio Nacional de Fauna Silvestre Barra del Colorado.** The refuge is home to critters like those at Tortuguero—monkeys, sloths, etc.—and even boasts a few marine turtle nesting sites, though Tortuguero is more renown for that turtle thang. There are lots of expensive tours to Barra, but access is difficult for the budget traveler. **Campo de Pesca Casa Mar** (tel. 221–8661), on the road by the canal, is the cheapest place to stay in the area. They charge $12 a person for cabinas with private bath, meals and a jungle guide—good thing, too, since there are no restaurants in the area.

Richard, one smooth limónense, says the best spot for dancing is Bar Acuarius in Hotel Acón. A good place for a quiet beer and some serious people-watching is Mares, next to the supermarket.

If you're hooked on getting here, the best way is to fly. **SANSA** (tel. 233–0397) flies to Barra del Colorado Monday–Saturday at 5:30 AM. The 30-minute flight costs $50 each way. Buy tickets at the SANSA office in San José on Calle 24, between Avenida 1 and Paseo Colón. You can also take a boat from Tortuguero—**Don Beto** in Tortuguero Village makes the 3-hour trip for $35 a person one way. Ask someone in the village where to find him.

CAHUITA

The brilliant white sands of **Parque Nacional Cahuita** sing a siren song to an international crowd of sun worshippers and balmy-evening revelers. Cahuita used to be *the* main destination for budget travelers from all over the world, but rumors of drugs and crime have scared most of them southward to Puerto Viejo (*see below*). Take advantage of the downswing, which is probably temporary. Cahuita remains beautiful and relaxed—if you keep your wits about you and don't go looking for trouble, you won't find it. The glistening beach and tangled jungle paths of the national park are lovely, but the park's true pride and joy is a living coral reef, the best on Costa Rica's Caribbean coast, about 500 meters off the elbow of Punta Cahuita. Slip on some snorkel or scuba gear and waltz with angelfish and sea urchins.

Cahuita's bad reputation is not wholly undeserved. You probably *will* see signs of Caribbean coast drug use in the form of a few crackheads muttering to themselves in the street. Another potential annoyance is the persistent attention women will get—and Cahuita men can be extremely aggressive. Scary stories abound—one woman had to wrestle with a potential rapist for an hour and a half before he finally let her go—but the majority of the men aren't dangerous, just very persistent. A sense of humor and the strength to not fall prey to seduction if you're really not interested are essential. Don't be scared away, just keep your head clear, your eyes wide open, and your back covered.

CAHUITA

Black-Sand Beach

Caribbean Sea

Soccer Field

TO LIMON

Post Office

N

Parque

Bus Stop

KEY

i Tourist Information

TO PUERTO VARGAS

TO PARQUE NACIONAL CAHUITA

White-Sand Beach

Lodging ○

Cabinas Anapola, **7**

Cabinas Margarita, **1**

Cabinas Palmer, **5**

Cabinas Safari, **4**

Cabinas Sea Side, **3**

Cabinas Sol y Mar, **6**

Cabinas Surfside, **2**

BASICS

Change traveler's checks and cash at **Cahuita Tours and Rentals** (tel. 755–0232; open daily 7–noon and 1:30–7), on the main road toward the black beach. Their rates are lousy, but around here it's your only option. Both Cahuita Tours and **Soda Uvita,** along the main road, have local and international phone service—rates are about 15¢ for a local call and 75¢ for collect or phone-card calls. Send mail from the **Cortel** office (open weekdays 8–noon and 1:30–5) on the main road near the crossroads on the north side of town—if you're not too concerned about when it gets there, that is. In an **emergency,** head to the police station next door; the closest hospital is in Bribri, half an hour away. Cahuita Tours and Rentals (*see above*) dishes out plenty of free visitor information and arranges local tours. **Turística Cahuita** (tel. 755–0071; open daily 7–6) also offers tours of the area and visitor information.

COMING AND GOING

Transportes MEPE (tel. 257–8129 or 758–1572) runs six buses daily from San José to Cahuita (4 hrs, $4). Take a bus marked SIXAOLA from the Terminal del Caribe (Calle Central, between Avs. 15 and 17) in Barrio Amon; they leave daily at 6, 8, and 10 AM and 1:30, 3:30, and 4 PM. Return buses supposedly pass through at 6:30 AM, 7:30 AM, 11 AM, and 4 PM. From Limón, six **Transportes MEPE** (tel. 758–1572) buses to Cahuita (1½ hrs, $1) leave daily 5 AM–6 PM from 200 meters north and 125 meters west of the San José bus stop. Take the bus from San José if you can—the trip from Limón is always hot and crowded. Buses make the return trip to Limón six times daily 6:30 AM–7 PM. Service to Limón and San José is not renowned for its punctuality, so be prepared to wait at the bus stop in the shady park. Buses pass through Cahuita on the way to the Puerto Vargas park entrance, Puerto Viejo, Bribri, and Sixaola at 6 AM, 11 AM, 2 PM, and 5 PM.

GETTING AROUND

Cahuita is a relatively small town, so it's pretty hard to get lost. The bus stops at an intersection bordered by a park and the town's two main discos: Salón Sarafina and Coco's Bar. The road perpendicular to the bus stop is the main drag, running from the national park and the **white-sand beach** at the southeast end of town toward the **black-sand beach** at the northwest end. Another semimain street is the ocean road, parallel to the main street but a block closer to the Caribbean coast. Several smaller streets cross these two. Most people will give directions relative to the beaches and local businesses. For us, east means toward the ocean, west away from it, north toward the black beach, and south is toward the national park—these aren't quite what your compass will tell ya.

WHERE TO SLEEP

There are two main lodging areas in Cahuita: one is in the village, and the other is near the black beach. The places close to town tend to fill up quickly, but the black beach is fairly remote and is a bad idea if you're alone. Staying in Cahuita is generally expensive, but prices are slightly lower in the village and during the June–August off-season. The solo traveler is particularly outta luck since room prices are generally fixed at a double rate. At least the quality is in line with the price; most places have private baths and come equipped with fans and/or mosquito nets. If the places below are full, try the $12 doubles at **Cabinas Surfside** (100 m east and 150 m north of bus stop, tel. 755–0246). If you prefer a bit more comfort, check out **Cabinas Safari** (75 m east of bus stop), which has fancy little doubles complete with fuzzy pink toilet-seat covers and ruffled bedspreads for $20 ($15 single). If they're full, cross the street to **Cabinas Palmer** (tel. 755–0243), which has much more spartan rooms for the same price, but they include breakfast.

You'll be much happier if you get a group together for a trip to Tortuguero—everything from the boat ride to various guided tours will be a great deal cheaper. Look for other confused gringos on buses to the volcanoes and at the Moín dock.

Cabinas Margarita. It's a bit removed from the action, but this group of cabinas clustered around a lush garden is near the black beach and refreshingly quiet at night. Clean, pretty doubles with private hot-water bath and fans go for $15. It might not be a good idea for solo travelers, especially women. *Tel. 755-2005. From bus stop, follow main road north to black beach; look for the sign. 10 rooms with bath.*

Cabinas Sea Side. To find the best beachside deal on the Atlantic coast, head straight for the shore when you get off the bus. Hammocks strung out in front invite you to kick back and enjoy the view. Roomy ground-floor doubles with ceiling fan, mosquito net, and private cold-water bath go for $16; rooms upstairs have semiprivate balconies and cost $22. The more nights you stay, the less they charge. Vanessa, the owner, and her partner Nan are friendly, chatty people who will hook you up with horseback rides and mountain bikes. *200 m east of bus stop, tel. 755–0210. 15 rooms with bath. Cash only.*

Cabinas Sol y Mar. This large cement building near the national park has cool, pleasant doubles with a fan and private bath for $16 ($14 for a single). The airy upstairs rooms are worth the extra $2 for the sea view and the cool wind. Downstairs, the restaurant serves tasty and quick breakfasts. The approachable management will keep your valuables locked up if you want to go for a swim; they also rent snorkel gear for $3. *200 m south of bus stop, tel. 755–0237. 11 rooms with bath. Restaurant.*

CAMPING • Theft, harassment, and vicious sand fleas make camping on the beach near Cahuita Village a bad idea. Instead, Cabinas Sea Side (*see above*) has $3 campsites with an outdoor kitchen, bathroom, and shower. Inside the national park, you can set up camp in the **Puerto Vargas** area on the other side of Punta Cahuita. To get there, you can either hike the beach/jungle trail about 7 km (4 mi) from the park entrance in Cahuita, or catch the Puerto Viejo bus (15¢) to the well-marked Puerto Vargas entrance (*see* Coming and Going, *above*) and hike or hitch in. Camping facilities are on **Playa Vargas,** 1 km (½ mi) from the entrance, near the **ranger station** (tel. 758–3996). The main disadvantage of camping in the park is that you have to pay the $6 entrance fee for every day you're there, on top of the $3 per person camping fee. The park has 50 campsites with access to potable water, pit toilets, and outdoor showers.

FOOD

You definitely won't starve in Cahuita, but you might spend more than you budgeted. Most restaurants have breakfast specials for around $3, but lunch and dinner can drain your wallet dry. To make those colones go their farthest, look for filling $3–$4 casados served at **Restaurant National Park** and **Vista del Mar,** both of which are south of the bus stop, right next to the entrance to the national park. Vista del Mar also serves Chinese food for $4–$5 a plate. For some of the best rice and beans on the Talamanca coast, wander over to the bus stop—Miss Mary dishes out heaping $3 plates weekend evenings starting at about 7 PM from outside the Salón Sarafina.

El Cactus. Just off the road to the black beach, this hot little Italian restaurant serves steaming pizza to an international crowd. The wine and beer flows as Germans, Italians, and North Americans pig out on enormous pizzas ($4–$5), spaghettis from clam to carbonara, and decent salads. Save room for a delicious lemon or chocolate crepes They have live music on Thursday nights. *Tel. 755–0276. Take main road to black beach; look for the sign 100 m down dirt road away from water. Closed Mon.*

Miss Edith's. It's is an important rite of passage to come here and wait for an hour at the long, family-style tables for a huge plate of Caribbean food. The house specialties include Jamaican jerk chicken and fish in coconut milk and rondon, which is only served on weekends. Miss Edith also makes great rice and beans every Sunday. Try traditional teas made with sweet basil or soursop leaves. *From bus station, follow main road north, turn right at police station. No phone.*

Restaurant Sol y Mar. This little restaurant below the Sol y Mar cabinas serves only breakfast, but it's a breakfast worth stopping by for, and it's right on the way to the national park. Pancakes and gorgeous fruit plates are available for around $2, whereas the traditional gallo pinto (black beans and rice) with eggs costs even less. Endless mix-it-yourself café con leche costs less than a buck, as do icy batidos (milkshakes) of papaya, pineapple, or melon. *Below Cabinas Sol y Mar, tel. 755–0237.*

Restaurant Típico Cahuita. This mellow soda-style restaurant is one of the cheapest and most pleasant places to eat in town. They serve good breakfasts and cheap and hearty casados all day long. Rice and beans simmer in rich coconut milk every Saturday and Sunday, and if you order it a few hours ahead of time, they'll whip up a batch of rondon for a small group. *Tel. 755–0224. From bus stop, south on main road, turn right at the Defi's sign; it's to your right before bend.*

AFTER DARK

When the sun sets, Cahuita's international crowd splashes on bug repellent and heads to one of the local bars to throw back a few cold ones. Favorite wells in town include **Restaurant National Park** (*see* Food, *above*) and **Bar Hannia,** on the main road in town, where groups of German students teach drinking games to onlookers. Weekends are the best time for dancing at warring discotheques **Salón Sarafina** and **Coco's Bar** (a.k.a. Salón Vaz), on the main road near the bus stop. If tropical rhythms and twinkling, colored lights aren't your scene, try **Soda Uvita,** on the main road in town, where you can watch locals play dominoes. Most nightspots open at sunset and rock into the wee hours.

OUTDOOR ACTIVITIES

You can hike in **Parque Nacional Cahuita.** You'll see the most wildlife in the early morning (around 5 AM), and howler monkeys and sloths are most common. The Kelly Creek entrance just south of town gives you free 24-hour access to the park. A 4-km (2½ mi) trail leads through the park to the reef. The Puerto Vargas station (open daily 8–4) is another 3 km (2 mi), down the same trail.

At the white-sand beach inside the park, you can swim or snorkel over the reef. If you're swimming, watch out for the dangerous rip currents common along the first 400 meters of the beach. Both **Cahuita Tours** and **Turistica Cahuita** (*see* Basics, *above*) rent snorkeling equipment, but if you really want to see what's out there, get a few people together and spring $15 for a boat tour, which will get you out to the best snorkelling spots. If the white-sand beach of the national park is too glaringly beautiful, head up to the black-sand beach northwest of town. It's more of a locals' beach, and when there's a swell, you can surf there, although you'll need your own board. Theft is an unfortunate problem at both beaches— bring a friend and take turns swimming or risk losing your clothes and valuables.

Both Cahuita Tours and Turistica Cahuita (*see* Basics, *above*) can set you up with guided **horseback tours** through the rain forest behind town; they cost $25–$35 according to how far you want to go. Cabinas Sea Side (*see* Where to Sleep, *above*) also offers horse rentals. If a live mount isn't your thing, rent a bike from Cahuita Tours or Turistica Cahuita (*see* Basics, *above*) for $1.50 an hour or $9 a day. The roads are rough, but this is a quick way to get to the black beach and do some exploring farther down the road north.

PUERTO VIEJO DE TALAMANCA

Only 16 km (10 mi) southeast of Cahuita, Puerto Viejo de Talamanca once offered a quiter, less developed atmosphere. No more. Puerto Viejo, or Old Harbor, as the old timers call it, is the closest thing the Caribbean coast has to a tourist mecca, with dozens of hotels and restaurants and some hoppin' nightlife on weekends. The influx of foreigners has taken its its cultural toll on this once-tranquil fishing village, but some residents are actively involved in developing tourism in harmony with the local lifestyle, an interesting mix of Afro-Caribbean and indigenous culture. Like Cahuita, Puerto Viejo has experienced problems with drugs and crime—there are several crack houses in and around town, and female tourists who have naively accompanied a local to the beach or his home for a friendly joint have ended up raped. That said, it is generally a safe and tranquil place, just watch who you hang out with.

Many Europeans and North Americans have settled in and around Puerto Viejo, some of whom work in the tourism industry—the very thing that might ruin the town they supposedly love—and others who live off money from far away. During the June–October low season, you'll share the beach with brilliant yellow crabs and locals gathering firewood; in the evening, when gentle mists wrap the surrounding blue-green mountains, you can admire the sunset from one of the most beautiful stretches of coast in the world. Surfers from around the world come to Puerto Viejo to test their skills on the pounding waves of **Salsa Brava.** Nonsurfers can enjoy the hot sun and sea, the coral reefs, or the lush jungle trails of the nearby **Reserva de Fauna Silvestre Gandoca-Manzanillo.**

BASICS

Comisario Manuel Leon (100 m south and 75 m east of bus stop), the local general store (often called El Chino), will change cash or traveler's checks daily 9–8. During the December–May high season, most hotels will also change money. At Hotel Maritza (*see* Where to Sleep, *below*), you can make international calls, use the fax machine, and pick up a good map of the town. **ATEC** (*see below*) has extensive **mail, phone, fax,** and **E-mail** services. In an **emergency,** you can try the police, although the residents seem to have little faith in them. The one doctor in town works at the hospital in Hone Creek, but is available for medical problems most nights and

At night, both Brisas del Mar and Salón La Culebra liven up Tortuguero with reggae and romantic tunes. Ask locals which is jamming hardest the night you're in town.

weekends. Go to the small cement house next to Casa Verde (*see* Where to Sleep, *below*), 100 meters south of the center road. Rent snorkeling equipment and buy your official Puerto Viejo T-shirt at **Color Caribe** (100 m south of bus stop, tel. 750–0284).

VISITOR INFORMATION • Asociación Talamanqueña de Ecoturismo y Conservación (ATEC). Created and run by local residents and visiting volunteers, ATEC seeks to develop socially responsible ecological tourism by educating residents and locals about the area's natural and cultural heritage. The bustling little office gives out information on the area, arranges tours to the Gondoca-Manzanillo refuge and the Kekõldi indigenous reserve, and provides phone and mail service for the town. *Center road, 100 m south and 175 m east of bus stop, tel. 750–0188. Open daily 7:30 AM–noon and 2–9 PM.*

COMING AND GOING

The road that enters Puerto Viejo from the highway splits into two roads at the town; the **ocean road** to the left (north) follows the shoreline, and the **center road** cuts straight through town. A handful of streets intersect these roads. Bus service in this part of the country is consistently behind schedule, and buses to Manzanillo are especially terrible. On the up side, there are plenty of them, especially between Perto Viejo and Cahuita. You're often better off hitching or biking. The 16 km (10 mi) between Cahuita and Puerto Viejo make for a good four- or five-hour walk along the beach, but don't attempt it with a backpack.

BY BUS • The Puerto Viejo **bus stop** is on the ocean road across from the supply store Abastecedor Priscilla, near the Sunset Reggae Bar (*see* After Dark, *below*). **Transportes MEPE** (tel. 257–8129 or 758–1572) runs two direct buses daily at 10 AM and 4 PM from San José to Puerto Viejo (4 hrs, $4) from the Terminal del Caribe (Calle Central, between Avs. 15 and 17) in Barrio Amon, returning at 6 and 10 AM. They also have daily buses to Sixaola at 6 AM, 8 AM, 1:30 PM, and 3:30 PM, which usually go all the way into Puerto Viejo, but which sometimes drop passegers off at the intersection on the main road, which is about 2 km (1½ mi) from the center of town. Return buses supposedly pass through at 6 AM, 7 AM, 10:30 AM, and 3:30 PM. From Limón, **Transportes MEPE** (tel. 758–1572) has six buses to Puerto Viejo (1½ hrs, $1) daily 5 AM–6 PM, leaving from 200 meters north and 125 meters west of the San José bus stop. Take the bus from San José if you can—the trip from Limón is always hot and crowded, and it adds at least an hour to your trip. Buses make the return trip to Limón six times daily 6 AM–7 PM. Buses from Limón to Manzanillo (30 min) depart at 6 AM and 2:30 PM and stop in Puerto Viejo at 7:15 AM and 3:45 PM; buses to Bribri and Sixaola come through seven times a day between 6 AM and 7 PM. Buy your tickets for San José at the office across from the bus stop—you'll definitely need to buy them ahead of time if you want to travel on Sunday afternoon.

HITCHING • Hitching is a relatively safe option between Cahuita, Puerto Viejo, and Punta Uva or Manzanillo. Getting someone to stop for you is half the battle—look respectable and you'll better your chances. Some of the trucks are self-proclaimed taxis, and others won't charge a penny. Within town, flagging down a passing vehicle is very common, especially for transportation to or from the cabinas outside town.

BY BIKE • Decent roads connect Puerto Viejo with outlying towns, and signs for bike rental abound. Try **Bela Bike Rental and Breakfast** (open daily 8–5:30), south of the center road, across from Casa Verde, or **Old Harbor Fresco Shop** (open daily 8–6), next to the Sunset Reggae Bar on the ocean road—they both rent bikes for $6 a day or $1.50 per hour. Don't expect to find any carbon-fiber, full-suspension rides around here—you'll be lucky if the tires are full and the brakes work.

WHERE TO SLEEP

Lodging in the area gets more expensive on the road east toward Punta Uva, and then disappears altogether. Puerto Viejo has seen the dollar signs of tourism; most doubles are about $15–$25 a night, although there are still a fair number of places where you can get a double for less than $15, and you can often bargain in the low season. If the places below are full, go to **Hotel Maritza** (on the ocean road after the bus stop, tel. 798–1844), which accepts all credit cards. Screened rooms with fans, private hot-water bath, and even soap and shampoo are $21 for two. **Cabinas Tamara** (50 m south of Hotel Puerto Viejo, tel. 758-0317) has seven small rooms, each with private bath and a soft double bed, that go for $12. At **Hotel Pura Vida** (tel. 750–0002) spacious doubles go for $20. To get there, follow the signs from the center road; it's across the street from the soccer field. Neither Tamara nor Pura Vida accepts credit cards. If you're really stuck, you can hit the local campgrounds, or try camping on the beaches east of town—watch out for thieves, sand fleas, and falling coconuts.

Casa Verde. Beautiful rooms are surrounded by art and greenery and have ceiling fans and those oh-so-romantic mosquito nets. Friendly owners René and Carolina charge $20 for a double ($15 a single) with a sink in the room and access to spotless communal bathrooms complete with hot water. For $30 you get a spacious double with private bath, a small fridge, and a porch with a hammock. *Follow signs from center road, 100 m south and 50 m east of Soda Tamara, tel. 750-0015. 14 rooms, 6 with bath. Laundry.*

Hotel Puerto Viejo. This three-story, Swiss Family Robinson–type house is the tallest building in town and the natural destination for budget travelers. Rooms vary in size, but all cost $6 per person except for two large double rooms with private baths that go for $14 and $16. Most of the singles are cave-like but clean, and the second-floor doubles are well lighted and airy. Stop in at the reception desk and slam tourism for a while with the expatriate owner—he seems to be unaware of the irony. *From the bus stop, follow ocean road to the crossroads by the little park; turn left just before Soda Tamara, and go straight 75 m. 31 rooms, 3 with bath. Cash only.*

Kiskadee. It's a bit of a hike from town, but at least you're in the wild. Beds in shared four-person rooms with communal bathroom go for just $6; the price includes coffee and use of the well-equipped kitchen. Proprietess Alice Noel is an intelligent, well-traveled woman with lots of stories to share. She might even whip up a fruit salad fresh for you from the surrounding trees. Kiskadee veterans say a flashlight is a must for the walk home at night. *Tel. 750–0075. From bus stop, take first road south (toward hills) to the far end of soccer field; look for the sign and follow path 200 m uphill. 8 beds, none with bath. Cash only.*

CAMPGROUNDS • Just past the Salsa Brava Cabinas on the road to Punta Uva is a grassy area where you can pitch your tent for about $3 a night. The fee includes the use of showers, toilets, and a waterproof shelter. The folks at **Hotel Puerto Viejo** (*see above*) will also let you camp in the backyard and use their showers for $2.50 a person, but only if they're completely full.

FOOD

The ultimate local food can be found at **Miss Sam's,** up the road from Hotel Puerto Viejo—she sells heaping casados for $2.50, as well as tasty gingerbread and banana cake. **Soda Isma** (100 m west of ATEC) is an excellent and inexpensive place to sample such local specialties as rice and beans and *scovitch* (pickled) fish. The owner, Isilma Baker, will prepare rondon if you order it a few hours ahead of time; she also serves great breakfasts, accompanied by homemade journey cake (coconut bread). Another good place for Caribbean cookin' is the red, gold, and green **Soda Tamara** (on the central road, near the ocean road intersection), which serves rice and beans almost every day of the week (closed Tues.). The heaping plates come with a choice of meat, chicken, fish, or egg for about $5; or try a whole fried fish with *patacones* (fried plantains) for the same price. On the weekends they have the best *paty* (spicy meat pastry) in town, as well as *pudín de maiz* (sweet, moist corn cake) or brownies. **El Parquecito** (100 m east of Soda Tamara) is a good spot to feast on fresh seafood or chicken in a spicy sauce. For the best pizza in town, head to **Carramba** (just east of Soda Tamara, tel. 750–0467), which also serves an array of pasta dishes, salads, and seafood (closed Wed.). Just up the road, **The Garden** (open daily 5 PM–10 PM) is highly recommended for Asian, Caribbean, and vegetarian food, although it's a bit more expensive that the other places.

AFTER DARK

After a hard day's surf and sun, survivors fill **Johnny's Place,** next to the old general store known as El Chino, or **Stanford's,** just outside town on the ocean road, where they bop and grind to an interesting mix of reggae, soca, salsa, funk, and techno. Both places start rocking at 7 PM and continue to the wee hours. On weekends and holidays, Johnny's is one of the most hoppin' dance spots in the country. Right next to Stanford's is **Bambú** (open Thurs.–Sat. at 5 PM), a surfer-stoner hangout with more drinking and less dancing, although they do have popular reggae Mondays and sometimes a live band. Facing the Caribbean on the ocean road, the **Sunset Reggae Bar** is a popular place with career alcoholics because it has the cheapest drinks in town, but the tables on the beach across the road are the perfect spot to sit and watch the sunset, and the bar also has live music. Lighter imbibers may want to hang out at **Restaurante El Parquecito** (open daily at noon), on the ocean road across from the spot where local fishermen keep their boats and the old guys gather to play dominoes.

Chat with any of Cahuita's older residents, and they'll tell you about the tranquil days when the only way to get there was by boat from Puerto Limón.

OUTDOOR ACTIVITIES

The famed **Salsa Brava break,** just off the point where Stanford's restaurant stands, is for skilled surfers only, who are willing to risk getting pounded on a coral reef in their search for the perfect tube. For wax, boogie board rental ($5 per day), surfboard rental ($10 per day), and excellent advice, drop by Hotel Puerto Viejo (*see* Where to Sleep, *above*). When the sea is calm, snorkelers will discover some amazing marine life on the reef, although the diving is much better down the coast, off Punta Uva and Manzanillo (*see* Near Puerto Viejo, *below*). You can rent snorkeling gear from ATEC (*see* Visitor Information, *above*) or **Terraventuras** (next door to El Chino, tel. 750–0236), which has scuba equipment available for certified divers and offers a number of dive tours to spots in the area, plus overnight packages to Bocas del Toro, in Panama. Swimmers will want to head to Playa Cocles, a gorgeous, palm-lined beach 1 km (½ mi) southeast of town; follow the trail that heads south along the coast behind Bambú. If there are any waves, beware of rip currents—if they're big, don't go in over your waist—several tourists have drowned there. Bikers may want to make the trip 13 km (8 mi) southeast to Manzanillo, in the Gandoca-Manzanillo Wildlife Reserve (*see below*), but if it's a busy weekend, it can be a dusty ride.

NEAR PUERTO VIEJO

PUNTA UVA AND MANZANILLO

Several beautiful, less-visited beaches stretch along the coast southeast of Puerto Viejo. **Playa Cocles,** 1 km (½ mi) away, and **Playa Chiquita,** 4 km (2½ mi) away, are the two closest ones. About 6½ km (4 mi) down the main road is the private white-sand harbor "town" of **Punta Uva.** Eight km (5 mi) farther down the road is **Manzanillo,** a small, unspoiled fishing town that lies near good diving and is surrounded by the rain forests of the **Reserva de Fauna Silvestre Gandoca-Manzanillo.** The trail that follows the coast south of town is an excellent route for exploring the reserve—ask someone to point you in the right direction, or look into guided tours at ATEC in Puerto Viejo. If you prefer peace and nature to the party scene of Pueto Viejo, head down to **Selvyn's Cabins,** a friendly, family-run lodge between Playa Chiquita and Punta Uva. Selvyn has nice rooms, each with a double bed, a mosquito net, and a communal bath, for about $10. His restaurant (closed Mon.–Tues.) serves tasty Caribbean cookin' for palatable prices.

In Manzanillo, **Cabinas Maxi** has doubles for about $10, but you'll be right in the heart of town, and it can be noisy on weekends. They also serve good seafood, including what is probably the cheapest lobster dinner in Costa Rica. Just before you get into Manzanillo proper, look for the signs to **El Rinconcito Alegre,** a family-run joint serving tasty rice and beans and casados for less than $3. The owner, Ronald Campbell, runs jungle tours for $6 an hour. Transportation is limited: the bus to Manzanillo, which stops in Punta Uva, leaves Puerto Viejo at 7:15 AM and 3:45 PM. Return buses leave Manzanillo at 8:30 AM and 4:30 PM. Renting a bike in Puerto Viejo is another option—except for a few hills, potholes, and log bridges, it's a fairly flat ride.

BRIBRI AND SIXAOLA (TO PANAMA)

Unless you're crossing the border, there is no good reason to venture into the heat and dust of Bribri and Sixaola. Bribri is named after the indigenous people who inhabit the surrounding Talamanca Mountains. The folks at ATEC in Puerto Viejo can arrange a tour of a nearby reserve with a Bribri guide. The only reason you might wind up in Bribri is to go to the **hospital** (yellow bldg. across from the bank, tel. 758–1393). Buses between Sixaola and San José stop there for a few minutes, but not long enough to eat at Soda Restaurant Bribri.

Sixaola has a similar lack of appeal as a town. You'll probably be hating life even before you get there after driving through hours of banana plantations and seeing how Chiquita and Dole aren't exactly sharing their profits with the workers. The border crossing to Guabito, Panama, is pretty cool, though—the bus drops you off in front of an old, rusty railroad bridge and you walk across the border. Be sure to get your passport stamped at the small immigration office on the left before the bridge. The immigration office (tel. 507/759–7019) on the Panama side will check your visa or sell you a tourist card for $5 (*see* Passports and Visas *in* Chapter 6). The immigration office is open daily 8–6, Panama time (7–5 Costa Rica time).

Transportes MEPE (tel. 257–8129) runs buses to Sixaola from San José (5 hrs, $3). They leave from Avenida 11, between Calles Central and 1 at 6 AM, 8 AM, 1:30 PM, and 3:30 PM. From the bus stop in Puerto Viejo, buses to Bribri (20 min, 50¢) and Sixaola (2 hrs, $1.50) leave daily at 6:30 AM, 9:30 AM, 5:20 PM, and 7:15 PM. Return buses leave from Sixaola at 5 AM, 7:30 AM, 9:30 AM, and 2:30 PM.

SOUTHWESTERN COSTA RICA

Travelers usually come to the southwest for a feeling of accomplishment—to climb the country's highest mountain, Cerro Chirripó, or surf the world's longest left-breaking wave at Playa Pavones. Other than these brave souls, not many tourists visit this region of Costa Rica. Cheap places to stay and eat exist, but you'll have to learn to go with the flow, since many have no phone, no address, no set hours, and no English speakers. Make the effort—you'll find vast, untapped, and untouristed stretches of tropical wilderness, silky-sand beaches, and sweeping valleys. Buses in the region, though punctual, are considerably less frequent than in other parts of the country—learn to love crowds and buy tickets well in advance where possible. Drivers should be especially careful on the Pan-American Highway in the southwest—fog and hairpin turns have caused many an accident—but once you get your sweaty, paranoid self here, you'll be glad you did.

SAN ISIDRO DE EL GENERAL

Around 135 stomach-turning km (85 mi) southwest of San José, the Pan-American Highway plunges down the aptly named Cerro de la Muerte ("Hill of Death") into the fertile valley surrounding San Isidro de El General. This medium-size commercial center is a convenient, if not thrilling, stop for travelers en route to the beaches of Uvita and Dominical, or Parque Nacional Chirripó. Inconvenient bus schedules may force you to spend a night here before moving on to bigger and better things, though you'd be wise to avoid it, since the nearby San Gerardo and Dominical are so much nicer. If you do get stuck here, San Isidro is laid-back and friendly enough to make your short stay a pleasant one. Most everything you'll need is near San Isidro's **Parque** (between Calles Central and 1, Avs. Central and 2)—use the white **cathedral** on the east side of the park as a landmark.

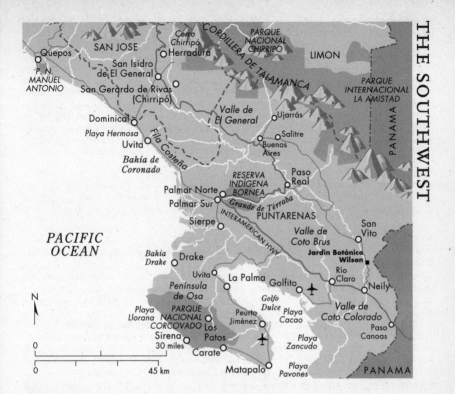

BASICS

Banco del Comercio (Av. Central, 125 m west of park, tel. 771–0629) changes cash and traveler's checks weekdays 8:30–3:45. **Banco Nacional** (Calle Central, at Pan-American Hwy., 100 m north of Parque central, tel. 771–3287) has the same hours and services, but also does cash advances on Visa. Look for **phones** around Parque central and inside Restaurant Chirripó, in front of Hotel Chirripó (see Where to Sleep, below). Drop off your mail or send a fax weekdays 7–5:30 at the **Cortel** office (Calle 1, 200 m south of cathedral, tel. 771–0345). The big blue-and-white **hospital** (250 m south of Cortel, tel. 771–3119 or 771–3115) has a few English-speaking doctors. Local **pharmacies** provide 24-hour service on a rotating schedule—ask at the hospital which one's on night duty.

VISITOR INFORMATION • The **Area de Conservación La Amistad-Talamanca** office has information about Parque Internacional La Amistad (see Near San Isidro, below) and is where you reserve cabin space in Parque Nacional Chirripó. Tel. 771–3155. From park, 200 m west on Av. 2, then 25 m south. Open weekdays 8–noon and 1–4.

COMING AND GOING

Apparently, San Isidro's five-year-old bus terminal hasn't really caught on yet, so buses come and go from various points in town. **Musoc** (tel. 222–2422) buses leave from San José from right next to the Coca-Cola bus station (3 hrs, $3.50) 10 times daily between 5:30 AM and 5 PM. Buy tickets in advance or you'll get stuck waiting around the bus terminal. **Transportes Blanco** (tel. 771–2550) runs buses from Quepos (3½ hrs, $4) at 5:30 AM and 1:30 PM. Transportes Blanco buses leave San Isidro from the **Centro Comercial Valle** (150 m south of cathedral); buy tickets at **Soda el Pionero.** The bus to Quepos travels via Dominical (2½ hrs, $1.50) and leaves at 7 AM and 1:30 PM. They also have buses to Dominical and Uvita (3½ hrs, $2) that leave at 8 AM and 4 PM. To get to Parque Internacional La Amistad, you'll have to catch a bus to Buenos Aires (1 hr, $2) first; they leave six times daily from outside **Hotel Amaneli** (Calle 2 at Av. 3, tel. 771–0352), across from the Musoc Terminal. **Tracopa** buses leave for San Vito (2 hrs, $3) daily at 9 AM, 11:30 AM, and 2:45 PM from behind the cathedral, on the highway. Buses to **San**

Gerardo de Rivas (1½ hrs, 75¢) and the trailhead for Chirripó leave from the north side of the park at 5 AM and from the market at 2 PM.

WHERE TO SLEEP

Even the cheapest hotels in San Isidro will claim to have hot water, but don't be fooled. The least offensive low-ender is **Hotel Astoria** (Av. Central, across from park, tel. 771–0914), which charges $9 for small but bright doubles with shared cold-water bath ($13 with private bath). Across the park, **Hotel Chirripó** (Av. 2 at Calle 1, tel. 771–0529) is popular with ticos and backpackers, with larger doubles for $9 ($15 with private bath); they've got a decent restaurant and accept credit cards. **Hotel Iguazú** (Calle Central, across from Banco Nacional, tel. 771–2571) is San Isidro's best kick-back luxury option. Huge $18 doubles have fans, TV, and hot-water baths (singles are $12); reservations are recommended.

FOOD

The best place in town is the **Restaurante El Tenedor** (Calle Central, 75 m north of park, tel. 771–0881), where you can chow down on an ample vegetarian pizza with real broccoli and other tasty pies; they close Mondays. **Restaurante El Jardín** (Av. Central, 50 m west of park, tel. 771–0349) is one of the cheapest spots, offering a filling casado with a wide variety of weird fried things for less than $3.

NEAR SAN ISIDRO DE EL GENERAL

DOMINICAL

Some 35 km (22 mi) southwest of San Isidro, this black-sand beach lined with coconut palms lies near several private rain-forest reserves and one of the country's most impressive waterfalls. Dominical is a surfer's wet dream, with one of the country's most consistent beach breaks, infamous for breaking many a board. Although surfing remains the town's main attraction, Dominical has plenty more to offer travelers. Try the horseback ride up to the gorgeous double waterfall of **Cataratas de Nauyaca**, a guided nature walk or ascent to a canopy platform in the protected rain forests of **Finca Barú**, or a simple tubing trip down the **Río Barú**. Robin Waters, at her store **Tropical Waters** (3 km [2 mi] east of town, tel. 787–0031; open daily 8–5), dishes out plenty of visitor info and can arrange any of the above tours. You can also book tours and rent surfboards from the San Clemente Bar and Grill (*see below*).

WHERE TO SLEEP AND EAT • Dominical's increasing popularity means that prices are high these days, but for now the budget traveler can still get by without too much wallet drainage. Camping on the beach is both free and mellow, with few thefts reported. **Cabinas San Clemente** (tel. 787–0026) offers a variety of lodging that ranges from a dorm-style surfer crash pad above the restaurant, for $8 a head, to nice rooms across the road from the beach, where doubles cost $15–$40; the expensive ones are excellent. Also on the main road, **Albergue Willdale** (tel. 771–1903 or 787–0023) offers rustic, eco-friendly cabins starting at $30 for two people. Try to strike a deal during the low season or if you're planning to stay for a while. The **San Clemente Bar and Grill** (main road, tel. 771–1972) is *the* spot to grab a beer and watch U.S. sports on the satellite TV while pigging out on awesome nachos, burritos, grilled fish, and big breakfasts. **Soda Nanyoa**, on the main road, has tasty *arepas* (sweet pancakes) for breakfast, and the *pupusas* (fried tortillas with cheese) make a filling snack. **Restaurante Maui**, farther up the main road, is a good place for seafood and other tasty concoctions, not to mention the *bocas* 'n' beer. Buy groceries at **Supermercado Dos Hermanos**, in the pink building on the highway just after the turnoff for Dominical. **La Escuelita Dominical** (tel. 771–1903), on the beach road near Cabinas San Clemente, is a hostel and school offering 15 hours a week of intensive Spanish taught by expert instructors. You'll get a 10% discount if you have a hostel card.

PARQUE INTERNACIONAL LA AMISTAD

Shared by Costa Rica and Panama, the International Friendship Park is part of a binational initiative to preserve some of Central America's most valuable land. On the Costa Rica side, the park is part of an integrated cluster reserve called the **Reserva Biósfera La Amistad**, which spans both sides of the Talamanca mountain range. Other areas in the reserve include Parque Nacional Chirripó (*see below*), Reserva Hitoy-Cerere in the Limón Province, and San Vito's Wilson Botanical Gardens, as well as eight indigenous reservations for the Bribri and Cabécar people. La Amistad is enormous—about 1.5 million acres—and the terrain ranges from lowland rain forests to subalpine savannas. Some 70% of Costa Rica's animal species live here, including jaguars, howler monkeys, quetzales, harpy eagles, and the rare giant anteater. The park also has more than 200 pre-Columbian archaeological sites. With so much to see, travelers are chomping at the bit to set out and explore. However, tourist development has been slow, and park access remains difficult. Indigenous guides in the town of **Ujarrás** offer six- to eight-day hikes through the park over the Talamanca range to **Shiroles,** a Bribri town near the Caribbean coast. For more info on the trip, talk to Agustín Mayorga; he lives 400 meters north of the school in Ujarrás. The most up-to-date information on the park itself can be found at San Isidro's **Area de Conservación La Amistad–Talamanca** (*see* Basics in San Isidro, *above*). Park admission costs $6. Accommodations are very limited in the area, but the two ranger stations at the **Las Nubes** and **Wetzo** entrances will let you stay in a bunk bed (they have six) for free if you ask nicely.

COMING AND GOING • To get to the Altamira section of the park from San Isidro, take a **Tracopa** (tel. 773–3410) bus heading toward San Vito (3 hrs, $3). They leave daily at 9 AM, 11:30 AM, and 2:45 PM from behind San Isidro's cathedral, on the highway. Ask the driver to let you off at Las Tablas, where you can catch another bus to the entrance by Finca Colorado (2½ hrs, $4). To get to Ujarrás (2 hrs, $4) from San Isidro, take a bus to Buenos Aires (not Argentina) and transfer there. Buses to Buenos Aires leave San Isidro six times daily from outside Hotel Amaneli on Calle 2.

PARQUE NACIONAL CHIRRIPÓ

The tiny village of San Gerardo de Rivas, 29 km (18 mi) northeast of San Isidro de El General, serves as the gateway to Chirripó. During the rainy season, the sight of a clear river rushing through green hills may inspire you to burst spontaneously into your best (or worst) John Denver imitation, but believe us, you're better off saving your breath for the area's most popular activity: mountain climbing. Several summits are available to appease that alpine spirit—**Cerro Crestones** is a difficult climb for experienced rock climbers only, while **Cerro Urán** is only feasible with a guide from the nearby town of **Herradura.** Call the community phone (tel. 771–1199) to reserve a guide in advance—they charge $12 a day. Most people come to tackle Costa Rica's highest mountain: 12,533-ft **Cerro Chirripó.** You should plan at least two days for the round-trip hike. The summit is 20 km (12½ mi) from San Gerardo, which works out to about eight mostly vertical hours. The trail is rough, rocky, and steep, but even beginners can make it if they don't go crazy during the first few kilometers. After your hike, check out the **thermal baths**—look for the wooden sign and dirt path 1 km (½ mi) up the road to Herradura. It costs $1 to use the pools. The site is beautiful and remote, but you'll probably share it with horny tico teens.

> *When the park service raised park entrance fees a few years ago, Cahuita residents, fearing a drop in tourism, protested by taking over the Kelly Creek entrance to the park, which they controlled for more than a year, letting people enter for a small donation.*

Camping isn't allowed in the park, but the Park Service has a large, new lodge at at **Base Crestones,** 6 km (3¾ mi) from the summit. During the dry season, the refuge fills up quickly, so reserve a spot as early as possible. In San José, you can reserve cabin space at the **Fundacion de Parques Nacionales** 300 m north and 175 m east of Iglesia de Santa Teresita, tel. 257–2239; open weekdays 8–5). Otherwise, go by the offices of the **Area de Conservación La Amistad-Talamanca** in San Isidro (tel. 771–3155; from park, 200 m west on Av. 2, then 25 m south; open weekdays 8–noon and 1–4). The park charges $8.50 per person per night. Before you begin the hike up from San Gerardo, you'll need to check in at the **administración** (tel. 233–4160; open daily 5–5), on the edge of town. They can answer your questions and will give all those last-minute lectures on things like sunburn and *mal de la montaña* (mountain sickness). Bring food, water, a gas stove, plenty of warm clothes, and a sleeping bag. Rain gear is essential in the rainy season. If you don't have enough gear, or if you don't feel like hauling your gear yourself, talk to Francisco at Posada El Descanso (*see* Where to Eat and Sleep, *below*). Not only does he rent out stoves and sleeping bags, but he can set you up with a porter to schlep your pack up the mountain. He also offers three-hour guided horseback tours of nearby waterfalls and lookout points, or he will rent you a horse to do your own exploring.

COMING AND GOING • Buses to San Gerardo (1½ hrs, 75¢) leave from San Isidro daily at 5 AM and 2 PM, with return buses at 8 AM and 4 PM. The morning bus leaves from the west side of San Isidro's parque central, but the afternoon bus leaves from the mercado, two blocks south of the park. San Gerardo's bus stop is about 50 meters from the administración. From here, walk north to the fork in the road; go left for Herradura and the thermal baths, and right for the rest of San Gerardo and the path to Cerro Chirripó.

WHERE TO SLEEP AND EAT • Although the refugio is your only option inside the park, you can camp in San Gerardo. At **Cabinas Marin,** next to the administración, you can pitch a tent for $2 per person, or bed down in one of several dark and dusty cabins for $4 per person. Up the hill toward the park, **Posada El Descanso** has better cabinas for $3.50 a person. Even farther up the hill, **Hotel Roca Dura** (formerly Cabinas Chirripó) has $3 rooms, as well as two groovy $13 rooms with private baths built against a rock for that caveman experience. Each of the places mentioned has a communal hot-water bath and small restaurants. Meals cost about $2–$4, but go to El Descanso for vegetarian fare. The general store next to Hotel Roca Dura sells camping food for your climb. During the high season, call the communal phone (tel. 771–1866; ask for the place you want) to make reservations or you'll be bedless.

GOLFITO

Surrounded by steep, forested mountains on the gorgeous eastern shore of the Golfo Dulce, Golfito should be a beautiful place to visit. Instead it's a dirty, lazy, scuzzy town—and it's all the United Fruit Company's fault. Early this century, the United Fruit Company made Golfito a base of its banana operation, giving out jobs right and left. When United Fruit left in 1984—blaming "communist" workers who were doing uppity things like forming unions—the town's economy floundered and collapsed. Since then, the local economy has improved a bit, thanks to the existence of a duty-free shopping zone and a new imperialist employer, the Stone Container Company. There is also some limited international tourism, as surfers and fishermen head through Golfito on their way to nearby Playa Zancudo and Playa Pavones. Many of the locals seem to spend all their time getting wasted and hustling prostitutes in the myriad bars along the main street of the *pueblo civil* (where the locals live). Unless you like conversing with the drunk, horny, and unemployed, you probably will want to steer clear of the nightlife. Women shouldn't even consider it.

Golfito looks (and smells) a lot better once you get out of the pueblo civil. On the north end of town—once the fruit company's housing compound for its U.S. managers—you'll find what every self-respecting capitalist should love: the bustling **depósito libre** (duty-free zone). It's open Tuesday–Sunday 8–4 and is especially busy during the first three weeks of December, when hoards of ticos crowd the place to spend their Christmas bonuses on various appliances and electronic equipment. Obviously, refrigerators and stereos won't fit into your backpack, but it's a kick to watch everyone else going nuts. The depósito libre also happens to be the best place in Costa Rica to pick up clothing at reasonable prices, so if a new pair of underwear is the only thing standing between you and utimate happiness, get down there and shop. All in all, Golfito is a mixed blessing. Beautiful beaches are minutes away by boat and the town itself even has a certain charm, especially in the morning while the drunks are sleeping off their hangovers. But, after a day of shopping and conversing with the locals, you'll probably want to move on to better times.

BASICS

Banco Nacional (100 m north of Tracopa terminal, tel. 775–1101; open weekdays 8:30–3:45) changes cash and traveler's checks and does cash advances on Visa. On weekends, try their branch in the duty-free zone (tel. 775–0616; open Tues.–Sat. 8:30–3:45, Sun. 8–noon). The **hospital** (tel. 775–1001, in emergency ask for ext. 236) is north of the pueblo civil, 1 km (½ mi) from the duty-free zone. The **post office** (tel. 775–0911; open weekdays 7:30–5:30) is in the pueblo civil on a side street 200 meters south of the Hotel Costa Rica (*see* Where to Sleep, *below*). Look for public **phones** in the pueblo civil, along the main street and on the road above the main street. **Lavendería** (open Mon.–Sat. 8–noon and 1:30–5), the local laundromat, is in the pueblo civil off the main road, across the street from Restaurante La Eurekita (*see* Food, *below*). They charge $1.50 a kilo.

VISITOR INFORMATION • Samoa del Sur (tel. 775–0233), on the main road on the north side of the pueblo civil, has a good free map of town. Ron, at **Golfito Centro** (across from Hotel Costa Rica, tel. 775–0449), arranges fishing trips and can help with lodging in outlying areas. Ron's son Cheech leads a $25 tour of their vanilla farm on the **Isla de Golfito.** This early morning hike through the jungle is for adventurous folks who want to see toucans and howler monkeys up close. He won't go unless there's at least two people, and you can't stay on the island. Golfito Centro is open Monday–Saturday 9–5.

COMING AND GOING

BY BUS • Tracopa (tel. 221–4214 or 775–0365 in Golfito) runs buses between Golfito and San José (8 hrs, $6), leaving the capital daily at 7 AM and 3 PM from Calle 14 between Avs. 3 and 5. Return buses leave Golfito daily at 5 AM and 1 PM from the main road on the north side of the pueblo civil. Buses coming from San José stop in San Isidro at 10 AM and 6 PM, but you may have to stand. The bus to Playa Pavones (3 hrs, $3) leaves at 2 PM from the La República newsstand in front of Hotel Golfito (*see* Where to Sleep, *below*), returning at 5 AM. To get to Playa Zancudo (3 hrs, $3), take the same bus to the town of Conte, where you can transfer to a Zancudo bus.

BY BOAT • The ferry to Playa Zancudo leaves daily at 7 AM and noon from the dock behind Hotel Golfito (*see* Where To Sleep, *below*). Another ferry goes to Puerto Jiménez daily at 11:30 AM. Both trips cost less than $5. There is no ferry service to Playa Pavones, and a taxi boat costs about $24 each way. The most feasible way to get to Playa Pavones is to try to corner the gringos that come into Golfito on Fridays to shop; they'll take you back with them for $5–$10. Look for them at **Soda Luis Bremes,** across the street from the docks on the main road.

BY PLANE • **SANSA** (tel. 775–0303) has the cheapest flights to and from San José. At $50 each way, they ain't that cheap, but you save yourself an eight-hour bus ride. Their ticket office is on the main road across from the docks. The trip takes 45 minutes, and there are several flights daily. Remember that you can only bring up to 12 kilograms (25 lbs) of luggage; surfers pay an extra $15 to bring their boards, but they must be shorter than 7 ft. Golfito's **airport** is 4 km (2½ mi) north of the pueblo civil, near the duty-free zone. Shared taxis run between the pueblo civil and the airport; the trip costs 75¢.

WHERE TO SLEEP

IN THE PUEBLO CIVIL • The only advantage to staying here is convenience to the boat dock and bus stop. And, hey, this part of town's so sleazy that you shouldn't worry about making reservations.

Hotel Golfito (tel. 775–0047), on the main road next to the Texaco station, has the best cheap rooms in town; bright doubles with private bath rent for $9, and they've got a balcony that overlooks the gulf. No hot water and no credit cards, but all the rooms have fans.

NEAR THE DEPOSITO LIBRE • This area is a safer and much more peaceful option. Several different families have expanded their wooden frame houses into comfy cabinas to accommodate travelers. **Jardin Alamedas** (100 m south of airport, tel. 775–0126) has big rooms packed with beds that are usually used by families of shoppers visiting the nearby Zona Libre. A room with private bath costs $18, whether you pack it with people or not. **Cabinas Casa Blanca** (tel. 775–0124), behind Cabinas Koktsur, charges $6 a person for older rooms with private bath and fans. Don't expect hot water, and don't bother pulling out your credit cards. Call to make reservations if you're planning to come during the weekend, or any time during the month before Christmas, when hotels near the duty-free zone are consistently full.

> *While you're waiting for your bus to get the hell out of Bribri, you can admire the murals at Soda Restaurant Bribri that teach you how to say "I am hungry. I am going to eat at Restaurant Bribri" in the Bribri language.*

FOOD

Sodas along the side road above the main highway offer cheap and decent eats. **Restaurante La Cubana** (25 m south of Hotel Costa Rica) is popular with locals and serves big casados for small prices. Next door, **Restaurante La Eurekita** (tel. 775–0916) is more of a gringo hangout, and therefore has higher prices. **Restaurante El Balcón,** above Hotel Costa Rica, has "American-style" meals for $5–$6. For late-night munchies, head to **Samoa del Sur** (*see* Basics, *above*), where the six-page menu will appease your hunger 24 hours daily. The restaurant at the **Jardin Alamedas** (*see* Where to Sleep, *above*) serves the best food in the deposito libre area, and does it in a pleasant atmosphere.

NEAR GOLFITO

PLAYA CACAO

Cacao is a convenient day trip from Golfito. It's not as stunning as Zancudo or Pavones, but it's close and ain't bad. If you want to stay the night, **Cabinas Las Palmas** has decent $20 doubles, while **Captain Tom's Place** has rooms for $5–$10. Bars and restaurants along the beach will keep your stomach occupied. To get here, take a taxi boat from Golfito ($3).

PLAYA PAVONES

Pavones, 35 km (22 mi) south of Zancudo, is famous for having either the largest or third-largest left-breaking wave in the world, depending on who you talk to. Needless to say, this is surfer heaven, to the point that permanent residents lie about the wave conditions to prevent more people from showing up. It's true that the surf is inconsistent, but you'll actually have to go there to find out what's up—Pavones has no phones. Beware of the extremely rocky beach, which has been known to mess with people's heads (literally). Camping on the beach is free, but **Hotel Restaurant La Esquina del Mar** is the town hot spot. It has rooms for $3 a person, cabins for $9–$12, as well as one of the only restaurants in town.

The place fills up fast, though, so you might want to check out the similarly priced rooms and cabins at **Pavones Surf Camp,** 1 km (½ mi) south of town. Pavones Surf Camp boasts a beautiful deck that was built into a huge rock on the beach; it's popular for sunbathing during the day and amorous encounters at night. The bus to Pavones (2 hrs, $3) leaves Golfito daily at 2 PM. You can also take a taxi boat from the Golfito dock. It'll cost at least $24 and you should be ready to swim or wade into shore; the boats won't land on the rocky beach.

PLAYA ZANCUDO

Zancudo, 16 km (10 mi) south of Golfito, spells tranquillity with a capital T. Nationals and gringos alike come to vegetate on the beach, while those with cash go sportfishing or take tours of the **Casa Orquídea** (Orchid House) or nearby canals. The mosquitoes and thousands of hermit crabs might make your stay a little less comfy, but it's all part of the beach fun. The beach is safe for swimming, although if there are waves, you should be careful. Anglers will want to stay at **Roy's Zancudo Lodge** (tel. 776–0008), which has its own fleet of charter boats and offers all-inclusive packages that cover everything from the beds to the bait to the beer. **Cabinas Sol y Mar** (tel. 776–0014) has several beachfront bungalows that rent for $30 a double. Their restaurant also serves good breakfasts, spaghetti, and seafood. Camping on the beach is free, or try **Cabinas el Coquito** (200 m from main dock), with basic $10 doubles. Farther down the beach, pleasant **Cabinas Los Cocos** (tel. 776–0012) has cabins for $35. The owners, Susan and Andrew Robertson, also offer taxi-boat service and tours of nearby sights. Since it's such a far trek, and there are few places to stay, you're best off making reservations at any of these places before leaving Golfito. A good eating option is **Soda Tranquilo,** way on the south side of the beach, where the specialty is walnut chicken ($5). To get to Zancudo, take the Pavones bus and transfer in Conte; take the ferry, which leaves Golfito daily at 7 AM and noon ($2.50); or get a few people together and hire a water taxi in Golfito ($20).

PUERTO JIMÉNEZ

On the western shore of Golfo Dulce, Puerto Jiménez is a less developed, more genuinely tico town than Golfito. While the town has its requisite share of traveling and resident gringos (after all, you're still in Costa Rica), it is basically a quiet agricultural community, and one of the only towns in Costa Rica where you'll see scarlet macaws flying over the rooftops. For the traveler, it is a base for trips to the not-so-nearby Parque Nacional Corcovado, or for kayak tours of the gulf and nearby estuaries. Since the town itself has very little to offer beyond food and lodging, your best bet is to get away from it all at **La Tierra de Milagros** (*see* Near Puerto Jiménez, *below*).

BASICS

Banco Nacional (tel. 735–5020; open weekdays 8:30–3:45) is behind the main road, 100 meters south of the strangely named Bar Anacin. Besides changing traveler's checks and cash, they process cash advances on Visa. After hours and on weekends, you can change traveler's checks and cash at **Supermercado El Tigre** (tel. 735–5075; open Mon.–Sat. 6 AM–7 PM), on the main street next to Restaurante Carolina. The **medical clinic** (tel. 735–5061) is across the street from the soccer field as you come into town. Near the clinic at **Cortel** (tel. 735–5045), you can buy stamps and send mail and faxes weekdays 7:30–11:30 and 1:30–5:30. Look for **phones** on the main street in front of Restaurante Carolina. On the main street, inside Restaurante Carolina, **Rainforest Trex** (tel. 735–5210) has good information about Puerto Jiménez and surrounding areas and offers substantial student discounts on guided hikes and kayaking and canoeing expeditions. Their hours are a little irregular, but if you leave a message on their door, they'll look for you at your hotel. If you plan to visit Corcovado National Park, you'll have to get a permit the **Area Conservación de Osa** (tel. 735–5036; open daily 8–11 and 1–4), next to Banco Nacional.

COMING AND GOING

Transportes Blanco (tel. 257–4121 or 771–2550) runs buses to and from San José (8 hrs, $6). To Jiménez, the bus leaves daily at 6 AM and noon from Calle 12, between Avenidas 7 and 9. The bus to the capital leaves daily at 5 AM and 11 AM from in front of Restaurante Carolina. Buy your tickets in advance, if possible. From Golfito (1½ hrs, $3), take the ferry that leaves from the dock behind Hotel Golfito daily at 11:30 AM. A passenger truck takes hikers to Carate, near the southern entrance of the national park, leaving from in front of Restaurante Carolina, Monday–Saturday at 6 AM. Fares are about $4. Hitching to nearby towns is also possible. **SANSA** (tel. 233–0397) has daily flights to Puerto Jiménez from the capital; the trip takes 1 hour and costs $50 each way. The **airstrip** is on the south end of town, disturbingly close to the cemetery.

WHERE TO SLEEP AND EAT

On the west side of the town's center, **Cabinas Marcelina** (tel. 735–5007) has decent $13 doubles ($7 singles) with private baths and an extremely friendly management that offers tours of their family farm during the high season. For the ultimate luxury splurge, **Cabinas Agua Luna** (tel. 735–5034), right by the dock, has rooms with TV, fridge, air-conditioning, and the only bathtubs you'll find in Costa Rica. Of course, the good life has its price: $36 for two or three people. For a more natural experience, or to pay with a credit card, head south of town to **Cabinas los Manglares** (tel. 735–5002), near the airstrip, where simple doubles with private baths ($30) are surrounded by a mangrove forest in which you are likely to see monkeys, racoons, macaws, and all kinds of other birds. **Restaurante Carolina** (tel. 735–5007), on the main street, is a good place to feast on fresh seafood and hearty típica food—they also have a few basic cabinas in back with private bath for $6. Breakfast on granola pancakes at **Restaurante Yessenia,** 50 meters west of Restaurante Carolina; they also serve lunch and dinner. For a good pizza, head over to **El Rancho** on the dirt road that curves east up from the docks.

NEAR PUERTO JIMÉNEZ

LA TIERRA DE MILAGROS

Golfito's restaurants are the best places in the region to exchange your English-language books. Tons of U.S. expats have left their reading material before you— Joseph Conrad's "Heart of Darkness" might be an interesting thematic choice.

The "Land of Miracles," 21 km (13 mi) from Puerto Jiménez, is a serene place with a communal atmosphere. The 10 open-air thatched huts are set inside a beautiful landscaped garden that attracts hundreds of butterflies, lizards, and frogs. Co-owners Nicki and Kia (a.k.a. Edy) are mellow women who make everyone feel at home, so much so that many people wind up staying for months. Here, you can hike to nearby jungle sights or go horseback riding. If you're lucky, you'll arrive for a full-moon ceremony or when people on work-exchange programs are giving massages or teaching meditation. Nicki and Kia also plan to do retreats in the near future. Rates are $40 per person per night, which includes three amazing meals. Short- and long-term work-exchange programs are available. For more information or to make reservations, fax the post office (fax 735–5045) to the attention of Tierra de Milagros. A taxi from Puerto Jiménez costs $15, so try to take the colectivo ($6) that leaves from in front of Restaurante Carolina Monday–Saturday at 6 AM.

PARQUE NACIONAL CORCOVADO

Covering one third of the Península de Osa, Corcovado National Park is one of the wildest, most beautiful spots in Costa Rica. You've got to be prepared to do some serious hiking to get in, though, and plan for at least three days there. The upside is that your trek through virgin rain forest will allow you to see animals you've never seen before—unless you happen to have a pet tapir at home. Corcovado gets an *enormous* amount of rainfall during the wet season, and everything is alive and busy. However, the trails are much harder to walk on, and you will definitely get soaked, either from the rain or by crossing one of the waist-high rivers, several of which can only be crossed at low tide. Only experienced backpackers should go solo. You need to make advanced reservations with the **Area Conservación de Osa** (tel. 735–5036) in Puerto Jiménez and register with them, paying your fees, before hiking in. You can also make reservations for the park in San José through the **Fundacion de Parques Nacionales** (300 m north and 175 m east of Iglesia de Santa Teresita, tel. 257–2239; open weekdays 8–5). Park admission is $6, and they have a limited beds and meal service at the Sirena ranger station, deep in the park. It can be a bit expensive, but it's a worthwhile investment if you can do it; jungle hiking is a lot easier if you don't have a tent and a bunch of food in your pack.

COMING AND GOING

Corcovado has three entrance points: **San Pedrillo** to the north, **Los Patos** to the east, and **La Leona** to the south. Getting to San Pedrillo is an expensive hassle, so most people start in La Leona and circle out to Los Patos via the **Sirena Station.** Cargo trucks from Puerto Jiménez will bring you as far as Carate (1 hr, $3); from there it's a short to walk up the beach to La Leona. The trucks leave Puerto Jiménez from Restaurante Carolina Monday–Saturday at 6 AM. A taxi from Puerto Jiménez to Carate costs $36; so if you miss the public transportation, you'd be better off entering though Los Patos, which will cost you about $15 to get close to in a taxi—have them take you to the Río Rincón, up the road from Las Palmas, and hike upriver 40 minutes to the park entrance.

GETTING AROUND

Important fact number one: you're not doing any swimming in the ocean—it's shark territory. Important fact number two: you're going to do a *prodigious* amount of walking. It's not really strenuous, but it's long. The 3½-km (2¼-mi) walk along the beach from Carate to the La Leona entrance takes 45 minutes. The park service has *puestos* (stations) at La Leona, Sirena, Los Patos, and San Pedrillo, where you can camp. The walk from the La Leona entrance to the Sirena Station takes six–eight hours, and you want to make sure the tide is low toward the end of your hike, or the river you have to wade through just before Sirena will be too high, and too shark-infested, to cross. The hike is entirely along the beach, and is it ever hot! From Sirena, hike all day through the jungle, up and down hills, to the Los Patos station, about an hour from the edge of the park. From there, it's another three–four hours to the tiny town of La Palma, from where you can catch a bus or taxi or hitch up to Puerto Jiménez. Your other option from La Sirena is a difficult 21-km (13-mi) hike north along Playa Llorona to the San Pedrillo station. You have to time three river crossings for low tide (ask the rangers at Sirena) if you want to make it to San Pedrillo before dark. Park rangers budget at least 10 hours for this difficult hike and its off-limits during the rainy season. From San Pedrillo, it takes four–six hours to hike along the coast to Bahía Drake, where you'll have to hire a boat to Sierpe. Lodging and the boat out of Bahía Drake are expensive, which is why most people leave through Los Patos.

WHERE TO SLEEP AND EAT

Since it's added torture to hoist food and a tent on your back, you're much better off paying for a bunk and meals at the Sirena station, deep inside the park. It costs $2 to stay the night, plus the $6 admission fee. Breakfast costs $4, and lunch and dinner are $6 each. You must make reservations at the Puerto Jiménez office (tel. 735–5036) well in advance if you plan to sleep or eat at Sirena. In the dry season, you're better off calling a couple of months in advance to get a space. Camping is another option. You can set up your tent near the puestos and use their "sanitary facilities" for $2 a night. You shouldn't camp anywhere but by the puestos, unless you want to be awakened by some animal trying to share your sleeping bag. Also, you could also find yourself floating in the river or the ocean if you underestimate the tides.

PANAMA

BY IAN SIGNER, UPDATED BY DAVID DUDENHOEFER

anama could be one of the world's most underrated travel destinations. Central America backpackers often skip the country on the premise that it's too expensive, or too Americanized, while many other travelers suffer the mistaken impression that Panama is anti-American. The truth is that you'd be hard-pressed to find a more pristine jungle than the vast Darién Gap in eastern Panama, or tropical shores more striking than those along the Caribbean coast. You could exhaust yourself reading anthropological surveys and not find a group of hunter-gatherers more removed from Western "civilization" than the Embera and Waunan of Darién, or more skilled artisans than the Kunas of San Blas. And if you think you can find another Panama Canal, well, good luck.

At first glance, Panama City may seem much like the Western urban melee you're probably trying to escape, but if you take the time to explore it, you'll discover a rich history, vibrant culture, and a wildly diverse population that includes indigenous peoples, Spanish, African, American, Chinese, and Indian among other ethnicities. The rest of the country has cool mountain retreats, coral-ringed islands, colonial monuments, timeless indigenous villages, Caribbean beaches, and more.

In addition to its varied sights and natural wonders, other things that make Panama an attractive place to visit include a well-developed infrastructure, good public transportation, and relatively few health risks. Panamanians rarely explore the natural wealth of their own nation, and there are still relatively few tourists in the country, so you may well have some places entirely to yourself. On the whole, Panama doesn't offer the cheapest room and board in Central America, but it does have its bargains.

Panama is most famous for its canal linking the Atlantic and the Pacific oceans. Built by the United States and well worth a visit, that monumental ditch is one of the world's great engineering marvels. The canal, together with Panama's role as the crossroads between North and South America, prompted the label "*el puente del mundo*" ("the world's bridge"). Ever since Balboa first "discovered" the Pacific Ocean by crossing the Panamanian isthmus, Panama has witnessed a constant stream of foreigners traveling from one ocean to the other.

Much of Panama's progress can be attributed to its role as a continental bridge: it has the highest per-capita income, the largest foreign investment, and the most highly developed economic infrastructure of any country in Central America. But its location also has drawbacks. After all, what do you do with a bridge? You walk on it, and Panama has had more than its share of getting trampled under the feet of invaders. Among the tramplers of Panama, you find the usual crowd: Spanish explorers claiming the

Caribbean Sea

PACIFIC
OCEAN

las Tablas
Cuabito
Changuinola
Isla
Colón
Bocas del Toro
PARQUE NACIONAL
MARINO ISLA BASTIMENTO

COSTA
RICA
Cerro
Punta
Volcán
Barú
Volcán
BOCAS DEL TORO

Paso Canoa
Internacional
PARQUE
INTERNACIONAL
LA AMISTAD
Almirante

Puerto
Armuelles
David
Concepción
Boquete
Caldera
Chiriquí
Grande

Golfo de Chiriquí

Golfo de
los Mosquitos

San Félix
Playa
las Lajas
CHIRIQUÍ

Isla de
Coiba

THE INTERAMERICAN HWY

Soná
Santa Fé
VERAGUAS
Santiago

Isla
Santa
Catalina
Isla
Cébaco

Playa
Santa
Catalina

Las Minas
Península
de Azuero
Divisa
HERRERA
Ocú

La Pintada
Penonomé
COCLÉ
La
COLÓN

Tonosí
SANTOS
LOS
Chitré
Los Santos
Aguadulce

El Valle
Nueva
Gorgona

Golfo de Panamá

Playa
Venado
Pedasí
Pocrí
Las Tablas
Isla Iguana

San Carlos
Farallón

Portobelo
Colón
Sabanitas
PARQUE
NACIONAL
SOBERANÍA
Gamboa
Lago
Gatún
Isla Grande
El Porvenir
Cartí
San Blas
Islands
Narganá
Río
Sidra
Ustupu

Panama City
Isla
Taboga
Bahía de
Panamá
Chepo
El Llano

Isla
San Miguel
Rey
Islas
las Perlas
Isla
Contadora

La Palma
Golfo de
San Miguel
Garachiné

COMARCA DE
SAN BLAS

Ailigandí
Mulatupu
Puerto
Obaldía

Río Sambú
Jaqué
Sambú
El Real
The Darién
Gap
Yaviza
Meteti

DARIÉN
PARQUE
NACIONAL
DARIÉN

COLOMBIA

land in the name of their God and a distant king and queen; French entrepreneur Ferdinand de Lesseps (of Suez Canal fame), who saw his plans to build a canal here crumble when thousands of his workers dropped dead from malaria and yellow fever; and President Teddy Roosevelt, who'd be damned if he'd let a minor concern like national sovereignty stand in the way of *his* canal.

Of all Panama's visitors, the United States distinguishes itself as champion usurper amid a competitive field. Since 1850, the United States has intervened militarily in Panama 18 times, most recently in 1989 to remove the country's wayward son: General Manuel Noriega. The U.S. government has exerted such influence over Panama's development that in many ways the nation resembles a U.S. colony more than an independent nation. U.S. greenbacks are the official currency, and the northwestern province of Bocas del Toro is largely owned by the Chiquita banana company. Panamanians have also heartily embraced U.S. consumerism: Nike shoes, rock music, and fast-food chains are everywhere.

It was the United States that fomented Panama's independence from Colombia in 1903, after Colombia refused a proposal that would have granted the United States control over a 3-mile zone on either side of the canal. The U.S. then signed a treaty with the new government of Panama, represented by Philippe-Jean Bunau-Varilla, a Frenchman left over from de Lesseps's bankrupt canal project. The treaty was negotiated and passed into law without a word of Spanish spoken or a single Panamanian signature. The treaty granted the United States 8 km (5 mi) on either side of the canal "in perpetuity" (i.e., forever), and the right to occupy lands outside the Canal Zone whenever such action was deemed "vital to the maintenance and defense of the water-way." Over the decades, Panamanian opposition to the "in perpetuity" clause grew steadily, and anti-American sentiment came to a head in 1964 with a series of riots and the tempo-rary suspension of diplomatic relations. Panamanian strong-man Omar Torrijos Herrera led an international campaign to make the canal Panamanian, and in 1977, he and U.S. President Jimmy Carter signed two treaties out-lining the gradual relinquishing of the canal to Panama—a process scheduled for completion on December 31, 1999.

Most Panamanians view their country's abundant natural resources as infinite and indestructible, and the streets are, apparently, a convenient garbage can.

A few years after signing the treaty, Torrijos Herrera died in a plane crash, and the void he left in Panama's military government was soon filled by Manuel Noriega: a CIA informant who eventually got on the bad side of his old friend Uncle Sam. Noriega was the kind of enterprising fellow for whom a CIA retainer and general's salary were not enough. His business ventures were as varied as selling guns to the contras to helping out the Colombian cocaine cartels. It was the latter that got him indicted in Miami, which eventually led to George Bush's invasion of Panama in December of 1989, long after Noriega had annulled a presidential election in which his candidate lost, and cracked down on all domestic opposi-tion. "Operation Just Cause," as the invasion was called, left thousands of Panamanians dead or wounded, and entire neighborhoods in rubble, though the U.S. government numbers made it look more like police action than the disaster it was. While Panama City burned, Noriega fled to the local Vatican embassy, and after negotiating an eventual surrender, he was taken to Miami, where he was convicted of drug trafficking and has since lived in a federal prison.

Although the U.S. invasion of Panama was a human disaster, the scars of which have not yet healed, Noriega's departure did give new life to a process of democratization demanded by the Panama Canal Treaties. Guillermo Endara, the opposition candidate whose election was annulled by Noriega, happily served out his term following the invasion, but the next president, Ernesto Balladares, was actually an old ally of Noriegas and the head of the PRD, the party founded by Torrijos Herrara. At press time, Panama was preparing for new presidential elections, and the political field, like the future of the nation, was wide open. On January 31, 1999, the entire canal and all former U.S. military bases will become Panamanian property, which means Panama enters the next millennium a renewed, complete nation, probably in a better position than it has occupied in its entire history.

BASICS

MONEY

Panama's national currency is the U.S. dollar. All the bills come in standard American denominations, although Panama also mints its own version of nickels, dimes, and quarters. Panamanians refer to dollars interchangeably as *dólares* or *balboas.* With more than 140 international banks, you can change almost any currency in the world here into American dollars. But by all means, carry your traveler's checks in American dollars. AmEx-issued checks can be changed without a commission at offices of the **Banco del Istmo,** although it's easier to use them to pay for rooms, meals, and merchandise, since they are widely accepted and the change is always in dollars. **Banco General** will change Visa and MasterCard traveler's checks with a 2% commission. ATM machines, found all over Panama City and in David, can be used for cash advances on most MasterCard and Visa cards, although you may have to get your PIN authorized for use abroad.

COMING AND GOING

BY PLANE • Tocumen International Airport (*see* Coming and Going in Panama City, *below*) outside Panama City handles flights from all the major airlines and a whole slew of smaller ones. International airlines include **American** (tel. 269–6022), **Continental** (tel. 263–9177), **United** (tel. 269–8555), **British Airways** (tel. 236–8335), **Iberia** (Spain, tel. 227–3966), and **COPA** (Panama, tel. 227–5000). All phone numbers listed are for offices in Panama City. The local airline **Aeroperlas** (tel. 269–4555), which has five flights weekly from San José, Costa Rica, lands at the Allbrook Airport, just north of the city. The Costa Rican airline **SANSA** (*see* Chapter 5) has daily flights from San José to Coto 47, which is a 20-minute taxi ride from the border post of Paso Canoas, from where buses regularly head to David. For airline phone numbers in the United States, *see* Air Travel *in* Chapter 1.

BY BUS • **Ticabus** (Calle 17, next to Hotel Ideal, tel. 262–2084 or 262–6275) and **Panaline** (Plaza Cinco de Mayo, 2nd floor of Hotel Internacional, tel. 262–1618 or 262–1589) both have daily luxury buses between Panama City and San José, Costa Rica. Ticabus departs San José at 10 PM and Panama City at 11 AM. Panaline departs both capitals at 2 PM. The journey takes 16 to 18 hours and costs $25 each way. The buses are air-conditioned (often too cold) and fairly comfortable. **Tracopa** (in David, tel. 775–0585) runs buses between David and San José. (10 hrs, $12.50). Direct buses also run from Changuinola to San José (7 hrs, $8) every morning at 10 AM. Buses are often full in July and November–March (Panamanian school holidays), so make reservations at least three days in advance; during the rest of the year you can probably get same-day seating.

CUSTOMS AND DUTIES • Visitors to Panama are allowed to import 500 cigarettes (or 500 grams of tobacco) and three bottles of alcohol duty-free. Panamanian customs are reputed to be very strict; even if you are only making an airline connection, make sure your papers are in order. Prescription drugs should always be accompanied by a doctor's authorization. When departing the country by land, travelers are *not* allowed to export any duty-free items.

GETTING AROUND

The Pan-American Highway spans the country from the Costa Rican border to the edge of the Darién; it is smooth and well maintained west of Panama City, but becomes a dirt road east of there. Roads connecting the highway with major towns tend to be in good condition, and most destinations enjoy excellent bus service. To reach some of the cool out-of-the-way destinations, however, you'll need your own ride or a plane ticket.

BY BUS • Buses and minibuses are the way to go in Panama. On the whole, they're clean and comfortable; they often have distorted stereos blasting and a couple of routes feature on-board TV. Not only do buses connect Panama City with the country's major towns, but there is also regular service between those towns, so you can pretty much go where and when you want. All buses are privately owned and operated, so there's no organized way to find out schedules except by asking around. Similarly, rates are not set in stone, but you can estimate $1–$2 per hour of travel. The most expensive bus ride is less than $25 (Panama City to Changuinola in Bocas del Toro). Panama City is the biggest transport hub and serves all points accessible by road. To get to smaller cities and beaches, you'll need to catch minibuses out of regional transit hubs.

BY CAR • Not only does Panama have the best roads in Central America, but they are amazingly well signposted as well, so it's easy to find your way around the countryside. Gas isn't too expensive (around $1.50 a gallon), and rental prices range from $30 a day for a sedan to $50 for a 4 x 4. Cars can be rented in Panama City and David.

BY BOAT • In the archipelagos of San Blas and Bocas del Toro, and much of the Darién, boats are the only way to get between points A and B. In the Darién, where people get around in dugouts with outboard motors, winding their way up narrow waterways, rides are extremely expensive ($60–$200), so try to get a large group together to reduce the cost. If you're willing to be patient and flexible, you may be able to get on a cargo boat from Panama City to Darién for only $10 (*see* Darién, *below*). Hiring private boats in Point San Blas is also expensive, but you might be able to catch a cheap ride on one of the small cargo boats heading out of Colón, if you are patient, flexible, and lucky. Bocas has a more structured system, with private boats island-hopping fairly regularly and inexpensively.

BY BIKE • If you plan to tour the country on a bike, be aware that you'll be sharing the road with drivers who view yielding as a sign of weakness. Not surprisingly, bikers rank low on the machismo scale. Nevertheless, mountain bikes can be rented in tourist towns such as Boquete and Bocas del Toro, which are actually quite conducive to biking.

BY PLANE • Domestic airlines leave from Allbrook Airport, just north of Panama City. **ANSA** (tel. 226–7891) and **Aerotaxi** (tel. 264–8644) fly to San Blas. **Mapiex** (tel. 270–2792) flies to David. **Aeroperlas** (tel. 269–4555) flies to destinations throughout the rest of the interior, with connections to San José, Costa Rica. Domestic flights are a good way to cut travel time way down, and are practically the only way to visit San Blas and much of the Darién. One-way flights from Panama City range from $28 (San Blas) to $54 (David).

WHERE TO SLEEP

Since tourism has yet to take off in Panama, there is a relatively small selection of accommodations available in some regions outside Panama City. In the city, there are plenty of moderately priced, quality accommodations alongside the more expensive, luxury establishments.

Remember that Panama is an hour ahead of Costa Rica and the rest of Central America.

Panama may not have the cheapest accommodations in Central America, but if you budget more than $15 a night, you'll be amazed by all the amenities the extra money buys. The cheapest rooms cost at least $5 per person, and often, closer to $10. Low-budget digs are particularly hard to come by in Panama City, but that's where you'll also find very nice doubles for less than $20, and a few more bucks can get you a swimming pool.

Camping here is a dream, especially compared to neighboring Costa Rica. To camp in a national park, you'll have to get a free permit from INRENARE (*see* Visitor Information, *below*) by telling them how long you plan to stay in a particular park. But once you do this, you can camp for *free*—often in bunk houses with mattresses, sheets, friendly rangers, and cooking facilities. Panamanians don't often camp, so most places are usually empty. Beaches are generally *not* a camping option, except in the more rural parts of western Panama.

FOOD

Panama has varied and delicious regional cuisines which will surprise the jaded taste buds of anyone who's getting a little sick of beans, rice, and chicken, though your typical Panamanian snack is seriously greasy. If you don't mind a bit of *grasa*, the following three snacks should be your first priorities once inside a Panamanian restaurant: *carimañolas* are fried treats made of diced and spiced meat surrounded by sticky yucca paste; *hojaldras* are crunchy, bubbly fried breads—the perfect quick breakfast food; and *bollos* are long corn tamales that come in a variety of flavors. Also sample the local tortillas, thick yellow-corn disks that are very different from their Mexican counterparts. Other great snack foods include *empanadas* (stuffed meat turnovers) and *ceviche* (marinated fish). Try the street stands for other local specialties, including beef lung and fried cow udders (which are a little chewy, but tasty).

When you sit down for a proper meal, the grease rating drops considerably. *Ropa vieja* (literally "old clothes"), one of the most popular Panamanian dishes, consists of shredded flank steak in a sauce of onions, peppers, and spices. *Sancocho* is a chicken stew made with vegetables, spices, and the starchy roots *yucca* and *naimey*. *Mondongo* (tripe) is another popular dish, as is *arroz con pollo* (rice which chicken), which is usually tastier than the Costa Rican version. Another popular poultry dish is *pollo guisado* (chicken stewed in a red sauce).

Panama City's cafeteria-style restaurants (try one of the many branches of Café Niko's; *see* Food, *below*) offer good, bargain local food. But the capital city also has a dizzying array of international restaurants, which offer everything from sushi and Cantonese dim sum to Greek satziki and Italian gelato. In the interior, you're usually limited to regional specialties and standard meat 'n rice fare, except in Bocas del Toro and the David area. Fresh lobster and crab are popular on the Caribbean coast. Darién and San Blas are another story altogether. If you're planning on staying with a native family, prepare yourself for bizarre (and sometimes stomach-churning) gastronomic frontiers.

HOW TO TALK LIKE A LOCAL

A 5-cent piece is called a "real" (pronounced "ray all"), a 25-cent piece a quarter, and a 50-cent piece a peso. Some other key words to memorize: "fulo/a" (pronounced "foolo/a") is a white, usually blond person; "chuleta" (pronounced "chooletta") literally means "pork chop" but is often used as a mild expletive (something like "darn it"); and "chucha" (that's "choocha"), a slang word for female genitalia, is used incessantly as an expletive (e.g., "I caught my hand in the thresher, and 'chucha,' talk about pain!").

DRINKS • On the beverage side of things, *chichas* (fresh-fruit drinks) are popular and come in a kaleidoscope of flavors: *maracuya* (passion fruit), *tamarindo* (a sour, brown seed coating), *maíz* (corn), *zarzamora* (blackberry), *saril* (a small, tart red fruit), and *guanabana* (a white-pulped fruit also known as soursop). Panamanian beers are nothing to write home about, although there are two local dark brews: *H B* (pronounced "ah chay bay") and *Steinbock*.

OUTDOOR ACTIVITIES

With coastline on two oceans, several mountain ranges, and plenty of jungle, Panama offers excellent conditions for an array of outdoor adventures. There are hiking trails into the rain and cloud forests and to the top of an extinct volcano; the bird-watching along these paths is some of the best in the world. For snorkeling and diving enthusiasts, the countless reefs and abundant marine life of two very different oceans can be enjoyed from some of the country's 1,600 islands. There are also dozens of surf breaks, most of which are rarely ever ridden, and world-class white-water rafting is available in the western province of Chiriquí, where horseback riding is yet another outdoor option. An amazing array of wildlife inhabits the jungles of the Darién and Bocas del Toro—even the area around the Panama Canal—and many rural areas are also home to indigenous cultures.

VISITOR INFORMATION

The people at **Instituto Panameño de Turismo (IPAT)** are helpful and will give you a nifty folder covered with pictures of Panama and some swell brochures. The main office is in Panama City (*see* Visitor Information in Panama City, *below*), but offices in the various provinces have much of the same literature, and the people who work at them can give you useful information about local attractions and services. *Focus* magazine is a digest-size guide packed with useful information and the best available maps of the country and capital city. English-language copies are available at the Costa Rican border station and all IPAT offices. *The Visitor* is a small, free tourist paper published by the same people that sometimes has interesting articles; it can be found at most hotels, travel agencies, and so forth. The national cartography center, **Instituto Geografico Tommy Guardia** (*see* Visitor Information in Panama City, *below*), is the place to go for detailed or topographic maps of the various provinces. However, unless you're planning to do some serious hiking or camping, it's not really worth the trouble—the map available at IPAT should be detailed enough to get you around. **INRENARE,** the National Resources Institute, has a national parks department in Curundú (Calle Acenio Villaluz, across from SINAPROC, tel. 232–7228) that has little in the way of visitor information, but would be the office to contact if you plan to do research. Permits required for visiting or camping in the parks must be solicited in regional offices (*see* David or Bocas del Toro, *below*). If you want to visit one of the parks near Panama City, just turn up.

ANCON, a private environmental organization based in the capital, works all over the country. They have short- and long-term volunteering opportunities in conservation, community development, and environmental education. They also have their own ecotourism company (Ancon Tours, tel. 269–9414 or 269–9414), which offers some of the country's best natural adventures. *Panama City: Calle 50 in El Cangrejo, opposite Floristería Marbella, tel. 264–8100. Mailing address: Apartado 1387, Panamá 1, República de Panamá. Open weekdays 8–4.*

VISAS AND TOURIST CARDS

The Panamanian consulate-general advises that all visitors obtain visas, issued by consulates and embassies throughout Central and North America. Technically, U.S. and Canadian citizens only need tourist cards ($5), which are issued at border posts and at the airport ticket counter. Citizens of Australia and New Zealand must obtain visas, while citizens of the United Kingdom only need a valid passport.

Visas are free and initially good for up to 30 days; officially everyone needs an onward or return ticket and proof of solvency, and though the requirement is not always enforced, you may be asked to show both money and a ticket at the Paso Canoas border with Costa Rica. To extend your stay (up to 90 days) you must visit an **immigration office** (Oficina de Migración, Av. Cuba and Calle 29, Panama City, tel. 225–8925; also in David, Changuinola, Santiago, and Chitré). Bring two photos, your passport, proof of onward passage, and $15. If you've stayed longer than 30 days, you'll need to visit the **Ministerio de Hacienda y Tesoro** (Calle 35 at Av. Perú, Panama City, tel. 227–3060) with your passport and 25¢ in hand to obtain a document called *paz y salvo* (peace and safety). Procure this right before you plan to leave, then see the folks at the immigration office for permission to exit the country (*permiso a salida*). The departure tax is $20 when leaving by plane; there's none if you're leaving by land.

PHONES & MAIL

AT&T, Sprint, and **MCI** offer direct-dial service from any phone in Panama. Dial 109 for AT&T, 108 for MCI, or 115 for Sprint to reach an English-speaking operator who will place a collect or calling-card call. Dial 106 to reach an international, Spanish-speaking operator. Panama's country code is 507.

A letter to the United States costs 35¢; to Europe or Australia it's 45¢. Letters take a *long* time to arrive, up to two months. If you hope to receive mail while you're in Panama, remember that mail is *only* delivered to post offices—there is no home delivery. If you're planning to stay awhile, it makes sense to get a post office box. Otherwise, most *correos* (post offices) will hold mail addressed to: Name on your passport, Entrega General, [city], [province], República de Panamá. There's a Panama City, Florida, so be sure to include the "República," unless you want some sun-loving granny knowing all your business.

You can drink the water from any tap in Panama; it's the best in the region, although in June 1995 some taps began curiously spouting yellow (but still potable) liquid—just after the president bought a company that sells bottled water. Hmmm . . .

DOS AND DON'TS

Because of decades of American military presence in Panama, most American travelers will be mistaken for Europeans, unless they sport a crew cut, tank top, shorts, and don't speak Spanish. As in the rest of Central America, you'll get a bit more respect from the locals if you look clean and wear decent clothing in good condition—with new clothes as cheap as they are here, only street people, and the odd foreign backpacker, would be caught dead in stained or torn clothing.

WHEN TO GO

The dry season (November–April) is presumed the best time to visit Panama, but the rains of *invierno* (winter; April–November) aren't much of an inconvenience unless you're trying to reach the Darién. There's no time of year when Panama is overrun with tourists, but the dry season coincides with Panamanian school vacations, when resorts and beaches are at their most crowded. During winter, you may have to spend some time waiting for the rains to stop, but you shouldn't have a problem finding a room.

The best time to visit Darién is immediately following the rainy season, when the jungles are still thick and all the rivers are high enough for dugout navigation. San Blas hosts huge cruise ships during the dry season, so you may want to visit in the rainy season or consider avoiding the touristy area around El Porvenir. Bocas del Toro, in the northwest, goes through two dry/rainy cycles annually: February–April is dry, May–July is wet, August–October is dry, and November–January is wet; but keep in mind that in Bocas "dry" doesn't mean no rain, it just means less rain. September is regarded as the best month to visit Bocas del Toro.

HOLIDAYS AND FESTIVALS • In addition to the major Central American holidays (*see* Chapter 1), Panamanian banks and shops are closed on the following days: **January 9** (Martyrs' Day); **February 15** and **April 10** (bank holidays); **May 1** (Labor Day); **August 15** (Anniversary of Panamá Viejo); **October 11–12** (Hispanic Days); **November 2–4** (Días de los Muertos y Santos); **November 10** (First Call for Independence); **November 28** (Independence Day); **December 8** (Mother's Day).

Carnaval is Panama's biggest party, especially in Las Tablas on the Azuero Peninsula; it's celebrated the five days prior to Ash Wednesday, and Tuesday is the high point. Otherwise, Panama goes crazy with minor festivals (*ferias*); you're bound to come across one sooner or later during your trip. Some of the most spectacular regional celebrations are the **Festival de Flores y Café** in Boquete in late January; the **Feria Internacional de David** in David on March 19; the **Feria Internacional de Azuero** in Los Santos at the end of April; **Corpus Christi** in Los Santos in mid- to late June; **Fiesta de los Congos** at the end of August on the Caribbean "Costa Arriba"; **Feria del Mar** in Bocas del Toro in mid-September; **Festival de la Mejorana** in Guararé at the end of September; and the **Celebración del Cristo Negro** in Portobelo at the end of October.

FURTHER READING

For further research into Panama, the following are good reads: *The Path Between the Seas: The Creation of the Panama Canal, 1870–1914,* by David McCullough (Simon and Schuster, 1977); *Getting to Know,* by M. Labrut (Focus Publications, 1992); *Legends from the Cuna,* by Tomás Herrera Porras (Three Continents Press, 1978); and *Panamá: A Country Study,* by Richard R. Nyrop (American University, 1981).

PANAMA CITY

The center of the country, and home to more than half the population, Panama City sits right next to the canal and is the transport hub for the Darién, San Blas, and Caribbean Costa Arriba, so you'll doubtless spend at least a few days here. Few places in Latin America have the history, vibrancy, and sophistication of Panama's capital; it's a living testament to the importance of the canal and to the tremendous variety of people lured to this tiny country. It also lies near some of the most accessible rain forest in the world, with lush foliage growing right up to the edge of the concrete sprawl.

Don't blow through town hell-bent on reaching Colombia—it's a great place to daydream and rejuvenate your taste buds before moving on to more isolated locales. This is not to say you won't find belching buses, rotting mango peels, and greasy food stands in the streets (it's still Central America). But if you brush away the grime, you find a city with a wealth of offerings.

The original Panama City was founded in 1519, the first European city on the Pacific Coast of the Americas. It was from here that Pizarro sailed south to conquer the Inca Empire in 1532, and it was to here he brought his plunder en route to Spain. Panama quickly became a key point in the Spanish Colonies, with most of the gold and silver captured in South America being shipped to Panamá Viejo, carried across the isthmus on mule trains, then loaded onto galleons for the trip across the Atlantic. The city grew into one of the richest in the continent, and that wealth soon attracted the attention of pirates. In 1671, it was sacked and completely destroyed by the English pirate Henry Morgan. (The ruins of Panamá Viejo show just how devastating this attack was.)

Two years later, the city relocated to a narrow peninsula, which was deemed easier to defend. Although this section of the city, now known as **Casco Viejo** (Old Crown), is grimy and run-down, the ruined churches and ornate architecture still bear testament to the glory and wealth of the 17th century. And here, among the crumbling walls, the city rings with vibrancy: soccer balls bounce off the ruins of 300-year-old cathedrals, families barbecue on the cobblestone streets, and old ladies peer through their clotheslines at the busy street below.

The baroque facades and iron grillwork of Casco Viejo appear frozen in time, while the rest of the city is vaulting into the 21st century. Gleaming silver skyscrapers tower over Vía España, where you can shop for some of the finest (and cheapest) goods in the world, and where you'll enjoy an eclectic range of cuisine. The constant flow of international traffic through the canal continually brings both wealth and a vibrant influx of people into the city.

Unfortunately, like most big cities, crime and violence are increasingly prevalent here. Certain parts of Panama City are *not* safe to walk around in, especially at night. The most dangerous area for gringos is El Chorrillo, which was hard-hit by the U.S. invasion: almost the entire neighborhood was burned down in 1989, and where ramshackle wood tenements once were, characterless pastel cement projects are now the rule. Unfortunately, neighboring Santa Ana, which borders the Casco Viejo, is also dicey. If you stay in Casco Viejo, take a taxi at night. This said, know that people are generally friendly and helpful, and if you're reasonably careful, you'll have a fine time in the city.

PANAMA CITY

Baha'i House of
Worship, **10**
El Catedral, **2**
Hindu Temple, **9**
Iglesia de
San José, **1**
Museo del Canal, **4**

Palacio Nacional, **5**
Panamá Viejo, **11**
Parque Natural
Metropolitano, **8**
Paseo de las
Bóvedas, **3**

Plaza de la
Independencia
(Plaza Central), **2**
Plaza Santa Ana, **6**
Reina Torres de
Araúz Anthropology
Museum, **7**

Canal de Panama

TO MIRAFLORES
LOCKS, SUMMIT
AND GAMBOA

Puente de
los Américas

Balboa
Yacht Club

TO THE
CAUSEWAY

Fort
Amador

Av. Roosevelt

Av. Amador

Av. de los Poetas

BALBOA

ANCON

EL
CHORRILLO

Av. de los Mártires

Av. A

Av. B

C. 11

CASCO
VIEJO

Calle Diablo

Allbrook
Domestic
Airport

Calle
Gaillard

Piquera

Calle Curundu

Plaza
Cinco de Mayo

Av. Central

Av. Perú

Av. Cuba

Av. J. Arosemena

C. 24

C. 25

C. 26

Av. Balboa

CALIDONIA

Av. España

Av. Simón Bolívar

37

C. 41

BELLA
VISTA

EL
CANGREJO

Via Argentina

Av. Juan Pablo II

8

Av. R. J. Alfaro

Hotel
El Panamá

Hotel
Continental

Av. España

Av. Samuel Lewis

EL
CARMEN

Via Transístmica

9

C. 49

C. 52

Via
Italia

PAITILLA

Via Brasil

Calle 67

Calle 72

Calle 74

Av. B. Porras

Via Israel

Atlapa
Convention
Center

Av. Ernesto T. Lefevre

Av. 11 de Octobre

TO
TOCUMEN
AIRPORT

10

11

Bahía de Panamá

0   1100 yards

0   1000 meters

N

311

WASH THAT DRUG RIGHT OUT OF MY CASH

You may notice there are far more towering apartment and office buildings than you'd expect in a city of only 1.5 million. Most of these are convenient shelters for shady characters to convert their illegitimate earnings into official income. How? First, someone with a lot of cash to burn will buy a hotel or apartment building. Then, they'll fill their register with fictitious names and pay themselves a ridiculous sum (say $750 per night) for each of the rooms. ¡Voila! Clean cash. At night, look up at the many apartment buildings and hotels and notice how few rooms are actually occupied.

BASICS

VISITOR INFORMATION

IPAT, the ministry of tourism, is on Vía Israel, across from the Marriott Caesar Park Hotel, far from everything but Panamá Viejo. To find it, go through a metal door in back of the Atlapa Convention Center. If you're lucky, you might come away with some glossy brochures and a map of Panama. *Atlapa Convention Center, tel. 226–7000. Take Bus 2 from Plaza Cinco de Mayo. Open weekdays 8:30–4:30.*

The **Instituto Geográfico Nacional Tommy Guardia** has useful maps of the interior for those headed toward the Darién and other outlying destinations. To reach the institute, take a Transísmica bus and get off at the university (second pedestrian bridge), and cross to the other side. *Tel. 236–2444. Open weekdays 8–4.*

AMERICAN EXPRESS

With an AmEx card, you can get up to $1,000 from your checking account every 21 days at either of the Travel-Related Services office. The office also holds mail for cardholders. *Agencia de Viajes Fidanque, Calle 50, Obarrio, tel. 264-2444. Open weekdays 8–5, Sat. 8–2:30.*

CHANGING MONEY

If you're not coming from the United States, get dollars before you arrive in Panama; it's *the* accepted currency and everything else is hard to change. If you do roll into town with another currency, **Panacambios** (ground floor of Plaza Regency on Vía España, tel. 223–1800) exchanges currency from all over the world, but at very poor rates. Otherwise, most international banks have branches here and will change their own currency into dollars (but it's a hassle).

EMBASSIES AND CONSULATES

If you plan to continue south from Panama, you may need to visit the **Colombian Consulate** on the 18th floor of the World Trade Center. *Calle 53 Este, Marbella, tel. 223–3535. Open weekdays 8–1.*

British Embassy. *Calle 53, 4th floor of Torre Swiss Bank, tel. 269–0866. Open weekdays 8–noon.*

Canadian Embassy. *Av. Samuel Lewis and Calle Gerardo Ortega, tel. 264–9731. Open weekdays 8:30–11.*

U.S. Embassy. *Calle 37 and Av. Balboa, tel. 227–1777. Open weekdays 8–12:30.*

EMERGENCIES

You can dial the national **police** (tel. 104) and the **fire department** (tel. 103) from most pay phones without depositing a coin. For **ambulance** service call the Red Cross (tel. 228–2786).

ENGLISH-LANGUAGE BOOKSTORES

Librería Argosy, a virtual clearinghouse of info on local cultural events, is owned by the jovial Gerasimos Kanelopulos. He stocks a wide variety of intellectual stimulants in a number of languages, including an amazing selection in English. *Vía Argentina at Vía España, tel. 223–5344. Open Mon.–Sat. 9–12:30 and 2–6.*

LAUNDRY

There are laundromats within walking distance of just about every hotel listed in this book; just ask the receptionist. In Casco Viejo, **Lavamatic** has coin-operated washers and dryers and charges 75¢ per load per machine. *Calle 3 and Av. Central. Open Tues.–Sat. 8:30–4:30, Sun. 8:30–2:30.*

PHONES AND MAIL

Cable and Wireless has an international calling center in the Banking/Hotel district; just down the Calle Eusebio A. Morales from Restaurante Jimmy, in the Dilido Building. You get discount rates—and increased crowds—weekdays after 6 PM and all day on weekends. *Calle Eusebio A. Morales, near Hotel Continental, tel. 264–8104. Open daily 7:30 AM–9:30 PM.*

If you want to send a letter, there are small post offices (Correo) scattered all over the city; just ask at your hotel for the nearest one. The main office of the **Correos Nacional** is located in Santa Ana, at the end of Avenida Balboa. It has telegraph, money-order, and 30-day poste restante services. Address poste restante mail to: Entrega General, Zona 3, Panamá, República de Panamá, Central America. *Tel. 262–1831. Open weekdays 7–5:30, Sat. 7–5.*

MEDICAL AID

The **Clinica Bella Vista** (Av. Perú and Calle 38, tel. 227–1266) is a private clinic with English-speaking doctors that is conveniently located in Caledonio. The **Centro Médico Paitilla** (Av. Balboa and Calle 53, tel. 265–8800), near Paitilla Point, is the country's best, and most expensive, hospital. To take advantage of Panama's socialized medical system, head to the public **Hospital Santo Tomás** (Av. Balboa at Calle 34 Este, tel. 227–4122). Two chains of 24-hour supermarket/pharmacies—**24, Arrocha** and **Rey**—have numerous branches: A convenient Arrocha farmacia is just off Vía España at the Banco Continental building.

COMING AND GOING

BY BUS

Ticabus (Calle 17, next to Hotel Ideal, tel. 262–2084 or 262–6275) and **Panaline** (Plaza Cinco de Mayo, 2nd floor of Hotel Internacional, tel. 262–1618 or 262–1589) both have daily luxu.y buses between Panama City and San José, Costa Rica. Ticabus departs San José at 10 PM and Panama City at 11 AM. Panaline departs both capitals at 2 PM. The journey takes 16 to 18 hours and costs $25 each way. Space is not a problem except during school vacations (Nov.–Feb. and Semana Santa), when you should make reservations at least three days in advance.

Most of the buses to the rest of Panama, commonly known as the "interior," depart from the **piquera** (bus terminal) in Curundú. Every taxi driver knows where the piquera is, and **SACA** buses travel to it from the Cinco de Mayo terminal. Most of those buses are minibuses, and no trip should cost more than $10. Lines are privately owned and there's a zillion of them, but buses to most places leave hourly if not more frequently, according to the destination, though those to the Darién leave only in the morning. Pay your fare on board. Buses to **Colón** and **Sabanitas,** where you catch buses for **Portobelo** and **Isla Grande,** leave every hour to half hour from Calle 30 Este at Avenida Perú, across the street from the Hotel Soloy. For **David,** Panafont (Calle 34 at Avenida Ecuador, tel. 227–4210) luxury buses depart from next to the Hotel Discover every hour or two. Direct Buses to **Bocas del Toro** leave from next to the Restaurante la Felicidad in Pueblo Nuevo (Via Fernandez de Cordoba 4161, tel. 229-6333) at 11 PM.

BY CAR

Driving a car in Panama City is not an undertaking for the meek, but renting a car can be an excellent way to explore the countryside. Rental cars are readily available and fairly affordable: $30–$40 a day, four-wheel-drive vehicles start at $53. **Hertz** (tel. 264–1111) has offices all over and is often the cheapest. **Budget** (tel. 263–8777) is also well established and competitive. Other companies include **Avis** (tel. 264–0722), **Central** (tel. 223–5745), **National** (tel. 265–2222), and **International** (tel. 264–4540). Shop around, you may find a deal. Rental cars cannot be taken out of the country.

BY PLANE

International flights arrive at **Tocumen** (tel. 238–4322), about 26 km (16 mi) northeast of Panama City, while domestic flights go through **Allbrook** (north of downtown). Tocumen has a tourist-info center, 24-hour luggage storage ($1 per day; look for the guys wearing brown pants, khaki shirts, and red caps), and car-rental agencies galore. There's also an Cable & Wireless calling center (tel. 238–4208). Allbrook is much more basic, but traveling in a small plane gives you a stunning view of the jungle, and the costs are fairly reasonable. Moreover, some of the most beautiful places in the country (like the Darién and San Blas) are most easily accessible by air. Domestic flights run from $60 to $110 round-trip. For more information on domestic and international airlines, *see* Chapter 1.

AIRPORT TRANSPORTATION • To reach Allbrook, catch a SACA bus at the terminal north of Plaza Cinco de Mayo, or hail a taxi ($1–$3) from anywhere in the city. Buses to Tocumen (30¢) run frequently from Plaza Cinco de Mayo, but it can be a big hassle to hoist your luggage onto them. Depending on traffic, it can take anywhere from 45 to 90 minutes to reach the Tocumen. A taxi from the city to Tocumen is $12–$20, depending on the size of the taxi and the time (night is more expensive). To get into the city from the airport, take a *colectivo,* a big, glorified taxi that carries groups for $8 per person.

GETTING AROUND

Panama City is your basic urban sprawl, stretching for 10 km (6 mi) along the Bahía de Panamá on the Pacific coast. The biggest chunk of the city is served by three roughly parallel east–west streets. **Avenida Balboa** runs along the Pacific Ocean and passes the Atlapa Convention Center and Paitilla Airport, changing names twice (first to Vía Israel and then to Vía Cincuentenario) before turning inland at the ruins of Panamá Viejo. **Vía Transístmica** runs out of the city across the isthmus, eventually reaching Colón. **Vía España** is in between the two and is packed with banks, restaurants, and fancy shopping malls. All three streets run into each other just before they reach Casco Viejo (the historic center of town) and Santa Ana (a huge bargain shopping area). The transport hub is the **Plaza Cinco de Mayo** on Avenida Central, in the western part of the city; from here you can catch almost any city bus.

The city is divided into dozens of *barrios* (neighborhoods): a bus with JUSTO AROSEMENA written on it will take you through the barrios of **Calidonia, Bella Vista,** and **El Cangrejo**—all home to budget food and lodging. The coolest old buildings and cheapest digs are in **Casco Viejo** (a.k.a. San Felipe), where Avenida Central ends on a little peninsula jutting into the Bay of Panama. To reach the Casco Viejo, you can get off any bus at the Plaza Santa Ana and head away from the pedestrian mall, following the old street car tracks. Between Plazas Santa Ana and Cinco de Mayo, the Avenida Central is a pedestrian zone planted with trees and lined with shops. Just north of Casco Viejo are **El Chorrillo** and **Santa Ana,** two very poor neighborhoods that were hit hard by the '89 invasion, and which should be avoided. The **Panama Canal** is west of the city proper and can be reached on buses headed for Balboa, Paraíso, or Gamboa. That former Canal Zone looks completely different from the rest of the city, with wide lawns, stately buildings, and plenty of rain forest.

If you navigate the city using a map, watch closely: sometimes one street will have two or three names. Avenidas with numbers are colloquially referred to by their officially forsaken names. For example, Avenida 3 Sur is Justo Arosemena, and Avenida 6 Sur is Balboa. By this reasoning, Avenida 4a should be Nicanor de Obarrio, but it's called Calle 50 instead. Neighborhoods, too, are only loosely defined. Do as the locals do and steer yourself by major landmarks: Plaza Cinco de Mayo, near the Santa Ana shopping area; the banks, malls, and overhead pedestrian walkway on Vía España near El Cangrejo; and Plaza Santa Ana, just north of Casco Viejo.

BY BUS

The buses alone almost make this city worth visiting. Not only are they cheap (15¢), they're also the best entertainment around. Each bus is independently owned and decorated with colorful airbrush art, and no holds are barred; the more outrageous the better. Images range from pinup girls and ghoulish creatures, to Paula Abdul and Rambo, to Jesus and stickers asking, "Did you just fart or do you always smell this bad?" Unfortunately, the trend in recent years has been to replace the original art with advertising, so those charming, typically Panamanian buses are increasingly being converted to rolling billboards, which is about the last thing needed in this city of rampant commercialism

Each bus has its destination and route painted broadly across the windshield. The word to remember when you want to get off is *parada* (stop). You pay your fare as you get *off* the bus. The central bus stop is Plaza Cinco de Mayo; from here you can catch buses to both airports and everywhere else in the city.

Buses run consistently until about 10 PM, with some routes running as late as 1–2 AM. Buses to the former Canal Zone leave from the SACA terminal, 1 block north of Plaza Cinco de Mayo.

BY TAXI

Fares are based on a zone system; the official charge is $1 per zone plus 25¢ for each additional person. Most trips coast $1–$2, but if it's a long trip, you may have to pay $3 or $4. If you think you're being cheated, all cabbies have to carry a map with zones and fares on it, which you can consult. Cabbies will usually pick up several passengers, if they're headed the same direction, so be prepared to share. Tips are not expected.

WHERE TO SLEEP

CASCO VIEJO/SANTA ANA

The turn-of-the-century hotels here are the ruins of a former glorious era, and they are surrounded by this city's most charming, historic architecture. It's a lively neighborhood by day, but unfortunately, safety, nourishment, and entertainment are hard to come by once the sun sets. Buses don't run directly into Casco Viejo. Most Vía España or Transístmica buses will take you as close as Plaza Santa Ana (always double-check with the driver), from where you'll have to walk a couple of blocks or take a taxi. Those arriving at night should take a taxi to their hotel.

Beware! Drivers will mow you down without touching the brake, then sue you for denting their grill with your head. Even worse are bus and taxi drivers, who obey no laws of God or man, carrying out their duties with distinct disregard for human life.

UNDER $12 • Hotel Central. Built around the turn of the century, this hotel is said to have housed Teddy Roosevelt on official state visits. Though truly dilapidated, it still has the feel of a stately manor—complete with wrought-iron balconies—but you can't ignore the creaking wood staircase, yellowing sheets, and potentially scary toilets. The nicest rooms face the noisy plaza in front and have private baths and balconies. Singles start at $8.30; doubles are $9.35 ($11.55 with bath). *Calle 5 at Plaza Catedral, tel. 262–8096. 140 rooms, 46 with bath. No credit cards.*

Pension Herrera. Occupying a beautiful blue-and-white colonial building, this former mansion has some lovely sitting areas and a few rooms with charming balconies or large windows overlooking Plaza Herrera. Unfortunately, most rooms are dim and musty, the sheets look as if they were last changed in 1925, and the worn mattresses are soft and tired. Still, the charming Herrera is extra-secure. Doubles are $8 ($11 with bath); Rooms 13 and 14 are a couple of the nicest. *Calle 9a, at Callejón on Plaza Herrera, tel. 228–8994. 47 rooms, 16 with bath. No credit cards*

UNDER $20 • Hotel Ideal. Located just off the Avenida Central pedestrian zone, about six blocks from the Casco Viejo, this tacky, busy hotel built in the '60s offers a safer, more convenient location and such amenities as air-conditioning and cable TV. There's even a small pool next to the snack bar. Singles start at $13, and doubles at $18 when two rooms share one bath ($20–$22 for a double with bath); there's a 10% discount for Tica Bus passengers; just show up around 4 PM and ask for it. *Calle 16, around the corner from Tica Bus station, tel. 262–2085. 173 rooms, 93 with bath. No credit cards.*

CALIDONIA/BELLA VISTA

This area is considerably safer than Casco Viejo, and close to the good restaurants and nightlife of El Cangrejo and Vía España. Many of the hotels fill up on weekends, when Panamanian couples move in and get those beds asqueaking. You can get to most of the hotels listed here by taking any AVENIDA JUSTO AROSEMENA bus: Look for the fine print on a Panamá Viejo Ruta 1 or Vía España bus.

UNDER $20 • Hotel Discovery. This place is one of the city's best deals, with small, modern, air-conditioned rooms complete with TV and telephone for just $15 a single or double with one bed and $20 for two beds. *Calle 34, between Av. Justo Arosemena and Av. Cuba, tel. 225–1140. 78 rooms with bath. No credit cards.*

Hostal Villa del Mar. Located on a side street in the safer part of Caledonio, this place is similar to the Discovery. The simple, modern rooms may lack personality, but they're quite comfortable, and the art-deco blue-and-red reception desk is truly groovy. *Calle 33, between Av. Justo Arosemena and Av. Cuba, tel. 225–3568. 33 rooms with bath. No credit cards.*

UNDER $30 • Hotel California. This place is conveniently located on the Vía España, a short walk from the restaurants of El Cangrejo. Spacious, bright, clean rooms have cable TV, air-conditioning, hot water, and firm beds for $20 (single) and $28 (a double with two beds). Those in back are much quieter. The hotel has its own restaurant and bar, serving some decent lunch specials, but there are definitely better places to eat in the area. *Vía España, at Calle 43, tel. 263–7736 or 263–8140. 60 rooms with bath.*

Hotel Covadonga. The Covadonga is an example of how a few more bucks can get you a lot more comfort. The small pool on the roof, which has a decent view of the city and ocean beyond, is the prize here. Rooms are also bigger and newer than the Montreal's. It's $22 for one bed (single or double) and $28 for two, and they all have cable TV, air-conditioning, telephone, and even the option of room service. *Calle 43 between Avs. Perú and Cuba (behind Hotel Soloy), tel. 225–3998. 65 rooms with bath. Restaurant.*

Hotel Montreal. This place has two selling points; location and the tiny pool on the roof. Although rooms are on the small side, they have TV, phone, and air-conditioning, and there's a decent restaurant downstairs. A single costs $18, and a double $20 for one bed and $30 for two. Avoid rooms in the front facing busy Vía España. *Vía España, at Av. Justo Arosemena, tel. 263–4422. 94 rooms with bath. Restaurant.*

FOOD

Dying for a vegetarian Greek salad with homemade pita bread? How about fresh pasta followed by a cup of homemade gelato, or genuine Cantonese dim sum? Food-lovers rejoice, for in Panama City you can sample the many flavors of a diverse population. In lieu of fast-food joints, follow your nose to the wide variety of ethnic restaurants; or try the local cafeterias, which serve a variety of traditional Panamanian dishes, plus credible sandwiches at palatable prices. The best restaurants are conveniently concentrated in an area along Vía España, Vía Argentina, and Calle 50.

CASCO VIEJO AND SANTA ANA

Although dominated by fast food-joints and greasy spoons, this area does have a few places to catch a decent meal at a very reasonable price. Centered around Avenida B between Calles 13 and 14, **China-town** encompasses a few blocks near the bay. Here you'll see stores selling roast whole ducks and a variety of dried fungus and animal parts labeled exclusively in Chinese. Come here for the best dim sum south of San Francisco.

Café Restaurante Coca Cola. Supposedly "the oldest café in Panamá," this place is popular with habitués, who patronize it well into the night. It's also the place to fill up on one of the best breakfasts in the city; try the pancakes ($1.75) with homemade syrup. It's not the safest place to be after dark. *Plaza Santa Ana, between Casco Viejo and shopping area on Av. Central, tel. 228–7687.*

Cafeteria Ideal. This simple cafeteria underneath the Hotel Ideal serves hearty, meaty lunches for $2–$2.50 a plate, which is why it is usually packed from noon to 2 PM. The menu is pretty basic, but the food is fresher and less greasy than most of the places in this neighborhood. They do only lunch. *Calle 16, 2 blocks west of pedestrian mall,, tel. 262–2085. Closed Sun.*

Restaurante Pizzeria Napoli. Around the corner and down the street is one of Panama's most popular Italian eateries, which has been packing 'em in since 1962. They haven't redecorated since then, nor have they done much to the prices—a 10-inch pepperoni pizza is $2.50, so is ravioli napolitana. Dozens of other tasty dishes won't run you a whole lot more. *Calle Estudiante, across from Instituto Nacional, tel. 262-2446. Closed Tues.*

CALIDONIA/BELLA VISTA

This area is safer to walk around than the Casco Viejo/Santa Ana neighborhoods. Restaurants here are slightly scattered, but many are good and have medium-to-low prices.

Mi Salud. "My Health" is the place to go for a meatless meal in Caledonia. About half a dozen hot dishes are served cafeteria style—you can get any three and a fruit drink for less than $3. They also bake whole-wheat bread and cakes, but the fresh ice cream and frozen yogurt (50¢) are probably the most provocative things on the menu. *Calle 31, near Av. Balboa, tel. 225–0972. Closed Sun.*

Restaurante Benidorm. It's no coincidence that this 24-hour restaurant around the corner from the Hotel Soloy is packed so much of the time—the food is consistentlly good and the portions larger than

ADVENTURES IN EATING: LA CASCADA

Come to La Cascada, the self-proclaimed biggest restaurant in Panama—where the phrase "We do not have it" is taboo—when you're really hungry and/or hurting for a laugh. Giant blue and yellow mushroom lights blossom between the tables, many of which look out on a carp-filled canal fed by a giant artificial waterfall with tacky painted statues and plastic dinosaurs. The portions are enormous, and the menu is an imposing 16-page tabloid monstrosity that reads like a choose-your-own adventure ("If you like to buy a fresh natural red rose for your female companion, look page No. 12"). The menu is dominated by seafood, but there are also a number of tasty meat dishes, and though most dishes cost more than $5, they give you so much food, it's well worth it. Even if you don't come away from this life experience with a souvenir Polaroid (see page 12 of menu, paragraph B), you are sure to leave stuffed with offerings like the mound of paella ($8), which could easily feed two. Avenida Balboa, at Calle 25, tel. 262–1297.

the prices. You can get half a fried chicken, fries, and a salad for $3.50, or simply nibble on a grilled cheese sandwich for $1. Drop $6, and you feast on paella or filet mignon. Wash it all down with a mug of draft beer (50¢). *Calle 30 Este between Avs. Perú and Cuba, next to Hotel Acapulco, tel. 226–8467.*

OBARRIO/EL CANGREJO

A huge concentration of good restaurants is found here in the commercial and banking center of the city. If you have the cash, you can dine on sushi at **Sushi Itto** (Av. Samuel Lewis, one block east of El Santuario, tel. 265-1222), or authentic Indian cuisine at **Calcutta** (Av. Federico Boyd, at Vía España, below the Hotel Costa Sol, tel. 263–8586), which is closed Monday. Meals at these places run $10–$15. For nouvelle cuisine, try **Golosinas** (Calle Ricardo Arias, across from Banco Aliado, tel. 269–6237), one of the finest restaurants in Panama, where entrées cost $10–$20. It is closed Sunday.

Athens. Athens offers delightful Greek food that's sure to please discriminating vegetarians and carnivores alike. Try the *pita satziki* (yogurt, garlic, red peppers, cucumbers, Greek olives, and dressing in homemade pita; $4) or a scrumptious Greek salad ($3.75). Carnivores can select from a number of yummy combinations of sliced beef or chicken with yogurt, tomatoes, and cucumbers in various types of homemade bread. *Calle 57, 2 blocks south of Vía España, tel. 223–1464. Closed Mon.*

Café Nikos. This giant, 24-hour restaurant dishes out an array of Panamanian and international dishes from a cafeteria line, while sandwiches are made to order, including juicy *gyros* (Greek-style lamb and veggies in pita bread). *Calle 51, ½ block from Vía España, near the Supermarket El Rey, tel. 264–0138.*

El Trapiche. Come here for a typically Panamanian meal like *ropa vieja* (strips of flank steak stewed with onions, peppers and tomatoes). It's a cozy place with both indoor and patio seating, but beware the piped-in music: Neil Diamond dominates the play list. An even better option for enjoying the same menu is the more elegant restaurant, located in the handcraft center next to the ruins of Panamá Viejo, that features an ocean view. *Vía Argentina, 2 blocks off Vía España, tel. 269–4353:.*

Restaurante La Mexicanita. La Mexicanita is one of the best restaurants in the city. It is owned and managed by a Mexican expat and is located in a former home on busy Calle 50, across from Josephine's

A ONE-DAY HISTORY TOUR

Start early, and spend the morning admiring the buildings, churches, and plazas of Casco Viejo, ending up at the air-conditioned Museo del Canal Interoceanico, where you'll want to linger. Then walk up the busy Avenida Central to the Museo Antropologico Reina Torres de Arauz, which deserves at least half an hour; don't leave without seeing the collection of pre-Columbian ceramics. Right behind the museum is the Mercado Artesanal (handicraft market), where you can buy the cheapest molas (embroidered panels) in the country. From Plaza Cinco de Mayo, catch a Panamá Viejo bus to the ruins of the original city, which are pretty dispersed (budget at least 90 minutes for this leg of your journey). There's another handicraft market in a cement building in Panamá Viejo, and it has a lot of things that you won't find at the one downtown. In the ground floor of the building is the restaurante El Trapiche, where you can enjoy a typical Panamanian lunch and an ocean view, but if you're on a tight budget, you'll want to eat in Santa Ana before heading to Panamá Viejo. Be forewarned that buses are super-crowded during commuter hours (noon–1:30 and 4:30–6).

Gold. The ample menu includes everything from soft tacos to mole poblano, and it's all authentic—they've even got Mexican beer and $3 margaritas. *Calle 50 No. 42, tel. 225–5806. Closed Mon.*

Restaurante Sorrento. Despite being located in the swanky El Cangrejo banking district, Sorrento is surprisingly affordable. They serve a wide selection of antipasto and pasta, as well as great pizzas, and the service is excellent. Try one of their salads ($1), followed by a heaping plate of fresh lasagna ($2.75), or perhaps a mushroom and olive pizza ($3.75). *Calle Ricardo Arias, down the street from the Hotel Continental, tel. 269–0055. Closed Mon.*

Restaurante Vegetariano Mireya. The wide selection of entrées changes every day, but they're always vegetarian and tasty. Mireya also has the best salad bar in the city. Choose your food from the cafeteria line, then sit down and eat it in the air-conditioned room. *Calle Ricardo Arias, down street from Hotel Continental, tel. 269–1876. Closed Sun.*

ON THE WATERFRONT

Don Samy's. This place is a land unto itself, especially on weekend nights when the parking lot—and the street for a half-mile in either direction—becomes a colossal festival of young drunken locals and car-speaker distortion. Through it all, Don Samy's serves up cheap, satisfying Panamanian food—the *sancocho* (chicken stew with vegetables and spices) is a perennial favorite for $1.50. Warning: passengers and drivers alike slake their thirst on cheap local beer. If you decide to do the same, just be careful as you stagger out the door into the street traffic. *Av. Balboa, across from Marriott Caesar's Park Hotel and Atlapa Convention Center, tel. 226–1309. Take Panamá Viejo–Ruta 2 bus from Plaza Cinco de Mayo.*

DESSERT AND COFFEEHOUSES

Java junkies will be in heaven in Panama City, where just about every restaurant grinds its own beans and makes every cup to order with an espresso machine. Unfortunately, the dessert selection is not always up to par with the quality of the coffee. One spot that usually has some good sweets to accompany the java is **Manolo** (Vía Veneto, near Hotel El Panamá, tel. 269–5414), which is a full-fledged restaurant but has a café feel to it, especially if you sit outside. It's a great place to watch the world go by no matter what you drink.

Café El Aleph. Panama's budding young poets, artists, and musicians exchange ideas over crepes and cappuccino at this superb café/art gallery/bar. Try the flavored coffees (70¢) or a vegetarian sandwich ($3.50). This is also one of the city's more popular nightspots, often presenting good films, live music, and other entertainment. *Vía Argentina at Vía España, tel. 264–2844.*

WORTH SEEING

Populated for almost five centuries, conquered and colonized by foreign powers, and lying on a major trade route, Panama City has a lot to offer sightseers. Unfortunately, little is organized for the tourist, and what few explanations are available are in Spanish. The good news is that most interesting sites are located within walking distance of each other, in the Casco Viejo and Santa Ana areas, with the exception Panamá Viejo, which is about half an hour away. If you stop by IPAT (*see* Basics, *above*), ask for a gold brochure titled "Conjunto Monumental Historico de Panamá," which has brief background information and small maps of Panamá Viejo, Casco Viejo, and Portobelo.

CASCO VIEJO

The narrow cobblestone streets, wrought-iron balconies, and ornate building facades evoke visions of Panama's glorious history as a major trade center. Starting at the Plaza Central, note the lovely cathedral, the ornate Palacio Municipal, on the third floor of which is the **History Museum of Panama** (admission 50¢; open weekdays 8:30–3:30), and the stately **Museo del Canal Interoceanico** (admission $2; open Tue.–Sun. 9:30–5:30). Continue down Avenida B toward the ocean,

If you were too young to experience the thrill of Saturday Night Fever firsthand, you can do it here—disco is king in Panama City. Don't forget to pack a pair of polyester bells and some platform shoes.

where you can veer left to check out the **Teatro Nacional**—if it's open, ask if you can peek inside. Just beyond the theater is Plaza Bolivar, which sits between the lovely old Hotel Colonial and the Church of San Francisco. Continue two blocks more, turn left, and walk another block to the see the **Palacio de las Garzas,** the Panamanian White House, if the security guards let you get that far.

Head back to Plaza Bolivar and continue walking out to the point, where you'll find **Las Bóvedas** (the old dungeons), now gentrified into an expensive restaurant and gallery. The shady park in front of Las Bóvedas is called the **Plaza de Francia** and is dedicated to the French effort to dig a canal. Wander back to Avenida A, turn left, and walk a block down to where the ruins of the **Iglesia y Convento de Santo Domingo** will appear on your right. Just inside the entryway is the baffling **Arco Chato.** Standing unsupported for three centuries, it was used as proof that the country was not subject to earthquakes, tipping the scales in favor of Panama over Nicaragua for a transoceanic canal.

Farther up on the left, on the corner of Calle 8, is the **Iglesia de San José.** The church is the resting place for a famous golden altar, which is supposedly the only piece of treasure left by the pirate Henry Morgan when he razed the old city. According to legend, either a wily priest painted the altar black or clever nuns covered it with mud in an effort to discourage its theft. Not only did pirate Morgan not pilfer it, he donated money to the priest for a new altar because he thought it was ugly.

MUSEO DEL CANAL INTEROCEANICO

Panama's newest and best museum is appropriately dedicated to the country's biggest attraction: the canal. A series of elaborate and educational exhibits traces the history of the canal and the country from the pre-Columbian and colonial eras, through France's disastrous attempt at digging a canal, America's successful construction, the signing of the treaty, and right up to its current operation. A collection of artifacts, paintings, photographs, and videos provides a thorough look at the history and importance of that monumental ditch. *Plaza Central, tel. 211–1649. Admission $2, free Sun. morning. Open Tues.– Sun. 9:30–5:30.*

TEATRO NACIONAL

The interior of this theater is truly posh, with painted ceilings, gold balconies, marble, and chandeliers— a little bit of Euro-heaven in the middle of Panama City. While you're here, check out what's playing at night; the national symphony orchestra is often featured. You can also ooh and aah at the **Palacio**

Nacional next door. Both buildings were designed by Ruggieri, who also did La Scala in Milan. *Av. B, at waterfront. Open Tues.–Sat. 9:30–4:15, Sun. 1:30–4:15.*

MUSEO ANTROPOLOGICO REINA TORRES DE ARAUZ

The Torres museum has an amazing array of artifacts, both indigenous and transplanted, dating back thousands of years and spanning numerous cultures. Most impressive is their collection of stone statues and pre-Columbian painted ceramics. There is also a small room with exquisite gold bells, pendants, and bracelets fashioned in the shape of fantastic insects, reptiles, and other creatures. All the signs are in Spanish, but you don't need translations to appreciate the artistry. *Plaza Cinco de Mayo, tel. 262–8338. Admission 50¢. Open Tues.–Sat. 9:30–4:15, Sun. 1:30–4:15.*

PANAMÁ VIEJO

About 6 km (4 mi) east of the city, these cool ruins are what's left of Old Panama, the first major Spanish settlement. In 1671, pirate Henry Morgan looted the city. According to legend, he overlooked only the famous golden altar, now in the Iglesia de San José (*see above*). In 1673, instead of rebuilding, residents opted to construct a new settlement on Panama City's present site. Today, the crumbling old ruins are mossy and impressive, but poorly marked. They lie scattered along the road, and it shouldn't take you more than an hour to see them. Keep your wits about you; the ruins are in the midst of a very poor neighborhood. *Take any Panamá Viejo bus from Plaza Cinco de Mayo.*

BAHA'I HOUSE OF WORSHIP

The Baha'i believe that all the world's religions are separate manifestations of a single religious process—which culminated with the appearance of their founder, Bahà'u'llàh, who preached about a new global society. They've built a gorgeous hilltop temple and grounds about 11 km (7 mi) north of the city; it's open to everyone for prayer, meditation, and subdued exploring. Check it out for a quiet afternoon and a 360° view. Men should wear long pants and women long skirts. *Transístmica Mile 8. Take a Transístmica bus, but first ask driver if he goes that far. Long driveway runs between Banco Nacional and Ron Bacardi Bldgs.; it's a 15-min walk to top of hill. Open daily 10–6.*

HINDU TEMPLE

Worshipers at this temple partake in millennia-old religious rituals; they welcome anyone who'd like to participate in polytheistic morning or evening prayer. The open-air building is an odd, heavy-looking, concrete contraption decorated with greenish-white images of Krishna, Vishnu, and Shiva, among others. *Calle Ricardo J. Alfaro (Tumba Muerto). Take a Tumba Muerto bus from Plaza Cinco de Mayo; ask driver where to get off. Bus stop and pedestrian overpass are next to driveway. Open daily 7:30–11 and 4:30–7:30.*

CHEAP THRILLS

Balboa, the heart of the old Canal Zone, is quite a switch from the rest of Panama City, with its wide lawns, big trees, and stately old buildings that have "made by Gringos" written all over them. It is a pleasant area to explore, with clean air, lots of greenery, and some great views of the canal. The foyer of the **Canal Commission Building**—an impressive structure set atop a hill—has a collection of murals depicting the canal's construction. The **Causeway,** which connects several former islands to the mainland, was made with the rocks removed from the Gailard Cut during canal construction. It features excellent views of the canal's entrance, the Bridge of the Americas, and Panama City. Cars aren't allowed on it on weekends, which is a great time to rent a bike at its entrance and ride out to the islands.

Mi Pueblo is the epitome of a cheesy tourist experience: a set of tile-roofed houses set around a small courtyard intended to depict life in a "typical" Panamanian village in the 1800s. A guide wearing a *pollera* (an intricately stitched, lacy dress) will take you around various refurbished rooms and to a lovely exhibit of typical clothing worn in the interior, including incredible *polleras*. The site's small restaurant is much less expensive than you'd expect ($3–$5 for comida tipica) and offers an incredible view of the city below. *Cerro Ancon: large green hill overlooking Balboa and El Chorrillo. Take a taxi ($1.50–$2). Admission 50¢. Open daily 10–10.*

FESTIVALS

Every March since 1914, the Panama Canal Commission has allowed a dugout **canoe race** to pass through the canal from Colón to Panama City. Entries range from traditional dugout tree trunks to high-tech, super-lightweight fiberglass jobbies. Ask around, since the exact date varies. **Carnaval** is *the* humdinger of all festivals. Starting the Friday before Mardi Gras, people party nonstop for five days. While many Panamanians recommend heading out to the western provinces for a really rocking fiesta, there's plenty going on in the city if you decide to stay. Vía España in the El Cangrejo area hosts an organized parade, but expect random hedonism wherever you go. The anniversary of the **Foundation of Panama,** August 15, is celebrated with parades, folk music, and dancing at Panamá Viejo. In October, look for the **Celebración del Cristo Negro,** a festival celebrating the Black Christ statue in a Portobelo church. This whing-ding attracts thousands of participants dressed in purple gowns, who start in Panama City and *walk* the 80-odd km (50 mi) to Portobelo, some on their knees. It's a serious religious occasion, especially for Panama's Afro-Caribbean citizens.

SHOPPING

MERCADO ARTESENAL

Shop at either of these two markets for souvenirs to take home; molas tend to be cheaper at the one near Plaza Cinco de Mayo, but the Panamá Viejo market tends to have more of the country's other handicrafts, such as masks from Chitré and Los Santos, pottery from La Arena, and baskets from the Darién. Both markets consist of a series of stalls occupied by individual families and artisans. Even if you're not interested in buying, this is a great place to meet people and see what are the crafts valued in the country. *Just off Plaza Cinco de Mayo, behind Reina Torres de Arauz Anthropology Museum, or next to the tower in Panamá Viejo. Open daily 9–6.*

The first track running between Colón and Panama City was built to take '49ers across the isthmus and on to the Gold Rush in California. What is left of that railroad now lies at the bottom of Gatún Lake.

LA CENTRAL

This pedestrian-only section of Avenida Central (between Plaza Santa Ana and Plaza Cinco de Mayo) is packed with shops offering especially good deals on watches, camera equipment, electronics, jewelry, fabrics, and clothing. It's worth checking out just to see how aggressive the salesmen can be, and to observe how they clap their hands and entice passersby to come on in.

MERCADO PUBLICO

Vendors at the public market hawk everything from incense and produce to whole sides of beef. The meat section is extensive and involves *no* refrigeration; in the tropical heat, the enclosed market is not for the queasy. You may not want to buy anything—hell, you may not be able to eat afterwards—but the market is an interesting part of Panamanian life, so it's worth a quick visit. *Av. E. Alfaro, between Calles 11 and 13. Open daily approximately 5 AM–6 PM.*

AFTER DARK

Panama City has a good selection of nightlife, conveniently accessible to the traveler. Most bars, dance clubs, and 24-hour restaurants are all within staggering distance of each other along Vía España; when it's time to pass out, it's a cheap taxi trek from the city's affordable lodging. Buses run until 10 PM, and if you're staying in Bella Vista, it's close and safe enough to walk.

As you would expect, Panamanians love their tropical music, which means there are plenty of places you can go to boogie to salsa, merengue, and other Latin rhythms. If you go to a dance club, though, be prepared for a high cover charge ($5–$15, according to the club), though in many cases you'll be treated to an open bar once inside—ask before you fork over your cash.

Teatro Alambra is a huge movie theater on Vía España, near Calle 52. If you're in Casco Viejo, you can see a $1.25 movie in the **Teatro Amador**; it's just up Avenida Central, half a block past Calle 11. The film selection in Panama tends to be dominated by the kind of visually spectacular and intellectually vacuous action flicks that Hollywood does such a good job of churning out.

Gambling is a popular pastime in Panama City, and there are **casinos** all over the place, ranging from fancy to seedy. The nicest ones are in the Hotels Caesar Park and El Panamá, although several of the medium-size hotels also have them, and if all you want to do is play the slots, you can hit one of the smaller ones on Vía España.

THE BAY
OF CHOLERA

Viewed from a distance, or at night, the Bay of Panama looks quite romantic, but stroll along the Malecón in the daytime—the waterfront promenade on Avenida Balboa—and you're likely to sniff some odors that will turn your stomach. The bay is extremely polluted, since all of Panama City's sewage is dumped directly into the ocean untreated. Over the years, environmental groups have made occasional fusses about the situation, and studies have outlined the multimillion-dollar job that cleaning up the bay would entail, but no government has been willing to bite that bullet.

A fine place to sip drinks and watch the sun set over the canal is the **Balboa Yacht Club**; take the SACA bus to Fort Amador (35¢) and ask for the club by name. Another option for a sunset cocktail is the bar on the roof of the **Hotel Costa Sol** (Vía España at Av. Federico Boyd). If you don't want to hit the bars or dance clubs after the sun sets, your best bet is to head to **Café El Aleph** (*see* Dessert and Coffeehouses, *above*), where they often have poetry readings, live music, or alternative films showing in a relaxed atmosphere.

BARS AND MUSIC

The El Cangrejo neighborhood off Vía España is seething with bars, all within crawling distance of each other. The underground **Casa de Cerveza** (Vía España east of Vía Argentina) is a no-frills bar that plays Latin music. **Ralph's Pool Place** has sort of a Gringo, sports-bar atmosphere (Via Argentina at Calle 52, tel. 265–2065). **Pavo Real** (Calle 51, near Calle Ricardo Arias, tel. 269–0504), a British-style pub in the heart of the banking district, holds an informal darts competition Tuesday nights. They offer live music—mostly classic rock on Wednesday and jazz on Friday. The pub is a good place to meet other English-speakers.

DANCE CLUBS

All dance places play a fair mix of U.S. and European pop, salsa, merengue, and reggae. They charge covers of between $5 and $10, according to the night, which usually includes two drinks, or sometimes, an open bar. Most clubs won't let you in if you're wearing a T-shirt or look scruffy. The dance clubs of Panama City are mostly flashy and expensive, but also relatively classy. Single women can expect no more machismo or scamming here than they would at home. Most clubs are open Tuesday–Sunday. **Bacchus** (Calle Elvira Mendez, off Vía España, tel. 263–9005) is probably the most agreeable of the straight dance places, with pool tables and dartboards in a glass-walled room if you're tired of dancing on their huge, air-conditioned dance floor. **Patatus** (Calle 50, tel. 217–7015) is another popular dance bar, slightly smaller than Bacchus but with a similar crowd of mostly young Panamanians. **Dreams** (Jardines Comerciales del Hotel Panamá, Vía España, tel. 263–4248) is a massive, split-level place with light shows and a clear waterfall between the bar and dance floor, but it has never been quite as popular as the other two. There are also two slick bars in the **Hotel El Panamá** open to the general public—a large bar off the lobby that often has a salsa band and a full-fledged discotheque on the top floor. **Cubares** (Calle 52, near Vía España, tel. 264–8905) is a simpler, cheaper, basement bar that attracts a more working-class clientele.

FOLK DANCING

If you want to see Panamanian folk dancing, your easiest option is to hit one of the presentations every Tuesday, Thursday, Friday, and Saturday at **Tinajas** (Calle 51 No. 22, tel. 269–3840), a slightly fancy restaurant specializing in Panamanian cuisine. The one-hour show starts at 9 PM and costs $5, but you have buy at least a drink. If you're not on a tight budget, it's also a good place to have dinner. You can often enjoy folk dancing for free on weekends at **Mi Pueblo** (*see* Cheap Thrills, *above*), and less frequently at **Panamá Viejo**. Check out the local tourist paper, *The Visitor*, for special events that often include traditional music and dancing.

GAY AND LESBIAN CLUBS

Gays and lesbians will be pleasantly surprised by the fairly open-minded, cosmopolitan atmosphere of the city. Expect to find a wild mélange of coeds making a lot of same-sex salsa moves at **Boy Bar** (Vía Ricardo Alfaro, tel. 230–3128), one of the most popular queer clubs in the city. It's open Friday–Sunday from 9 PM until the wee hours of the morning, and charges a $5 cover. If you're interested in a more subdued bar-like setting, **Hidalgo** (Vía Brasil, in front of Texaco station, tel. 269–0317) tends to attract thirtysomething men and women. It's open Thursday–Sunday, and the cover runs $3–$5 (it's free on Thursday). Don't miss their drag show at 11 PM on Sundays.

OUTDOOR ACTIVITIES

Panama City offers a wealth of activities for outdoorsy types, including the largest chunk of urban rain forest in the world. **ANCON Expeditions** (Calle Elvira Mendez, Edificio El Dorado, tel. 269–9414) has an excellent selection of day tours to protected areas near the capital, plus longer packages that visit some of its five field stations scattered around the country. Other good companies for day trips to the many wilderness areas near Panama City are **Pesantez Tours** (Paitilla, tel. 263–8771) and **Iguana Tours** (Av. Porras, across from Parque Omar, tel. 226–8738).

PARQUE NATURAL METROPOLITANO

This 655-acre patch of jungle on the northern edge of the city holds an amazing array of wildlife, making it a must-visit for anyone interested in tropical nature. Head there at the crack of dawn—it's a mere 10- to 15-minute taxi ride from most hotels—when you have a good chance of spotting parrots, tanagers, toucans, tiny simians known as red-naped tamarinds, and terrier-sized rodents called agoutis, among dozens of other interesting animal species. The park's flora is equally

Tolls for passing through the Panama Canal are based on weight. The average toll is about $30,000 per ship, but the unsuspecting Richard Halliburton was charged $36 when, in 1928, he swam the canal.

impressive, ranging from massive barrigón to delicate heliconia flowers. The Mono Tití Road—a good place to start—ends atop a hill that affords a great view of the city, the Pacific mouth of the canal, and cargo ships in the Bay of Panama. Guides can be arranged for a small fee. *Off Calle Curundu, at Av. Juan Pablo II, tel. 232–5552. From Plaza Cinco de Mayo, take SACA bus toward Fort Clayton; ask driver for park's visitor center. Admission free. Open daily 6–5:30.*

BEACHES

The closest beaches to Panama City, aside from the one on **Isla Naos** at the end of the Causeway, are **Kobbe** and **Veracruz,** both of which are located on the other side of the Canal. SACA buses leave for here from Plaza Cinco de Mayo station infrequently during the week, but fairly regularly on weekends. The water around Isla Naos is really too polluted to swim in, but the ocean off the other two is probably safe, though quite murky. The closest beach with clear water is found on Isla Taboga, a 90-minute ferry ride from the city (*see below*).

DIVING

If you're a certified diver, you can rent scuba gear from **Scuba Panamá,** at the Hotel Taboga on Isla Taboga ($30 for a one-tank beach dive). During the dry season, check into diving in Gatun Lake, in the Panama Canal, where you can see submerged towns and machinery. They also offer PADI and NAUI certification courses in English and have a dive center and hotel at Isla Mamey, on the Caribbean coast. *Urbanización Herbruger El Carmen, across from Teatro en Círculo, tel. 261–3841. Open weekdays 8–6, Sat. 8–1.*

NEAR PANAMA CITY

THE CANAL ZONE

From 1904, only one year after Panama declared its independence from Colombia, till the Canal Treaties began to take effect, the United States controlled and maintained an area skirting the sides of the canal—approximately 48 km (30 mi) wide—that included a number of military bases and housing for canal workers and military families. The forests in this area, together with those of several nearby national parks, were protected as a watershed to support the huge lakes (Gatún and Alajuela) that provide the freshwater needed to raise and lower ships the 85 ft that the bulk of the canal sits above sea level. So, while the star attraction may be the canal itself, that waterway is flanked by some of the most accessible rain forest anywhere in the world. In fact, just minutes from the capital a smooth, paved road winds through completely undeveloped forest filled with a mind-boggling diversity of tropical flora and fauna. You can reach the trails that lead into that forest by taking a SACA bus (35¢) to Gamboa or Paraíso; the buses leave every half hour or so from near the Plaza Cinco de Mayo.

THE PANAMA CANAL

Connecting the Pacific Ocean and the Caribbean Sea, the Panama Canal runs 80 km (50 mi) across the narrowest part of the isthmus, passing through Lago Gatún, an enormous artificial lake created by the damming of the Río Chagres. The first ship traversed the Panama Canal in 1914, after 10 years of construction—and a little international wheeling and dealing—by the United States. The canal is just minutes from the city and can easily be toured as a morning or afternoon trip.

Spain developed plans for a canal here as early as the 16th century. In the 1880s, France started serious work under Ferdinand de Lesseps (the architect responsible for Suez), but his Compagnie Universelle du Canal Interocéanique went bankrupt in 1889 (see chapter introduction, above for more canal history). Soon after, the Americans took over and completed the canal at a cost of $352 million, a staggering sum at that time. Its realization was more than financial, though. Especially during the French years, workers on the canal dropped like flies from disease: malaria, yellow fever, bubonic plague, beriberi, and typhoid felled as many as 25,000 people during the 30-odd years of construction—that's 500 deaths for every mile of the Panama Canal.

Despite the gruesome death toll and the legacy of imperialism that the canal has left Panama, there's no getting around the fact that this is one amazing piece of engineering. The amount of dirt excavated for the canal could have filled a train stretching three times around the equator. Under de Lesseps's plan, which called for an ocean-level canal right through the isthmus, the amount of dirt excavated would have been even greater. To the American engineers this seemed unfeasible. Instead, they opted for a lock system that would raise and lower ships over the highly varied terrain of the isthmus. They constructed three sets of locks—**Miraflores, Pedro Miguel,** and **Gatún**—each measuring 1,000 ft by 110 ft.

The locks act as aquatic elevators by opening doors that let the lock either fill with water or drain. As the water level rises, a ship is raised (or conversely, lowered). Each door of each lock weighs 80 tons, yet they float and thus require only about 40 watts of power to open and close. Gravity does all the necessary water transfer, so the locking process uses no pumps. "Panamax" ships are designed specifically for the canal to maximize the cargo capacity. Watching a ship 106 ft wide and 950 ft long passing with only inches to spare is probably the most awesome sight on the canal.

COMING AND GOING • The canal is conveniently accessible from Panama City: take a SACA bus (35¢) toward Gamboa or Paraíso and get off at the Miraflores Locks. Follow the signs to the visitor center, where bilingual guides explain what's happening over loud speakers as you gawk at the ships passing through.

GETTING AROUND • The best way to see the canal is from a boat, which is why you might want to consider signing on for a tour. **Argotours** (Pier 18, tel. 228–4348) offers one or two ocean to ocean canal trips once a month, which are definitely the best, though the $99 price is a bit steep. It has the best view of Gaillard Cut, where engineers had to cut through solid rock to get across the isthmus, and the jungle-cloaked islands of Gatún Lake. The other option is the half-day tour, which takes you through the Miraflores Locks for $55 per person. Canal tours are offered only on weekends. Another way to get onto the canal is on one of the tours to Barro Colorado (see below), which lies within the canal route, in Gatún Lake. A cheap and convenient option is to take the ferry out to Taboga, at the canal's Pacific entrance, passing big ships en route. If you've got time and are willing to work, you may be able to navigate the canal on a private boat, since they often have to hire one or two people to handle the lines at the locks. Ask around at the Balboa Yacht Club (see After Dark, above), leave your name and contact info at the bar if you don't hook up with anyone while you're there. Canal passage usually takes one–two days.

ISLA BARRO COLORADO

This island in Lago Gatún was created when the Río Chagres was dammed during construction of the Panama Canal. Today it's a center for environmental research, and only a few visitors are allowed at a time. On your way out to the island, you pass over a surreal underwater forest of trees submerged when the dam was built. Also lost in the depths are the remains of the first transisthmus railroad. The underwater world is the exclusive territory of Lago Gatún's famous peacock bass, a species introduced to the area as a sportfishing experiment that went awry. The invasive latecomer now dominates all the indigenous species of fish. When the lake flooded the surrounding jungle, many large mammals retreated to the safety of the island, so there's a much larger concentration of monkeys, coatis, agoutis, and other jungle animals there than in other areas, and they're much less frightened of people.

The **Smithsonian Tropical Research Institute** (tel. 227–6022) administers the Barro Colorado preserve and grants permission to visit. They take groups out to the island on Tuesdays, Saturdays, and Sundays, but since these tours tend to fill up from five months to a year ahead of time, your best bet is to call when you arrive in Panama City and ask if there have been any cancellations, which are frequent enough. The $28 tour is well worth it, since the island is home to an array of rain-forest fauna, and the English-speaking guides do an excellent job. Wear long pants, shoes, and socks to combat the island's mean chigger contingency. If you can't get in with the Smithsonian, consider a trip with Iguana Tours (see Outdoor Activities, *above*) which at $90 is considerably more expensive, but actually offers more opportunities to see wildlife.

PARQUE NACIONAL SOBERANIA

Soberanía protects 54,000 acres of tropical rain forest starting less than 25 km (16 mi) from Panama City, making it one of the most accessible jungles on the planet. Within that lush wilderness live more than 100 species of mammals—including the howler monkey, tamandua anteater, and jaguarundi—and more than 350 bird species. The Pipeline Road, which heads north out of Gamboa, is one of the best bird-watching spots in the world. You can head up that paved road on foot or bicycle, or if you take a tour, in a car. The **Sendero el Charco,** on the right about 1 km (½ mi) past Summit Gardens (*see below*), is another excellent route for seeing animals, although it can get seriously muddy during the rainy months—"charco" means puddle. Either trail can be reached on a Gamboa bus,

The American-built Panama Canal was completed ahead of schedule and under budget. When was the last time you heard of a government project that could make either claim? It should give you an idea of how old the canal is.

which leaves from the Plaza Cinco de Mayo terminal, although you'll see and understand a lot more if you go with an experienced guide. Pesantez Tours, Iguana Tours, and Ancon Expeditions (see Outdoor Activities, *above*) all offer guided trips to Soberania. The best time to see animals is first thing in the morning or early evening; these are also the coolest times to hike in the jungle. Be sure to wear shoes with good traction, and bring insect repellent. *Ranger station, Gamboa, tel. 229–7885. Admission free. Open weekdays 8–5.*

The **Jardín Botánico Summit** (Summit Botanical Garden and Zoo) is surrounded by the national park, and locked in its cages are all those monkeys, birds, and jaguars that may elude you on your hike. Although the zoo is a bit small, it has some rare animals, such as the impressive harpy eagle, Panama's national bird. You can also while away your time in the fragrant botanical gardens, and if you stray from the cages, you may see such wild animals as agoutis (large jungle rodents), parrots, and other birds in the nearby forest. On weekends you can rent bicycles just inside the entrance for $2 an hour. *Tel. 232–4854. Open weekdays 8–4, weekends 8–5.*

ISLA TABOGA

The "Island of Flowers," as Taboga is known, is an excellent day or overnight trip from Panama City, reached by an enjoyable 90-minute ferry ride. Taboga itself is a beautiful, tranquil isle, with beaches washed by aquamarine waters and a charming little village. On weekends, the main beach may have an excess of radios and screaming kids, but during the week, it's almost deserted. The nicest beach on the island lies within the grounds of the Hotel Taboga, which charges $5 to spend the day on the beach. However, they give you $5 in play money that you can use for food and drink at their overpriced snack bar, which makes it fairly worthwhile. **Scuba Panama** has a stand at the hotel, where you can rent snorkeling or scuba gear. If visibility is good in the ocean, you may see some big fish out there. If you don't want to pay $5, follow the trail that veers left at the hotel entrance and runs along the back fence. This leads to a smaller, more isolated beach that almost never sees tourists. Another option is to hike to the top of the nearby hill, which is topped by a huge white cross. You'll get a dazzling view of the town, the bay, and even Panama City on a clear day.

COMING AND GOING • Argo Tours (Pier 7 in Balboa, Panama City, tel. 228–4348) has a ferry to the island that costs $7 per person round-trip. Boats leave for Taboga on weekdays at 8:30 AM and 3 PM (return trips at 10 AM and 4:30 PM), on weekends at 8:30 and 11:30 AM and 4 PM (return trips at 10 AM, 2:30 PM, and 5 PM). To reach the boats, take the SACA bus (15¢) from the Cinco de Mayo terminal to Pier 7. Once you're on the island, you'll be able to walk everywhere. You can see everything on a day trip except for the thousands of frogs that come out only at night.

WHERE TO SLEEP AND EAT • Lodging on Taboga is expensive for what you get, though not outrageous. **Hotel Chu** (left of pier, tel. 250–2035) is an old wooden building on the water, where simple rooms run $19 a single and $24 a double. Their restaurant serves decent Chinese food ($5–$8) daily 8–7. The much nicer **Hotel Taboga** (right off the pier, tel. 264–2122) has a big beach, swimming pools, and large, air-conditioned rooms for $66 a double. To stay the night without spending any moolah, hoof it up to the top of the hill. It's completely secluded, so you shouldn't have any hassles camping, and you'll have a gorgeous sunrise all to yourself.

COLÓN

Basically, the only reason you should stay here is if you get stuck traveling from Panama City to Portobelo or San Blas. This happens more frequently than you might think, so make actual plans to avoid it. You can do so easily by taking a Panama City–Colón bus and getting off in **Sabanitas,** a town on the eastern edge of Lago Gatún; from there, you can catch a bus to Portobelo or beyond. Here is where you'll find the lovely beaches and lively towns that make the Caribbean coast of the province of Colón such a great place to visit.

With unemployment around 40%–50%, Colón is a wasteland in which the average traveler walking down the street might as well have a sign around the neck reading, "I have money and valuables, please mug me." Such is the desperation in Colón that not even daylight or crowds necessarily protect you. It's a great pity, not only for the residents of Colón, who are almost entirely descendants of African slaves or Jamaicans brought for railroad and canal work, but for Panama as a whole. In the early 20th century, Colón was an important shipping center and one of the world's most beautiful ports. If you visit Colón, preferably from the security of a car, you'll see the decaying remnants of what was once a gorgeous city, with wide boulevards and stylish old buildings, all now gone to pot.

Behind huge gated walls, impervious to the blight outside, is the Zona Libre, a duty-free micro-city with huge international stores drawing in $4 billion a year. It sells mainly to retailers, so you only get good prices if you buy in bulk. With all that money pouring into the Zona Libre and with so much poverty just outside, you might sympathize a little with those Colón residents willing to rob you on a busy street in the middle of the day. The Zona Libre is on the eastern edge of the city; take a taxi from the terminal rather than attempting to walk. It's open weekdays 9–5, and you need your passport to enter the zone.

BASICS

Spending the night in Colón is not something to look forward to. Luckily, it isn't necessary since buses to Panama City leave from Avenida Bolívar and Calle 13, two streets west of Amador Guerrero, at almost all hours for less than $2. Regular buses (90 min, $1.75) run 4 AM–1 AM; express buses (1 hr, $2) run 5 AM–9 PM. Buses to Colón from Panama City leave from the corner of Avenida Central and Calle P, four blocks north of Plaza Cinco de Mayo, and from Calle 30 Este at Avenida Perú, across the street from the Hotel Soloy.

THE CARIBBEAN COAST

Beautiful beaches, coral reefs, colonial ruins, and the predominant Afro-Caribbean culture make Panama's Caribbean coast a superb place to visit. This is where people from Panama City come to dive, relax, and enjoy quiet white sand and Creole lobster and conch concoctions. One of the main cultural attractions of the area is the typical dance and performances, known as *congos.* Men wear elaborate costumes covered with beads, feathers, and mirrors, and dance to wild drum music. These displays are performed in many towns along the coast, but the most spectacular is in Portobelo on its Patron Saint Day (March 20), at New Year's, and during Carnaval.

FORT SAN LORENZO

Perched on a cliff overlooking the mouth of the Chagres River are the ruins of this ancient Spanish fort, which was destroyed by Henry Morgan. You drive through some serious rain forest to get there (the U.S. army's old jungle-warfare training site), and the cliff it's perched on offers a stunning view of the

Caribbean coast and jungle covering the hinterlands. Unfortunately, San Lorenzo is a tough place to visit—you can only reach it in a private car or on a tour, which are infrequent. If you have a vehicle, drive toward Colón, veering left past Fort Davis to the Gatún Locks. After driving across the canal, veer right on the main road, following it to Fort Sherman, where you may have to check in with a U.S. Army guard (just tell him you're headed to Fort San Lorenzo). From there, stay on the main dirt road through the jungle (the side roads are, for the most part, marked with signs saying stuff like AMBUSH TRAINING SITE–STAY OUT). Bring a flashlight to explore the nifty nooks and crannies. Also, bring bug repellent or risk being devoured.

PORTOBELO

Sitting on a clear-water bay bordered by jungle, Portobelo ("beautiful port") lives up to its name. It's home to some of the most inspiring colonial ruins in Panama, with rusty cannons still lying in wait for an enemy assault and decaying fortress walls yielding to the advancing jungle. Also in Portobelo is the church that houses the statue of the Black Christ (see Festivals in Panama City, above). You can easily see all of this on a day trip, or during a stop on your way to Isla Grande.

Portobelo is also the site of a national marine park, and there are several dive centers located along the road just before the town, and they all run boats out to nearby reefs. Most offer the same prices: $30 to rent diving equipment, $5 per tank, $5 each for snorkel/mask/fins, and $4 per boat ride. Several of them also have dorm-style sleeping quarters for $8–$10. **Aquatic Park** (tel. 448–2175) and **Diver's Haven** (tel. 448–2003) offer weekend packages that include dives and accommodations. Bring your own food, or be gouged by their restaurants. You need to be certified to dive, but most places also offer quick and inexpensive certification courses.

The buildings at El Farallon, Noriega's former base, are in ruins—pockmarked with bullet holes, painted with vultures shooting from tanks, and adorned with slogans like "loyalty or death." Gives you an idea of just how power-crazy Noriega was.

Direct buses run from Colón, 48 km (30 mi) southwest, about every half hour (90¢). You should skip Colón by getting off the Panama City–Colón bus at Sabanitas and catching the Colón–Portobelo bus as it passes through. Buses run until about 9 PM.

ISLA GRANDE

A smashing little island located just off the Caribbean coast, Isla Grande has about half a dozen hotels and a town so small you don't need addresses, or even directions, to get around. The cheapest place to stay, **Cabañas Jackson** (no phone), charges $25 per night ($35 with air-conditioning) and does not accept credit cards. **Villa Ensueño** (tel. 269–5819) is a newer place with a view of Isla Grande's famous cross on top of a coral reef, where air-conditioned rooms rent for $44–$55. The spacious grounds of the **Hotel Isla Grande** (tel. 225–6722) overlook the western end of the island, where bungalows shaded by coconut palms rent for $60. Since Isla Grande has little in the way of beaches, and the surrounding reef has suffered years of abuse, it's worthwhile to organize a group and hire a boat for a day trip to nearby beaches and reefs.

Several buses daily travel from Colón to the tiny town that is the jumping-off point for the island (a 10-minute, $1 boat trip). Take the bus for Colón to Sabanitas, where you can catch a bus to the island, or to Portobelo, where there is plenty to see while waiting for the next Isla Grande bus.

BEACHES OFF THE PAN-AMERICAN HIGHWAY

A couple of hours west of Panama City along the Pan-American Highway are some nice beaches, which are traditionally the domain of Panamanian families, who come in droves on holidays and dry-season weekends to picnic and watch their kids romp on the sand. Buses heading west from Panama City leave from the main piquera (called Curundú) regularly; those to Santiago, Penonomé, Chitré, Las Tablas, and Aguadulce pass the entrances to all beaches listed below (2–3 hrs, $2–$3). However, most of the beaches are a 20- or 30-minute walk from the highway, so if you don't rent a car, bring good shoes and a light load.

Hotels here aren't cheap, but outside of the holiday season, prices are often negotiable. Because prices go up on the weekend, it's best to come during the week, when the cheaper rooms are complemented by greater solitude. Camping is not permitted at many beaches, the exceptions being **Corons, Santa Clara,** and **El Farallon.**

SAN CARLOS

Less than two hours west of Panama City on the Pan-American Highway, this cute little village has everything you could want, from a supermarket to tons of bizarre shrines to Jesus and the Virgin Mary. The partially black-sand beach is a pleasant 10-minute walk from town. On one half of the beach, IPAT's huge contrived *turicentro* charges admission ($6–$8 for a palapa on the beach), which includes lunch and soda. To get in, you walk through a giant hut with a huge cement replica of a pre-Columbian jaguar over the entrance—a truly bizarre creation. The other half belongs to the town council, which charges $2 per car to enter, although it's free if you're on foot. On the highway is the **Hotel San Carlos** (tel. 240–8185), which has basic rooms with a private bath and fan for $11.

PLAYA RIO MAR

Just 2 km (1 mi) past San Carlos is the entrance to this small, grey-sand beach that spends most of the year deserted. Perched on a hill with an ocean view is the **Hotel Playa Rio Mar** (tel. 240–8027), eight small cement buildings that hold two simple, air-conditioned rooms each and an open-air restaurant that overlooks the beach and swimming pool. Rooms cost $30 Monday–Thursday, and $60 on weekends, but the second night is half price, and you can probably bargain after that.

PLAYA CORONA

One of the nicest beaches in the area, Corona lies 3 km (2 mi) from the highway, about a dozen clicks past San Carlos. The **Hotel Playa Corona** (tel. 240–8037) sits on a forested ridge overlooking the beach and has an array of options, ranging from spacious suites to musty little trailers. Large standard rooms ($65) have air-conditioning, two double beds, and small fridges. Trailers go for $25 and include use of communal baths. You can pitch a tent for $10. The more nights you spend, the lower the rates.

PLAYA SANTA CLARA

This beautiful stretch of almost deserted beach faces the cross-topped Farallon islands, just offshore. Here you'll find the absolutely gorgeous **Cabañas Sirena** (tel. 993–3235), where you can get a tile-floored room with a stove, fridge, little bar, lounge, upper-story bedroom, and use of the beautiful hammocks for $77 a night; it's not too expensive if you can rustle up five people (the maximum occupancy). Bring in all your own food, because there's only one grimy beach-side comedor. You can also camp at the comedor for $3 per night (under a palapa), plus an extra $2 if you want to use their skanky bathroom and cold shower.

Just before you get to **Río Hato**, you'll cross an abandoned airstrip. Turn left on the road to **El Farallon**, formerly Noriega's most powerful base and training center (the ruins are immense and pretty creepy). IPAT wants to develop a major resort on this long, beautiful beach, but for now it's still a quiet fishing village where you'll see boats bringing in the day's catch (and vultures scarfing down the leftovers). **Hospedaje Turistico Farallon** (tel. 993–3484), located right on the beach, charges $25–$45 for simple rooms with air-conditioning and kitchenettes, some of which can fit a lot of people. The beach is clean and the people are friendly, so you should have no problem camping here, if you ask nicely.

THE AZUERO PENINSULA

The whitewashed tile-roofed houses, scrubby rolling countryside, and colonial churches and plazas of the Azuero Peninsula are a piece of old colonial Spain. It is here that Panama raised its first cry for independence from Spain (it was then a part of Colombia). The people speak with a distinctly Spanish accent, and their festivals (which feature swirling dances with masks and ribbons) have a distinctly European flavor. The pace of life here is slow; unless you come during one of the many festivals, the main attractions are the southern beaches, which offer secluded sunbathing and surfing galore.

The peninsula, considered the "cradle of national folklore," is a must-see for those interested in Panama's history and culture. Many exquisite crafts are made here, including handmade drums, ornate devil masks, fish-scale jewelry, and polleras. However, other than in the few museums and "casas artesenales," the only places to see these crafts are at festivals or in the homes of the artists. Few tourists pass this way, so just ask around and you'll find yourself led from one master's home to another, where you can watch them ply their trade and possibly even commission them to make something for you.

GETTING AROUND

One main road runs south through the Azuero Peninsula, originating at the intersection with the Pan-American Highway, just west of the town of Divisa (about 32 km or 20 mi east of Santiago). In the unlikely event you find someone who uses street names, they might call this road Avenida Nacional. Buses regularly head down it to Chitré, Las Tablas, and Pedasí, and minibuses connect those small cities to outlying towns. The peninsula's main routes are well marked, making navigation easy for travelers who rent cars. If you bus out into the sticks, be sure to ask your driver when buses return; some places (like Playa Venado) are serviced only once a day.

FESTIVALS

Throughout the year, the Azuero Peninsula's towns and cities throw festivals where you can enjoy traditional music, dance, and costume. The most famous is **Carnaval,** which is celebrated all over, but particularly in Las Tablas) in February and March. Other big-name festivals include:

January 19–23: San Sebastián in Ocú, considered the most "typical" fair with costumes, music, and dance.

April 26–May 2: The Feria de Azuero in Los Santos.

May and June: Corpus Christi, which takes place 60 days after Easter and features the "dance of the devils."

June 24: San Juan Bautista in Chitré.

July 20: Santa Librada in Las Tablas. This is where you'll see the pollera, the national dress, being worn most frequently.

August 15: Ocú's Manito Festival features typical music, folk dancing, and horse parades.

September 24: Festival de la Mejorana in Guararé.

October 19: Celebration of the founding of Chitré.

November 10: The "first cry for independence" is celebrated in Los Santos.

The Panama City side of the canal is called the "boca," or mouth in Spanish. As one Panamanian resident quips, "Like most animals, the canal has a mouth at one end and a colon at the other."

CHITRÉ AND LOS SANTOS

Chitré and its neighboring town, Los Santos, throw more parties than your average fraternity. People from all over the country rendezvous here for the famous fêtes. Although most festivals take place in Los Santos, accommodations are more abundant in nearby Chitré (4 km or 2½ mi away).

BASICS

At the **INTEL** building (Av. Perez, at Belarmino Oriola, tel. 996–2355) in Chitré, make international calls and attend to your mail needs daily 8 AM–9 PM. Call **police** (tel. 996–4333), **fire** (tel. 103), or the **hospital** (tel. 996–4444) in an emergency.

COMING AND GOING

Chitré, about 96 km (60 mi) south of Divisa, is a transportation hub for the peninsula: you can catch buses to almost every town from the terminals near the cathedral. To get to Los Santos, you can either walk about 20 minutes along Avenida Nacional, or catch a bus (10 min, 20¢). **Tuasa** (near central plaza, tel. 996–2661) has eight buses departing for Panama City (4 hrs, $6) 7–5. Buses for Santiago (90 min, $3) and Aguadulce (2 hrs, $3) leave fairly often from the end of Calle Manuel M. Correa near the Banco Nacional.

WHERE TO SLEEP

If you plan to come here for Carnaval, make reservations well in advance. Most of the area's hotels and pensiónes are clustered around Chitré's Avenida Herrera.

UNDER $10 • Pensión Herrerana. Although pretty basic, this place has some of the cheapest clean rooms in town; they charge a mere $5 per person with a communal bath ($6 per person with private bath). *4072 Av. Herrera, tel. 996–4356. 2 blocks west of cathedral. 16 rooms, 13 with bath. No credit cards.*

PANAMANIAN HAT COUTURE

The hats preferred by Panamanian campesinos are finely woven "sombreros pintados" (straw hats) with black stripes. You can tell where someone comes from by the way they bend their sombrero. In Los Santos, for example, the front and back rims are turned up, while in Penonomé, the rim is worn down. Most hats are made in the tiny villages of Coclé, Herrera, and Los Santos, where women weave "bellota" (a fine straw) around a wooden plug that forms the crown of the hat. Loosely woven hats can be as cheap as $5 while more intricate, finer hats can sell for up to $250.

UNDER $20 • Hotel El Prado. For just $14 a single or $18 a double you'll have cold drinking water (taken to your room), fresh towels, hot running water, a TV, a fan, and even a little balcony. A few more bucks gets you air-conditioning. There's also a nice little second-story restaurant/lounge where you can sit and watch the activity on the avenida below. *3946 Av. Herrera, tel. 996–4620. 1 block west of cathedral. 25 rooms with bath. No credit cards.*

Hotel La Villa. Located on the western edge of Los Santos, this country-style hotel has seen better days but is quite a deal. Spacious doubles with private baths and fans start at $16.50, ($24 with air-conditioning) and include the use of the swimming pool. It also holds the town disco, which means it can get a bit noisy on weekends. *5 blocks west of highway (follow signs), tel. 966–9321. 38 rooms with bath. No credit cards.*

Hotel Santa Rita. Second-floor rooms overlooking the street here are bright, with big windows and high ceilings; some even have tiny balconies. The down side could be the cold-water showers and, at certain hours, street noise. A double with a private bath costs $15 ($11 for a single). *Av. Herrera at Calle Manuel María Correa, tel. 996–4610. 12 rooms with bath. No credit cards.*

FOOD

Café y Restaurante Chiquito. Right behind the cathedral, where buses depart for Las Tablas, Chiquito serves up a good selection of Panamanian food. They also offer everything on the menu of the adjacent, air-conditioned China Internacional, from fried wontons to bok choy and fish in black bean sauce. Most meals are less than $5 and scrumptious. Top it off with a cookies 'n' cream shake for $1. *Av. Herrera, tel. 996–0408. 1 block behind cathedral.*

Productos Manolos. Most popular for its pizzas, which can be ordered to go or by the slice, Manolos also has a cafeteria line, a small menu of Mexican and Chinese dishes, and an array of fresh baked goods. *Calle Manuel María Correa, tel. 996–5668. 2 blocks from Museo Herrera.*

WORTH SEEING

In Chitré, **Museo de Herrera** (Av. Manuel M. Correa, at Parque La Bandera, tel. 996–0077) has some good displays of pre-Columbian pottery and regional clothing. Come here to see the polleras and incredible devil masks used in festivals. Admission is 25¢ and all signs are in Spanish.

Los Santos' Parque Central is dominated by the **Church of Augustinas and Anastasias,** one of the oldest churches in Panama. The **Museo de la Nacionalidad,** housed in an impressive colonial building also overlooking the Parque Central, contains a small collection of religious art, antique tools, and household utensils; check out the museum's meticulously tended garden (closed Sunday afternoon and Monday). The **Humboldt Ecological Station,** a refuge for migratory birds, is at Playa El Aguillito, a 20-minute bus ride from Chitré.

LAS TABLAS

It's hard to believe this quiet community some 24 km (15 mi) south of Chitré is home to the most raging Carnaval party in Panama. Fifty-one weeks out of the year, Las Tablas is a small colonial town without much going for it except its church, **Santa Librada,** which sports a painted gold altar and the title of national monument.

If you come for Carnaval, don't expect to find housing at the last minute. Make reservations far in advance, even if you're planning to stay in Chitré and bus into Las Tablas. Wear clothes you don't mind getting drenched with water, booze, and paint. This is a five-day humdinger, in which Chitré consumes its weight in Seco (the 40-proof domestic liquor sold at the bargain price of $8 per half-gallon). The town divides into two sides, an "up street" and a "down street," for the ensuing four-day competition. Las Tablas also hosts the **Festival de Santa Librada,** also known as "fiesta de la pollera" after the traditional dress, on July 20. The pollera party isn't nearly as hedonistic a melee as Carnaval, but there is something appealing about seeing people dressed in intricately woven, colorful clothing.

COMING AND GOING

Buses to Las Tablas (1 hr, $1) depart from behind the cathedral in Chitré. Buses leave for Chitré from the edge of town, on Avenida Nacional toward the hospital. The last bus for Chitré leaves at 7 PM, but get on it early (around 6:45) or risk being stuck in Las Tablas.

Panama hats aren't made in Panama at all—they're from Ecuador. Ante-canal, almost all South American goods came north via Panama. So Teddy Roosevelt and his cronies, when asked where they got those cool hats, responded "Panama," and the name stuck.

WHERE TO SLEEP AND EAT

One of the cheapest places to stay is **Pensión Marta** (off Av. Central, at Glidden store, tel. 994–6547), which has simple, clean rooms with fans for $8 and a manager who considers guests a nuisance in her life. The much nicer **Hotel Piamonte** (Av. Central, tel. 994–6372) has air-conditioning, hot water, and private baths for $14 a single ($19 a double), and a popular restaurant downstairs. The best food in town, however, is found at **Restaurante El Caserón** (Calle Augustín Batista, at Av. Moises Espino), which serves such unusual delicacies as *pollo tabogana* (chicken in a plum, grape, and pineapple sauce) for a mere $4.

OUTDOOR ACTIVITIES

Beaches are the best hangouts in the area, although you'll probably have to endure a lengthy bus ride to get to one. One good choice is **Playa Venado** (the "d" is silent), a surf haven about 64 km (40 mi) from Las Tablas on the southern tip of the peninsula. The only bus leaves Las Tablas (2 hrs) daily around 2:30 PM and returns in the morning, but the schedule depends on whether there are enough passengers to make the trip worthwhile; you may have to wait. Cabañas that sleep up to three people (and an indefinite number of unobtrusive frogs) go for $11 per night. You can also camp for free on the beach; ask the owners, but they'll probably say it's okay. Surfers, unless they bring their own boards, have to rely on the kindness of others for a loan, because rentals haven't caught on yet. Weekends are the best time to find other surfers. Santa Catalina, in the province of Veraguas, comes highly recommended by local surfers.

CHIRIQUÍ

Ask any Panamanian to name the most beautiful region of Panama and he or she is likely to say Chiriquí. Although its rolling lowlands are similar to what you'll find on the Azuero Peninsula, its two highland valleys are incredibly lush and refreshingly cool areas where the scenery might have you imagining you're in the Alps, till the squawking of parakeets snaps you back to reality. Panama City's wealthy have long been heading to Boquete and the surrounding area to pick strawberries and frolic in the crisp, clean air outside their vacation cottages. But foreign travelers all too often buzz through Chiriquí without even stopping. Those who do take the time to experience the province's cool cloud forests, sweeping vistas, raging white water rivers, and charming people invariably find themselves wishing they had more time to hang around.

DAVID

The capital of Chiriquí province, this is western Panama's biggest city. Hot and grimy, it serves as the region's major transportation hub. Buses regularly depart from David for the mountain towns of Cerro Punta and Boquete, while several rent-a-car agencies are available for those who prefer to drive. So unless you get there late, or have to catch an early bus or flight, you're best off heading straight for the hills. Although David appears sprawling on a map, the city center is fairly compact. **Parque Cervantes** (between Av. 3 Este and Av. 4 Este, Calle A Norte and Calle B Norte) is roughly the center of town; all practicalities lie within several blocks. Few of the streets are marked, and locals don't know them by name. The **Feria Internacional de David** (week of March 19) is one of the biggest in the country, with carnival rides, rodeos, and traditional music and dance—one of the few times you may want to stay in this town, but it won't be easy to find a room. Kill time between buses at the **Museo José de Obaldía** (Av. 8 Este, tel. 775–7839), a tiny museum full of religious icons, housed in the old home of Chiriquí's founder. Admission is 25¢, and it's open Tuesday–Saturday 8:30–4:30.

BASICS

For an **ambulance** dial 775–2162, for **fire department** 103, or for **police** 104. Make international calls at **Cable & Wireless** (Calle B Norte, 1 block from Parque Cervantes, tel. 775–0369) daily 8 AM–9:30 PM. The **post office** (between Av. 4 and Av. 5, tel. 775–4136) is open weekdays 7–5:45, Saturday 7–4:45. The regional **tourist office** (2nd Floor, Edificio Gahlerna, on Av. 3 across from Parque Cervantes, tel. 775–4120) has free maps of David. **Farmacia Gonzales Ruiz** (Calle C Norte, tel. 775–3519) is open 24 hours.

COMING AND GOING

BY BUS • The bus terminal, the hub for all points near David, lies at the northern end of Avenida 2 Este-Cincuentenario, on Avenida del Estudiante north of Avenida Obaldiá. It's a 15-minute walk (or a $1 cab ride) from Parque Cervantes. From the terminal, **Padafront** (tel. 774–9205) buses depart every hour or two for Panama City (7 hrs, $10). The bus for San José, Costa Rica (8 hrs, $12.50), leaves from **Tracopa** (tel. 775–0585) at 8:30 AM. Buses coming from San José to David depart daily at 7:30 AM. Remember that Costa Rica is one hour behind Panama.

BY PLANE • **Aeroperlas** (Panama City, tel. 263–5363; David, tel. 775–4362) has several flights daily for Panama City ($55 one way) and five flights per week to Bocas del Toro and San José, Costa Rica. **Mapiex** (Panama City, tel. 270–2792; David, tel. 775–0812) has several flights daily to Panama City. The **Malek Airport** is about 4 km (2½ mi) outside David; a taxi from Parque Cervantes ($2) is your only transportation option.

WHERE TO SLEEP

David's accommodations are better value than what comparable digs would run you in Panama City. If you want to attend the annual feria (see above), you'll want to book well in advance or stay in nearby Boquete.

Hotel Alcala. This new hotel near the market may have little in the way of personality, but its clean, modern rooms have all the amenities, including cable TV, air-conditioning, and tacky art on the walls, all for $24 a double. There's a restaurant next to the lobby and a parking lot out back. Av. 3 Este, Calle D Norte, tel. 774–9018. 57 rooms with bath.

Hotel Iris. Dog-eared as it may be, the Hotel Iris has plenty of good attributes; a convenient location across from Parque Cervantes; clean rooms with hot water baths, telephones, fans, and a TV; and a cost of $12 a single and $15 a double ($18 with air-conditioning). Calle A Norte, across from Cervantes Park, tel. 775–2251. 62 rooms with bath.

Pensión Costa Rica. Located just two blocks from Parque Centenario, this place doesn't offer a whole lot of privacy or space, but you get what you pay for. Labyrinthine hallways of wood and stucco lead to clean rooms with fans for only $4 a single ($6.50 with bath) and $9 a double ($12 with bath). You can pay a little extra for a private bath. Calle 5, at Av. 5 Este, tel. 775–1241. 50 rooms, 40 with private bath.

FOOD

David has few places that offer much beyond the basic menu found everywhere outside Panama City: con pollo (chicken), con puerco (pork), or con carne (meat). Reap the benefits of the great fruit and veggie **market** on the corner of Calle D Norte and Avenida 2 Este, two blocks north of Parque Cervantes.

Cafetería La Campiña. This cafeteria serves decent breakfasts (scrambled eggs for 80¢) and the basic meat, rice, and vegetable lunches for $2–$3. Locals head here for the *sancocho* (chicken soup) or to sit sipping coffee, reading newspapers, and enjoying the air-conditioning. *Calle 3, tel. 774–5695. In front of Banco General.*

Churrasco's Place. One of the few places in David open 24 hours a day, its tables are sheltered from the street by a little tropical foliage. For additional air-conditioned comfort, head up the back stairs to cool your heels in the bar. The *churrasco* (a barbecued beef steak) comes with a fresh salad and fries for $5. *Av. 2 Este, tel. 774–0412. Next to Mister Pollo, 2 blocks from Parque Cervantes.*

Pizzeria Hotel Nacional. Located across the street from the venerable hotel for which it was named, this large, sterile eatery serves everything from *chicharón de calamar* (deep-fried squid) to lasagna, but the pizza is definitely your best bet. *Calle Central at Av. Central, tel. 775–1042.*

OUTDOOR ACTIVITIES

Balneario Majagua is a pleasant waterfall along the river where you can escape the afternoon heat. You can even camp here for free. Take a Boquete-bound bus (10 min, 40¢) and ask to be let off at the *balneario.* **ANCON** (on road to Boquete, tel. 744–6020) provides information on the natural wonders of Chiriquí. They're open weekdays 8–noon and 2–4. Call **INRENARE** (tel. 775–2055) if you are headed to Parque Internacional La Amistad or Volcán Barú for info on required permits.

The 1st and 15th of each month are big party days in Panama, because that's when most people receive their paychecks.

BOQUETE

Boquete is a tranquil, traditional town set at the bottom of a vast, verdant valley in the mountains north of David. Overshadowed by dormant Barú Volcano, the region is famous for its strong coffee, juicy oranges, and abundant flowers. Panamanians head here to revel in the cool mountain air (extremely refreshing after the heat of David), but Boquete has plenty more to offer than an agreeable climate. The valley holds enough trails and rural roads to keep you hiking for weeks on end, and the mosaic of farms and forest provides excellent bird-watching—the upper slopes are home to such rare birds as the resplendent quetzal and the three-wattled bellbird. Trails lead into the forest along boulder-strewn streams to hidden waterfalls or unforgettable vistas. If you're willing to undergo some strenuous hiking, do the all-day climb to the summit of Barú Volcano, where you'll be rewarded with an amazing view of the surrounding countryside, the Pacific Ocean and, on those rare clear days, the Caribbean.

Besides the lush fields of sunflowers, geraniums, roses, and other flowers, you'll see row upon row of coffee plants as you walk the outlying roads of Boquete. Flower fetishists are drawn by the town's **Festival de Flores y Café** held annually in mid-January, but the fairgrounds' flower beds can be admired any time of year. Flower gardens abound in Boquete, although none are as extensive, and bizarre, as **Mi Jardin es su Jardin,** the private garden of an eccentric millionaire that is open to the public (just north of town on main road). If you're on the north side of town, be sure to take the free, 15-minute tour of the **Cafe Ruiz** coffee processing plant (north Boquete, tel. 720–1392), which produces a staggeringly wide assortment of gourmet blends and flavors. It's open Monday to Saturday. If you're really interested in coffee, you can take a more extensive tour, which includes a visit to the Ruiz family coffee farm; it's free, but you have to reserve at least half a day ahead of time.

BASICS

Banco Nacional (Av. Los Fundadores, tel. 720–1328) changes traveler's checks and is open weekdays 8–3 and Saturday 8–noon. Clean your drawers at **Lavamático Mar de Plata** in front of the church (open Mon.–Sat. 8–6, Sun. 8–noon). You'll find the **post office** as well as some good **phones** in the municipio on the central plaza. For visitor information and a great view of Boquete, check out the new **visitor's center** on the hill south of town.

COMING AND GOING

Buses from David ($1.25) stop at Parque Domingo Médica (a.k.a. Parque Central) in the center of town. The main road from David, (Avenida Los Fundadores) branches into two main loops above town that wind through the mountains north of Boquete, past coffee farms, sundry small communities, and cloud forest. Vans that leave from the Casa Bruña supermarket, two blocks north of the Parque Central, go

WHITE-WATER MADNESS

Few people realize it, but two excellent rafting rivers churn their ways down valleys in the mountains of western Panama. The Chiriquí is an invigorating Class III river that approaches Class IV during the rainy season, while its cousin, the Viejo, is a consistently invigorating Class IV ride. Although some white-water experience is recommended for the Viejo, the Chiriquí River is usually easy enough for neophytes, although quite exciting. Rafting doesn't cost any less in Panama than in Costa Rica, but at least you don't have to share the river with a bunch of other paddlers. The oldest and most experienced rafting outfitter is Chiriquí River Rafting (tel. 720–1505); if you can't arrange a trip with them, try Panama Rafting (tel. 774–1236).

around either of the loops, charging $1 for most trips. There are also plenty of four-wheel-drive taxis that can take you to out-of-the-way spots for $1 to $5 a trip.

WHERE TO SLEEP

UNDER $25 • Hotel Fundadores. A creek runs right through the rambling grounds of the Hotel Fundadores, which has a decent restaurant and a basement bar complete with tiny dance floor. Doubles with private bath start at $22. *Av. Los Fundadores, in front of Texaco station, tel. 720–1298. 37 rooms with bath.*

Pensión Marilos. This small, family-run place is one of the best deals in Panama. Super-clean, comfortable, quiet rooms cost $10 for two people ($16 with bath), and use of the kitchen is included. The helpful owners speak perfect English. *Av. A Este, at Calle 6 Sur (across from Hotel Rebequet), tel. 720–1380. 7 rooms, 5 with bath. No credit cards.*

Pensión Topaz. Another family operation, the Topaz has large, attractive rooms with private baths for $26 a double, as well as two smaller rooms that share a separate bath for $16. Most rooms open onto a covered patio where optional breakfasts are served; there's even a small pool. *Behind Texaco station, tel. 720–10. 5 rooms, 4 with bath. No credit cards.*

UNDER $30 • Hotel Rebequet. Spacious rooms with parquet floors, private baths, and small refrigerators cost $30 a double ($20 single) and include the use of a communal kitchen. *Calle 6 Sur, at Av. A Este. (look for sign on Av. Central), tel. 720–1365. 9 rooms with bath. No credit cards.*

UNDER $70 • Villa Marita. This collection of charming bungalows spread along a ridge high above Boquete may be a splurge, but you get what you pay for. Bungalows can sleep up to three for $66 (the second night is $55); each one has a bedroom, a separate sitting room with a single bed that doubles as a couch, and big windows to take advantage of the gorgeous view. *3 km (2 mi) north of Boquete, tel. 720–2164. 6 bungalows with bath.*

FOOD

Pizzeria La Volcanica. Build your own pie at this simple pizzeria, where you pay according to the size, no matter how many ingredients you want on it. They also serve roast chicken and a few other dishes. *Av. B Este, tel. 720–1857. Behind police station. Closed Mon.*

Punto de Encuentro. At the Punto de Encuentro, a small café on the porch of a private home, the charming owner serves an excellent selection of inexpensive breakfasts. *Calle 6 Sur, just off Av. Central, no phone.*

Restaurante La Conquista. This simple restaurant in the heart of town serves hearty lunch specials, often typical Panamanian dishes, complete with soup or salad for $2.25. Or spring for the local specialty, *trucha* (trout) prepared in a mouth-watering butter-garlic-celery sauce ($6.50). *Av. Los Fundadores, tel. 720–1864. 1 block south of central plaza.*

NEAR BOQUETE

If you're feeling adventurous, you can try the following excursions on your own. If you can get a few people together it's worthwhile to hire a guide who will help you get a lot more out of your hike. The public transportation vans that make the loops above town pass countless dirt roads that head higher into the hills, all of which are worthy hiking and bird-watching routes. **Expediciones Tierras Altas** (2 blocks west of Texaco station, tel. 720–1342) offers half a dozen guided trips through the cloud forest to waterfalls and areas where you're likely to spot quetzals, as well as tours to Caldera and the summit of Barú Volcano. They also offer a guided hike from Cerro Punta to Boquete on the Sendero los Quetzales, which includes transportation from Cerro Punta and pick-up in the hills above Boquete. Most of their tours cost $50–$75 for a guide and transportation, which is a deal if you get four people together.

PARQUE NACIONAL VOLCÁN BARÚ

Barú Volcano, Panama's only volcano (now extinct), is also the country's highest peak at 11,467 ft. The climb up is tough, the air is thin, and the view from the top is often obscured by fog— but on a clear day you can see spectacular jungle-covered mountains falling into both oceans. **Expediciones Tierras Altas** (*see above*) can take you up to the summit to watch the sunrise for $120 (up to four people), or will provide transportation to and from the park entrance and a guide for the hike ($45 for up to four people; around 12 hours). The hike takes you through lush cloud forest, home for all kinds of birds, but the barren summit holds an ominous communications installation that serves the whole country. If you want to spend the night near the peak, be prepared for wet, extremely cold weather. The campsite, 1–2 km (½–1 mi) down the road from the summit (look for the CAMPAMENTO sign), offers shelter from the wind. Call INRENARE (tel. 775–2055) for the lowdown on camping permits.

Most people of African descent here speak Guari Guari, an autochthonous mix of creole English and Spanish that can be tough to follow. Thankfully, they address foreigners in an English more akin to the queen's.

EL EXPLORADOR

This is Latin American kitsch at its finest. Meandering paths lead you past painted Snoopies, Charlie Browns, and Woodstocks spouting gems of wisdom like "Happiness has to be cultivated, like the art of playing the violin." Every turn brings a surprise, from the recycled butterfly-shaped speakers to the old televisions filled with dolls. The place *is* cheesy, but the views of Boquete are spectacular and the *trapezios* (huge rope swings) confirm the old adage: flirtation with death is an affirmation of life. *In hills above Boquete, tel. 720–1989. Take van from Casa Bruña, then walk ½ km (¼ mi) along dirt road. Admission $1. Open weekends.*

CALDERA

The village of Caldera, nestled amid a surreal landscape of palm trees and giant black-lava rocks, is famous for **Las Piedras Pintadas**: a set of cool petroglyphs carved into a huge black stone at the far end of a lava field. Farther out of town are **Las Aguas Termales**, a grouping of tiny hot springs. To reach these natural bathing pools, you must take about a 45-minute hike along a dirt path; once there, immerse yourself in the knee-deep water for around 10 minutes at a time (any longer and you may burn yourself). Buses from Boquete to Caldera (45 min, $1.25) leave from near the central park. Buses from David ($1.50) take about an hour. The last bus for David out of Caldera leaves at 2 PM. There are no hotels in Caldera.

CERRO PUNTA

This gorgeous, highland agricultural community surrounded by forested mountains can get *cold*—you'll be sorry if you don't bring a thick sweater or jacket—but the scenery more than makes up for any discomfort. It's not only the climate that's jarringly alpine, the landscape sometimes evokes the Alps, and

THE CERRO PUNTA–BOQUETE TRAIL

The towns of Cerro Punta and Boquete lie about 24 km (15 mi) apart as the crow flies, but the hiking trail that connects the towns is anything but direct, winding its way over the back side of Barú Volcano through a cloud forest that holds dozens of rare bird species, including the resplendent quetzal. People usually hike from Cerro Punta to Boquete, which means walking mostly downhill. The footpath itself winds though the forest from Alto Quiel, which can be reached in a four-wheel-drive taxi from Cerro Punta, to Bajo Mono, which sits high above Boquete, making it important to have someone to pick you up on that side. The trail is poorly marked, which is why most people hire a guide. Juan Fernandez (tel. 771–2233), in Cerro Punta, often leads hikers along the trail, and Expediciones Tierras Altas (tel. 720–1342) provides a guide and transportation for hikers staying in Boquete. Bring rain gear, plenty of water, and something to eat.

the town was founded by immigrants from central and eastern Europe, who left the countryside speckled with chalets. As incongruous as some of the details may be, the valley is spectacularly verdant, and the amazing scenery—horse pastures, flower gardens, rocky peaks, and patches of cloud forest—is often shrouded in mist or topped by a rainbow.

For outdoor enthusiasts, this place is a dream. The valley sits between Parque Internacional La Amistad (PILA) and Parque Nacional Volcán Barú, two vast protected areas that hold lush forests and a wealth of wildlife. Those parks are incredibly devoid of tourists; if beds are available, you can stay at PILA for free—the next morning, you might even find yourself invited on a hunt for jaguar tracks. For a spectacular view, climb the limestone monolith that gives the town its name; if you prefer a less strenuous option, stroll past the valley's many flower gardens, check out some of the resident bird life, or visit the phenomenal orchid collection at Finca Dracula.

BASICS

There's a tiny clinic and pharmacy in Cerro Punta, but you're better off taking care of business down the hill in Volcán. Everything is conveniently located in a large building right where the road turns up to Cerro Punta: **Clínica Medico-Dental Alfa** offers $7 consultations daily 2–7 PM (24 hrs in emergencies, tel. 771–4963); next door is **Farmacia Don Bosco** (tel. 771–4317), open daily 8–8. Change traveler's checks at **Banco del Istmo** (next to pharmacy) weekdays 8–3:30, Saturday 9–noon.

Amisconde (tel. 771–2171), which is open weekdays 8–noon and 2–5, a conservation group working in and around La Amistad, provides maps and information about Barú and PILA—in English! Stop by their artists' cooperative, Zorzal, down the hill from the main road; their office lies a little farther down the road.

COMING AND GOING

Buses from David to Cerro Punta (90 min, $3) follow the loop created by Calle Principal and Calle Central, which intersect in town and then again several miles away. Buses are $1 from Volcán.

WHERE TO SLEEP

Cerro Punta has a more limited selection than Boquete, but it does have some interesting options. All you usually need is a sleeping bag to stay at the PILA ranger station (*see* Near Cerro Punta, *below*); there may even be a bed available. Los Quezales offers more expensive, and more comfortable, options for staying in or near the park, and if you can get four or five people together, it won't be too expensive to sleep at one of the accommodations inside the cloud forest at Los Quetzales.

Hotel Cerro Punta. Located in the town of Cerro Punta, this older, pleasant hotel has small, clean rooms with views of the surrounding valley ($22 single, $27.50 double with hot water and private bath) and a good little restaurant. The staff and owners are extremely pleasant and will delight in telling you about the many attractions in and around town. *Cerro Punta, tel. 771–2020. 10 rooms with bath.*

Los Quetzales. There are several lodging options available at this novel ecotourism resort: two houses inside the PILA, two-bedroom cabañas at the edge of the cloud forest, and a hotel a short hike from it, in the community of Guadelupe. A double in Guadelupe costs $28 and lies close to the pizzeria and bakery, while the cabañas ($55) have fully equipped kitchens; you have to bring in your own food, but they'll sell you fresh trout. The houses rent for $100, but they sleep between five and 10 people and are surrounded by cloud forest where you may spot quetzals and other rare birds. *Barrio Guadelupe, tel. 771–2182. 10 rooms, 2 cabañas, 2 houses with bath.*

Pension La Primavera. Here you'll find mushy beds in musty rooms for $12.50 with communal bath, $15.50 with private bath. It does have a nice garden with a little tram that leads to a big tree house (the "honeymoon suite") at the back. No lack of ambience here! The only problem is that the woman who owns it sometimes leaves town for several days at a time, shutting down the whole place. *Down hill from center of town, no phone. 5 rooms, 3 with bath.*

At the Mangrove Inn office (see below) you can pick up the free newsletter, "Islas de Bocas," published by local diving expert Angel Gonzales Diaz. That simple publication includes a local map and gobs of useful info.

FOOD

M . . . Mama Lolas (tel. 771–2053), down the hill from the main drag on the right-hand side, has great pizzas on soft french bread, homemade yogurt with fresh fruit, and scrumptious strawberry and raspberry shakes. On a chilly evening, try a *chocoña* (hot chocolate with cognac) for 90¢. They are open daily 8–7. The restaurant at the **Hotel Cerro Punta** (*see* Where to Sleep, *above*) offers typical Panamanian fare for $3–$5 a plate; the best deals are the hearty lunch specials. Los Quetzales (*see* Where to Sleep, *above*) has a pizzeria and a large restaurant upstairs, although it usually opens only weekends.

WORTH SEEING

Jardín Mary (tel. 771–2003), in Barrio Guadalupe, is a lovely, family-run garden where a colorful collection of flowers blooms year-round. The nearby **Haras Cerro Punta** horse ranch has some beautiful animals; they sometimes offer free tours. **Finca Dracula** (tel. 771–2223), located above Barrio Guadalupe on the road to Los Quetzales, is a small, private farm that has the largest collection of orchids in Central America. For a $5 donation, they'll give a guided tour that includes lots of information about local species and orchid propagation and a chance to see dozens of rare and beautiful flowers.

NEAR CERRO PUNTA

PARQUE INTERNACIONAL LA AMISTAD

PILA, or International Friendship Park, is so named because it encompasses parts of both Panama and Costa Rica. At the main intersection in Cerro Punta, a sign directs you down Calle Central; from there, another sign points you toward the park entrance, about 6 km (4 mi) north in the mountains. If you don't have a car, it's best to hire a taxi to the park entrance (about $3). You can stay overnight with a permit from the INRENARE office in David (tel. 775–7840 or 775–4937). Officially, you're supposed to get a permit just to visit the park, but few people bother with that detail. An easier way to visit is to take a guided tour at Los Quetzales (*see* Where to Sleep, *above*), which costs a few dollars per person for nonguests.

BOCAS DEL TORO

The white-sand beaches, forest-covered islands, and laid-back pace of "Bocas" (as the region is referred to by locals) make it one of the most fulfilling destinations in Panama. Located in the far northwestern corner of the country—and connected by only one long road to the capital—Bocas del Toro is one of the most isolated provinces in the interior. For those visiting from Costa Rica, however, it is a short jaunt from the beaches along the Caribbean coast and only seven hours from San José. It follows that you will probably find more budget tourists here than in the rest of Panama *combined*.

Most people come to Bocas to snorkel and dive in and around Bastimentos Marine Park, Panama's first underwater wildlife sanctuary—home to mangroves, spectacular reefs, and long, deserted beaches used as nesting sites by several species of endangered sea turtles. The park covers just a few of the dozens of islands scattered around Chiriquí Lagoon, the most striking geographic feature of the province. The region includes vast expanses of virgin forest, protected in La Amistad National Park and Palo Seco Forest Reserve, as well as the territory of the Teribe, Bokota, and Bugle (Guaymi) Indians, most of whom still live in stilted houses in tiny villages that line the rivers that flow out of the Talamanca Mountains. Bocas has almost no roads and, except for the lowlands just near the coast, is completely undeveloped.

Expect to meet some of the friendliest folk in all of Panama in the towns of Bocas del Toro, Bastimentos, and Almirante. These folk are largely the descendants of Jamaicans, who were brought here to work on the banana plantations. Almost everyone here is in some way tied to the banana business. For an enlightening, if not lighthearted, look at the history of the industry, check out Clyde Stephens's book *Bananeros in Central America,* which you should be able to find for sale at Las Brisas (*see* Where to Sleep, *below*).

The provincial capital, located on the island of Colón, is called Bocas del Toro (Bocas Town); the other major towns are Almirante, a banana port on the mainland, and Changuinola, the ultimate ugly banana town. Chiriquí Grande, a tiny port town to the east, used to be at the end of the road into the province, where a ferry departed for Almirante and Bocas del Toro, but since the completion of a coastal road to Almirante, it is much less of a transportation hub.

BASICS

If you're coming from Costa Rica, change your colones in Guabito or Changuinola with someone in the street or marketplace—*none* of the banks in the province will accept them. You can, however, change U.S. traveler's checks at most banks during normal banking hours (weekdays 9–3, Sat. 9–1). Ring 103 in case of **fire** and 104 for **police.** The town of Bocas has several phones from which you can make international calls collect or with a calling card. Mail is faster out of San José or Panama City, so hang on to those postcards.

COMING AND GOING

Most travelers enter the province by bus or boat, but it can be much quicker to fly. **Aeroperlas** (tel. 269–4555 in Panama City, 757–9341 in Bocas) has direct flights daily from Panama City ($47 one way) and David, and several times a week from San José, Costa Rica.

BY BUS • Union de Buses Panamericano (Pueblo Nuevo, Vía Fernandez de Cordova, next to Restaurante La Felicidad, tel. 229–6333) runs direct buses from Panama City to Changuinola (9 hrs, $27). At press time, departures were daily at 11 PM (9:30 AM from Chaguinola), because the buses were still boarding a daily ferry at Chiriquí Grande, but the completion of the road to Almirante implies changes in bus schedules and frequency, so you'll have to call. Minibuses depart Canguinola every 20 minutes for Almirante, from where water taxis head to the town of Bocas about once an hour. Buses leave from Changuinola for Panama City at 7 AM. Buses leave from Changuinola for San José, Costa Rica (7 hrs, $8), at 10 AM daily. There are also half a dozen buses per day between David and Changuinola (5 hrs, $9).

BY BOAT • A car ferry makes the one-hour trip between Almirante and Bocas town every day, but unless you're driving, you'll want to take a **water taxi:** small motorboats that make the same trip in about 20 minutes. Water taxis run hourly from sunup to sundown and charge $3 each way between Almirante and Bocas, and if there are enough people, they make a stop at Bastimentos. A free, though slow, alternative is the fruit-company ferry, which runs twice a day from a small pier in Almirante, right near the abandoned train station, and heads to both the towns of Bocas and Bastimentos (Mon.–Sat. 5 AM and 5 PM). Private dugouts sporadically make the trip between the towns of Bocas and Bastimentos, charging $2 each way.

WHERE TO SLEEP AND EAT

Focus your stay on the towns of Bocas del Toro and Bastmentos, both of which are within walking distance of nice beaches. An array of interesting accommodations are available in both towns, often in old wooden buildings or private homes. Except in the more expensive places, expect cold-water showers, which are actually perfect for this climate.

It's said by some that the name Panamá comes from the Kuna "bannaba" (far away)—the response Kunas would give (while pointing to the thickest and most inhospitable jungle) when the Spanish asked where their villages were.

BOCAS TOWN

Connected to the rest of Isla Colón (a large, sparsely inhabited island) by a causeway, Bocas del Toro is picturesque in a ramshackle sort of way. It's the capital of the province and has plenty of affordable lodging and dining options and basically functions as a base for exploring the surrounding area: a playground for outdoorsy explorers that includes beautiful beaches, extensive coral reefs, rain forest, and small villages.

BASICS

The only bank in town, **Banco Nacional** (Parque Bolívar), changes traveler's checks weekdays 8–3, Saturday 9–noon. The **post office** (Parque Bolívar, tel. 757–9273) handles your basic mail, and you can make international calls at the **Cable & Wireless** office on Calle 1 (tel. 757–9308). For an **ambulance**, call 757–9201. The regional **tourist office** is housed in a small green building over the water, on Calle 3, which is the main drag. **INRENARE** (Calle 1, tel. 757–9244), which issues permits for visiting Bastimentos National Park, is located behind the park, near the fire station.

COMING AND GOING

Bocas is only accessible by boat. Water taxis leave from Almirante (25 min, $3) just about every hour from 6 AM to 6 PM. If you are driving a vehicle, you'll have to take the daily car ferry.

GETTING AROUND

You can walk to most places you need to reach in this tiny, commodious town. Calle 3a serves as the main drag, and it runs from the pier straight to Pensión Las Brisas. Basics are all located on Parque Bolívar. If you walk all the way to the end of Calles 1 or 3, you'll reach Avenida Norte, which connects the peninsula with the rest of Isla Colón—mostly undeveloped beaches and forest. If you want to explore the rest of the island, you're best off renting a bike from Las Brisas or La Ballena (*see below*).

WHERE TO SLEEP

Botel Las Brisas. No, it's not a typo; the *B* refers to the fact that you can tie your boat up to the back of this old, wooden hotel built over the water. The deck is a great place to hang out in a hammock and enjoy the ocean view. Rooms vary, but all have fans and private baths, except for two that share a bath; some have air-conditioning. More rooms are located in a similar building across the street, where the restaurant is to be found. Singles start at $8 ($13 with bath), while most doubles are around $15–$17. *Av. Norte, at end of Calle 3, tel. 757–9248. 37 rooms, 35 with bath.*

Hospedaje E. y L. It may be too close to the disco, but this mom-&-pop pensión makes up for weekend noise by making guests feel like part of the family. The friendly owners can help with travel arrangements, will let you use their kitchen, and even give Spanish classes. A spacious, clean single with bath costs $8 (doubles are $10–$12). *Calle 3, near banana-company dock, tel. 757–9206. 6 rooms with bath. No credit cards.*

Pensión Las Delicias. This second-floor pensión on the main drag has some of the cheapest accommodations in town, with singles starting at $5 ($7–$9 with bath) and doubles at $9 ($12 with bath). They're clean and centrally located, but the proximity to the local disco make this a tough place to get shut-eye on weekends. The restaurant downstairs serves cheap and tasty Creole lunches—worth hitting no matter where you sleep. *Calle 3, close to banana-company dock, tel. 757–9318. 9 rooms, 7 with bath. No credit cards.*

FOOD

Baia Paradiso. You can't miss this big, Italian restaurant across the street from the park, and you wouldn't want to. They have something for every appetite: fresh bread and pastries, an array of pizzas ($5–$10), lasagna ($5), salads, seafood, ice cream, an espresso machine, and a full bar. *Calle 3, tel. 757–9170. Closed Tues.*

Restaurante don Chicho. Also called "El Lorito," this popular local hangout serves basic "comida corriente," such as *pollo guisado* (chicken in a red sauce), *carimañolas* (meat fried in yucca paste), and thick yellow-corn tortillas, cafeteria style. It's all greasy, and many dishes start to look scary as the night drags on, but it's cheap and authentic. *Calle 3, near park, tel. 757–9288.*

Restaurante La Ballena. If you're not on a tight budget and your taste buds need a break, head for this colorful restaurant behind the Muncipal Building for a fresh salad ($3.50) and maybe even some pasta with lobster ($10). The friendly French owners also rent bikes and horses. *Av. F, between Calles 3 and 2, tel. 757–9089.*

FESTIVALS

In mid-September, Bocas celebrates the **Feria del Mar,** a huge fair held on the beach between town and the rest of the island. Like most Panamanian ferias, it is marked by dancing, parades, drunkenness, and loud music into the wee hours. If you plan on coming, be sure to make hotel reservations well in advance.

OUTDOOR ACTIVITIES

There is plenty to keep you busy in Bocas: you can rent a bike and ride up Avenida Norte to the rain forests and beaches of **Isla de Colón.** The island is connected to Bocas Town by a strip of land on the north side of which is a small beach where the annual feria is held. If you head left at the fork in the road, you will cross the island (1- to 2-hour ride) to Bocas del Drago (*see below*). If you veer right at the fork, you'll soon reach tiny Paunch Beach, where a nearby reef has some decent snorkeling. A 10-minute ride beyond Paunch is beautiful Bluff Beach (*see below*). Botel Las Brisas and Baia Paradiso both rent **kayaks** for the paddle over to nearby Carenero Island and points beyond.

The big activity in this area is **skin diving,** and Bocas Town is the departure point for half a dozen excellent scuba or snorkeling excursions. A 10-minute boat ride from town takes you to Hospital Point, one of the best dive spots in the region. You're better off scheduling a full day to hit Olas Chicas, on the north side of Isla Bastimentos, or the famous Cayos Zapatillas, protected within Parque Marino Isla Bastimentos (*see below*). The **Mangrove Inn** (tel. 757–9594), a dive resort located 10 minutes by boat from town, has a small reef just behind it and offers trips to all the area's dive spots as well as inexpensive certification courses. **Starfleet Eco-Adventures** (Calle 1, tel. 757–9630) rents scuba and snorkeling equipment and runs day trips on a small catamaran; they also offer certification courses. **Bocas Water Sports** (Calle 3, tel. 757–9541) rents snorkeling and scuba equipment and offers a similar selection of dive trips.

NEAR BOCAS TOWN

BLUFF BEACH

A gorgeous, golden-sand beach, Bluff is a short bike ride or drive north of town. From March to July, massive leatherback sea turtles crawl onto the sand at night to lay their eggs—an amazing event that can be witnessed with local guides (contact Caribaru, next to the library). By day, it's a tranquil, beautiful spot perfect for swimming and sun bathing. The Pension Las Delicias has half a dozen rustic cabañas on the beach ($3 per person) and can arrange transportation for $1; bring bottled water and food or arrange for them to cook meals.

BOCAS DEL DRAGO

This secluded beach on the western tip of the island, backed by a small fishing community, features good snorkeling and lots of tranquillity. You can reach it by crossing the island by bicycle, bus, or taxi, or on boat excursions that also visit nearby Bird Island: a seabird nesting site. A minibus makes the trip between the two Bocas ($1.50) every Monday, Wednesday, and Friday, and sometimes on weekends, leaving Bocas del Drago at 7 AM and returning around 1 PM, which implies spending a couple of nights. You can camp here for $5, or rent a bungalow with a kitchen and several beds for $28. A round-trip taxi should cost $25.

About halfway to Bocas del Drago, you'll find **La Gruta,** a small group of houses behind which (on the right) lies a path leading through several caves. You won't get lost in the caves, but you will disturb the sleeping bats and you may get wet up to the knees. Be sure to bring a flashlight and a hat to protect your head. To get back to the road, backtrack through the caves or look for the overgrown path to your right as you leave the third cave.

If you want to photograph someone, be sure to ask permission first. In more touristy areas, people will demand anywhere from 25¢ to $1 per photo.

PARQUE MARINO ISLA BASTIMENTOS

Panama's first marine park covers part of Bastimentos Island—including the sea-turtle nesting beach of Playa Larga, rain forest, and mangrove estuaries—and the two Cayos Zapatillas: idyllic islets surrounded by large coral reefs. Most people visit the Cayo Zapatillas on day trips out of Bocas Town that cost $20–$30 per person, according to the size of the group. **ANCON** (next to Pensión Las Brisas, Bocas del Toro, tel. 757–9367) has a field station on Playa Larga that sometimes takes long-term volunteers. To visit the park, you need a permit from **INRENARE** (Calle 1, tel. 757–9244), which charges $10; tours to the island stop there on the way out of town.

BASTIMENTOS

This friendly little community comprised almost entirely of Guari-Guari speakers of African descent is located on the island of the same name, 15 minutes by boat from Bocas Town. A crowded collection of wooden buildings propped up on cement posts, Bastimentos overlooks a calm bay on the southern side of the island. It's a colorful, funky little town where everyone knows everyone else's business, and people often crowd the local bars to dance the night away. There is no beach near town, and the abundance of garbage and raw sewage in the bay make it an unappetizing place for a swim, but a 20-minute walk across the island takes you to one of the province's nicest beaches, washed by crystalline waters. Bastimentos is an excellent base for snorkeling trips to Hospital Point, Olas Chicas, and other spots. You can make collect and calling-card calls from the pay phones near the public dock. The bank, clinic, and government offices are located in Bocas Town.

SAN BLAS

Also known as Kuna Yala (Conmarca de San Blas), Panama's northeastern Caribbean coast is a stretch of some of the most beautiful green-forested mountains and reef-encircled islands on Earth. It's also a trip to another cultural world. This area is owned and administered exclusively by the Kuna Indian people, who essentially run it as an autonomous republic. Here, anyone who's not Kuna (including Panamanians) is a *waga* (foreigner); from the time you step off your boat or plane, you'll be subject to the laws, folkways, and mores of the Kuna people.

HOLY MOLAS

The Kunas of San Blas are famous for their molas, many-layered hand-stitched panels (in a dizzying assortment of colors) depicting animals, mythical scenes, or abstract patterns. Kuna women wear blouses with molas on the front and back, but most are put on shirts, bags, dresses, and other touristy stuff. Some simple patches sell for as little as $1, while more complex designs can go for more than $50. Besides molas, the Kunas design intricate gold necklaces and extended bracelets, which—when wrapped around the arms and legs—form interlocking patterns.

When Christopher Columbus arrived on the Caribbean coast of Panama in 1502, most of the Kuna lived on the mainland, in what is now eastern Panama and northwestern Colombia. You'll still find some Kuna villages in the forest (like Paya in the Darién, near the Colombian border). When the Spanish began their conquest of the Americas, the Kuna managed to distance themselves and thus maintained their language and customs. Several hundred years ago, they began migrating to the islands of San Blas—this not only protected them from diseases that ravaged mainland villages (particularly malaria), but it also saved their culture and society from Spanish domination. There are now Kuna villages on about 40 of the more than 350 San Blas Islands, the rest of which are covered with either Kuna coconut plantations or jungle.

Ships from all over the world passed through San Blas, and some Kuna men crewed on New England whaling ships or traveled to France and England, where a few stayed and studied. Those early travelers established a tradition of adapting to the outside world while protecting their territory and culture. When Panama attempted to take over the Comarca in the 1920s, the Kuna rebelled, and thanks to certain backing from the U.S. military, they managed to establish an independent province that is governed by their own laws and customs. Today, Kuna Yala (Land of the Kuna), as they call San Blas, is one of the best-organized and most culturally intact Indian nations in the Americas.

A trip to San Blas is consequently exactly the kind of cross-cultural adventure that foreign travel should be. The Kuna are proud of their culture and happy to share it with outsiders, but be aware that you are expected to follow their rules while in the province, and that they demand respect for their culture and laws. Some islands won't even allow you to step off the boat, while at others you'll be asked to register with local authorities. Most people visit the western end of the province, around El Porvenir, which is regularly overrun by tourists and has consequently become pretty commercialized. Nevertheless, it still offers beautiful beaches shaded by coconut palms, superb snorkeling, and exposure to the way of life and unique culture of a fascinating people.

BASICS

Change all the money you need into cash *before* you get here; you won't find any banks in this region. If you get sick, the larger islands have **Centros de Salud,** which will patch you up for a minimal charge. There's *one* phone in the region, on the island of El Porvenir, but police stations on larger islands have radios to call for help in an emergency.

COMING AND GOING

The easiest way to get to San Blas is to fly. **ANSA** (tel. 226–7891) and **Aerotaxi** (tel. 264–8644) have daily flights to almost a dozen airstrips scattered along the coast. The closest is El Porvenir ($56 round-trip) and the farthest is Puerto Obaldia ($88 round-trip). If you plan to island-hop, you'll want to buy a one-way ticket, so you can board a plane at any of those tiny airports.

If you're thinking about hiring a private boat to go between islands, keep in mind that it's *really* expensive (it can be cheaper to wait at the airstrip and ask pilots if they can take you to nearby islands). One option for adventurers is to get off a bus heading toward the Darién at El Llano and walk two days to the airport at Carti. Midway there, you can stay at the Pemasky Lodge in Nusagandi, where you'll probably want to spend at least two nights; catch the first bus and hike hard if you want to reach it in one day. You'll have to wade across a river just before Carti, where you can catch a boat to the islands.

WHERE TO SLEEP AND EAT

The province's three best-value hotels are located on or near El Porvenir and are owned and operated by Kuna peoples. The price of a room at any one includes three meals (often fresh lobster for dinner), use of snorkeling gear, and boat trips to nearby islands for diving and sunbathing or to see villages. The cheapest, and most rustic, is the **Hotel San Blas** on the island of Nalunega (tel. 262–5410), with 15 rooms, none with bath. The property is owned by the venerable Luis Burgos, who charges $27 per person per night for a thatched hut with a sand floor or a room in a nearby building. The **Hotel Porvenir** (tel. 226–2644 or 270–1748), with eight rooms, all with bath, is located on the island of the same name, which also holds the landing strip and a Panamanian police station. They charge $35 a single ($60 a double) for small rooms with cement floors. The **Hotel Anai** (tel. 239–3025), with 30 rooms, all with bath, is on nearby Wichub Huala Island and has nicer rooms, but it charges $55 per person. A much better option in that price range is **Kuanidup** (tel. 227–7661 or 227–1396), with 10 rooms, none with bath, which charges $60 per person for thatched huts on a private island near Rio Sidra, surrounded by great snorkeling, and near communities that have seen fewer tourists than the others.

If you're adventurous, speak decent Spanish, and have lots of time, you can explore Kuna Yala on a low budget, by camping on deserted islands or staying with families. Wherever you go outside of the hotel islands, you'll have to ask permission to stay from the local *Saila* (chief). If you stay with families, you should pay them about $5 per night and prepare your stomach—Kuna food is greasy and takes some getting used to, and you'll be expected to eat lots of it.

Don't even think about hiking through the Darién on your own. Indian footpaths wind in a zillion directions, and a fair number of fugitives and Colombian drug-runners use this as their main hangout. Get a guide!

THE DARIÉN

Crisscrossed by rivers and blanketed by thick jungle, Darién is Panama's largest and most isolated province. The Pan-American Highway stops 48 km (30 mi) short of the Colombian border—this is the only break in its path from Alaska to Tierra del Fuego—and beyond it lies the Darién Gap, a wild and beautiful area that holds dozens of Indian villages and the incomparable Parque Nacional Darién, covering 1.5 million acres along the border. For the adventurer, nature-lover, or anyone interested in indigenous culture, the jungles and villages of the Darién are nonpareil.

The Darién is also home to the Waunan and Embera Indians, who live in stilt houses in villages scattered along the region's main rivers, hunting and practicing small-scale agriculture. In isolated villages, the men may still be seen wearing loincloths, while the women often go topless, wearing colorful skirts and lots of necklaces. Both men and women often paint their chests and faces with a black dye made from charcoal and plant juices, which serves both as decoration and protection from biting insects. These tribes share two *comarcas* (Indian reservations): Comarca Cemaco, to the north of the highway, and Comarca Sambú, which runs along the Sambú River in the southern part of the province. In addition to the Embera and less-numerous Waunan communities, the Darién also has a few Kuna villages (Paya, Ucurganti, and Púcuro).

The Darién's major towns are completely different from the Indian villages and are inhabited mostly by Cimarrones, Spanish-speaking descendants of slaves who escaped during the colonial era. The towns of Yaviza, La Palma, El Real, Pinogana, and Boca de Cupe are largely inhabited by Cimarrones and Latinos who have migrated from other parts of Panama or Colombia.

Some towns are accessible only by long, expensive boat rides or arduous hikes through miles of steamy jungle. Rest assured, there is a way to get to almost any town or village, although you may have to go through hell and (literally) high river water to get there.

BASICS

WHEN TO GO • The end of the rainy season, December or January, is the best time to experience the Darién, since the jungle is lush and the rivers are high enough to navigate deep into the jungle. Ticks dominate in the late dry season (Feb.–Apr.), but that's when the trails are the least muddy, and the bus may actually reach Yaviza without getting stuck in a giant mud hole. Mosquitoes are thick year-round, but worst in the rainy season, when you'll also be walking in thick mud and getting soaked to the bone by daily torrential downpours. Guides are always available ($10–$20 a day) and are recommended for jungle treks.

WHAT TO PACK • Pack as little as possible; the tropical heat makes even the smallest backpack feel like a ton of bricks. That said, you will need the following: boots (to trudge through mud) and sandals (so your feet can dry when you get there), at least two changes of clothes, bathing suit, rain poncho, insect repellent, sunscreen, flashlight, mosquito net, a tent or hammock, a light sleeping bag or blanket, lots of food, soap, several water bottles, some sort of water purifier, and lots of plastic bags. If you plan to go overland into Colombia, consider bringing batteries, lighters, machetes, and watches for bartering. Did someone say pack light?

COMING AND GOING

Since the bus trip to Yaviza is long and bumpy, and sometimes doesn't even make it, it's worthwhile to fly to the Darién. El Real, which is near the entrance to Parque Nacional Darién, lies a short boat trip from Yaviza, but La Palma and Sambú are so isolated you either have to fly or boat there. **ANCON Expeditions** (Calle Elvira Mendez, Edificio El Dorado #3, Bella Vista, tel. 269–9414) has field stations in Punta Patiño, near La Palma, and Cana, on the edge of Darién National Park. Cana is expensive, since it is reached by a charter flight, but Punto Patiño isn't so dear. They also run two-week trans-Darién expeditions that retrace Balboa's route when he discovered the Pacific; these are very expensive.

BY BUS • From the main piquera in Panama City, Tito Gomez (tel. 266–2474) runs four buses daily to Yaviza (9–12 hrs, $14). The buses lack air-conditioning, and your arrival time may vary. In the rainy season, buses often get stuck in mud bogs, which sometimes means you spend the night on it.

BY BOAT • The Darién is crisscrossed by a host of muddy rivers, and most settlements lie along those waterways, which is why boats are the best way to get around. Motorized dugouts called *piraguas* are expensive to rent (around $50 for a boat and driver, plus $20 for each hour). Talk to people when you arrive in a town, and with luck, there might be a boat already heading where you want to go.

Boats for Garachine and Sambú leave from the pier near the main market in Casco Viejo (Panama City). The boats (12 hrs, $12) go at night about every five days—you'll have to walk over there and find out their schedule, or call them at 262–9124. They also have a boat called the *Darién Express* (10 hrs, $10) that goes to La Palma, El Real, and Yaviza.

BY PLANE • From Allbrook Airport, **Aeroperlas** (tel. 269–4555) has flights to Jaque, Garachiné, Sambú, La Palma, and El Real ($70–$80 round-trip).

WHERE TO SLEEP AND EAT

The towns of **La Palma, Yaviza,** and **El Real** all have little hotels that may look dingy if you're arriving from Panama City, but if you're coming back from the woods, they'll feel like the Ritz. None of them take credit cards. **Baiquira Bagara** (El Real, tel. 299–224) is the nicest hotel in the region—a wooden building over the water—and most of its rooms have private baths. **Pension Las Tres Americas** (Yaviza, no phone) is a collection of dusty rooms with shared bath and located above a store. Camping in Parque Nacional Darién is free, when its open to the public. If you stay and eat with an indigenous family, you should pay them $5 per night to cover costs. About half the Indians, mostly the younger ones, speak Spanish. If you don't know any Spanish, you'd better brush up on your charades, because English is useless here.

METETI AND CONMARCA EMBERA—CEMACO

If you want to visit an Indian village, but aren't up for long stints of travel, your best option is to take the bus to Meteti (7–9 hrs, $10), about 48 km (30 mi) before Yaviza. Here, you can hire a guide to the Chucunaque River ($10), or you can get a boat to villages like Rancho Ahogado and Lajas Blancas.

EL REAL AND PARQUE NACIONAL DARIÉN

At press time, Darién National Park was closed to the public because government officials considered it too dangerous due to drug trafficking and Columbian rebel activity. Contact INRENARE (Curundú, Calle Acenio Villaluz, across from SINAPROC, tel. 232–7228) for the park's current status. If it's open, you'll reach it via El Real, a teeny town with a couple of stores and one hotel, **El Nazareño,** which is a minor house of horrors—you may have to share your room with giant cockroaches and bats, but that's life in the jungle. The one place to eat is a little set of tables behind a women's bathroom.

There are three ranger stations in the park. **Rancho Frio** is the closest to El Real (4-hr hike) and is the best one to camp in. It's got a beautiful river and an incredible waterfall just a 15-minute walk away. From here, you can climb **Cerro Pirre,** the highest mountain in Darién, and home to more species of birds than anywhere else in the country, including three kinds of macaws and harpy eagles. Other than paying for a guide ($10 each way) and bringing food for yourself and the park guards (really), your stay here is free. They have beds, sheets, water, and cooking facilities. **Cruce Mono** is six hours from Boca de Cupe; you'll have to rent a boat (about $95) and pay $10 (plus food) for a guide. This is the most isolated station, but it's the best place to see big animals. The station at **Río Sabalo-Balsas** is a seven-hour boat ride away (about $180).

GARACHINE AND RIO SAMBU

If you're getting off in Sambú, you'll have to register with local authorities; you'll be a guest of the Embera Indians.

This is the place to see the most traditional Embera and Waunan villages. There are villages within a one-hour hike from Sambú, and unless you take expensive boats up the Río Sambú, you'll be able to get around on a minimum budget. Garachine is where you'll find the most exquisite traditional arts, including the incredibly beautiful *tagua* carvings, made from a hard palm fruit that looks and feels like ivory. Before you stay in a village, you must ask permission from the *nocó* (chief). Bring food for your hosts, as well as small gifts.

INDEX

Fodor's Travel Publications

Available at bookstores everywhere. For descriptions of all our titles and a key to Fodor's guidebook series, visit www.fodors.com/books

Gold Guides

U.S.

Alaska

Arizona

Boston

California

Cape Cod, Martha's Vineyard, Nantucket

The Carolinas & Georgia

Chicago

Colorado

Florida

Hawai'i

Las Vegas, Reno, Tahoe

Los Angeles

Maine, Vermont, New Hampshire

Maui & Lāna'i

Miami & the Keys

New England

New Orleans

New York City

Oregon

Pacific North Coast

Philadelphia & the Pennsylvania Dutch Country

The Rockies

San Diego

San Francisco

Santa Fe, Taos, Albuquerque

Seattle & Vancouver

The South

U.S. & British Virgin Islands

USA

Virginia & Maryland

Washington, D.C.

Foreign

Australia

Austria

The Bahamas

Belize & Guatemala

Bermuda

Canada

Cancún, Cozumel, Yucatán Peninsula

Caribbean

China

Costa Rica

Cuba

The Czech Republic & Slovakia

Denmark

Eastern & Central Europe

Europe

Florence, Tuscany & Umbria

France

Germany

Great Britain

Greece

Hong Kong

India

Ireland

Israel

Italy

Japan

London

Madrid & Barcelona

Mexico

Montréal & Québec City

Moscow, St. Petersburg, Kiev

The Netherlands, Belgium & Luxembourg

New Zealand

Norway

Nova Scotia, New Brunswick, Prince Edward Island

Paris

Portugal

Provence & the Riviera

Scandinavia

Scotland

Singapore

South Africa

South America

Southeast Asia

Spain

Sweden

Switzerland

Thailand

Toronto

Turkey

Vienna & the Danube Valley

Vietnam

Special-Interest Guides

Adventures to Imagine

Alaska Ports of Call

Ballpark Vacations

The Best Cruises

Caribbean Ports of Call

The Complete Guide to America's National Parks

Europe Ports of Call

Family Adventures

Fodor's Gay Guide to the USA

Fodor's How to Pack

Great American Learning Vacations

Great American Sports & Adventure Vacations

Great American Vacations

Great American Vacations for Travelers with Disabilities

Halliday's New Orleans Food Explorer

Healthy Escapes

Kodak Guide to Shooting Great Travel Pictures

National Parks and Seashores of the East

National Parks of the West

Nights to Imagine

Orlando Like a Pro

Rock & Roll Traveler Great Britain and Ireland

Rock & Roll Traveler USA

Sunday in San Francisco

Walt Disney World for Adults

Weekends in New York

Wendy Perrin's Secrets Every Smart Traveler Should Know

Worlds to Imagine

Fodor's Special Series

Fodor's Best Bed & Breakfasts
America
California
The Mid-Atlantic
New England
The Pacific Northwest
The South
The Southwest
The Upper Great Lakes

Compass American Guides
Alaska
Arizona
Boston
Chicago
Coastal California
Colorado
Florida
Hawai'i
Hollywood
Idaho
Las Vegas
Maine
Manhattan
Minnesota
Montana
New Mexico
New Orleans
Oregon
Pacific Northwest
San Francisco
Santa Fe
South Carolina
South Dakota
Southwest
Texas
Underwater Wonders of the National Parks
Utah
Virginia
Washington
Wine Country
Wisconsin
Wyoming

Citypacks
Amsterdam
Atlanta
Berlin
Boston
Chicago
Florence
Hong Kong
London
Los Angeles
Miami
Montréal
New York City
Paris

Prague
Rome
San Francisco
Sydney
Tokyo
Toronto
Venice
Washington, D.C.

Exploring Guides
Australia
Boston & New England
Britain
California
Canada
Caribbean
China
Costa Rica
Cuba
Egypt
Florence & Tuscany
Florida
France
Germany
Greek Islands
Hawai'i
India
Ireland
Israel
Italy
Japan
London
Mexico
Moscow & St. Petersburg
New York City
Paris
Portugal
Prague
Provence
Rome
San Francisco
Scotland
Singapore & Malaysia
South Africa
Spain
Thailand
Turkey
Venice
Vietnam

Flashmaps
Boston
New York
San Francisco
Washington, D.C.

Fodor's Cityguides
Boston
New York
San Francisco

Fodor's Gay Guides
Amsterdam
Los Angeles & Southern California
New York City
Pacific Northwest
San Francisco and the Bay Area
South Florida
USA

Karen Brown Guides
Austria
California
England B&Bs
England, Wales & Scotland
France B&Bs
France Inns
Germany
Ireland
Italy B&Bs
Italy Inns
Portugal
Spain
Switzerland

Languages for Travelers (Cassette & Phrasebook)
French
German
Italian
Spanish

Mobil Travel Guides
America's Best Hotels & Restaurants
Arizona
California and the West
Florida
Great Lakes
Major Cities
Mid-Atlantic
Northeast
Northwest and Great Plains
Southeast
Southern California
Southwest and South Central

Pocket Guides
Acapulco
Aruba
Atlanta
Barbados
Beijing
Berlin
Budapest
Dublin
Honolulu
Jamaica
London

Mexico City
New York City
Paris
Prague
Puerto Rico
Rome
San Francisco
Savannah & Charleston
Shanghai
Sydney
Washington, D.C.

Rivages Guides
Bed and Breakfasts of Character and Charm in France
Hotels and Country Inns of Character and Charm in France
Hotels and Country Inns of Character and Charm in Italy
Hotels of Character and Charm in Paris
Hotels of Character and Charm in Portugal
Hotels of Character and Charm in Spain
Wines & Vineyards of Character and Charm in France

Short Escapes
Britain
France
Near New York City
New England

Fodor's Sports
Golf Digest's Places to Play (USA)
Golf Digest's Places to Play in the Southeast
Golf Digest's Places to Play in the Southwest
Skiing USA
USA Today The Complete Four Sport Stadium Guide

Fodor's upCLOSE Guides
California
Europe
France
Great Britain
Ireland
Italy
London
Los Angeles
Mexico
New York City
Paris
San Francisco